May 31–June 4, 2016
Kyoto, Japan

I0028746

**Association for
Computing Machinery**

Advancing Computing as a Science & Profession

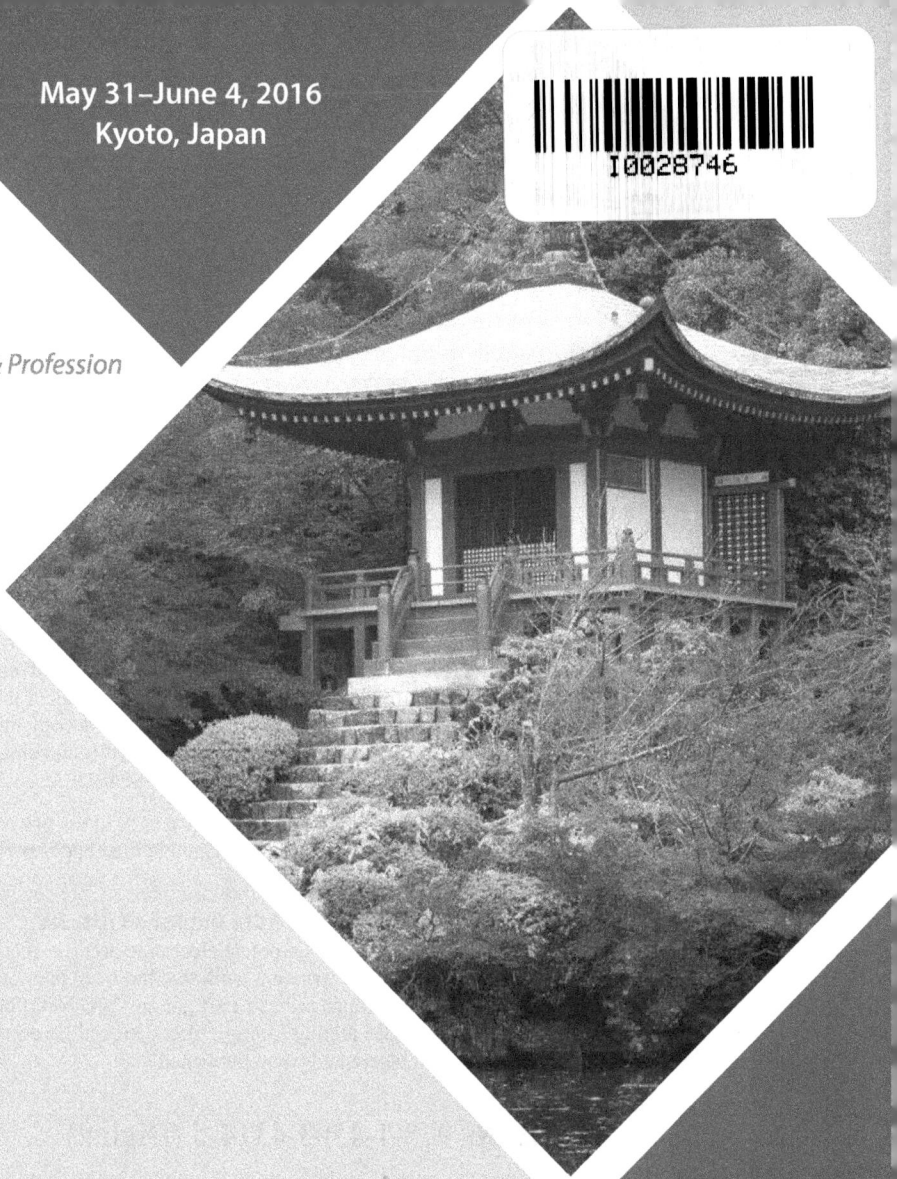

HPDC'16

Proceedings of the 25th ACM International Symposium on
High-Performance Parallel
and Distributed Computing

Sponsored by:
ACM SIGARCH & The University of Arizona

Supported by:
**NSF, Fujitsu, University of Tsukuba, iTC - University of Tokyo,
Tokyo Institute of Technology, Kyoto University, JHPCN, & Cray**

In-cooporation with:
ACM SIGHPC

Association for Computing Machinery

Advancing Computing as a Science & Profession

The Association for Computing Machinery
2 Penn Plaza, Suite 701
New York, New York 10121-0701

Notice to Past Authors of ACM-Published Articles
ACM intends to create a complete electronic archive of all articles and/or other material previously published by ACM. If you have written a work that has been previously published by ACM in any journal or conference proceedings prior to 1978, or any SIG Newsletter at any time, and you do NOT want this work to appear in the ACM Digital Library, please inform permissions@acm.org, stating the title of the work, the author(s), and where and when published.

ISBN: 978-1-4503-4314-5 (Digital)

ISBN: 978-1-4503-4595-8 (Print)

Additional copies may be ordered prepaid from:

ACM Order Department
PO Box 30777
New York, NY 10087-0777, USA

Phone: 1-800-342-6626 (USA and Canada)
+1-212-626-0500 (Global)
Fax: +1-212-944-1318
E-mail: acmhelp@acm.org
Hours of Operation: 8:30 am – 4:30 pm ET

Printed in the USA

HPDC'16 Chairs' Welcome

Welcome to the 25th ACM Symposium on High-Performance Parallel and Distributed Computing (HPDC'16). HPDC'16 follows the tradition of previous versions of the conference by providing a high-quality, single-track forum for presenting new research results on all aspects of the design, implementation, evaluation, and application of parallel and distributed systems for high-end computing. The HPDC'16 program features eight sessions that cover wide range of topics including high performance networking, parallel algorithms, algorithm-based fault tolerance, big data processing, I/O optimizations, non-volatile memory, cloud, resource management, many core systems, GPUs, graph processing algorithms, and more. In these sessions, not only full papers but also short papers are presented to give a mix of novel research directions at various stages of development, which also is exhibited by a number of posters. This program is complemented by an interesting set of six workshops, FTXS, HPGP, SEM4HPC, DIDC, ROSS and ScienceCloud, on a range of timely and related systems and application topics.

The conference program also features three keynote/invited talks given by Dr. Jeffrey Vetter of Oak Ridge National Laboratory, Professor Jack Dongarra of University of Tennessee, and Professor Ada Gavrilovska of Georgia Tech to memorialize the late Professor Karsten Schwan of Georgia Tech.

Jack Dongarra is the recipient of the 5th HPDC Annual Achievement Award. The purpose of this award is to recognize individuals who have made long lasting, influential contributions to the foundations or practice of the field of high-performance parallel and distributed computing, to raise the awareness of these contributions, especially among the younger generation of researchers, and to improve the image and the public relations of the HPDC community. The Award Selection Committee followed the formalized process established in 2013 to select the winner with an open call for nominations.

The HPDC'16 call for papers attracted 129 paper submissions. In the review process this year, we followed two established methods that were started in 2012: a two-round review process and an author rebuttal process. In the first round review, all papers received at least three reviews, and based on these reviews, 71 papers went on to the second round in which most of them received another two reviews. In total, 514 reviews were generated by the 54- member Program Committee along with a number of external reviewers. For many of the 71 second-round papers, the authors submitted rebuttals. Rebuttals were carefully taken into consideration during the Program Committee deliberations as part of the selection process. On March 10-11, the Program Committee met at University of Pittsburgh (Pittsburgh, PA) and made the final selection. Each paper in the second round of reviews was discussed at the meeting. At the end of the 1.5-day meeting, the Program Committee accepted 20 full papers, resulting in an acceptance rate of 15.5%. In addition, the committee accepted 9 submissions as short papers. We would like to thank all contributing authors, regardless of the results of their submissions. We are very grateful to the Program Committee members for their hard work and for providing their reviews, in what was a very tight review schedule and a very rigorous review process.

HPDC 2016 has been generously sponsored by ACM SIGARCH and The University of Arizona. We would also like to acknowledge the support of the US National Science Foundation and the cooperation of ACM SIGARCH.

Enjoy the conference and your stay in Kyoto!

Hiroshi Nakashima
HPDC'16 General Chair
Kyoto University

Kenjiro Taura
HPDC'16 Program Co-Chair
The University of Tokyo

Jack Lange
HPDC'16 Program Co-Chair
University of Pittsburgh

Table of Contents

Keynote Address

Session: Systems, Networks, and Architectures for High-end Computing

Session: Cloud and Resource Management

Session: Massively Multicore Systems

Keynote Address

Session: Graph Algorithms

Session Chair: Shuaiwen Song *(Pacific Northwest National Lab)*

Session: Potpourri

Session Chair: Naoya Maruyama *(RIKEN Advanced Institute for Computational Science)*

HPDC 2016 Organization

General Chair: Hiroshi Nakashima *(Kyoto University, Japan)*

Program Chairs: Kenjiro Taura *(The University of Tokyo, Japan)*
Jack Lange *(University of Pittsburgh, USA)*

Workshop Co-Chairs: Naoya Maruyama *(RIKEN Advanced Institute of Computational Science, Japan)*
Ioan Raicu *(Illinois Institute of Technology/Argonne National Laboratory, USA)*

Poster Chair: Kento Aida *(National Institute of Informatics, Japan)*

Publicity Co-Chairs: Masaaki Kondo *(The University of Tokyo, Japan)*
Shuaiwen Leon Song *(Pacific Northwest National Laboratory, USA)*
Torsten Hoefler *(Eidgenössische Technische Hochschule Zürich, Switzerland)*

Publications Chair: Brian Kocoloski *(University of Pittsburgh, USA)*

Sponsorship Chair: Toshio Endo *(Tokyo Institute of Technology, Japan)*

Travel Award Chair: Patrick Bridges *(University of New Mexico, USA)*

Local Arrangements Chair: Takeshi Iwashita *(Hokkaido University, Japan)*

Webmaster: Hideyuki Jitsumoto *(Tokyo Institute of Technology, Japan)*

Steering Committee: Franck Cappello *(Argonne National Lab, USA and INRIA, France)*
Andrew A. Chien *(University of Chicago, USA)*
Peter Dinda *(Northwestern University, USA)*
Dick Epema *(Delft University of Technology, The Netherlands)*
Renato Figueiredo *(University of Florida, USA)*
Salim Hariri *(University of Arizona, USA)*
Thilo Kielmann *(VU University Amsterdam, The Netherlands)*
Arthur "Barney" Maccabe *(Oak Ridge National Laboratory, USA)*
Manish Parashar *(Rutgers University, USA)*
Matei Ripeanu *(University of British Columbia, Canada)*
Karsten Schwan *(Georgia Tech, USA)*
Doug Thain *(University of Notre Dame, USA)*
Jon Weissman *(University of Minnesota, USA)* (Chair)
Dongyan Xu *(Purdue University, USA)*

HPDC'16 Sponsors & Supporters

Sponsors:

Supporters:

In-Cooperation with:

Preparing for Supercomputing's Sixth Wave

Jeffrey S. Vetter

Oak Ridge National Laboratory

Abstract

After five decades of sustained progress, Moore's law appears to be reaching its limits. In order to sustain the dramatic improvements to which we have become accustomed, computing will need to transform to Kurzweil's sixth wave of computing. The supercomputing community will likely need to re-think most of its fundamental technologies and tools, spanning innovative materials and devices, circuits, system architectures, programming systems, system software, and applications. We already see evidence of this transition in the move to new architectures that employ heterogeneous processing, non-volatile memory, multimode memory hierarchies, and optical interconnection networks. In this talk, I will recap progress in these areas over the past three decades, discuss current solutions, and contemplate various future technologies that our community will need for continued progress in supercomputing.

CCS Concepts

• **Computer systems organization~Architectures**
• **Hardware~Emerging technologies**

Keywords

Moore's Law; supercomputing; emerging technologies;

Short Bio

Jeffrey Vetter, Ph.D., is a Distinguished R&D Staff Member at Oak Ridge National Laboratory (ORNL). At ORNL, Vetter is the founding group leader of the Future Technologies Group in the Computer Science and Mathematics Division. Vetter also holds joint appointments at the Computational Science and Engineering School of the Georgia Institute of Technology, and at the Electrical Engineering and Computer Science Department of the University of Tennessee-Knoxville. The coherent thread through his research is developing rich architectures and software systems that solve important, real-world high performance computing problems. Recently, he has been investigating the effectiveness of next-generation architectures, such as graphics processors, non-volatile memory systems, heterogeneous multicore processors, and field-programmable gate arrays (FPGAs), for important science applications. His papers have won awards at the International Parallel and Distributed Processing Symposium and EuroPar; he was awarded the ACM Gordon Bell Prize in 2010. His recent books "Contemporary High Performance Computing (Vols. 1 and 2)" survey the international landscape of HPC. Vetter is a Senior Member of the IEEE, and a Distinguished Scientist Member of the ACM. See his website for more information: http://ft.ornl.gov/~vetter/.

HPDC'16, May 31–June 4, 2016, Kyoto, Japan.
ACM ISBN 978-1-4503-4314-5/16/05.
DOI: http://dx.doi.org/10.1145/2907294.2911994

Routing on the Dependency Graph: A New Approach to Deadlock-Free High-Performance Routing

Jens Domke
Institute of Computer
Engineering
TU Dresden, Germany
jens.domke@tu-dresden.de

Torsten Hoefler
Computer Science
Department
ETH Zurich, Switzerland
htor@inf.ethz.ch

Satoshi Matsuoka
Global Scientific Information
and Computing Center
Tokyo Tech, Japan
matsu@is.titech.ac.jp

ABSTRACT

Lossless interconnection networks are omnipresent in high performance computing systems, data centers and network-on-chip architectures. Such networks require efficient and deadlock-free routing functions to utilize the available hardware. Topology-aware routing functions become increasingly inapplicable, due to irregular topologies, which either are irregular by design or as a result of hardware failures. Existing topology-agnostic routing methods either suffer from poor load balancing or are not bounded in the number of virtual channels needed to resolve deadlocks in the routing tables. We propose a novel topology-agnostic routing approach which implicitly avoids deadlocks during the path calculation instead of solving both problems separately. We present a model implementation, called Nue[1], of a destination-based and oblivious routing function. Nue routing heuristically optimizes the load balancing while enforcing deadlock-freedom without exceeding a given number of virtual channels, which we demonstrate based on the InfiniBand architecture.

Keywords

Deadlock-free, destination-based, routing, virtual channels

1. INTRODUCTION

Today's HPC and data center network architectures increasingly embrace functions that enable a tighter interaction between networking hardware and programming models. The best example is Remote Direct Memory Access (RDMA) that enables the programmer to directly instruct the network interface to read and write remote memory. This functionality commonly requires reliable hardware transport between sender and receiver, which can be achieved using iWARP or more recently using lossless Layer 2 network protocols. Such advanced functions have been prevalent in the high-speed networking area, such as InfiniBand [18] or Cray's Cascade [9]. Ethernet was recently extended with Priority Flow Control

---

[1] Japanese chimera combining the advantages of existing routings

HPDC'16, May 31–June 04, 2016, Kyoto, Japan.

© 2016 Copyright held by the owner/author(s). Publication rights licensed to ACM.
ISBN 978-1-4503-4314-5/16/05. . . $15.00

DOI: http://dx.doi.org/10.1145/2907294.2907313

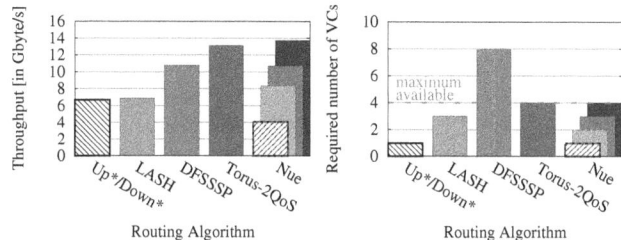

(a) Throughput for all-to-all   (b) Required VCs (DL-free)

Figure 1: Simulated throughput for an all-to-all operation and required VCs for deadlock-freedom for different routing algorithms (hatched bars indicate that only 1 VC is used) — Simulated network: 4x4x3 3D-torus, 4 terminals per switch, 1 faulty switch, QDR InfiniBand, maximum of 4 VCs available

at Layer 2 to enable the reliable transport needed for RDMA. Indeed, the RoCE protocol enables RDMA for Ethernet.

The downside of lossless Layer 2 networking is that the needed protocols can create deadlock situations [4], where a group of packets cannot be forwarded because of unavailable resources, such as buffers or channels, and the group is circularly depended on each other. Such deadlocks (DL) can be avoided algorithmically for many regular topologies, e.g., by restricting the routing to use only a subset of all available channel dependencies, as it is implemented by dimension-order routing (DOR) [26]. Another well-known technique for HPC and on-chip networks (NoC) is the use of virtual channels (VCs, different sets of buffers) to break deadlocks in arbitrary topologies and routing functions [1,30,32]. Dally et al. [6] described this method of conditionally switching between virtual channels along a route, so called virtual channel transition, to obtain a DL-free routing. For example, a k-ary n-cube network needs two VCs if virtual channel transition is possible. However, not all network technologies, e.g., InfiniBand, support this method, in which case the routing functions, such as the layered shortest path routing (LASH) [32], can combine VCs into virtual layers—imagine multiple virtual copies of the actual network—and assign all routes to different layers. Hence, the routing is DL-free, if the combination of routes within each layer is deadlock-free.

Yet, all these concepts have limitations: (1) Topology-aware routings assume perfect topologies and often do not support switch/link failures [7]. (2) Cycle-avoiding routings often cannot balance routes and thus limit global bandwidth [28]. (3) Routings based on virtual channel isolation fail when the required number of VCs is not available [11].

Assume, for example, a 4x4x3 InfiniBand torus network with four terminals per switch and one failed switch (i.e., 47 switches in total) and network support for four VCs. The throughput for various deadlock-free routing strategies, as implemented in InfiniBand's subnet manager, is shown in Fig. 1a, provided that all terminals participate in an all-to-all send operation with 2 KiB messages. Fig. 1b shows the needed number of VCs for these deadlock-free routing algorithms. The topology-aware Torus-2QoS routing [25] enables a high throughput within the virtual channel limit, but will fail if a second switch failure occurs in the same torus ring. Up*/Down* routing and LASH [32] are inefficient in comparison to Torus-2QoS. The throughput of the topology-agnostic routing DFSSSP [8] is in-between, however the deadlock-free single-source shortest-path routing (DFSSSP) exceeds the given VC limit and is therefore inapplicable. The achievable throughput while using our new routing approach, Nue, for the 4x4x3 torus is included in Fig. 1a for every number of VCs within the 4-VC limit, showing Nue's resiliency to network faults and ability to offer competitive throughput.

We now describe the underlying idea for Nue routing, i.e., a routing function that overcomes all mentioned limitations (1)–(3), meaning the routing is capable of distributing the paths across the network to increase the throughput. Furthermore, the objectives for our routing function should be to work on arbitrary topologies with all possible numbers of available virtual channels, including network technologies without support for VCs. We assume destination-based routing as is used in many of today's technologies, e.g., InfiniBand.

2. DEFINITIONS AND ASSUMPTIONS

We define a network as a multigraph assuming that each pair of network devices can be connected with multiple duplex channels (or links). In this regard, all duplex channels of the interconnection network are logically split into two directed channels of opposite direction, see Fig. 2a. Furthermore, we assume that the channel capacity is uniform and constant over time. If exact device information is required, e.g., for figures, then we use ordered pairs (n_x, n_y) or c_{n_x,n_y}, otherwise a simpler c_i notation is used for channels.

Definition 1 (Interconnection Network). *An **interconnection network** $I := G(N, C)$ is a connected multigraph with the node set N and multiset C of directed (multi-)channels. We call $n_x \in N$ a **terminal**, if and only if it exists exactly one n_y with $(n_y, n_x) \in C$, otherwise n_x is called a **switch**.*

Definition 2 (Cycle-free Route). *A **route** (or **path**) P_{n_x,n_y} of length h from node n_x to n_y in $I = G(N,C)$ is defined as a sequence of channels $(c_1, \ldots, c_h) =: P_{n_x,n_y}$ under the condition that $\{c_1, \ldots, c_h\} \subseteq C$, $c_1 := (n_x, \cdot)$, $c_h := (\cdot, n_y)$, and if $c_q = (\cdot, n_z)$ then $c_{q+1} = (n_z, \cdot)$ for all $1 < q < h$. P_{n_x,n_y} is considered to be **cycle-free**, if from $p \neq q$, with $1 \leq p, q \leq h$ and $c_p = (\cdot, n_u)$, $c_q = (\cdot, n_v)$, it follows that $n_u \neq n_v$. Let ${}^s P_{n_x,n_y}$ denote a shortest path from n_x to n_y.*

Definition 3 (Destination-based and Cycle-free Routing). *A **routing function** $R : C \times N \to C$ for a network $I := G(N,C)$ assigns the next channel c_{q+1} of the route depending on the current channel c_q and the destination node n_y. For multigraphs, we assume that the next channel c_{q+1} is unique among the existing parallel channels of a multi-channel. Furthermore, a routing R is considered to be **destination-based** if the channel c_{q+1} is unique (denoted by the $\exists!$ sign) at each*

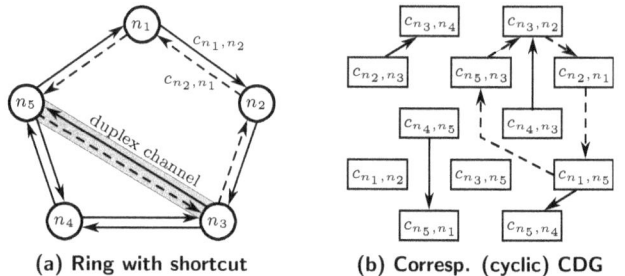

(a) Ring with shortcut   (b) Corresp. (cyclic) CDG

Figure 2: Using a shortest-path, counter-clockwise routing for network I (2a) induces the channel dependency graph D (2b); dashed channel dependencies in D form a potential deadlock (induced by paths, with $h = 2$, using dashed channels of I)

node, i.e., $\forall n_x \in N \ \exists! c \in C : R\big((\cdot, n_x), n_y\big) = c$. The routing R is **cycle-free** if all paths induced by R are cycle-free.

Although our definition of the routing function is equivalent to $R' : N \times N \to C$, we will use R to express channel dependencies later on. We consider a routing function for a given network I to be valid, if and only if (iff) the routing has these three properties: cycle-free, destination-based, and deadlock-free, so that the routing is applicable to InfiniBand, Ethernet, and many NoC designs. Especially, the InfiniBand standard demands the use of DL-free routing algorithms, see Section C14-62.1.2 [18]. Dally et al. [6] postulate Theorem 1, which sets the necessary and sufficient condition for the deadlock-freedom of a destination-based routing function.

Theorem 1. *A routing function R for an interconnection network I is deadlock-free if and only if there are no cycles in the corresponding channel dependency graph.*

The channel dependency graph (CDG) is induced by the used routing function R for a given network I as follows:

Definition 4 (Channel Dependency Graph). *The **channel dependency graph** for a given network I and routing function R is defined as a directed graph $D := G(C, E)$ whose node set consists of the channel set of I. The edge set of D, denoted by ordered channel pairs $(\cdot, \cdot)$, is induced by the routing function, i.e., $(c_p, c_q) \in E$ iff $\exists n_y \in N : R(c_p, n_y) = c_q$.*

Fig. 2b shows the CDG for the network shown in Fig. 2a assuming a shortest-path, counter-clockwise routing function is used (with "shortest-path" as primary path selection criterion). If VCs are supported, but no VC transition, then the alternative way to achieve DL-freedom is the use of virtual channels and to combine them into virtual layers, as mentioned in Section 1. Routes are then assigned to individual layers, so that all routes within one layer induce an acyclic CDG. This technique is used by DFSSSP [8] and LASH [32] routing (among others). However, assuming shortest-path routing, then the minimum number of virtual layers required to achieve deadlock-freedom can exceed the available number of virtual layers, see Section 5.3, and an optimal assignment of routes to layers is an NP-complete problem [8].

Definition 5 (Virtual Layer). *Assume each network channel $c \in C$ can be split into k virtual channels $\{c_1^{virt}, \ldots, c_k^{virt}\}$, with $k \in \mathbb{N}$, then we can determine the i-th **virtual layer** $L_i := G(N, C_i)$ of the interconnection network $I = G(N, C)$ with $C_i := \{c_i^{virt} \mid c_i^{virt} \in c \text{ for } c \in C\}$. The network I and virtual layer L_i are identical for $k = 1$.*

4

Our routing algorithm, as we explain hereafter, will use a similar approach, i.e., using virtual layers for deadlock-freedom, but to the best of our knowledge is the first routing function which can be used for every topology and any given number of virtual channels, including $k = 1$.

3. ROUTING IN A DEPENDENCY GRAPH

The current best practice, e.g., as implemented by DFSSSP and LASH, is to decouple the two problems of path creation and deadlock-free assignment to virtual channels. The reason is that both problems require a different graph representation of the network and routes. The deadlock-free assignment needs the CDG, an abstract graph induced by the routes, while the route calculation has to take place beforehand and is usually performed on a graph identical to the network. Assume, we can combine the information required to solve both problems within one graph, then we can impose routing restrictions to the path creation on-demand, because the effects of a partial or full path on the CDG can be checked simultaneously. Hence, we can avoid closing cycles in the CDG while calculating the paths instead of breaking the cycles later. Assume, this new graph represents one virtual layer, then a graph search algorithm, such as Dijkstra's algorithm, can traverse the graph and construct routes from all nodes to all other network nodes and the routes are deadlock-free within this layer. The type of graph search and the information assigned to this graph influence the resulting routes, e.g., source-routing or destination-based routing could be possible. Furthermore, assuming the used network technology supports an arbitrary, but fixed, number of virtual channels, $k > 1$, then individual destination nodes can be assigned to different virtual layers. As a consequence, the graph search algorithm within one layer is able to calculate DL-free routes for all source nodes to the destination nodes assigned to this virtual layer. Therefore, all routes in all virtual layers are deadlock-free without exceeding the VC constraint.

4. NUE ROUTING

In the following, we will show how to construct the complete channel dependency graph. Based on this graph, we will develop our deadlock-free, oblivious, and destination-based Nue routing as one example for the general idea of routing within the dependency graph.

4.1 Complete Channel Dependency Graph

To create paths within the CDG, we need a complete representation of all possible channel dependencies, instead of a graph induced by a specific routing. Therefore, we define the complete CDG using the adjacency of channels as follows:

Definition 6 (Complete Channel Dependency Graph). *Let $I = G(N, C)$ be a network according to Definition 1, then the **complete CDG** $\overline{D} := G(C, \overline{E})$, with $\overline{E} \subseteq C \times C$, is defined by $\forall (n_x, n_y), (n_y, n_z) \in C, n_x \neq n_z : ((n_x, n_y), (n_y, n_z)) \in \overline{E}$. We define that the graph $\overline{D}$ is **cycle-free**, if $D \subseteq \overline{D}$ is acyclic, for any CDG D induced by a routing function according to Definition 4. Assuming, the network technology supports $k > 1$ VCs, then the definition of the i-th complete channel dependency graph $\overline{D}_i := G(C_i, \overline{E}_i)$, with $\overline{E}_i \subseteq C_i \times C_i$, is equivalent to the definition of $\overline{D}$.*

The CDG D induced by a routing function does not have to be stored separately, and can be saved indirectly by assigning

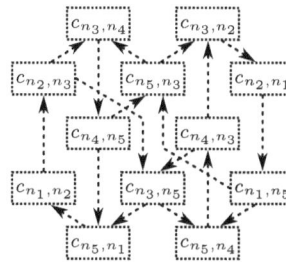

Figure 3: Complete CDG $\overline{D}$ for the 5-ring network with shortcut, see Fig. 2a, assuming $k = 1$; all channels are in *unused* state ($\Rightarrow$ no routing applied, yet)

states to the vertices, i.e., channels of I, and edges of the complete CDG $\overline{D}$. These states are *unused*, *used*, or *blocked*, whereby the *blocked* state is only used for edges. We consider $e \in \overline{E}$ to be *used* iff $e \in E$, i.e., e is induced by a routing R. We mark an edge $e \in \overline{E}$ as *blocked* iff $G(C, E \cup \{e\})$ forms a cyclic graph for an acyclic CDG $D = G(C, E)$. Fig. 3 shows the complete CDG for the 5-node ring network with shortcut, previously shown in Fig. 2a, for $k = 1$. Each vertex/edge of $\overline{D}$ is in the *unused* state, i.e., no routing has been applied.

4.2 Escape Paths

Cherkasova et al. [3] made an important observation: An incremental algorithm calculating paths and adding routing restrictions at the same time, i.e., prohibiting the assignment $R(c_q, \cdot) = c_{q+1}$ for any destination node, can lead to an impasse. Hence, further progress in the algorithm is impossible due to previously added restrictions. While Cherkasova et al. [3] report that this state was observed only rarely for their investigated networks, our experiments show that it is a permanent problem for larger networks.

For adaptive routing algorithms it is common to avoid deadlocks by utilizing a separate set of buffers, similar to a virtual layer, which acts as "escape paths" [4, 13]. Within this layer a fixed deadlock-free routing, such as Up*/Down*, is employed, and switches transfer a blocked packet into the escape paths for the remainder of the route to its destination.

We adapt the concept of escape paths[2] for our oblivious routing to ensure that at least one valid path—not necessarily shortest—between every given node pair exists, which does not induce a cycle in the CDG. The disadvantages of fixed and predefined escape paths are the imposed channel dependencies which cannot act as routing restrictions. Meaning, Nue assigns the *used* state to a subset of vertices and edges of $\overline{D}$, even so these are not necessarily induced by R. Escape paths inevitably serve as potential imaginary paths which influence the generation and balancing of real paths by Nue. Therefore, the escape paths should induce as few channel dependencies as possible while minimizing the average path length across the escape paths. We are using a spanning tree of I to define the escape paths in $\overline{D}$, since a spanning tree does not induce a cyclic CDG while minimizing the number of channels required to connect all nodes in I.

Definition 7 (Escape Paths). *Let $N^d \subseteq N$ be a set of destination nodes for Nue within the network $I = G(N, C)$ and let $S = G(N, C^s)$, with $C^s \subseteq C$, be a spanning tree*

---

[2]Not in the sense of a separate set of buffers, but available fall back paths in layer L_i.

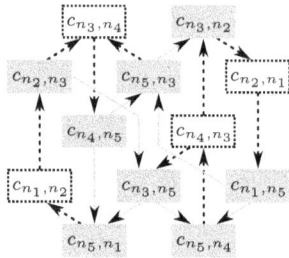

Figure 4: Acyclic escape paths D^s for the 5-node ring network with shortcut, see Fig. 2a, are marked as solid boxes/lines within the complete CDG $\overline{D}$, assuming $k = 1$, destination set $N^d = N$, root node $n_r = n_5$, and spanning tree $S = G(N, C \setminus \{(n_1, n_2), (n_2, n_1), (n_3, n_4), (n_4, n_3)\})$

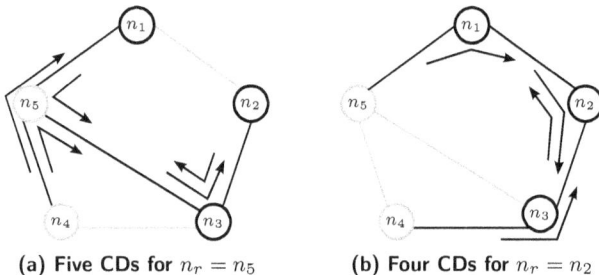

(a) Five CDs for $n_r = n_5$　　　**(b) Four CDs for $n_r = n_2$**

Figure 5: Initial channel dependencies (CDs) of the escape paths shown for the node set $N_i^d = \{n_1, n_2, n_3\}$ and root node n_5 (left) or root node n_2 (right) of the spanning tree (marked as black channels)

*of network I with root node $n_r \in N$. Then, the **escape paths** $D^s := G(C^s, E^s)$ are a subgraph of $\overline{D}$ induced by a routing $R^s : N \times N^d \to C^s$. Assuming $k > 1$, then D_i^s for virtual layer L_i and root $n_{r,i}$ is defined equivalently, with the substitution of C^s by $C_i^s \subseteq C_i$.*

The term "spanning tree" in this context refers to the originally undirected duplex channels of I, and therefore $(n_x, n_y) \in C^s \implies (n_y, n_x) \in C^s$. Evidently, all cycle-free, destination-based routings R^s induce the same escape paths D^s or D_i^s, respectively, for a given spanning tree. Fig. 4 shows the escape paths marked in the complete CDG for $N^d = N$ when n_5 is used as the root node for S.

The escape paths for our Nue routing have two functions: The first, as mentioned above, is to define an initial set of channel dependencies, which once added cannot be removed to resolve cyclic states in the CDG. Therefore, the escape paths ensure a deadlock-free path from all nodes in N to all nodes in N_i^d within virtual layer L_i. Hence, escape paths for each layer are needed. Despite of having escape paths D_i^s, Nue can end up in an impasse due to the iterative nature of the path creation, as we will see in Sections 4.6.2 and 4.6.3. Therefore, secondly and more importantly, the escape paths are to be actively used by Nue after reaching an unsolvable impasse for a destination node, see Section 4.6.2.

4.3 Choosing Root Node for the Spanning Tree

Nue routing is using escape paths when encountering an impasse, illustrated in Section 4.6.2. Therefore, Nue should ensure that the paths in S are as short as possible. This will reduce latency and oversubscription of individual channels.

Assuming $N_i^d \subset N$, then an observation is, that the number of initial channel dependencies derived from the escape paths depends on the location of the root node as well. To illustrate this property, we use our previously investigated 5-node ring with shortcut, see Fig. 2a. If n_5 is chosen as root node, since it allows for the shortest average path length in the spanning tree, then the escape paths for $N_i^d = \{n_1, n_2, n_3\}$, as specified in Definition 7, induce five initial channel dependencies. However, if $n_r = n_2$ is chosen instead, then we only have four initial channel dependencies, as shown in Fig. 5.

As a consequence, we propose to use a root node which is the most central with respect to the subset $N_i^d \subset N$ to reduce the initial channel dependencies within virtual layer L_i. Freeman et al. [12] introduced the metric of betweenness centrality, which is ideal for our purpose to determine the root node for the spanning tree. If we assume a graph $G(N, C)$, then the betweenness centrality $C_B(n)$ for a node $n \in N$ is defined via the absolute number of shortest paths between the two nodes s and t, called σ_{st}, and the number of shortest paths $\sigma_{st}(n)$ which include node n, i.e.,

$$C_B(n) := \sum_{s \neq n \neq t \in N} \frac{\sigma_{st}(n)}{\sigma_{st}}$$

Brandes et al. [2] developed an algorithm to compute the betweenness centrality of every node in the graph. The algorithm for unweighted graphs has a $\mathcal{O}(|N| \cdot |C|)$ time complexity. Unfortunately, the algorithm is not directly applicable to our problem, since we are seeking the most central node with respect to the subset $N_i^d \subset N$ to reduce the initial channel dependencies of the escape paths towards nodes of N_i^d. To adapt our problem, we calculate the convex subgraph for the node set N_i^d, and apply Brandes' algorithm on the convex subgraph.

Definition 8 (Convex Subgraph). *The **convex subgraph** $H_i := G(N_i^H, C_i^H)$ for a set N_i^d includes all nodes of N_i^d as well as some nodes of $N \setminus N_i^d$, which are intermediate nodes of the shortest paths ${}^sP_{\cdot, \cdot}$ between nodes of N_i^d. Therefore, $N_i^H := \{n \in N \mid \forall n_x, n_y \in N_i^d : n = n_x \lor (\cdot, n) \in {}^sP_{n_x, n_y}\}$ and the edge set C_i^H of the convex subgraph is defined analogously.*

The fact that our networks are represented by an unweighted graph allows us to compute the convex subgraph with a time complexity of $\mathcal{O}(|N_i^d| \cdot (|N| + |C|))$ with a breadth-first search (forward step) and an inverse traversal of the graph to find all shortest paths (backward step).

After we compute the convex subgraph H_i, Brandes' algorithm is executed on H_i instead of I to find $n_{r,i} \in N_i^H$ which maximizes the betweenness centrality $C_B(n)$ w.r.t. N_i^d. This node will be used as the root node of the spanning tree for the escape paths from all nodes towards the destination nodes in N_i^d. As a remark, for $k = 1$ Nue assigns all destination nodes N_i^d to one virtual layer, i.e., it follows that $H_1 = I$ and Brandes' algorithm can be executed directly on I.

4.4 Dijkstra's Algorithm for the complete CDG

Domke et al. [7, 8] and Hoefler et al. [17] showed the effectiveness, in terms of balancing the paths across the available channels, of a routing algorithm based on Dijkstra's single-source shortest-path algorithm. Their modified Dijkstra algorithm, using a Fibonacci heap to lower the time complexity and extended to work on multigraphs, is combined

Algorithm 1: Dijkstra's Algorithm within $\overline{D}$

Input: $I = G(N,C)$, $\overline{D} = G(C, \overline{E})$, source $n_0 \in N$
Result: P_{n_y, n_0} for all $n_y \in N$ (and $\overline{D}$ is cycle-free)

1 **foreach** *node* $n \in N$ **do**
2    $n.\text{distance} \leftarrow \infty$
3    $n.\text{usedChannel} \leftarrow \emptyset$
4 **foreach** *channel* $c \in C$ **do**
5    $c.\text{distance} \leftarrow \infty$
   /* Need source channel c_0 to start Dijkstra's algorithm: if n_0 is terminal then use unique $(n_0, \cdot)$; if n_0 is switch then $\overline{D}$ has multiple $(n_0, \cdot) \Rightarrow (\emptyset, n_0)$ connects to all */
6 **if** n_0 *is switch* **then** $c_0 \leftarrow (\emptyset, n_0)$ **else** $c_0 \leftarrow (n_0, \cdot)$
7 $n_0.\text{distance} \leftarrow 0$
8 $c_0.\text{distance} \leftarrow 0$
9 FibonacciHeap $Q \leftarrow \{c_0\}$
10 **while** $Q \neq \emptyset$ **do**
11    $c_p \leftarrow Q.\text{findMin}()$
12   **foreach** $(c_p, c_q) \in \overline{E}$ *with* $(c_p, c_q).\text{state} \neq \text{blocked}$ **do**
     // Let $n_{c_q} \in N$ be the tail of directed channel c_q
13   **if** $c_p.\text{distance} + c_q.\text{weight} < n_{c_q}.\text{distance}$ **then**
14        $(c_p, c_q).\text{state} \leftarrow \text{used}$ // modifies $\overline{D}$
15   **if** $\overline{D}$ *is cycle-free (see Algorithm 3)* **then**
16   **if** $n_{c_q}.\text{usedChannel} \neq \emptyset$ **then**
17            $Q.\text{remove}(n_{c_q}.\text{usedChannel})$
18          $Q.\text{add}(c_q)$
19          $c_q.\text{distance} \leftarrow c_p.\text{distance} + c_q.\text{weight}$
20          $n_{c_q}.\text{distance} \leftarrow c_p.\text{distance} + c_q.\text{weight}$
21          $n_{c_q}.\text{usedChannel} \leftarrow c_q$
22   **else**
23          $(c_p, c_q).\text{state} \leftarrow \text{blocked}$
   // Optimizations are explained in Sections 4.6.2/4.6.3
24 **if** n_0 *is switch* **then**
25   remove fake channel c_0 from $\overline{D}$ and $(c_0, (n_0, \cdot))$ from $\overline{E}$

Algorithm 2: Nue routing calculates all paths within a network I for a given number of virtual channels $k \geq 1$

Input: $I = G(N,C)$, $k \in \mathbb{N}$
Result: Path P_{n_x, n_y} for all $n_x, n_y \in N$

1 Partition N into k disjoint subsets $N_1^d, \ldots, N_k^d$ of destinations
2 **foreach** *Virtual layer* L_i *with* $i \in \{1, \ldots, k\}$ **do**
   // Check attached comments for details about each step
3   Select a subset of nodes $N_i^d \subseteq N$ for virtual layer L_i
4   Create a convex subgraph H_i for N_i^d // Section 4.3
5   Identify central $n_{r,i} \in N_i^H$ of H_i // Section 4.3
6   Create a new complete CDG $\overline{D}_i$ // Section 4.1
7   Define escape paths D_i^s for root $n_{r,i}$ // Section 4.2
8   **foreach** *Node* $n \in N_i^d$ **do**
9   Identify deadlock-free paths $P_{\cdot, n}$ // Section 4.4
10   Store these paths, e.g., in forwarding tables
11   Update channel weights in $\overline{D}_i$ for these paths

---

with positive weight updates for the used channels after all paths to one destination node are computed.

We use a similar approach, but within the complete CDG $\overline{D}$ or $\overline{D}_i$, respectively. For convenience, we describe Algorithm 1 for $\overline{D}$ only, but it can easily be extended for $\overline{D}_i$. Algorithm 1 computes shortest paths from one source node $n_0 \in N$ to all other nodes in the complete CDG while complying to the cycle-free constraint. Meaning, these paths are not necessarily shortest paths w.r.t. the actual network I. Following the paths in opposite direction along the used channels, i.e., nodes of $\overline{D}$, results in the paths for the destination-based routing. Nue routing initializes and updates the channel weights similar to DFSSSP [8]. However, the fact that channels are the vertices of $\overline{D}$ changes the computation, see line 13, and weights are stored at the adjacent channel instead of the edge between two channels. The advantage of our approach is that channel dependencies are directly considered, see line 15, and routing restrictions can be identified instantaneously, as outlined in Section 3. Therefore, paths do not have to be recomputed to avoid the routing restriction afterwards, as it is the case with smart routing [3], for example.

4.5 Nue Routing Function

Combining the knowledge of Section 4.1–4.4 into one routing function, see Algorithm 2, allows us to achieve our objectives, i.e., to be able to balance the paths globally while not exceeding a given number of VCs, $k \geq 1$, used for deadlock-freedom. In the first step, Nue routing partitions the nodes of the network I into k disjoint subsets, $N_1^d, \ldots, N_k^d$. Each subset N_i^d will denote a set of destinations for calculated paths, i.e., $P_{\cdot, n}$ for $n \in N_i^d$, within virtual layer L_i. While the exact partitioning of N will not influence whether Nue can

calculate deadlock-free routes for I or not, the partitioning affects the path balancing. Nue routing uses a multilevel k-way partitioning algorithm [19] with $\mathcal{O}(|C|)$ time complexity to partition the network I. Moreover, we implemented a random partitioning and partial clustering, i.e., all terminals connected to a switch are assigned to the same partition. However, Nue with the multilevel k-way partitioning outperformed the other two partitioning algorithms w.r.t. the evaluations carried out in Section 5. An optimal partitioning algorithm, i.e., a partitioning which results in a maximized path balancing and which minimizes the edge forwarding indices for the switches, is beyond the scope of this paper and requires further research. For future versions of Nue, we envision improved (optimal) partitioning algorithms that result in an even better path balancing.

The node set N_i^d is used to calculate a convex subgraph H_i. Brandes' algorithm is executed on H_i to determine the betweenness centrality for each node of H_i ensuring the selection of an appropriate root node $n_{r,i}$ for the escape paths, see Section 4.3 for more details. After creating a complete CDG $\overline{D}_i$ for virtual layer L_i, which complies to Definition 6, Nue routing determines the escape paths D_i^s. The acyclic escape paths are derived from a spanning tree rooted at $n_{r,i}$ according to Definition 7, i.e., the channels C_i^s and edges E_i^s are changed into the *used* state. This completes the initialization phase of the complete CDG $\overline{D}_i$ to perform the graph search algorithm within $\overline{D}_i$ with our modified Dijkstra algorithm, see Algorithm 1. Each node of N_i^d is used as a source for Algorithm 1. The subsequent weight update for the used channels aims for an improved global balancing of the paths.

4.6 Optimizations for Nue Routing

4.6.1 Numbering of Subgraphs and Cycle Search

Algorithm 1 has an $\mathcal{O}(|C_i| \cdot \log |C_i| + |\overline{E}_i|)$ time complexity, if applied on virtual layer L_i, and if the search for cycles in $\overline{D}_i$ is omitted. However, Algorithm 1 potentially needs to check $\overline{D}_i$ for cycles every time the state of an edge $(c_p, c_q) = e \in \overline{E}_i$ changes, see line 15. The time complexity of each full cycle search in $\overline{D}_i = G(C_i, \overline{E}_i)$ is $\mathcal{O}(|C_i| + |\overline{E}_i|)$.

If we can distinguish between vertex-disjoint, *used* subgraphs of $\overline{D}_i$, induced by a routing R as explained in Section 4.1, then it is possible to avoid a cycle search by applying memorization, since connecting two disjoint, acyclic, and *used* subgraphs with an *used* edge creates a new acyclic subgraph. Therefore, we incorporate an identification number ω for *used* and cycle-free subgraphs of $\overline{D}_i$, which is an extension of the three states we utilized before, see Section 4.1. The function $\omega : C_i \cup \overline{E}_i \to \mathbb{Z}_0^+ \cup \{-1\}$, with

$$\omega(x) = \begin{cases} -1 & \text{if } D_i \cup x \text{ form cycle in } \overline{D}_i, \text{ i.e., } x \text{ is } \textit{blocked}, \\ 0 & \text{if } x \notin D_i \wedge x \notin D_i^s, \text{ i.e., } x \text{ is } \textit{unused}, \\ \geq 1 & \text{if } x \text{ is in the } \textit{used} \text{ state} \end{cases}$$

is used to identify the vertex-disjoint, cycle-free subgraphs and *blocked* edges, i.e., $\omega(e) = -1$. An example is shown in Fig. 6a with $\omega = 1$ pointing to the escape paths of the complete CDG $\overline{D}$, i.e., $\omega(C^s \cup E^s) = 1$ for $D^s = G(C^s, E^s)$ assuming $k = 1$.

The advantage of this is to identify conditions during the routing with Dijkstra's algorithm where a cycle search is needed or can be omitted. Hence, at node $c_p \in C$ of the complete CDG with assigned $\omega(c_p) \geq 1$ and adjacent node $c_q \in C$, with $(c_p, c_q) =: e \in \overline{E}$, there are four possible conditions and three of them do not require a cycle search:

(a) $\omega(e) = -1 \implies$ no cycle search needed, because the result is known already (these edges are ignored by the conditional loop in line 12 of Algorithm 1);

(b) $\omega(e) \geq 1 \implies \omega(c_p) = \omega(c_q) = \omega(e) \implies$ no cycle search needed, because e was used before and is therefore part of an acyclic subgraph;

(c) $\omega(e) = 0 \wedge \omega(c_p) \neq \omega(c_q) \implies$ no cycle search needed, because directed edge e connects two disjoint acyclic subgraphs and therefore cannot close a cycle;

(d) $\omega(e) = 0 \wedge \omega(c_p) = \omega(c_q) \implies$ cycle search is needed, because e adds an used edge in an acyclic subgraph and might induce a cycle.

Algorithm 3 shows the handling of these conditions, inclusive the performed cycle search with a depth-first search (DFS). For simplicity, the algorithm shows the procedure for $\overline{D}$, i.e., $k = 1$. The depth-first search is only performed within a selected subgraph of $\overline{D}$ identified by $\omega(c_p)$. Since this subgraph is acyclic without (c_p, c_q), this edge must be part of a new cycle if it exists. Therefore, one depth-first search starting from c_q and searching for c_p is sufficient. Hence, Nue potentially omits to traverse parts of the subgraph, which leads to a more efficient algorithm.

We will illustrate the conditions (b) to (d) with our previously investigated example of the ring topology with shortcut for $k = 1$. Initially, we assign $\omega = 1$ to the escape paths identifying one cycle-free subgraph. Assume, we start the first routing step with Algorithm 1 at node c_{n_1,n_2} and assign $\omega(c_{n_1,n_2}) = 2$ to it, which will identify the second *used* and cycle-free subgraph of $\overline{D}$, as shown in Fig. 6a. Node c_{n_1,n_2} has only one adjacent node c_{n_2,n_3} available via an *unused* directed edge. Since $\omega(c_{n_1,n_2}) \neq \omega(c_{n_2,n_3})$ we can omit a cycle search, see condition (c). According to lines five to eight of Algorithm 3, both subgraphs, with $\omega = 1$ and $\omega = 2$, are merged into one acyclic subgraph with $\omega = 2$. Now, the adjacent nodes of c_{n_2,n_3} are c_{n_3,n_5} and c_{n_3,n_4} whereby the conditions (b) and (c) apply, respectively. Assuming, Algorithm 1 considers node c_{n_3,n_4} next, then the only available adjacent node is c_{n_4,n_5}, which results in condition (d), where a depth-first search is needed. A DFS from c_{n_4,n_5} for node c_{n_3,n_4} checks a total of three nodes, i.e., c_{n_5,n_1}, c_{n_5,n_3}, and c_{n_3,n_2}. Since the starting node is not found, it is possible to use $(c_{n_3,n_4}, c_{n_4,n_5})$ without closing a cycle. The intermediate state of $\overline{D}$ during Algorithm 1, after these steps have been performed, is shown in Fig. 6b.

Algorithm 3: Search for cyclic *used* subgraphs in $\overline{D}$

Input: $\overline{D} = G(C, \overline{E})$, channels $c_p, c_q \in C$
Result: true if a cycle was found; **false** otherwise

```
1  if ω(c_p, c_q) = −1 then
2   |   return true                    // State described in condition (a)
3  else if ω(c_p, c_q) ≥ 1 then
4   |   return false                   // State described in condition (b)
5  else if ω(c_p) ≠ ω(c_q) then
        /* Merge two disjoint subgraphs                         */
6   |   if ω(c_q) = 0 then ω(q) ← ω(c_p) and return false
7   |   foreach x ∈ C ∪ E̅, with ω(x) = ω(c_q) do
8   |    |   ω(x) ← ω(c_p)
9   |   return false                   // State described in condition (c)
10 else
        /* Perform depth-first search for c_p in subgraph G with
           ω(G) = ω(c_p) starting from c_q, see condition (d)   */
11  |   if the D̅.DFS(c_q, ω(c_p)) does not find c_p then
12  |    |   ω(c_p, c_q) ← ω(c_p)
13  |    |   foreach x ∈ C ∪ E̅, with ω(x) = ω(c_q) ≠ 0 do
14  |    |    |   ω(x) ← ω(c_p)
15  |    |   ω(c_q) ← ω(c_p)
16  |    |   return false
17  |   else
18  |    |   ω(c_p, c_q) ← −1
19  |    |   return true
```

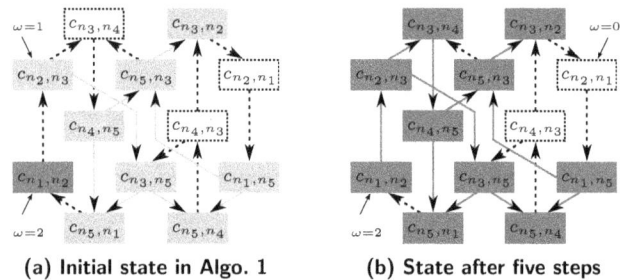

(a) Initial state in Algo. 1   **(b) State after five steps**

Figure 6: State change of $\overline{D}$ after five steps with Algorithm 1, starting from c_{n_1,n_2}; Fig. 6a: initial state (line 14) before the while loop is executed; Fig. 6b: state of $\overline{D}$ after five iterations of the loop

4.6.2 Solving Impasses for Isolated Nodes/Clusters

The approach of either randomly removing channel dependencies, as explained in Section 4.2 and mentioned by Cherkasova et al. [3], can lead to impasses during an iterative routing algorithm. Incrementally calculating routes and placing routing restrictions on-demand, as we do, can lead to similar impasses. Meaning, creating isolated parts of the network, we call them *islands*, where no path can be assigned to without creating a cycle in the CDG, based on previously calculated routes for other destinations. Even the escape paths, as introduced in Section 4.2, for our iterative, destination-based routing function cannot prevent impasses.

To illustrate the problem, we consider a large network I, with a small subnetwork I^* connected as a binary tree, as shown in Fig. 7a, and $k = 1$. The subgraph of the complete CDG $\overline{D}$ for the relevant parts of the network, i.e., for I^*, is shown in Fig. 7b. Assume, our iterative algorithm has calculated all routes for $i - 1$ destinations and is at an intermediate step to calculate the routes towards the ith destination. Therefore, parts of $\overline{D}$ will have $\omega = i$ assigned to it, i.e., $\omega = 1$ for the escape paths plus $i - 1$ destinations. Algorithm 1 reaches n_3 and n_5 on the shortest path via the channels c_{n_1,n_3} and c_{n_7,n_5}, respectively. Due to previous routing decisions, the channel dependencies $(c_{n_1,n_3}, c_{n_3,n_4})$

8

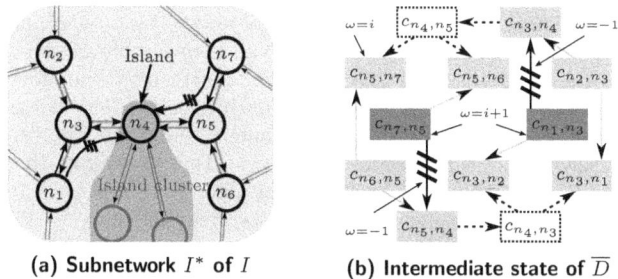

(a) Subnetwork I^* of I (b) Intermediate state of $\overline{D}$

Figure 7: Impasse of Algorithm 1 to reach n_4 based on previously placed routing restrictions for channels dependencies $(c_{n_1,n_3}, c_{n_3,n_4})$ and $(c_{n_7,n_5}, c_{n_5,n_4})$, which are shown as crossed out edges in I^* and $\overline{D}$

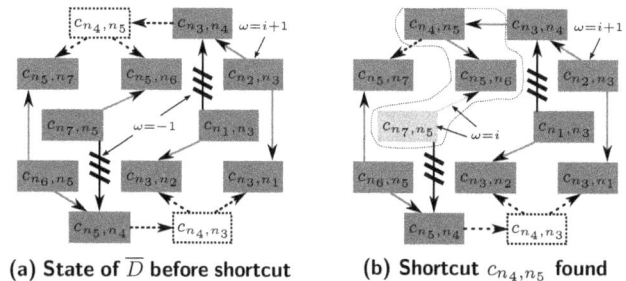

(a) State of $\overline{D}$ before shortcut   (b) Shortcut c_{n_4,n_5} found

Figure 8: The states of the channel dependency graph $\overline{D}$, of the subnetwork I^* of Fig. 7a are shown; Fig. 8a shows the state after solving the island problem for n_4; Fig. 8b highlights the change to $\overline{D}$ when n_4 is used as a shortcut to reach n_5

and $(c_{n_7,n_5}, c_{n_5,n_4})$ are in the *blocked* state, as illustrated by the crossed out edges. Hence, the routing algorithm reached an impasse and cannot calculate valid routes for node n_4.

There are multiple options to solve the impasse, we will list three of them in the following. The easiest among them is to simply fall back to the escape paths for the entire routing step, i.e., all routes to one specific destination node will use the escape paths instead of the paths calculated by Algorithm 1. Remember, falling back to the escape path for only a subset of the paths to one destination can violate the destination-based property of Nue. The first option is the least preferred, because impasses happen regularly, hence the escape paths will be overloaded with routes.

Another option is a backtracking algorithm starting from the current intermediate state of Nue routing and revert previous decisions about chosen paths. However, this means that potentially all previous chosen (partial) paths to the current destination have to be changed, due to the channel dependencies. This results in a brute-force algorithm, because the algorithm has no knowledge which "wrong decision" in the beginning leads to the impasse. The method would guarantee a solution, since at least one valid solution, i.e., the escape paths, exists, but it greatly increases the runtime.

We propose to use a local backtracking algorithm, as the third option, whereby we check only the surrounding nodes of distance of 2 hops for alternative routes to the island. This can be accomplished both time- and memory-efficient[3]. If no alternative path can be found, which happens less frequent, then Nue falls back to the escape paths as described in the first option. So, instead of having Algorithm 1 to overwrite the used channel, see line 21, we store the used channels in a stack. Hence, the stack[4] of valid alternatives, potentially using a longer path, to reach a certain node are stored and is accessible in a backtracking step. Continuing the example from Fig. 7: If Algorithm 1 reaches the impasse at node n_4, then it checks the stack of alternative routes to the nodes n_3 and n_5, and determines whether or not these can be used to reach n_4. For example, an alternative path to n_3, stored in the stack, is to use channel c_{n_2,n_3}. As Fig. 7b illustrates (upper right corner), the channels c_{n_2,n_3} and c_{n_3,n_4}, and the edge between them, already belong to the same acyclic subgraph identified by $\omega = i$. Therefore, using the channel dependency $(c_{n_2,n_3}, c_{n_3,n_4})$ is a valid al-

ternative for our modified Dijkstra algorithm to reach n_4. If multiple valid alternatives exist, then Nue selects the shortest among them—w.r.t. the weight/distance parameters of the channels. After a valid alternative is found for one island node, Algorithm 1 continues to operate as before to ensure that paths into clusters of island nodes are calculated.

4.6.3 Using Formerly Isolated Nodes as Shortcut

In the previous section, we explained how to use a local backtracking to solve routing impasses and how to find paths into island nodes/clusters. Furthermore, these island nodes can be used to shorten the distance to previously discovered nodes. For instance, assume, Algorithm 1 reaches an impasse for the network presented in Fig. 7a and the algorithm cannot find a path to node n_4, as described in Section 4.6.2. However, the nodes n_3 and n_5 have already been discovered and have a certain distance from the source node of the current routing step performed with Algorithm 1. Assume, the distance of node n_3 from the current source node is six hops and the distance of n_5 is nine hops when Algorithm 1 reaches the impasse. The local backtracking algorithm, see Section 4.6.2, enables a valid path to n_4 via n_3. Node n_4 can now be used as a potential "shortcut" to reach node n_5, which shortens the distance of n_5 to eight hops.

However, to make use of shortcuts during the routing within the complete CDG, existing channel dependencies have to be considered. While, in theory, it would be possible to invalidate decisions and dependencies for paths which use n_5 as an intermediate node, it will increase the runtime of the routing algorithm. Since the channel dependencies are built incrementally by Algorithm 1, changing an intermediate dependency (c_p, c_q) potentially invalidates all existing dependencies $(c_q, \cdot)$, as well as subsequent dependencies. To avoid the recalculation of paths, we incorporate the following optimization into Nue: Using islands as shortcuts is only allowed if existing local channel dependencies can be kept in place. This avoids the need to reconsider subsequent dependencies.

We exemplify this algorithm[5] by using the example network of Fig. 7a. Assume, after the impasse of Algorithm 1 and the solution for a path to the island node $n_4 = n_{c_q}$, the current state of $\overline{D}$ is shown in Fig. 8. So, we first have to check whether n_4 can be used as a shortcut to reach n_5 or not, i.e., we must verify that changing the channel dependency $(c_{n_3,n_4}, c_{n_4,n_5})$ into the *used* state does not induce a cycle in $\overline{D}$. Assume further, that n_7 and n_5 were used as

---

[3]The detailed algorithms for the optimizations explained in Sections 4.6.2 and 4.6.3 are not needed to understand the underlaying concept, and are therefore omitted.

[4]For simplicity, the handling of the stack in Algorithm 1 is omitted.

[5]See footnote 3.

intermediate nodes to reach n_6 and subsequent nodes, not shown in Fig. 7a. Therefore, the usedChannel variable of n_6 is set to (n_5, n_6) and the channel dependency $(c_{n_7,n_5}, c_{n_5,n_6})$ is in the *used* state. Our shortcut algorithm determines all dependent channels of n_5, i.e., all channels dependencies $(c_{\cdot,n_5}, c_{n_5,\cdot})$ calculated in the current routing step. Afterwards, the algorithm checks for all dependent channels $(n_5, \cdot)$ whether changing the dependency $(c_{n_4,n_5}, c_{n_5,\cdot})$ via the previous island induces a cycle or not. If no cycle is induced in $\overline{D}$, then n_4 is a valid shortcut for n_5 and any subsequent path decisions. The usedChannel variable for n_5 can be changed to c_{n_4,n_5}, and previous changes to ω of c_{n_7,n_5} and $(c_{n_7,n_5}, c_{n_5,n_6})$ can be reversed.

4.7 Correctness, Completeness & Complexity

In the following, we prove that Nue routing is destination-based and cycle-free, see Definition 3, and we prove Nue's deadlock-freedom. Meaning, the CDG D induced by the calculated paths is acyclic, independently of the underlying network or the predefined number of available VCs. Afterwards, we summarize Nue's time and memory complexity.

Lemma 1. *Nue routing is destination-based and cycle-free.*

Proof. Assume, Nue is not destination-based, and therefore the next channel c_{q+1} at a certain node is not unique for one destination. Algorithm 1 calculates the paths P_{n_y,n_x} for a source node n_x and all other nodes in the network in the opposite direction of the spanning tree created by the modified Dijkstra algorithm, i.e., that the paths follow the usedChannel variable towards the source node. The fact that the algorithm either assigns $\emptyset$ to usedChannel, see line 3, or one specific channel for each node, see line 21, contradicts our assumption. Hence, Nue routing is destination-based. The fact that Nue is cycle-free follows directly from the fact that Nue is destination-based and the use of positive channel weights: Let P_{n_u,n_v} be a cyclic path, then either n_v is part of the cycle or not. The former case implies that n_v has a usedChannel $\neq \emptyset$ assigned to it by Algorithm 1, i.e., $\exists c_p, c_q \in C : c_p.\text{distance} + c_q.\text{weight} < 0 = n_v.\text{distance}$. This is only possible when weights are negative, which contradicts the fact, that initial weights are positive and weight updates of channels are positive as well. In the later case, that n_v is not part of the cycle, at least one channel $(\cdot, n_w)$ of the path has to contradict the destination-based property of Nue routing. Hence, Nue routing is cycle-free. $\square$

Lemma 2. *Nue routing is deadlock-free.*

Proof. According to Theorem 1, the routing function is deadlock-free iff the corresponding CDG is acyclic. For each virtual layer, Nue creates a new complete CDG $\overline{D}_i$ and changes the states of the channels and channel dependencies of the escape paths to the *used* state. Since the escape paths are derived from a spanning tree, no cycle is induced in $\overline{D}_i$ after adding the escape paths. The cycle checks, see Algorithm 1 line 15, and Sections 4.6.2 and 4.6.3, before any of the usedChannel variables are changed, are preventing Nue from creating a cycle in the acyclic $\overline{D}_i$. As a result, the complete CDG $\overline{D}_i$ for virtual layer L_i, for all $1 \leq i \leq k$, is cycle-free, see Definition 6, and Theorem 1 is applicable. $\square$

Lemma 3. *The Nue routing function ensures connectivity between any pair of two nodes $n_u, n_v \in N$ in the interconnection network $I = G(N, C)$, i.e., $P_{n_u,n_v} \neq \emptyset$.*

Proof. Assume, there exists a pair of nodes, $n_u, n_v \in N$, for which the path $P_{n_u,n_v} = \emptyset$, i.e., Nue is incapable of calculating the path under the given VC constraint. Therefore, either the network I is disconnected, which contradicts Definition 1, or the variable $n_u.\text{usedChannel} = \emptyset$ and the modified Dijkstra algorithm reaches an impasse. Due to the fact that $P_{n_u,n_v} = \emptyset$, the local backtracking algorithm falls back to the escape paths, see Section 4.6.2. Meaning, if $n_v \in N_i^d$, then from Definition 7 it follows that for every $n_w \in N$ there exists a $(n_w, \cdot) \in C_i^s$ with $R^s((n_w, \cdot), n_v) \in C^s$, i.e., a path $P_{n_u,n_v} = \{(n_u, \cdot), \dots, (\cdot, n_v)\}$ exists using only channels in C_i^s. This contradicts the initial assumption $P_{n_u,n_v} = \emptyset$, hence Nue routing ensures full connectivity. $\square$

Most terms of the below shown Proposition 1 follow directly from the explanations in previous Sections 4.1–4.6. Therefore, we will focus the following explanations on the most complex and most time consuming term $\mathcal{O}(\dots)_{\text{Routing}}$, i.e., Algorithm 1 of our Nue routing.

For the complexity analysis, let Δ denote the maximum degree of the interconnection network $I = G(N, C)$, then it follows that $|C| \leq \Delta \cdot |N|$ and $|\overline{E}| \leq \Delta \cdot |C| \leq \Delta^2 \cdot |N|$. The time complexity, excluding the acyclicity check, for our modified Dijkstra algorithm, as presented in Algorithm 1, is $\mathcal{O}(|C_i| \cdot \log |C_i| + |\overline{E}_i|)$ when executed on a complete CDG $\overline{D}_i$. A heap with $\mathcal{O}(1)$ time complexity for the "decrease-key" operation is needed to achieve this complexity. The optimization, see Section 4.6.1 and conditions (a)–(d), results in a differentiated time complexity for the acyclicity check of $\overline{D}_i$, see line 15 of Algorithm 1. In the best case, i.e., condition (a) or (b) are applied, the time complexity is $\mathcal{O}(1)$. The same applies to the "merge" of the two acyclic subgraphs assuming that $\omega(c_q)$ is zero, see line 6 of Algorithm 3. An actual merge, see lines 7 and 8, of two vertex-disjoint and acyclic subgraphs with varying identification numbers can only be performed $|N|$ times throughout the execution of Nue routing. Hence, the time complexity of all merge steps is at most $\mathcal{O}(|N| \cdot (|C_i| + |\overline{E}_i|))$. The time complexity for any depth-first search within a subgraph of $\overline{D}_i$ is $\mathcal{O}(|C_i| + |\overline{E}_i|)$. However, the DFS has to be executed at most once per edge $e \in \overline{E}_i$ and per virtual layer L_i, because afterwards the state of e is either *used* or *blocked*, and condition (d) cannot be applied again.

Proposition 1. *The time complexity of Nue routing for a given interconnection network I, with a fixed maximum switch radix Δ, with $\Delta \in \mathbb{N}$, and a fixed number of supported virtual channels k, with $k \in \mathbb{N}$, is*

$$\mathcal{O}(|C|)_{Partitioning} + k \cdot \mathcal{O}(\Delta|C_i|)_{Build\ complete\ CDG} +$$
$$k \cdot \mathcal{O}(\Delta|N|^2)_{Convex\ H_i} + k \cdot \mathcal{O}(|N|\log|N| + |C|)_{Spanning\ Tree} +$$
$$\mathcal{O}(|N|(|C_i|\log|C_i| + |C_i| + |\overline{E}_i|) + k|\overline{E}_i|(|C_i| + |\overline{E}_i|))_{Routing} +$$
$$\mathcal{O}(|N|^2)_{Forwarding\ Tables} + \mathcal{O}(|N|^2)_{Weight\ Updates}$$
$$= \mathcal{O}(|N|^2(\Delta\log(\Delta|N|) + k\Delta^4)) = \mathcal{O}(|N|^2 \cdot \log|N|)$$

while its memory complexity (including storing the result) is

$$\mathcal{O}(|N| + \Delta \cdot |N| + \Delta^2 \cdot |N| + |N|^2) = \mathcal{O}(|N|^2)$$

assuming that the number of channels of I can be approximated by $\Delta \cdot |N|$ and assuming that $|\overline{E}_i| \leq \Delta^2 \cdot |N|$.

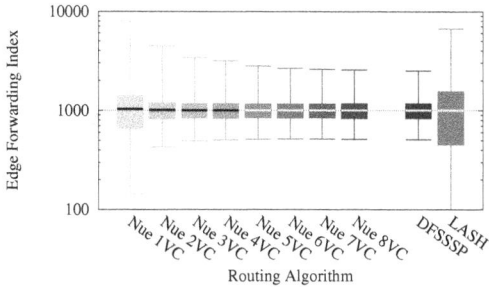

Figure 9: Averaged edge forwarding index metrics: minimum Γ^r_{min} and maximum Γ^r_{max} for the whiskers, and average Γ^r_{avg} ($\pm$ standard deviation Γ^r_{SD}) for the box; for 1,000 random topologies with 125 switches, 1,000 terminals and 1,000 switch-to-switch channels

5. EVALUATION OF NUE ROUTING

We apply Nue to the InfiniBand network technology. We use a publicly available simulation toolchain [7], based on InfiniBand tools and a flit-level simulator written with the OMNeT++ framework. We create different topologies and route these with multiple routing algorithms which are implemented in the production-quality InfiniBand network manager OpenSM version 3.3.16 [25]. The simulator estimates the communication throughput of an all-to-all traffic pattern. Most of the routing algorithms either omit the calculation of switch-to-switch paths entirely, e.g., fat tree routing [33] or Up*/Down* routing [29], or ignore these paths during the DL-avoidance calculation phase, e.g., DFSSSP, since switch-to-switch paths are only used for management messages and not data messages. Therefore, for a fair comparison, we exclude switches from the set of destination nodes for Nue routing while performing the following evaluations.

5.1 Path Length and Edge Forwarding Index

Nue routing does not always create routes along the shortest-paths, depending on the available number of VCs and whether the escape path is used or not. However, non-minimal routes increase latency and may cause higher network congestion. We first analyze the path length of routes created by Nue and compare them to shortest-path algorithms. Additionally, we investigate the edge forwarding index γ for inter-switch ports in the network [15]. This metric allows us to analyze and compare the quality of the routing function in terms of path balancing. A high minimum γ and low maximum γ are indicators for a well balanced routing algorithm.

To evaluate both metrics, we create 1,000 random topologies. Each topology consists of 125 switches interconnected by 1,000 channels, and eight terminals connected to each switch. We apply our Nue routing, with $1 \leq k \leq 8$ virtual channels, as well as LASH and DFSSSP routing, to create DL-free forwarding tables. We collect the following metrics for each topology/routing combination: minimum, maximum, and average edge forwarding index and the standard deviation, i.e., $\gamma^{t,r}_{min}$, $\gamma^{t,r}_{max}$, $\gamma^{t,r}_{avg}$, and $\gamma^{t,r}_{SD}$ for topology t and routing r. These metrics are then arithmetically averaged for all 1,000 topologies: $\Gamma^r_{min} = \frac{\sum^{1,000}_{t=1} \gamma^{t,r}_{min}}{1,000}$ and so forth.

Fig. 9 shows the result as box plots, with whiskers indicating Γ^r_{min} and Γ^r_{max}, and with the box indicating the average Γ^r_{avg} and $\Gamma^r_{avg} \pm \Gamma^r_{SD}$. As we can see, Nue routing performs almost similar to DFSSSP, for $k \geq 4$. It is worth

mentioning, that DFSSSP needs at least four VCs to calculate DL-free routes for these topologies, or five VCs in some exceptional cases. LASH's VCs requirement is lower compared to DFSSSP and ranges between two and four. However both, Nue and DFSSSP, clearly outperform LASH w.r.t. the edge forwarding index metric. Even so Fig. 9 indicates that DFSSSP slightly outperforms Nue, we have to keep in mind that Nue routing is designed for arbitrary topologies and supports every given number of VCs. Therefore, Nue will be able to calculate DL-free paths even if we scale up the size of the topologies, while the other routings, such as DFSSSP, will fail due to VC limitations, as we will see in Section 5.3.

The increased γ for $k < 4$ has two reasons: one is the concentration of paths on certain channels to bypass routing restrictions, and the other are longer paths due to the use of the escape paths or parts of them. It is clear that a longer path changes γ for more ports in the network. For all 1,000 random topologies, we measured the maximum path length in the network. For the best case, Nue routing needs only two VCs to support the same maximum path length as the shortest-path algorithms DFSSSP and LASH. On average, Nue routing achieves the same maximum path length—arithmetic average of 5.3—as DFSSSP, if Nue distributes the paths among at least seven virtual layers. The worst case length of the longest path for Nue is 7–10, depending on the given number of VCs, while it is 6 for DFSSSP/LASH.

The number of fall backs to escape paths depends on many factors, such as topology type, size, number of VCs, and the chosen root node for the spanning tree. For our random topologies with no additional VCs, Nue did fall back for 0%–9.7% of the destinations, with an average of 0.95% across all 1,000 simulations for this case. For 8 VCs this average is below 0.006%. A general prediction of the number of times Nue uses the escape paths is beyond the scope of this paper.

5.2 Throughput for (Ir-)regular Topologies

Additionally to the random topologies from Section 5.1, we use the simulation toolchain to measure the throughput for four standard topologies (i.e., fat tree, torus, Kautz graph [23], Dragonfly [20]) and two real-world topologies, namely Cray's Cascade [9] and Tsubame2.5's fat tree [14] (2nd rail; connecting 1,407 compute node). For the Cascade topology, we configured 192 global channels to connect the two Cascade electrical groups. An arbitrary random topology has been chosen among the 1,000 created random topologies for this throughput measurement. All topologies accommodate roughly 1,000 terminals[6] to allow comparison between topologies as well. Each switch is connected to at least one terminal for all topologies, except for the two fat tree topologies. Detailed topology configurations, utilizing 36-port switches (exception: 48 ports for Cascade), are given in Tab. 1. We assume QDR InfiniBand and a limit of eight VCs for the simulations. The redundancy r listed in Tab. 1 refers to a multiplication of switch-to-switch channels w.r.t. the usual topology definition to increase the port usage.

The flit-level simulator performs an all-to-all send operation with 2 KiB message size between all terminals of the network. An exchange pattern of varying shift distances[7] is used at each terminal to communicate with all other ter-

---

[6] High memory consumption for the detailed/accurate flit-level simulations prevents us from analysing much larger topologies.

[7] Simulating uniform random injection traffic yields similar behaviour of Nue, and showing these results will not provide further insight.

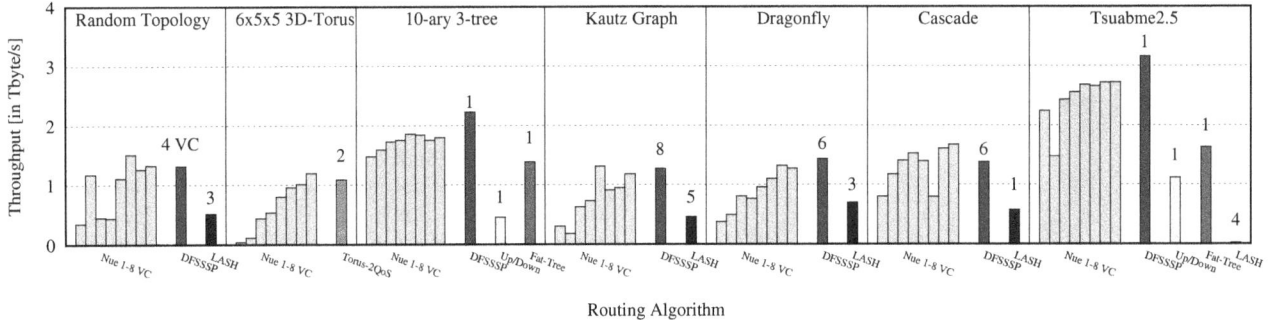

Figure 10: Simulated throughput for all-to-all operation on five standard and two real-world topologies, as configured according to Tab. 1; Nue routing shown for all numbers of VCs between 1 and 8 (from left to right); VC requirement by other routings for deadlock-freedom are shown atop the individual bars

Table 1: Topology configurations (w/ link redundancy r) used for throughput simulations in Fig. 10

Topology	Switches	Terminals	Channels	r
Random	125	1,000	1,000	1
6x5x5 3D-Torus	150	1,050	1,800	4
10-ary 3-tree	300	1,100	2,000	1
Kautz ($d = 7, k = 3$)	150	1,050	1,500	2
Dragonfly ($a = 12$, $p = 6, h = 6, g = 15$)	180	1,080	1,515	1
Cascade (2 groups)	192	1,536	3,072	1
Tsubame2.5	243	1,407	3,384	1

minals [7]. We measure the throughput of all eight routing algorithms that are available in OpenSM version 3.3.16. Impossible topology/routing combinations, such as Torus-2QoS routing for the 10-ary 3-tree, are ignored. We compare Nue routing, for the number of virtual channels $1 \leq k \leq 8$, for a given topology to the other usable algorithms, see Fig. 10.

Besides the simulated throughput for each topology and routing combination, we give the number of needed VCs atop of the bars in Fig. 10. For example, DFSSSP routing needs four VCs for a deadlock-free routing of the random topology. However, DFSSSP usually uses all eight available VCs to optimize the path balancing across the virtual layers, a technique to increase the throughput slightly [5].

We see two trends for all investigated topologies: First, an increase of used VCs for Nue also increases the throughput for the all-to-all communication. This is a result of the decreased $\gamma_{max}^{t,\text{Nue}}$ when we use multiple VCs, as reported in Section 5.1. The outliers from this pattern, e.g., the decrease in throughput for the random topology and four VCs, are correlated to a sudden increase in fall backs to the escape paths. In this particular example, Nue had to fall back for 14 of the 1,000 destinations, while Nue with two and more than four VCs was able to route the topology without any fall back. A second trend is, that Nue shows a slight variance in throughput after reaching a certain peak, usually for about $k \geq 5$ in our examples, but this generally depends on topology type and size. We account this behavior to a mismatch between the static routing and the execution order of the point-to-point communications, which assemble the all-to-all traffic pattern. A mismatch can cause temporary congestion

in the network which slows down the entire communication process as a result, which is a known problem [7, 16].

In general, Fig. 10 shows that Nue routing is competitive to the best performing routing for each individual topology, i.e., offers between 83.5% (10-ary 3-tree) and 121.4% (Cascade network) throughput in comparison to Torus-2QoS for the torus and DFSSSP for the other topologies. Occasionally, depending on the given number of VCs, Nue is able to outperform the best competitor. For example, for the random topology Nue, with $k \geq 6$, offers up to 15% higher throughput than DFSSSP, and for the Cascade network up to 21% higher throughput, with $k \geq 3$ but excluding $k = 6$. Furthermore, given enough VCs, Nue is able to outperform the other routings, such as fat-tree routing or LASH, to a great extent. Therefore, we consider Nue routing to be a adequate alternative to the other investigated algorithms, or at least a suitable fall back in case the best performing algorithm becomes inapplicable, as we will discuss in Section 5.3.

5.3 Runtime and Practical Considerations

In Proposition 1 we mathematically derived the time complexity of Nue routing. To put this into perspective, we compare the runtime of Nue (with 8 VCs) for tori topologies to other deadlock-free routing algorithms implemented in OpenSM. Therefore, we extend the current OpenSM (version 3.3.19) with our Nue routing to achieve a fair comparison and integrate Nue into the toolchain, described in Section 5.

We create 25 3D torus networks with a difference in dimension of at most one, i.e., we start with a grid size for the switches of 2x2x2, 2x2x3, 2x3x3, ..., and go up to 10x10x10. Each of these switches connects to four terminals, hence the 10x10x10 torus accommodates 4,000 terminals. Furthermore, the assumption for this test is that the maximum of available VCs is 8, adjacent switches utilize no channel redundancy, and we randomly inject 1% link/channel failures into the topology. The 1% link failures have been chosen according to the observed annual failure rate of production HPC systems [7]. Besides Nue, we evaluate the runtime of DFSSSP, LASH, and Torus-2QoS routing to calculate deadlock-free routing tables for the same faulty topology. The testbed used is a dual-socket Intel Xeon E5-2620 server with 64 GiB RAM and we pin the InfiniBand fabric simulator (ibsim) to socket 0 and OpenSM to socket 1 to minimize disturbances.

From the results, as shown in Fig. 11, we can draw two main conclusions: First, Nue is competitive in terms of runtime. Nue routing calculates the forwarding tables faster

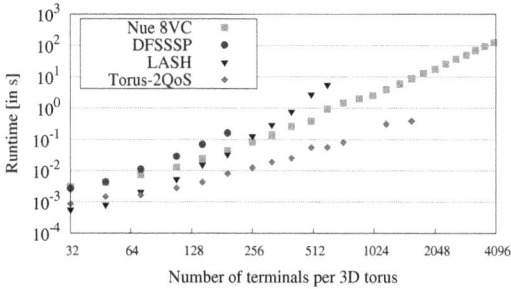

Figure 11: Runtime comparison of DL-free routings for 3D tori (w/o channel redundancy) of various topology sizes with 1% injected link failures; Four terminals per switch (e.g., smallest: 2x2x2 torus with 32 terminals, largest topology: 10x10x10 torus with 4,000 terminals); Missing dots: routing failed

than the topology-agnostic DFSSSP, which has the same time complexity of $\mathcal{O}(|N|^2 \cdot \log |N|)$, see [8]. Nue outperforms the runtime of LASH routing for tori larger than 4x4x4 with 256 terminals attached. Only the topology-aware Torus-2QoS routing is on average 9x faster than Nue, which is as expected since Torus-2QoS is able to avoid deadlocks analytically. The second important result is an applicability of 100%, i.e., Nue routing scales with the topology size. The other three deadlock-free algorithms fail, notice the missing data points in Fig. 11, either because the algorithms run out of VCs (DFSSSP and LASH exceed the 8 VC limit) or because the failures prevent an analytical solution for the deadlock-free paths problem (Torus-2QoS). Only Nue routing is always applicable while offering good path balancing.

6. RELATED WORK

A well-known example for algorithms avoiding to create cycles in the CDG is the Up*/Down* routing [29]. Up*/Down* prohibits a route to use an 'up' direction after a 'down' directions. This approach does not necessarily use shortest paths or load-balances routes efficiently. Indeed, the root often becomes a bottleneck in practice. The algorithms UD_DFS routing [28], L-turn routing [22] and segment-based routing (SR) [24] are based on Up*/Down* and try to reduce or balance the routing restrictions to increase the path balancing across the network. For network technologies where the next channel in each routing step is chosen based on the source and destination node the Multiple Up*/Down* routing [10] can increase the path balancing. For similar network technologies without virtual channel support the Tree-turn routing [34] or FX [27] routing can be used. For example, Tree-turn adds two more directions to the four directions used by L-turn routing, which reduces the number of prohibited turns further to increase the balancing.

Another set of routing algorithms breaks cycles in the CDG with virtual channels. The destination-based DFSSSP [8] and LASH [32] routings operate similarly in terms of breaking the cycles, i.e., searching for cycles in the CDG and moving individual paths to other virtual layers. Albeit, both algorithms might suffer from a limited number of available VCs. Therefore, LASH-TOR [31] enhanced LASH routing to use Up*/Down* in the last virtual layer if the routes in this layer form an unresolvable cycle. This can result in multiple

outgoing ports at a switch for a single destination, hence LASH-TOR is not destination-based in the general case.

Kinsy et al. [21] proposed two application-aware routings, called bandwidth-sensitive oblivious routing (with minimal routes), or BSOR(M). While BSOR operates similar to our approach, meaning its calculates the routes within the CDG, the BSORM routing calculates the routes within the network and breaks cycles afterwards, resembling the method of DFSSSP and LASH. However, the difference between Nue and BSOR is that BSOR randomly deletes edges from the CDG to form an acyclic CDG and solves a multi-commodity flow problem, based on the demands of the application, with a MILP algorithm for small networks. For large networks, BSOR uses Dijkstra's algorithm as a heuristic on a weighted and acyclic CDG for each source/destination pair to balance the application traffic. BSOR(M) is designed for network technologies with forwarding based on source and destination, and therefore are inapplicable to InfiniBand for example. The same holds for smart routing [3]. The approach of smart routing is to calculate the shortest paths and investigate the induced CDG for cycles, while storing which path induced which edge in the CDG. A cycle search in the CDG subsequently cuts the edges of a cycle which minimizes the average path length after recalculating the paths inducing this edge. While smart routing can be used for technologies without VCs, the computational cost, which is $\mathcal{O}((\#\text{switch})^9)$, is too high for a practical use in large scale networks.

7. CONCLUSION

The InfiniBand interconnect is currently the #1 network technology—w.r.t. the number of systems in the Top500 list—for high performance computing. Lossless networks, such as InfiniBand or Converged Enhanced Ethernet (CEE), also become more common in data center environments. The main features of these networks are lossless transmission using either credit based flow control in InfiniBand or Priority Flow Control (PFC) with pause frames in Ethernet. Both technologies require deadlock-free routing to function reliably. The same is true for many network-on-chip architectures.

Our approach of applying a graph search algorithm within the complete channel dependency graph instead of the actual network, and our implementation of it, called Nue, is the first reliable strategy to route arbitrary topologies with a limited number of virtual channels, or even in the absence of VCs. Nue routing is tailored for the deadlock-free, oblivious, and destination-based routing needed in CCE and InfiniBand and can directly be employed for both, e.g., using InfiniBand's virtual lanes or using PFC together with Priority Code Point for CEE. Possible applications of Nue for NoC architectures include, but are not limited to, the routing between tiles connected by virtual channel routers in a fault-tolerant manner.

Furthermore, Nue's capability of arbitrarily limiting the number of used VCs allows the combination of DL-freedom and quality of service (QoS), which could be based on the same technology feature. E.g., InfiniBand's service levels are mapped to virtual lanes, which are used by LASH/DFSSSP to avoid deadlocks. So, previously, the choice was either having QoS with topology-aware routing or ignoring QoS and using topology-agnostic routings based on VLs (LASH or DFSSSP). With Nue routing, one could use two VLs for DL-freedom while having four QoS levels, for example.

All these characteristics and advantages, combined with Nue's low time complexity of $\mathcal{O}(|N|^2 \cdot \log |N|)$ and memory complexity of $\mathcal{O}(|N|^2)$, make Nue routing a suitable algorithm to route modern large-scale HPC systems, lossless data center fabrics, and NoC architectures. Therefore, we expect a wide adoption of Nue routing and of the concept of routing on the complete channel dependency graph in these fields.

8. REFERENCES

[1] T. Bjerregaard and S. Mahadevan. A Survey of Research and Practices of Network-on-chip. *ACM Comput. Surv.*, 38(1), June 2006.

[2] U. Brandes. A Faster Algorithm for Betweenness Centrality. *Journal of Mathematical Sociology*, 25:163–177, 2001.

[3] L. Cherkasova, V. Kotov, and T. Rokicki. Fibre channel fabrics: evaluation and design. In *Proceedings of the Twenty-Ninth Hawaii International Conference on System Sciences*, volume 1, 1996.

[4] W. Dally and B. Towles. *Principles and Practices of Interconnection Networks*. Morgan Kaufmann Publishers Inc., San Francisco, CA, USA, 2003.

[5] W. J. Dally. Virtual-channel Flow Control. In *Proceedings of the 17th Annual International Symposium on Computer Architecture*, ISCA '90, New York, USA, 1990. ACM Press.

[6] W. J. Dally and C. L. Seitz. Deadlock-Free Message Routing in Multiprocessor Interconnection Networks. *IEEE Trans. Comput.*, 36(5):547–553, 1987.

[7] J. Domke, T. Hoefler, and S. Matsuoka. Fail-in-place Network Design: Interaction Between Topology, Routing Algorithm and Failures. In *Proceedings of the International Conference for High Performance Computing, Networking, Storage and Analysis*, SC '14, Piscataway, NJ, USA, 2014. IEEE Computer Society.

[8] J. Domke, T. Hoefler, and W. E. Nagel. Deadlock-Free Oblivious Routing for Arbitrary Topologies. In *Proceedings of the 25th IEEE International Parallel & Distributed Processing Symposium (IPDPS)*, Washington, DC, USA, 2011. IEEE Computer Society.

[9] G. Faanes, A. Bataineh, D. Roweth, T. Court, E. Froese, B. Alverson, T. Johnson, J. Kopnick, M. Higgins, and J. Reinhard. Cray Cascade: a Scalable HPC System based on a Dragonfly Network. In *Proceedings of the International Conference on High Performance Computing, Networking, Storage and Analysis*, SC '12, pages 103:1–103:9, Los Alamitos, CA, USA, 2012. IEEE Computer Society Press.

[10] J. Flich, P. López, J. C. Sancho, A. Robles, and J. Duato. Improving InfiniBand Routing Through Multiple Virtual Networks. In *Proceedings of the 4th International Symposium on High Performance Computing*, ISHPC '02, London, UK, UK, 2002. Springer-Verlag.

[11] J. Flich, T. Skeie, A. Mejia, O. Lysne, P. Lopez, A. Robles, J. Duato, M. Koibuchi, T. Rokicki, and J. C. Sancho. A Survey and Evaluation of Topology-Agnostic Deterministic Routing Algorithms. *IEEE Trans. Parallel Distrib. Syst.*, 23(3):405–425, 2012.

[12] L. C. Freeman. A Set of Measures of Centrality Based on Betweenness. *Sociometry*, 40(1):35–41, 1977.

[13] M. Garcia, E. Vallejo, R. Beivide, M. Odriozola, and M. Valero. Efficient Routing Mechanisms for Dragonfly Networks. In *42nd International Conference on Parallel Processing (ICPP)*, 2013.

[14] GSIC. TSUBAME2 Hardware Architecture. http://tsubame.gsic.titech.ac.jp/en/hardware-architecture, Jan. 2016.

[15] M. C. Heydemann, J. Meyer, and D. Sotteau. On Forwarding Indices of Networks. *Discrete Appl. Math.*, 23(2):103–123, May 1989.

[16] T. Hoefler, T. Schneider, and A. Lumsdaine. Multistage Switches are not Crossbars: Effects of Static Routing in High-Performance Networks. In *Proceedings of the 2008 IEEE International Conference on Cluster Computing*. IEEE Computer Society Press, 2008.

[17] T. Hoefler, T. Schneider, and A. Lumsdaine. Optimized Routing for Large-Scale InfiniBand Networks. In *17th Annual IEEE Symposium on High Performance Interconnects (HOTI 2009)*, 2009.

[18] InfiniBand Trade Association. *Infiniband Architecture Specification Volume 1, Release 1.2.1*, 2007.

[19] G. Karypis and V. Kumar. Multilevel K-way Partitioning Scheme for Irregular Graphs. *J. Parallel Distrib. Comput.*, 48(1):96–129, 1998.

[20] J. Kim, W. J. Dally, S. Scott, and D. Abts. Technology-Driven, Highly-Scalable Dragonfly Topology. In *Proceedings of the 35th Annual International Symposium on Computer Architecture*, ISCA '08, pages 77–88, Washington, DC, USA, 2008. IEEE Computer Society.

[21] M. A. Kinsy, M. H. Cho, T. Wen, E. Suh, M. van Dijk, and S. Devadas. Application-aware deadlock-free oblivious routing. In *Proceedings of the 36th annual international symposium on Computer architecture*, ISCA '09, New York, NY, USA, 2009. ACM Press.

[22] M. Koibuchi, A. Funahashi, A. Jouraku, and H. Amano. L-turn routing: an adaptive routing in irregular networks. In *International Conference on Parallel Processing*, 2001.

[23] D. Li, X. Lu, and J. Su. Graph-Theoretic Analysis of Kautz Topology and DHT Schemes. In *NPC*, pages 308–315, 2004.

[24] A. Mejia, J. Flich, J. Duato, S.-A. Reinemo, and T. Skeie. Segment-based routing: an efficient fault-tolerant routing algorithm for meshes and tori. In *20th International Parallel and Distributed Processing Symposium (IPDPS)*, 2006.

[25] Mellanox Technologies. *Mellanox OFED for Linux User Manual*, rev 2.0-3.0.0 edition, 2013.

[26] T. Rauber and G. Rünger. *Parallel Programming: for Multicore and Cluster Systems*. Springer-Verlag, 2013.

[27] J. C. Sancho, A. Robles, and J. Duato. A Flexible Routing Scheme for Networks of Workstations. In *ISHPC '00: Proceedings of the Third International Symposium on High Performance Computing*, London, UK, 2000. Springer-Verlag.

[28] J. C. Sancho, A. Robles, and J. Duato. A new methodology to compute deadlock-free routing tables for irregular networks. In *Network-Based Parallel Computing. Communication, Architecture, and Applications*, volume 1797 of *Lecture Notes in Computer Science*, pages 45–60. Springer Berlin Heidelberg, 2000.

[29] M. D. Schroeder, A. Birell, M. Burrows, H. Murray, R. Needham, T. Rodeheffer, E. Satterthwaite, and C. Thacker. Autonet: A High-speed, Self-Configuring Local Area Network Using Point-to-Point Links. *IEEE Journal on Selected Areas in Communications*, 9(8), 1991.

[30] K. S. Shim, M. H. Cho, M. Kinsy, T. Wen, M. Lis, G. E. Suh, and S. Devadas. Static Virtual Channel Allocation in Oblivious Routing. In *Proceedings of the 2009 3rd ACM/IEEE International Symposium on Networks-on-Chip*, NOCS '09, pages 38–43, Washington, DC, USA, 2009. IEEE Computer Society.

[31] T. Skeie, O. Lysne, J. Flich, P. López, A. Robles, and J. Duato. LASH-TOR: A Generic Transition-Oriented Routing Algorithm. In *ICPADS '04: Proceedings of the Tenth International Conference on Parallel and Distributed Systems*, Washington, DC, USA, 2004. IEEE Computer Society Press.

[32] T. Skeie, O. Lysne, and I. Theiss. Layered Shortest Path (LASH) Routing in Irregular System Area Networks. In *IPDPS '02: Proceedings of the 16th International Parallel and Distributed Processing Symposium*, Washington, DC, USA, 2002. IEEE Computer Society Press.

[33] E. Zahavi, G. Johnson, D. J. Kerbyson, and M. Lang. Optimized InfiniBand fat-tree routing for shift all-to-all communication patterns. *Concurr. Comput. : Pract. Exper.*, 22(2):217–231, 2010.

[34] J. Zhou and Y.-C. Chung. Tree-turn routing: an efficient deadlock-free routing algorithm for irregular networks. *The Journal of Supercomputing*, 59(2):882–900, 2012.

Network-Managed Virtual
Global Address Space for Message-driven Runtimes

Abhishek Kulkarni, Luke Dalessandro, Ezra Kissel
Andrew Lumsdaine, Thomas Sterling, Martin Swany
Center for Research in Extreme Scale Technologies, Indiana University
{adkulkar, ldalessa, ezkissel, lums, tron, swany}@indiana.edu

ABSTRACT

Maintaining a scalable high-performance virtual global address space using distributed memory hardware has proven to be challenging. In this paper we evaluate a new approach for such an active global address space that leverages the capabilities of the network fabric to manage addressing, rather than software at the endpoint hosts. We describe our overall approach, design alternatives, and present initial experimental results that demonstrate the effectiveness and limitations of existing network hardware.

1. INTRODUCTION

Abstraction of local resources is a fundamental capability of modern operating systems. An elegant example of resource abstraction is virtualization of memory which separates the logical address space unique to each process from the physical address space provided by the computer's memory hardware. Most operating systems provide this indirection separately for contiguous regions of the address space ("pages"). Powerful features are enabled by the combination of abstraction and paging: memory that is not being actively used can be stored to disk, regions of physical memory can be shared among processes, files can be mapped directly into the logical memory space, etc. To adapt to varying resource demands (among other reasons), a logical address mapped to one location in physical memory can later map to a different address [5].

This paper explores extending the separation of logical and physical memory addresses to an ensemble of systems to create an *active global address space* (AGAS). Where distributed shared memory systems attempt to transparently create a logical shared address space using distributed memory hardware at the OS level [2], the approach we present here is primarily a programming abstraction separate from local program memory and is implemented in user space. Our address space is "active" in two senses. It is virtualized and dynamically relocatable (unlike some existing static models, discussed in Section 2), and it is used is primarily through the use of active messages [10] and *put/get* operations (often implemented with active messages),

HPDC'16, May 31–June 04, 2016, Kyoto, Japan.
© 2016 ACM. ISBN 978-1-4503-4314-5/16/05. . . $15.00
DOI: http://dx.doi.org/10.1145/2907294.2907320

as opposed to the local *read/write* model in current distributed shared memory models.

In this paper we make the following contributions:

- We propose an *active* global address space (AGAS) for a message-driven runtime system to dynamically balancing load and data during execution.

- We introduce network-managed global virtual memory where the AGAS runtime programs the network fabric to adaptively route messages based on memory locations rather than host identifiers.

- We demonstrate that the overheads of address translation and global memory accesses of our hardware implementation are comparable, and at times better, than a performant software implementation.

2. BACKGROUND & RELATED WORK

A global address space (GAS) provides a uniform way to refer to memory in a distributed system. Distributed shared memory (DSM) systems sought to completely abstract the distributed memory and present it as shared memory [2]. These approaches suffered from a number of limitations, however, including dependencies on subtle models of memory consistency and locality. A partitioned GAS (PGAS) is a non-uniform global address space where the representation of a global address statically encodes the physical address of the memory. PGAS approaches attempt to find a compromise between exposing locality while also presenting global access to data [11]. Address translation in PGAS implementations is efficient as address mappings are static. This static distribution maps well to remote direct memory access network hardware but restricts the system's ability to load balance computation and communication. PGAS has been effective for problems that are amenable to static mappings but do not directly support dynamic data distributions.

A number of current extreme-scale runtime systems [1,3,7,9] target many of the same issues as an active-message global virtual address space, but do not as explicitly support dynamic data mappings. More importantly, all existing efforts for providing a global address space are host based. None provide an approach based on leveraging the network fabric to manage the mappings.

We envision an active GAS in which the mapping is dynamic and managed in hardware. The functionality of network switching elements is analogous to that of memory management units. Logically, a table must be consulted to bind a virtual address to a physical destination. Software Defined Networking (SDN) enables fine-grained programming of a network by defining a clear separation between the "control" and "data" plane of a switch, and it is a powerful approach that is shaping future network

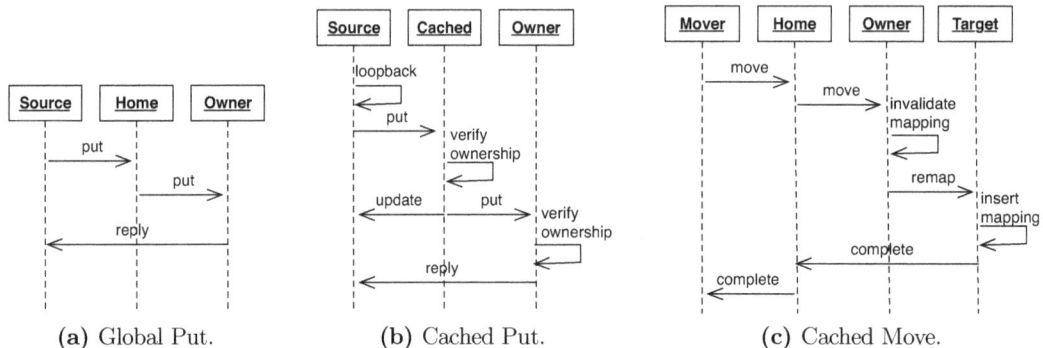

Figure 1: AGAS algorithms: (a) Requests are forwarded through a global directory (Get is equivalent), (b) Put to an invalid cached rank results in a forwarded message and an updated owner for the cache (multiple forwards may be required), (c) Equivalent to the naive move, but annotated with the local ownership modifications at the old owner and new target.

architectures. OpenFlow [8] is the burgeoning protocol for implementing SDN, which enables a software controller to define the forwarding decisions of switching hardware, with the ability to implement custom policies and packet handling behavior while still processing "flows" at line rate. As SDN switch implementations continue to improve, the interest to HPC applications will grow as support for large, hierarchical flow tables, faster switching speeds, and hardware-assisted rewriting of arbitrary packet headers becomes commonplace in data center networks.

3. APPROACH

We present three algorithms for AGAS management in an event-driven active message runtime, resulting in a two-sided networking implementation. While our experimental evaluation focuses on the get/put model described in Section 4, these algorithms can support arbitrary active message interaction with the global address space—indeed our put/get implementation uses active messaging internally.

Software Global Directory: Our naive software AGAS implementation maintains a distributed global directory that maps global virtual addresses (GVA) to owner ranks. GVAs are distributed statically and cyclically, so that each has a "home" rank. Put and get requests are forwarded to the GVA's owner through the home rank; replies are returned directly back to the initiating rank. This protocol is diagrammed in Figure 1a. Move operations are performed at the GVA's home, which initiates a move operation at the current owner, copying the data to the target rank, and then updating the owner mapping once the move has completed. While ranks can optimize ownership lookup for their home pages, there is no optimized path for loopback.

Software Cached Global Directory: The global directory stores the minimum amount of data for GVA translation, however it requires a hop through the home in the common case for get and put operations. This increases the number of network messages by 50%, and leads to higher bandwidth overheads as large put payloads may be copied during forwarding.

We eliminate this extra hop with per-rank software caches of the global directory. Rather than forwarding requests through the home rank of a GVA, we use the cached mapping directly. While this can eliminate the common case extra hop, the caches represent instruction overhead, memory pressure, and synchronization contention (when ranks are multithreaded), and complicate the put, get, and move operations.

The directory caches could be kept coherent with an expensive

coherence protocol. Instead we leverage the underlying active message model and forward invalid messages to their correct current owner. This requires that each rank keep an ownership table for pages that it currently owns. This was not necessary in the naive algorithm because messages are always forwarded to correct locations. It is natural, though not necessary, to keep this ownership information in the software cache. Given these local ownership tables a rank can optimize loopback checks.

Each rank stores a table of the pages that it currently owns, and a cache of known remote owners. The put and get operations consult this table for an optimized loopback check before querying their cache for an owner for the page. On a miss, the source forwards the request to the home for the page, which will reply with the current owner. The next time this source wants to access the page, it will find the mapping locally.

The target of a put request must validate its ownership of incoming requests—a failed ownership check means that the page has moved. In this situation the original target must forward the request either to the page's home rank, which always knows the correct mapping, or to a more recent owner if it has one cached. It will also reply to the source with an updated owner to cache. This is shown in Figure 1b. These update operations ensure that the cache stabilizes after a move operation takes place, and a quiescent map will incur only local table space and lookup overheads.

As with the software global directory, a move operation is managed by the page's home. The primary differences are the "disown" and "own" events that update the local ownership tables at the two nodes. During the period of time between when the original owner invalidates its local mapping, and the destination inserts its local mapping, the page is in "limbo," i.e., no rank believes that they own it. Requests arriving at the original owner after the page is invalidated will continue to be forwarded until the destination inserts its mapping, at which point they will be received at the destination.

Hardware Directory: An ideal hardware implementation would eliminate the common case overheads of the software directory without imposing the space or lookup constraints of the cache, while still providing optimized loopback operations. Software-defined networking provides the opportunity to push the directory into the network itself, allowing requests to be routed to the appropriate rank based on their page ids. However, storing the directory in the network makes loopback optimization difficult. A hardware solution supporting low-latency loopback would require integration with the CPU memory infrastructure.

16

4. IMPLEMENTATIONS

We adopt a simple `put/get` GAS model. This provides us a limited interface to implement and optimize and is implemented internally through active messages and captures their behavior. Put and get operations are asynchronous and fences ensure that preceding operations have completed. We extend this simple interface with the `agas_remap()` operation that allows explicit data movement. Data is remapped at page granularity, and r emapping a page that is currently being accessed is considered a data race and will result in undefined behavior.

Global data is allocated collectively or from a single rank, and can initially be distributed either cyclically, where the pages are striped across the ranks, or blocked, where the allocation is partitioned into equal blocks of pages and these blocks are placed on the ranks. Any distribution is realizable using the remap operation. Byte-based address arithmetic is performed directly on the global address representation. In addition to these global memory operations, the runtime supports normal SPMD operations including topology queries, barriers, and collectives.

Software-Based AGAS: Our implementation of the AGAS interface is built on our custom implementation of GASNet's core two-sided active message API [4]. Core GASNet provides a basic interface for global memory registration, byte transfer and active message instantiation, and message dependency. Each rank is modeled as a sequential process. GASNet has been shown to be scalable and high performance and serves as the networking implementation of Berkeley Unified Parallel C [6]. The core conduit uses GASNet's segment as the physical memory for our global heap and Doug Lea's *dlmalloc* memory allocator to manage allocation within the global address space. As a simplification, the heap tested here is symmetric, however the AGAS implementations do not require this in general. The heap is divided into single size relocatable pages of 4 KB in order to support consistency between the software and hardware implementation. Dynamic allocation is currently performed at rank 0, which is also the home rank for all of the pages. The AGAS put and get operations are implemented as simple request-forward-reply active message handlers.

We do not expect a software AGAS to be an effective option at scale or when remapping is common. The purpose is to present an idealized implementation for use as a reference point for our hardware system during quiescent execution. The core of this algorithm is the local ownership table and cache. Common across our implementations is a single table that provides the local ownership table and owner cache in one data structure.

Our implementation uses a direct-mapped table where, after initial cache population, each rank stores a mapping for every page in the system. This structure minimizes lookup overheads at the expense of table size and likely memory and cache pressure. Arriving put and get requests check for valid mapping using a simple array index operation, and move operations atomically update locations using hardware compare-and-swap primitives.

Hardware-Based AGAS: The InfiniBand unicast protocol, and specifically the reliable connection (RC) IB mode, require pairwise *Verbs* queue pair (QP) establishment via peer exchange and knowledge of the target endpoint before initiating send operations. Since AGAS addresses are resolved in the network, a sender has no prior knowledge about the destination QP to which a message will eventually be delivered. Fortunately, IB's multicast over unreliable datagram (UD) allows receivers to accept packets from any potential source node in the network and is the target of our AGAS implementation. In particular,

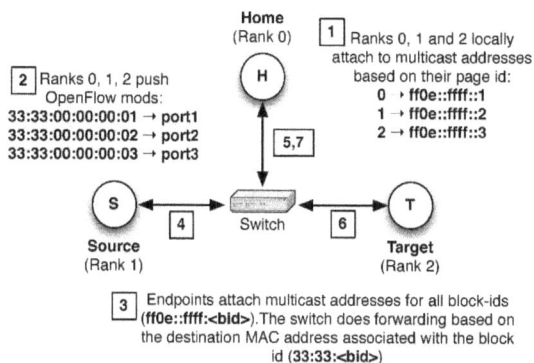

Figure 2: Use of multicast addressing in RoCE.

we leverage IB's multicast capabilities available through RDMA over Converged Ethernet (RoCE).

In the RoCE case, although the multicast control interfaces are identical, the resulting behavior is different due to the lack of a subnet manager (SM) within an Ethernet network. Using RoCE, IB multicast GIDs are mapped to multicast Ethernet MAC addresses when operations are posted to QPs by senders. These frame headers are matched on within the OpenFlow switch and the active flow, or AGAS "remap", entries enable unicast behavior from multicast frames. For our evaluation we developed a new GASNet conduit, called *Photon*, employing this IB multicast mechanism. Photon operates in conjunction with address-to-port mapping rules in an OpenFlow switch to forward a message sent to a given global address towards the current address "owner", performing global address resolution within the network.

Figure 2 outlines this approach. During block initialization, the AGAS layer registers local blocks as multicast groups via Photon (1) and pushes flow entries to the discovered switch(es) in the network (2,3). Step (1) allows the receiver to accept messages destined to that block from any sender, while steps (2,3) allow the switch to direct a given AGAS block, identified by its mapped multicast Ethernet MAC address, to the appropriate port. In our example, node A owns block 1, and when nodes B and C send a message to destination block 1, the destination node A is unknown at the time of the send operation. Only when the switch matches on the flow entry for block 1 is the destination node determined, steps (5,7) and (6,7), and the message delivered to the current owner of the block. When a block moves, the AGAS remapping operation updates the flow entry(ies) in the switch along with the receiver multicast groups.

5. EXPERIMENTAL RESULTS

Experiments were run on a cluster of 16 nodes with 32GB of RAM and two 6-core Intel Xeon E5-2620v3 processors running at 2.40GHz. Each node contained a Mellanox ConnectX-3 EN 10 Gbs Ethernet network adapter. Networking is provided by a NoviFlow 2128, an OpenFlow v1.3-capable 10 Gbps Ethernet switch. Compute nodes ran Ubuntu 14.04.3 (kernel version 3.13) and Mellanox's OFED release 2.4-1.0.4. Our runtime is based on GASNet 1.26.0 and all compilation was done with gcc 5.2.0 with `-O3` optimization.

Dynamic Remapping of Global Memory: The GUPS microbenchmark was used to evaluate the impact of dynamically "remapping" pages by initializing an experiment with a small table size that resulted in a total of four logical pages and a million global updates. Since GUPS performs updates on random

17

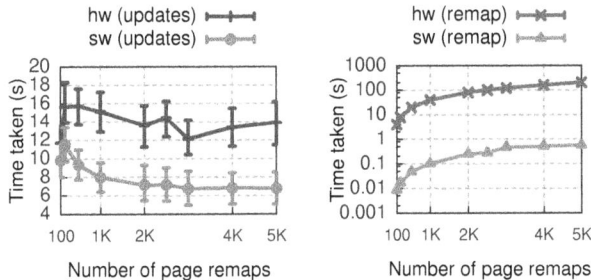

(a) Global update, no move. **(b)** Move and remap.

Figure 3: Effect of active dynamic remapping on random access performance for Software and Hardware AGAS.

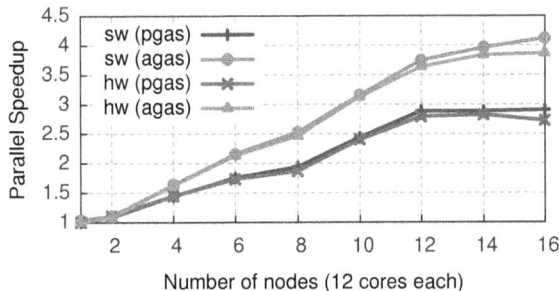

Figure 4: Benefit of AGAS to the overall stencil computation time in the simplified AMR application.

global data, the impact of remapping is difficult to discern at larger scales, and our motivation in constraining the table size is to force frequent movement of a sizeable segment of the total address space. Distributed across 192 cores, remapping these pages ensures that at least 25% of all subsequent global updates will target a different process.

Figure 3a shows only the total global random update time (discounting the remap operation itself) between software and hardware cases over increasing numbers of remap operations. As page movement frequency increases, the raw communication performance of the hardware approach is affected as the switch has to keep up with concurrent flow updates. The direct lookups afforded by the hardware case however ensure a constant, or improved, run time as remaps increase. In our small-scale evaluation, the overall time trend even decreases for hardware as pages frequently become local to a single physical node that would otherwise require a network hop.

On the other hand, the limitations of our OpenFlow-based implementation become apparent in Figure 3b. For each remap operation, the time needed to update the switch table via out-of-band signaling, as opposed to updating the software owner cache with an in-band active message, is considerably higher.

Adaptive Mesh Refinement (AMR): We now evaluate a simplfied AMR implementation where a 2D grid of 500x500 cells is cyclically allocated by rank 0. Each rank at random discretizes the parent grid into finer children grids of 100x100 cells. In a real AMR application, this spatial discretization is often done dynamically at runtime based on the requirements of the simulation. The child grids are also allocated cyclically starting from rank 0. Each processor, in a SPMD fashion, performs parallel stencil computations on the cells in the region that it owns. This example get heavily load-imbalanced due to the randomly added finer grids and benefits from the AGAS remap capability. Eight 5-point stencil operations are performed on parts of the

child grid followed by a reduction of the computed values. This amortizes the cost of remapping child grids by increasing their reuse. Figure 4 plots the parallel speedup in the stencil computation time ignoring the time it took to update the switch flows. As the child grids are remapped locally, both software and hardware AGAS achieve close to $4x$ speedup at 192 cores.

6. CONCLUSION

We have presented a novel approach to implementing an active global address space by using the network fabric to manage mappings of global addresses to hosts. The network-assisted design simplifies the address resolution protocols on each host and provides potential performance benefits when data migrates. Our results with the current switch hardware generation are mixed. We have demonstrated the benefit of hardware AGAS over software alternatives in terms of reduced common-case overheads due to memory pressure and synchronization penalties, however hardware remapping remains an expensive operation due to the cost to program flows. Hardware-assisted memory management opens up a number of new areas to explore. The complete network fabric consists of not only centrally located switching devices within the topology, but also the host adapters, at each endpoint. Offloading local address resolution to embedded controllers and programmable host adapters has the potential to further offload the lookup and synchronization overheads involved with AGAS.

Acknowledgment

This work was supported by the Department of Energy, National Nuclear Security Administration under Award Number(s) DE-SC0008809 and DE-NA0002377 and NSF Award CNS-1446950.

7. REFERENCES

[1] P. An, A. Jula, et al. STAPL: An adaptive, generic parallel C++ library. In *Languages and Compilers for Parallel Computing*, pages 193–208. Springer, 2003.

[2] H. Attiya and J. Welch. Distributed shared memory. *Distributed Computing: Fundamentals, Simulations and Advanced Topics, Second Edition*, pages 189–205, 2004.

[3] M. Bauer, S. Treichler, E. Slaughter, and A. Aiken. Legion: Expressing locality and independence with logical regions. In *High Performance Computing, Networking, Storage and Analysis (SC), 2012 International Conference for*, pages 1–11. IEEE, 2012.

[4] D. Bonachea. GASNet specification, v1. *Univ. California, Berkeley, Tech. Rep. UCB/CSD-02-1207*, 2002.

[5] P. J. Denning. The working set model for program behavior. In *the ACM symposium*, pages 15.1–15.12, New York, New York, USA, 1967. ACM Press.

[6] T. El-Ghazawi, W. Carlson, T. Sterling, and K. Yelick. *UPC: Distributed shared memory programming*, volume 40. John Wiley & Sons, 2005.

[7] L. V. Kale and S. Krishnan. *CHARM++: A portable concurrent object oriented system based on C++*, volume 28. ACM, 1993.

[8] N. McKeown, T. Anderson, et al. OpenFlow: Enabling innovation in campus networks. *ACM SIGCOMM Computer Communication Review*, 38(2):69–74, 2008.

[9] V. Sarkar, B. Chapman, W. Grop, and R. Knauerhase. Birds-of-a-feather session: Building an open community runtime (OCR) framework for exascale systems, November 2012.

[10] T. von Eicken, D. E. Culler, S. C. Goldstein, and K. E. Schauser. Active messages: A mechanism for integrated communication and computation. In *International Symposium on Computer Architecture*, pages 256–266, New York, NY, USA, 1992. ACM.

[11] K. Yelick, D. Bonachea, et al. Productivity and performance using partitioned global address space languages. In *Proceedings of the 2007 international workshop on Parallel symbolic computation*, pages 24–32. ACM, 2007.

High-Performance Distributed RMA Locks

Patrick Schmid*
Department of Computer
Science
ETH Zurich
patrick.schmid@ieffects.com

Maciej Besta*
Department of Computer
Science
ETH Zurich
bestam@inf.ethz.ch

Torsten Hoefler
Department of Computer
Science
ETH Zurich
htor@inf.ethz.ch

ABSTRACT

We propose a topology-aware distributed Reader-Writer lock that accelerates irregular workloads for supercomputers and data centers. The core idea behind the lock is a modular design that is an interplay of three distributed data structures: a counter of readers/writers in the critical section, a set of queues for ordering writers waiting for the lock, and a tree that binds all the queues and synchronizes writers with readers. Each structure is associated with a parameter for favoring either readers or writers, enabling adjustable performance that can be viewed as a point in a three dimensional parameter space. We also develop a distributed topology-aware MCS lock that is a building block of the above design and improves state-of-the-art MPI implementations. Both schemes use non-blocking Remote Memory Access (RMA) techniques for highest performance and scalability. We evaluate our schemes on a Cray XC30 and illustrate that they outperform state-of-the-art MPI-3 RMA locking protocols by 81% and 73%, respectively. Finally, we use them to accelerate a distributed hashtable that represents irregular workloads such as key-value stores or graph processing.

Code: spcl.inf.ethz.ch/Research/Parallel_Programming/RMALocks

1 INTRODUCTION

The scale of today's data processing is growing steadily. For example, the size of Facebook's social graph is many petabytes [7, 45] and graphs processed by the well-known HPC benchmark Graph500 [37] can have trillions of vertices. Efficient analyses of such datasets require distributed-memory (DM) machines with deep *Non-Uniform Memory Access* (NUMA) hierarchies.

Locks are among the most effective synchronization mechanisms used in codes for such machines [6]. On one hand, if used improperly, they may cause deadlocks. Yet, they have intuitive semantics and they often outperform other schemes such as atomic operations or transactions.

Designing efficient locks for machines with deep hierarchical memory systems is challenging. Consider four pro-

cesses competing for the same lock. Assume that two of them (A and B) run on one socket and the remaining two (C and D) execute on the other one. Now, in a naive lock design oblivious to the memory hierarchy, the lock may be passed between different sockets up to three times, degrading performance (e.g., if the order of the processes entering the critical section (CS) is A, C, B, and D). Recent advances [9,15] tackle this problem by reordering processes acquiring the lock to reduce inter-socket communication. Here, the order of A, B, C, and D entails only one inter-socket lock transfer, trading fairness for higher throughput. Extending such schemes to DM machines with weak memory models increases complexity. Moreover, expensive inter-node data transfers require more aggressive communication-avoidance strategies than those in intra-node communication [17]. To our best knowledge, no previous lock scheme addresses these challenges.

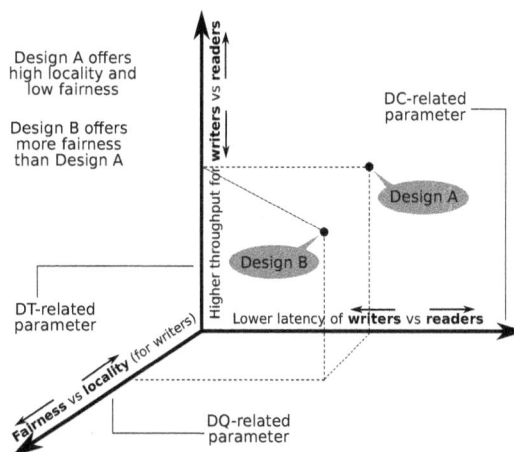

Figure 1: The space of parameters of the proposed Reader-Writer lock.

Another property of many large-scale workloads is that they are dominated by reads (e.g., they constitute 99.8% of requests to the Facebook graph [45]). Here, simple locks would entail unnecessary overheads. Instead, the Reader-Writer (RW) lock [35] can be used to reduce the overhead among processes that only perform reads in the critical section (CS). Initial RW *NUMA-aware* designs have recently been introduced [8], but they do not address DM machines.

In this work, we develop a lock that addresses the above challenges. Its core concept is a modular design for adjusting performance to various types of workloads. The lock consists of three key data structures. First, the distributed counter (DC) indicates the number of readers or the presence of a writer in the CS. Second, the distributed queue

---

Publication rights licensed to ACM. ACM acknowledges that this contribution was authored or co-authored by an employee, contractor or affiliate of a national government. As such, the Government retains a nonexclusive, royalty-free right to publish or reproduce this article, or to allow others to do so, for Government purposes only.

HPDC'16, May 31-June 04, 2016, Kyoto, Japan
Copyright is held by the owner/author(s). Publication rights licensed to ACM.
ACM 978-1-4503-4314-5/16/05...$15.00
DOI: http://dx.doi.org/10.1145/2907294.2907323

(DQ) synchronizes writers belonging to a given element of the memory hierarchy (e.g., a rack). Finally, the distributed tree (DT) binds together all queues at different levels of the memory hierarchy and synchronizes writers with readers. Each of these three structures offers an adjustable performance tradeoff, enabling high performance in various settings. DC can lower the latency of lock acquire/release performed by either readers or writers, DQ can be biased towards improving either locality or fairness, and DT can increase the throughput of either readers or writers. The values of these parameters constitute a three dimensional space that is illustrated in Figure 1. Each point is a specific lock design with selected performance properties.

Most DM machines offer Remote Direct Memory Access (RDMA) [39], a hardware scheme that removes the OS and the CPU from the inter-node communication path. RDMA is the basis of many Remote Memory Access (RMA) [17] programming models. Among others, they offer a Partitioned Global Address Space (PGAS) abstraction to the programmer and enable low-overhead direct access to remote memories with put/get communication primitives. RMA principles are used in various HPC languages and libraries: Unified Parallel C (UPC) [44], Fortran 2008 [27], MPI-3 [36], or SHMEM [4]. We will illustrate how to utilize RMA in the proposed locks for DM machines, addressing the above-mentioned challenges. In the following, we use MPI-3 RMA but we keep our protocols generic and we discuss (§ 6) how other RMA languages and libraries can also be used.

In summary, our key contributions are as follows:

- We develop a topology-aware distributed Reader-Writer lock that enables various tradeoffs between fairness, throughput, latency, and locality.

- We offer a topology-aware distributed MCS lock that accelerates the state-of-the-art MPI-3 RMA codes [17].

- We illustrate that our designs outperform the state-of-the-art in throughput/latency (7.2x/6.8x on average) and that they accelerate distributed hashtables used in key-value (KV) stores or graph processing.

2 RMA AND LOCKS

We start by discussing RMA (§ 2.1), our tool to develop the proposed locks. Next, we present traditional (§ 2.2) and state-of-the-art (§ 2.3, § 2.4) locks that we use and extend.

Notation/Naming: We denote the number of processes as P; we use the notion of a *process* as it occurs frequently in DM codes such as MPI [36]. Still, our schemes are independent of whether heavyweight processes or lightweight threads are incorporated. Each process has a unique ID called the *rank* $\in \{1,...,P\}$. A process in the CS is called *active*. A null pointer is denoted as $\varnothing$. Then, N is the number of levels of the memory hierarchy of the used machine. Here, the selection of the considered levels depends on the user. For example, one can only focus on the nodes connected with a network and racks that contain nodes and thus $N = 3$ (three levels: the nodes, the racks, and the whole machine). We refer to a single considered machine part (e.g., a node) as an *element*. We refer to a node that is a shared-memory cache-coherent domain connected to other such domains with a non-coherent network as a *compute node* (or just *node*). One compute node may contain smaller elements that

are cache-coherent and together offer *non-uniform memory access (NUMA)*. We refer to such elements as *NUMA nodes*; an example NUMA node is a socket with a local DRAM. We present symbols used in the paper in Table 1.

P	Number of processes.
p	Rank of a process that attempts to acquire/release a lock.
N	Number of levels of the considered machine.
N_i	Number of machine elements at level i; $1 \leq i \leq N$.
i	Index used to refer to the ith machine level.
j	Index used to refer to the jth element at a given machine level.

Table 1: Symbols used in the paper.

2.1 RMA Programming

In RMA programming, processes communicate by directly accessing one another's memories. Usually, RMA is built over OS-bypass RDMA hardware for highest performance. RMA non-blocking *put*s (writes to remote memories) and *get*s (reads from remote memories) offer low latencies, potentially outperforming message passing [17]. Remote *atomics* such as compare-and-swap [21,36] are also available. Finally, RMA *flushes* ensure the consistency of data by synchronizing respective memories. RDMA is provided in virtually all modern networks (e.g., IBM PERCS [3], IBM's on-chip Cell, InfiniBand [43], iWARP [18], and RoCE [26]). Moreover, numerous libraries and languages offer RMA features. Examples include MPI-3 RMA [36], UPC [44], Titanium [22], Fortran 2008 [27], X10 [11], or Chapel [10]. The number of RMA codes is growing steadily.

RMA Windows: In RMA, each process explicitly exposes an area of its local memory as shared. In MPI, this region is called a *window*. Once shared, a window can be accessed with puts/gets/atomics and synchronized with flushes. We will refer to such an exposed memory in any RMA library/language as a window.

RMA Functions: We describe the syntax/semantics of the used RMA calls in Listing 1. All ints are 64-bit. For clarity, we also use the bool type and assume it to be an int that can take the 0 (false) or 1 (true) values, respectively. Values returned by Get/FAO/CAS are only valid after the subsequent Flush. The syntax is simplified for clarity: we omit a pointer to the accessed window (we use a single window). We use an *origin*/a *target* to refer to a process that issues or is targeted by an RMA call.

```
1  /* Common parameters: target: target's rank; offset: an offset
2   * into target's window that determines the location of the
3   * targeted data; op: an operation applied to a remote piece of
4   * data (either an atomic replace (REPLACE) or a sum (SUM));
5   * oprd: the operand of an atomic operation op.*/
6
7  /* Place atomically src_data in target's window.*/
8  void Put(int src_data, int target, int offset);
9
10 /* Fetch and return atomically data from target's window.*/
11 int Get(int target, int offset);
12
13 /* Apply atomically op using oprd to data at target.*/
14 void Accumulate(int oprd, int target, int offset, MPI_Op op);
15
16 /* Atomically apply op using oprd to data at target
17  * and return the previous value of the modified data.*/
18 int FAO(int oprd, int target, int offset, MPI_Op op);
19
20 /* Atomically compare cmp_data with data at target and, if
21  * equal, replace it with src_data; return the previous data.*/
22 int CAS(int src_data, int cmp_data, int target, int offset);
23
24 /* Complete all pending RMA calls started by the calling process
25  * and targeted at target.*/
26 void Flush(int target);
```

Listing 1: The syntax/semantics of the utilized RMA calls.

2.2 Traditional Hardware-Oblivious Locks

We now present hardware-oblivious locks used in this work.

2.2.1 Reader-Writer (RW) Locks

Reader-Writer (RW) locks [12] distinguish between processes that only perform reads when in the CS (*readers*) and those that issue writes (*writers*). Here, multiple readers may simultaneously enter a given CS, but only one writer can be granted access at a time, with no other concurrent readers or writers. RW locks are used in OS kernels, databases, and present in various HPC libraries such as MPI-3 [36].

2.2.2 MCS Locks

Unlike RW locks, the MCS lock (due to Mellor-Crummey and Scott) [34, 40, 42] does not distinguish between readers or writers. Instead, it only allows one process p at a time to enter the CS, regardless of the type of memory accesses issued by p. Here, processes waiting for the lock form a queue, with a process at the head holding the lock. The queue contains a single global pointer to its tail. Moreover, each process in the queue maintains: (1) a local flag that signals if it can enter the CS and (2) a pointer to its successor. To enter the queue, a process p updates both the global pointer to the tail and the pointer at its predecessor so that they both point to p. A releasing process notifies its successor by changing the successor's local flag. The MCS lock reduces the amount of coherence traffic that limits the performance of spinlocks [2]. Here, each process in the queue spin waits on its local flag that is modified once by its predecessor.

2.3 State-of-the-Art NUMA-Aware Locks

We now discuss lock schemes that use the knowledge of the NUMA structure of the underlying machine for more performance. We will combine and extend them to DM domains, and enrich them with a family of adjustable parameters for high performance with various workloads.

2.3.1 NUMA-Aware RW Locks

Many traditional RW locks (§ 2.2.1) entail performance penalties in NUMA systems as they usually rely on a centralized structure that becomes a bottleneck and entails high latency when accessed by processes from remote NUMA elements. Calciu et al. [8] tackle this issue with a flag on each NUMA node that indicates if there is an active reader on that node. This reduces contention due to readers (each reader only marks a local flag) but may entail additional overheads for writers that check for active readers.

2.3.2 Hierarchical MCS Locks

Hierarchical locks tackle expensive lock passing described in § 1. They trade fairness for higher throughput by ordering processes that enter the CS to reduce the number of such passings. Most of the proposed schemes address two-level NUMA machines [9, 14, 31, 38]. Chabbi et al. consider a multi-level NUMA system [9]. Here, each NUMA hierarchy element (e.g., a socket) entails a separate MCS lock. To acquire the global lock, a process acquires an MCS lock at each machine level. This increases locality but reduces fairness: processes on the same NUMA node acquire the lock consecutively even if processes on other nodes are waiting.

2.4 Distributed RMA MCS Locks

Finally, we present a distributed MCS (D-MCS) lock based on an MPI-3 MCS lock [19]. We will use it to accelerate state-of-the-art MPI RMA library foMPI [17] and as a building block of the proposed distributed topology-aware RW and MCS locks (§ 3).

2.4.1 Summary and Key Data Structures

Here, processes that wait for the D-MCS lock form a queue that may span multiple nodes. Each process maintains several globally visible variables. A naive approach would use one window per variable. However, this would entail additional memory overheads (one window requires $\Omega(P)$ storage in the worst case [17]). Thus, we use one window with different offsets determining different variables: a pointer to the next process in the MCS queue (offset NEXT, initially $\varnothing$) and a flag indicating if a given process has to spin wait (offset WAIT, initially false). A selected process (rank tail_rank) also maintains a pointer to a process with the queue tail (offset TAIL, initially $\varnothing$).

2.4.2 Lock Protocols

We now describe the protocols for acquire/release. We refer to respective variables using their offsets in the window.

Lock Acquire (Listing 2) First, p atomically modifies TAIL with its own rank and fetches the predecessor rank (Line 6). If there is no predecessor, it proceeds to the CS. Otherwise, it enqueues itself (Line 10) and waits until its local WAIT is set to false. Flushes ensure the data consistency.

```
1  void acquire() {
2     /* Prepare local fields. */
3     Put(∅, p, NEXT);
4     Put(true, p, STATUS);
5     /* Enter the tail of the MCS queue and get the predecessor. */
6     int pred = FAO(p, tail_rank, TAIL, REPLACE);
7     Flush(tail_rank); /* Ensure completion of FAO. */
8     if(pred != ∅) { /* Check if there is a predecessor. */
9        /* Make the predecessor see us. */
10       Put(p, pred, NEXT); Flush(pred);
11       bool waiting = true;
12       do { /* Spin locally until we get the lock. */
13          waiting = Get(p, WAIT); Flush(p);
14       } while(waiting == true); } }
```

Listing 2: Acquiring D-MCS.

Lock Release (Listing 3) First, p checks if it has a successor in the queue (Line 3). If there is none, it atomically verifies if it is still the queue tail (Line 5); if yes, it sets TAIL to $\varnothing$. Otherwise, p waits for a process that has modified TAIL to update its NEXT field (Lines 9-11). If there is a successor, the lock is passed with a single Put (Line 14).

```
1  void release() {
2     int succ = Get(p, NEXT); Flush(p);
3     if(succ == ∅) {
4        /* Check if we are waiting for the next proc to notify us.*/
5        int curr_rank = CAS(∅, p, tail_rank, TAIL);
6        Flush(tail_rank);
7        if(p == curr_rank)
8           return; /* We are the only process in the queue. */
9        do { /* Wait for a successor. */
10          successor = Get(p, NEXT); Flush(p);
11       } while (successor == ∅);
12    }
13    /* Notify the successor. */
14    Put(0, successor, WAIT); Flush(successor);}
```

Listing 3: Releasing D-MCS.

3 DISTRIBUTED RMA RW LOCKS

We now present a distributed *topology-aware* RW lock (RMA-RW) for scalable synchronization and full utilization of parallelism in workloads dominated by reads. For brevity, we focus on the RW semantics and only briefly discuss the topology-aware MCS lock (§ 3.5); full algorithm listings for

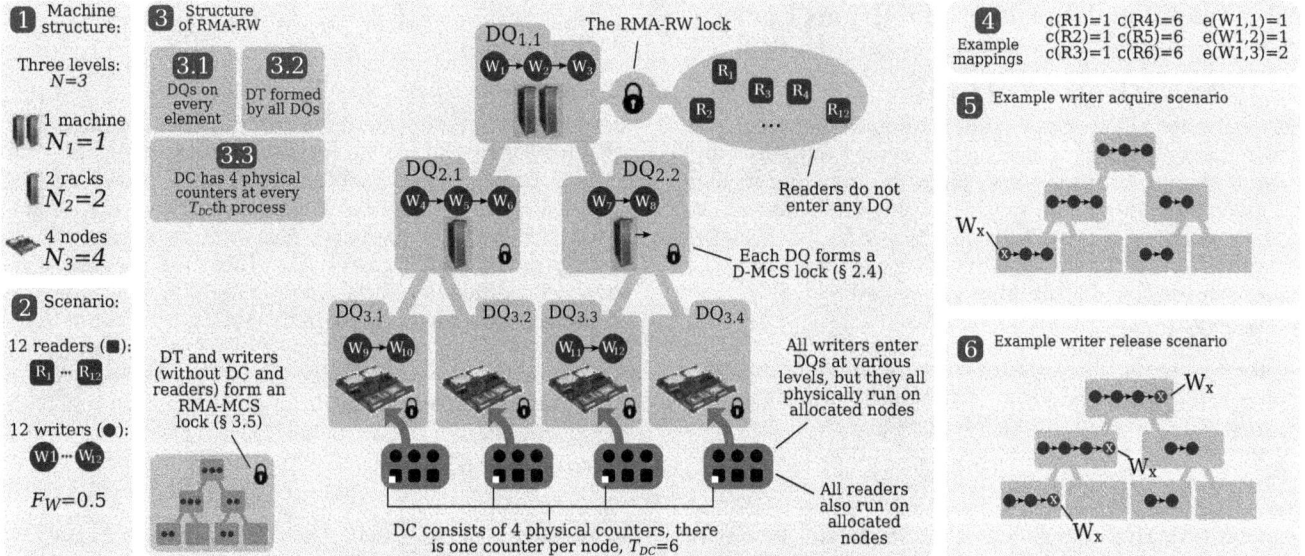

Figure 2: An example RMA-RW on a three-level system.

the latter can be found in an extended technical report[1]. Symbols specific to RMA-RW are presented in Table 2.

Lock Abbreviations We always refer to the proposed topology-aware distributed RW and MCS lock as RMA-RW and RMA-MCS, respectively. Both RMA-RW and RMA-MCS use as their building block a simple distributed topology-oblivious MCS lock (§ 2.4) denoted as D-MCS.

Example In the whole section, we will use the example shown in Figure 2. Here, $N = 3$ and the considered levels are: compute nodes, racks, and the whole machine.

T_{DC}	The *Distributed Counter* threshold (§ 3.2.1).
$T_{L,i}$	The *Locality* threshold at level i (§ 3.2.2).
T_R	The *Reader* threshold (§ 3.2.3).
T_W	The *Writer* threshold; $T_W = \prod_{i=1}^{N} T_{L,i}$ (§ 3.2.3).
$c(p)$	Mapping from a process p to its physical counter (§ 3.2.1).
$e(p,i)$	Mapping from a process p to its home machine element at level i (§ 3.2.2).
F_W	The fraction of writers in a given workload (the fraction of readers: $1 - F_W$).

Table 2: Symbols used in RMA-RW.

3.1 Design Summary and Intuition

As explained in § 1, RMA-RW consists of three types of core data structures: distributed queues (DQs), a distributed tree (DT), and a distributed counter (DC). They are illustrated in Figure 2. First, every machine element (at each considered level) has an associated DQ and thus a D-MCS lock *local* to this element (as opposed to the *global* RMA-RW lock). In our example, every node, rack, and the whole machine have their own DQ (and thus a local MCS lock). Note that some DQs that are associated with elements such as nodes are not necessarily distributed, but we use the same name for clarity. Second, all the DQs form a DT that corresponds to the underlying memory hierarchy, with one DQ related to one tree vertex. For example, DQs associated with nodes that belong to a given rack r constitute vertices that are children of a vertex associated with a DQ running on rack r. Third, DC counts active readers and writers and consists of several physical counters located on selected processes. DT on its own (without DC and any readers) constitutes RMA-MCS.

Writers A writer that wants to acquire a lock starts at a leaf of DT located at the lowest level N (a node in our

---

[1] http://spcl.inf.ethz.ch/Research/Parallel_Programming/RMALocks

example). At any level i ($2 \leq i \leq N$), it acquires a local D-MCS lock that corresponds to a subtree of D-MCS locks (and thus DQs) rooted at the given element. Here, it may compete with other writers. When it reaches level 1, it executes a different protocol for acquiring the whole RMA-RW lock. Here, it may also compete with readers. RMA-RW's locality-aware design enables a *shortcut*: some writers stop before reaching level 1 and directly proceed to the CS. This happens if a lock is passed within a given machine element.

Readers Readers do not enter DQs and DT and thus have a single acquire protocol. This design reduces synchronization overhead among readers.

3.2 Key Data Structures

We now present the key structures in more detail.

3.2.1 Distributed Counter (DC)

DC maintains the number of active readers or writers. It enables an adjustable performance tradeoff that accelerates readers or writers. For this, one DC consists of multiple physical counters, each maintained by every T_{DC}th process; T_{DC} is a parameter selected by the user. To enter the CS, a reader p increments only one associated physical counter while a writer must check each one of them. Thus, selecting more physical counters (smaller T_{DC}) entails lower reader latency (as each reader can access a counter located on a closer machine element) and contention (as each counter is accessed by fewer readers). Yet, higher T_{DC} entails lower latency for a writer that accesses fewer physical counters.

A physical counter associated with a reader p is located at a rank $c(p)$; $c(\cdot) \in \{1, ..., P\}$ can be determined at compile- or run-time. In a simple hardware-oblivious scheme, one can fix $c(p) = \lceil p/T_{DC} \rceil$. For more performance, the user can locate physical counters in a topology-aware way. For example, if the user allocates x processes/node and a node s hosts processes with x successive ranks starting from $(s - 1)x + 1$, then setting $T_{DC} = kx$ in the above formula results in storing one physical counter every kth node. This can be generalized to any other machine element.

To increase performance, we implement each physical counter as two 64-bit fields that count the readers (assigned to this counter) that arrived and departed from the CS, re-

22

spectively. This facilitates obtaining the number of readers that acquired the lock since the last writer and reduces contention between processes that acquire and release the lock. We dedicate one bit of the field that counts arriving readers to indicate whether the CS of RMA-RW is in the READ mode (it contains readers) or the WRITE mode (it contains a writer).

RMA Design of DC: Each physical counter occupies two words with offsets ARRIVE (for counting arriving readers) and DEPART (for counting departing readers); physical counters together constitute an RMA window.

3.2.2 Distributed Queue (DQ)

DQ orders writers from a single element of the machine that attempt to enter the CS. DQs from level i have an associated threshold $T_{L,i}$ that determines the maximum number of lock passings between writers running on a machine element from this level before the lock is passed to a process from a different element. We use a separate threshold $T_{L,i}$ for each i because some levels (e.g., racks) may need more locality (a higher threshold) than others (e.g., nodes) due to expensive data transfers. This design enables an adjustable tradeoff between fairness and throughput at each level.

DQ extends D-MCS in that the local flag that originally signals whether a process can enter the CS now becomes an integer that carries (in the same RMA operation) the number of past lock acquires within a given machine element. We use this value to decide whether to pass the lock to a different element at a given level i (if the value reaches $T_{L,i}$) or not (if the value is below $T_{L,i}$).

RMA Design of DQ: All DQs at a given level constitute an RMA window. Respective offsets in the window are as follows: NEXT (a rank of the next process in the queue), STATUS (an integer that both signals whether to spin wait and carries the number of past lock acquires in the associated machine element), and TAIL (a rank of the process that constitutes the current tail of the queue). TAIL in DQ at level i associated with jth element is stored on a process tail_rank[i,j].

3.2.3 Distributed Tree of Queues (DT)

DT combines DQs at different memory hierarchy levels into a single structure. This enables p to make progress in acquiring/releasing RMA-RW by moving from level N to level 1. Then, at the tree root, writers synchronize with readers. Specifically, the lock is passed from writers to readers (if there are some waiting) when the total number of lock passings between writers reaches a threshold T_W. In our design, $T_W = \prod_{i=1}^{N} T_{L,i}$. To avoid starvation of writers, we also introduce a threshold T_R that is the maximum number of readers that can enter the CS consecutively before the lock is passed to a writer (if there is one waiting). Increasing T_R or T_W improves the throughput of readers or writers because more processes of a given type can enter the CS consecutively.

While climbing up DT, a writer must determine the next DQ (and thus D-MCS) to enter. This information is encoded in a mapping $e(\cdot,\cdot)$ and structure tail_rank[i,j]. $e(p,i) \in \{1,...,N_i\}$ returns the ID of a machine element associated with a process p at level i. An expression tail_rank[i,e(p,i)] returns the rank of a process that points to the tail of a DQ at level i within a machine element assigned to p. This enables p to enter D-MCS at the next level on the way to the CS. Similarly to $c(p)$, $e(p,i)$ can be determined statically or dynamically.

Depending on $T_{L,i}$, some writers do not have to climb all DT levels and can proceed directly to the CS. Thus, we fur-

ther extend the STATUS field used in DQ with one more special value ACQUIRE_PARENT. This indicates that p cannot directly enter the CS and should continue up DT.

3.2.4 Discussion on the Status Field

A central part of DQ and DT is the STATUS field that enables processes to exchange various additional types of information in a single RMA communication action, including: (1) if a lock mode changed (e.g., from READ to WRITE), (2) if a given process should acquire a lock at a higher DT level, (3) if a given process can enter the CS, and (4) the number of past consecutive lock acquires. Two selected integer values are dedicated to indicate (1) and (2). All the remaining possible values indicate that the given process can enter the CS (3); at the same time the value communicates (4).

3.3 Distributed Reader-Writer Protocol

We now illustrate how the above data structures play together in the acquire and release protocols. A writer starts at the leaf of DT (level N) both for acquiring and releasing. At any level i ($2 \leq i \leq N$), it proceeds up the tree executing a protocol for a partial acquire/release of the respective part of the tree (§ 3.3.1, § 3.3.2). At level 1, it executes a different protocol for locking or releasing the whole lock (§ 3.3.3, § 3.3.4). Readers do not follow such a hierarchy and thus have single acquire (§ 3.3.5) and release (§ 3.3.6) protocols.

3.3.1 Writer Lock Acquire: Level N to 2 (Listing 4)

Intuition: p enters the DQ associated with a given level i and its home element $e(p,i)$; it then waits for the update from its predecessor. If the predecessor does not have to hand over the lock to a process from another element (i.e., has not reached the threshold $T_{L,i}$), the lock is passed to p that immediately enters the CS. Otherwise, p moves to level $i-1$.

Details: p first modifies its NEXT and STATUS to reflect it spin waits at the DQ tail (Lines 2-3). Then, it enqueues itself (Line 5). If there is a predecessor at this level, p makes itself visible to it with a Put (Line 8) and then waits until it obtains the lock. While waiting, p uses Gets and Flushes to check for any updates from the predecessor. If the predecessor reached $T_{L,i}$ and released the lock to the parent level, p must itself acquire the lock from level $i-1$ (Line 23). Otherwise, it can directly enter the CS as the lock is simply passed to it (Line 18). If there is no predecessor at level i, p also proceeds to acquire the lock for level $i-1$ (Line 23).

```
1  void writer-acquire<i>() {
2    Put(∅, p, NEXT);
3    Put(WAIT, p, STATUS); Flush(p);
4    /* Enter the DQ at level i and in this machine element. */
5    int pred = FAO(p, tail_rank[i,e(p,i)], TAIL, REPLACE);
6    Flush(tail_rank[i,e(p,i)]);
7    if(pred != ∅) {
8      Put(p, pred, NEXT); Flush(pred); /* pred sees us. */
9      int status = WAIT;
10     do { /* Wait until pred passes the lock. */
11       status = Get(p, STATUS); Flush(p);
12     } while(status == WAIT);
13     /* Check if pred released the lock to the parent level. This
14        would happen if T_L,i is reached. */
15     if(status != ACQUIRE_PARENT) {
16       /* T_L,i is not reached. Thus, the lock is passed to
17          p that directly proceeds to the CS. */
18       return; /* The global lock is acquired. */
19     }
20   }
21   /* Start to acquire the next level of the tree.*/
22   Put(ACQUIRE_START, p, STATUS); Flush(p);
23   writer-acquire<i-1>();}
```

Listing 4: Acquiring the RMA-RW lock by a writer; levels N to 2.

3.3.2 Writer Lock Release: Level N to 2 (Listing 5)

Intuition: p passes the lock within $e(p,i)$ if there is a successor and $T_{L,i}$ is not yet reached. Otherwise, it releases the lock to the parent level $i-1$, leaves the DQ, and informs any new successor that it must acquire the lock at level $i-1$.

Details: p first finds out whether it has a successor. If there is one and $T_{L,i}$ is not yet reached, the lock is passed to it with a Put (Line 8). If $T_{L,i}$ is reached, p releases the lock for this level and informs its successor (if any) that it has to acquire the lock at level $i-1$. If there is no known successor, it checks atomically if some process has already entered the DQ at level i (Line 15). If so, the releaser waits for the successor to make himself visible before it is notified to acquire the lock at level $i-1$.

```
1  void writer-release<i>() {
2    /* Check if there is a successor and get the local status. */
3    int succ = Get(p, NEXT);
4    int status = Get(p, STATUS); Flush(p);
5    if(succ != ∅ && status < T_{L,i}) {
6      /* Pass the lock to succ at level i as well as the number
7         of past lock passings within this machine element. */
8      Put(status + 1, succ, STATUS); Flush(succ); return;
9    }
10   /* There is no known successor or the threshold at level i is
11      reached. Thus, release the lock to the parent level. */
12   writer-release<i-1>();
13   if(succ == ∅) {
14     /* Check if some process has just enqueued itself. */
15     int curr_rank = CAS(∅, p, tail_rank[i,e(p,i)], TAIL);
16     Flush(tail_rank[i,e(p,i)]);
17     if(p == curr_rank) { return; }
18     do { /* Otherwise, wait until succ makes itself visible. */
19       succ = Get(p, NEXT); Flush(p);
20     } while(succ == ∅);
21   }
22   /* Notify succ to acquire the lock at level i-1. */
23   Put(ACQUIRE_PARENT, succ, STATUS); Flush(succ); }
```

Listing 5: Releasing an RMA-RW lock by a writer; levels N to 2.

3.3.3 Writer Lock Acquire: Level 1 (Listing 7)

Intuition: This scheme is similar to acquiring the lock at lower levels (§ 3.3.1). However, the predecessor may notify p of the *lock mode change* that enabled readers to enter the CS, forcing p to acquire the lock from the readers.

Details: p first tries to obtain the lock from a predecessor (Lines 2-18). If there is one, p waits until the lock is passed. Still, it can happen that the predecessor hands the lock over to the readers (Line 14). Here, p changes the mode back to WRITE before entering the CS (Line 16); this function checks each counter to verify if there are active readers. If not, it switches the value of each counter to WRITE (see Listing 6). If there is no predecessor (Line 19), p tries to acquire the lock from the readers by changing the mode to WRITE (Line 21).

3.3.4 Writer Lock Release: Level 1 (Listing 8)

Intuition: p first checks if it has reached T_W and if there is a successor waiting at level 1. If any case is true, it passes the lock to the readers and notifies any successor that it must acquire the lock from them. Otherwise, the lock is handed over to the successor.

Details: First, if T_W is reached, p passes the lock to the readers by resetting the counters (Line 6). Then, if it has no successor, it similarly enables the readers to enter the CS (Line 12). Later, p appropriately modifies the tail of the DQ and verifies if there is a new successor (Line 17). If necessary, it passes the lock to the successor with a Put (line 23) and simultaneously (using next_stat) notifies it about a possible lock mode change.

```
1  /****** Change all physical counters to the WRITE mode ******/
2  void set_counters_to_WRITE() {
3    /* To simplify, we use one counter every T_DC th process. */
4    for(int p = 0; p < P; p += T_DC) {
5      /* Increase the arrival counter to block the readers.*/
6      Accumulate(INT64_MAX/2, p, ARRIVE, SUM); Flush(p);
7  } }
8
9  /**************** Reset one physical counter ****************/
10 void reset_counter(int rank) {
11   /* Get the current values of the counters.*/
12   int arr_cnt = Get(rank, ARRIVE), dep_cnt = Get(rank, DEPART);
13   Flush(rank);
14   /* Prepare the values to be subtracted from the counters.*/
15   int sub_arr_cnt = -dep_cnt, sub_dep_cnt = -dep_cnt;
16
17   /* Make sure that the WRITE is reset if it was set.*/
18   if(arr_cnt >= INT64_MAX/2) {
19     sub_arr_cnt -= INT64_MAX/2;
20   }
21   /* Subtract the values from the current counters.*/
22   Accumulate(sub_arr_cnt, rank, ARRIVE, SUM);
23   Accumulate(sub_dep_cnt, rank, DEPART, SUM); Flush(rank);
24 }
25
26 /**************** Reset all physical counters ****************/
27 void reset_counters() {
28   for(int p = 0; p < P; p += T_DC) { reset_counter(p); } }
```

Listing 6: Functions that manipulate counters.

```
1  void writer-acquire<1>() {
2    Put(∅, p, NEXT); Put(WAIT, p, STATUS);
3    Flush(p); /* Prepare to enter the DQ.*/
4    /* Enqueue oneself to the end of the DQ at level 1.*/
5    int pred = FAO(p, tail_rank[1,e(p,1)], TAIL, REPLACE);
6    Flush(tail_rank[1,e(p,1)]);
7
8    if(pred != ∅) { /* If there is a predecessor...*/
9      Put(p, pred, NEXT); Flush(pred);
10     int curr_stat = WAIT;
11     do { /* Wait until pred notifies us.*/
12       curr_stat = Get(p, STATUS); Flush(p);
13     } while (curr_stat == WAIT);
14     if(curr_stat == MODE_CHANGE) { /* The lock mode changed...*/
15       /* The readers have the lock now; try to get it back.*/
16       set_counters_to_WRITE();
17       Put(ACQUIRE_START, p, STATUS); Flush(p);
18     } }
19   else { /* If there is no predecessor...*/
20     /* Change the counters to WRITE as we have the lock now.*/
21     set_counters_to_WRITE();
22     Put(ACQUIRE_START, p, STATUS); Flush(p); } }
```

Listing 7: Acquiring an RMA-RW lock by a writer; level 1.

3.3.5 Reader Lock Acquire (Listing 9)

Intuition: Here, p first spin waits if there is an active writer or if p's arrival made its associated counter $c(p)$ exceed T_R. Then, it can enter the CS. If $c(p) = T_R$, then p resets DC.

Details: In the first part, p may spin wait on a boolean barrier variable (Line 5), waiting to get the lock from a writer. Then, p atomically increments its associated counter and checks whether the count is below T_R. If yes, the lock mode is READ and p enters the CS. Otherwise, either the lock mode is WRITE or T_R is reached. In case of the latter, p checks if there are any waiting writers (Line 17). If there are none, p resets the DC (Line 20) and re-attempts to acquire the lock. If there is a writer, p sets the local barrier and waits for DC to be reset by the writer.

3.3.6 Reader Lock Release (Listing 10)

Releasing a reader lock only involves incrementing the departing reader counter.

```
1  void reader-release() {
2    Accumulate(1, c(p), DEPART, SUM); Flush(c(p)); }
```

Listing 10: Releasing an RMA-RW reader lock.

3.4 Example

Consider the scenario from Figure 2. Here, there are three machine levels, 12 readers, and 12 writers ($F_W = 0.5$).

```
1  void writer-release<1>(){
2    bool counters_reset = false;
3    /* Get the count of consecutive lock acquires (level 1).*/
4    int next_stat = Get(p, STATUS); Flush(p);
5    if(++next_stat == T_W) { /* Pass the lock to the readers.*/
6      reset_counters();/* See Listing 6.*/
7      next_stat = MODE_CHANGE; counters_reset = true;
8    }
9    int succ = Get(p, NEXT); Flush(p);
10   if(succ == ∅) { /* No known successor.*/
11     if(!counters_reset) { /* Pass the lock to the readers.*/
12       reset_counters(); next_stat = MODE_CHANGE;/* Listing 6.*/
13     }
14     /* Check if some process has already entered the DQ.*/
15     int curr_rank = CAS(∅, p, tail_rank[1,e(p,1)], TAIL);
16     Flush(tail_rank[1,e(p,1)]);
17     if(p == curr_rank) { return; } /* No successor...*/
18     do { /* Wait until the successor makes itself visible.*/
19       succ = Get(p, NEXT); Flush(p);
20     } while (succ == ∅);
21   }
22   /* Pass the lock to the successor.*/
23   Put(next_stat, succ, STATUS); Flush(succ); }
```

Listing 8: Releasing an RMA-RW lock by a writer; level 1.

```
1  void reader-acquire() {
2    bool done = false; bool barrier = false;
3    while(!done) {
4      int curr_stat = 0;
5      if(barrier) {
6        do {
7          curr_stat = Get(c(p), ARRIVE); Flush(c(p));
8        } while(curr_stat >= T_R);
9      }
10
11     /* Increment the arrival counter.*/
12     curr_stat = FAO(1, c(p), ARRIVE, SUM); Flush(c(p));
13     if(curr_stat >= T_R) { /* T_R has been reached...*/
14       barrier = true;
15       if(curr_stat == T_R) {/* We are the first to reach T_R.*/
16         /* Pass the lock to the writers if there are any.*/
17         int curr_tail = Get(tail_rank[1,e(p,1)], TAIL);
18         Flush(tail_rank[1,e(p,1)]);
19         if(curr_tail == ∅) { /* There are no waiting writers.*/
20           reset_counter(c(p)); barrier = false;/* Listing 6.*/
21         }
22       }
23       /* Back off and try again.*/
24       Accumulate(-1, c(p), ARRIVE, SUM); Flush(c(p));
25   } } }
```

Listing 9: Acquiring an RMA-RW lock by a reader.

Writer Acquire Assume a new writer W_x running on a node related to $DQ_{3.1}$ attempts to acquire RMA-RW (Figure 2, Part 5). First, it enters $DQ_{3.1}$ (Listing 4). As this queue is not empty, W_x spins locally (Lines 10-12) until its predecessor W_9 modifies W_x's STATUS. Now, if W_9 has not yet reached $T_{L,3}$, W_x gets the lock and immediately proceeds to the CS (Lines 15-19). Otherwise, it attempts to move to level 2 by updating its STATUS (Line 22) and calling writer-acquire<$i-1$>(). Thus, it enters $DQ_{2.1}$ and takes the same steps as in $DQ_{3.1}$: it spins locally until W_4 changes its STATUS and it either directly enters the CS or it proceeds up to level 1. Assuming the latter, W_x enters $DQ_{1.1}$ and waits for W_1 to change its STATUS (Listing 7, Lines 10-12). If STATUS is different from MODE_CHANGE (Line 17), W_x can enter the CS. Otherwise, the lock was handed over to the readers and W_x calls set_counters_to_WRITE() to change all physical counters to the WRITE mode (Line 15), which blocks new incoming readers. At some point, the readers reach the T_R threshold and hand the lock over to W_x.

Writer Release Assume writer W_x occupies the CS and starts to release RMA-RW (Figure 2, Part 6). It begins with level 3 (Listing 5). Here, it first checks if it has a successor in $DQ_{3.1}$ and if $T_{L,3}$ is not yet reached (Line 5). Its successor is W_{10} and assume that the latter condition is true. Then, W_x passes the lock to W_{10} by updating its STATUS so that it contains the number of lock acquires within the given element.

If $T_{L,3}$ is reached, W_x releases the lock at level 2 (Line 12). Here, it repeats all the above steps (its successor is W_6) and then starts to release the lock at level 1 (Listing 8). Here it hands the lock over to the readers if T_W is reached (Lines 5-8). Finally, it notifies its successors at each level (N to 2) to acquire the lock at the parent level (Listing 5, Line 23).

Reader Acquire A reader R_x that attempts to acquire RMA-RW first increments $c(R_x)$ (Listing 9, Line 12) and checks if T_R is reached (in the first attempt Lines 6-8 are skipped). If yes, it sets barrier (Line 14), backs off (Line 24), and reattempts to acquire the lock. In addition, if R_x is the first process to reach T_R, it also checks if there are any waiting writers (Lines 15-21). If not, it resets $c(R_x)$ and sets barrier to false so that it can enter the CS even if T_R was reached. Then, it reexecutes the main loop (Line 3); this time it may enter the loop in Lines 6-8 as the lock was handed over to a writer (if T_R was reached). In that case, R_x waits until its $c(R_x)$ is reset (Listing 9, Lines 6-8).

Reader Release This is a straightforward scenario in which R_x only increments DEPART at $c(R_x)$.

3.5 RMA-RW vs. RMA-MCS

We now outline the design of RMA-MCS; the details are in the technical report. RMA-MCS consists of DQs and DT but not DC. T_R and T_W are excluded as the are no readers. Similarly, $T_{L,1}$ is not applicable because there is no need to hand the lock to readers. The acquire/release protocols are similar to the ones in Listings 4 and 5 for any $i \in \{1, ..., N\}$.

4 CORRECTNESS ANALYSIS

We now discuss how RMA-RW ensures three fundamental correctness properties: mutual exclusion (ME), deadlock freedom (DF), and starvation freedom (SF) [21]. At the end of this section, we show how we use model checking to verify the design.

4.1 Mutual Exclusion

ME is violated if two writers or a reader and a writer enter the CS concurrently. We now discuss both cases.

Writer & Writer: We distinguish between writers that are in the same DQ (case A) or in different ones (case B). In case A, they operate on the same TAIL. Thus, they could only violate ME if both writers do not see any predecessor. This is prevented by using FAO for atomically modifying TAIL. In case B, two writers competing in different DQs have a common DQ in DT where they or their predecessor compete for the lock. Similarly as above, the MCS lock must be acquired at each DT level. If a predecessor has to compete for the lock, a writer waits until he gets notified by its predecessor and thus does not interfere in the lock acquiring process.

Reader & Writer: A reader and a writer can be active at the same time if the lock mode is READ and about to change to WRITE. This is because the reader on its own cannot change the mode and as a consequence cannot acquire a lock while a writer is active. However, a writer can alter the mode to WRITE while a reader is active. This is prevented by a writer that checks each counter again for active readers after changing all of them.

4.2 Deadlock Freedom

Here, we also differentiate two base cases: two writers deadlock or a reader and a writer deadlock.

Writer & Writer The only way how writers deadlock is if there is a cycle in a queue. For two writers it means that

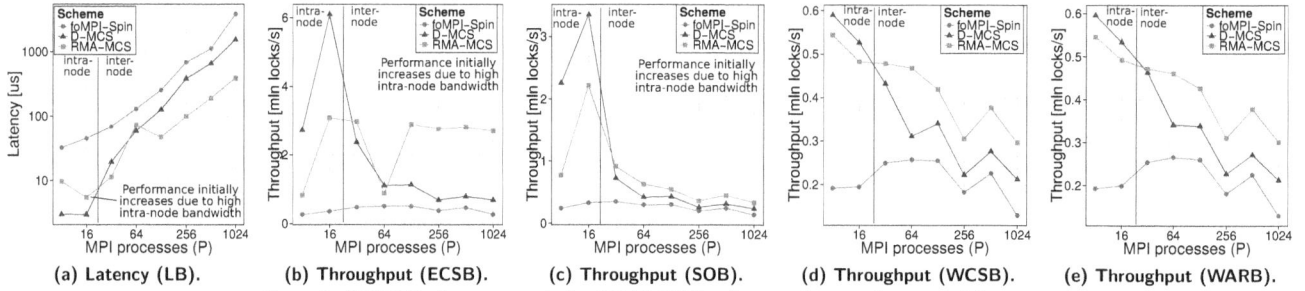

| (a) Latency (LB). | (b) Throughput (ECSB). | (c) Throughput (SOB). | (d) Throughput (WCSB). | (e) Throughput (WARB). |

Figure 3: (§ 5.1) Performance analysis of RMA-MCS and comparison to the state-of-the-art.

one becomes the predecessor of the other. Therefore, both wait on the other to get notified. This cannot happen as the processes use an atomic FAO to obtain their predecessor. As explained, this function is atomic and thus we can order the uses of FAO in a timeline. This contradicts that the writers have a cycle in their waiting queue.

Reader & Writer A reader may deadlock after T_R is reached (case A) or the mode goes into WRITE (case B). In case A, either there is no writer active and the reader resets the DC or a writer is waiting and a reader backs off. Thus, the writer changes the mode to WRITE after all readers back off which is done in a finite time. As writers do not deadlock and the last writer changes the mode back to READ, no reader will deadlock in case B either.

4.3 Starvation Freedom

Finally, we show that no writer or reader can starve.

Writers A writer may starve while other writers or readers are active. We prevent it with different thresholds. First, there is $T_{L,i}$ at each DT level i. After reaching $T_{L,i}$, writers in one of the associated DQs at i release the lock to the next DQ at the same level. Thus, we only need to show that one DQ is starvation-free which is already provided by the underlying MCS queue lock design. Yet, there is the T_R threshold that regulates the number of lock acquires by readers for one counter before the readers associated to the counter back off. We already showed that the readers make progress. Thus, at some point, all counters have reached T_R and a writer changes the mode to WRITE.

Readers There are two ways how readers could starve. First, other readers are active while processes associated with a certain counter back off to let writers acquire the lock. However, there is the T_R threshold for each counter after which the readers associated with this counter back off. Thus, eventually, all readers wait on the writers to take over. This leads us to the second case where the writers have the lock and do not pass it to the waiting readers. This is not possible since there is the $T_{L,i}$ threshold at each level of the writer hierarchy and at most after $T_W = \prod_{i=1}^{N} T_{L,i}$ lock passings between writers the lock goes to readers; we have also already illustrated that the writers will make progress until this threshold is reached.

4.4 Model Checking

To confirm that RMA-RW provides the desired correctness properties, we also conduct model checking with SPIN [24] (v6.4.5), a software tool for the formal verification of multi-threaded codes. The input to SPIN is constructed in PROMELA, a verification modeling language that allows for the dynamic creation of concurrent processes to model, for example, distributed systems. We evaluate RMA-RW for up to $N \in \{1, ..., 4\}$ and a maximum of 256 processes. The machine elements on each level of the simulated system have the same number of children. Thus, for $N = 3$ and four subelements per machine element, the system would consist of 4^3 processes. Each process is defined randomly either as a reader or a writer at the beginning and after that, it tries to acquire the lock 20 times. We choose this value as it generates a feasible number of cases that SPIN has to check even for a high count of processes. During the execution of a test, we use a designated process that verifies that either only one writer or multiple readers hold a lock. All the tests confirm mutual exclusion and deadlock freedom.

5 EVALUATION

We now illustrate performance advantages of RMA-MCS and RMA-RW over state-of-the-art distributed locks from the foMPI implementation of MPI-3 RMA [17].

Comparison Targets We consider D-MCS and both foMPI locking schemes: a simple spin-lock (foMPI-Spin) that enables mutual exclusion, and an RW lock (foMPI-RW) that provides both shared and exclusive accesses to the CS.

Selection of Benchmarks We conduct six series of experiments. The latency benchmark (LB) measures the latency of both acquiring and releasing a lock; an important performance metric in workloads such as real-time queries. Four other analyses obtain throughput under varying conditions and parameters. The empty-critical-section benchmark (ECSB) derives the throughput of acquiring an empty lock with no workload in the CS. The single-operation benchmark (SOB) measures the throughput of acquiring a lock with only one single operation (one memory access) in the CS; it represents irregular parallel workloads such as graph processing with vertices protected by fine locks. Next, the workload-critical-section benchmark (WCSB) covers variable workloads in the CS: each process increments a shared counter and then spins for a random time (1-$4\mu s$) to simulate local computation. The wait-after-release benchmark (WARB) varies lock contention: after release, processes wait for a random time (1-$4\mu s$) before the next acquire. The throughput experiments represent data- and communication-intensive workloads. Finally, we integrate and evaluate the proposed locks with a distributed hashtable (DHT) to cover real codes such as key-value stores.

Varied Parameters To evaluate various scenarios, we vary: T_{DC}, $T_{L,i}$, and T_R. Unless stated otherwise, we set the fraction of writers $F_W = 0.2\%$ as it reflects Facebook workloads [45]; however, we also evaluate other values.

Experimentation Methodology To calculate the latency, we derive the arithmetic mean of 100,000 operations per process (for each latency benchmark). Throughput is the aggre-

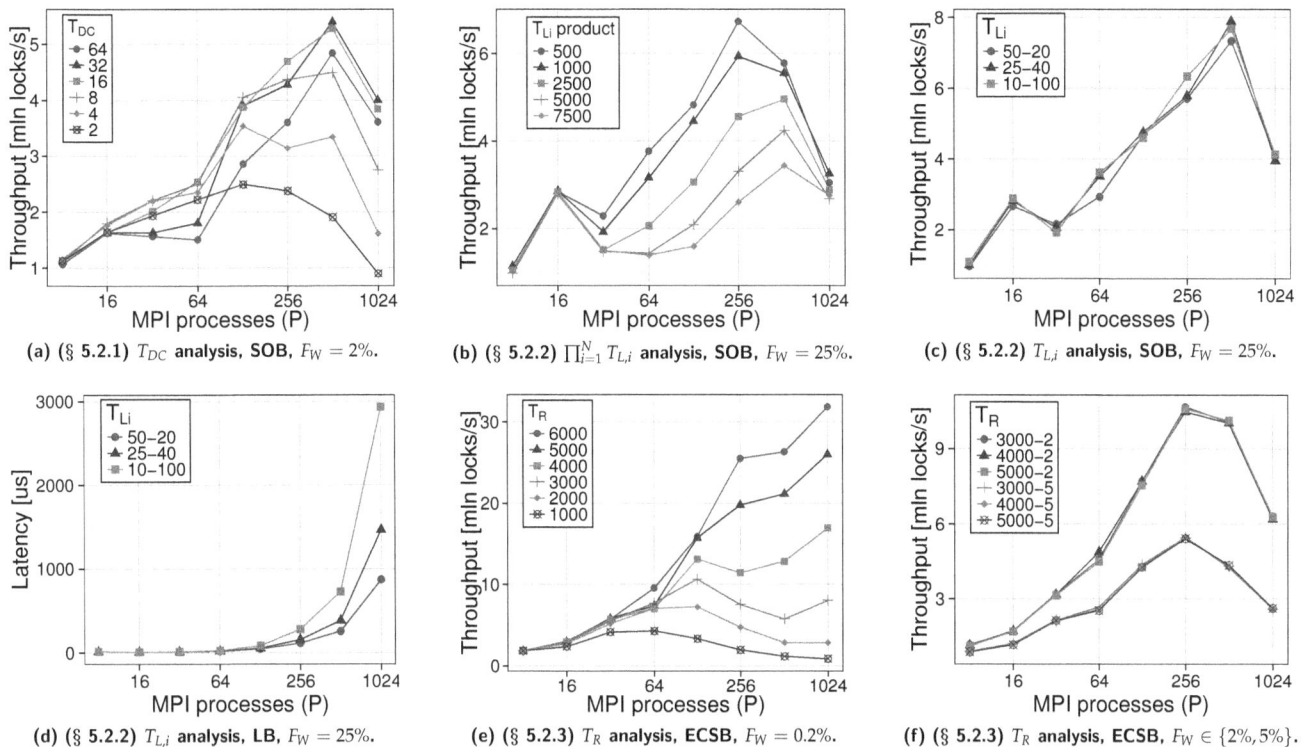

(a) (§ 5.2.1) T_{DC} analysis, SOB, $F_W = 2\%$.

(b) (§ 5.2.2) $\prod_{i=1}^{N} T_{L,i}$ analysis, SOB, $F_W = 25\%$.

(c) (§ 5.2.2) $T_{L,i}$ analysis, SOB, $F_W = 25\%$.

(d) (§ 5.2.2) $T_{L,i}$ analysis, LB, $F_W = 25\%$.

(e) (§ 5.2.3) T_R analysis, ECSB, $F_W = 0.2\%$.

(f) (§ 5.2.3) T_R analysis, ECSB, $F_W \in \{2\%, 5\%\}$.

Figure 4: Analysis of the performance impact of various thresholds.

gate count of lock acquires or releases divided by the total time to run a given benchmark. 10% of the first measurements are discarded (warmup). All time measurements are taken using a high precision rdtsc timer [23].

Experimental Setup We conduct experiments on CSCS Piz Daint (Cray XC30). Each node has an 8-core HT-enabled Intel Xeon E5-2670 CPU with 32 GiB DDR3-1600 RAM. The interconnection is based on Cray's Aries and it implements the Dragonfly topology [16, 28]. The batch system is slurm 14.03.7. We use C++ and the GNU 5.2.40 g++ compiler with -O3 optimizations. The utilized Cray DMAPP is 7.0.1-1.0501.8315.8.4.ari. Unless stated otherwise, we use all the compute resources and run one MPI process per one HT resource (16 processes per one compute node).

Machine Model We consider two levels of the hierarchy: the whole machine and compute nodes, thus $N = 2$.

Implementation Details We use the *libtopodisc* [20] library for discovering the structure of the underlying compute nodes and for obtaining MPI communicators that enable communication within each node. We group all the locking structures in MPI allocated windows to reduce the memory footprint [17].

5.1 Performance Analysis of RMA-MCS

We present the results in Figure 3. The latency of RMA-MCS is lower than any other target. For example, for $P = 1,024$, it is $\approx$10x and $\approx$4x lower than foMPI-Spin and D-MCS, respectively. This is because foMPI-Spin entails lock contention that limits performance. In addition, both foMPI-Spin and D-MCS are topology-oblivious. Then, the throughput analysis confirms the advantages of RMA-MCS across all the considered benchmarks. The interesting spike in ECSB and SOB is because moving from $P = 8$ to $P = 16$ does not entail internode communication, initially increasing RMA-MCS's and

D-MCS's throughput. We conclude that RMA-MCS consistently outperforms the original foMPI design and D-MCS.

5.2 Performance Analysis of RMA-RW

We now proceed to evaluate RMA-RW. First, we analyze the impact of various design parameters (Figure 4) and then compare it to the state-of-the-art (Figure 5). Due to space constraints, we only present a subset of the results, all remaining plots follow similar performance patterns and are included in the technical report[2].

5.2.1 Influence of T_{DC}

We first discuss how different T_{DC} values impact performance. We consider $T_{DC} \in \{1, 2, 4\}$ (one physical counter on each compute node and every 2nd and 4th compute node, respectively). We also vary the number of counters on one node $(1, 2, 4, 8)$. The results are presented in Figure 4a. First, lower T_{DC} entails more work for writers that must access more counters while changing the lock mode. This limits performance, especially for high P, because of the higher total number of counters. Larger T_{DC} increases throughput (less work for writers), but at some point (e.g., $P = 512$ a counter on every 2nd node) the overhead due to readers (contention and higher latency) begins to dominate. We conclude that selecting the proper T_{DC} is important for high performance of RMA-RW, but the best value depends on many factors and should be tuned for a specific machine. For example, higher T_{DC} might entail unpredictable performance penalties on Cray XE because the job scheduler does not enforce contiguous job allocations [5].

5.2.2 Influence of $T_{L,i}$

Next, we analyze the performance impact of $T_{L,i}$ in the considered system $i \in \{1, 2\}$. We fix $F_W = 25\%$ to en-

---

[2]http://spcl.inf.ethz.ch/Research/Parallel_Programming/RMALocks

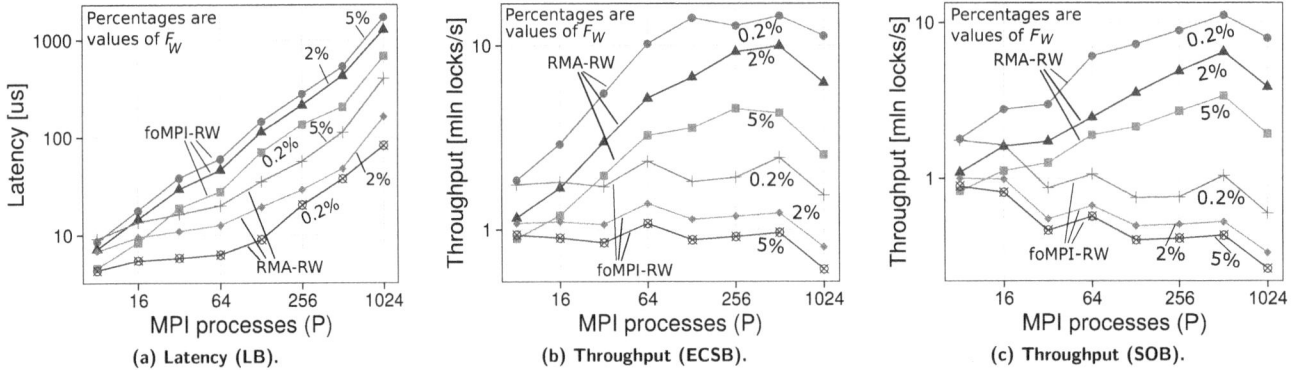

(a) Latency (LB). (b) Throughput (ECSB). (c) Throughput (SOB).

Figure 5: (§ 5.2.4) Performance analysis of RMA-RW and comparison to the state-of-the-art.

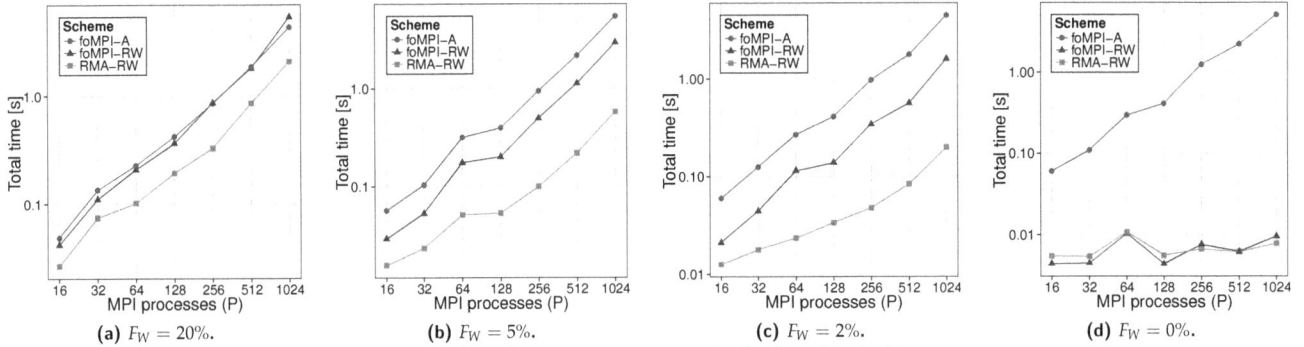

(a) $F_W = 20\%$. (b) $F_W = 5\%$. (c) $F_W = 2\%$. (d) $F_W = 0\%$.

Figure 6: (§ 5.3) Performance analysis of a distributed hashtable.

sure that there are multiple writers per machine element on each level. We start with various $\prod_{i=1}^{N} T_{L,i}$: the maximal number of writer acquires before the lock is passed to the readers; see Figure 4b. As expected, smaller product increases throughput because more readers can enter the CS, but reduces fairness as writers wait longer. In the second step, we analyze how varying each $T_{L,i}$ impacts performance. We first fix $\prod_{i=1}^{N} T_{L,i} = 1000$. As $N = 2$, we use $T_{L,2} \in (10, 25, 50)$ and $T_{L,1} \in (100, 40, 20)$. The outcome is shown in Figure 4c. When more writers consecutively acquire the lock within one node (higher $T_{L,2}$), the throughput increases. Still, the differences between the considered options are small (up to 25% of the relative difference), especially for lower P. This is because of smaller amounts of inter-node communication. Interestingly, options that increase throughput (e.g., 50-20) also increase latency, see Figure 4d. We conjecture this is due to improved fairness caused by smaller $T_{L,2}$ (more processes from different nodes can acquire the lock). However, the average latency increases because other writers have to wait for a longer time.

5.2.3 Influence of T_R

Next, we analyze the impact of T_R; see Figure 4e. We first use $F_W = 0.2\%$. The throughput for $T_R \in \{1,000 ; 2,000\}$ drops significantly for $P > 512$ due to the higher overhead of writers. Contrarily, increasing T_R improves the throughput significantly. This is because the latency of readers is lower than that of writers and a higher T_R entails a preference of readers. However, the larger T_R the longer the waiting time for writers is. Finally, we analyze the relationship between T_R and F_W in more detail; see Figure 4f. Here, we vary $F_W \in \{2\%, 5\%\}$. The results indicate no consistent significant advantage (<1% of relative difference for most P) of one threshold over others within a fixed F_W.

5.2.4 Comparison to the State-of-the-Art

We now present the advantages of RMA-RW over the state-of-the-art foMPI RMA library [17]; see Figure 5. Here, we consider different F_W rates. As expected, any RW distributed lock provides the highest throughput for $F_W = 0.2\%$. This is because readers have a lower latency for acquiring a lock than writers and they can enter the CS in parallel. The maximum difference between the rates $F_W = 0.2\%$ and $F_W = 2\%$ is 1.8x and between $F_W = 0.2\%$ and $F_W = 5\%$ is 4.4x. We then tested other values of F_W up to 100% to find out that for $F_W > 30\%$ the throughput remains approximately the same. At such rates, the throughput is dominated by the overhead of writers that enter the CS consecutively.

In each case, RMA-RW always outperforms foMPI by >6x for $P \geq 64$. One reason for this advantage is the topology-aware design. Another one is the presence of $T_{L,i}$ and T_R that prevent one type of processes to dominate the other one resulting in performance penalties.

5.3 Case Study: A Distributed Hashtable

We now illustrate how RMA-RW accelerates a distributed hashtable (DHT) that represents irregular codes. Our DHT stores 64-bit integers and it consists of parts called local volumes. Each local volume consists of a table of elements and an overflow heap for elements after hash collisions. The table and the heap are constructed with fixed-size arrays. Every local volume is managed by a different process. Inserts are based on atomic CASes. If a collision happens, the losing thread places the element in the overflow list by atomically incrementing the next free pointer. In addition, a pointer to the last element is also updated with a second CAS. Flushes are used to ensure memory consistency.

We illustrate a performance analysis in Figure 6. In the benchmark, $P - 1$ processes access a local volume of a se-

28

	UPC (standard) [44]	Berkeley UPC [1]	SHMEM [4]	Fortran 2008 [27]	Linux RDMA/IB [33,43]	iWARP [18,41]
Put	UPC_SET	bupc_atomicX_set_RS	shmem_swap	atomic_define	MskCmpSwap	masked CmpSwap
Get	UPC_GET	bupc_atomicX_read_RS	shmem_mswap	atomic_ref	MskCmpSwap	masked CmpSwap
Accumulate	UPC_INC	bupc_atomicX_fetchadd_RS	shmem_fadd	atomic_add	FetchAdd	FetchAdd
FAO (SUM)	UPC_INC, UPC_DEC	bupc_atomicX_fetchadd_RS	shmem_fadd	atomic_add	FetchAdd	FetchAdd
FAO (REPLACE)	UPC_SET	bupc_atomicX_swap_RS	shmem_swap	atomic_define*	MskCmpSwap	masked CmpSwap
CAS	UPC_CSWAP	bupc_atomicX_cswap_RS	shmem_cswap	atomic_cas	CmpSwap	CmpSwap

Table 3: Illustration of the feasibility of using libraries/languages other than MPI RMA for RMA-MCS/RMA-RW. * indicates the lack of an atomic swap in Fortran 2008, suggesting that some of RMA-RW protocols that depend on it would have to be adjusted to a different set of available atomics.

lected process with a specified number of inserts and reads targeted at random hashtable elements. We compare the total execution time of foMPI-A (a variant that only synchronizes accesses with CAS/FAO), foMPI-RW, and RMA-RW. For $F_W \in \{2\%, 5\%, 20\%\}$ RMA-RW outperforms both the remaining variants. For $F_w = 0\%$, foMPI-RW and RMA-RW offer comparable performance.

6   DISCUSSION

Using Different RMA Libraries/Languages In our implementation, we use MPI RMA. Still, the proposed schemes are generic and can be implemented using several other existing RMA/PGAS libraries/languages that support the required operations described in Listing 1. We illustrate this in Table 3 (we omit the distinction between blocking and non-blocking operations as any type can be used in the proposed locks). The analysis indicates that RMA-MCS and RMA-RW can be used in not only traditional HPC domains (by utilizing UPC, SHMEM, or RDMA/IB), but also in TCP/IP-based settings (by using iWARP).

Selecting RMA-RW Parameters To set the parameters, we first find an appropriate value for T_{DC}. This is because our performance analysis indicates that T_{DC} has on average the highest impact on performance of both readers and writers. Here, our evaluation indicates that placing one counter per compute node results in a reasonable balance between reader throughput and writer latency. In the second step, we further influence the reader/writer performance tradeoff by manipulating with T_R and $T_{L,i}$. To reduce the parameter space, we fix T_W as indicated in Table 2. Selecting $T_{L,i}$ depends on the hardware hierarchy and would ideally incorporate several performance tests before fixing final numbers. One rule of the thumb is to reserve larger values for $T_{L,i}$ associated with components with higher inter-component communication costs, such as racks; this may reduce fairness, but increases throughput.

7   RELATED WORK

Queue-Based Locks The well-known traditional examples of this family are CLH [13,32] and MCS [34]. Yet, they are oblivious to the memory hierarchy and cannot use this knowledge to gain performance. More recently, Radovic and Hagersten [38] proposed a hierarchical backoff lock that exploits memory locality: a thread reduces its backoff delay if another thread from the same cluster owns the lock. This increases the chance to keep the lock within the cluster, but introduces the risk of starvation. Luchangco et al. [31] improved this scheme by introducing a NUMA-aware CLH queue that ensures no starvation. Yet, it considers only two levels of the memory hierarchy. Chabbi et al. [9] generalized it to any number of memory hierarchy levels. Similarly to our scheme, they introduce an MCS lock for each level. Yet, they do not target DM machines. None of these protocols can utilize the parallelism of miscellaneous workloads where the majority of processes only read the data.

RW Locks There exist various traditional RW proposals [25,29]. Recently, Courtois et al. [12] introduced different preference schemes that favor either readers (a reader can enter the CS even if there is a writer waiting) or writers (a writer can enter the CS before waiting readers). Yet, this protocol neither prevents starvation nor scales well. Mellor-Crummey and Scott [35] extended their MCS lock to distinguish between readers and writers. This algorithm however does not scale well under heavy read contention. Next, Krieger et al. [29] use a double-linked list for more flexibility in how processes traverse the queue. Yet, there is still a single point of contention. Hsieh and Weihl [25] overcome this by trading writer throughput for reader throughput. In their design, each thread has a private mutex; the readers acquire the lock by acquiring their private mutex but the writers need to obtain all mutex objects. This introduces a massive overhead for the writers for large thread counts. Other approaches incorporate elaborate data structures like the Scalable Non-Zero Indicator (SNZI) tree [30] that traces readers in the underlying NUMA hierarchy for more locality. Yet, writers remain NUMA-oblivious. Calciu et al. [8] extend this approach with an RW lock in which both readers and writers are NUMA-aware. This design improves memory locality but it only considers two levels in a NUMA hierarchy. None of these schemes address DM environments.

Distributed Locks To the best of our knowledge, little research has been performed into locks for DM systems. Simple spin-lock protocols for implementing MPI-3 RMA synchronization were proposed by Gerstenberger et al. [17]. Some other RMA languages and libraries (e.g., UPC) also offer locks, but they are not RW, their performance is similar to that of foMPI, and they are hardware-oblivious.

We conclude that our work offers the first lock for DM systems that exploits the underlying inter-node structure and utilizes the RW parallelism present in various data- and communication-intensive workloads.

8   CONCLUSION

Large amounts of data in domains such as graph computations require distributed-memory machines for efficient processing. Such machines are characterized by weak memory models and expensive inter-node communication. These features impact the performance of topology-oblivious locks or completely prevent a straightforward adoption of existing locking schemes for shared-memory systems.

In this work, we propose a distributed topology-aware Reader-Writer (RMA-RW) and MCS lock that outperform the state-of-the-art. RMA-RW offers a modular design with three parameters that offer performance tradeoffs in selected parts of the lock. These are: higher lock fairness or better locality, larger throughput of readers or writers, and lower latency of readers or writers. This facilitates performance tuning for a specific workload or environment. RMA-RW could also be extended with adaptive schemes for a runtime selection and tuning of the values of the parameters. This might be used in accelerating dynamic workloads.

Microbenchmark results indicate that the proposed locks outperform the state-of-the-art in both latency and throughput. Finally, RMA-RW accelerates a distributed hashtable that represents irregular workloads such as key-value stores.

Acknowledgements

This work was supported by Microsoft Research through its Swiss Joint Research Centre. We thank our shepherd Patrick G. Bridges and the anonymous reviewers for their insightful comments. We thank the CSCS team granting access to the Piz Dora and Daint machines, and for their excellent technical support. MB is supported by the 2013 Google European Doctoral Fellowship in Parallel Computing.

9   References

[1] Berkeley UPC User's Guide version 2.22.0. http://upc.lbl.gov/docs/user/.

[2] T. E. Anderson. The performance of spin lock alternatives for shared-memory multiprocessors. *IEEE Trans. Parallel Distrib. Syst.*, 1(1):6–16, Jan. 1990.

[3] B. Arimilli et al. The PERCS High-Performance Interconnect. In *Proc. of the IEEE Symp. on High Perf. Inter.*, HOTI '10, pages 75–82, 2010.

[4] R. Barriuso and A. Knies. *SHMEM user's guide for C*, 1994.

[5] A. Bhatele et al. There goes the neighborhood: performance degradation due to nearby jobs. In *Proc. of the ACM/IEEE Supercomputing*, page 41. ACM, 2013.

[6] C. Bienia. *Benchmarking Modern Multiprocessors*. PhD thesis, Princeton University, January 2011.

[7] N. Bronson et al. TAO: Facebook's Distributed Data Store for the Social Graph. In *USENIX Annual Technical Conference*, pages 49–60, 2013.

[8] I. Calciu et al. NUMA-aware Reader-writer Locks. In *Proc. of the ACM Symp. on Prin. and Prac. of Par. Prog.*, PPoPP '13, pages 157–166, 2013.

[9] M. Chabbi, M. Fagan, and J. Mellor-Crummey. High Performance Locks for Multi-level NUMA Systems. In *Proc. of the ACM Symp. on Prin. and Prac. of Par. Prog.*, PPoPP 2015, pages 215–226, 2015.

[10] B. Chamberlain, S. Deitz, M. B. Hribar, and W. Wong. Chapel. Technical report, Cray Inc., 2005.

[11] P. Charles et al. X10: an Object-Oriented Approach to Non-Uniform Cluster Computing. *SIGPLAN Not.*, 40(10):519–538, Oct. 2005.

[12] P. J. Courtois, F. Heymans, and D. L. Parnas. Concurrent control with "readers" and "writers". *Commun. ACM*, 14(10):667–668, Oct. 1971.

[13] T. S. Craig. Building FIFO and Priority-Queuing Spin Locks from Atomic Swap. Technical report, 1993.

[14] D. Dice, V. J. Marathe, and N. Shavit. Flat-combining NUMA Locks. In *Proc. of the ACM Symp. on Par. in Alg. and Arch.*, SPAA '11, pages 65–74, 2011.

[15] D. Dice, V. J. Marathe, and N. Shavit. Lock Cohorting: A General Technique for Designing NUMA Locks. In *Proc. of the ACM Symp. on Prin. and Prac. of Par. Prog.*, PPoPP '12, pages 247–256, 2012.

[16] G. Faanes et al. Cray cascade: a scalable HPC system based on a Dragonfly network. In *Proc. of the ACM/IEEE Supercomputing*, page 103, 2012.

[17] R. Gerstenberger, M. Besta, and T. Hoefler. Enabling Highly-scalable Remote Memory Access Programming with MPI-3 One Sided. In *Proc. of ACM/IEEE Supercomputing*, SC '13, pages 53:1–53:12, 2013.

[18] R. Grant, M. Rashti, A. Afsahi, and P. Balaji. RDMA Capable iWARP over Datagrams. In *Par. Dist. Proc. Symp. (IPDPS), 2011 IEEE Intl.*, pages 628–639, 2011.

[19] W. Gropp, T. Hoefler, R. Thakur, and E. Lusk. *Using Advanced MPI: Modern Features of the Message-Passing Interface*. MIT Press, 2014.

[20] W. D. Gropp. Personal exchange, 2013.

[21] M. Herlihy and N. Shavit. *The Art of Multiprocessor Programming*. Morgan Kaufmann Publishers Inc., 2008.

[22] P. N. Hilfinger et al. Titanium Language Reference Manual, version 2.19. Technical report, UC Berkeley Tech Rep. UCB/EECS-2005-15, 2005.

[23] T. Hoefler et al. Netgauge: A Network Performance Measurement Framework. In *Proc. of High Perf. Comp. and Comm.*, HPCC'07, volume 4782, pages 659–671, 2007.

[24] G. J. Holzmann. The Model Checker SPIN. *IEEE Trans. Softw. Eng.*, 23(5):279–295, May 1997.

[25] W. C. Hsieh and W. W. Weihl. Scalable reader-writer locks for parallel systems. In *Proc. of Par. Proc. Symp.*, pages 656–659, Mar 1992.

[26] InfiniBand Trade Association. *Supplement to InfiniBand Architecture Spec., Vol. 1, Rel. 1.2.1. Annex A16: RDMA over Converged Ethernet (RoCE)*. 2010.

[27] ISO Fortran Committee. Fortran 2008 Standard (ISO/IEC 1539-1:2010). 2010.

[28] J. Kim, W. J. Dally, S. Scott, and D. Abts. Technology-driven, highly-scalable dragonfly topology. In *ACM SIGARCH Comp. Arch. News*, volume 36, pages 77–88, 2008.

[29] O. Krieger, M. Stumm, R. Unrau, and J. Hanna. A fair fast scalable reader-writer lock. In *In Proc. of the Intl. Conf. on Par. Proc.*, pages 201–204, 1993.

[30] Y. Lev, V. Luchangco, and M. Olszewski. Scalable reader-writer locks. In *Proc. of the Symp. on Par. in Alg. and Arch.*, SPAA '09, pages 101–110, 2009.

[31] V. Luchangco, D. Nussbaum, and N. Shavit. A Hierarchical CLH Queue Lock. In W. Nagel, W. Walter, and W. Lehner, editors, *Euro-Par 2006 Par. Proc.*, volume 4128 of *Lecture Notes in Computer Science*, pages 801–810. 2006.

[32] P. S. Magnusson, A. Landin, and E. Hagersten. Queue Locks on Cache Coherent Multiprocessors. In *Proc. of the Intl. Symp. on Par. Proc.*, pages 165–171, 1994.

[33] Mellanox Technologies. Mellanox OFED for Linux User Manual, 2015.

[34] J. M. Mellor-Crummey and M. L. Scott. Algorithms for scalable synchronization on shared-memory multiprocessors. *ACM Trans. Comput. Syst.*, 9(1):21–65, Feb. 1991.

[35] J. M. Mellor-Crummey and M. L. Scott. Scalable reader-writer synchronization for shared-memory multiprocessors. In *Proc. of the ACM SIGPLAN Symp. on Prin. and Prac. of Par. Prog.*, PPOPP '91, pages 106–113, 1991.

[36] MPI Forum. MPI: A Message-Passing Interface Standard. Ver. 3, 2012.

[37] R. C. Murphy, K. B. Wheeler, B. W. Barrett, and J. A. Ang. Introducing the graph 500. *Cray User's Group (CUG)*, 2010.

[38] Z. Radovic and E. Hagersten. Hierarchical backoff locks for nonuniform communication architectures. In *Proc. of the Intl. Symp. on High-Perf. Comp. Arch.*, HPCA '03, pages 241–, 2003.

[39] R. Recio et al. A remote direct memory access protocol specification, Oct 2007. RFC 5040.

[40] M. L. Scott and W. N. Scherer. Scalable Queue-based Spin Locks with Timeout. In *Proc. of the ACM SIGPLAN Symp. on Prin. and Prac. of Par. Prog.*, PPoPP '01, pages 44–52, 2001.

[41] R. Sharp et al. Remote Direct Memory Access (RDMA) Protocol Extensions. 2014.

[42] H. Takada and K. Sakamura. Predictable spin lock algorithms with preemption. In *Real-Time Operating Systems and Software. RTOSS '94, Proc., IEEE Workshop on*, pages 2–6, 1994.

[43] The InfiniBand Trade Association. *Infiniband Architecture Spec. Vol. 1-2, Rel. 1.3*. InfiniBand Trade Association, 2004.

[44] UPC Consortium. UPC language spec., v1.3. Technical report, Lawrence Berkeley National Laboratory, 20013. LBNL-6623E.

[45] V. Venkataramani et al. TAO: How Facebook Serves the Social Graph. In *Proc. of the ACM Intl. Conf. on Manag. of Data*, SIGMOD '12, pages 791–792, 2012.

Towards Practical Algorithm Based Fault Tolerance in Dense Linear Algebra

Panruo Wu
Department of Computer
Science and Engineering
University of California,
Riverside
pwu011@cs.ucr.edu

Qiang Guan,
Nathan DeBardeleben and
Sean Blanchard
Ultrascale Systems Research
Center
Los Alamos National
Laboratory[*]
{qguan,ndebard,seanb}
@lanl.gov

Dingwen Tao, Xin Liang,
Jieyang Chen and
Zizhong Chen
Department of Computer
Science and Engineering
University of California,
Riverside
{dtao001,xlian007,jchen098,chen}
@cs.ucr.edu

ABSTRACT

Algorithm based fault tolerance (ABFT) attracts renewed interest for its extremely low overhead and good scalability. However the fault model used to design ABFT has been either abstract, simplistic, or both, leaving a gap between what occurs at the architecture level and what the algorithm expects. As the fault model is the deciding factor in choosing an effective checksum scheme, the resulting ABFT techniques have seen limited impact in practice. In this paper we seek to close the gap by directly using a comprehensive architectural fault model and devise a comprehensive ABFT scheme that can tolerate multiple architectural faults of various kinds. We implement the new ABFT scheme into high performance linpack (HPL) to demonstrate the feasibility in large scale high performance benchmark. We conduct architectural fault injection experiments and large scale experiments to empirically validate its fault tolerance and demonstrate the overhead of error handling, respectively.

1. INTRODUCTION

The extreme scale high performance computing (HPC) systems that are expected by the end of this decade poses several challenges including performance, power efficiency, and reliability. Due to the large amount of components in these systems and the shrinking feature size, the probability that an extreme scale application experiences faults during its execution is projected to be non negligible. Resilience to faults have been widely accepted as critical for exascale HPC applications[21, 6, 3].

---

[*]This work was performed at the Ultrascale Systems Research Center (USRC) at Los Alamos National Laboratory. The publication has been assigned the LANL identifier LA-UR-16-20226.

HPDC'16, May 31-June 04, 2016, Kyoto, Japan
© 2016 ACM. ISBN 978-1-4503-4314-5/16/05. . . $15.00
DOI: http://dx.doi.org/10.1145/2907294.2907315

Faults are malfunctions of the hardware or software, and are the underlying causes for observable errors. When the fault does not interrupt the execution of a process the program can continue execution normally, but the results may be corrupted. Such silent data corruptions cannot be tolerated by checkpoint/restart (C/R) alone unless they can be frequently detected. Silent data corruptions may be the consequence of soft faults caused by cosmic rays and radiation from packaging materials, and are usually one time events that corrupt the state of the machine but not its overall functionality. We restrict our scope to silent data corruptions (SDC) in this work. Note that since soft errors which are caused by single event upset frequently corrupt data silently, SDC handling is also often discussed in context of soft errors.

Faults in storage and communication systems are often effectively tolerated by error correction codes (ECC) because the data stored or communicated are not changing. However, faults in logic units that transform the data are harder to detect and tolerate. Typically some kind of double modular redundancy (DMR) is needed to detect soft faults in logic units and triple modular redundancy (TMR) is needed to tolerate SDCs. Although modular redundancy requires at least 100% resource overhead and often incurs significant execution time overhead, it is sometimes the only general system level solution to tolerate SDCs [1, 22].

System level SDC solutions can be prohibitively expensive for HPC systems. An alternative solution is to implement fault tolerance in applications, which can take advantage of the semantics and structure of a specific application resulting in much lower cost. Algorithm based fault tolerance (ABFT) represents a middle ground between application specific fault tolerance and architecture fault tolerance. At one end application specific fault tolerance is highly diverse that often require ad-hoc solutions, at the other end system fault tolerance is general but too costly and unscalable. Algorithms thus presents just enough semantics to take advantage and structure to be generally useful.

ABFT has first been proposed in a seminal work by Huang and Abraham [14] for matrix-matrix multiplication on systolic arrays. The idea of ABFT can be seen as an adaption of ECC to numeric structures like matrices or vectors. The significant difference is that for ECC the data is static but for ABFT the data is under transformation. In ABFT the central problem is that the codes must maintain after transformation in order to be able to detect errors using the codes. The fault model is a deciding factor in the design of ABFT codes and adaption to the associated algorithm. However the fault models used in existing ABFT research are either too abstract [, ,] or too simplistic [, ,] limiting their use where the architectural fault models do not fit. In this work we rethink the fault model and explore the challenges if we use a comprehensive architectural fault model that allows both logic/arithmetic faults and storage faults in main memory, on-chip memory, and other datapaths. We demonstrate that with this fault model we still can design highly efficient and resilient ABFT techniques for dense linear algebra and use high performance linpack (HPL) to show that the new techniques can be implemented efficiently in complex real world high performance and highly scalable applications. The design is validated empirically by a QEMU [ ] based architectural fault injector, F-SEFI [ ], which implements the comprehensive fault model. We incorporate the new ABFT techniques into the latest Netlib HPL-2.1 and empirically show that the resulting FT-HPL incurs low overhead and maintains high scalability of the original HPL.

The contributions of this paper are:

New fault model We use a fault model that allows logic faults and memory system faults that are comprehensive temporally and spatially and design ABFT schemes that can effectively detect and correct errors caused by these faults.

New checksum scheme We propose a novel process local checksum scheme, multiple checksums for error detection and correction by studying the syndrome (error patterns) caused by the faults.

Validation and software implementation We test and validate the resilience using an architectural fault injector. We implement the new ABFT schemes in the latest Netlib HPL-2.1.

The rest of the paper is organized as follows. In section 2 we survey the techniques to handle SDCs in computing systems especially the algorithm based approach. In section 3 we propose the architectural fault model and the errors it causes in the eyes of application. In section 4, we present our new designs to handle the proposed fault model. In section 5, fault tolerance capability, various sources of overheads, and optimization methods are discussed. In section 6, we present empirical study of the fault tolerance of the proposed design and implementation through error injection, and the overheads in large scale runs. Section 7 concludes the paper.

2. RELATED WORK

The first report on soft errors due to alpha particles in computer chips was from Intel in 1978 [ ]. The first report on soft errors due to cosmic radiations in computer chips was in 1984 [ ]. In 1996, Norman [ ] studied error logs of several large computer systems and reported a number of incidents of cosmic ray strikes. In 2005, Hewlett-Packard admitted that the ASC Q supercomputer located in Los Alamos National Laboratory experienced frequent crashes because of cosmic ray strikes to its parity protected cache tag arrays. The machine is particularly susceptible because

of the 7000ft altitude of the installation location [ ]. The book by Mukherjee [ ] surveys extensively the architectural techniques to design architectures for soft errors.

In the HPC context much effort has been spent on techniques to detect and tolerate soft errors. System level approaches usually involves some kind of modular redundancy. RedMPI [ ] is a general MPI level solution that replicates each MPI rank to form double modular redundancy (DMR) for soft error detection or triple modular redundancy (TMR) for error correction. The difficulty is the silent nature of soft errors; error detection must be active and in a timely manner. RedMPI does the error detection when MPI ranks communicate: the replicas should send out the same message otherwise a soft error is detected. According to the paper, MPI rank level replication incurs 20% to 60% execution time overhead in addition to 100% to 200% computing resource overheads. Another approach is algorithmic error detection coupled with checkpointing for recovery. In [ ], the intrinsic orthogonality of some Krylov linear solvers is used for error detection. A study by [ ] proposes to turn many interesting problems into optimization problems that can be solved iteratively which is naturally resilient to soft errors.

In the following texts the most relevant related works are discussed and special attention is paid to the fault models and the influence fault model on the design of algorithm based fault tolerant schemes. ABFT has been researched extensively for many algorithms but we will narrow our scope to those that are checksum based and applicable on dense matrix multiplication and triangularization.

Algorithm based fault tolerance was first proposed by Abraham and Huang [ ]. The original ABFT was proposed for matrix multiplication and LU on systolic arrays for real time signal processing. The fault model used is logic faults that produces erroneous results. Storage cell faults such as in memory, latch, and registers are assumed to be handled by traditional error correction codes. In matrix multiplication, as a single arithmetic fault causes only a single error in the result matrix, this ABFT scheme can effectively detect and correct it. In LU decomposition, because of error propagation, a single fault will cause an overwhelmingly large amount of errors in the results, thus making this ABFT scheme unable to tolerate a single fault algorithmically. The limited correction capability is due to three factors: 1) inability to tolerate multiple errors in the checksum scheme, 2) massive error propagation in matrix triangularization, and 3) offline error correction. These three factors conspire to make algorithmic error correction difficult in matrix triangularization.

Later Luk and Park [ ] described an elegant analytical model for ABFT in matrix triangularization. The analytical model assumes an abstract fault model that a transient error occurs at some intermediate iteration in the triangularization. Even though the single error will propagate in later stages and become uncorrectable at the end, it can be shown that the error can be cast back as a single rank perturbation to the original input matrix, much like the widely used backward error analysis [ ]. Then assuming two row checksums the correct result can be derived based on the backward fault model. This is a powerful technique that avoids the error propagation problem but it has three limitations: 1) the fault model assumes single error not necessarily single fault, as we have seen that single fault may cause multiple errors; 2) this checksum scheme has no column checksums thus may fail to even detect certain faults as pointed out by a recent work by Yao [ ]; and 3) the method can only tolerate at most one fault during the decomposition. As the scale of supercomputing marches towards exascale, fault tolerance is becoming a key aspect in achieving the required performance at reasonable cost [, ,]. And assuming only one fault during the application run seems not appropriate in future large scale systems any more. To address more than one error in matrix triangularization, Du [,] proposed a technique to tolerate two errors in solving linear system using partial pivoting LU decomposition. In this case, the decomposition cannot be corrected, but the result to the linear system can be recovered using the Sherman-Morrison-Woodbury formula. Handling beyond two errors would be more expensive than the LU decomposition itself. The fault model used is the same as in Luk and Park [ ] thus suffers from the same problem.

Some researchers went in another direction in order to tolerate more faults effectively. Realizing that the offline approach taken by the traditional ABFT techniques have to face catastrophic error propagation at the end, researchers attempted to adapt checksum schemes for online error detection and correction [, ,]. The idea is that online ABFT catches errors early on when they are not propagated far away, therefore making it easier to correct. Online ABFT also can tolerate more errors that spread in time by avoiding errors compounding each other. The fault model used however is still arithmetic faults, and there still is no column checksums due to the difficulty in row pivoting.

A recent study [ ] discovers that the fault models used in the previous ABFT works are not adequate even in detecting faults (Section 3 in [ ]). This work proposes a global row and column checksums that can effectively detect errors and it is also an online approach. However error correction is not considered.

In this work we do not use an abstract fault model; rather we assume an architectural fault model and aim to detect and correct multiple errors. The architectural fault model is closer to what happens in real world and not only include all the fault models discussed above but also more improvements.

3. FAULT MODEL

The fault model for silent soft errors includes arithmetic faults that result in a wrong answer, for example 1+1=3. The other important fault is the memory system fault, manifesting as corrupted bits in storage cells. Memory faults could happen in main memory, in caches, registers, and other datapaths. We suppose one memory fault only affects one memory word; it can be multiple bits or single bit corruption.

It is useful to see how the architectural level faults manifest themselves in the algorithm level. Typically numerical algorithms deal with scalar numbers, vectors, and matrices. A variable may be mapped to multiple memory devices. For example the variable may be mapped to main memory, and cached in on-chip cache. It may also live in a register temporarily. The fault that affects the variable may be caused by corruptions in one of the mapped physical devices, and manifest themselves differently. For example if the main memory is corrupted, the mapped variable may read the corrupted value continuously until the memory is overwrit-

ten. If the corruption happens in cache, the variable may read incorrect value until the cache line is flushed. Therefore, a corrupted data element in program may sometimes read correct value but at other times read corrupted value.

4. THE CHECKSUM SCHEME

It is important to make a distinction between fault and error. For our purpose, a fault is a malfunction in the architecture, such as a bit flip in memory, cache, or registers. An error is the symptom due to the fault. Thus faults are the cause and errors are what we observe that are not correct. In designing numerical algorithms, errors are erroneous floating point variables. A single bit fault may lead to multiple errors, depending on how the faulty value is used. For algorithm designers and implementers, the problem to design fault tolerant algorithms is to find ways to detect and tolerate errors. In online ABFT framework, the problem can be further specified as to detect and tolerate errors resulting from one for *every error handling interval*. In this section, we will first study the error patterns of a single fault and how to tolerate them; then we will discuss how to design checksum schemes in LU decomposition; we will discuss how to put this technique in use in the very high performance LU decomposition package HPL; last we drop the assumption of precise arithmetic and deal with finite precision floating point arithmetic.

4.1 Error patterns and correction

We begin by studying the error patterns caused by a single fault in matrix multiplication, as matrix multiplication is the simplest dense matrix operation and it is an important part of the LU decomposition. We will see that memory faults may lead to multiple errors, while in contrast one arithmetic fault will only lead to one error in matrix multiplication.

Figure 1 shows four cases when one fault strikes. The fault could be an arithmetic fault or a silent data corruption (SDC). The red elements indicate errors. In subfigure (a), a single arithmetic error can only corrupt one element in the result, because the intermediate value produced by the faulty arithmetic operation is only used to calculate one element. In subfigure (b), a SDC in matrix A corrupts the whole row in the result C, because the corrupted element in A is used to calculate the whole row. In subfigure (c), the SDC occurs not in memory but in for example cache, or occurs later during the matrix multiplication. In this case a single SDC in matrix A causes partial row corruptions in C. In subfigure (d) a single SDC in matrix B causes partial column corruption in C. The important observation here is that *a single fault cannot cause errors in more than one row or column*. This observation enables us to design checksums that can correct all the error patterns caused by a single fault.

Next we discuss how to design checksum schemes to detect and correct up to one fault based on the fault patterns in figure 1. A matrix can have two types of checkums along its two dimensions: the checksum at the bottom of a matrix is called column checksum and the checksum to the right of a matrix is called row checksum. The column checksum encoded matrix is often denoted by a superscript A^c and the row checksum encoded matrix by superscript A^r. If a matrix has both then it is called fully checksummed and denoted by A^f. Mathematically, let e be the weight vector (or matrix

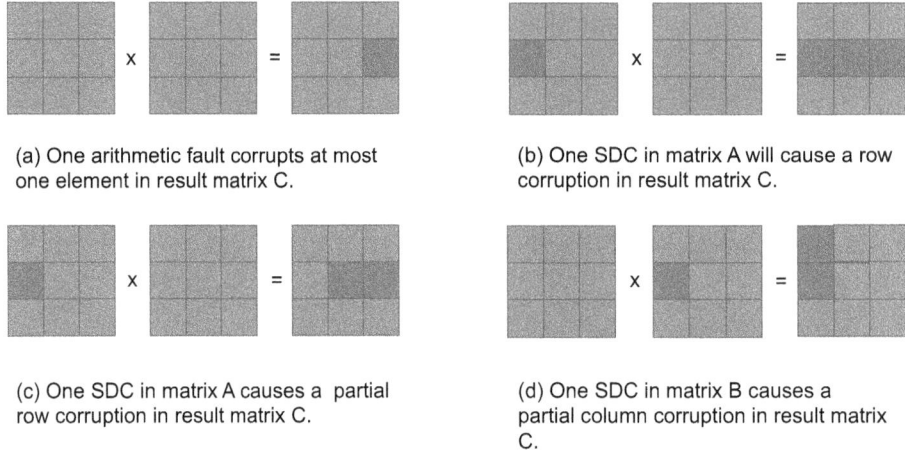

(a) One arithmetic fault corrupts at most one element in result matrix C.

(b) One SDC in matrix A will cause a row corruption in result matrix C.

(c) One SDC in matrix A causes a partial row corruption in result matrix C.

(d) One SDC in matrix B causes a partial column corruption in result matrix C.

Figure 1: Error patterns for a single fault in matrix multiplication

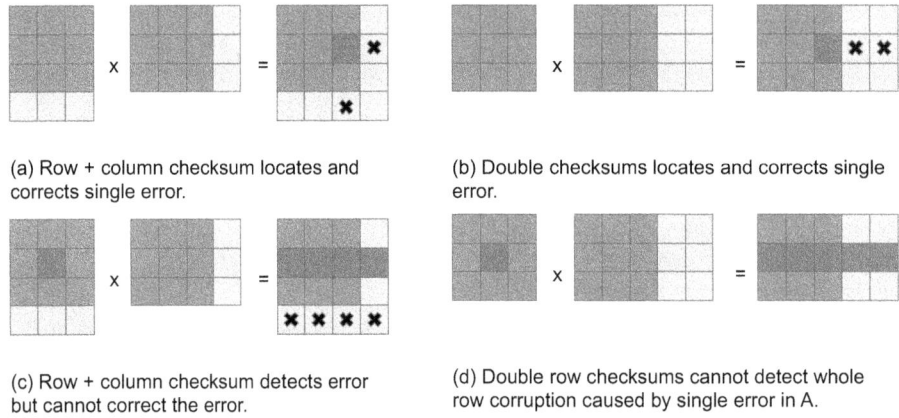

(a) Row + column checksum locates and corrects single error.

(b) Double checksums locates and corrects single error.

(c) Row + column checksum detects error but cannot correct the error.

(d) Double row checksums cannot detect whole row corruption caused by single error in A.

Figure 2: Checksums for matrix multiplication

in the case of multiple checksums) then:

$$A^c = \begin{bmatrix} A \\ e^T A \end{bmatrix}, \quad B^r = \begin{bmatrix} B & Be \end{bmatrix}, \quad C^f = \begin{bmatrix} C & Ce \\ e^T C \end{bmatrix}$$

As shown in figure 2, we have multiple configurations of checksums. The yellow blocks are row or column checksums associated with the matrix. The red block indicates an incorrect element, and a black cross on a row/column checksum indicates that the row/column checksum is inconsistent with the respective row/column in matrix. We need at least two checksums to correct up to one error because the location and the magnitude of the error are two unknowns. For a single error in a matrix, either two row checksum, two column checksum, or one row plus one column checksums can detect and correct one error in matrix C. In subfigure (a), the error can be located at the intersection of the inconsistent row and column. The error can be recovered using either the row or column checksum [13], because the *checksums are correct*. In subfigure (b), a single error in matrix C can be detected and corrected using two row (weighted) checksums with different weights [21]. The location of the error and the magnitude of the error can be solved from the two checksums. In subfigure (c), a single SDC in matrix A causes a whole row corruption that result in an incorrect but consistent row. Because the row checksum is corrupted,

it leaves us with only one column checksum which is inadequate to correct the errors. In subfigure (d), a single SDC in matrix A causes a whole row corruption with incorrect but consistent checksums. In this case the checksum scheme cannot detect the errors.

It is now clear that we need both row and column checksums to avoid the error detection failure. And to correct row/column corruptions we need two row checksums and column checksums, as shown in figure 3. In figure 3, a SDC in matrix A causes a whole row corruption in C detectable by the column checksums. The errors can be located and corrected on per column basis using the two correct column checksums. The row checksums are neither able to locate the errors nor correct them.

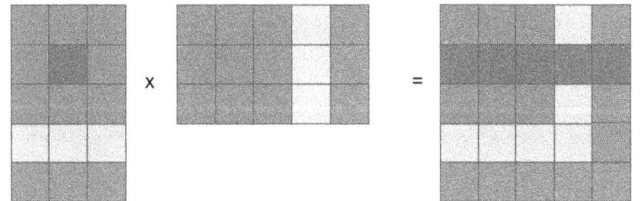

Figure 3: The checksum scheme that can tolerate single arithmetic fault or memory fault

Specifically, how do we locate and correct one erroneous element using two checksums? There is an easy to use encoding method. Suppose we encode a vector using two different weights $e_1 = [1, 1, \ldots, 1]^T, e_2 = [1, 2, \ldots, n]^T$. The vector is $a = [a_1, \ldots, a_n]$ and we have two correct encoded checksums of a:

$$r_1 = ae_1 = \sum_{i=1}^{n} a_i, \quad r_2 = ae_2 = \sum_{i=1}^{n} ia_i$$

Now suppose the computed $a' = [a'_1, \ldots, a'_n]$ has up to one erroneous element $a'_j \neq a_j$, where the location j is unknown to us. However when we verify the checksums:

$$\delta_1 = \sum_{i=1}^{n} a'_i - r_1 = a'_j - a_j \neq 0$$

$$\delta_2 = \sum_{i=1}^{n} ia_i - r_2 = j(a'_j - a_j) \neq 0$$

Then a simple division δ_2/δ_1 gives us the location j. The correct value of a_j can then be recovered using the correct checksum and the other correct elements of a: $a_j = a'_j - \sum_{i=1, i \neq j}^{n} a'_i$.

In this subsection the error patterns in matrix multiplication are discussed and checksums are devised to detect and correct errors, given that we have the desired checksums available. In the following subsection, how to maintain the checksums online is discussed in LU decomposition. Note that in LU decomposition the matrix multiplication is actually $C \leftarrow C - A \times B$ instead of $C \leftarrow A \times B$ so *correction through re-computation cannot be used* because the original C is overwritten.

4.2 Checksum scheme in LU decomposition

In this subsection the right-looking LU decomposition is briefly introduced. We first show that LU decomposition maintains global row and column checksums. Then we discuss the two adaptions to the LU decomposition that are essential in achieving good performance on modern cache based system and parallel computing.

LU decomposition factors a matrix A into the product of two triangular matrices (lower) L and (upper) U: $A \rightarrow L \times U$. The tiled right-looking variant of the LU algorithm works as shown in figure 4.

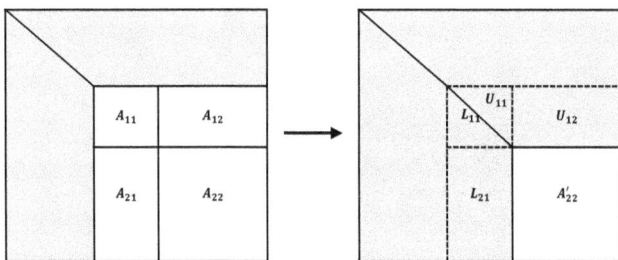

Figure 4: Tiled right-looking LU algorithm, one iteration

Figure 4 shows the state before and after an iteration in the algorithms. The algorithm is a series of iterations that keeps shrinking the trailing matrix until done. The yellow parts of the matrix indicate areas that have been factored and not active. For a certain iteration, the algorithms follows three steps: left panel factorization, top panel update,

and trailing matrix update, described by the following equations:

$$\begin{bmatrix} A_{11} \\ A_{21} \end{bmatrix} \rightarrow \begin{bmatrix} L_{11} \\ L_{21} \end{bmatrix} \times U_{11} \tag{1}$$

$$A_{12} \rightarrow L_{11} \times U_{12} \tag{2}$$

$$A'_{22} \leftarrow A_{22} - L_{21} \times U_{12} \tag{3}$$

The maintenance of checksums offline: In the original Huang and Abraham ABFT paper [13] it has been shown that if we LU decompose a full checksummed matrix A^f, we will end up with column checksummed L^c and row checksummed U^r:

$$\begin{bmatrix} A & Ae \\ e^T A & \end{bmatrix} \rightarrow \begin{bmatrix} L \\ e^T L \end{bmatrix} \times \begin{bmatrix} U & Ue \end{bmatrix} \tag{4}$$

where vector e is the checksum weights vector. This relationship can only be used to detect errors but not correct errors because in LU the errors will propagate to checksums too.

The maintenance of checksums online: If LU decompose a full checksum matrix, we will end up with a column checksummed L and row checksummed U. However multiple errors compound each other resulting in algorithmically uncorrectable errors. It would be desirable to detect and correct errors frequently during the factorizations to handle errors in a timely manner. In fact, we will show that at the end (or beginning) of each iteration, the factored left panel and top panel will be column checksummed and row checksummed, and the trailing matrix will be fully checksummed. We will show this claim inductively by first assuming the condition holds at the beginning of a certain iteration and prove that the condition holds at the end of the iteration. The initial condition clearly holds as we have a fully checksummed initial matrix.

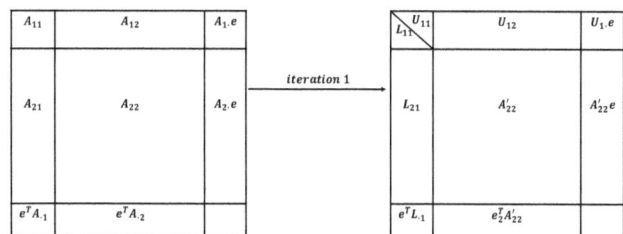

Figure 5: Tiled right-looking LU algorithm with checksums, one iteration

For simplicity we only examine the first iteration. As shown in figure 5, before the iteration we have the full checksums. After the left panel has been factorized according to equation (1), the column checksum associated with the left panel turns into the checksum of the factorized panel: $e^T A_{.1} \rightarrow e^T L_{.1}$. To see why this is true one only has to observe: 1) the factorized left panel will not be updated again therefore will stay unchanged through the end; 2) from equation (4) we know that at the end the left panel will be column checksummed. Thus we proved that the left panel factorization maintains column checksum. Similarly, the second step according to equation (2) maintains the row checksum of the top panel. Next we need to prove that after the trailing matrix update according to equation (5), the trailing matrix will be fully checksummed. To see that we only have to apply the matrix multiplication to the checksums. Take the column checksums for example. The transformation done to the column checksums is depicted by:

$$
\begin{aligned}
&= e^T \begin{bmatrix} A_{12} \\ A_{22} \end{bmatrix} - e^T \begin{bmatrix} L_{11} \\ L_{21} \end{bmatrix} \times U_{12} \\
&= e_1^T (A_{12} - L_{11}U_{12}) + e_2^T (A_{22} - L_{21}U_{12}) \\
&= e_2^T (A'_{22})
\end{aligned} \tag{5}
$$

which proves that the trailing matrix is fully checksummed by the second part of the checksum weights vector e_2.

4.3 The complete picture as in HPL

The previous subsection discusses the algorithmic structure of tiled right-looking LU decomposition, and the maintenance of checksums at each iteration in fault free execution. In this subsection we discuss what happens when faults strikes, namely the error patterns. Once we know the error patterns we can describe correction procedures. We will also deal with two more complications in HPL: partial row pivoting for numerical stability and 2d cyclic block distributions of matrix for load balance in distributed computing.

Error patterns: We examine the error patterns in the three steps during one iteration, and discuss detection and correction procedures. First, we look at the first step and the second step according to equations (1) and (2), namely the left and top panel factorization. Our first claim is that *any single fault that occur during the left and top panel factorization will lead to inconsistent checksums*, provided that the arithmetic are precise, i.e. no round-off errors. In other words, the error detection by checksums is precise. The reason that the error detection is precise is because we have both row and column checksums. If for example only row checksums are used, as pointed out by figure 5 in [26], certain faults strike in lower triangular L will not be detected. In our case the fault will be detected by the inconsistent column checksums. Depending on the location and timing of the fault, the error pattern could be very complex and both the row and column checksums will be contaminated and there is no easy algorithmic corrections, as shown in figure 6 (a). For this case we can use in-memory checkpointing and rollback specifically for the left and top panels. Once the checksum inconsistency is detected the computation can be rolled back to the beginning of the iteration. In HPL the in-memory checkpoint can be stored in the communication buffer for broadcasting L thus do not consume extra memory space. The overhead of memory copy of two panels is not significant.

For the trailing matrix update, as discussed earlier a single arithmetic fault only affects one element in the result thus easily correctable. More interesting cases are memory faults within L_{21} or U_{12}. For a single SDC in L_{21} or U_{12}, *the errors cannot be in more than one row or one column.* Assuming precise arithmetic, a single fault will trigger at least one row checksum inconsistency and one column checksum inconsistency. Therefore the error detection in trailing matrix update is precise, and furthermore the error patterns are within our capability to correct. For example in the case shown in figure 6 (b) a memory fault associated with an element in L_{21} causes partial row corruptions. In this

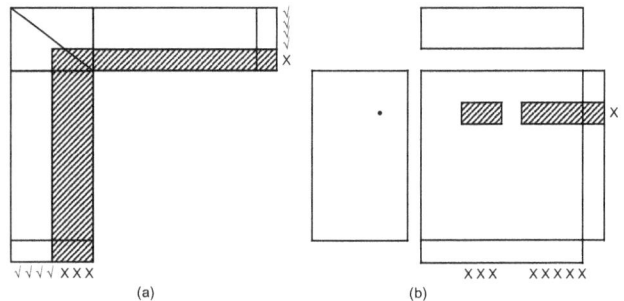

Figure 6: Tiled right-looking LU algorithm with checksums, one iteration. Shaded area are incorrect due to error propagation. Note that the affected checksums are also incorrect but the checksums are inconsistent therefore can be used to detect errors.

case the errors are easily located by the intersection of the inconsistent row and column checksums and corrected by the correct column checksums. It seems that one row checksum and one column checksum is sufficient to locate and correct any single fault in the trailing matrix update. However this is not true and will be explained next.

Parallel LU decomposition and 2d cyclic block distribution: On a multiprocessor machine a matrix is usually distributed onto a PxQ grid of processes according to 2d block cyclic scheme for load balance and scalability. As shown in figure 7, a 4x4 block matrix is distributed onto four processes. In the previous discussion we only look at the logical (global) view of the matrix and the checksum scheme is applied to the whole matrix. This view has some drawbacks. First, the fault tolerance capability is not scalable with the size of the matrix. Second, as the checksums are associated with the global matrix that are distributed, the error detection and correction requires inter process communication. To avoid these two drawbacks, we instead apply checksums to the process local matrix rather than the global matrix. In this way, the fault tolerance capability is fixed per process, and increases proportionally with the number of processes or the size of the matrix. Error detection and correction only involve local information.

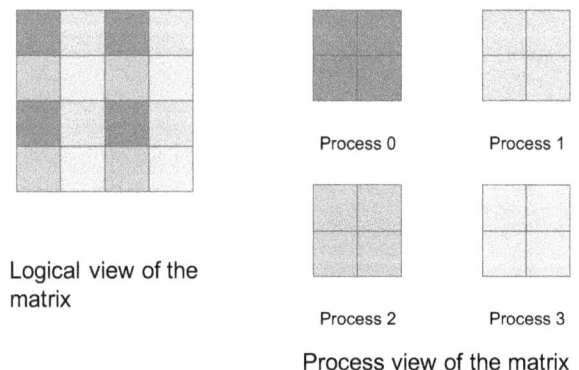

Figure 7: 2D block cyclic matrix distribution.

The online maintenance of the process local checksums are very similar to the global checksums. The error patterns can exhibit more patterns than that of global checksums. For

36

example, consider the first iteration and the matrix distribution in figure 7. In the trailing matrix update, for process 0 and 2, a memory fault in left panel will always produce one inconsistent row checksum but that is not the case for process 1 and 3. For process 1 and 3, a persistent memory corruption in L causes the trailing matrix update to exhibit the error pattern shown in figure 2 (d) where all row checksums are incorrect but consistent. In this case a single column checksum can only detect error; two column checksums are required to correct the errors. For process 0 and 2 we show that even a persistent memory fault in L can produce one inconsistent incorrect checksums. Similar to equation (5) and figure 5, suppose after the left panel is factorized it is corrupted in one element $L_{21} \rightarrow \widehat{L_{21}} := L_{21} + \alpha e_i e_j^T$. Then the trailing matrix A_{22} and its row checksums will be updated by the corrupted $\widehat{L_{21}}$ in the following way (the symbol with a hat indicates a corruption):

$$\widehat{A'_{22}} \leftarrow A_{22} - \widehat{L_{21}}U_{12}$$
$$\widehat{CS(A'_{22})} \leftarrow \begin{bmatrix} A_{21} & A_{22} \end{bmatrix} \begin{bmatrix} e_1 \\ e_2 \end{bmatrix}$$
$$= (A_{21} - \widehat{L_{21}}U_{11})e_1 + (A_{22} - \widehat{L_{21}}U_{12})e_2 \quad (6)$$
$$CS(\widehat{A'_{22}}) = \widehat{A'_{22}}e_2 = (A_{22} - \widehat{L_{21}}U_{12})e_2$$
$$\widehat{CS(A'_{22})} - CS(\widehat{A'_{22}}) = (A_{21} - \widehat{L_{21}}U_{11})e_1$$
$$= \alpha e_i e_j^T U_{11}e_1$$

with the last equation indicating one inconsistent row checksum. Note that the equations confirm that only one row in the trailing matrix will be affected; the whole row is corrupted and so is the associated row checksum, but they are corrupted in a way that makes them inconsistent. The single row corruption can be handled by the double column checksum effectively. The above analysis also shows that the Example 3 in [ ] is incorrect.

Partial row pivoting in LU: In practice unpivoted LU can easily break down due to numerical instability. To reduce the instability while not incur prohibitively high overhead, partial row pivoting is commonly used. However the row swapping in the pivoting disrupts the maintenance of the checksums. If the row checksums are swapped together with their respective rows the row checksums still maintain. Column checksums need to be fixed and not swapped. In process local checksums however, maintaining column checksums require more care. One row may be swapped with a row from another process, thus invalidating both checksums. Therefore the checksums must be updated when inter process swapping happens.

Putting them together The pseudo code algorithm 1 summarizes the error detection and correction logic. For brevity it is in the point of view of global matrix.

4.4 Round-off error bounds

In the last section we have shown that if we limit the faults to one per error handling interval and assume precise arithmetic, the error detection is both sound and precise. In practice the floating point arithmetic are not precise, soundness and precision cannot be attained simultaneously. As lack of soundness is not acceptable in fault tolerance, we thus strive to maintain soundness at some expense of precision. To do that, we derive *a priori* norm based error bounds for the

---

Algorithm 1 The fault tolerant HPL algorithm, global view.

Require: Fully checksummed matrix A^f and right hand side b
Ensure: $x = A^{-1}b$ in the presence of floating point soft errors, or signal errors
  n is the size of A, B the blocking factor
  for $i = 0$ to n step B **do**
    $A(i:n, i:n) =: \begin{bmatrix} A_{11} & A_{12} \\ A_{21} & A_{22} \end{bmatrix}$
    Factorize left panel $\begin{bmatrix} A_{11} \\ A_{21} \\ CS(A_{\cdot 1}) \end{bmatrix} \rightarrow \begin{bmatrix} L_{11}\backslash U_{11} \\ L_{21} \\ CS(L_{\cdot 1}) \end{bmatrix}$
    Factorize top panel $\begin{bmatrix} A_{12} & CS(A_{12}) \end{bmatrix} \rightarrow \begin{bmatrix} U_{12} & CS(U_{12}) \end{bmatrix}$
    Check column checksums for L and row checksums U
    if Errors not algorithmically correctable **then**
      Rollback to the start of this iteration
    end if
    Update the trailing matrix $A_{22}^f \leftarrow A_{22}^f - L_{21}^c U_{12}^r$
    Check and correct full checksum matrix A_{22}^f
  end for

---

round-off error, and use the upper bound as the threshold to distinguish architectural faults from floating point round-off errors. If the architectural faults alters the less significant bits in a floating point number and the result is still within round-off error bounds, no errors will be detected and the fault is deemed indistinguishable from round-off errors.

Specifically, when we are verifying the checksums we need to compare the calculated sums to the checksums. Because floating point arithmetic has finite precision, those two may differ even in fault free execution. Our problem is now to bound the difference that round-off errors alone would not violate the bound. Consider the matrix multiplication $C = AB$. A well known norm bound of the round-off errors in matrix multiplication is as follows [ ].

$$||fl(AB) - AB||_\infty \leq \gamma_n ||A||_\infty ||B||_\infty \quad (7)$$

Assuming that the encoded matrix multiplication $C^f = A^c B^r$ is carried correctly, and the variable with a hat represents its floating point representation, we have the following result:

$$\left| \sum_{j=1}^n \widehat{c_{ij}} - \widehat{c_{i,n+1}} \right| = \left| \sum_{j=1}^n (\widehat{c_{ij}} - c_{ij}) - (\widehat{c_{i,n+1}} - c_{i,n+1}) \right|$$
$$\leq \left| \sum_{j=1}^n (\widehat{c_{ij}} - c_{ij}) \right| + |(\widehat{c_{i,n+1}} - c_{i,n+1})|$$
$$\leq ||fl(C^f) - C^f||_\infty$$
$$\leq \gamma_n ||A^c||_\infty ||B^r||_\infty$$

$$\quad (8)$$

where $\gamma_n = nu/(1 - nu)$ and u is the unit round-off error of the machine. For IEEE 754 64bit floating point number $u = 10^{-16}$. We thus obtained a bound of round-off errors that can be used as a threshold to distinguish architectural faults from floating point round-off errors. There is a similar bound to verify the row checksums.

5. OVERHEAD, PERFORMANCE, SCALABILITY, AND FAULT TOLERANCE CAPABILITY

In this section we model the fault tolerance capability, the execution time overhead, the scalability, and optimization of the proposed fault tolerant HPL.

5.1 Fault tolerance capability

For the error correction capability provided that errors can be detected, a natural question is how many errors or faults can be corrected? For each process in each error handling interval, any number of errors during the left and top panel factorization can be tolerated by the rollback. Multiple errors or one fault can be tolerated during the trailing matrix update, provided that the errors are within one row or one column. Note that the number of faults that can be tolerated is scalable with the number of processes and problem size, so at large scale enormous number of errors or faults can be tolerated as long as the faults do not burst into one error handling interval.

Compared to online ABFT (FT-ScaLAPACK) [,]: Online ABFT may fail to detect memory error in the trailing matrix update where the process is not engaging in the left panel factorization. FT-ScaLAPACK cannot correct the errors caused by faults in the left panel during the matrix multiplication.

Compared to offline ABFT (Du, Luk) [, ,]: Our FT-HPL is resilient to much more faults. For non permanently sticky memory fault, for example faults in cache or registers, offline ABFT correction based on casting the fault back to low rank perturbations to the initial matrix no longer work. In fact, any fault that do not corrupt a variable for its entire lifespan will fail in offline ABFT fault tolerance scheme, as the fault do not fit in the abstract fault model. Thus the tolerable faults in offline ABFT schemes is a small subset of the more comprehensive fault models considered in this paper.

5.2 Execution time overhead

The fault tolerant LU decomposition introduces overheads in maintaining checksums, checking checksums periodically, and correcting errors if detected. As the analysis here only serves as a first order approximation of the performance, we use a widely used simple machine model. The communication time is modeled as $T = \alpha + \beta L$ where α is network latency and β is the reciprocal of network bandwidth. The computation of matrices and vectors can be modeled by the product of compute rate γ and number of floating point operations (FLOPs). The compute rate of BLAS3 operation such as matrix multiplication is γ_3 and the compute rate of BLAS2 operation such as matrix vector multiplication is γ_2. On modern architectures γ_2 is much lower than γ_3 so it is important to make the distinction. Let N be the size of the matrix A, B be the blocking factor, $P \times Q$ be the dimension of the process grid, then the run time of HPL LU decomposition is as follows [ ]:

$$T_{\text{hpl}} = 2\gamma_3 \frac{N^3}{3PQ} + \beta N^2 \frac{3P+Q}{2PQ} + \alpha N \frac{(B+1)\log P + P}{B} \tag{9}$$

Checksum maintenance overhead: The overhead of checksum maintenance can be considered as the effectively increased matrix size. Adding two row checksums and two column checksums to the process local matrix, the global checksum matrix is bounded by $\max(N(1 + 2P/N), N(1 + 2Q/N))$. In a reasonable configuration of HPL, N/P and N/Q are the local dimensions of process local matrix that are around 10,000 therefore the enlargement of the global matrix size is around 0.02%. The resulting relative increase run time in equation 9 will be less than 0.1%, thus not a significant contribution to the run time overheads.

Checksum verification overhead: The periodical verification of the checksums is one major contribution to the run time overhead. The verification of checksums is a BLAS2 operation. The overhead of the verifications are:

$$\begin{aligned} T_{\text{check}} &= \frac{4\gamma_2}{PQ}(N^2 + (N-B)^2 + (N-2B)^2 + \cdots + B^2) \\ &= 4\gamma_2 \frac{N^3}{3BPQ} \end{aligned} \tag{10}$$

Compared to equation 9 the relative overhead is

$$\frac{T_{\text{check}}}{T_{\text{hpl}}} < \frac{2\gamma_2}{B\gamma_3} \tag{11}$$

Assuming a blocking factor B around 200 and BLAS2 operation is 5x slower than BLAS3 operations, the overhead is less than 5%. Different machines will have different ratio and different relative overhead.

5.3 Error correction overhead

This overhead is only present when errors are detected and correctable. The algorithmic error correction using checksums are non-significant. For the errors that are not algorithmically correctable by the checksums, the overhead is the lost work and rollback and recompute of the left panel factorization, which is empirically a small relative to the whole factorization.

5.4 Memory overhead

The fault tolerance needs extra memory space to store the checksums and the left panels. The extra space to store the checksums are less than 0.1% so not a significant overhead. The memory overhead of storing the left panel is more significant at $\frac{B}{N/Q}$. Again assuming a typical HPL configuration $B = 200, N/Q = 10,000$ the overhead is at 2%.

5.5 Impact on scalability

If we measure scalability by the parallel efficiency $\frac{T_{\text{ser}}}{PQT_{\text{hpl}}}$ which indicates how close it is to ideal parallel speedup, because the execution time overhead is bounded if memory usage per process is fixed and regardless of P, Q, the scalability of the fault tolerant HPL will remain the same as the original HPL which is excellent.

5.6 Tradeoffs between resilience and overhead

According to the overhead analysis and the detailed timing result from the experiments we found that the verification of the trailing matrix is one major overhead to the execution time. In fact when the trailing matrix verification is disabled the fault free execution time overhead dropped by half. In this section we discuss the tradeoff between fault tolerance and overhead, and the insights to allow such trade-offs to happen.

Let us take the point of view of one particular process. Suppose there is a grid of $P \times P$ processes and the matrix is distributed in 2d cyclic blocked manner. Since the LU decomposition works factorizes left and top panel sequentially from left to right and from top to bottom, the particular process engages into panel factorization every P iterations (in figure 8 $P = 4$). As we have discussed in the error patterns in matrix-matrix multiplication (TU), the errors propagate in a controlled way. In fact, if we skip the trailing matrix verification procedure at the end of iteration 1 and 2, we still can correct up to 1 fault happening during iteration 1,2, and 3 at the end of iteration 3. In this way we trade fault tolerance for reduced error checking overhead. The observation that allows us to make this tradeoff is that faults during iteration 1 will not propagate during iteration 2 and 3. However this is not true for PF as one fault in PF will propagate and cause massive errors in subsequent TU making the single fault uncorrectable. Thus the error handling procedure after each PF cannot be skipped to reduce fault tolerance.

The overhead analysis in the last section takes a global workload approach and assumes perfect load balance between the processes. But in parallel LU there is load imbalance during the panel factorizations where only a column of processes engage and other processes are waiting for the factorization result. It can be seen that PF is likely to be on the critical path. As PF depends on the TU immediately before, that TU is also likely to be on the critical path. The TU verification before PF thus is likely to be on the critical path. In fact from the experiments we found that by disabling only the TU verification immediately before a PF (shown in figure 8 OPT) the overall execution time drops almost as much as by disabling *all* TU verifications altogether. This significant reduction in overhead is therefore highly desirable, however it seems to break the promise that single fault during one error handling interval is tolerable. To remedy this problem, we only need to observe that, one fault in the last TU will cause the immediate subsequent PF verification to fail. The PF can be made non-destructive and once the PF fails the checksum verification, the error handling procedure for the previous TU is automatically invoked and the PF will restart. Therefore, the best tradeoff

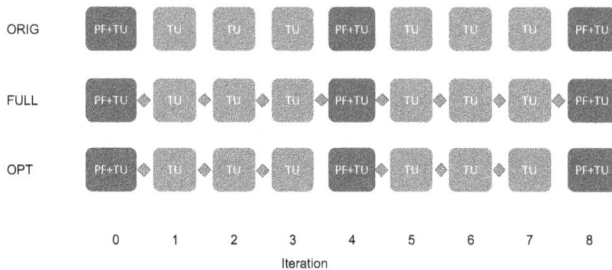

Figure 8: One process view in a 4x4 process grid: PF stands for (left and top) panel factorization and TU for trailing matrix update. The red diamond represents checksum verification point.

between fault tolerance and overhead is to disable only the TU verification immediately before a PF for every process. In this way the error handling interval remains short and the critical TU verification overhead is reduced significantly.

6. EXPERIMENTAL STUDY

In this section we empirically evaluate: 1) the fault coverage of the proposed FT-HPL in comparison to the state-of-the-art ABFT techniques by targeted fault injection; 2) the resilience of the FT-HPL scheme and implementation by randomly injecting various faults; 3) the cost of introducing such fault tolerance by measuring large scale executions.

6.1 Fault injection for fault coverage

In this subsection we experimentally compare the fault coverage of the state-of-the-art ABFT techniques that can apply to LU decomposition and HPL. We inject both arithmetic faults and memory faults to various locations in code and data at various times during the execution. We select several representative stages in one iteration to inject faults. Specifically, during the first iteration of LU algorithm, we inject faults right before the iteration and in the middle of the iteration (at iteration 2 of trailing matrix update). The arithmetic fault is simulated by modifying the output of a floating point multiplication. The memory fault is injected to matrix element (2,1) by modifying the data value. To precisely control where and how to inject a fault, we use the debugger GDB to stop the program and modify the program and data. During each run, we only inject one fault.

The fault coverage are summarized in table 1. As can be seen in table 1, no previous ABFT techniques provide as complete coverage to both arithmetic faults and memory faults happening at any time.

Table 1: Fault coverage for different ABFT techniques. "Before" means the fault affects data that is produced but not yet used. "Middle" means the fault affects data that is undergoing repeated use.

Fault category	Arithmetic	Memory	
Fault timing		Before	Middle
FT-HPL (this paper)	✓	✓	✓
FT-ScaLAPACK[21] /FTLU[5]	✓	✗	✗
FT-DGESV[8, 7]	✗	✓	✗

6.2 Fault injection experiments

We use a architectural fault injector F-SEFI [1] to implement the fault model and reveal the resilience of the FT-HPL implementation. Faults are injected at random time to a random instruction or memory locations that is to be used. Note that we inject faults into active memory to avoid masked faults that are never used. We model both floating point arithmetic faults and memory system faults. F-SEFI is based on QEMU, an architecture emulator. It works by intercepting the instructions of the application and alter the effect of the instructions to simulate arithmetic faults and memory faults. The application runs unmodified in the virtual machine and F-SEFI effectively simulate architecture correct execution (ACE) faults [17]. Memory system faults are modeled in detail: different level of stickiness associated with a memory address is used. In a cache based architecture, a variable in the program is mapped to multiple physical spaces in the memory hierarchy. When the image of the variable in different physical spaces is corrupted, the program perceives a certain stickiness of the error. For example, a corrupted main memory word is very sticky as it

Table 2: Fault tolerant for dense linear algebra: costs and fault tolerance capability. "Yes" means the faults can be tolerated; "No" means otherwise. The percentage indicates the execution time overhead against non fault tolerant LU implementation (PDGESV/PDGESV in ScaLAPACK, HPL_pdgesv in HPL).

Fault category	No Error	Arithmetic Faults		Memory Faults	
Number of faults	0	≤ 2	many	≤ 2	many
FT-HPL	5%	Yes, 5%	Yes, 5-35%[a,b]	Yes, 5%	Yes, 5-35%[a,b]
FT-ScaLAPACK[ ]/FTLU[ ]	8%	Yes, 8%	Yes, >8%[b]	No	No
FT-DGESV[,]	1%	Partial[c], 1%	No	Partial[c], 1%	No
RedMPI[ ][d]	$\geq 20\%$	Yes, $\geq 20\%$	Yes, $\geq 20\%$	Yes $\geq 20\%$	Yes,$\geq 20\%$

[a] Overhead depends on the impacted phase in HPL.
[b] To tolerate multiple faults they must be spaced out in time thus not overwhelming one error handling interval.
[c] The fault must happen in specific time and location to fit the algebraic model in [,]. See table 1.
[d] To tolerate faults RedMPI need 200% more processors to form TMR at MPI rank level.

will read corrupted value until overwritten. On contrast, a corrupted cache word may only read corrupted value temporarily until it is flushed out, and subsequent read to the variable will read from main memory or lower level cache which has the correct value.

The configurations of the fault injection experiments are as follows. Four virtual machines are used with one MPI rank in each virtual machine. The problem size is 200x200 with blocking factor $B = 5$, which means that there are 40 intervals. During each run of the experiment, 5 faults are injected at random times to a random memory locations that are active. We take care not to inject two faults into one error handling interval which our FT-HPL cannot handle. Note that this setting injects a considerable amount of faults into a small problem size to stress the fault tolerance mechanism.

In total 300 repetitions of the experiment are performed. Among them, 252 cases (84%) successfully tolerated the injected faults and passed the residual check of the HPL application. In all passed cases, the injected faults are detected and corrected by our algorithms. Another 21 cases (7%) run to completion but failed to pass the residual check because in HPL application not all data structures and operations can be protected by our algorithm. The remaining 27 (9%) cases crashed or hung. In contrast, when subject to 5 random memory faults both FT-ScaLAPACK/FTLU and FT-DGESV would have success rate of 0%.

6.3 Overheads of fault free execution and error correction

In this section we evaluate how much execution time overhead is during fault free execution, and the cost of error correction in the presence of faults. The experiments are conducted on two clusters: 1) a small cluster TARDIS (up to 512 cores) for detailed overhead reduction experiments, and 2) TACC Stampede for large scale (up to 4096 cores) scalability and overhead experiments. The TARDIS is a 16 node cluster; each node is equipped with two sockets AMD 6272 processors (32 cores) clocked at 2.1GHz. Each node has 64 GB memory. The interconnect is Mellanox QDR InfiniBand. The TACC Stampede is currently the #10 on Top500.org November 2015 list. Each node has two Intel E5 8-core (Sandy Bridge) processors with core frequency 2.7GHz and 32 GB memory. Each core is capable to deliver 21.6GFLOP/s at maximum. The interconnect is FDR 56Gbps InfiniBand Mellanox switches using the 2-level Clos fat tree topology. Table 2 provides summarized comparison

to state-of-the-art ABFT techniques in terms of overhead and fault coverage.

6.3.1 Overhead reduction and correction overhead

This set of experiments are done on TARDIS to investigate the overhead reduction effect discussed in subsection 5.6. In the fault free execution mode, four variants of implementations are measured: ORIG is the original unmodified Netlib HPL-2.1[ ]; FULL implements the fault tolerance described in the last section; OPT implements an optimization technique that partially removes the trailing matrix checksum verification from the critical path; and FAULT is essentially FULL plus injected error that triggers all error correction procedures. In the non fault free execution, faults are injected via source code instrumentation to trigger all error checking and correction, thus demonstrating the maximum overhead of error correction. The process local matrix size is fixed at around 3000x3000, lower than a typical 10000x10000 configuration which will take much longer to complete. We use process grids $N \times 32$, with the number of nodes N being from 2 to 10, and the matrix size N being from 24000 to 51000 The block size is fixed at $B = 200$.

Figure 9 thus shows the execution time in weak scaling experiments. It can be seen that with fault free execution, the execution time overhead can be as low as 6% compared to the non fault tolerant original HPL implementation. This is the cost paid to be able to tolerate faults that can occur during the execution. Also the error correction procedures are very cheap and cost between 25% to 35% execution overhead at the maximum of its fault tolerance capability. Note that this is the time it takes to handle hundreds of faults or thousands of errors caused by the faults.

It is also worth noting that the OPT configuration has almost 50% overhead reduction over the FULL configuration which confirms the analysis that the trailing matrix verification immediately before panel factorization is on the critical path.

6.3.2 Scalability experiments

In the following texts we adopt the OPT strategy and look at the fault free overhead at large scale on TACC Stampede using up to 4096 cores (256 nodes, the maximum allowed scale without special request). For HPL the efficiency in terms of floating point operations per second (FLOP/s) per core increases when memory usage per process increases. In the first set of experiments we use only a small fraction of memory available to avoid exceedingly long experiment

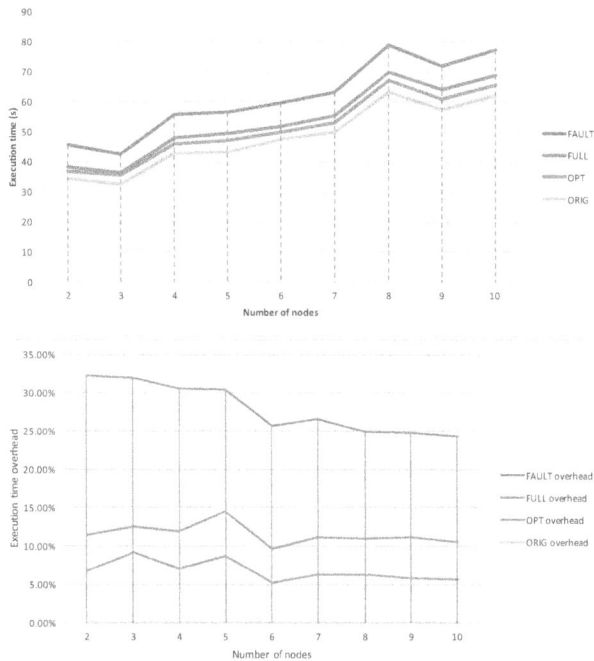

Figure 9: The execution time of FAULT, FULL, OPT, and ORIG HPL with varying number of nodes as X-axis. Each node comes with 32 computing cores.

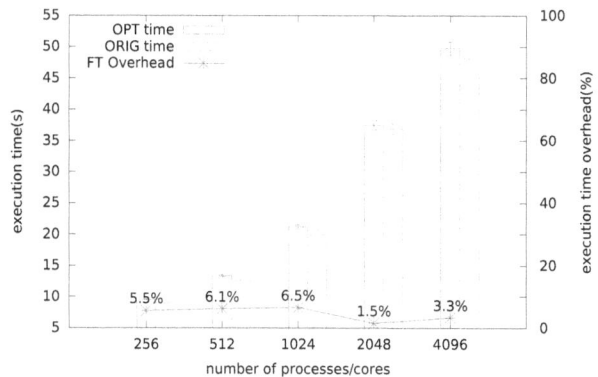

(a) Fault free execution time for optimized fault-tolerant HPL (OPT) and the original HPL (ORIG). The process local matrix size is fixed at 2000×2000 while the number of processes/cores is scaling from 256 to 4096.

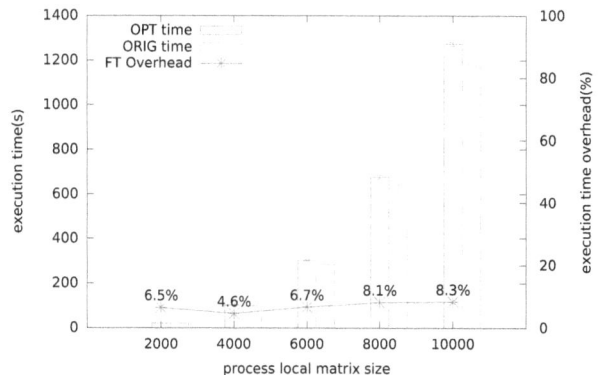

(b) Fault free execution time for optimized fault-tolerant HPL (OPT) and the original HPL (ORIG). The number of processes/cores is fixed at 1024 while the process local matrix size scales from 2000×2000 to 10000×10000.

Figure 10: Fault free execution time for optimized fault-tolerant HPL.

execution time (a single HPL run at its maximum problem size could take hours for 4096 cores). In the second set of experiments we fix the number of computing elements at 1024 cores and increase the problem size to observe the trend of overhead. From these two sets of experiments we can get an empirical idea of the overhead in introducing the resilience into HPL. The results are shown in figure 10

Reproducing large scale parallel experiments is difficult; so we strive to improve the interpretability [12] by providing more contexts and data. Since the execution time of HPL on a typical computing cluster is slightly indeterministic on Stampede, we collected enough measurements until the 99% confidence interval is around 5% of the reported mean measurements, following the recommendations from [12]. Also for this particular experiments on TACC Stampede we strongly suspect that there was an abnormal node with significantly slower network interface. If such node is included in the resource allocation the job will be significantly delayed by at least 20%. We base this conclusion on the following two reasons: 1) the measurements strongly exhibit two clusters around two modes. Any one measurement belonging to one cluster will appear as outlier for the other cluster using Tukey's outlier classification method. 2) jobs involving more nodes have a higher portion of such abnormally slow measurements: for 1024 cores we got 1 every 20 measurements; for 2048 cores we got 1 every 10 measurements; for 4096 cores 1 every 2 measurements. To eliminate the interference of such slow node we remove the measurements that are abnormally slow.

7. CONCLUSION

Fault model is the deciding factor on design of ABFT algorithms. In this work we seek to close the gap between what occurs at the architecture level and what the algorithm expects. We explore the challenges in designing ABFT algorithms under a general architectural fault model that allows both arithmetic and memory system faults comprehensive both temporally and spatially. By dividing the execution into many error handling intervals and aim at tolerating single fault in each error handling interval, we build a process local checksum scheme that achieves scalable fault tolerance (one fault per iteration per process) at around 5% fault free execution time overhead and less than 35% execution time overhead when facing maximum number of faults. Targeted fault injection shows that the comprehensive fault model cannot be handled by existing state-of-the-art ABFT techniques but will be effectively tolerated by FT-HPL scheme. Random fault injection shows that our FT-HPL implementation can tolerate 84% of the cases where 5 faults occur within less than 1 second. Such low overhead and high fault tolerance under comprehensive fault model makes the new ABFT in dense linear algebra practical and attractive in extreme scale systems, on unreliable commodity hardwares, or in hostile environments.

Acknowledgments

The authors would like to thank the anonymous reviewers for their insightful comments and valuable suggestions. This work is partially supported by the NSF grants CCF-1305622, ACI-1305624, CCF-1513201, the SZSTI basic research program JCYJ20150630114942313, and the Special Program for Applied Research on Super Computation of the NSFC-Guangdong Joint Fund (the second phase).

8. REFERENCES

[1] F-SEFI: A Fine-Grained Soft Error Fault Injection Tool for Profiling Application Vulnerability. In *IPDPS'14*.

[2] F. Bellard. QEMU, a Fast and Portable Dynamic Translator. In *USENIX Annual Technical Conference, FREENIX Track*, pages 41–46, 2005.

[3] F. Cappello, A. Geist, W. Gropp, S. Kale, B. Kramer, and M. Snir. Toward Exascale Resilience: 2014 update. *Supercomputing frontiers and innovations*, 1(1):5–28, June 2014.

[4] Z. Chen. Online-ABFT: An Online Algorithm Based Fault Tolerance Scheme for Soft Error Detection in Iterative Methods. In *Proceedings of the 18th ACM SIGPLAN Symposium on Principles and Practice of Parallel Programming*, PPoPP '13, pages 167–176, New York, NY, USA, 2013. ACM.

[5] T. Davies and Z. Chen. Correcting soft errors online in LU factorization. In *Proceedings of the 22nd international symposium on High-performance parallel and distributed computing*, pages 167–178. ACM, 2013.

[6] N. DeBardeleben, J. Laros, J. T. Daly, S. L. Scott, C. Engelmann, and B. Harrod. High-end computing resilience: Analysis of issues facing the HEC community and path-forward for research and development. *Whitepaper*, 2009.

[7] P. Du, P. Luszczek, and J. Dongarra. High Performance Dense Linear System Solver with Soft Error Resilience. In *2011 IEEE International Conference on Cluster Computing (CLUSTER)*, pages 272–280, Sept. 2011.

[8] P. Du, P. Luszczek, and J. Dongarra. High Performance Dense Linear System Solver with Resilience to Multiple Soft Errors. *Procedia Computer Science*, 9:216–225, 2012.

[9] D. Fiala, F. Mueller, C. Engelmann, R. Riesen, K. Ferreira, and R. Brightwell. Detection and Correction of Silent Data Corruption for Large-scale High-performance Computing. SC '12, pages 78:1–78:12, Los Alamitos, CA, USA, 2012.

[10] P. Fitzpatrick and C. Murphy. Fault tolerant matrix triangularization and solution of linear systems of equations. In *Proceedings of the International Conference on Application Specific Array Processors, 1992*, pages 469–480, Aug. 1992.

[11] G. H. Golub and C. F. V. Loan. *Matrix Computations*. JHU Press, Dec. 2012.

[12] T. Hoefler and R. Belli. Scientific Benchmarking of Parallel Computing Systems: Twelve Ways to Tell the Masses when Reporting Performance Results. SC '15, pages 73:1–73:12, New York, NY, USA, 2015.

[13] K.-H. Huang and J. Abraham. Algorithm-Based Fault Tolerance for Matrix Operations. *IEEE Transactions on Computers*, C-33(6):518–528, June 1984.

[14] F. T. Luk and H. Park. An Analysis of Algorithm-based Fault Tolerance Techniques. *J. Parallel Distrib. Comput.*, 5(2):172–184, Apr. 1988.

[15] T. May and M. H. Woods. Alpha-particle-induced soft errors in dynamic memories. *IEEE Transactions on Electron Devices*, 26(1):2–9, Jan. 1979.

[16] S. E. Michalak, K. W. Harris, N. W. Hengartner, B. E. Takala, S. Wender, and others. Predicting the number of fatal soft errors in Los Alamos National Laboratory's ASC Q supercomputer. *Device and Materials Reliability, IEEE Transactions on*, 5(3):329–335, 2005.

[17] S. Mukherjee. *Architecture design for soft errors*. Morgan Kaufmann, 2011.

[18] E. Normand. Single event upset at ground level. *IEEE transactions on Nuclear Science*, 43(6):2742–2750, 1996.

[19] A. Petitet, R. C. Whaley, J. Dongarra, and A. Cleary. HPL - A Portable Implementation of the High-Performance Linpack Benchmark for Distributed-Memory Computers.

[20] J. Sloan, D. Kesler, R. Kumar, and A. Rahimi. A numerical optimization-based methodology for application robustification: Transforming applications for error tolerance. In *2010 IEEE/IFIP International Conference on Dependable Systems and Networks (DSN)*, pages 161–170, June 2010.

[21] M. Snir and et. al. Addressing failures in exascale computing. *International Journal of High Performance Computing Applications*, 28(2):129–173, May 2014.

[22] J. Von Neumann. Probabilistic logics and the synthesis of reliable organisms from unreliable components. *Automata studies*, 34:43–98, 1956.

[23] J. H. Wilkinson, J. H. Wilkinson, and J. H. Wilkinson. *The algebraic eigenvalue problem*, volume 87. Clarendon Press Oxford, 1965.

[24] P. Wu and Z. Chen. FT-ScaLAPACK: Correcting Soft Errors On-line for ScaLAPACK Cholesky, QR, and LU Factorization Routines. In *Proceedings of the 23rd International Symposium on High-performance Parallel and Distributed Computing*, HPDC '14, pages 49–60, New York, NY, USA, 2014. ACM.

[25] P. Wu, C. Ding, L. Chen, T. Davies, C. Karlsson, and Z. Chen. On-line soft error correction in matrix–matrix multiplication. *Journal of Computational Science*, 4(6):465–472, Nov. 2013.

[26] E. Yao, J. Zhang, M. Chen, G. Tan, and N. Sun. Detection of soft errors in LU decomposition with partial pivoting using algorithm-based fault tolerance. *International Journal of High Performance Computing Applications*, page 1094342015578487, Apr. 2015.

[27] J. F. Ziegler and H. Puchner. *SER–history, Trends and Challenges: A Guide for Designing with Memory ICs*. Cypress, 2004.

New-Sum: A Novel Online ABFT Scheme For General Iterative Methods

Dingwen Tao
University of California, Riverside
dtao001@cs.ucr.edu

Shuaiwen Leon Song
Pacific Northwest National Laboratory
Shuaiwen.Song@pnnl.gov

Sriram Krishnamoorthy
Pacific Northwest National Laboratory
sriram@pnnl.gov

Panruo Wu
University of California, Riverside
pwu011@cs.ucr.edu

Xin Liang
University of California, Riverside
xlian007@cs.ucr.edu

Eddy Z. Zhang
Rutgers University
eddy.zhengzhang@cs.rutgers.edu

Darren Kerbyson
Pacific Northwest National Laboratory
Darren.Kerbyson@pnnl.gov

Zizhong Chen
University of California, Riverside
chen@cs.ucr.edu

ABSTRACT

Emerging high-performance computing platforms, with large component counts and lower power margins, are anticipated to be more susceptible to soft errors in both logic circuits and memory subsystems. We present an online algorithm-based fault tolerance (ABFT) approach to efficiently detect and recover soft errors for general iterative methods. We design a novel checksum-based encoding scheme for matrix-vector multiplication that is resilient to both arithmetic and memory errors. Our design decouples the checksum updating process from the actual computation, and allows adaptive checksum overhead control. Building on this new encoding mechanism, we propose two online ABFT designs that can effectively recover from errors when combined with a checkpoint/rollback scheme. These designs are capable of addressing scenarios under different error rates. Our ABFT approaches apply to a wide range of iterative solvers that primarily rely on matrix-vector multiplication and vector linear operations. We evaluate our designs through comprehensive analytical and empirical analysis. Experimental evaluation on the Stampede supercomputer demonstrates the low performance overheads incurred by our two ABFT schemes for preconditioned CG (0.4% and 2.2%) and preconditioned BiCGSTAB (1.0% and 4.0%) for the largest SPD matrix from UFL Sparse Matrix Collection. The evaluation also demonstrates the flexibility and effectiveness of our proposed designs for detecting and recovering various types of soft errors in general iterative methods.

ACM acknowledges that this contribution was authored or co-authored by an employee, or contractor of the national government. As such, the Government retains a nonexclusive, royalty-free right to publish or reproduce this article, or to allow others to do so, for Government purposes only. Permission to make digital or hard copies for personal or classroom use is granted. Copies must bear this notice and the full citation on the first page. Copyrights for components of this work owned by others than ACM must be honored. To copy otherwise, distribute, republish, or post, requires prior specific permission and/or a fee. Request permissions from permissions@acm.org.

HPDC'16, May 31-June 04, 2016, Kyoto, Japan

© 2016 ACM. ISBN 978-1-4503-4314-5/16/05. . . $15.00

DOI: http://dx.doi.org/10.1145/2907294.2907306

Keywords

Algorithm-Based Fault Tolerance (ABFT); Resilience; Iterative Methods; Online Error Detection; Silent Data Corruption (SDC); Checksum; Checkpoint; Rollback Recovery

1. INTRODUCTION

Supercomputers are being built with an increasing number of complex components, each of which has growing on-chip transistor density [20]. Together with a renewed emphasis on limiting power and energy consumption, this is anticipated to result in these systems being increasingly susceptible to soft errors [5, 15], errors that do not lead to noticeable system crashes, but to silent data corruption (SDC). This phenomenon has already been observed on several real-world leadership-class supercomputers [5, 15].

Algorithm-based fault tolerance (ABFT) is an approach to detect and possibly correct errors at a lower cost than double- or triple-modular redundancy. These approaches exploit the characteristics of an algorithm to encode a small amount of redundancy into the computation. This redundancy is later used to detect and correct errors. In this paper, we present an ABFT approach to tolerate soft errors in general iterative methods. These methods, used in a wide variety of applications [1], primarily consist of matrix-vector multiplication (MVM) and vector linear operations (VLOs).

Novel checksum-encoding scheme. The effectiveness and efficiency of an ABFT scheme depends on the checksum-encoding mechanism employed and its coverage in terms of number and type of errors detected. Much existing work on ABFT strategies is built on a checksum-encoding scheme designed for matrix-matrix multiplication [11]. While this scheme has been extended to cover a wide range of related algorithms [18, 19, 23], we show that it is not sufficient to construct ABFT schemes for matrix-vector multiplication (MVM) due to its inability to detect soft errors if the input vector is corrupted. We present a novel checksum-encoding scheme that can tolerate soft errors in both logic circuits (e.g., arithmetic operations) and the memory subsystems (e.g., memory, cache and register bit-flips). Our new scheme separates the checksums from their corresponding encoded matrix and vectors, enabling checksum updates across multiple operations to improve overall performance. We show that our checksum scheme also can be used in the context of preconditioners employed in iterative methods.

Flexible detection latency. Error detection latency refers to the latency between the manifestation of an error and its detection. In general, longer error detection latencies enable reduced detection costs but might lead to increased recovery overhead due to the error corrupting a larger fraction of the application state. ABFT schemes for iterative methods often require error detection after each matrix-vector multiplication (MVM) or each iteration. We show that our checksum scheme supports eager (immediate) and lazy (after several iterations) error detection by detecting an arbitrary number of errors across multiple operations.

Two-level ABFT. ABFT schemes often employ redundancy proportional to the number of errors to be detected and corrected. This requires careful consideration of anticipated error rates and performance penalties proportional to the number of errors that need to be corrected. Alternatively, checkpoint-rollback incurs significant recovery penalties to recover even from one error, say impacting one arithmetic operation. We present a two-level ABFT algorithm that combines the best aspects of both strategies. In the most compute-intensive component of iterative methods, the matrix-vector multiplication (MVM), we employ a low-cost inner-level recovery scheme to efficiently correct one error and detect multiple errors. When multiple errors are detected, the algorithm resorts to immediate rollback. Multiple errors in an MVM as well as errors in the VLOs are protected by an outer-level rollback strategy that is invoked every few iterations. This two-level approach protects the most compute-intensive parts efficiently while ensuring sufficient coverage for other parts of the computation.

Contributions. The proposed ABFT schemes in this paper are applicable to all the iterative methods constructed from matrix-vector multiplication and vector linear operations. In particular, all the Krylov solvers, including Richardson, Chebyshev, CG variants, quasi-minimal residual (QMR), conjugate residuals (CR), generalized conjugate residuals (GCR), variations of GMRES, minimum residual (MINRES), SYMMLQ, and LSQR, can be protected using the presented ABFT approaches.

We compare our online ABFT designs with the state-of-the-art techniques and demonstrate benefits in terms of coverage for different types of soft errors, generality for addressing iterative methods, and overhead introduced. We also evaluate the overall performance of our two schemes (i.e., *basic online ABFT* and *two-level online ABFT*) under various error scenarios on a leadership-class supercomputer. Experimental results show that our proposed designs encounter trivial overhead for both erroneous (single error or multiple errors) and error-free execution. Additionally, we compare the two schemes through theoretical and empirical analysis, demonstrating the scenario under which each scheme should be applied to achieve the better overall performance.

The primary contributions of this paper are:

- A novel checksum encoding scheme for matrix-vector multiplication and preconditioners, separating the check-

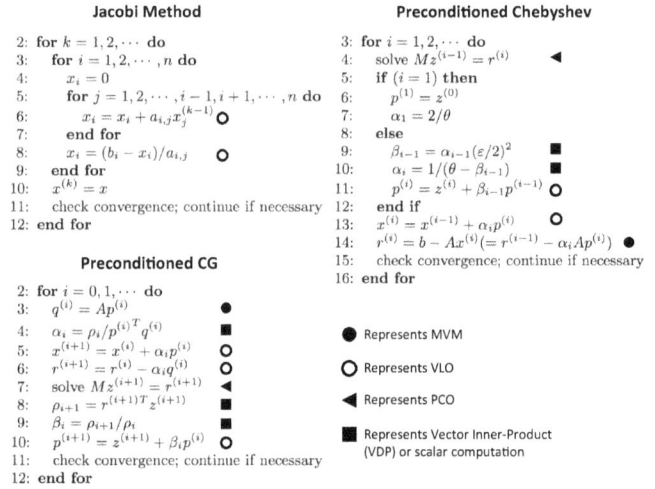

Figure 1: Main loops of several representative iterative methods: Jacobi, preconditioned conjugate gradient (PCG), preconditioned Chebyshev.

sums from their corresponding encoded matrix and vectors, leading to schemes that compute the output checksum directly from the inputs' checksums;
- Proof that the new checksum scheme can detect soft errors in both the logic circuits and the memory subsystem;
- An ABFT scheme for iterative methods that allows the errors to be detected eagerly or lazily;
- A technique to efficiently correct one error and detect the presence of multiple errors in a vector;
- Two online ABFT designs based on the new encoding mechanism;
- Detailed theoretical and empirical comparison between the proposed designs and state-of-the-art approaches.

2. ALGORITHM-BASED FAULT TOLERANCE FOR ITERATIVE METHODS

Iterative methods are widely used for solving systems of equations or computing eigenvalues of large sparse matrices. The key feature of iterative methods is the use of matrix-vector multiplication (MVM) to iteratively compute approximations to the solution vector until desired accuracy is achieved. Figure 1 shows three representative iterative methods: Jacobi, preconditioned CG, and preconditioned Chebyshev. As illustrated, iterative methods consist of a few key operations: matrix-vector multiplications (MVM), vector linear-operations (VLOs), and solving preconditioned systems (PCO). Among them, MVM and PCO consume the largest fraction of the total computation time, making them particularly vulnerable to soft errors.

Algorithm-based fault tolerance (ABFT) techniques exploit specific algorithmic properties of a given computation to detect and possibly locate/correct errors. More commonly, ABFT techniques for matrix computations augment the input matrices with a *checksum* computed from the rows or columns of the matrices. It is then shown that performing a matrix operation on this augmented matrix automatically computes the checksum for the output matrix as part of the computation, as shown in Figure 2(a). Any error in the computation will result in the encoding relationship between the

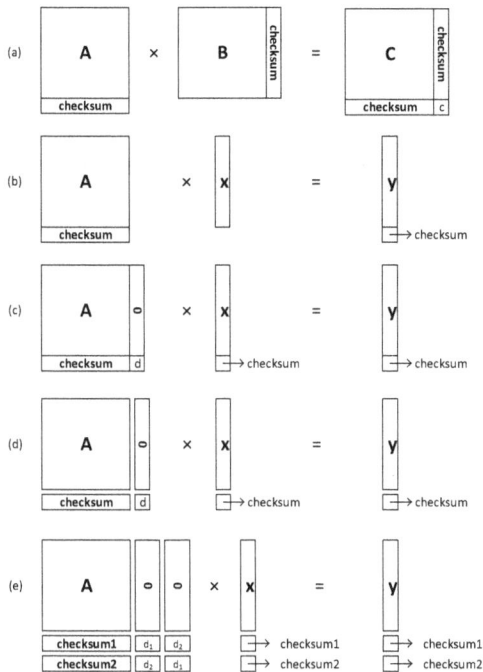

Figure 2: Checksum encoding mechanisms discussed in this paper: (a) Traditional checksum; (b) Traditional checksum applied to matrix-vector multiplication; (c) Our proposed checksum encoding; (d) Separation scheme of our new checksum; (e) Multiple-checksums encoding for our new checksum.

output matrix and its checksum being violated. Variants of this scheme have been designed to verify the encoding relationship online—at intermediate steps within the execution rather than at the end.

The notion of ABFT was introduced by Huang and Abraham [11] in the form of a checksum-based approach to verify matrix-matrix multiplication and LU decomposition. Several subsequent ABFT techniques employ the same encoding strategy [16, 18, 19, 23] illustrated for matrix A as follows:

$$A \xrightarrow{encode} A^* := \begin{bmatrix} A \\ c^T A \end{bmatrix}$$

where c is a predefined vector with all non-zero entries and $c^T A$ is matrix A's checksum. A matrix-vector multiplication $y = Ax$ is replaced with a multiplication of the encoded operands, $y^* = A^* x$, shown in Figure 2(b). We use $checksum(y)$ to denote the checksum computed in y^* as part of the operation. In this example, $checksum(y)$ is the last entry of the vector y^*. In the absence of faults, $checksum(y) = c^T y$[1]. This checksum relationship can be used to detect errors in the computation of y. For example, consider an error in an arithmetic operation resulting in y'^* that is not equal to y^*. In this case, it can be shown that $checksum(y') \neq c^T y$.

This encoding was designed for matrix-matrix multiplication and has some limitations when applied to iterative methods. For example, consider an error in x before the operation, resulting in an erroneous vector x'. The encoded

matrix-vector multiplication $y = Ax$ becomes:

$$y'^* = A^* x' = \begin{pmatrix} A \\ c^T A \end{pmatrix} x' = \begin{pmatrix} Ax' \\ c^T Ax' \end{pmatrix}$$

We observe that the checksum relationship for y holds even in the presence of an error in x. In the absence of additional protection, this can lead to silent data corruption, making the encoding scheme unusable in detecting faults in the input vector. In other words, under this encoding scheme, the output vector's checksum relationship cannot be used to identify all soft errors.

Dealing with cache errors. Although adding additional checksum verification cost for x may capture the erroneous output vector sometimes, a more insidious case is a cache error in x. Consider an error that affects a value of x in cache (e.g., a cache bit-flip while memory still holds the correct value). This erroneous value then resides in cache for the duration of the calculation, corrupting the computation of both the matrix-vector multiplication and the associated checksums. Given that the entire calculation consistently used the incorrect input value, the output checksums will be consistent, which makes verifying output checksum useless. Now if we add extra cost to verify x, it may still not detect the error because cache lines can be evicted and the erroneous value x is replaced by the correct value loaded from the main memory. This error will now escape detection. Manifestation of this error depends on various factors such as compiler optimizations that reorder instructions, cache replacement and eviction policies, hardware cache configurations, etc. Tolerating faults in cache or registers in this scheme requires verifying every access to the vectors, which could be much more expensive. Because matrix-vector multiplication is invoked in every iteration of the iterative methods, and the traditional encoding scheme may lead to undetected errors, these errors need to be effectively detected every iteration.

Protecting preconditioners. Another limitation of the preceding checksum scheme is its inability to deal with preconditioned systems (PCOs) used to accelerate convergence in iterative solvers. For example, when solving preconditioned system $Mz = r$ in CG, where matrix M and vector r are input operands, the above encoding scheme cannot compute the checksum for z as part of the encoded computation.

State-of-the-art online ABFT schemes. The two most related state-of-the-art online ABFT schemes are from Chen [6] and Sloan et al. [19]. Chen proposed to exploit the vectors' orthogonal relationship to detect soft errors for *a subset of algorithms* in Krylov subspace methods. Every several iterations, the algorithm will check if the orthogonality relationship or the residual relationship $r^{(i+1)} = b - Ax^{(i+1)}$ is valid. If either relationship is broken, execution is rolled back to the nearest checkpoint. Although good in terms of coverage for many operations (MVM, VLO, PCO, vector dot product, etc), this method has several limitations. First, it is not general enough to cover all iterative methods because some of them do not have orthogonal relationship of vectors, e.g., Jacobi and Chebyshev methods shown in Figure 1. Even if there are orthogonality relations between vectors, it still cannot detect soft errors that do not propagate to these vectors. Checking the residual requires an expensive MVM operation. This higher error detection overhead necessitates less frequent error checking, leading to a higher rollback recovery cost when errors are detected.

---

[1]This holds subject to the inexactness of floating point arithmetic, which we account for in the overall algorithm.

45

Sloan et al. [19] apply the traditional checksum discussed above to identify only arithmetic errors in the MVM operation (detection), and then use binary search to locate and partially correct the erroneous element(s) in the output vector (recovery). However, several issues can occur when this approach is used in the context of iterative methods. First, they focus on MVM and assume that no soft errors occur in other operations such as VLOs and PCOs. Second, they assume the input vector to the MVM is correct. As demonstrated previously, the traditional checksum cannot detect the error(s) by verifying the output vector's checksum relationship if the input vector is corrupted (e.g., memory bit-flips before MVM or arithmetic errors carried from the previous iteration). If the detection technique fails, all the benefits from the recovery scheme disappear. Third, to avoid such undetectable propagation of errors, Sloan's method needs to conduct expensive checksum verification for error detection every iteration, and then apply binary search to locate and correct the errors. This might be only beneficial under high error rates. While soft errors are more likely to occur in future systems, errors affecting the computation every few iterations is not a common or practically anticipated scenario. We present theoretical and empirical evaluation of Sloan's approach in Sections 6.2 and 6.3.

These issues motivate the design of new online ABFTs scheme that can be applied to general iterative methods to effectively tolerate various types of soft errors.

3. ERROR MODEL

We focus on errors affecting matrices and vectors employed in iterative methods. Specifically, we focus on errors in matrix-vector multiplication (MVM), vector linear operations (VLOs)—addition, scaling, assignment, etc.—and solving preconditioned systems (PCOs). We assume other low-computation operations (e.g., scalar operations, vector dot-product, etc.) not amenable to general ABFT checksum-encoding are protected using other schemes (e.g., duplicated execution or definition-use checksums [22]).

We consider errors in arithmetic operations or values used in these operations. These correspond to soft errors in the ALU or the memory subsystem. We consider errors in any part of the memory subsystem—main memory, caches, registers, etc.—that can affect the result of multiple (but not necessarily all) arithmetic operations.

We only consider errors that affect the data in the matrices and vectors used in the iterative method. As is the case with other ABFT schemes, we assume that errors do not affect scalar variables, control flow, program stack, etc. We model an error as a random additive contribution e to a value. For example, an error in x before computing Ax can be represented as $A(x + e)$ where e represents the error introduced. We assume that errors do not get canceled or get hidden during the algorithm execution. This notion is specified in the form of the following assumptions:

Non-zero scaling factor assumption: In any operation $y = \alpha x$, we assume that $\alpha \neq \vec{0}$. We exploit this property to ensure that any error in x is reflected in the output of the operation, enabling efficient detection by checking only y. A complete solution needs to check, at runtime, the scaling factor α and detect errors in x if α is close to zero.

Cancellation-less error assumption: $\forall x, e_1, e_2 : x + e_1 \neq \vec{0}$ and $x \cdot e_1 \neq \vec{0}$ and $e_1 + e_2 \neq \vec{0}$, where x is an arbitrary program variable and e_1 and e_2 are the errors introduced. This assumption ensures that existing errors in a variable do not get canceled out by subsequent errors.

4. ERROR PRESERVING CHECKSUM FOR MATRIX-VECTOR MULTIPLICATION

In this section, we present our checksum scheme that addresses the aforementioned limitations. Given an $N \times N$ matrix A, we define $checksum(A)$ (Figure 2(c)) as:

$$checksum(A) = c^T A - dc^T,$$

where c is a predefined $N \times 1$ vector and d is a predefined non-zero scalar larger than $n||c||_\infty||A||_\infty/min(c)$ (see Lemma 2). Here $min(c) = \min_{1,\cdots,n} |c_i|$ and c_i is the i-th element of the vector c.

We encode matrix A to matrix A^* as

$$A^* = \begin{pmatrix} A & \vec{o} \\ c^T A - dc^T & d \end{pmatrix}. \quad (1)$$

As shown in Figure 2(c), we encode all the vectors x with their own column checksums:

$$x^* = \begin{bmatrix} x \\ c^T x \end{bmatrix}$$

The ABFT form of a given operation, such as matrix-matrix multiplication, often performs the same operation on the encoded matrix (Figure 2(c)). For example, $A \cdot B$ is replaced with $A^* \cdot B^*$. In the case of our checksum scheme, encoding the symmetric matrix A leads to A^* that is no longer symmetric. This will cause some iterative methods (e.g., CG) that solve symmetric and positive-definite (SPD) systems to converge slowly, or even diverge. Therefore, we develop a different scheme on ABFT that separates the checksum(s) from the encoded input matrix and vectors, shown in Figure 2(d). This allows the original operation to proceed unchanged while the checksum of the output vector computed directly from the checksums of the input operands. For example,

$$
\begin{aligned}
y^* = A^* x^* &= \begin{pmatrix} A & \vec{o} \\ c^T A - dc^T & d \end{pmatrix} \begin{pmatrix} x \\ checksum(x) \end{pmatrix} \\
&= \begin{pmatrix} Ax \\ (c^T A - dc^T)x + d \cdot checksum(x) \end{pmatrix} \\
&= \begin{pmatrix} Ax \\ checksum(A) \cdot x + d \cdot checksum(x) \end{pmatrix}
\end{aligned}
$$

As can be seen, the output checksum $checksum(y)$ can be computed as $(checksum(A)x + d \cdot checksum(x))$. In this way, computing the output vector's checksum does not rely on the operations of the encoded input operands (i.e., $checksum(y)$ and $y^* = A^* x$ can be computed separately). The output checksum for MVM, VLO and PCO operations are computed as follows:

Matrix-vector multiplication $y = Ax$:

$$checksum(y) = checksum(A)x + d \cdot checksum(x) \quad (2)$$

Vector linear-operation $z = \alpha x + \beta y$:

$$checksum(z) = \alpha \cdot checksum(x) + \beta \cdot checksum(y) \quad (3)$$

Preconditioner Say the preconditioned system $Mz^{(i)} = r^{(i)}$ needs to be solved to compute the preconditioned system's residual vector $z^{(i)}$, where M is a preconditioner and r is the original system's residual. The preconditioner M can be expressed either explicitly as a matrix or implicitly as a sequence of operations. If M is expressed explicitly, according to the Equation (2), the checksum of z can be computed from r as:

$$checksum(z) = \frac{(checksum(M)^T z^{(i)} - checksum(r))}{d} \tag{4}$$

If the preconditioner M is expressed implicitly, e.g., incomplete factors or algebraic multigrid, it will be composed of several matrix-vector multiplications (MVMs) and vector-linear operations (VLOs). Thus, even if the preconditioner M cannot be directly encoded, the checksum of z can be computed through updating each checksum of the output vector after these MVMs and VLOs using Equations (2) and (3).

Since the implicitly expressed preconditioner can be encoded as a composition of encoded MVMs and VLOs, we only consider the explicit expression of M in the following discussion. However, we note that implicit preconditioners composed of MVMs and VLOs can also be efficiently protected by the schemes described in this paper.

We now prove that this checksum scheme can detect soft errors for the key operations in iterative methods, even if the input vectors of these operations are corrupted. We refer to the following operations that can generate a vector in iterative methods as *vector-generating operations*:

Table 1: Vector-generating operations and their expression

Vector-generating operations	Expression
MVM	$w := Au$
PCO	$Mw := u$
VLO scaling	$w := \alpha u$
VLO addition	$w := u + v$

M is a preconditioner and ':=' is assignment. Note that iterative methods are primarily composed of these vector-generating operations (e.g., shown in Figure 1).

Lemma 1. *For any vector-generating operation, if the checksum relationship holds for the input operands and there is no soft error during the operation, the checksum relationship of the output vector is maintained.*

Proof. We prove for each vector-generating operation:

1. Consider an MVM, $w := Au$. We have $w = Au$ and, from Equation (2), $checksum(w) = c^T Au + d(checksum(u) - c^T u)$. Combining the two:

$$checksum(w) - c^T w = d(checksum(u) - c^T u).$$

If $checksum(u) = c^T u$, $checksum(w) = c^T w$.

2. Consider a PCO, $Mw := u$. Together with Equation (4), we have

$$checksum(w) - c^T w = \frac{checksum(u) - c^T u}{d}.$$

If $checksum(u) = c^T u$, $checksum(w) = c^T w$.

3. Consider a VLO, $w = \alpha u$. We have $w = \alpha u$ and, from Equation (2), $checksum(w) = \alpha \cdot checksum(u)$. Therefore,

$$checksum(w) - c^T w = \alpha(checksum(u) - c^T u).$$

If $checksum(u) = c^T u$, $checksum(w) = c^T w$.

4. Consider a VLO, $w := u + v$. We have $w = u + v$ and, from Equation (3), $checksum(w) = checksum(u) + checksum(v)$, thus,

$$checksum(w) - c^T w = (checksum(u) - c^T u)$$
$$+ (checksum(v) - c^T v)$$

If $checksum(u) = c^T u$ and $checksum(v) = c^T v$, $checksum(w) = c^T w$. $\square$

Lemma 2. *For any vector-generating operation, any composition of the following soft errors results in the checksum relationship of output vector being broken:*

1. *Arithmetic error affecting the operation;*
2. *Memory bit flips or arithmetic errors in input vectors carried from the previous operations;*
3. *Cache or register bit flips that affect the input vector(s) during the operation.*

Proof. Due to space constraints, we only present the proof for the MVM operation. The proof of the PCO operation is similar. The proof for the VLO operations is the same as in the case of traditional checksum schemes.

Using our new checksum mechanism, we perform an MVM $w := Au$ with checksum update.

1. If there are arithmetic errors during the operation and e_a represents arithmetic errors, the erroneous output vector w can be represented as $Au + e_a$.

2. If the input vector is corrupted by memory bit flips or arithmetic errors (possibly carried from previous operations) before its first use in this operation and e_m represents the errors, the erroneous output vector can be represented as $w = A(u + e_m)$.

3. If cache or register bit flips corrupt the input vector during the operation and $e_{c1}, \cdots, e_{ck}$ are cache or register errors, assume $A = A_{ne} + A_{e1} + \cdots + A_{ek}$, where A_{ne} represents the rows that are used in the computation without being affected by soft errors and A_{ei} $(i = 1, \cdots, k)$ represents the i-th row of A if it is affected by a combination of $e_{c1}, \cdots, e_{ck}$ in the computation. Then the erroneous output vector w can be represented as $A_{ne}u + \sum_{i=1}^{k} A_{ei}(u + \sum_{j=1}^{k} \alpha_{ij} e_{cj}) = Au + \sum_{i=1}^{k} \sum_{j=1}^{k} \alpha_{ij} A_{ei} e_{cj}$, where $\alpha_{ij} \in \{0, 1\}$.

Under any composition of these soft errors, the erroneous output vector w can be represented as

$$w = A(u + e_m) + e_a + \sum_{i=1}^{k} \sum_{j=1}^{k} \alpha_{ij} A_{ei} e_{cj}$$

Because the checksum update is calculated after a soft error occurs, we have two scenarios:

1. If the checksum update is not affected by the soft error,

$$checksum(w) = checksum(A)(u + e_m) + d \cdot checksum(u)$$
$$= c^T A(u + e_m) - dc^T e_m$$

Thus, $checksum(w) - c^T w = -c^T(\sum_{i=1}^{k} \sum_{j=1}^{k} \alpha_{ij} A_{ei} e_{cj})$ $- dc^T e_m - c^T e_a$.

47

2. If checksum update is affected by the soft error,

$checksum(\boldsymbol{w}) =$

$checksum(\boldsymbol{A})(\boldsymbol{u} + \boldsymbol{e_m} + \sum_{i=1}^{k} \boldsymbol{e_{ci}}) + d \cdot checksum(\boldsymbol{u})$

$= \boldsymbol{c^T A}(\boldsymbol{u} + \boldsymbol{e_m} + \sum_{i=1}^{k} \boldsymbol{e_{ci}}) - d\boldsymbol{c^T}(\sum_{i=1}^{k} \boldsymbol{e_{ci}} + \boldsymbol{e_m})$

Thus, $checksum(\boldsymbol{w}) - \boldsymbol{c^T w}$ is

$\sum_{i=1}^{k}(\boldsymbol{c^T A} - d\boldsymbol{c^T} - \boldsymbol{c^T}\sum_{j=1}^{k}\alpha_{ji}\boldsymbol{A_{ej}})\boldsymbol{e_{ci}} - d\boldsymbol{c^T e_m} - \boldsymbol{c^T e_a}$

$= \sum_{i=1}^{k}(\boldsymbol{c^T A_e} - d\boldsymbol{c^T})\boldsymbol{e_{ci}} - d\boldsymbol{c^T e_m} - \boldsymbol{c^T e_a}$

Since $\boldsymbol{A_e}$ is a part of $\boldsymbol{A}$, the absolute value of each element in vector $\boldsymbol{c^T A_e}$ is no larger than $n||\boldsymbol{c}||_\infty||\boldsymbol{A}||_\infty$, which means $||\boldsymbol{c^T A_e}||_\infty \leq n||\boldsymbol{c}||_\infty||\boldsymbol{A}||_\infty$. Moreover, we choose d to be larger than $n||\boldsymbol{c}||_\infty||\boldsymbol{A}||_\infty/min(\boldsymbol{c})$, thus, the absolute value of each element in vector $d\boldsymbol{c^T}$ is larger than $n||\boldsymbol{c}||_\infty||\boldsymbol{A}||_\infty$, which means $min(d\boldsymbol{c^T}) > n||\boldsymbol{c}||_\infty||\boldsymbol{A}||_\infty$. Therefore, $min(d\boldsymbol{c^T}) > ||\boldsymbol{c^T A_e}||_\infty$. It demonstrates that $\boldsymbol{c^T A_e}$ can not be equal to $d\boldsymbol{c^T}$, thus, $\boldsymbol{c^T A_e} - d\boldsymbol{c^T} \neq \vec{\boldsymbol{o}}$.

Therefore, if any of $\boldsymbol{e_a}, \boldsymbol{e_m}, \boldsymbol{e_{c1}}, \cdots, \boldsymbol{e_{ck}}$ is not equal to $\vec{\boldsymbol{o}}$, according to our error model, $checksum(\boldsymbol{w}) \neq \boldsymbol{c^T w}$. $\square$

Theorem 3. *For any vector-generating operation, the checksum relationship of the output vector is preserved if and only if there are no soft errors before or during the operation.*

Proof. The proof follows from Lemma 1 (if part) and Lemma 2 (only-if part). $\square$

Based on Theorem 3, if the checksum relationship of the output vector from a vector-generating operation is broken, soft errors must have occurred before (memory bit flips or arithmetic errors carried from the previous operations) or during (memory bit flips of the input vector or arithmetic errors) the operation. On the other hand, if the checksum relationship of the output vector is maintained, the checksum relationship of any input vector is held and this can guarantee that no soft error (arithmetic errors, or bit flips in memory, caches or registers) happened before or during the operation. *This provides an efficient approach to soft error detection for all the vector-generating operations: we only need to identify if the checksum relationship of the output vector is broken.*

As mentioned in Section 2, the traditional checksum and its encoding for MVM and PCO does not propagate the inconsistency of the input vector to the output vector when the input vector is corrupted before the operation. In order to get better coverage for error detection, ABFT approaches based on prior checksum schemes need to check every input and output vector in all operations, incurring large detection overheads. This is evaluated in greater detail in Section 6.

5. NEW ONLINE ABFT SCHEMES

We now use the checksum encoding scheme described above to design efficient online ABFT solutions for iterative methods. While widely applicable to iterative solvers, for simplicity and clarity, we will illustrate the designs in the context of the widely-used preconditioned conjugate gradient (PCG).

5.1 "Lazy" Detection: Low-Cost Online ABFT Algorithm Using Checksum Update

The *preconditioned conjugate gradient (PCG)* method is one of the most commonly used iterative methods to solve

Table 2: Computation relationships among various vectors in PCG.

Output Vector	Input Vector(s)	Operation
z	r	$z = M^{-1}r$
p	z, p	$p = z + \beta p$
q	p	$q = Ap$
x	x, p	$x = x + \alpha p$
r	r, q	$r = r - \alpha q$

the sparse linear system $\boldsymbol{Ax} = \boldsymbol{b}$ when the coefficient matrix $\boldsymbol{A}$ is symmetric and positive definite (SPD). PCG consists of three major computation components: successive approximations to the solution, residuals corresponding to the approximate solution, and search directions used to update both the approximate solutions and the residuals [13]. Each iteration consists of one sparse MVM, three vector updates, and two vector inner-products (Figure 1). Figure 3 outlines our first proposed online ABFT algorithm (**Algorithm 1**) for PCG based on the proposed checksum mechanism. The figure also illustrates the cost (in terms of operation count) for the added code lines. In **Algorithm 1**, after each vector-generating operation (i.e., MVM, VLO and PCO), we efficiently update the checksum for each output vector according to Equations (2), (3), and (4).

To detect soft errors, the simplest method is to *verify the checksum relationship* of each output vector after every vector-generating operation. However, this incurs high detection overhead. The most practical recovery strategy for iterative solvers involves checkpoint/rollback. When any soft error is detected, the program will be rolled back to the nearest checkpoint. Minimizing the fault tolerance cost requires balancing the checkpointing overheads with the potential to lose significant amount of work in the event of an error-induced rollback. To reduce the overall error checking and recovery overhead, we analyze the computational relationships among all the involved vectors in the vector-generating operations and see if their checksums really need to be verified after every operation.

We make the following three observations based on the summarized computational relationships between the vectors in PCG, shown in **Table 2**:

- Soft errors, if present, in vectors $\boldsymbol{z}$, $\boldsymbol{p}$, or $\boldsymbol{q}$ will eventually propagate to the vectors $\boldsymbol{x}$ and $\boldsymbol{r}$. Therefore, verifying the checksum relationship of the vector $\boldsymbol{x}$ and $\boldsymbol{r}$ is adequate to cover all the other vectors.
- Computing vectors $\boldsymbol{p}$, $\boldsymbol{x}$, and $\boldsymbol{r}$ requires their results from the previous iteration, which means that soft errors in $\boldsymbol{p}$, $\boldsymbol{x}$ and $\boldsymbol{r}$, if presented in an iteration, will propagate to the subsequent iterations.
- At each iteration, we can use vectors $\boldsymbol{p}$ and $\boldsymbol{x}$ to compute the other three vectors $\boldsymbol{q}$, $\boldsymbol{r}$, and $\boldsymbol{z}$.

Corresponding to these three observations, we identify **three optimizations** to significantly reduce the overhead of the error detection and recovery for PCG:

1. Rather than verifying each output vector's checksum relationship after every vector-generating operation, we only need to **verify** two checksum relationships, namely $checksum(\boldsymbol{x}) = \boldsymbol{c^T x^{(i)}}$ and $checksum(\boldsymbol{r}) = \boldsymbol{c^T r^{(i)}}$, to detect the soft errors in any vector (line 6 in Algorithm 1);
2. We only need to **verify** the checksum relationship between $\boldsymbol{x}$ and $\boldsymbol{r}$ *every several iterations* rather than every iteration (line 5 in Algorithm 1);
3. We only need to **checkpoint** two vectors, $\boldsymbol{p}$ and $\boldsymbol{x}$. In

Algorithm 1 Online-ABFT Preconditioned Conjugate Gradient Algorithm Based on New Checksum with checkpoint/restart Technique

1: Compute $r^{(0)} = b - Ax^{(0)}, z^{(0)} = M^{-1}r^{(0)}, p^{(0)} = z^{(0)}$ and $\rho_0 = r^{(0)T}z^{(0)}$ for some initial guess $x^{(0)}$
2: Compute $checksum(A) = c^T A - dc^T$, $checksum(M) = c^T M - dc^T$, $checksum(b) = c^T b^{(0)}$, $checksum(x) = c^T x^{(0)}$, $checksum(r) = c^T r^{(0)}$, $checksum(z) = [(checksum(r) - checksum(M)z^{(0)})]/d$, $checksum(p) = checksum(z)$
3: Checkpoint A, M
4: **for** $i = 0, 1, \cdots$ **do**
5:     **if** $((i > 0)$ and $(i\%d = 0))$ **then**
6:       **if** $(\|checksum(r) - c^T r^{(i)}\|/n > \theta)$ or $(\|checksum(x) - c^T x^{(i)}\|/n > \theta)$ **then**   `2 VDP (4n FLOPS)`
7:         Rollback: recover $A, M, i, \rho_i, p^{(i)}, x^{(i)}, r^{(i)}$ `2 Mcpy + 4 Vcpy`
8:       **else if** $(i\%(cd) = 0)$ **then**
9:         Checkpoint: $i, \rho_i, p^{(i)}, x^{(i)}$ `2 Vcpy`
10:       **end if**
11:     **end if**
12:     $q^{(i)} = Ap^{(i)}$ `1 MVM (nnz FLOPS)`
13:     $checksum(q) = checksum(A)p^{(i)} + d \cdot checksum(p)$ `1 VDP (2n FLOPS)`
14:     $\alpha_i = \rho_i / p^{(i)T}q^{(i)}$ `1 VDP (2n FLOPS)`
15:     $x^{(i+1)} = x^{(i)} + \alpha_i p^{(i)}$ `1 VLO (2n FLOPS)`
16:     $checksum(x) = checksum(x) + \alpha_i \cdot checksum(p)$ `2 FLOPS`
17:     $r^{(i+1)} = r^{(i)} - \alpha_i q^{(i)}$ `1 VLO (2n FLOPS)`
18:     $checksum(r) = checksum(r) - \alpha_i \cdot checksum(q)$ `2 FLOPS`
19:     solve $Mz^{(i+1)} = r^{(i+1)}$ `1 PCO`
20:     $checksum(z) = \frac{(checksum(r) - checksum(M)z^{(i+1)})}{d}$ `1 VDP (2n FLOPS)`
21:     $\rho_{i+1} = r^{(i+1)T}z^{(i+1)}$ `1 VDP (2n FLOPS)`
22:     $\beta_i = \rho_{i+1}/\rho_i$ `1 FLOPS`
23:     $p^{(i+1)} = z^{(i+1)} + \beta_i p^{(i)}$ `1 VLO (2n FLOPS)`
24:     $checksum(p) = checksum(z) + \beta_i \cdot checksum(p)$ `2 FLOPS`
25:     check convergence; continue if necessary
26: **end for**

MVM: Matrix-Matrix Multiplication   **VDP:** Vector Dot-Product
VLO: Vector Linear Operation   **PCO:** Preconditioned Operation
Mcpy: Matrix Copy   **Vcpy:** Vector Copy

Figure 3: online ABFT algorithm for preconditioned conjugate gradient (PCG) based on our new checksum mechanism. The operation count for checksum updates, error detection, and recovery (checkpoint/restart) are also listed.

the event of an error, we can use the checkpointed version of the two vectors to recover all the other vectors and checksums (line 9 in Algorithm 1) .

Algorithm 1 in Figure 3 shows a low-cost online ABFT-based PCG algorithm that includes these optimizations. In Figure 3 and 4, black represents the original code of PCG; pink represents the checkpoints; red represents the checksum updates; blue represents the error detection and rollback. Pink, red, and blue show the extra operations introduced over the original code. This scheme enables "lazy" error detection mode that only checks errors every several iterations based on the assumption that under a lower error rate, immediate checksum verification after every vector-generating operation is too expensive. Note that we still update the checksums of the output vector after each operation using the low-cost scheme described earlier. For error detection in Algorithm 1, we verify the checksum relationship of x and r every error detection interval (d), based on the optimization (1) and (2) above. The overhead of such detection is only the checksum verification for two VLOs (line 6), which is $O(n)$ FLOPS. For error recovery, according to optimization (3), we only need to checkpoint the two vectors p and x every checkpoint interval (cd), which can significantly reduce the checkpointing overhead and the large memory space requirements. Note that for the purpose of high scalability in parallel computation, all the checkpoints and checksums are saved locally in our proposed designs. We will discuss error

detection interval d and checkpoint interval cd in the later section.

We use $\theta = 10^{-10}$ as threshold in our experimental evaluations. In reality, we perform all the operations using floating-point arithmetics with round-off errors. When the checksum relationships of x and r are used to detect errors, the effects of round-off errors need to be carefully investigated. In Algorithm 1, as the problem size n increases, the accuracy of the round-off error (i.e., $checksum(x) - c^T x$) decreases. When verifying checksum relationship, we apply $(checksum(x) - c^T x)/n$ to reduce the accuracy loss for round-off errors. When the errors are close to the machine accuracy ϵ, we cannot detect them. However, because we only focus on numerically stable solvers and well-conditioned problems, these errors do not need to be detected since they will not significantly impact the performance of numerically stable algorithms and well-conditioned problems.

5.2 "Eager" Online Recovery for MVM Using Triple Checksums

In order to reduce the chances of a rollback, we would like to correct errors as soon as possible without requiring rollback. In iterative methods, since MVM operations are the most computation-intensive, and therefore the most vulnerable operations, they could benefit from a faster recovery under a high error rate.

According to coding theory, $2m + 1$ checksums (i.e., independent equations) can be used to locate and correct m errors. For instance, Figure 2(e) shows the case of two separate checksums in our scheme for detection and correction. However, this requires a strong assumption of a bound m on the maximum number of soft errors in an MVM. A larger number of errors than m can lead to the recovery mechanism mis-identifying some locations as erroneous and correcting them, resulting in cases of "fake correction". We illustrate this scenario and present a solution.

Consider a double-checksum used to detect errors and correct up to one error in the output vector. Shown in Figure 2(e), let the output vector be $y = (y_1, y_2, \cdots, y_n)^T$. We encode it with double checksums as $y^* = (y, c_1^T y, c_2^T y)^T$. In this example, we use $c_1 = (1, 1, \cdots, 1)^T$ and $c_2 = (1, 2, \cdots, n)^T$. The double checksums $checksum_1(y)$ and $checksum_2(y)$ can be represented as

$$checksum_1(y) = c_1^T y = \sum_{i=1}^n y_i$$
$$checksum_2(y) = c_2^T y = \sum_{i=1}^n iy_i$$

Now, say the output vector $y' = (y_1', y_2', \cdots, y_n')^T$ has one erroneous element. Specifically, $y_j' \neq y_j$, where the error position j is to be determined to locate the error. The presence of the error can be detected as:

$$\delta_1 = \sum_{i=1}^n y_i' - checksum_1(y) = y_j' - y_j \neq 0$$
$$\delta_2 = \sum_{i=1}^n iy_i' - checksum_1(y) = j(y_j' - y_j) \neq 0$$

One common way to locate the error position j is to calculate a simple division $\delta_2/\delta_1 = j$, and then apply $\delta_1 = y_j' - y_j$ to correct the erroneous computed value y_j' through $y_j' = y_j' - \delta_1$. In reality, we do not know the number of soft errors that has affected a given MVM. For instance, *one error could occur in the input vector and propagate to the output, forming multiple errors*. Using the two checksums, we can only tell if the MVM result is erroneous, but cannot know if it has only one soft error. If there are actually k erroneous elements $y_{j_1}', \cdots, y_{j_k}'$ ($k > 1$), but the assumption is that there is only one error, we calculate δ_1 and δ_2 as

$$\delta_1 = \sum_{i=1}^{k}(y'_{j_i} - y_{j_i}), \delta_2 = \sum_{i=1}^{k} j_i(y'_{j_i} - y_{j_i})$$

If $y'_{j_1} - y_{j_1} = \cdots = y'_{j_k} - y_{j_k}$ and $j_1 + \cdots + j_k$ is multiples of k, $\delta_2/\delta_1 = (j_1 + \cdots + j_2)/k$ is an integer. Therefore, the double-checksum mechanism will lead to a fake correction of y', which may result in slow convergence or divergence of the underlying iterative method.

Inspired by Fasi et al. [10], we propose a triple-checksum detection and correction mechanism to identify if there is only one error, and if so, correct it. Specifically, we introduce a different third checksum with vector $c_3 = (1, \frac{1}{2}, \cdots, \frac{1}{n})^T$. Assuming that there are k erroneous elements $y'_{j_1} \cdots y'_{j_k}$. δ_1, δ_2 and δ_3 are computed as:

$$\delta_1 = \sum_{i=1}^{k}(y'_{j_i} - y_{j_i}), \delta_2 = \sum_{i=1}^{k} j_i(y'_{j_i} - y_{j_i}), \delta_3 = \sum_{i=1}^{k}\frac{y'_{j_i}-y_{j_i}}{j_i}$$

Now we can use the relationship between δ_1, δ_2 and δ_3 to identify if there is only one error, eliminating the fake correction case above. Since in the fake correction case, $y'_{j_1} - y_{j_1} = \cdots = y'_{j_k} - y_{j_k}$, we have

$$\delta_2/\delta_1 = \frac{j_1 + \cdots + j_k}{n}, \delta_1/\delta_3 = \frac{n}{\frac{1}{j_1} + \cdots + \frac{1}{j_k}}$$

Therefore, δ_2/δ_1 and δ_1/δ_3 are the arithmetic mean and harmonic mean, respectively, of $j_1, \cdots, j_k$. The relation between the two means requires that $\delta_2/\delta_1 = \delta_1/\delta_3$ **if and only if** $j_1 = \cdots = j_k$. However, since the position indices $j_1, \cdots, j_k$ are all different, $\delta_2\delta_3 = \delta_1^2$ **if and only if** $k = 1$. Therefore, we are able to use this simple verification $\delta_2\delta_3 = \delta_1^2$ to identify if the output vector is erroneous when there is only a single error. If it is a single error, we can locate and correct the error right away using this triple-checksum mechanism.

In order to match the triple-checksum encoding in the vectors, the matrices are encoded in the following fashion:

$$A^* = \begin{pmatrix} A & \vec{o} & \vec{o} & \vec{o} \\ c_1^T A - d_1 c_1^T - d_2 c_2^T - d_3 c_3^T & d_1 & d_2 & d_3 \\ c_2^T A - d_2 c_1^T - d_3 c_2^T - d_1 c_3^T & d_2 & d_3 & d_1 \\ c_2^T A - d_3 c_1^T - d_1 c_2^T - d_2 c_3^T & d_3 & d_1 & d_2 \end{pmatrix}$$

Therefore, applying triple-checksum encoding, we can: (1) detect if there is any error, (2) identify whether or not there is more than one error, and (3) if there is only one error, locate and correct it.

5.3 "Hybrid" Detection: Two-Level Online ABFT Algorithm Using Triple-Checksum

Based on this triple-checksum protection mechanism and **Algorithm 1**, we present a *two-level online ABFT* scheme for iterative methods that uses the triple-checksum for immediate single error detection and recovery in MVM (inner-level), and the checksum relationship verification to recover from multiple errors (outer-level). The general procedure to construct a two-level online ABFT version of a given iterative solver is as follows:

1. Encode matrices and vectors using triple-checksum;
2. Form the checksum update formulas for the output vectors based on the encoded matrices and vectors;
3. Compute these checksum updates after each vector-generating operation (MVM, VLO, PCO);
4. Analyze the dependency relationships between vectors;
5. Every d iterations, invoke the outer-level protection: verify the checksum relationships of the vectors that

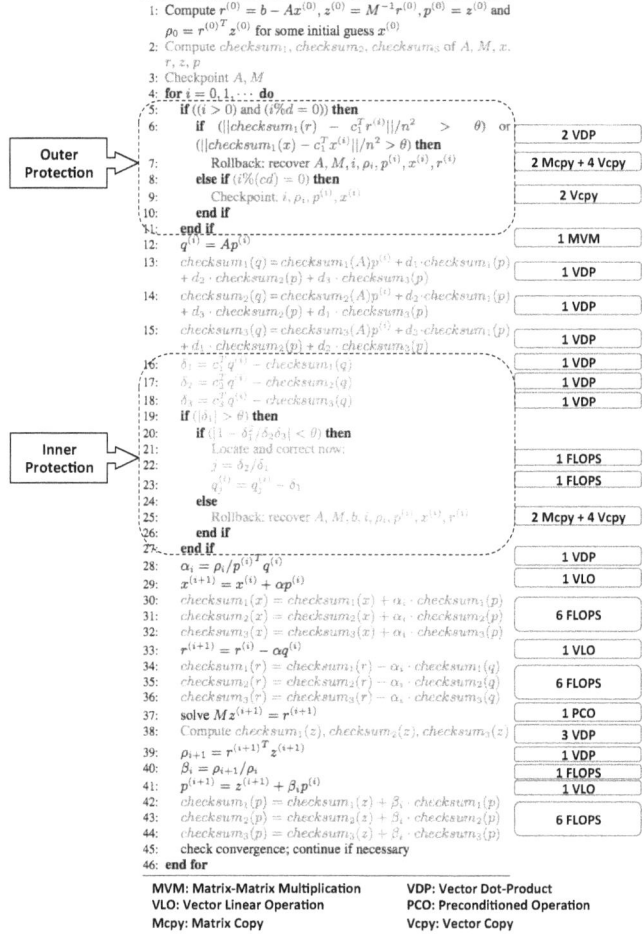

Figure 4: Two-level online ABFT algorithm for preconditioned conjugate gradient (PCG)

the other vectors will eventually propagate to every d iterations;

6. At the beginning of every cd iterations, checkpoint the minimum number of the vectors based on the dependency relationships from **Step 4** and scalars that can calculate the other vectors;
7. After each MVM, add the inner-level protection:

   (a) Use one out of the three checksums of the output vector to identify if there is any error in MVM
   (b) If there are no errors, update the vector checksums and continue the execution
   (c) If the output vector is erroneous, use the tripe-checksum mechanism to identify if it is one error or multiple errors
   (d) If there is one error in MVM, apply triple-checksum to correct immediately
   (e) If there are multiple errors, rollback to the previous checkpoint

We illustrate this procedure for the PCG solver in **Algorithm 2**. For the **outer-level** protection (lines 5–11), we verify the checksum relationship of the vectors x and r for detecting the potential error(s) in VLOs and multiple errors that cannot be recovered in MVM, and then rollback to the latest secure state if the condition is not satisfied (recov-

50

ery). For the **inner-level** protection (lines 16–27), after the MVM operation $q = Ap$, we verify the checksum relationship of the output vector q (line 19). If it does not hold, it indicates that soft error has affected the MVM. Then we use the simple check $\delta_2\delta_3 = \delta_1^2$ (line 20) to determine the cause of the inconsistency in q: a single error or multiple errors. If the verification fails, it indicates that there are multiple errors. Since our triple-checksum mechanism cannot correct more than one error, the program is rolled back to the closest checkpoint immediately for recovery, in order to avoid the waiting till the beginning of the next d interval. If the verification passes, it indicates that there is only one error and the error is corrected immediately via triple-checksum.

This two-level algorithm effectively protects all the vector-generating operations in an iterative method. Specifically, we identify the essential vectors that need to be checkpointed, recover from the most common case of single error by locating and correcting the error rather than rolling back, while ensuring that the outer-level detector catches possible errors from the other operations. In the common case, where there are no errors, the inner-level detector checks for errors with a single checksum. This operation incurs $O(n)$ cost per MVM operation per time step. For sparse matrices with number of non-zeros being much larger than vector length, say $nnz > 10n$, this check adds very little overhead. The efficient check and correction employed by the inner-level scheme enables us to reduce the frequency of the outer-level protection (i.e., increasing the outer protection interval d). Additionally, since the outer protection is using the higher-cost checkpoint/restart technique for recovery, at a high error rate, our two-level protection mechanism may significantly lower the overhead introduced by checkpoint/restart and, therefore, the overall overhead (see Section 6.2 and 6.3).

6. RESULTS AND ANALYSIS

In this section, we start by comparing the following five soft-error tolerating schemes in terms of features and coverage: (1) the offline residual checking at the end of computation (denoted by **offline residual**), (2) the state-of-the-art online matrix-vector multiplication (MVM) scheme using the traditional checksum proposed in [11] (denoted by **online MV**), (3) the online orthogonality checking proposed in [6] (denoted by **online orthogonality**), (4) our proposed "lazy" online ABFT scheme using checksum updates and checkpoint/rollback (**Algorithm 1** in Section 5.1, denoted by **basic online ABFT**), and (5) our proposed two-level online ABFT algorithm using triple-checksum mechanism (**Algorithm 2** in Section 5.3, denoted by **two-level online ABFT**). After that, we theoretically compare the cost of applying online-MV scheme with that of applying our two schemes, assuming they have the same error coverage. Finally, we empirically evaluate our two schemes on a leadership supercomputer under different error scenarios, and compare their costs with those using online MV.

We conduct our evaluation with the widely used preconditioned conjugate gradient (PCG) solver and preconditioned biconjugate gradient stabilized (PBiCGSTAB) solver [17]. The former has the orthogonality relations between essential vectors, but the latter does not. For input, we use the sparse matrix 'G3_circuit', the largest SPD matrix available from the University of Florida Sparse Matrix Collection [7]. It contains 1,585,478 rows and columns with 7,660,826 non-zero elements. We implement our proposed online ABFT schemes in PETSc [1], one of the most popular toolkits pro-

Table 3: Comparison of features and error coverage among different fault-tolerance techniques for iterative methods

	Offline residual	Online MV	Online orthogonality	Basic/two-level online ABFT method
Can protect arithmetic error	Yes	Yes	Yes	Yes
Can protect memory bit flips	Yes	Yes	Yes	Yes
Can protect cache or register bit flips	Yes	No	No	Yes
Can be applied to all iterative methods	Yes	Yes	No	Yes
Not necessary to check every iteration	Yes	No	Yes	Yes
Not necessary to check every operation	Yes	No	Yes	Yes

viding parallel solutions of scientific applications modeled by PDEs. All of our experiments are conducted using 2048 cores (i.e., 256 nodes, each node with two Intel Xeon E5-2680 processors) on the Stampede supercomputer at Texas Advanced Computer Center (TACC).

6.1 Error Coverage and Feature Comparison

Table 3 compares features and error coverage of different fault tolerance schemes for iterative methods. The table clearly shows that only the offline residual scheme and our proposed two designs have all the six soft-error tolerance features. The offline-residual scheme simply verifies the residual at the end of computation to identify if there is any error. If there is, the offline-residual scheme has to recompute the entire program. Under the best-case scenario where the convergence iteration number is set to that of the correct execution, the offline-residual scheme incurs 100% overhead. Therefore, the offline-residual scheme will most likely perform worse than the well-designed online schemes if any soft error occurs during the program execution [6]. Therefore, it is excluded from the following performance evaluation. For the online-MV scheme, we will evaluate it both theoretically (Section 6.2) and empirically (Section 6.3) against our approaches. To further demonstrate better coverage of our schemes over the online-orthogonality approach, we will use the preconditioned biconjugate gradient stabilized (PBiCGSTAB) solver in addition to PCG, to evaluate our designs in Section 6.3.

6.2 Theoretical Performance Comparison

As previously discussed in Section 4 and Table 3, although the **online MV** approach (i.e., using the traditional checksum encoding schemes) cannot protect cache or register bit-flips, we still would like to explore the performance of applying it to iterative methods when those error scenarios are absent. We also want to conduct theoretical performance comparison between online MV and our two approaches under different error rates. We select the recent online ABFT scheme from Sloan et al. [19] that uses traditional checksum encoding method for comparison. Note that Sloan's method only considers soft errors in matrix-vector multiplication (MVM). For the purpose of a fair comparison, we apply the standard triple modular redundancy (TMR) to protect other operations in iterative methods such as VLOs and PCOs, since the traditional encoding mechanism cannot encode PCOs. We also exclude cache or register bit-flips from the error scenarios for this comparison because the online-MV approach cannot protect them. To be consistent with the use case in [19], we use PCG as the candidate iterative method. The algorithm cost analysis for our approaches are

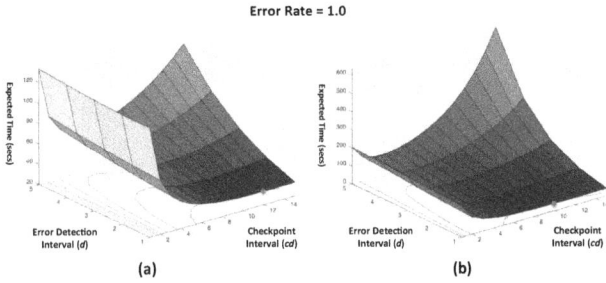

Figure 5: Expected execution time of our basic online ABFT scheme for (a) PCG and (b) PBiCGSTAB for G3_circuit with error rate $\lambda = 1.0$.

shown in Figures 3 and 4. Due to space limitation, we refer the reader to [19] for the details of Sloan's algorithm.

We denote the error detection interval as d (i.e., outer-loop error detection happens every d iterations in our approaches) and checkpoint interval as cd (i.e., checkpointing necessary data every cd iterations). d and cd are integers and $cd > d$. We use I to denote the total number of iterations and assume $I = k \times cd$ where $k \geqslant 1$. Since Sloan's approach is not based on checkpoint/rollback technique, d does not exist in Online-MV. The following three error-rate scenarios are explored in this comparison:

- Scenario 1: One error in MVM during the entire execution (I iterations).
- Scenario 2: One error in MVM every cd iterations.
- Scenario 3: One error in MVM every iteration.

These three scenarios correspond to low error rate, medium or high error rate, and extremely high error rate, respectively. Table 4 shows the performance overhead per iteration for basic online ABFT (O_1), two-level online ABFT (O_2) and online MV (O_3) under the three scenarios in PCG. Note that $c_0 = nnz/n$ represents the sparsity of the matrix $\boldsymbol{A}$; and ∞ illustrates that the execution will not terminate due to the repeated rollbacks. Also, all the costs shown in Table 4 are the average values from different error locations in cd. From Table 4, we can make the following conclusions:

1. Under low or extremely low error rate (Scenario 1), **basic online ABFT (O_1)** approach has the lowest overhead: $O_1 < O_2 < O_3$. This is because PCO consumes much more time than vector-vector multiplication (VDP) and vector-linear operation (VLO) in CG.
2. Under medium/high error rate (Scenario 2), the performance overhead of **two-level online ABFT (O_2)** is the lowest among the three. However, the performance comparison between our basic online ABFT and online MV is unclear, depending on if PCO is more time consuming than MVM. For example, if the matrix $\boldsymbol{A}$ is highly sparse, $O_1 < O_3$ because PCO in this case consumes more time. Otherwise, if PCO is less time-consuming, e.g., the preconditioner $\boldsymbol{M}$ is well selected, $O_3 < O_1$.
3. Under extremely high error rate (Scenario 3), **two-level online ABFT (O_2)** wins: $O_2 < O_3 < O_1$. The basic online ABFT (O_1) will not terminate.

To summarize, no matter the error rate, one of our approaches will outperform the online MV method implemented with [19] for PCG. The methodology used here can also be applied to analyze other iterative methods.

6.3 Empirical Performance Evaluation

We implement our proposed online ABFT schemes in PETSc, and use its default preconditioner (block Jacobi with ILU/IC) and convergence tolerance. We simulate an arithmetic or storage error by significantly increasing the value of a random element in matrices or vectors.

6.3.1 Determining Optimal cd and d

As discussed previously, the expected execution time of an application depends on the error detection interval (d) and checkpoint interval (cd), which are commonly determined by the system's error rate (λ). However, it is often difficult to determine their optimal values for different designs. In order to conduct a fair evaluation and comparison, we first estimate their optimal values under a certain error rate. Because both our proposed designs are based on (or partially based on) loop-level checkpoint/rollback, it is similar to Chen's online orthogonality approach [6]. Therefore, we modify the expected execution time formula from that work to accommodate our scenarios. The following equation shows the expected time for basic online ABFT:

$$E(c,d) = \min_{c,d} \frac{I}{cd} [(e^{\lambda cd(t+t_u+t_d/d)} - 1)(\frac{d \cdot (t+t_u)+t_d}{1-e^{-\lambda cd(t+t_u+t_d/d)}} + t_r) + t_c]$$
(5)

where λ denotes the error rate, t_d denotes the time to detect an error (i.e., loop-level detection), t_c denotes the overhead for one checkpoint, t_r denotes checkpoint recovery overhead, t denotes the time for each iteration, d denotes the error detection interval (in iterations), cd denotes the checkpoint interval (in iterations), and I is the total number of iterations. Additionally, we add t_u to represent the overhead for checksum updates per iteration in basic online ABFT. We assume the time to failure for all processes follows an independent and identically distributed exponential distribution. Due to space limitations, please refer to [6] for details on how the equation is derived.

Based on Equation (5), Figure 5 demonstrates the simulated correlations between error detection interval (d), checkpoint interval (cd) and the expected execution time under a medium/high error rate, denoted as $\lambda = 1.0$. All the input parameters used to construct Figure 5, such as t_d, t_c, t_r, and t_u, are the average measurements from 50 runs on Stampede. Based on Figure 5, we can estimate the optimal pairs of (cd, d) for both PCG and PBiCGSTAB algorithms implemented with basic online ABFT as (12, 1) and (10, 1). Similarly, when the error rates are low and extremely high, e.g., $\lambda = 10^{-2}$ and $\lambda = 10$, the optimal (cd, d) pairs for PCG and PBiCGSTAB implemented with basic online ABFT can be found in Table 5. Since the goal of the empirical analysis is to compare the overhead induced by different techniques, optimal (cd, d) is not required for two-level online ABFT as long as they are consistent between our two designs (see Table 4). Thus, for simplicity, we use the same (cd, d) from basic online ABFT for error injection in two-level online ABFT in the following comparative analysis. Note that, since the proposed ABFT algorithms conduct a low-cost error detection every d iterations for only two vector-dot products, our detection overhead is small under these scenarios, therefore, the optimal strategy is to detect errors at every iteration.

6.3.2 Overhead Comparison Between Techniques

In order to validate the conclusions from the theoretical comparison in Section 6.2, we will use the same error

Table 4: Theoretical cost analysis for three schemes under different error-rate scenarios.

	Basic online ABFT (O_1)	Two-level online ABFT (O_2)	Online MV (O_3)
Scenario 1	(2/d+2)VDP+2VLO/cd	(2/d+9)VDP+2VLO/cd	1PCO+2VDP+3VLO
Scenario 2	0.5MVM+(2/d+5)VDP+0.5PCO+($6(1+c_0)$/cd + 1.5)VLO	(2/d+9)VDP+2VLO/cd	1PCO+(5/cd+2)VDP+3VLO
Scenario 3	$+\infty$	(2/d+9)VDP+2VLO/cd	1PCO+7VDP+3VLO

Table 5: Optimal pairs of (cd, d) for PCG and PBiCGSTAB algorithms implemented with basic online ABFT.

	PCG	PBiCGSTAB
$\lambda = 10^{-2}$	(1000, 1)	(1000, 1)
$\lambda = 1$	(12, 1)	(10, 1)
$\lambda = 10$	(1, 1)	(1, 1)

scenarios to conduct our empirical analysis for PCG and PBiCGSTAB, denoting them as O_1, O_2, and O_3. As discussed in Section 6.3.1, in corresponding to the three error scenarios, we will use the optimal (cd, d) for three error rates (i.e., low, medium/high, extremely high) from Table 5 to setup the experiments. It is worth noting that, unlike PCG, PBiCGSTAB does not exhibit the orthogonal property within its essential vectors and it is more compute-intensive than PCG (i.e., two MVMs and two PCOs every iteration). The implementations of the basic PCG and PBiCGSTAB algorithms are from PETSc. We use their default preconditioners. All the results are the average values from different error locations in cd.

Figure 6 shows the overall performance comparison between three online ABFT implementations of PCG under different error scenarios. We make the following observations. (1) The performance overhead for all three designs is low (i.e., 0.4%, 2.2% and 1.3% respectively) when the execution is error-free. (2) Under low error rate (Scenario 1), basic online ABFT has the lowest overhead: $O_1 < O_2 < O_3$. (3) Under medium/high error rate (Scenario 2), two-level online ABFT performs the best: $O_2 < O_3 < O_1$. As the preconditioner M is well-selected for PCG, PCO is less time-consuming than MVM, causing $O_3 < O_1$. (4) Under extremely high error rates (Scenario 3), two-level online ABFT outperforms the other two again and our basic online ABFT is unable to terminate. The overhead of online MV is 48% higher than two-level online ABFT. Observations (2), (3) and (4) are consistent with our theoretical analysis from Section 6.2.

For the performance comparison among PBiCGSTAB implementations shown in Figure 7, we observe behaviors different from those in PCG. (1) When the execution is error-free, our proposed two techniques still incur low overhead (1.0% and 4.0%, respectively), but much higher than those of PCG. This is because the overhead of checksum updates increases with more involved vectors in PBiCGSTAB. Also, our techniques' overhead is much lower than that of online MV (29% lower), indicating that the triple-checksum updates encounter much lower overhead than the more expensive binary search and partial computation. (2) In Scenario 1, two-level online ABFT has the lowest overhead: $O_2 < O_1 < O_3$, which is different from the case for PCG. This is because average execution time per iteration of PBiCGSTAB (9.1×10^{-2} seconds) is much higher than that of PCG (4.8×10^{-2} seconds). Therefore, the rollback recovery overhead in PBiCGSTAB becomes more significant than when using the triple-checksum scheme. (3) Unlike the case with PCG, basic online ABFT outperforms online MV in Scenario 2 of PBiCGSTAB. This is because the choice of M

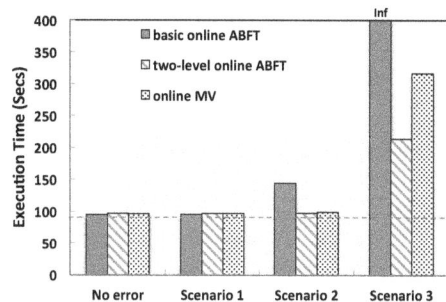

Figure 6: Performance comparison of PCG and (b) PBiCGSTAB implemented with three online ABFT techniques on Stampede. 'Inf' means it doesn't terminate. Red dotted lines represent the baseline cases.

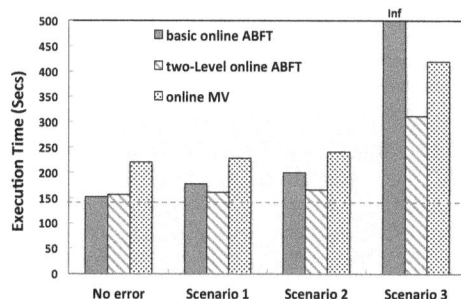

Figure 7: Performance comparison of PBiCGSTAB implemented with three online ABFT techniques on Stampede.

in PBiCGSTAB is not optimal, making PCOs to consume much higher time than MVMs. (4) The performance improvement of our two designs over online MV is more significant than that in PCG. This is because the fraction of time involving in updating the checksums shrinks as the computation intensity of the algorithm increases. This indicates that our designs will benefit computation intensive solvers with more MVMs and PCOs.

Figure 8 and 9 show the overall performance comparison between the three online ABFT implementations of PCG and PBiCGSTAB, respectively, under those three different error scenarios on the supercomputer Tianhe-2. Figure 8 and 9 indicate that the peformance overhead on Tianhe-2 is similar to Stampede.

6.3.3 Scenario with Multiple Errors

We evaluate our two techniques under a relatively high error-rate scenario, where multiple errors occur in different MVMs within different cd and one error occurs in a randomly selected VLO during the entire execution. This scenario is built on the rationale that MVM dominates most of the execution time in PCG, so it is highly likely that several soft errors arrive one after another, spreading out in different checkpoint intervals (cd) during the execution when error rate is high [23]. Figure 10 shows three scenarios of errors: (1) 4 errors occur one after another in four different MVMs of different checkpoint intervals; (2) 2 errors occur one after

53

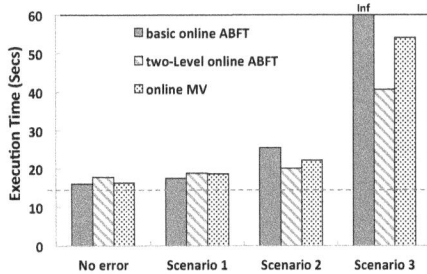

Figure 8: Performance comparison of PCG implemented with three online ABFT techniques on Tianhe-2.

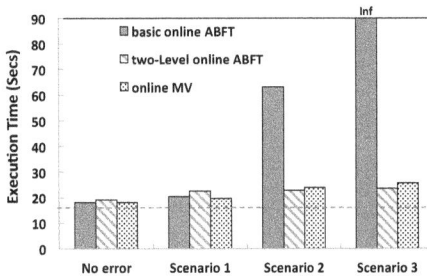

Figure 9: Performance comparison of PBiCGSTAB implemented with three online ABFT techniques on Tianhe-2.

another in two different MVMs of different checkpoint intervals; and (3) 1 error occurs in a randomly selected MVM. For the purpose of fair comparison, each of these three cases will be accompanied with a scenario in which an error occurred in a randomly selected VLO. As shown, the two-level online ABFT, on average, outperforms the basic online ABFT by 32.1% under the high error rate scenario, even though it suffers from a one-time rollback cost from the outer-level protection on the VLO's error. Furthermore, because of the inner-level protection, we can reduce the frequency of the error detection in the outer-level (i.e., increasing d), which may even gain further performance improvement. Determining d to achieve global optimal performance will be our future work.

7. RELATED WORK

Bronevetsky et al. [5], Shantharam et al. [15] and Li et al. [21] characterized and predicted the impact of soft errors on scientific applications. Di et al. [8] and Bautista-Gomez et al. [2] focused on combating SDC problems for general HPC applications. The most straightforward method to tolerate soft errors is triple modular redundancy (TMR) [12]. While generally applicable, it incurs high overheads.

Algorithm-based fault tolerance (ABFT) is a checksum-

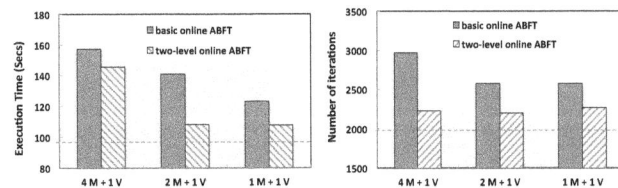

Figure 10: Performance comparison of our proposed techniques under a relatively high error-rate scenario, where multiple errors occur in different MVMs at different checkpoint intervals, and one error occurs in a randomly selected VLO.

based technique developed by Huang and Abraham [11], commonly used to locate and sometimes correct soft errors for matrix operations. The basic check for absence of soft errors involves verifying if the checksum relationships in output are maintained in the final results. Using their checksum encoding mechanism, Wu et al.[23] presented a design and implementation of a fault tolerant version of the ScaLA-PACK[3] to support online error detection and possibly recovery for *dense linear algebra* routines such as Cholesky, QR, and LU factorizations. This traditional checksum encoding mechanism has also been applied to the realm of iterative methods. Sloan et al. [18, 19] proposed techniques specifically for soft error detection and correction in matrix-vector multiplications (MVM), which can be applied to iterative methods under some strong assumptions (discussed in Section 2). As discussed in Sections 2 and 6, the traditional checksum-encoding mechanism cannot correctly detect soft errors in the input vectors in MVM and PCO without additional expensive verification. Even with such verification, it cannot protect the computation from input vector corruption due to cache or register errors. Chen [6] developed a highly efficient online ABFT approach for soft error detection by leveraging the orthogonality relationship of two vectors. This approach, however, only covers a subset of the Krylov methods that can offer such orthogonality. Shantharam et al. [16] proposed an ABFT-SpMxV algorithm for PCG that guarantees the detection of a single error striking in either computation or memory representation of the two input operands. This method requires A to be strictly diagonally dominant, a condition that will restrict the practical applicability of this techniques. Unlike these approaches, our proposed designs can be applied to general iterative methods without the aforementioned limitations while providing significantly improved error coverage and efficient online error detection and recovery.

In [4] and [9], the authors target GMRES based on its special characteristics and proposed a fault tolerant version via selective reliability, which can run through soft errors in the preconditioning phase without the need for detection and recovery. Similar to theirs, Sao and Vuduc[14] studied self-stabilizing corrections after error detection for CG algorithm. However, these approaches potentially affect the speed of the convergence for the underlying algorithms in an error- and input-specific fashion. Moreover, these solutions target specific features of certain iterative algorithms and are not general enough to address the larger class of iterative methods addressing by the our work.

8. CONCLUSION

To enable high error-detection coverage and low overhead, we proposed a new checksum encoding mechanism that guarantees that only the checksum relationship of the output vector needs to be verified to detect any soft error in MVM or VLO operations in iterative methods. Unlike traditional checksum schemes, our design can tolerate cache and register bit-flips and does not require additional checksum verifications after every vector-generating operation. Based on this new checksum encoding scheme, we developed two online ABFT algorithms—basic and two-level—for general iterative methods, allowing errors to be detected eagerly or lazily based on system error rates. Experimental results demonstrated that our proposed designs are efficient and effective in tolerating various error scenarios in general iterative methods.

Acknowledgments

The authors would like to thank the anonymous reviewers for their insightful comments and valuable suggestions. This work is partially supported by the NSF grants CCF-1305622, ACI-1305624, CCF-1513201, the SZSTI basic research program JCYJ20150630114942313, and the Special Program for Applied Research on Super Computation of the NSFC-Guangdong Joint Fund (the second phase). This work was also supported in part by the U.S. Department of Energy's (DOE) Office of Science, Office of Advanced Scientific Computing Research, under awards 66905 and 59921. Pacific Northwest National Laboratory is operated by Battelle for DOE under Contract DE-AC05-76RL01830.

9. REFERENCES

[1] S. Balay, S. Abhyankar, M. F. Adams, J. Brown, P. Brune, et al. PETSc Web page. http://www.mcs.anl.gov/petsc, 2015.

[2] L. A. Bautista-Gomez and F. Cappello. Detecting and correcting data corruption in stencil applications through multivariate interpolation. In *CLUSTER, Chicago, IL, USA, September 8-11, 2015.*

[3] L. S. Blackford, J. Choi, A. J. Cleary, J. Demmel, I. S. Dhillon, J. Dongarra, S. Hammarling, G. Henry, A. Petitet, K. Stanley, D. W. Walker, and R. C. Whaley. Scalapack: A portable linear algebra library for distributed memory computers - design issues and performance. In *SC, November 17-22, 1996, Pittsburgh, PA, USA.*

[4] P. G. Bridges, K. B. Ferreira, M. A. Heroux, and M. Hoemmen. Fault-tolerant linear solvers via selective reliability. *CoRR*, abs/1206.1390, 2012.

[5] G. Bronevetsky and B. R. de Supinski. Soft error vulnerability of iterative linear algebra methods. In *ICS, Island of Kos, Greece, June 7-12, 2008.*

[6] Z. Chen. Online-abft: an online algorithm based fault tolerance scheme for soft error detection in iterative methods. In *ACM SIGPLAN Symposium on Principles and Practice of Parallel Programming, PPoPP '13, Shenzhen, China, February 23-27, 2013,* pages 167–176, 2013.

[7] T. A. Davis and Y. Hu. The university of florida sparse matrix collection. *ACM Trans. Math. Softw.*, 38(1):1, 2011.

[8] S. Di and F. Cappello. Adaptive impact-driven detection of silent data corruption for hpc applications. *TPDS*, to appear, 2016.

[9] J. Elliott, M. Hoemmen, and F. Mueller. Evaluating the impact of SDC on the GMRES iterative solver. In *2014 IEEE 28th International Parallel and Distributed Processing Symposium, Phoenix, AZ, USA, May 19-23, 2014,* pages 1193–1202, 2014.

[10] M. Fasi, Y. Robert, and B. Uçar. Combining backward and forward recovery to cope with silent errors in iterative solvers. In *2015 IEEE International Parallel and Distributed Processing Symposium Workshop, IPDPS 2015, Hyderabad, India, May 25-29, 2015,* pages 980–989, 2015.

[11] K. Huang and J. A. Abraham. Algorithm-based fault tolerance for matrix operations. *IEEE Trans. Computers*, 33(6):518–528, 1984.

[12] R. E. Lyons and W. Vanderkulk. The use of triple-modular redundancy to improve computer reliability. *IBM Journal of Research and Development*, 6(2):200–209, 1962.

[13] Y. Saad. *Iterative methods for sparse linear systems.* SIAM, 2003.

[14] P. Sao and R. W. Vuduc. Self-stabilizing iterative solvers. In *Proceedings of the Workshop on Latest Advances in Scalable Algorithms for Large-Scale Systems, ScalA 2013, Denver, Colorado, USA, November 17-21, 2013,* pages 4:1–4:8, 2013.

[15] M. Shantharam, S. Srinivasmurthy, and P. Raghavan. Characterizing the impact of soft errors on iterative methods in scientific computing. In *Proceedings of the 25th International Conference on Supercomputing, 2011, Tucson, AZ, USA, May 31 - June 04, 2011,* pages 152–161, 2011.

[16] M. Shantharam, S. Srinivasmurthy, and P. Raghavan. Fault tolerant preconditioned conjugate gradient for sparse linear system solution. In *International Conference on Supercomputing, ICS'12, Venice, Italy, June 25-29, 2012,* pages 69–78, 2012.

[17] G. L. Sleijpen and D. R. Fokkema. Bicgstab (l) for linear equations involving unsymmetric matrices with complex spectrum. *Electronic Transactions on Numerical Analysis*, 1(11):2000, 1993.

[18] J. Sloan, R. Kumar, and G. Bronevetsky. Algorithmic approaches to low overhead fault detection for sparse linear algebra. In *IEEE/IFIP International Conference on Dependable Systems and Networks, DSN 2012, Boston, MA, USA, June 25-28, 2012,* pages 1–12, 2012.

[19] J. Sloan, R. Kumar, and G. Bronevetsky. An algorithmic approach to error localization and partial recomputation for low-overhead fault tolerance. In *2013 43rd Annual IEEE/IFIP International Conference on Dependable Systems and Networks (DSN), Budapest, Hungary, June 24-27, 2013,* pages 1–12, 2013.

[20] J. C. Smolens, B. T. Gold, J. Kim, B. Falsafi, J. C. Hoe, and A. G. Nowatzyk. Fingerprinting: Bounding soft-error detection latency and bandwidth. In *Proceedings of the 11th International Conference on Architectural Support for Programming Languages and Operating Systems, ASPLOS 2004, Boston, MA, USA, October 7-13, 2004,* pages 224–234, 2004.

[21] L. Tan, S. L. Song, P. Wu, Z. Chen, R. Ge, and D. J. Kerbyson. Investigating the interplay between energy efficiency and resilience in high performance computing. In *2015 IEEE International Parallel and Distributed Processing Symposium, IPDPS 2015, Hyderabad, India, May 25-29, 2015,* pages 786–796, 2015.

[22] S. Tavarageri, S. Krishnamoorthy, and P. Sadayappan. Compiler-assisted detection of transient memory errors. In *ACM SIGPLAN Conference on Programming Language Design and Implementation, PLDI '14, Edinburgh, United Kingdom - June 09 - 11, 2014,* page 24, 2014.

[23] P. Wu and Z. Chen. FT-ScaLAPACK: correcting soft errors on-line for ScaLAPACK cholesky, QR, and LU factorization routines. In *The 23rd International Symposium on High-Performance Parallel and Distributed Computing, HPDC'14, Vancouver, BC, Canada - June 23 - 27, 2014,* pages 49–60, 2014.

SDS-Sort: Scalable Dynamic Skew-aware Parallel Sorting

Bin Dong   Surendra Byna   Kesheng Wu

Lawrence Berkeley National Laboratory, 1 Cyclotron Road, Berkeley, CA 94720

{DBin, SByna, KWu}@lbl.gov

ABSTRACT

Parallel sorting is an essential algorithm in large-scale data analytics using distributed memory systems. As the number of processes increases, existing parallel sorting algorithms could become inefficient because of the unbalanced workload. A common cause of load imbalance is the skewness of data, which is common in application data sets from physics, biology, earth and planetary sciences. In this work, we introduce a new scalable dynamic skew-aware parallel sorting algorithm, named *SDS-Sort*. It uses a skew-aware partition method to guarantee a tighter upper bound on the workload of each process. To improve load balance among parallel processes, existing algorithms usually add extra variables to the sorting key, which increase the time needed to complete the sorting operation. SDS-Sort allows a user to select any sorting key without sacrificing performance. SDS-Sort also provides optimizations, including adaptive local merging, overlapping of data exchange and data processing, and dynamic selection of data processing algorithms for different hardware configurations and for partially ordered data. SDS-Sort uses local-sampling based partitioning to further reduce its overhead. We tested SDS-Sort extensively on Edison, a Cray XC30 supercomputer. Timing measurements show that SDS-Sort can scale to 130K CPU cores and deliver a sorting throughput of 117TB/min. In tests with real application data from large science projects, SDS-Sort outperforms HykSort, a state-of-art parallel sorting algorithm, by 3.4X.

1. INTRODUCTION

Parallel sorting is a commonly used function by scalable data management systems and scientific applications. For example, data management systems, such as SciDB [7] and Scientific Data Services (SDS) framework [12], sort large-scale data records in parallel to improve the locality of data accesses. Data clustering applications, such as BD-CATS[21], use parallel sorting to order cosmological particles. Well-known parallel sorting algorithms include bitonic sort [4],

radix sort [30], and parallel sort by sampling (PSS) [24]. Among them, PSS minimizes the interprocess data movement and communication, both of which are expensive operations in distributed memory systems [2]. Because of the reduced communication, PSS algorithm has been used by multiple data analytics methods [12, 21] and has been extensively optimized [24, 28, 19]. Implementations of PSS, however, generally target at a certain dataset or a specific hardware. Hence, existing PSS algorithms could be ineffective on some computing hardware and exhibit significant load-imbalance on real-world datasets that are highly skewed. In this research, we aim to explore a new PSS algorithm, which can efficiently sort various datasets, including skewed data and partially ordered data, and also can take into account the features of the hardware of current supercomputers, i.e., high throughput network interconnect and multicore CPUs.

On a distributed memory computing system with p parallel processes and enough memory to hold data in core, classical PSS algorithm [19] has three steps. 1) *Pivot selection*: using a random sample of the data to choose $p-1$ ordered global pivots. These $p-1$ global pivots partition the value space of the data into p ranges and each range is assigned to a single process. 2) *Exchange*: perform all-to-all data exchange to gather the data records belonging to a value range onto a single process. 3) *Local ordering*: order the data records within each process. This is the final ordering step that produces a globally ordered output.[1]

It is widely accepted that partitioning the data (i.e., load or workload) evenly among processes will significantly benefit the overall sorting performance by reducing the time of exchange and local ordering step [28]. Applying existing PSS algorithms in sorting uniformly distributed data with N records, the upper bound on the workload for a process is $O(2N/p)$ [24, 28, 19]. But, when applying these methods to sort the skewed data, which widely appears in physics, biology, earth, and planetary sciences [20, 21, 12], this upper bound increases linearly as the skewness of data increases [19]. A dataset is said to be skewed when its value distribution is not uniform, for example, having a cluster of very popular values toward one end of its distribution function [14]. Often, a skewed dataset contains many duplicated values and the amount of duplicates represents the skewness of data. These duplicated values might produce duplicated global pivots, which eventually cause existing PSS al-

HPDC'16, May 31-June 04, 2016, Kyoto, Japan

© 2016 ACM. ISBN 978-1-4503-4314-5/16/05...$15.00

DOI: http://dx.doi.org/10.1145/2907294.2907300

---

[1]The pivot selection step might also employ the local ordering operation. When it is necessary distinguish these two ordering steps, we will call the one in pivot selection the initial ordering step and step 3 the final ordering step.

gorithms to assign more data to a single process than others leading to significant load imbalance. In some applications, users might also require stable sorting algorithm to maintain the relative order of duplicated values[19]. Using secondary sorting keys, such as payload [18] or the rank of data record [28], could alleviate these issues. However, the presence of these secondary sorting keys increases the amount of work in all three steps of PSS, increasing both CPU time and communication time. Moreover, requiring secondary sorting might also let users have limited sorting keys to choose or spend extra efforts to pick up secondary sorting keys. Thus, it is highly desirable to develop parallel stable sorting algorithms that do not require such secondary sorting keys.

In order for a PSS to execute efficiently, it must be able to take advantage of the new hardware. For example, current supercomputers typically have multicore CPUs and high-throughput interconnect network. However, existing PSS algorithms [28] are generally optimized for slow network through merging the data from multiple CPU cores on the same node to avoid slow data exchange step. New research indicates that using multiple CPU cores to saturate high-throughput network is equally important in reducing the time of the data exchange [8, 17]. At the same time, because the high-throughput interconnects could reduce the data transfer time so much that the benefit of overlapping data exchange and local ordering, widely used by existing PSS algorithms [24, 28], might also be significantly reduced.

In the local ordering step, if we use a straightforward sorting algorithm, its time complexity would be $O(N log(N))$. If we view the data as p ordered chunks received from p process, we might achieve a lower time complexity of $O(N log(p))$ using merging [28]. However, if the data records are partially ordered, the complexity of sorting might reduce from $O(N log(N))$ to $O(N)$ [9]. In some cases the input data might be partially ordered [9], or the data produced by the data exchange step might be nearly sorted [28]. Therefore, it would be useful to recognize the partially ordered data and use efficient approaches for the local ordering step.

To achieve the design goals above, we propose a novel scalable dynamic skew-aware parallel sorting algorithm, called SDS-Sort. SDS-Sort only needs to exchange data once among processes in the whole sorting procedure. More importantly, based on the characteristics of the data and the computing hardware, SDS-Sort employs adaptive idea to dynamically select the most appropriate subroutine for each step. Specifically, SDS-Sort has following unique features:

- SDS-Sort achieves tight upper bound of $O(4\frac{N}{p})$ on the workload of each process and achieves balanced load among processes in sorting skewed datasets without rely on secondary sorting keys.

- SDS-Sort performs various optimizations dynamically to make use of multicore processing and high-speed interconnects. SDS-Sort has dynamic optimizations in local ordering and in overlapping data exchange and local ordering.

- SDS-Sort is capable of performing parallel stable sorting algorithm to maintain the relative order of same values. To the best of our knowledge, this is the first sampling-based stable parallel sorting algorithm for distributed memory systems.

- SDS-Sort uses the local pivots-based parallel partition to further reduce the overhead of data partition.

We provided theoretical analysis for the workload on each process. On Edison, a Cray XC30 supercomputer, we evaluated SDS-Sort with both synthetic and real datasets. We show that SDS-Sort outperforms HykSort, a state-of-art parallel sorting algorithm, by 3.4× in sorting highly skewed Palomar Transient Factory data, which contains around 28% duplicated values. We have scaled SDS-Sort up to 128K CPU cores and where it delivers ~ 117TB/min throughput in sorting highly skewed data.

The rest of the paper is organized as follows. In Section 2, we present the details of SDS-Sort and its design considerations. Section 3 describes our experimental setups. In Section 4, we evaluate the performance of SDS-Sort algorithm. In Section 5, we provide related research efforts of parallel sorting algorithm. We conclude the paper with a discussion of future work in Section 6.

2. SDS-SORT ALGORITHM DESIGN

2.1 SDS-Sort algorithm overview

With the goal of developing a parallel sorting algorithm that works on skewed and partially ordered datasets, uses multicore processors efficiently, and preserves the order of duplicate values, we propose **SDS-Sort**, a scalable dynamic skew-aware parallel sorting algorithm. We introduce a new skew-aware partition strategy to ensure the balanced load of all parallel processes in sorting highly skewed data. Through the same skew-aware partition method, SDS-Sort can also preserve the order of duplicated values scattered across different compute nodes. By supporting dynamic node level merging and overlapping of data exchange and local ordering phases, we devise SDS-Sort to take full advantage of hardware features on HPC systems such as high-throughput network interconnect and multicore CPUs. Our algorithm also incorporates strategies to work with partially ordered data, which can be ordered more quickly than random data. We allow using different local ordering strategies based on the characteristics of the data.

The overall SDS-Sort algorithm is shown in Fig. 1. We follow the single instruction and multiple data (SIMD) pattern used by MPI [16] to describe the algorithm. All the functions shown in Fig. 1 run in parallel on multiple cores or on multiple computing nodes or both. The standard functions of MPI (prefixed with *"MPI"*) are used to clearly express the operations. The functions prefixed with *"Sdss"* are defined in this paper and will be discussed in the following sections.

Let A be a vector of data records to be sorted and each record has a key for sorting and an arbitrary number of non-key values (also called payload). B is a vector to hold the sorted output data. Assume that there are N records in the input array to be sorted using p MPI processes. Each MPI process works on n data records, where $n = N/p$. The size of B on each MPI process, referred as m, is dynamically determined based on the data partition of global pivots. The MPI communicator $comm$ and the number of cores per node c are passed into SDS-Sort for communication and adaptive merging, respectively. Theoretically, c might be any number from 1 to p. In our implementation, we set c to be the number of CPU cores per node, which can avoid merging data cross nodes. We provide a flag s_f to specify whether SDS-Sort needs to perform stable sorting. If $s_f =$ **TRUE**, SDS-Sort preserves the order of duplicate keys, and if $s_f =$ **FALSE**, SDS-Sort ignores the stability in the output. Ad-

```
function SDS-Sort(A[1,...,n], B[1,...,m], com, c, s_f, τ_m, τ_o, τ_s)
        A : data array with size n to sort          s_f : flag of stable sorting (TRUE or FALSE)
        B : sorted data array with size m            τ_m : merging parameter
        com : MPI communicator for all process       τ_o : overlapping parameter
        c : the number of CPU cores per node         τ_s : local ordering parameter
0.   p = MPI_Comm_size(com)      ▷ get the number of processes used to sort data ◁
1.   r = MPI_Comm_rank(com)      ▷ get the rank of current process, ( 0, p − 1) ◁
2.   A = SdssLocalSort(A, 1, s_f)      ▷ SdssLocalSort is described in § 2.2 ◁
3.   if (n/p ≤ τ_m) then      ▷ merge data when the average size of all-to-all exchange is small ◁
4.        (c_g, c_l )= SdssRefineComm(com)      ▷ SdssRefineComm is described in § 2.3 ◁
5.        A = SdssNodeMerge(A, c_l)      ▷ SdssNodeMerge is described in § 2.3 ◁
6.        n = n × c, p = p/c, com = c_g, c = 1      ▷ update parameters, n, p, com, and c ◁
7.   end if
8.   P_l[0, ..., p-1] = A[1+⌊n/p⌋, ..., 1+(p − 1)⌊n/p⌋]      ▷ local sampling ◁
9.   P_g[0, ..., p-1] = SdssSelectPivots(p_l)      ▷ SdssSelectPivots is described in § 2.4 ◁
10.  (sdisp[0,...,p], scount[0,...,p]) = SdssPartition(A, P_l, P_g, p, r, s_f, com)      ▷ SdssPartition is described in § 2.5 ◁
11.  MPI_Alltoall(scont, p, rcont, p, com)      ▷ exchange the size of data to receive ◁
12.  rdisp[0,...,p] = Accumulate(rcont)      ▷ compute the displacement of received data ◁
13.  m = rdisp[p − 1] + rcount[p − 1]
14.  B = Memory_Alloc(m)
15.  if( s_f == TRUE or p > τ_o ) then      ▷ no overlapping for stable sorting and larger number of processes ◁
16.      MPI_Alltoallv(A, B, sdisp, scont, rdisp, rcont, comm)      ▷ all-to-all data exchange ◁
17.      if( p < τ_s ) then
18.          B = SdssMergeAll(B, rdisp, rcont, p, c)      ▷ SdssMergeAll is described in § 2.6 ◁
19.      else
20.          B = SdssLocalSort(B, s_f, c)      ▷ SdssLocalSort is described in § 2.6 ◁
21.      endif
22.  else      ▷ overlap all-to-all exchange and local sorting ◁
23.      C = Memory_Alloc(m)
24.      aid[0,...,p]=SdssAlltoallvAsync(A, C, sdisp, scont, rdisp, rcont, comm) ▷ SdssAlltoallvAsync is described in § 2.6 ◁
25.      while( (id_1, id_2) = SdssFinished(aid) != (NULL, NULL) ) do      ▷ SdssFinished is described in § 2.6 ◁
26.          B = SdssMergeTwo(C, rdisp, rcont, (id_1 ,id_2), c)      ▷ SdssMergeTwo is described in § 2.6 ◁
27.      end while
28.  end if
```

Figure 1: SDS-Sort algorithm overview

ditionally, SDS-Sort accepts three parameters, $τ_m$, $τ_o$, and $τ_s$, to determine the merging for data exchange, overlapping data exchange with local ordering, and choosing sorting or merging to perform local ordering. Even though determining optimal values for these parameters is out the scope for this paper, we will provide their empirical optimal values in our test results section § 4.1.1.

To ensure the quality of global pivots selected, SDS-Sort starts a local pivots selection process on each MPI process by first sorting the local content of A with the function *SdssLocalSort*. This function is described in § 2.2. Then, SDS-Sort detours to merge the data from all processes located at the same node when the average message size ($\frac{n}{p}$) is smaller than $τ_m$. Merging the data before actual local pivot selection can determine the number of local pivots to select. More importantly, local node based merging provides SDS-Sort adaptive capability for the network with different throughput and the computing node with different numbers of CPU cores. To support the merging at each node, SDS-Sort refines its communication through *SdssRefineComm* (discussed in § 2.3) and updates the number of processes (p), that would be processing data from there onwards. The function *SdssNodeMerge* (see § 2.3) is used to merge data at each node. In step 8 of Fig. 1, SDS-Sort selects local pivots (stored in p_l) using equal striping length $\lfloor \frac{n}{p} \rfloor$, also called regular sampling [19]. Based on local pivots, the global pivots (stored in vector p_g) are chosen using the function *SdssSelectPivots* which is described in § 2.4.

After the global pivots are determined, the data is partitioned with function *SdssPartition*(described in § 2.5). Es-

pecially, SDS-Sort uses local pivots (p_l) to speedup the partition function *SdssPartition*. Meanwhile, *SdssPartition* is skew-aware and therefore it can partition the skewed data evenly among the processes. From steps 10 to 13, the displacements (i.e., *sdisp* and *rdisp*) and amounts (i.e., *scount* and *rcount*) required for the data exchange are computed. In step 14, the memory space for storing the sorted data in B is allocated. When one requires stable sorting or the number of processors is larger than $τ_o$, SDS-Sort does not overlap data exchange and local ordering steps. In this case, SDS-Sort uses *MPI_alltoallv* to exchange data in step 16. After the data exchange is finished, the received data is local ordered. The local ordering step uses *SdssMergeAll* (described in § 2.6) when the number of processes is less than $τ_s$. Otherwise, it calls *SdssLocalSort* to obtain globally ordered data. Choosing different methods for local ordering enables SDS-Sort to efficiently work on partially ordered data. When the number of processes is smaller than $τ_o$ and the stable sorted is not required, SDS-Sort calls *SdssAlltoallvAsync* and *SdssFinished* (§ 2.6) to overlap data exchange and local ordering. In this case, SDS-Sort uses *SdssMergeTwo* (§ 2.6) to merge the received data. We elaborate the steps involved in SDS-Sort in the following subsections.

2.2 Skew-aware merging based local sorting

In line 2 and line 20 of SDS-Sort (Fig. 1), a shared memory parallel sorting algorithm (*SdssLocalSort*) is required. Sorting local data at the beginning of SDS-Sort (line 2) helps the sampling step (line 8) to thoroughly measure the value distribution and also the final local ordering step (line

20) to quickly process the partially ordered data. A popular strategy to sort an array on a shared memory machine with c CPU cores is to divide the array into c chunks; sort each chunk in parallel; and then merge these chunks in parallel [11]. As sorting on each core is a straight forward method, it is important to design an efficient parallel merging method, especially for skewed data. The designed $SdssLocalSort$ function can quickly merge sorted chunks from multiple cores via its skew-aware partition.

Our implementation of $SdssLocalSort$ accepts three parameters: a vector of data to sort (A), the number of CPU cores (c), and the stable sorting flag (s_f). In line 2 of SDS-Sort with $c = 1$, the sequential version of $SdssLocalSort$ is used. Internally, $SdssLocalSort$ partitions its input A into c chunks. Then, depending on stable flag s_f, $SdssLocalSort$ calls $std::sort$ (when s_f=**FALSE**) or $std::stable\_sort$ (i.e., s_f=**TRUE**) of C++ library [27] to sort each chunk. Finally, these sorted chunks are merged to be a single vector in parallel using OpenMP. A sampling based parallel merging for shared memory local sorting was proposed in previous research [28]. This method could suffer from load imbalance issue in merging skewed data as it might cause one CPU core to be assigned with more data to merge than the others. In $SdssLocalSort$, we use the same skew-aware partition method as described in the following sub-section (§ 2.5) to partition each sorted chunk into subchunks and then merge these subchunks in parallel. Hence, basically, $SdssLocalSort$ is a shared memory version of SDS-Sort without network connection.

2.3 Node-level merging

When sorting data on low-throughput network, merging sorted data from all CPU cores on a single node can reduce the number of messages and therefore reduce the network initialization overhead for the data exchange step. However, the same approach might not fully utilize the high bandwidth network available on the current-generation supercomputer systems because a single process running on a CPU core does not have the processing power to saturate the network. To address this issue, SDS-Sort adaptively decides whether or not merging the data at each node before the data exchange process (from line 3 to line 7 of Fig. 1). Specifically, we assume the average exchange size for data exchange is $\frac{n}{p}$. When $\frac{n}{p}$ is smaller than τ_m, SDS-Sort merges the data package at each node. This approach is suitable for low-throughput network. When the average data volume is larger than τ_m, each process sends its own data records to their respective destinations. This approach allows SDS-Sort to quickly feed all data into high throughput network.

To implement node level merging, we use function $Sdss-RefineComm$ to create two MPI communicators: c_g and c_l. $SdssRefineComm$ uses $MPI\_Comm\_split\_type^2$ of MPI with the $MPI\_COMM\_TYPE\_SHARED$ parameter. The local communicator c_l is used by $SdssNodeMerge$ to merge the data from all CPU cores into a single core. $SdssNodeMerge$ shares the same idea as the skew-aware merging used in local sorting in previous section. One difference is that $SdssNode-Merge$ uses network communication instead of memory copying. At line 8, the global communicator $comm$ that is used for the following all-to-all data exchange phase that occurs later is replaced with global communicator c_g.

---

^{2}http://www.open-mpi.org/doc/v1.8/man3/MPI_Comm_split_type.3.php

2.4 Regular sampling and pivots selection

Sampling method is used to choose local pivots on each process and global pivots at the global scale. The local pivots are chosen from original data and global pivots from local pivots. SDS-Sort uses equal-striped sampling method (also called regular sampling [19]) to choose both local and global pivots. In line 8 of Fig. 1, $p - 1$ local pivots are selected at regular striping size $\lfloor \frac{n}{p} \rfloor$. Since each node sorts the data at the beginning, these $p - 1$ local pivots can represent its local value distribution very well. In this case, each local pivot represents at most $2\frac{N}{p^2}$ values. To choose $p - 1$ global pivots from local pivots, a popular method is to gather all local pivots onto a single process, sort all local pivots, and choose the global pivots at equal-striped distance p. In this case, each global pivot represent at most $2\frac{N}{p^2} \times p = 2\frac{N}{p}$ values. SDS-Sort uses this regular sampling to select pivots and incorporates new optimizations from existing work in implementations, as discussed in next paragraph.

Such sampling method is simple and efficient but when p is large, these $p(p-1)$ local pivots might overflow the memory of single process. There are two solutions to address this issue. The first one is histogram sorting [24], where each node builds a histogram for a common global pivot vector and uses a single node to gather the histograms to choose global pivots. In sorting the non-skewed data that has a small number of replicated values, histogram sorting is useful as it can choose distinctive global pivots easily. But for the skewed data with highly replicated values, histogram sorting might need secondary sorting keys to distinguish the same values. The second method is to use the parallel sorting algorithms, which do not require gathering local pivots onto single node [28]. In SDS-Sort, we use the second approach and choose bitonic sort [4] to select pivots ($SdssSelectPivots$). Although bitonic sort needs a few data communications, the performance of botonic sort is acceptable in sorting $p(p - 1)$ local pivots with p processes.

2.5 Fast and skew-aware partition

Equally partitioning data among all processes is key to ensure the load balance in the final ordering step. In sorting skewed data with highly replicated values, the selected global pivots might be replicated too. Using replicated global pivots to partition the data will cause serious load imbalance. Specifically, among all the processes that share the same global pivot, one of the processes could be assigned with all the data belonging to these same global pivots, while the other processes are assigned with no data. The process that is assigned all data ends up being the bottleneck while other processes will be idle in the final ordering step. Even worse, this might cause out-of-memory (OOM) errors and crash the sorting program. Adding the original rank or the non-key value (named secondary sorting key) of each data record to distinguish the replicated global pivots can avoid this issue, but it increases extra overhead of comparing and communicating one or more secondary sorting keys. Such limitation might let users have limited sorting keys to choose or spend extra efforts to pick up secondary sorting keys. Our SDS-Sort does not rely on secondary sorting keys to ensure the load balancing of local ordering. We also propose to use local pivots to partition data and reduce the overhead of data partition. Our partition method named $SdssPartition$ is summarized in Fig. 2 and its details are discussed in below subsections.

```
function SdssPartition(A, P_l, P_g, p, r, s_f, com)
    A : sorted data with size n        p : number of processes
    P_l : local pivots                 r : rank of processes
    P_g : global pivots                s_f : flag of stable sorting
    com : MPI communicator for all process
0.   rdisp[0] = 0        ▷ Initialization ◁
1.   for i = 0, ..., p - 2 do
2.       p_i = std::upper_bound(P_l[0], P_l[p-1], P_g[i])
3.       p_d = std::upper_bound(A[p_i⌊n/p⌋], A[(p_i+1)⌊n/p⌋], P_g[i])
4.       (f_r, r_s, r_r, pp_v) = SdssReplicated(P_g, p, i)
5.       if f_r == TRUE then ▷ Replicated pivots detected ◁
6.           pp_i = std::upper_bound(P_l[0], P_l[p-1], pp_v)
7.           pp_d = std::upper_bound(A[pp_i⌊n/p⌋],
                     A[(pp_i+1)⌊n/p⌋], pp_v)
8.           if s_f != TRUE then ▷ Fast version ◁
9.               rdisp[i + 1] = pp_d + (p_d − pp_d)/r_s (r_r + 1)
10.          else     ▷ Stable version ◁
11.              c_r = pp_d - p_d + 1
12.              MPI_Allgather(c_r, 1, c_v, p, com)
13.              s_b = sum(c_v[0, r − 1])
14.              s_a = sum(c_v[0, p − 1])/r_s
15.              r_t = s_b/s_a        ▷ skip r_t process ◁
16.              for k = 0, ..., (r_t -1) do
17.                  rdisp[i + k + 1] = pp_d
18.              for
19.              for k = r_t, ..., r_s do
20.                  if s_b%s_a + c_r ≤ s_a then
21.                      rdisp[i + k + 1] = pp_d + c_r
22.                  else     ▷ Split replicated on a node ◁
23.                      rdisp[i + k + 1] = pp_d + s_a
24.                      s_b = s_b + s_a, c_r = c_r − s_a
25.                  end if
26.              for
27.              i = i + r_s;
28.          end if
29.      else     ▷ No replicated pivots ◁
30.          rdisp[i + 1] = p_d
31.      endif
32.  endfor
33.  scount[0, ..., p − 1] = difference(rdisp)
34.  return (rdisp, scount)
```

Figure 2: SdssPartition Algorithm.

```
function SdssReplicated(P_g, p, i)
    P_g : global pivots vector        i : target process index
    p : number of processes
0.   f_r = FALSE, r_s = 1, r_r = 0, pp_v = P_g[0], j = i − 1
1.   while (j >= 0) and P_g[j] == P_g[i] do
2.       j − −, r_s + +, f_r = TRUE
3.   end while
4.   pp_v = P_g[j]
5.   r_r = r_s - 1, j = i + 1
6.   while (j < p − 1 and P_g[j] == P_g[i] ) do
7.       j + +; r_s + +; f_r = TRUE
8.   end while
9.   return (f_r, r_s, r_r, pp_v)
```

Figure 3: SdssReplicated Algorithm

ing procedure is the presence of replicated global pivots. To enable *SdssPartition* to detect replicated global pivots dynamically (line 5 of Fig. 2), we designed an algorithm named *SdssReplicated* (in Fig. 3). For a specific global pivot $P_g[i]$, *SdssReplicated* scans all $p-1$ global pivots once and identifies that "is $P_g[i]$ duplicated with its neighborhood pivots?" If $P_g[i]$ is not a replicated pivot (f_r=**FALSE**), SDS-Sort partitions the data as traditional method [19] (line 30 of Fig. 2). Once $P_g[i]$ is found replicated (f_r=**TRUE**), *SdssReplicated* continues to find "what is the number (i.e., r_s) of pivots that are equal to $P_g[i]$?" and "what is the rank (i.e., r_r) of $P_g[i]$ in its replicated pivots?" When *SdssReplicated* detects replicated pivots, it also finds the pivot (pp_v) right before all replicated $P_g[i]$. The r_r, r_s, and pp_v are used to evenly partition the skewed data among processes, as discussed in rest of this subsection.

Since the requirement to maintain stability requires us to handle the same key value differently, next we discuss the two cases of partitioning with and without stability requirement separately. We will refer to the version without stability requirement as the **"fast version"** and the version with stability requirement as the **"stable version"**.

Fast version of skew-aware partitioning. Without duplicated keys, the theoretical upper bound for the number of data records for each process in local ordering step is $O(2\frac{n}{p})$ [19]. When sorting skewed data, this upper bound of existing methods will increase proportionally as the number of replicates increases [19]. Using secondary sorting key can alleviate this issue, but, as mentioned above, requires extra overhead in comparing and communicating. Without rely on secondary keys in sorting skewed data, we device a more efficient partitioning method in SDS-Sort. More importantly, this new partition method has fixed upper bound of $O(4\frac{n}{p})$ for the number of data records for each process in local ordering step (see proof in §2.8). The partitioning method is presented from line 6 to line 9 of Fig. 2. First, SDS-Sort finds the index (pp_i) and the displacement (pp_d) of pp_v in P_l and A, respectively. Combined with the displacement p_d found in line 3, SDS-Sort knows that all replicated values fall between pp_d and p_d. As the fast version of SDS-Sort does not require to maintain the relative order of replicated data, SDS-Sort equally partitions the replicated values between pp_d and p_d among all r_s process (at line 9 of Fig. 2). In other words, the partitioning method is equal to implicitly adding the rank of replicated pivots (i.e, r_r) to distinct the replicated values between pp_d and p_d. A simple example of this partition method is presented in Fig 4.

Stable version of skew-aware partitioning. In the stable version of SDS-Sort, the replicated values in output must have the same order as they have in the input. Especially,

2.5.1 Local pivots based partition

The data partitioning step uses the $p - 1$ global pivots (line 11 of Fig. 1) to partition the whole data space into p chunks. Specifically, the goal of data partition is to find the pairs of *sdisp* and *scount* for all-to-all data exchange. The *sdisp* variable is the starting displacement of data in A and the *scount* is the amount of the data after *offset*. A widely used data partitioning method is to shift through the total $O(n)$ local data once. When n is large, shifting all data may have significant overhead. To reduce this overhead, SDS-Sort uses local pivots-based partition to reduce its shift space from $O(n)$ to $O(\frac{n}{p})$. It is because local pivots and their associated displacements provide good representation and partition of the sorted local data space. The algorithm to perform this partition is shown in Fig. 2 (from line 1 to line 4). For a global pivot $P_g[i]$, SDS-Sort firstly ranks it among $p - 1$ local pivots via *std::upper_bound* function of C++, which is based on binary search [27]. Then, SDS-Sort uses *std::upper_bound* again to find the actual displacement of pivot $P_g[i]$ between $P_{ld}[p_i]$ and $P_{ld}[p_i + 1]$ of A.

2.5.2 Skew-aware partitioning

Next, we describe the skew-aware data partition method. A key factor affecting the partition sizes in a parallel sort-

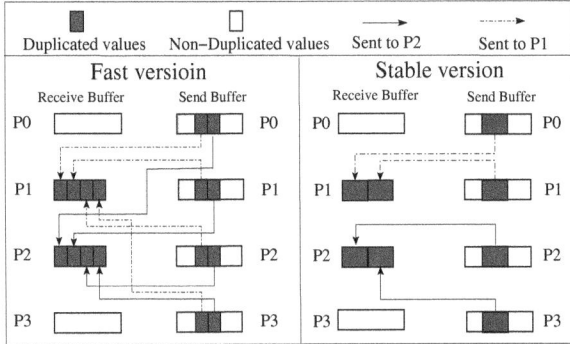

Figure 4: A simple example of skew-aware partition for four processes: P0, P1, P2, and P3; where two global pivots (out of three) are the same. In the fast version, each process partitions its own replicated values evenly into two chunks, denoted with brown boxes. The first brown box of all four processes is gathered onto P1 and the second brown box of all four processes onto P2. In the stable version, all replicated values are partitioned into two groups. P0 and P2 belongs to the first group and P2 and P3 the second group. All brown boxes on P0 and P1 are sent to P1 and all brown boxes on P2 and P3 are sent to P2.

the duplicated values located on different processes must be ordered by their MPI process rank in final output. The partition method used by the fast version of SDS-Sort can not guarantee this stability request. For instance, in the fast version example of Fig 4, process P3 sends its replicated values to both P1 and P2. In the final output, the replicated value sent from P0 to P2 could be placed between these replicated values sent by P3, which breaks the requirement of stable parallel sorting.

To address this issue, SDS-Sort uses a new partitioning method for the stable version. The main idea of our method is to consider all duplicated values from the first MPI process to the last MPI process as a contiguous 'replicated value space', to evenly partition this space into groups, and then to designate an MPI process in each group for gathering and storing all the replicated values in its respective group. When there are r_s replicated pivots, the number of groups is set equal to r_s. These designated processes are the processes assigned with duplicated global pivots. As each designated process only gathers equally sized replicated values inside its group, the load on these processes will be very small and balanced. The upper bound on the load of each process of this partition method is $O(4\frac{n}{p})$, the same as the fast version (see proof in Section 2.8). The implementation details are presented from line 11 to 25 of Figure 2. SDS-Sort first lets each process gather duplicated value count (c_r) of all p processes into a vector (sv), which has the size equal to p. Since we have r_s groups and also r_s designated processes, the average size of replicated values for each designated process is calculated as $s_a = \text{sum}(c_v[0, p-1])/r_s$. The first designated process will gather s_a duplicated values from the first process p_0 until the process p_i, where $i \geq 0$ and $\text{sum}(c_v[0, i-1]) \leq s_a \leq \text{sum}(c_v[0, i])$. Note that when a single process has more replicated values than s_a, these replicated values will then be divided into different groups (line 23 and line 24). By applying the same idea, each designated process can find its s_a contiguous duplicated values within its group. In the gathering process, we preserve the order of value as their MPI process rank by taking advantage of the blocking (non-

asynchronous) MP_alltoallv function (line 16 of Fig. 1). A very simple example of the partition method is also shown in Fig 4, where the number of replicated values on P0 and P2 is equal to that on P2 and P3.

2.6 Adaptive all-to-all data exchange

When performing the data exchange, SDS-Sort can dynamically choose between two options: synchronous and asynchronous. The asynchronous data exchange is used to overlap data exchange and local ordering phases. This option is effective when CPU is relatively fast compared to the network, where the CPU could process the data to be sent without waiting for the receiver to acknowledge the message, and then wait to perform the local ordering operations as soon as the data arrives. On HPC systems with relatively weak CPUs, the CPUs might have to devote a large portion of its computing power to feed the network with no opportunity to conduct other operations. Furthermore, asynchronous communication requires the senders nad receivers to dedicate a certain amount of system resources to monitor the progress of the messages. In a large scale all-to-all data exchange, the competition for these system resources could introduce unexpected delays and reduce the overall performance. In such a case, using synchronous communication might be faster. In the current implementation, we use a threshold τ_s, certain number of processes, to choose synchronous and asynchronous data exchange adaptively.

As the asynchronous might break the order of data exchange but the stable sorting requires to maintain relative order, SDS-Sort uses synchronous to perform all-to-all data exchange for stable sorting. SDS-Sort uses *MPI_Alltoallv* to perform synchronous data exchange (line 16 of Fig. 1) and *MPIAlltoallvAsync* (line 24 of Fig. 1) to perform asynchronous data exchange. Note that *MPIAlltoallvAsync* is not a standard MPI function, but a function we implemented with *MPI_Isend*, *MPI_Irecv*, and *MPI_Test* functions. *MPIAlltoallvAsync* returns two received data chunk ids: id_1 and id_2, corresponding to the ranks of two processes. Function *SdssMergeTwo*, a special case of *SdssMergeall* reported in following subsection 2.6, is used to merge two received data chunks.

2.7 Adaptive local ordering

After the all-to-all data exchange, SDS-Sort performs the final local ordering within each process to place the data records in their output order. In this process, SDS-Sort could dynamically decide to use a number of different procedures as shown from line 17 to line 21 of Fig. 1. By design, the input to this final ordering step on each MPI rank is a list of p ordered chunks. Currently, we only consider two options named merging and sorting, where the first option merges the p ordered chunks into a single order array and the second option simply invoke a standard sorting algorithm on the incoming data. The reason is that the complexity of merging increases as the number of processes p increases, but the complexity of sorting decreases as p increases. Specifically, the time complexity of merging p sorted chunks (received from p processes) is $O(n log(p))$, which highly depends on the number of sorted chunks. On the other hand, p sorted chunks form a partially ordered data. The best complexity of sorting partially ordered reduces from $O(n log(n))$ to $O(n)$ [9]. It is obviously that given certain number of processes p, choosing sorting or merging wisely can reduce the time spent on local ordering. In implementation, we uses two functions: *SdssMergeAll* and *SdssLocalSort*. Both can run in parallel on shared memory if its input parameter c is larger than one. *SdssMergeAll* takes advantage of sorted order of the chunks from other processes and uses *std::merge* of C++ to obtain globally sorted data. As described in previous Section 2.2, *SdssLocalSort* is a shared memory sorting algorithm which is based on *std::sort* or *std::stable_sort* of C++.

2.8 Analysis of workload on each process

Following the analysis by Li et al. [19], we use m_i to denote the number of data records on the ith process in the final local ordering step and

$$U = \max_{1 \le i \le p} m_i = 2\frac{N}{p} - \frac{N}{p^2} - p + 1 + d$$

where N is the number of data records, p is the number of processes used, and d is the number of the records whose key value is duplicated most. In the analysis done by Li et al., the big O notation is also used to denote the dominant term (also called the 'upper bound') in the expression. Assuming both p and d are much smaller than N, Li et al. express the upper bound of U as $O(2\frac{N}{p})$. Using these conventions, we have the following theorem:

THEOREM 1. *The upper bound of workload on each process (U) with SDS-Sort in sorting N data records using p processes is $O(4\frac{N}{p})$.*

PROOF. We divide the proof into two parts based on whether or not there are any duplicated global pivots.

When there are no duplicated global pivots, the worst case bound on U is same as given by the analysis of Li et al. [19]. In this case, the worst case value for d can be computed as follows. Since there is no duplicated global pivot, there are at most $p-1$ replicated local pivots. Since SDS-Sort orders original data before choosing local pivots, each local pivot represents at most $2\frac{N}{p^2}$ replicated values. Hence, we have $d < 2\frac{N}{p^2} \times (p-1) < 2\frac{N}{p^2} \times p = 2\frac{N}{p}$. Thus, $U < 2\frac{N}{p} - \frac{N}{p^2} - p + 1 + 2\frac{N}{p} = 4\frac{N}{p} - \frac{N}{p^2} - p + 1 + 2$, which gives that the upper bound of U as $O(4\frac{N}{p})$.

When there are duplicated global pivots, SDS-Sort denotes the number of duplicated global pivots with r_s and the rank of each replicated global pivot with r_r, where $1 \le r_s \le p-1$ and $0 \le r_r \le r_s - 1$. As the fast version and the stable version of SDS-Sort partition the data with different methods, we prove the upper bound for them separately as below:

- The fast version SDS-Sort uses r_s and r_k to partition the replicated values equally among r_s processes. In this partition method, a replicated global pivot implicitly assigns its rank value (i.e., r_r) to all duplicated values which are represented by it. This will make the duplicated values represented by different replicated global pivots are distinct from each other. Meanwhile, we have that each global pivot represents at most $2\frac{N}{p^2} \times p = 2\frac{N}{p}$ duplicated data records. Hence, the maximum number of the duplicated values reduce from d to $2\frac{N}{p}$. As indicating in above steps, the upper bound of sorting data with at most $2\frac{N}{p}$ values is $O(4\frac{N}{p})$. Therefore, we have that the upper bound of U is equal to $O(4\frac{N}{p})$ in this case.

- The stable version of SDS-Sort partitions the number of processes into r_s groups and uses a designated process within a group to gather the duplicated values. This partition method implicitly attach a rank value r_k to all the duplicated values within a single group. Thus, it can distinct the values belonging to different groups. As the number of duplicated values of a single group is at most $2\frac{N}{p^2} \times (p) = 2\frac{N}{p}$, which is also equal to the number of data records represented by a single pivot, the maximum number of the duplicated values reduce to be $2\frac{N}{p}$. As indicating in above steps, we have that upper bound of U is equal to $O(4\frac{N}{p})$ in this case. This completes the proof.

□

3. SYSTEM CONFIGURATION

We have conducted all the experiments reported in this paper on Edison [3], a Cray XC30 supercomputer at the National Energy Research Scientific Computing Center (NERSC). Edison is equipped with 133,824 compute cores and 357 terabytes of aggregate memory. Each compute node of Edison is configured with two 12-core Intel "Ivy Bridge" processors at 2.4 GHz and 64 GB DDR3 1600 MHz memory. Edison uses Cray Aries [6] high-speed interconnect, which has $0.25\mu s$ to $3.7\mu s$ MPI latency and 8GB/sec MPI bandwidth. The high-speed interconnect of Edison uses Dragonfly topology, which is able to deliver 23.7TB/s global bandwidth. Our SDS-Sort implementation code is written in C++ and is compiled with Intel Compiler version 16.0 and Cray's implementation of MPI. We have scaled our sorting experiments up to $131,072$ CPU cores. The measured performance in this paper does not include the time to read the data from the parallel file system, i.e., the measured time includes sorting time after the data is loaded into memory.

4. EXPERIMENTAL EVALUATION

In this section, we conduct an in-depth evaluation of SDS-Sort, and compare it with the most efficient in-memory sorting algorithm known as Hyksort [28]. The evaluation uses two synthetic data sets and two real scientific data sets from cosmology and astronomy.

4.1 Performance evaluation of SDS-Sort

Two synthetic data sets, a Uniform data set and a Skewed data set, are used to evaluate SDS-Sort. Uniform data set is generated by standard Uniform distribution, which is widely used in previous research to test various parallel sorting algorithms [28]. The Skewed data set is generated by Zipf distribution: $p(i) = \frac{C}{i^\alpha}$, where $i = 1$ to N, α is the Zipf exponent, and C is the normalization constant [26]. Since the number of duplicates is a critical parameter to the performance of parallel sample sorting algorithms, we next introduce a parameter δ as the maximum replication ratio. For a data set with d denoting the number of the records whose key value is duplicated most, δ is defined as $\frac{d}{N} \times 100\%$, where N is the number of data records to sort. All tests were repeated three times and the best performing values are reported.

Using these synthetic workloads, we first explore the optimal values for the parameters τ_m, τ_o, τ_s that are used by SDS-Sort. Next, we explore the performance characteristics

---

[3]http://www.nersc.gov/users/computational-systems/edison/

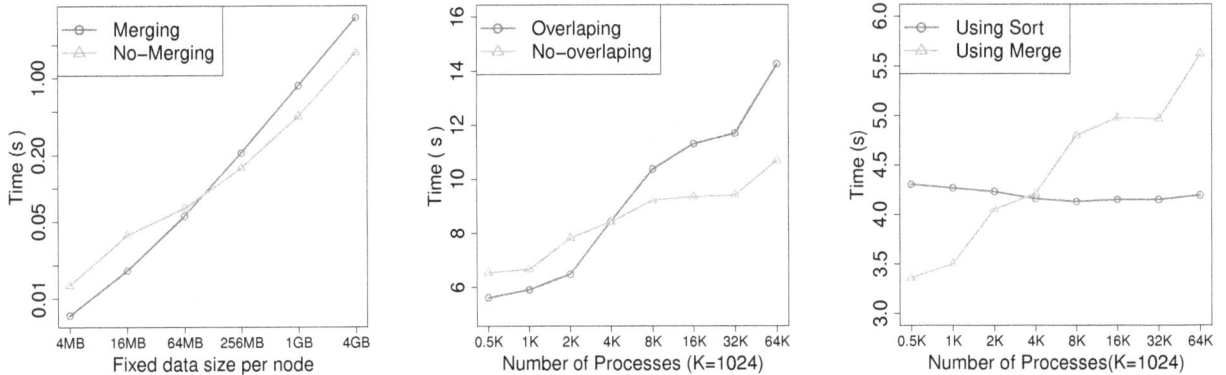

(a) All-to-all data exchange with or without merging.

(b) Overlapping and not-overlapping data exchange with local-sorting.

(c) Final local ordering using sorting vs. using merging.

Figure 5: Performance test results of exploring optimal value for parameters τ_m, τ_o, and τ_s.

of *std::sort* and *std::stable_sort* from C++ Standard Template Library as SDS-Sort uses them to perform sequential sorting on a CPU core. Finally, we compare SDS-Sort with a state-of-art parallel sorting algorithm, namely HykSort [28]. HykSort has a parameter, k, representing k-way communication. Previous study [28] shown that 128 is the optimal for k, which is used in our evaluation. Specifically, we compare SDS-Sort and HykSort in terms of different replication ratio values (i.e., δ) and varying number of MPI processes.

4.1.1 Evaluation with varying parameters

The SDS-Sort algorithm has a number of parameters, such as the threshold τ_m for merging data in the exchange phase, the threshold τ_o for overlapping communication with computation, and the threshold τ_s in the local ordering phase. Next, we use the synthetic data sets to find the optimal values of these parameters.

Performance with merging data before the exchange phase (τ_m). The merging parameter (τ_m) of SDS-Sort decides whether to merge data of each CPU node for the all-to-all data exchange phase. Fig. 5a reports the execution time for all-to-all data exchange with varying message size. It is clear that when the message size is small (i.e., less than 160MB), merging data at each node is beneficial. On the other hand, when the message size is larger than 160MB, merging data at each node has high overhead. The main reason is that merging small messages on each node can avoid the overhead of establishing all-to-all communication. But, when the message size is large, using all the CPU cores to feed data individually into the network without merging can take advantage of high bandwidth of the network. Our test results indicate that setting τ_m to be 160MB is reasonable on our test bed, Edison.

Overlapping of the exchange and the local ordering phases (τ_o). The threshold τ_o decides whether overlapping the all-to-all exchange with the local sorting phases of SDS-Sort. To explore the optimal values of τ_o, we tested the time for overlapping and not overlapping using different numbers of MPI processes. The results reported in Fig. 5b show that overlapping all-to-all data exchange with local ordering is faster than not overlapping when the number of processes is smaller than 4096. A reason for this behavior is that when the number of processes is small, the network bandwidth that the sorting phase obtains is small. As a re-

Table 1: Time (s) of using *std::sort* and *std::stable_sort* of C++ to sort $1GB$ data.

	Uniform	Zipf (a (δ%))		
		0.7 (2)	1.4 (32)	2.1 (63)
std::sort	26.1	14.6	8.9	6.6
std::stable_sort	35.2	24.3	16.5	12.5

sult, when data is transferred on network, the CPU might be idle and overlapping data exchange and local ordering can reduce the overall time. As the number of processes increases, the workload that local ordering phase requires to do increases too. Hence, overlapping the all-to-all data exchange and local ordering phases can delay the rate of feeding the data into network. As a result, the performance with overlapping degrades. Through our tests on Edison, we decide the optimal τ_o to be 4096.

Merging vs. sorting (τ_s). In SDS-Sort, τ_s decides whether to use merging or sorting to perform the local ordering phase. In our analysis in Section 2.6, we argue that the time for using merging to perform local ordering phase will increase as the number of processes increases. On the other hand, the time to sort partially sorted data will reduce. We report the time used by sorting and merging with different number of processes in Fig. 5c. As expected, the time for using merging to perform local ordering phase increases sharply from 512 processes to 64K processes. On the other hand, the time for using sorting on CPU cores to perform local ordering is much more stable and decreases gradually. Hence, the test results are consistent with theoretical analysis. 4000 MPI processes is the turning point where using merging becomes more expensive than sorting. Hence, in following tests on Edison, τ_s is set to be 4000.

Evaluation of *std::sort* and *std::stable_sort*. The standard C++ functions *std::sort* and *std::stable_sort* are used as the sequential sort algorithm in SDS-Sort. In Table 1, we show the performance of sorting 1 GB data (268 millions float values) from both uniform and skewed data sets. In the skewed data set tests, we used skewed data sets with different Zipf distribution settings. As expected, *std::sort* is faster than *std::stable_sort*. The time to sort highly skewed data is smaller than sorting the uniform distributed data set. Moreover, the time to sort skewed data gradually decreases as the replication ratio (δ) increases.

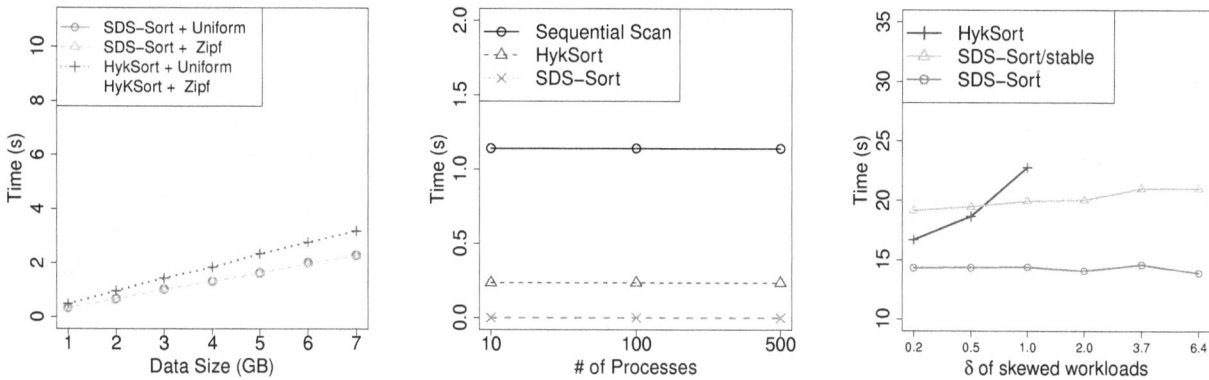

(a) Time to merge data in parallel for different workloads on a single node.

(b) Time to partition data using different methods

(c) Time to sort skew data with varying replication ratios (δ, %).

Figure 6: Micro performance comparison of different optimizations: skew aware merging, local pivots based parallel partition, and skew aware sorting.

Table 2: Relatioship between δ and α.

α	0.4	0.5	0.6	0.7	0.8	0.9
δ (%)	0.2	0.5	1.0	2.0	3.7	6.4

4.1.2 Large-scale comparison with HykSort

In this section, we compare SDS-Sort and HykSort[24] using the synthetic data sets. We first compare their two components: shared memory parallel merging and data partition methods. Then we compare SDS-Sort with HykSort to sort the skewed data set with different replication ratios and to run using on different numbers of CPU cores. We label *SDS-Sort* to denote the fast version and *SDS-Sort/stable* to denote the stable stable version of SDS-Sort.

Skew-aware parallel merging. Parallel merging is an important step in functions *SdssLocalSort*, *SdssMergeSort* and *SdssNodeMerge*. Compared with the parallel merging used by HykSort, SDS-Sort uses a skew aware partition method to support parallel merging. In Fig. 6a, we compare the time to merge different data workloads and different data sizes. The parallel merging used in HykSort uses more time when merging skewed data represented by Zipf distribution. This is consistent with the analysis by Li et al [19], which indicates that a high number of duplicated values would increase the load imbalance. On the other hand, the skew-aware parallel merging used in SDS-Sort delivers stable performance in both Uniform and Zipf workloads because the skew-aware parallel merging is better at maintaining load balance.

Local pivots-based data partition. In Section 2.5, we propose the function *SdssPartition* that uses local pivots to partition data. Here we evaluate this idea experimentally. In this test, we fix the data size for each process at 2GB and test different number of processes. The test results are reported in Fig. 6b. In this test, we compared the performance of full scan partition, parallel partition used by HykSort, and local pivot based partition used in SDS-Sort. As the test results indicate that using local pivots can reduce the time for data partition to almost zero. Hence, the proposed local pivots based data partition is an efficient method to reduce the data partition overhead.

Replication ratios δ scaling tests. Next, we compare

SDS-Sort with HykSort using the skewed workloads of different replication ratios. The performance comparison is shown in Fig. 6c. The α and δ values in the test data are reported in Table 2. The timing results in Fig. 6c indicate that both SDS-Sort and SDS-Sort/Stable deliver scalable performance with different replication ratios. On the other hand, Hyk-Sort can only work when the replication value is less than 1.0% (δ=0.6). The reason is that skewed data causes load imbalance in HykSort. When the replication ratio is too high, certain nodes will be assigned so much data that the processes running on those nodes run out of memory.

Scalability of SDS-Sort. We show weak-scaling performance of SDS-Sort on uniform and skewed data sets in Fig. 7 and Fig. 8, respectively. In these tests, we fix the data size per process at 400MB (i.e., 100 millions records) and increase the number of CPU cores from 512 (0.5K) to 131,072 (128K). The data size for sorting with 128K cores is 52.4TB (i.e., 10^{13} data records). For uniform workload, HykSort takes 42.6 seconds to sort the 52.4TB. Using sorting throughput, a popular metric [29], to express this performance number, HykSort archives at most 73.8TB/min sorting throughput using 128K cores. SDS-Sort takes 28.25 seconds to sort the same data, resulting in 111TB/min sorting throughput. SDS-Sort is 51% faster than HykSort. For the SDS-Sort/stable, it delivers 54TB/min in sorting the same data. The reason for SDS-Sort/Stable is slower than both HykSort and SDS-Sort is that it takes more time to select pivots and to perform local ordering as discussed in the previous sections. For the skewed workload, HykSort fails to execute due to the Out-of-Memory (OOM) error because of the load imbalance issue after the all-to-all data exchange phase. Both SDS-Sort and SDS-Sort/stable deliver performance similar to that of sorting the uniform data set. Using 128K processes, SDS-Sort delivers 117TB/min sorting throughput, and SDS-Sort/stable delivers 55.8TB/min sorting throughput.

We now evaluate the impact of load balancing of different sorting algorithms in the above scaling tests. Popular metric used to compare the load balancing of sorting algorithms is $RDFA$, which is the Relative Deviation of the size of the largest partition From the Average size of the p processes, and is defined as: $RDFA = \frac{\max_{i=1}^{p}(m_i)}{ave_{i=1}^{p}(m_i)}$ [19], where m_i de-

Table 3: RDFA of different parallel sorting algorithms

		Number of Cores								
		512	1024	2048	4096	8192	16384	32768	65536	131072
Uniform	HykSort	1.0692	1.0433	1.0232	1.0145	1.0126	1.0096	1.0085	1.0073	1.2051
	SDS-Sort	1.0025	1.0044	1.0049	1.0076	1.011	1.0177	1.0264	1.0353	1.0546
	SDS-Sort/stable	1.0025	1.0044	1.0049	1.0076	1.011	1.0177	1.0264	1.0353	1.0546
Zipf(0.7-2.0)	HykSort	∞	∞	∞	∞	∞	∞	∞	∞	∞
	SDS-Sort	1.6816	1.8172	1.8411	1.9222	1.9552	1.9556	1.9732	1.4889	2.6753
	SDS-Sort/stable	1.6816	1.8172	1.8411	1.9222	1.9552	1.9556	1.9732	1.4888	2.6753

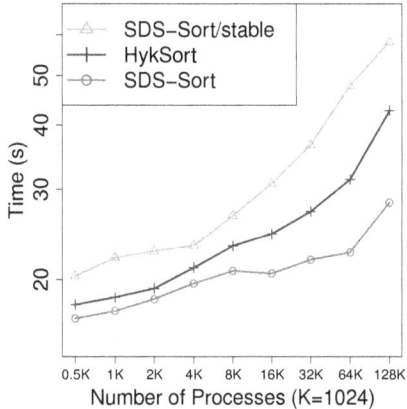

Figure 7: Scaling test of Uniform distribution

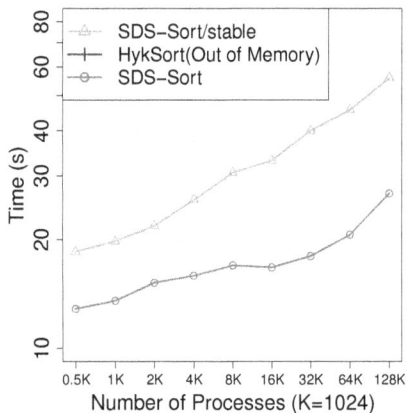

Figure 8: Scaling test of Zipf distribution

note the load on the ith processes. The $RDFA$ of all scaling tests are reported in Table 3. HykSort uses histogram sampling to choose pivots. SDS-Sort uses striped-equal sampling (also called regular sampling) to choose pivots. For the Uniform distribution workload, we can see that HykSort, HykSort/stable and SDS-Sort have almost equal RDFA values. The difference of RDFA values between these sorting methods is negligible. For the skewed data set generated using Zipf distribution, both SDS-Sort and SDS-Sort/stable deliver almost similar RDFA values. But, histogram sampling used in HykSort assigns a lot of replicated values to single node, which causes out-of-memory errors. Hence, we denote the RDFA values for HykSort as ∞ in these tests. Using external values or rank of replicated values to distinct the replicated one can turn HykSort to allocate replicated val-

ues among processes [29]. But, it requires extra overhead to store, exchange, and process external values. Also, user's objective selection for secondary sorting keys can impact the tests results. Hence, we only compare the method without using secondary sorting keys here. In summary, we can see that SDS-Sort works on different workloads and also show good scalability to different number of processes.

4.2 Evaluation of SDS-Sort with Real Application Data Sets

We next compare SDS-Sort with HykSort using two real scientific data sets from Palomar Transient Factory (PTF) observations and a Cosmology simulation of billion particles.

Palomar Transient Factory (PTF) data. The PTF is an automated survey system of the sky for identifying supernova and other transient events in the universe [5]. An important component of the survey is the automated transient detection pipeline to enable the early detection of these events. One task among this pipeline is to make automated real/bogus decision about each detected objects based on image and context features using real-bogus (RB) classifier [5]. In the PTF data sets, the RB classifier is represented by real-bogus score as a real number. Hence, sorting the objects by real-bogus score is one typical method used by the RB classifier. In our sorting tests, we used a 27GB data set (with 1 billion records) for measuring the performance of SDS-Sort and HykSort. Before SDS-Sort and HykSort starts to work, the time to read the data into memory is 19.6 seconds.

The PTF data shows high skewness as its replication ratio (δ) of real-bogus score is 28.02%. We show the performance of sorting PTF data using HykSort and SDS-Sort in Fig. 9[4]. The RDFA values of different sorting methods are reported in Table 4, where load imbalance with HykSort for PTF data is significantly larger than that of SDS-Sort. As each node of Edison has 64GB memory, the whole data can be stored on a single node. Hence even though HykSort has serious load imbalance (RDFA=32.68), it can still finish the sorting without out-of-memory (OOM) issues. Overall, SDS-Sort is 3.4× faster than HykSort in sorting PTF data and SDS-Sort/stable is 2.2× faster than HykSort.

Cosmology simulation data. Large-scale cosmological simulations such as GADGET-2 [25] and NyX [1] play critical roles in exploring the unknown structure formation process of the universe. Analyzing the data generated by cosmological simulations is essential step to extract its insights of cosmological discoveries. Recently, researchers proposed BD-CATS, a KD-tree based clustering method, to analyze the particle data from GADGET-2 [21]. An important step in BD-CATS is to sort the particles based its clustering ID.

---

[4]The Exchange time for HykSort also contains the time for local ordering as it uses overlapping inside

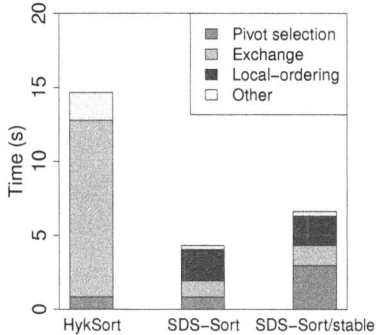

Figure 9: Sorting 27GB PTF data with 192 cores.

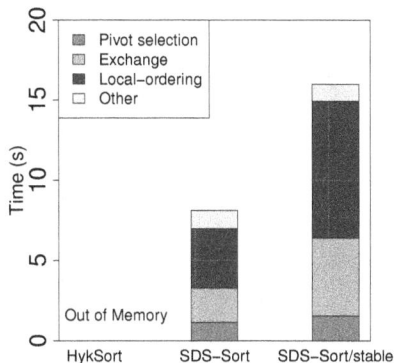

Figure 10: Sorting 2.1TB Cosmology data with $16K$ cores.

In this test, we apply both SDS-Sort and HykSort to sort a 2.1TB particle data by using its clustering ID as the sorting key. Before SDS-Sort and HykSort starts to work, the time to read the data into memory is 438.1 seconds. Specifically, the 2.1TB data contains 68 billion particles and we sort these particles by their clustering IDs. Meanwhile, each particle data record also contains spatial location (x, y, and z), and particle velocities (vx, vy, and vz). In sorting tests, we trade these extra attributes as payload. In the data, the replication ratio (δ) for clustering ID is 0.73. Hence, the cosmology data used in this test is a typical example of skewed data. The performance of sorting is reported in Fig. 10. The RDFA values of sorting this 2.1TB data are reported in Table 4, which are small for SDS-Sort. The RDFA value for HykSort is ∞ because that HykSort fails to sort the cosmology data set due to OOM errors. Both SDS-Sort and SDS-Sort/stable can sort the Cosmology data quickly, giving 15.63TB/min and 7.87TB/min sorting throughput, respectively.

5. RELATED WORK

Non-sampling based parallel sorting algorithms include bitonic sort[4], radix sort [30], bubble sort[3], merging sort[11], and so on. Bitonic sort [4] focuses on converting a random sequence of numbers into a bitonic sequence which monotonically increases and then decreases. Radix sort [30] is a non-comparative integer sorting algorithm that sorts data with integer keys by grouping keys by the individual digits

Table 4: RDFA values of sorting Cosmology and PTF data

	HykSort	SDS-Sort	SDS-Sort/stable
PTF	32.6759	1.9908	1.6908
Cosmology	∞	1.3962	1.3962

that share the same significant position and value. Bubble sort [3] repeatedly steps through the data to be sorted, compares each pair of adjacent items and swaps them if they are in the wrong order. Merge sort [11] divides data list into the small unit, then compare each element with the adjacent list to sort and merge the two adjacent lists. Generally, these non-sampling based parallel sorting algorithms need a significant amount of communication and data exchange, which are expensive operations on parallel systems [28].

Sampling based sorting algorithm was invented in 1970s [15] and it is based on the divide and conquer idea. Parallel sampling sorting [24] was then devised to sort large-scale data on distributed memory systems. A theoretical study on the load balancing of parallel sampling sorting algorithms was conducted in [19], where authors proved $O(2\frac{n}{p})$ upper bound for load balancing without highly duplicated keys. Parallel sorting by sampling was compared with other algorithms [2], e.g radix sort and bitonic sort. Authors found that sampling sorting is good at the distributed memory machine where interprocess communication and data movement are expensive.

To reduce the sampling size and improve scalability of parallel sampling sorting, Solomoik et al [24] use histogram-based method to choose pivots and propose to overlap data exchange and local ordering to reduce its overhead. In out-of-core parallel sorting, similar idea have been employed to overlap computation and disk I/O operations [28, 10]. CloudRAMSort [18] performs multi-node optimizations by carefully overlapping computation with inter-node communication. CloudRAMSort uses payload to be part of the key to deal with skewed data.

HykSort was devised to reduce all-to-all communication overhead via avoiding network transmission contentions [28]. As HykSort divides all process into groups to reduce transmission contention, the global pivots used in HykSort are reduced to k, a user controlled parameter. Based on the number of pivots, HykSort is general sampling sorting algorithm of quick sort [23] and standard parallel sampling sort [19]. To the best of our konwledge, HykSort is the fastest and the most scalable parallel sorting algorithm so far.

Other sorting algorithms, e.g., TritonSort [22] and NTOSort [13], also exist. Being different from the above sorting algorithms and from our SDS-Sort, these sorting algorithms are generally disk-based sorting algorithms, or usually called out-of-core sorting. These out-of-core sorting algorithms mainly focus on optimizing the I/O performance and cache efficiency in sorting.

6. CONCLUSIONS

The SDS-Sort algorithm, we introduced in this paper, addresses the issues inherited in parallel sorting algorithms on common application data sets, such as skewed data and partially ordered data. Furthermore, existing parallel sorting algorithms are not designed for heterogeneous architecture of current generation of supercomputers. SDS-Sort uses skew-aware partitioning method to address the load imbalance issue in working with skewed data. To run efficiently on new computing and networking hardware and to sort partially ordered data, SDS-Sort is capable of decide many aspects of its execution dynamically, such as merging data at each node, overlapping communication and computation, and selecting different approaches for local ordering. Through extensive experiments with both uniformly distributed and skewed synthetic workloads, SDS-Sort scaled to $131,072$ cores and was shown to be at 50% faster than a state-of-the-art parallel sorting algorithm, HykSort. On two sets of scientific data from astronomy and cosmology, SDS-Sort outperformed HykSort by 3.4X. In the future, we plan to systematically study the configuration parameters τ_m, τ_o, and τ_s. We plan to perform more comparisons against various parallel sorting methods and carry out more tests with well-known sorting benchmarks and scientific data sets. We are also interested in exploring the new hardware such as general graphics processing unit (GGPU).

Acknowledgment

This work was supported by the DOE Office of Science, Advanced Scientific Computing Research, under contract number DE-AC02-05CH11231 (Program manager: Lucy Nowell). This research used resources of the National Energy Research Scientific Computing Center (NERSC).

7. REFERENCES

[1] A. Almgren, J. Bell, M. Lijewski, Z. Lukic, and E. Van Andel. Nyx: A Massively Parallel AMR Code for Computational Cosmology. *Astrophys. J.*, 765:39, 2013.

[2] N. Amato, R. Iyer, S. Sundaresan, and Y. Wu. A comparison of parallel sorting algorithms on different architectures. Technical report, TX, USA, 1998.

[3] O. Astrachan. Bubble sort: An archaeological algorithmic analysis. *SIGCSE Bull.*, 35(1):1–5, Jan. 2003.

[4] G. Bilardi and A. Nicolau. Adaptive bitonic sorting: An optimal parallel algorithm for shared memory machines. Technical report, Ithaca, NY, USA, 1986.

[5] J. S. Bloom, J. W. Richards, P. E. Nugent, R. M. Quimby, M. M. Kasliwal, D. L. Starr, D. Poznanski, E. O. Ofek, S. B. Cenko, N. R. Butler, S. R. Kulkarni, A. Gal-Yam, and N. Law. Automating discovery and classification of transients and variable stars in the synoptic survey era. *Publications of the Astronomical Society of the Pacific*, 124(921):pp. 1175–1196, 2012.

[6] L. K. Bob Alverson, Edwin Froese and D. Roweth. Cray XC (R) Series Network. Technical report, Cray Inc., 2012.

[7] P. G. Brown. Overview of SciDB: Large Scale Array Storage, Processing and Analysis. In *ACM SIGMOD*, pages 963–968, 2010.

[8] A. Chan, P. Balaji, W. Gropp, and R. Thakur. Communication analysis of parallel 3d fft for flat cartesian meshes on large blue gene systems. In *Proceedings of the 15th International Conference on High Performance Computing*, HiPC'08, pages 350–364, Berlin, Heidelberg, 2008. Springer-Verlag.

[9] B. Chandramouli and J. Goldstein. Patience is a virtue: Revisiting merge and sort on modern processors. In *Proceedings of the 2014 ACM SIGMOD International Conference on Management of Data*, SIGMOD '14, pages 731–742, New York, NY, USA, 2014. ACM.

[10] M. Clement and M. Quinn. Overlapping computations, communications and i/o in parallel sorting. *Journal of Parallel and Distributed Computing*, 28(2):162 – 172, 1995.

[11] R. Cole. Parallel merge sort. *SIAM J. Comput.*, 17(4):770–785, Aug. 1988.

[12] B. Dong, S. Byna, and K. Wu. Expediting scientific data analysis with reorganization of data. In *Cluster Computing (CLUSTER), 2013 IEEE International Conference on*, pages 1–8, Sept. 2013.

[13] A. Ebert. Ntosort. Technical report, April, 2013.

[14] C. Faloutsos, Y. Matias, and A. Silberschatz. Modeling skewed distribution using multifractals and the 80-20 law. In *VLDB'96, Proceedings of 22th International Conference on Very Large Data Bases, September 3-6, 1996, Mumbai (Bombay), India*, pages 307–317, 1996.

[15] W. D. Frazer and A. C. McKellar. Samplesort: A sampling approach to minimal storage tree sorting. *J. ACM*, 17(3):496–507, July 1970.

[16] W. Gropp, R. Thakur, and E. Lusk. *Using MPI-2: Advanced Features of the Message Passing Interface*. MIT Press, Cambridge, MA, USA, 2nd edition, 1999.

[17] M. Howison, E. W. Bethel, and H. Childs. Mpi-hybrid parallelism for volume rendering on large, multi-core systems. In *Proceedings of the 10th Eurographics Conference on Parallel Graphics and Visualization*, EG PGV'10, pages 1–10, Aire-la-Ville, Switzerland, Switzerland, 2010. Eurographics Association.

[18] C. Kim, J. Park, N. Satish, H. Lee, P. Dubey, and J. Chhugani. Cloudramsort: Fast and efficient large-scale distributed ram sort on shared-nothing cluster. In *SIGMOD '12*, pages 841–850, New York, NY, USA, 2012. ACM.

[19] X. Li, P. Lu, J. Schaeffer, J. Shillington, P. S. Wong, and H. Shi. On the versatility of parallel sorting by regular sampling. *Parallel Comput.*, 19(10):1079–1103, Oct. 1993.

[20] M. E. J. Newman. Power laws, pareto distributions and zipfâĂŹs law. *Contemporary Physics*, 2005.

[21] M. M. A. Patwary, S. Byna, N. R. Satish, N. Sundaram, Z. Lukić, V. Roytershteyn, M. J. Anderson, Y. Yao, Prabhat, and P. Dubey. Bd-cats: Big data clustering at trillion particle scale. In *Proceedings of the International Conference for High Performance Computing, Networking, Storage and Analysis*, SC '15, pages 6:1–6:12, New York, NY, USA, 2015. ACM.

[22] A. Rasmussen, G. Porter, M. Conley, H. V. Madhyastha, R. N. Mysore, A. Pucher, and A. Vahdat. Tritonsort: A balanced and energy-efficient large-scale sorting system. *ACM Trans. Comput. Syst.*, 31(1):3:1–3:28, Feb. 2013.

[23] R. Sedgewick. Implementing quicksort programs. *Commun. ACM*, 21(10):847–857, Oct. 1978.

[24] E. Solomonik and L. Kale. Highly scalable parallel sorting. In *Parallel Distributed Processing (IPDPS), 2010 IEEE International Symposium on*, pages 1–12, April 2010.

[25] V. Springel. The cosmological simulation code GADGET-2. Technical report, 2005.

[26] M. H. Stanley, S. V. Buldyrev, S. Havlin, R. N. Mantegna, M. A. Salinger, and H. E. Stanley. Zipf plots and the size distribution of firms. *Economics Letters*, 49(4):453 – 457, 1995.

[27] B. Stroustrup. *The C++ Programming Language*. Addison-Wesley Longman Publishing Co., Inc., Boston, MA, USA, 3rd edition, 2000.

[28] H. Sundar, D. Malhotra, and G. Biros. Hyksort: A new variant of hypercube quicksort on distributed memory architectures. In *Proceedings of the 27th International ACM Conference on International Conference on Supercomputing*, ICS '13, pages 293–302, New York, NY, USA, 2013. ACM.

[29] H. Sundar, D. Malhotra, and K. W. Schulz. Algorithms for high-throughput disk-to-disk sorting. In *Proceedings of the International Conference on High Performance Computing, Networking, Storage and Analysis*, SC '13, pages 93:1–93:10, New York, NY, USA, 2013. ACM.

[30] K. Thearling and S. Smith. An improved supercomputer sorting benchmark. In *Supercomputing '92*, pages 14–19, Los Alamitos, CA, USA, 1992. IEEE Computer Society Press.

Scalable I/O-Aware Job Scheduling for Burst Buffer Enabled HPC Clusters

Stephen Herbein
University of Delaware
Newark, DE, United States
sherbein@udel.edu

Dong H. Ahn
Lawrence Livermore National
Laboratory
Livermore (CA), United States
ahn1@llnl.gov

Don Lipari
Lawrence Livermore National
Laboratory
Livermore (CA), United States
lipari1@llnl.gov

Thomas R.W. Scogland
Lawrence Livermore National
Laboratory
Livermore (CA), United States
scogland1@llnl.gov

Marc Stearman
Lawrence Livermore National
Laboratory
Livermore (CA), United States
stearman2@llnl.gov

Mark Grondona
Lawrence Livermore National
Laboratory
Livermore (CA), United States
grondona1@llnl.gov

Jim Garlick
Lawrence Livermore National
Laboratory
Livermore (CA), United States
garlick1@llnl.gov

Becky Springmeyer
Lawrence Livermore National
Laboratory
Livermore (CA), United States
springmeyer1@llnl.gov

Michela Taufer
University of Delaware
Newark, DE, Un/ited States
taufer@udel.edu

ABSTRACT

The economics of flash vs. disk storage is driving HPC centers to incorporate faster solid-state burst buffers into the storage hierarchy in exchange for smaller parallel file system (PFS) bandwidth. In systems with an underprovisioned PFS, avoiding I/O contention at the PFS level will become crucial to achieving high computational efficiency. In this paper, we propose novel batch job scheduling techniques that reduce such contention by integrating I/O awareness into scheduling policies such as EASY backfilling. We model the available bandwidth of links between each level of the storage hierarchy (i.e., burst buffers, I/O network, and PFS), and our I/O-aware schedulers use this model to avoid contention at any level in the hierarchy. We integrate our approach into Flux, a next-generation resource and job management framework, and evaluate the effectiveness and computational costs of our I/O-aware scheduling. Our results show that by reducing I/O contention for underprovisioned PFSes, our solution reduces job performance variability by up to 33% and decreases I/O-related utilization losses by up to 21%, which ultimately increases the amount of science performed by scientific workloads.

Keywords

High performance computing; Resource management; Scheduling algorithms; Nonvolatile memory

HPDC'16, May 31-June 04, 2016, Kyoto, Japan

© 2016 ACM. ISBN 978-1-4503-4314-5/16/05. . . $15.00

DOI: http://dx.doi.org/10.1145/2907294.2907316

1. INTRODUCTION

High performance storage is critical to achieving computational efficiency on high performance computing (HPC) systems. For over a decade, HPC has met this need by separating compute systems from parallel file systems (PFS) [25, 14, 32] that are built from an array of disks for both capacity and bandwidth. As the capacity growth of disks continues to outpace increases in their bandwidth, disks will meet capacity demands but fail to deliver bandwidth cost-effectively [12, 5]. Large HPC centers have begun to face this challenge by using solid-state burst buffers [23, 31], a new storage media that is cost-effective for bandwidth while not yet viable for capacity, between the compute nodes and the PFS. As HPC applications alternate between computationally dominant and I/O-dominant execution phases, the burst buffers can absorb their bursty I/O requests and turn them into a constant I/O stream, as seen by the PFS. This approach can not only offer better performance for the applications but also reduce the requisite PFS bandwidth. The PFS no longer needs to be provisioned for the worse-case scenario where multiple jobs happen to enter their I/O-dominant phases simultaneously. This trend is already apparent in recent leadership-class system procurements [1]. Next-generation systems will deliver 7 to 10× higher peak floating-point performance with only 1 to 2× higher PFS bandwidth compared to previous generation systems [18, 28]. The underprovisioning level is expected to increase, as system software technologies (e.g., smart checkpoint staging) will more effectively exploit the burst buffers. Similarly, a desire for global mounts (i.e., mounting all of the PFSes on all of the clusters) [33, 19] will increasingly split the already underprovisioned bandwidth across multiple clusters.

This paper targets next-generation HPC centers characterized by large-scale systems with burst buffers, reduced I/O network bandwidth, and underprovisioned PFS bandwidth. These characteristics require scheduling techniques that use I/O awareness to make informed decisions at the batch scheduling level and reduce PFS contention caused by over-allocated I/O resources. Unfortunately, the dynamicity and uncertainty of batch jobs (i.e., which jobs happen to be scheduled and burst into I/O phases) as well as the sheer scale of the largest centers have long made the definition of effective, yet scalable, I/O-aware scheduling a hard problem to solve. As a result, I/O awareness within batch schedulers in use for today's large centers remains largely rudimentary (e.g., Moab [2] can only hold dependent jobs when a file system is marked as being down). Our work tackles the I/O-aware scheduling problem within batch schedulers and complements existing work that manages the I/O contention problem by coordinating and optimizing the I/O performed at runtime [9, 34, 10, 36]. While these runtime techniques have shown promising results at maximizing the use of the PFS and minimizing I/O contention, they are ultimately constrained by the I/O requests of the specific running applications. If many I/O-intensive jobs are running concurrently, these runtime techniques are unable to prevent a slowdown of the applications. On the other hand, because we tackle I/O contention at batch job scheduling time, our work prevents applications' slowdown by ensuring that many I/O-intensive jobs are not run concurrently.

Our I/O-aware scheduling takes advantage of two emerging technologies for next-generation systems: (1) burst buffers and (2) center-wide resource management and job scheduling frameworks. The burst-buffer layer absorbs random I/O bursts and thus makes the bandwidth requirement of a job constant over its lifetime. A center-wide resource and job management framework enables schedulers to model the global I/O subsystem and view jobs beyond cluster boundaries, enabling global scheduling decisions for shared file systems. We integrate the knowledge of the I/O subsystem including burst buffers and I/O-aware algorithms directly into Flux [4], one of the few resource and job managers for next-generation centers. Exploiting a global view in Flux, however, comes with multidimensional scale challenges. Our hierarchical representation of the system must cope with unprecedented numbers of jobs and individual resources. By using a Flux emulator, this paper explores the effectiveness and costs of this large-scale constrained scheduling. Our exploration includes the degree of resource utilization under the I/O-aware scheduling as well as the computational costs of the scheduling itself, as it must consider both compute nodes and available bandwidth at every level of the I/O hierarchy. Specifically, the paper makes the following contributions:

- Modeling of the hierarchical nature of real-world I/O subsystems using a resource description language;

- Scheduling algorithms that integrate I/O awareness as a driving scheduling factor into one of the most popular scheduling policies (i.e., EASY backfilling);

- Exploration of the cost-effectiveness space of I/O-aware scheduling relative to the I/O-ignorant baselines.

Our results show that by reducing I/O contention for underprovisioned PFSes, our solution reduces job performance variability by 33% and decreases I/O-related utilization losses by 21% on a system underprovisioned by 30%. In addition, our solution offers these benefits over I/O-ignorant

scheduling policies with negligible scheduling cost, making deployment of our solution practical for next-generation environments.

The rest of this paper is organized as follows: Section 2 explains the need for I/O awareness; Section 3 presents our I/O subsystem model and I/O-aware scheduling algorithms; Section 4 describes the Flux emulator along with the system and workload models used in our tests; Section 5 presents the results of our tests and demonstrates the benefits of I/O-aware scheduling; Section 6 discusses related work; and Section 7 concludes this paper.

2. NEED FOR I/O AWARENESS

Due to the economics of flash vs. disk storage media, the HPC community has long predicted that flash-based burst buffers (BBs) must be included in the next-generation storage hierarchy, and recent high-end system procurements have attested to this prediction [1, 3, 23, 31, 24]. Initially, burst buffer enabled systems [3, 1] will still provision a reasonably high bandwidth PFS to ensure expedient draining of jobs' last checkpoints from the burst buffers to the PFS. This will allow a quick turnaround time even though, for simplicity, the system may require draining a job's burst buffers before scheduling the following job. Over time, smart staging, in conjunction with advancements in relevant system software, will remove this requirement. The system will stage the new job's data into the burst buffers while the previous job's last checkpoint is still being drained to the PFS, hiding the latency [21]. With the support of BB and smart staging, the PFS and the I/O links no longer need to be provisioned for worst-case scenarios (i.e., the I/O-dominant phases of many independent jobs overlap). Instead, the I/O links and the PFS will be provisioned to handle the average case (i.e., the average egress bandwidth of the burst buffers). Under this scenario, when multiple data-intensive applications run in concert on a cluster that has burst buffers and uses I/O-ignorant scheduling, the applications' cumulative average bandwidths can exceed the PFS bandwidth, causing I/O contention. In other words, the applications spend time blocking on I/O rather than performing computation.

With a significantly underprovisioned PFS, it will be crucial to avoid scheduling any combination of jobs that can create I/O contention at the lower storage levels. Fortunately, next-generation technologies present a practical opportunity to address this challenge at the batch job scheduling layer through I/O-aware scheduling.

3. I/O-AWARE JOB SCHEDULING

This section describes our approach. We begin with the enablers of our approach and progressively add core techniques until we can fully describe our methodology.

3.1 Constant Job-Lifetime I/O Bandwidth

Researchers have long observed that the common I/O patterns of HPC applications are bursty: they alternate between computationally dominant and I/O-dominant execution phases. Thus, the actual bandwidth used by a job during its lifetime is not a quantity that can easily be scheduled. Even if a batch system schedules jobs in accordance with their average bandwidth, the I/O dominant execution phases of these jobs can still often overlap, and utilization can oscillate widely, often exceeding the threshold. Burst buffers (BBs) naturally address this challenge: they turn the bursty I/O requests into a *constant* I/O stream. The BB layer absorbs applications' I/O bursts and the applications' I/O requests are then drained in the background into the parallel file system (PFS) from the BBs. As also proposed in [27], we assume that the BBs are placed either at the compute nodes (CNs) or on the same high-speed interconnect as the CNs, thus minimizing the probability of I/O contention occuring on resources in-between the CNs and the BBs. This architectural assumption allows us to focus our study on the I/O contention in-between the BBs and the PFS. In the rest of this paper, when we refer to I/O contention between the nodes and the PFS, we mean the CNs+BBs and the PFS.

The BB write-behind scheme is the first enabler for the design and implementation of practical I/O-aware scheduling. Batch job schedulers can use the draining rate of the BB as the overall bandwidth requirement of a job, a constant that machine learning algorithms trained on historical job records can provide. Work of McKenna and coworkers indicates that by using decision trees, we can predict, within 16MB, the I/O produced over the lifetime of a job, 80% of the time [26].

3.2 Global View

With a strong desire to mount a PFS to multiple clusters [33, 19], effective I/O-aware schemes also require a global view over all compute resources from which jobs can access the PFS. Without global knowledge, many jobs from multiple scheduler domains can request the shared resources concurrently, which precludes the scheduler from being able to manage bandwidth allocation reliably. Thus, practical schemes need advanced resource and job management software (RJMS) that can provide the scheduler with visibility into both jobs and resources across system boundaries. Fortunately, demand has grown to have an RJMS to schedule jobs at levels above these boundaries using hierarchical approaches. Flux [4] is among a few of the already available next-generation resource and job management software systems. Being developed at Lawrence Livermore National Laboratory (LLNL), Flux responds to the aforementioned need and presents an opportunity for our methodology to be developed.

3.3 I/O Subsystem Modeling

Using these enablers (i.e., burst buffers and Flux), we first model the full I/O subsystem including the BBs and I/O switches into the RJMS so that our scheduler can reason about key bandwidth constraints. We consider an I/O architecture based on an approach used by the Tri-Laboratory Linux Capacity Cluster (TLCC) [1]. A TLCC cluster is built on the notion of a scalable unit (SU). A large cluster can be built by scaling out and replicating SUs, each of which consists of a certain number of compute nodes, a few gateway nodes that can route I/O traffic to global parallel file system, and one or two login nodes. A multilevel system of switches connects nodes within a single SU and across SUs. For example, at LLNL, an SU is composed of 154 compute nodes, 6 gateway nodes, and 2 login nodes; one or multiple high level Infiniband switches connect multiple lower

---

[1]Tri-Laboratory refers to the NNSA's (National Nuclear Security Agency) three national laboratories: Livermore, Sandia, and Los Alamos National Laboratory.

level Infiniband switches. Figure 1 shows an example of a TLCC cluster containing 12 SUs with its low and high level switches.

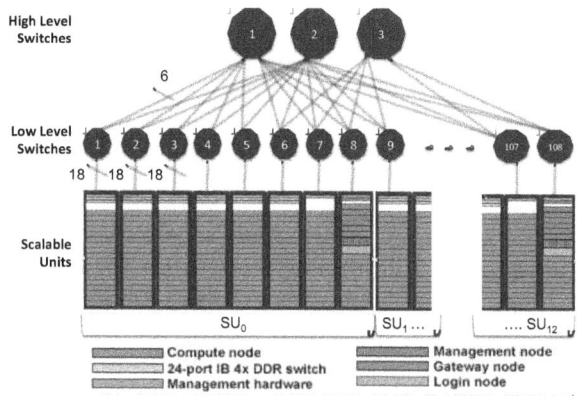

Figure 1: Example of 12 SU cluster with high and low level switches.

Any effective job scheduling is based on a rigorous but efficient model of the cluster resources and must include the resource relationships pertaining to the scheduler's capabilities. In the case of I/O-aware scheduling, a resource model must also capture the essential attributes of the I/O subsystem of clusters in addition to their compute resources (e.g., compute nodes and cores). We use the Resource Description Language (RDL) within Flux [4] to model the I/O subsystems as a hierarchy of network switches and gateway nodes leading to a parallel file system (PFS) and establish hierarchical relationships between them. Figure 2 shows a simple example of an RDL-based model with its compute nodes, each with a BB at the fringes of the hierarchy. Nodes are connected to their leaf switches before accessing the PFS through the gateway nodes (e.g., in the case of Lustre file system, LNET routers run across the gateway nodes). Since I/O traffic is routed round-robin across the high-level switches and the gateway nodes, we aggregate these resources into pools, where the BW of the pool is the sum of the individual resources' BWs. This model still matches well with the high-level architecture of a TLCC SU as shown in Figure 1, maintains a reasonable computational cost, and can easily be extended when multiple large clusters share a PFS.

When modeling how a job's I/O affects the I/O hierarchy and vice versa, we consider each level in the I/O hierarchy (i.e., PFS, switches, and compute nodes). When placing a job on the I/O hierarchy, BW is allocated at every level in the hierarchy. When modeling the impact of the I/O hierarchy on a job's I/O BW, we consider both the state of the I/O hierarchy and the job's position within the hierarchy using a contention model described in detail in Section 4.4. Figure 3 shows an example of I/O contention for the hierarchical resources considered in Figure 2 when two jobs with different BW requirements are executed. In Figure 3, Job1 runs on three nodes. Job1's required I/O rate is 192 MB/s per process, while the upper limit of the low level switches is only 256 MB/s (or 128 MB/s per child). If we assume that Job1's I/O pattern is highly synchronous, which is a dominant I/O pattern at HPC centers [23], Job1's overall I/O rate is limited to 128 MB/s, despite one of its processes

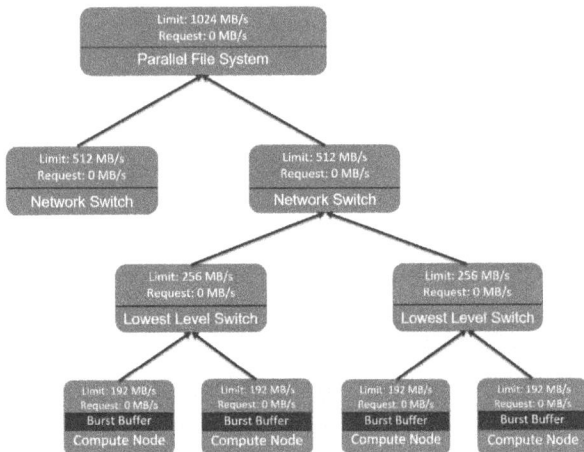

Figure 2: Example of an I/O-resource hierarchy in RDL.

having access to the full 192 MB/s. Job1 is over-utilizing bandwidth not only at the low level switches but at the higher level switches. If a new job, Job2 arrives and tries to use additional bandwidth, on the higher level switch, the job can further steal BW from Job1. Our tests inject job arrivals and their bandwidth requests into the models that represent real clusters at LLNL in a similar but larger scale than in the example presented above.

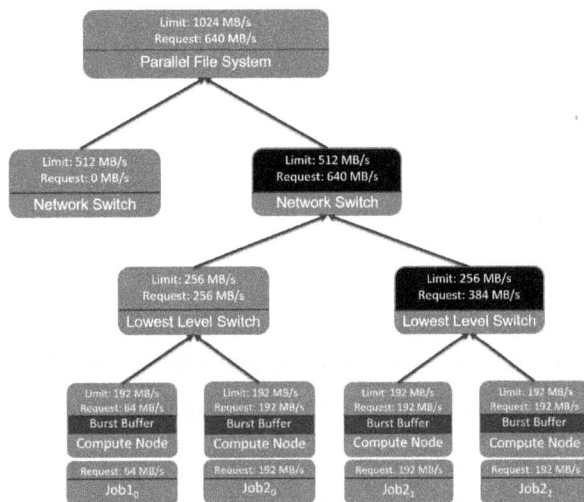

Figure 3: Example of I/O contention in action for our I/O-resource hierarchy.

3.4 Making a Scheduler I/O-Aware

We use our I/O subsystem and the integrated I/O contention model to extend popular batch job scheduling algorithms. We consider two existing scheduling policies: First-Come First-Served (FCFS) and EASY backfilling [22]. We select these policies because they represent algorithms with increasing complexity and expected efficiency in real resource managers [7]. The base scheduling schemes of the FCFS and EASY backfilling algorithms are currently without I/O awareness.

As part of the FCFS algorithm, jobs are scheduled in the order they are submitted. Thus, the algorithm may suffer

from head-of-line blocking, where a large job can delay every other job in the queue from running. The EASY backfill algorithm is similar to FCFS except that if a job at the front of the queue cannot be scheduled, lower priority jobs are scheduled on resources reserved for the highest priority job - as long as doing so does not delay the projected start time of the highest priority job. We assume that jobs are ordered in the queue based on their submission time. Under this assumption, both FCFS and EASY backfilling will not delay high bandwidth jobs infinitely (i.e., starve). The problem of job starvation associated to different job sorting (e.g., priority-based) is addressed elsewhere [17].

Defining a scheduler as I/O-aware means that the I/O is used as an additional constraint when determining if a job can be scheduled. The I/O subsystem described in Section 3.3 allows us to add I/O awareness to the two schedulers. This additional I/O constraint means that if scheduling a job over-allocates any of the I/O resources available, the job should not be scheduled even though compute resources are idle. Our I/O-aware schedulers keep track of over-allocations by updating the state of the I/O model based on each job's I/O BW requirements and make scheduling decisions accordingly. Scenarios like the one in Figure 3 should never occur on a system that relies on our I/O aware scheduler.

To add I/O awareness to either of the two scheduling algorithms (i.e., FCFS and EASY backfilling), we extend the scheduler to consider both available compute nodes and the I/O BW available to the nodes themselves. Consequently, our I/O-aware scheduler assigns a job to a node only when the available BW at each level in the I/O switch hierarchy, from the PFS to the node itself, meets the BW requirements. For example, let's assume we have an empty system similar to the one modeled in Figure 2 and two jobs to be scheduled (i.e., Job 1 and Job 2 with Job 1 at the head of the queue). Job 1 only requires a single node and 64 MB/s of BW, and Job 2 requires three nodes, with each node requiring 128 MB/s of BW. The scheduler starts with Job 1 and attempts to schedule the job on Node 1. The scheduler also checks the feasibility of the job by ensuring that the node is free and that 64 MB/s of BW are available at Node 1 and Node 1's ancestors (i.e., Lowest Level Switch 1, Network Switch 2, and the PFS). Since there is enough bandwidth, Job 1 is scheduled on Node 1 and the BW is allocated at Node 1 and at all of the ancestors. The scheduler then attempts to schedule Job 2. The same process applied to Node 1 is repeated for Nodes 2 and 3, but this time, the scheduler must ensure that 128 MB/s are available. If both feasibility checks succeed, Nodes 2 and 3 are reserved for Job 2. Finally, the scheduler attempts to reserve Node 4 for Job 2. Node 4 is available, but there is not enough available BW at Lowest Level Switch 2 or Network Switch 2. Thus, the scheduler does not reserve Node 4 for Job 2. Because the scheduler now has no nodes left to consider in order to satisfy Job 2's requirements, it deems Job 2 unschedulable with the current state of the entire system and releases the reservations on Nodes 2 and 3. Figure 3 demonstrates the overallocation thats occur if Job 2 is scheduled. This does not mean that Job 2 cannot run; once Job 1 finishes, the scheduler is be able to schedule Job 2. If a job's requirement are not satisfiable even on an empty system, the job is deemed unsatisfiable and an error is returned to the user when they submit the job.

4. EVALUATION METHODOLOGY

This section describes our evaluation methodology including the modeling of an expected large next-generation system and of job workloads, as well as our metrics.

4.1 A Large Next-Gen. System Model

We test our approach against the model of a large, realistic system. We construct such a model by analyzing the request for proposal (RFP) for next-generation systems. Specifically, we build the node and I/O components of our modeled system after a large system that will be built as part of the Commodity Technology System 1 procurement (CTS-1) [20]. The CTS-1 cluster model consists of 3,888 compute nodes (24 SUs); 216 GB/s per edge IB switch (i.e., 4x EDR 36-port switch); and a 70 GB/s parallel file system (PFS) with perfect provisioning [2] as well as 432 GB/s core switch pool (i.e., the bandwidth available in routing I/O requests to the LNET routers). We assume that no significant I/O contention occurs when applications write to the burst-buffer (BB), which requires that the BB is either located at the compute node or close enough such that the probability of contention is minimal, as discussed in Section 3.3.

We define the bandwidths for the edge switch and core switch pool based on the requirements in the draft RFP and the latest IB technologies [20]. The bandwidth of the PFS is determined based on the checkpointing patterns captured in the CORAL RFP [1], as CTS-1 does not capture these requirements in the presence of the burst buffers. We assume that applications need to be able to write a checkpoint every hour with a per-node checkpoint size of 1/2 of the available node memory. We use the same frequency and size for the checkpointing on CTS-1 whose nodes are each assumed to have 128GB of memory. With this setting, a CTS-1 node will need to checkpoint at least 64GB/hour with an average I/O bandwidth of $\sim$18MB/s per compute node and $\sim$70GB/s for the entire system (i.e., 18MB/s $\times$ 3,888 nodes). We model the BW of the PFS either as perfectly provisioned (i.e., perfectly matching the applications' requirements) or as underprovisioned (i.e., less than the applications' requirements), as further described in Section 5.1.

4.2 Workload Model

As CTS-1 does not exist yet, we extrapolate the job traces from two other clusters at LLNL: the 1,200 compute-node Cab and the 2,740 compute-node Zin. We feed the same traces to both the I/O-aware and I/O-ignorant versions of our tests. We statistically generate the profiles of job workloads in terms of job submission times/rate, job request size per node, requested time limit and elapsed times by using real traces from LLNL's current resource and job management system: Slurm (cluster resource manager) and Moab (scheduler).

At LLNL, jobs are submitted to Moab which stores the submission times and queues the jobs up until they are ready to launch. When a set of jobs are ready to be executed, Moab sends these jobs to Slurm which then launches them on its cluster. Since Slurm only receives jobs when they are ready to launch, only Moab has the correct submit time in its database. Slurm records the start and end times of the jobs but does not return these times back to Moab. The

net effect is that an individual database does not contain all of the needed information, and thus we relate the two data sets. Because these data sets do not have common unique identifiers, we relate them by generating statistical patterns from the two sets of data and then merge these statistics to get a holistic view of the data.

From these statistics, we derive representative job workloads for our tests. Specifically, we model the *arrival rates of jobs* as random events by using a Poisson distribution. There are two assumptions underlying the use of the Poisson distribution: the event occurrences are all independent and the events occur at a constant, average rate. Previous work by Dinh *et al.* [8] shows, however, that it is inaccurate to model job submission times directly as they are not independent events: a single user normally submits multiple jobs at the same time. Instead, we use a method proposed by Dinh *et al.*: modeling "user arrivals." In the existing traces, we find all the instances where a user submitted many jobs in quick succession (i.e., less than 10 seconds between each job) and bundle those job submissions up into one "user arrival." We also build a distribution that models the number of jobs that a user is expected to submit when they arrive. This binning into "user arrivals" makes our I/O profiles satisfy the independence assumption of Poisson distributions. However, this approach can still violate the constant, average rate assumption. It is well-known that user arrival is more common during the day on a weekday than at night on a weekend. To satisfy the constant, average rate requirement, we extend the previous work done by Dinh *et al.* as follows. We break the job data into four ranges: weekday day from 6:00am to 6:59pm; weekday night from 7:00pm to 5:59am; weekend day from 6:00am to 6:59pm; and weekend night from 7:00pm to 5:59am. These four ranges represent periods of time where the user arrivals are mostly constant. By chunking our data into these four ranges, we now satisfy the constant, average rate requirement of Poisson distributions as well. We record the lambda value for user arrival in each time range and build a Poisson distribution for each range.

We model the *job request size* in terms of the number of nodes requested by each job. These values are recorded by both Moab and Slurm, so either data set is sufficient. The analysis of the distribution of node request sizes shows a rapidly decreasing function that is heavily biased towards smaller sizes requests. We also notice that request sizes are biased towards powers-of-two values. To model the population distribution of node request sizes both accurately and automatically, we use a sampling distribution. We bin the data where the size of each bin is a monotonically increasing power of two and then record the number of jobs in each bin — much like a histogram. We then build a sampling distribution from these values.

We model the *time limit* and *elapsed time* in terms of the wall-time requested for a job and the job's actual execution time. These values are taken from the Slurm data set since it contains the execution time information. There is a correlation between the amount of time requested by the user and how long the job ran (i.e., elapsed time). Thus, instead of modeling the values separately, we model them together. We again build a sampling distribution of these values by collecting all of the unique tuples of the form (time limit, elapsed time) and counting the frequency at which they oc-

---

[2]We expect that the initial PFS BW provisioning of such a system will be much larger because not all needed system software including smart staging will have matured [21].

cur. From these frequencies, we calculate the probability density function for time limit and elapsed time.

Finally, we build our I/O workloads by sampling values from the aforementioned distributions. Jobs (i.e., the smallest unit of input for our tests) consist of the following information: (1) a monotonically increasing identifier starting from one; (2) the number of nodes requested by the user generating the job; (3) the number of cores requested by the user generating the job; (4) the time limit (i.e., how much time is requested by the user) sampled from the sampling distribution that is generated using the Slurm data; (5) submit time (i.e., when is the job submitted) sampled from the appropriate Poisson distribution (i.e., from weekday day, weekday night, weekend day, or weekend night traces); (6) elapsed time sampled simultaneously with time limit from the sampling distribution that is generated using the Slurm data; and (7) an average I/O Rate of 18MB/s per node in the job. We use 18MB/s as the average I/O rate per node under the assumption that all jobs will follow the checkpointing pattern outlined in Subsection 4.1. This means that the total I/O rate of a job is correlated with the number of nodes in the job. For future work, we are investigating the effects of a more diverse mix of job I/O rates.

4.3 Emulation Environment

To test our approach without having to launch real jobs, we developed a scheduling emulator within Flux. Figure 4.a depicts Flux in real use. Users submit jobs to the scheduler which launches them based on a defined scheduling policy. Our emulation mode entirely removes any user interaction and replaces it with an auto-submission module as shown in Figure 4.b. Moreover, the emulator does not rely on the direct execution of jobs but on the simulation of their execution. It can use the Slurm database of submitted jobs to generate the profile of simulated job executions. As real time is too slow for the testing, the emulator triggers events synthetically by extending Flux as shown in Figure 4.b. By using the emulator, we can rapidly study critical questions associated with the scheduler.

For the schedulers themselves, we take an incremental approach in implementing them into the Flux emulator for a fair comparison. We start with the simple FCFS scheduler and extend it to support EASY backfill scheduling. We adapt these schedulers to become I/O-aware by adding I/O as an additional constraint when determining if a job can be scheduled and executed. To this end, our adapted scheduler allocates and deallocates I/O bandwidth within the I/O hierarchy to work correctly within the I/O-aware emulator. When adding I/O to schedulers that use a priority function, we include the I/O requirements of a job in the scheduler's priority function.

4.4 Contention Model

To quantify the effect of I/O contention, we model the contention and calculate the slowdown that applications experience when running on an over-allocated PFS.

We first model the contention that occurs at every resource within the I/O hierarchy (i.e., nodes, switches, and PFS). For each resource, we consider the amount of I/O BW that is being requested by its children in the hierarchy. The child requests ($ReqBW$) are sorted based on their BW size from least to greatest (i.e., given n children, $ReqBW_i \leq ReqBW_{i+1}$, for each $0 \leq i < n-1$). We calcu-

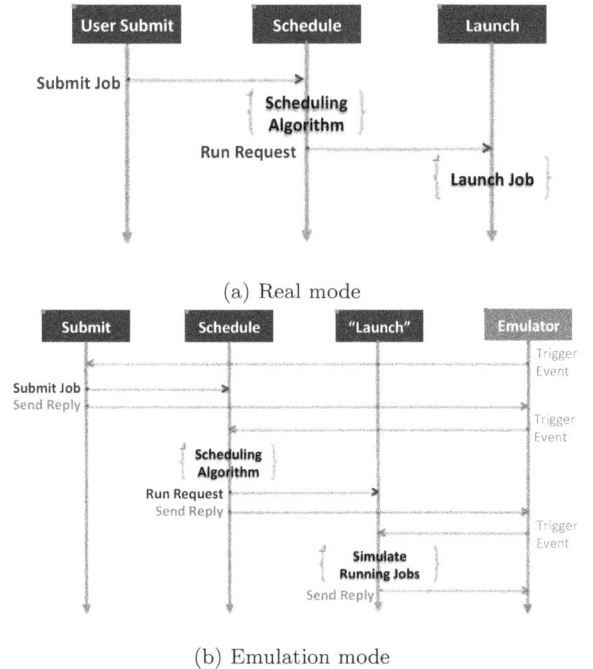

(a) Real mode

(b) Emulation mode

Figure 4: Flux in real vs. emulation mode.

late the actual bandwidth that each child receives as:

$$ActualBW_i = min(ReqBW_i, AvgRemainingBW_i)$$

where $AvgRemainingBW_i$ is a function of the parent's peak BW ($PeakBW$) and is defined as:

$$AvgRemainingBW_i := \frac{PeakBW - \sum_{j=0}^{i-1} ActualBW_i}{n-i}$$

Two cases can be observed. First, the sum of the requests BWs is smaller than the available. Thus, all children get their requested BW and any extra BW remains at the parent. Second, the sum of the requests BWs is greater than the available. Thus, the smaller requests are completely satisfied but for larger requests the remaining BW is distributed equally. Contention only occurs in the second case. In our contention model, we assume that the number of children and the degree of overallocation has no effect on the aggregate bandwidth. In reality, the aggregate bandwidth of a resource decreases w.r.t. the number of children and degree of overallocation due to increased cache thrashing, extra seeks at the PFS, and additional dropped packets. Our assumption is still valid for our tests because it minimizes the effects of contention, which is expected to occur only under I/O-ignorant scheduling. Thus, we do not introduce any positive bias towards our I/O-aware scheduling.

Each job comes with a required BW ($JobActualBW$) but receives an actual BW ($JobActualBW$). The actual job BW is the minimum of the actual BW of the resource the job is running on. We use the interference factor (I) as defined in [9] to determine the time an application spends performing computation or blocking on I/O, where the interference factor is defined as:

$$I = \begin{cases} 1, & \text{if } JobActualBW = JobReqBW \\ \frac{JobActualBW}{JobReqBW}, & \text{otherwise} \end{cases}$$

When a job's actual BW equals its requested BW, I is equal to one; otherwise, the job experiences contention and I ranges between zero and one. As the jobs running on the system change, the interference factor for each job also changes; we discretize time into intervals (Δ_i), during which each job's interference factor (I_i) can be considered constant. The time an application spends performing computation is defined by:

$$T(computing) = \sum_i (I_i \times \Delta_i) \qquad (1)$$

and the time an application spends blocking on I/O is defined by:

$$T(I/O) = \sum_i (\Delta_i - (I_i \times \Delta_i))$$
$$= (\sum_i \Delta_i) - T(computing)$$

Under our model, jobs under I/O contention ($I < 1$) perform less computations than jobs not suffering from contention ($I = 1$) in the same period of time. For our tests in Section 5.1, we observe that the percentage of time that the interference factor is less than one ranges between 55% and 65% for underprovisioned PFSes with an I/O-ignorant scheduler; the percentage of time is 0% in the other cases.

5. RESULTS

In this section we provide empirical evidence that I/O-aware scheduling can increase the PFS efficiency and reduce job performance variability due to I/O contention.

5.1 Critical Questions and Test Settings

We address four critical questions: (1) Does I/O-aware scheduling impact the percentage of time that nodes spend in computation? (2) Does I/O-aware scheduling impact the variability of each individual job's performance? (3) Does I/O-aware scheduling affect the time to make a scheduling decision? and (4) What is the trade-off between system efficiency and turnaround time when comparing I/O-ignorant with I/O-aware schedulers? To answer these questions, we run tests with an EASY Backfilling scheduler on CTS-1 using four levels of PFS underprovisioning: no underprovisioning or 0% (70GB/s), an underprovisioning of 10% (63GB/s), an underprovisioning of 20% (56GB/s), and an underprovisioning of 30% (49GB/s). The sets of tests with the FCFS schedulers displayed similar trends as the EASY backfilling scheduler and thus are not shown in this section. Each test consists of 2500 jobs built from the workload model described in Section 4.2 and executed with the Flux emulator using the model of CTS-1 described in Section 4.1. For our tests, we assume that there are no external sources of I/O outside the control of the scheduler (e.g., interactive users). However if the system does have external sources of I/O, our scheduler can still work by reserving a fraction of the parallel filesystem (PFS) bandwidth (BW) for these external sources of I/O. Our results can support system administrators in deciding how much BW to reserve for these external sources. For example, a system with a perfectly provisioned PFS that reserves 30% of the PFS BW for extraneous I/O will produce the same results as a system with a PFS that has been underprovisioned by 30% and does not have extra-

neous sources of I/O, which is one of the scenarios that we show in our results.

5.2 Impact on Total Performance

To assess whether I/O-aware scheduling impacts the percentage of time that nodes spend in computation, we measure the total time that allocated nodes spend performing computation versus blocking on I/O. Figure 5.a refers to the set of tests in which the I/O-ignorant scheduler is used; Figure 5.b refers to the tests where the I/O-aware scheduler is used. For each level of underprovisioning, the figures report the percentage of time that nodes spend in computing (i.e., the blue bar) and in blocking on I/O (i.e., the red bar). As shown in Figure 5.a, under I/O-ignorant scheduling, nodes spend 100% of the jobs' time in computation only if the PFS is perfectly provisioned. However, as the PFS bandwidth decreases due to underprovisioning, the percentage of time allocated to computation also decreases. This is due to the fact that the reduced PFS bandwidth increases the probability that I/O contention occurs. For example, when the PFS is underprovisioned by 30%, only 79.1% of the nodes are executing jobs' computations; the rest are blocking on I/O. On the other hand, Figure 5.b shows that regardless of the PFS underprovisioning, I/O-aware scheduling keeps the nodes in computation 100% of the time. This is because jobs are scheduled only when sufficient resources (both CPU and I/O) are available. These results support the need for I/O-aware scheduling in order to prevent I/O contention when data-intensive jobs are simultaneously run on an underprovisioned PFS.

5.3 Impact on Individual Job Performance

To assess the impact of the I/O-aware scheduling on each individual job's runtime, we measure the performance variability of jobs launched on the model of CTS-1 under I/O-ignorant and I/O-aware EASY backfilling scheduling. Performance variability is measured as the percentage of time spent by each individual job doing computations versus blocking on I/O. In Figure 6, we present the variability of the 2500 jobs run under the four different levels of PFS underprovisioning (i.e., 0%, 10%, 20%, and 30%). Under I/O-ignorant scheduling in Figure 6.a, we observed that only when the PFS is perfectly provisioned do the jobs not exhibit any variability in performance. As the degree of PFS underprovisioning increases, the variability of job performance also increases. For example, when the PFS is underprovisioned by 30%, the amount of time that individual jobs spend in computation ranges from 66.7% to 100%. On the other hand, in Figure 6.b we do not observe any performance variability under I/O-aware scheduling. The conclusions are twofold. First, we observe that under an I/O-ignorant scheduling, there is no guarantee on job performance and each job's performance varies wildly. In contrast, under an I/O-aware scheduling, every job is guaranteed to receive the required I/O, thus resulting in no variability. Second, as the PFS is being increasingly underprovisioned, individual jobs' performance variability grows larger under I/O-ignorant scheduling but remains zero under I/O-aware scheduling. This consistency under I/O-aware scheduling means that users fully receive the requested resources and thus their jobs are not unexpectedly slowed down by other jobs on the system. In other words, I/O-aware scheduling

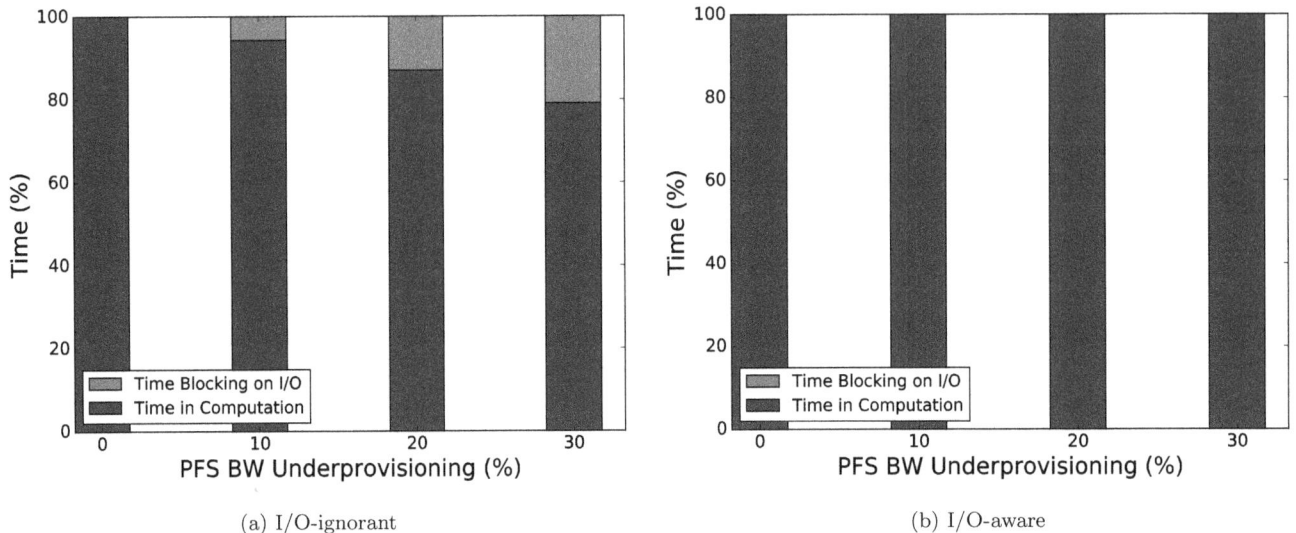

(a) I/O-ignorant   (b) I/O-aware

Figure 5: Percentage of total time spent by the entire CTS-1 cluster in computation and blocking on I/O.

resolves the variability in job performance due to I/O contention.

5.4   Impact on Scheduling Decision Time

The benefits of I/O-aware scheduling do not come without a cost. The additional checking that the I/O-aware scheduler performs when deciding which jobs to place on the system increases the time to make a scheduling decision versus an I/O-ignorant scheduler. The scheduling decision time is the number of seconds between when a job state change occurs and when the scheduler makes a decision based on that state change. Intuitively, a more computationally-expensive scheduling algorithm, such as our I/O-aware scheduling, can cause a longer scheduling decision time. The decision time of a scheduler becomes a major concern when it is longer than the time between state changes. In the job workloads described in Section 4.2 and used for our tests, the average time between state changes is 31.7 seconds.

Figures 7.a and 7.b summarize the observed additional cost in terms of the scheduler's decision time (in seconds) for EASY backfilling running on the emulated model of CTS-1 under the four different underprovisioning levels with I/O-ignorant and I/O-aware schedulers respectively. The number of sampled times in each scenario is on average 9,580 (roughly four times the number of jobs). This is expected since there are four state transitions that each job goes through, and each state transition causes the scheduler to run. Jobs that transition states together cause only one single invocation of the scheduler and are counted as a single sample time.

In Figures 7.a and 7.b, we represent the sampled times with box plots. Traditionally a box plot consists of six different pieces of information. The whiskers on the bottom extend from the 5th percentile to the top 95th percentile. The top, bottom, and line through the middle of the box correspond to the 75th percentile (top), 25th percentile (bottom), and 50th percentile (middle). A square indicates the arithmetic mean. Due to the distribution of the times in our tests, only the 75th and 95th percentiles are visible. With I/O-ignorant scheduling, 75% of the decision times are be-

low 0.07 seconds and the 95th percentile times are ∼1.43 seconds. With I/O-aware scheduling, 75% of the decision times are below 0.12 seconds and the 95th percentile times range between 1.97 and 6.64 seconds.

The critical comparison of Figures 7.a and 7.b outlines the following three trends. First, when we consider the lowest 75% of the decision times for I/O-ignorant and I/O-aware scheduling, scheduler decision times differ by at most 0.04 seconds. Second, the variability of the decision times under I/O-ignorant scheduling remains constant irrespective of PFS BW underprovisioning. This is not the case for I/O-aware scheduling, for which we observed that the variability of the largest 25% decision times increases when the PFS is underprovisioned. Third, for both schedulers, the 95th percentile decision time is still shorter than the average time between state changes, which is on the order of 10s of seconds.

Preliminary analysis of the longest 25% of decision times under both schedulers suggests that these times occur after the completion of a job with either large compute or I/O requirements followed by the scheduling of many smaller jobs. The fact that I/O-aware scheduling with an underprovisioned PFS exhibits larger variability indicates that the problem is exacerbated by the additional I/O constraints. The additional variability can potentially be alleviated with the introduction of new mechanisms such as caching, preemptive scheduling, and hierarchical scheduling [13].

5.5   System Efficiency vs. Turnaround Time

Users running applications want a system that maximizes the total useful computation performed on the allocated nodes (system efficiency) and minimizes the time between when a job is submitted and when the job completes (turnaround time). The turnaround time is the time the job spends in the scheduler's queue plus the time the job spends in execution. To ensure that jobs obtain their required I/O bandwidth, the I/O-aware scheduler may delay the execution of some jobs until more I/O resources become available. In other words, jobs obtain the exactly required resources, achieving 100% system efficiency, in exchange for a poten-

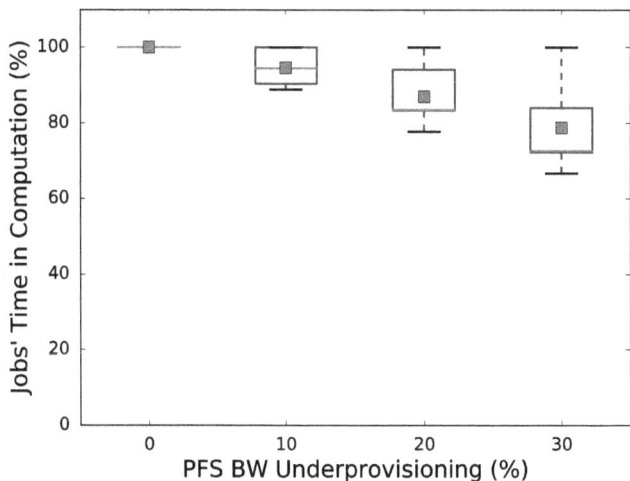

(a) I/O-ignorant

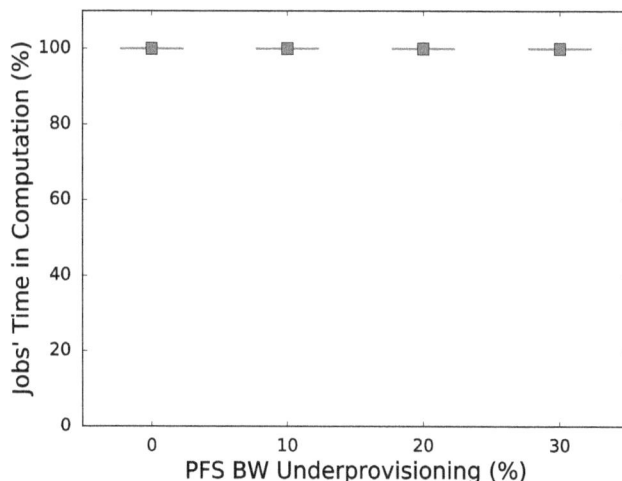

(b) I/O-aware

Figure 6: Variability of individual jobs' time spent in computation.

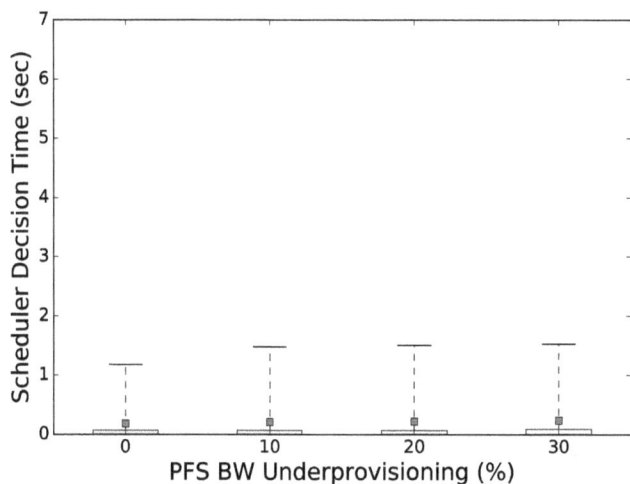

(a) I/O-ignorant

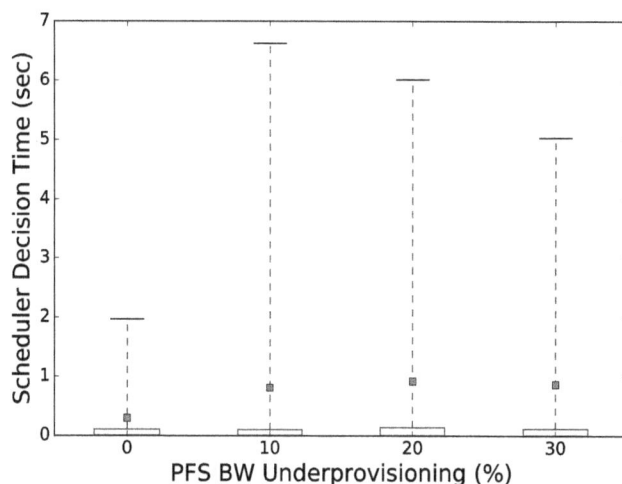

(b) I/O-aware

Figure 7: Scheduler decision time distributions.

tially longer time in the queue and consequently, a longer turnaround time. To quantify this trade-off, we measure the lower-bound ratio of I/O-aware system efficiency over I/O-ignorant system efficiency as well as the upper-bound ratio of I/O-aware turnaround time over I/O-ignorant turnaround time for the same CTS-1 tests as in Figures 5-7 when using EASY backfilling scheduling. For the system efficiency ratio, the higher, the better for I/O-aware scheduling; for the turnaround time ratio, the lower, the better for I/O-aware scheduling. The ratio of system efficiencies is defined as a lower-bound since we expect this ratio to be higher in real systems. This is because the contention model that we use for our tests is quite conservative and underpenalizes I/O contention, which only occurs in I/O-ignorant simulations, as we discussed in Section 4.4. A greater penalty on contention can further reduce the overall system efficiency under I/O-ignorant scheduling and consequently increase the

system efficiency ratio. On the other hand, the turnaround time ratio is an upper-bound since we expect this ratio to be lower in real systems. This is because in real workloads we can observe a greater diversity in job I/O requirements; this diversity allows the I/O-aware scheduler to fill idle nodes with jobs that have a low I/O requirement, decreasing the turnaround time of jobs under I/O-aware scheduling, and consequently decreasing the ratio.

In Figure 8, we observe how in a perfectly provisioned PFS, I/O-ignorant and I/O-aware scheduling have the same system efficiency and turnaround time (i.e., the ratios are equal to one). As the level of PFS underprovisioning increases, the ratios increase. For example, in our tests we observed that at 30% underprovisioning, I/O-aware scheduling has, on average, a 1.29 times greater lower-bound system efficiency ratio and a 1.52 times greater upper-bound turnaround time ratio. This means that for real-world workloads, the system under I/O-aware scheduling can perform at least 29% more science (lower bound) as the nodes are fully utilized for computation but, at the same time, the turnaround time can be up to 52% longer (upper bound). These observations support our claim that I/O-aware scheduling boosts the amount of science performed by scientific workloads despite a longer turnaround time.

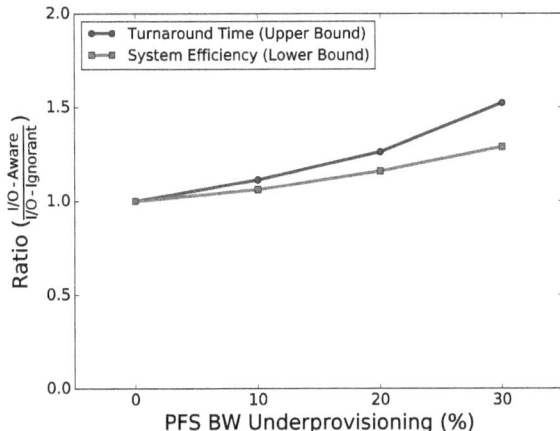

Figure 8: System efficiency versus job turnaround time.

6. RELATED WORK

I/O-aware scheduling is still in its infancy. First efforts have extended existing scheduling policies by using heuristics in application-specific domains. For example, the extended FCFS scheduling in [11] integrates heuristics to deal with irregular I/O-intensive jobs. The heuristics search for I/O parameter values among the parameter ranges using testing. The work builds upon and extends previous work [6]. In this paper, we move away from individual heuristics and applications.

More recent efforts on runtime scheduling of I/O contention include [35, 10, 9, 36]. Specifically, work in [35] addresses I/O contention with a PFS access controller: the controller provides a single application exclusive access to the PFS for a time window. Work in [9] analyzes the I/O contention between two applications and investigates the use of runtime application coordination in order to avoid congestion. Work in [10] analyzes the impact of congestion on applications' I/O bandwidth and assesses a variety of runtime techniques designed to either maximize system efficiency or minimize application slowdown. Finally, work in [36] presents an I/O-aware scheduling framework that coordinates I/O requests at runtime on petascale computing systems driven by either user-oriented metrics or system performance. Our work aligns with and complements these four runtime methods by targeting next-generation large-scale systems and defining a method that operates at batch schedule time to mitigate I/O contention.

IBM defines network-aware scheduling within their production resource manager and scheduler [15]. Our I/O-aware scheduling can directly apply to network-aware scheduling by extending our I/O subsystem resource model to include the full switch hierarchy and making schedulers consider the network bandwidth requirement of a parallel or distributed application.

When looking at resource allocations in a broader spectrum of systems, including grid and batch systems, many do not target I/O bandwidth as constraints, although they have begun to consider increasingly diverse resource types beyond compute nodes and cores. For example, work in [16] deals with multiple resource scheduling (MRS) algorithms aiming for the minimal execution schedule through efficient management of available grid resources (i.e., memory, disk and CPUs of a wide area distributed computing platform).

Finally, dynamic scheduling work such as [29, 30] can complete our approach by enabling the extension of our solutions to more traditional systems without burst buffers. Dynamic scheduling extends a batch system with dynamic allocation facilities to support on-the-fly resource allocation to elastic jobs; although dynamic scheduling does not currently target any non-traditional constraints, including I/O bandwidth.

7. CONCLUSIONS

The economics of flash vs. disk storage is increasingly motivating large HPC centers to underprovision parallel file system bandwidth. With such underprovisioned parallel file systems (PFSes), avoiding an I/O storm at the PFS level is critical to achieving computational efficiency and to avoiding any disruption of the entire HPC center.

In this paper we present a novel solution that allows us to meet these challenges at the batch job scheduler layer. Our technique reduces I/O contention by incorporating I/O-awareness directly into scheduling policies such as FCFS and EASY backfilling. We model the links between all levels in the storage hierarchy and use this model at schedule time to avoid I/O contention.

We explore the effectiveness and scalability of our method using schedulers and an emulator built on top of the Flux resource and job management framework. We show that I/O-aware scheduling eliminates all I/O contention on the system, regardless of the level of underprovisioning. In addition, it ensures that all jobs receive the I/O bandwidth they require. Furthermore, we observed that our solution reduces job performance variability by up to 33% and increases system utilization by up to 21%.

Our results suggest that I/O-aware scheduling can scale to handle the next-generation of HPC systems and ultimately improve the amount of science performed on these systems.

8. ACKNOWLEDGMENTS

The authors thank Jay Lofstead for his insights and feedback during the review process. Prepared by LLNL under Contract DE-AC52-07NA27344 (LLNL-CONF-679271). The UD authors acknowledge the support of NSF grants CCF-1318445/1318417.

9. REFERENCES

[1] CORAL. Retrieved Jan 3, 2015 from https://asc.llnl.gov/CORAL/.
[2] The Moab workload manager. http://www.adaptivecomputing.com/resources/docs/mwm/help.htm#topics/0-intro/productOverview.htm. Retrieved Jan 3, 2015.

[3] Trinity and NERSC-8 Computing Platforms Draft Technical Requirements. Retrieved Jan 3, 2015 from http://www.lanl.gov/business/vendors/_assets/docs/Trinity-NERSC-8-DRAFT-technical-requirements.pdf.

[4] D. H. Ahn, J. Garlick, M. Grondona, D. Lipari, B. Springmeyer, and M. Schulz. Flux: A Next-Generation Resource Management Framework for Large HPC Centers. In *Proc. of the 10th International Workshop on Scheduling and Resource Management for Parallel and Distributed System (SRMPDS)*, Sep. 2014.

[5] J. Bent, S. Faibish, J. Ahrens, G. Grider, J. Patchett, P. Tzelnic, and J. Woodring. Jitter-free Co-Processing on a Prototype Exascale Storage Stack. In *Proc. of 2012 IEEE 28th Symposium on Mass Storage Systems and Technologies (MSST)*, April 2012.

[6] M. Beynon, R. Ferreira, T. Kurc, A. Sussman, and J. Saltz. DataCutter: Middleware for Filtering Very Large Scientific Datasets on Archival Storage System. In *Proc. of the 2000 Mass Storage Conference*, March 2000.

[7] A. Chandio, C.-Z. Xu, N. Tziritas, K. Bilal, and S. Khan. A Comparative Study of Job Scheduling Strategies in Large-Scale Parallel Computational Systems. In *Proc. of the 2013 12th IEEE International Conference on Trust, Security and Privacy in Computing and Communications (TrustCom)*, July 2013.

[8] T. Dinh, L. Andrew, and P. Branch. Exploiting per User Information for Supercomputing Workload Prediction Requires Care. In *Proc. of the 2013 13th IEEE/ACM International Symposium on Cluster, Cloud and Grid Computing (CCGrid)*, May 2013.

[9] M. Dorier, G. Antoniu, R. Ross, D. Kimpe, and S. Ibrahim. CALCioM: Mitigating I/O Interference in HPC Systems Through Cross-Application Coordination. In *Proc. of the 2014 IEEE 28th International Parallel and Distributed Processing Symposium (IPDPS)*, May 2014.

[10] A. Gainaru, G. Aupy, A. Benoit, F. Cappello, Y. Robert, and M. Snir. Scheduling the I/O of HPC Applications Under Congestion. In *Proc. of the 2015 29th IEEE International Parallel and Distributed Processing Symposium (IPDPS)*, May 2015.

[11] L. F. Goes, P. Guerra, B. Coutinho, L. Rocha, W. Meira, R. Ferreira, D. Guedes, and W. Cirne. AnthillSched: A Scheduling Strategy for Irregular and Iterative I/O-Intensive Parallel Jobs. In *Job Scheduling Strategies for Parallel Processing*, volume 3834 of *Lecture Notes in Computer Science*, pages 108–122. Springer Berlin Heidelberg, 2005.

[12] G. Grider. Speed Matching and What Economics Will Allow. In *HEC FSIO Research and Development Workshop*, August 2010.

[13] S. Herbein, D. H. Ahn, and M. Taufer. Poster: Exploring the Trade-Off Space of Hierarchical Scheduling for Very Large HPC Centers. In *Proc, of the 27th ACM/IEEE International Conference for High Performance Computing and Communications Conference (SC)*, November 2015.

[14] IBM. General Parallel File System. http://www-03.ibm.com/software/products/en/software. Retrieved 10 Nov, 2015.

[15] IBM. Network-aware scheduling. https://www-01.ibm.com/support/knowledgecenter/#!/SSETD4_9.1.2/lsf_admin/pe_network_aware_sched.dita. Retrieved 12 Nov, 2015.

[16] B. B. Khoo, B. Veeravalli, T. Hung, and C. S. See. A Multi-dimensional Scheduling Scheme in a Grid Computing Environment. *Journal of Parallel and Distributed Computing*, 67(6):659 – 673, 2007.

[17] D. Klusáček and Š. Tóth. On Interactions among Scheduling Policies: Finding Efficient Queue Setup Using High-Resolution Simulations. In *Proc. of the 2014 20th International Euro-Par Conference on Parallel Processing*, August 2014.

[18] Lawrence Livermore National Laboratory. Advanced Simulation and Computing Sequoia. https://asc.llnl.gov/computing_resources/sequoia. Retrieved 16 May, 2015.

[19] Lawrence Livermore National Laboratory. Linux @ Livermore. https://computing.llnl.gov/linux/projects.html. Retrieved 10 Nov, 2015.

[20] Lawrence Livermore National Laboratory. Tri-Laboratory Commodity Technology System 1. https://asc.llnl.gov/computers/cts1-rfp. Retrieved 11 Nov, 2015.

[21] Lawrence Livermore National Laboratory. Trinity / NERSC-8 Use Case Scenarios. https://www.nersc.gov/assets/Trinity--NERSC-8-RFP/Documents/trinity-NERSC8-use-case-v1.2a.pdf. Retrieved 10 Nov, 2015.

[22] D. A. Lifka. The ANL/IBM SP Scheduling System. In *Proc. of the Workshop on Job Scheduling Strategies for Parallel Processing (IPPS)*, May 1995.

[23] N. Liu, J. Cope, P. Carns, C. Carothers, R. Ross, G. Grider, A. Crume, and C. Maltzahn. On the Role of Burst Buffers in Leadership-class Storage Systems. In *Proc. of the 2012 IEEE Conference on Massive Data Storage (MDS)*, Apr. 2012.

[24] J. Lofstead, I. Jimenez, and C. Maltzahn. Consistency and Fault Tolerance Considerations for the Next Iteration of the DOE Fast Forward Storage and IO Project. In *Proc. of the 6th Workshop on Interfaces and Architectures for Scientific Data Storage (IASDS)*, Sep. 2014.

[25] Lustre. Lustre. http://lustre.org. Retrieved 10 Nov, 2015.

[26] R. Mckenna, T. Gamblin, A. Moody, and M. Taufer. Poster: Forecasting Storms in Parallel File Systems. In *Proc, of the 27th ACM/IEEE International Conference for High Performance Computing and Communications Conference (SC)*, November 2015.

[27] NERSC. Burst buffer architecture and software roadmap. http://www.nersc.gov/users/computational-systems/cori/burst-buffer/burst-buffer/. Retrieved 01 Apr, 2016.

[28] Oak Ridge National Laboratory. Introducing Titan - Advancing the Area of Accelerated Computing. https://www.olcf.ornl.gov/titan/. Retrieved 16 May, 2015.

[29] S. Prabhakaran, M. Iqbal, S. Rinke, C. Windisch, and F. Wolf. A Batch System with Fair Scheduling for Evolving Applications. In *Proc. of the 43rd International Conference on Parallel Processing (ICPP)*, pages 351–360, Sep. 2014.

[30] S. Prabhakaran, M. Neumann, S. Rinke, F. Wolf, A. Gupta, and L. V. Kalé. A Batch System with Efficient Adaptive Scheduling for Malleable and Evolving Applications. In *Proc. of 2015 IEEE International Parallel and Distributed Processing Symposium (IPDPS)*, May 2015.

[31] K. Sato, K. Mohror, A. Moody, T. Gamblin, B. de Supinski, N. Maruyama, and S. Matsuoka. A User-Level InfiniBand-Based File System and Checkpoint Strategy for Burst Buffers. In *Proc. of the 14th IEEE/ACM International Symposium on Cluster, Cloud and Grid Computing (CCGrid)*, May 2014.

[32] F. Schmuck and R. Haskin. GPFS: A Shared-Disk File System for Large Computing Clusters. In *Proc. of the 1st USENIX Conference on File and Storage Technologies*, FAST '02, Jan 2002.

[33] G. M. Shipman, D. A. Dillow, S. Oral, and F. Wang. The Spider Center Wide File System: From Concept to Reality. In *Proc. of the Cray User Group (CUG) Conference*, 2009.

[34] S. Thapaliya, P. Bangalore, J. Lofstead, K. Mohror, and A. Moody. IO-Cop: Managing Concurrent Accesses to Shared Parallel File System. In *Proc. of the 6th Workshop on Interfaces and Architecture for Scientific Data Storage (IASDS)*, Sep. 2014.

[35] S. Thapaliya, P. Bangalore, J. Lofstead, K. Mohror, and A. Moody. IO-Cop: Managing Concurrent Accesses to Shared Parallel File System. In *Proc. of 2014 43rd International Conference on Parallel Processing Workshops (ICCPW)*, Sept 2014.

[36] Z. Zhou, X. Yang, D. Zhao, P. Rich, W. Tang, J. Wang, and Z. Lan. I/O-Aware Batch Scheduling for Petascale Computing Systems. In *Proc. of 2015 IEEE International Conference on Cluster Computing (CLUSTER)*, Sept 2015.

SWAT: A Programmable, In-Memory, Distributed, High-Performance Computing Platform

Max Grossman
Rice University
6100 Main St, Houston, TX, USA
jmg3@rice.edu

Vivek Sarkar
Rice University
6100 Main St, Houston, TX, USA

ABSTRACT

The field of data analytics is currently going through a renaissance as a result of ever-increasing dataset sizes, the value of the models that can be trained from those datasets, and a surge in flexible, distributed programming models. In particular, the Apache Hadoop [1] and Spark [5] programming systems, as well as their supporting projects (e.g. HDFS, SparkSQL), have greatly simplified the analysis and transformation of datasets whose size exceeds the capacity of a single machine. While these programming models facilitate the use of distributed systems to analyze large datasets, they have been plagued by performance issues. The I/O performance bottlenecks of Hadoop are partially responsible for the creation of Spark. Performance bottlenecks in Spark due to the JVM object model, garbage collection, interpreted/-managed execution, and other abstraction layers are responsible for the creation of additional optimization layers, such as Project Tungsten [4]. Indeed, the Project Tungsten issue tracker states that the "majority of Spark workloads are not bottlenecked by I/O or network, but rather CPU and memory" [20].

In this work, we address the CPU and memory performance bottlenecks that exist in Apache Spark by accelerating user-written computational kernels using accelerators. We refer to our approach as Spark With Accelerated Tasks (SWAT). SWAT is an accelerated data analytics (ADA) framework that enables programmers to natively execute Spark applications on high performance hardware platforms with co-processors, while continuing to write their applications in a JVM-based language like Java or Scala. Runtime code generation creates OpenCL kernels from JVM bytecode, which are then executed on OpenCL accelerators. In our work we emphasize 1) full compatibility with a modern, existing, and accepted data analytics platform, 2) an asynchronous, event-driven, and resource-aware runtime, 3) multi-GPU memory management and caching, and 4) ease-of-use and programmability. Our performance evaluation demonstrates up to 3.24× overall application speedup relative to Spark across six machine learning benchmarks, with a detailed investigation of these performance improvements.

Keywords

distributed, heterogeneous, Spark, GPU, OpenCL, data analytics

1. INTRODUCTION

The introduction of the Apache Hadoop [1] and Spark [5] programming systems to the data analytics community has greatly simplified the task of processing large datasets. While users celebrate the programmability of Hadoop, Spark, and the frameworks built on top of them, performance tuning of these systems is non-trivial. Their construction on an interpreted, managed runtime improves the flexibility of Spark and Hadoop, but this added layer of abstraction makes it difficult to tune locality, instruction scheduling, memory allocation, disk and network access, and other low-level performance knobs. Indeed, Spark's creation was partially motivated by criticisms of Hadoop's disk bottlenecks, while Project Tungsten [4] is motivated by CPU and memory bottlenecks in Spark.

Therefore, while the problem of building distributed applications to operate on large datasets is being addressed effectively, the challenge of achieving computational efficiency in large-scale systems without sacrificing programmability remains open. In particular, much of the existing work in the open source community has focused on fixing the I/O bottlenecks of these distributed programming systems, which has led to the computational inefficiencies becoming more pronounced. One recent approach to improving the computational performance of these big data analytics platforms has been the exploration of the use of accelerators, such as GPUs. We call these accelerator-based platforms *accelerated data analytics platforms* (ADAs).

Both of the leading data analytics platforms listed above (Hadoop and Spark) are JVM-based, but supporting full JVM execution on accelerators is infeasible. To bridge this gap, past work has taken a number of approaches. We characterize these approaches along four axes: the generality of the API exposed to the user, the degree to which low-level accelerator details are exposed to the user, compatibility with existing frameworks, and the flexibility/efficiency of the framework's runtime.

To one extreme, fixed-function frameworks offer high-level, domain-specific APIs which are highly programmable but also inherently inflexible. Some well-known examples are

BIDMach [8], Caffe [14], and HeteroSpark [17]. The specialization of fixed-function frameworks allows them to optimize both their performance and programmability for the domain they target, but limit their applicability to any others.

On the other hand, fully programmable ADA frameworks such as HeteroDoop [21] or HadoopCL [11] enable the implementation of novel algorithms and are more generally useful, but often pay the price of added overhead. For example, HadoopCL uses runtime code generation of accelerator kernels from JVM bytecode to support accelerated execution. This code generation step adds overhead to each job's execution, but augments the framework's overall flexibility.

While most ADAs choose to expose high-level accelerator-agnostic APIs, SparkCL [22], GPMR [23], and Glasswing [10] expose low-level details of accelerator hardware to the user, such as thread IDs and accelerator-specific address spaces. In our work, we follow the trends we observe in the community and hide hardware details from the user. This approach limits some user optimizations, but improves programmability.

While compatibility with existing frameworks is partly a software engineering concern, it is also an important constraint on the research problem. In past work, HadoopCL and SparkCL required modifications to the core code of Hadoop or Spark. While this approach enables applications to run unmodified and leverage optimizations that are not possible from outside of these frameworks, there are major barriers to broad acceptance in the long term if these extensions are not incorporated in the main development trunk of the underlying open source projects. Frameworks like HeteroDoop introduce entirely new APIs that sit on stop of other frameworks but which require a complete rewrite of any existing applications. Frameworks like MapCG [13] construct entirely new APIs and runtimes, limiting both the portability of legacy applications and the ability to co-locate them with existing frameworks like Spark and Hadoop. In this work, we build our solution as a third-party library which maintains the look and feel of Apache Spark and runs on top of Spark without requiring modifications to the internals of Spark.

Finally, the runtime system of an ADA is an important factor in its performance and stability. Related work like HadoopCL and HeteroDoop place a heavy emphasis on the efficient management of resources on behalf of the user, addressing out-of-memory errors and efficient scheduling without bothering the user with such low-level concerns. HadoopCL even includes a component to automatically determine at runtime which kernels to run in the JVM, on an accelerator, or on the CPU natively. Other work minimizes the safety for the user 1) by allowing them to allocate arbitrary amounts of accelerator memory, 2) by using blocking operations rather than asynchronous tasks, and 3) by generally requiring the user to do more manual resource management without protecting them from mistakes. We focus on building a flexible, asynchronous, and event-driven runtime that transparently handles resource management for the user.

In this paper we describe the open-source Spark With Accelerated Tasks (SWAT) framework, available at https://github.com/agrippa/spark-swat. Table 1 compares the relevant characteristics of SWAT with those of several related ADAs. SWAT accelerates the user-written computational kernels of Apache Spark jobs using OpenCL-supporting GPUs. SWAT is not fixed function: it allows Spark programmers to write custom kernels in high level JVM languages like Scala. SWAT is high-level: it does not expose accelerator hardware details, maintaining the same APIs as Spark. It fully integrates with the Spark framework as a third-party JAR, requiring only minimal code re-write for existing Spark applications. SWAT uses an asynchronous, event-driven, and resource-aware runtime to accurately and efficiently manage intra-node resources for the programmer.

The remainder of this paper is structured as follows. Section 2 will briefly describe Apache Spark, as well as explain the characteristics of GPU accelerators that make them relevant to data analytics workloads. Section 3 will describe the techniques and contributions of this work in detail. Section 4 will evaluate the performance benefits of those methods experimentally. Section 5 will conclude with a discussion of our approach and a summary of future work.

2. BACKGROUND

In this work, we combine Apache Spark and GPU accelerators to produce a programmable and high-performance data analytics system. This section briefly provides background on Spark and GPUs, and puts this work in the context of our past work on combining Hadoop MapReduce and GPUs.

2.1 Apache Spark

Apache Spark is a distributed, multi-threaded, in-memory programming system. The core abstraction of Apache Spark is that of a resilient distributed dataset (RDD). An RDD represents a distributed vector of elements. Elements in an RDD can be of any serializable type. RDD creation is lazy: creating an RDD object in a Spark program does not necessarily evaluate and populate that RDD. Only certain operations in Spark programs force evaluation, resulting in long chains of lazily evaluated RDDs as one RDD is transformed into another. RDD resiliency derives from their ancestry tracking. By persisting information on how RDDs were created rather than their actual contents, Spark guarantees that lost data can be recovered through recomputation without storing large amounts of intermediate data on disk.

A single RDD is split into multiple partitions. All elements in the same partition are stored on the same machine, but different partitions may be stored on different machines. Hence, partitions are the granularity of distribution in Spark.

One of Spark's strengths is its API, i.e. the transformations that it supports on RDDs. Spark transformations run in parallel across the machines that an RDD is stored on. Transformations are functional: they are applied to one RDD and produce another. This generally leads to long chains of lazily evaluated RDDs, linked by functional transformations. The transformations that Spark supports include `map`, `reduce`, `filter`, `reduceByKey`, `groupByKey`, `join`, and `distinct`. This variety of transformations greatly expands the flexibility of Spark relative to its predecessor, Hadoop MapReduce.

Transformations generally take some Scala lambda `f`, apply it to the input RDD using the semantics of the transformation, and produce some output RDD. For example, the `map` transformation applies `f` to each element of the input RDD, producing the corresponding element in the output RDD.

Framework	Fixed Function	Low-Level	Compatibility	Runtime Flexibility
SWAT	No	No	No code change, No data transorms	Asynchronous runtime, Full platform management
HadoopCL	No	No	Small code change, Major data transforms	Pipelined runtime, Auto-scheduling
HeteroDoop	No	No	No code compatibility, shared runtime with Spark	Transparent resource management
MapCG	No	No	None	Assumes fixed memory usage, work partitioned across CPU + GPU
GPMR	No	Yes	None	Efficient support of many-GPU execution through augmentation of the MapReduce pipeline
Glasswing	No	Yes	None	Low-level OpenCL-based APIs
SparkCL	No	Yes	No code compatibility, shared runtime with Spark	None
HeteroSpark	Yes	No	Callable from Spark jobs	Unspecified
BIDMach	Yes	No	None	Minimal
Caffe	Yes	No	None	Minimal

Table 1: A comparison of relevant characteristics of various ADAs, including whether they are fixed-function, whether they expose low-level hardware details to the user, how much code rewrite is necessary for an existing Hadoop/Spark application, and the flexibility of the underlying runtime system.

In this paper, we refer to the processing of a single RDD partition by a single transformation as a Spark "task".

In-memory caching is also an important feature of Spark. Spark allows users to explicitly mark certain RDDs as "cached", indicating that the programmer would like Spark's runtime to make a best-effort at keeping the partitions of this RDD in memory. This may benefit performance when the output of one transformation is immediately fed into another as input, or when a single RDD is accessed repeatedly.

Spark also supports broadcast variables. Spark broadcast variables are read-only data structures accessible on every node of a Spark cluster. Broadcast variables are an efficient way to share read-only data among all tasks in a Spark job.

2.2 GPUs

It should be apparent that Spark is a highly parallel framework for processing large amounts of data. This computational pattern fits well with GPUs.

GPUs are throughput-optimized devices which are generally attached to a host processor (i.e., CPU) but physically separate from it. They perform best relative to multi-core CPUs on highly parallel workloads with simple control flow (i.e. minimal conditional divergence between threads) and large memory bandwidth requirements.

GPU memory hierarchies also contain special-purpose memory that allow programmers to manually place data with certain characteristics in appropriate parts of the hierarchy. For example, GPU constant memory is useful for constant data structures read by all threads on the GPU. GPU shared (or scratchpad) memory is on-chip and useful for storing frequently accessed, small data structures.

Programming GPUs requires the use of low-level, data parallel programming models such as CUDA or OpenCL. These models allow programmers to manage GPU memory, GPU communication, and massively parallel kernel creation. They are generally considered by be verbose, especially when compared to high-level languages like Scala and Java.

The data parallelism, memory bandwidth, and low-level programming models of GPUs make them complementary

to data analytics platforms like Spark. Both exhibit wide parallelism, either across many cores in a chip or across a whole distributed system. Spark processes large datasets in a streaming model, which matches well with GPUs' high memory bandwidth. Spark offers a high-level programming model but suffers from performance bottlenecks, while GPUs suffer from low-level programming models but have a high peak computational performance.

2.3 HadoopCL

In past work called HadoopCL, we explored accelerating Hadoop MapReduce using GPUs. While the motivations of HadoopCL and SWAT are similar, the constraints and resulting systems are not. Hadoop and Spark are different programming models that expose different abstractions and are entirely disjoint in their backend implementations. As a result, the accelerated frameworks HadoopCL and SWAT are also entirely disjoint. HadoopCL simplified the problem of building an efficient ADA by modifying core Hadoop code, introducing custom data structures, requiring the programmer to use HadoopCL-specific APIs, and significantly limiting the logic that could be written in accelerated kernels. On the other hand, SWAT is constructed entirely as a third-party library, does not introduce custom data structures, has an API that consists of a single method, and uses new techniques in code generation to broaden the JVM features that can be used in accelerated kernels. SWAT's runtime system is also novel, doing a better job of seamlessly combining multi-threaded JVM and OpenCL execution in an event-driven model than HadoopCL's runtime was able to.

2.4 Contributions

In this work, we build a novel accelerated data analytics platform, called SWAT, by accelerating Apache Spark with GPUs. Our main contributions beyond past work include:

1. Full compatibility with a modern data analytics platform, Apache Spark, by minimizing user-visible changes to the API.

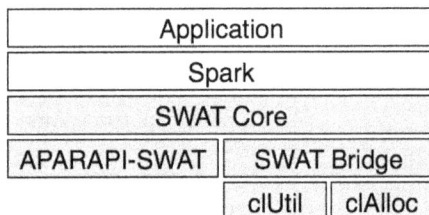

Figure 1: The SWAT software stack. Colored boxes indicate components that are novel contributions of this work.

2. Extensions to the bytecode-to-OpenCL code generation work from [12] to support Spark-specific data structures, such as dense and sparse vectors from MLlib [24].

3. An asynchronous, event-driven, resource-aware runtime for managing JVM and accelerator resources.

4. A multi-GPU memory management and caching layer, with experiments in device locality-aware scheduling.

5. An evaluation of SWAT on six diverse machine learning benchmarks with detailed analysis to explain performance improvements and losses.

3. METHODS

The software stack of SWAT is illustrated in Figure 1. In this section, we start by describing the SWAT API and then discuss each of these layers, starting at the bottom with the clAlloc and clUtil modules and moving progressively higher in the stack.

3.1 SWAT API

In a vanilla Spark program, RDDs are created by applying transformations or operations to other RDDS. In the example code snippet below, an RDD of integers is created from a file stored in HDFS, and a new RDD is created where element `i` contains the value of element `i` in the first RDD, multiplied by two:

```
val input = sc.objectFile[Int](hdfsPath)
val doubled = input.map(i => 2 * i)
```

To run this kernel on an accelerator, SWAT simply requires that the `input` RDD be wrapped by a custom SWAT RDD object using a `cl` API call (shown below). No other code change is required, and this is the only method exposed by SWAT.

```
val input = cl(sc.objectFile[Int](hdfsPath))
val doubled = input.map(i => 2 * i)
```

SWAT currently supports intercepting and accelerating calls to Spark `map` and `mapValues` transformations. Other transformations could be supported, but we have not found motivating application kernels that use other transformations and would benefit from acceleration. For example, `filter` kernels tend to be short-lived and the GPU offload time would be dominated by overheads. Future work could investigate the use of kernel fusion across chained transformations to produce larger GPU kernels. These fused kernels might offset the offload overheads, making offload of lightweight transformations like `filter` profitable.

3.2 clUtil and clAlloc

clUtil is a simple utility library written by the authors that simplifies management of OpenCL devices. It makes tasks like device selection, device setup, querying device information, and kernel launches less verbose than the lower-level OpenCL APIs.

clAlloc is a thread-safe, single-accelerator memory management library built on top of the OpenCL APIs. It exposes two data structures: 1) an `allocator` object for each OpenCL device in a platform that serves as a context/handle for clAlloc operations on that device, and 2) `region` objects which represent a contiguous block of allocated memory on a single OpenCL device. Its API is as follows:

1. `clalloc_init(device)`: Initialize an `allocator` instance for the selected device.

2. `cl_allocate(nbytes, allocator)`: Allocate `nbytes` bytes on the device associated with `allocator`, returning a `cl_region` handle for the allocated memory or `NULL` if the allocation failed.

3. `cl_free(region, try_to_keep)`: Release the device memory represented by `region` for future allocations. If `try_to_keep` is true, clAlloc will make a best-effort to not use that memory to satisfy future allocations as it may be re-used soon.

4. `cl_reallocate(region)`: Using the provided `region`, attempt to re-allocate the same device memory. Successfully re-allocating memory guarantees that it has not been used to satisfy another allocation since `region` was originally allocated, and so its state is consistent with previous operations performed on the same `region`. If the `region` is not already free this simply increments a reference counter, allowing multiple kernels to share the same `region`.

5. `get_pinned(region)`/`release_pinned(buf)`: Fetch or release a page-locked buffer `buf` in host memory that matches the size of `region`. Page-locked buffers are necessary for performing asynchronous communication to or from accelerators.

6. `set_region(region, buf, nbytes)`/`get_region(buf, region, nbytes)`: Fill or fetch the contents of a region on an OpenCL device using a corresponding host buffer.

clAlloc adds a higher-level API on top of the standard OpenCL APIs, including features that enable higher layers of the software stack to perform inter-kernel data sharing and efficient data communication. clAlloc pre-allocates all device memory when it is initialized and partitions memory up for allocation requests on-demand using the OpenCL `clCreateSubBuffer` API.

Free device memory is represented by a free list, sorted by offset into the device memory address space. When a clAlloc `region` is freed with `cl_free` and with `try_to_keep` set to false, it is merged into any neighboring regions to reduce fragmentation. If `try_to_keep` is set to true, it is not merged.

clAlloc also stores free regions in buckets for efficient allocation. For a single device, `B` buckets are created. Each bucket `b` from 0 to `B-1` stores all free regions on that device with a size between 2^b (inclusive) and 2^{b+1} (exclusive). A special-purpose bucket is used to store any regions larger than $2^B - 1$. The free regions in each bucket are kept sorted by size, from smallest to largest. Regions freed with `try_to_keep` set to true are not kept in these buckets, only in the global free list for each device.

When allocating `nbytes`, clAlloc starts with the smallest bucket that may have a region of size `nbytes`, searching larger buckets until a free region that is large enough to satisfy this allocation is found. The free region is then trimmed to `nbytes`, any leftover space is re-inserted in the free list and free buckets, and the allocated region is returned.

If no free region is found in the buckets list, the allocator reverts to a linear search of the device-global free list for adjacent free regions that can be merged to produce a sufficiently large free region to satisfy this allocation. This step will only succeed where the previous one failed if some regions freed with `try_to_keep` set to true can be merged with neighboring free regions to de-fragment device memory. If this step fails, a `NULL` region is returned.

Note that clUtil and clAlloc are only exposed to the internals of SWAT, and not used directly by a SWAT programmer.

3.3 APARAPI-SWAT

APARAPI is an open source, general-purpose framework that enables transparent execution of Java programs on OpenCL devices through an API similar to Java's `Runnable`. APARAPI includes a runtime code generator from JVM bytecode to OpenCL kernels and handles all OpenCL memory allocation, data transfer, and kernel execution for the programmer.

In this work, we use APARAPI's code generator to translate the Scala lamdbas passed to Spark transformations (illustrated in Section 3.1) into OpenCL kernels that can be executed on an accelerator. This code generation is performed at runtime, converting dynamically loaded JVM bytecode into the OpenCL kernel language.

In past work, we have extended APARAPI's code generator to support 1) dynamic memory allocation inside OpenCL kernels through a retry-on-failure approach, and 2) JVM object references in bytecode translated to OpenCL kernels through generation of equivalent native structs and automatic serialization of those objects. For more details, see our previous work in [12].

In this work, we build on [12] to also support references to Spark-specific data structures in kernels. In particular, we support the `SparseVector` and `DenseVector` classes from Spark's MLlib, and the Scala `Tuple2` class used to store key-value pairs in Spark. An example of the OpenCL kernel code generated to store and manipulate a `DenseVector` object is shown below:

```
typedef struct __attribute__ ((packed)) dv {
  __global double*  values;
  int  size;
  int  stride;
} DenseVector;

static int DenseVector__size(
    __global DenseVector *this) {
  return (this->size);
}
```

```
static double DenseVector__apply(
    __global DenseVector *this, int index) {
  return (this->values)[this->stride * index];
}
```

One important item to note in the definition of the DenseVector struct is the addition of a `stride` field. During serialization of `DenseVector` JVM objects to native structs that can be accessed on the GPU, we tile and stride `DenseVector` objects to improve memory access coalescing on the GPU. This transformation places the `ith` element of neighboring `DenseVector` objects adjacent to each other. In our implementation, we tile 32 `DenseVector` objects together before striding them because NVIDIA GPUs schedule threads in "warps" of 32 threads. However, the implementation is structured so that this can be easily tuned when porting to new architectures. These same optimizations are also performed on `SparseVector` objects.

The automatic optimization of the user-written kernels during code generation is beyond the scope of this work, but ideas from related work [25][16][7] could be integrated into this code generator in the future.

3.4 SWAT Bridge

Sitting on top of clAlloc and clUtil is the SWAT Bridge, a bridge between the components of SWAT running in the JVM and those sitting on top of OpenCL. As such, SWAT Bridge's upward exposed APIs are expressed in terms of JVM or Spark objects, which it then translates into commands to the OpenCL-centric layers below.

The Bridge's primary responsibilities are the caching of data on OpenCL devices across kernels and tasks, the creation and management of native SWAT contexts, the setting of arguments to OpenCL kernels, and the management of asynchronously executing OpenCL operations (including kernel executions and data communication). It exposes APIs to the JVM that enqueue work for accelerators and block or poll on their completion. At a high level, the Bridge accepts input buffers from the JVM, places them on the accelerator, launches computation on those buffers at the JVM's request, retrieves outputs, and signals the JVM on completion of various stages and as resources are released.

Described in Section 2.1, Spark uses in-memory caching to address I/O bottlenecks in past frameworks without losing resiliency guarantees. Logic in the Bridge supports similar caching of data on OpenCL devices. In particular, we investigated caching RDD partitions and broadcast variables on the GPU.

The Bridge stores two mappings for caching data on OpenCL devices: one mapping from unique RDD partition IDs to their clAlloc regions, and another from unique broadcast variable IDs to their clAlloc regions. When layers higher in the software stack indicate that a partition or broadcast variable should be allocated and populated on a device, the Bridge first checks if an entry already exists for it in one of the cached mappings. If it does and a call to `cl_reallocate` succeeds on it, the Bridge can skip creating a separate allocation. This saves space on the device through deduplication, and reduces data communication to the device. When freeing regions associated with cacheable data, the `try_to_keep` flag is set to true.

In practice, we found that caching partitions of RDDs on the device was not useful. The limited size of device memory and the scale of Spark datasets meant that RDD partitions were never re-used before being evicted from device memory: the memory used to store them had to be allocated to store other data before the application came back around to a re-use of that partition. In fact, the increased fragmentation of device memory and added overhead of managing the Bridge's RDD cache mapping generally hurt performance. Broadcast variables, on the other hand, are frequently used, may be shared across multiple stages of a Spark application, and are usually smaller than an RDD partition. We generally see benefits from caching them. For the evaluation conducted in Section 4, we do not cache RDD partitions in device memory but do cache broadcast variables.

SWAT does not make use of GPU constant or scratchpad memory for a number of reasons. The OpenCL APIs for accessing GPU constant memory severely restrict the ability of our runtime to store general, dynamically initialized data in constant memory. We could not design a general technique to make use of constant memory for arbitrary data and so, rather than impinging on the generality of our framework by asking programmers to explicitly handle constant memory, we classify it as future work.

Preliminary experiments with scratchpad memory did show performance benefits from using it to store certain thread-local, SWAT internal data structures or broadcast variables. However, the OpenCL kernel language requires annotating every pointer with the address space it points to. The small size of GPU scratchpad memory meant that storing even moderately sized broadcast variables would require some sort of tiling or partitioning, where part of the broadcasted variable was stored in scratchpad memory with the remainder stored in global device memory. This would have meant generating multiple versions of any OpenCL kernel function that used broadcast variables with different signatures depending on the address space of the data being referenced. This approach would have also caused thread divergence as different threads went down the scratchpad memory code path or the device memory code path. Further experiments showed that this added complexity negated the performance benefits of scratchpad memory for the cases where we could automatically identify good candidates for storage in scratchpad. Again, rather than ask the programmer to explicitly manage scratchpad memory or reduce the generality of our framework, we classify its use as future work.

Besides caching, the bridge's other main responsibility is exposing an API that allows higher layers to enqueue asynchronous OpenCL operations and check for their completion. In support of this, the bridge implements an asynchronous runtime that coordinates asynchronous OpenCL operations with the host application using pthreads condition variables, OpenCL events, and OpenCL event callbacks. This runtime is illustrated in Figure 2. Below the dotted line in Figure 2 are OpenCL operations managed by the OpenCL runtime including data communication, kernel execution, and SWAT-specific callbacks. These callbacks are identified by the light gray boxes. All of these operations are asynchronous with respect to the host JVM, with OpenCL events being used to maintain inter-operation dependencies.

The functions that the SWAT Bridge exposes to higher layers in SWAT are listed below:

1. `setPinnedArrayArg`: This function initiates the transfer of the contents of a host page-locked buffer to a buffer on an OpenCL device. It also sets the appropriate arguments of an OpenCL kernel to point to the

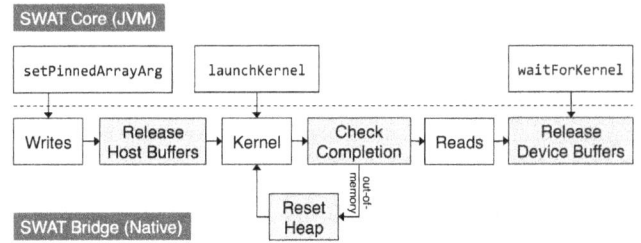

Figure 2: The flow of event-driven actions in the SWAT Bridge at runtime.

same OpenCL buffers. This call is non-blocking, and creates OpenCL events for later operations to depend on.

2. `launchKernel`: This function launches a new kernel processing data initialized using `setPinnedArrayArg`. This kernel is made dependent on the writes started by `setPinnedArrayArg` using OpenCL events. Each kernel launch is uniquely identified by a 64-bit sequence number, which is incremented by one on each kernel launch.

3. `waitForKernel`: This function forces the current JVM thread to wait for a specific kernel launch to complete, identified by its sequence number. This involves a wait on a condition variable which is set by the box labelled "Release Device Buffers" in Figure 2.

4. `waitForInputBuffersRelease`: This function forces the current JVM thread to wait for a set of transfers to the device to complete, signalling that the host buffers they originate from are now available for re-use by the host.

All of these APIs are thread-safe as they may be concurrently called by multiple JVM threads.

3.5 SWAT Core

SWAT Core refers to the components of SWAT that sit inside the JVM. SWAT Core runs inside a Spark Worker JVM. The interface between Spark and SWAT is a custom SWAT RDD class (illustrated in Figure 3). When Spark has a partition to process it calls a `compute` method on the custom RDD, passing it an iterator over an input partition. The `compute` method returns an iterator over output items. SWAT currently adds two custom RDD classes: one each for the Spark `map` and `mapValues` transformations. Both of these classes hand off processing of the input partitions to a shared code base in `CLProcessor`.

`CLProcessor` has four main responsibilities: 1) setup and configuration of the SWAT environment, 2) input buffering and serialization, 3) launching a GPU batched kernel, and 4) output deserialization and writing. At a high level, `CLProcessor` accumulates many input items from the input iterator, launches a batched OpenCL kernel on the accumulated inputs, and returns the accumulated outputs to Spark through the iterator which was returned by the RDD `compute` method.

There are five categories of objects that the `CLProcessor` is responsible for initializing:

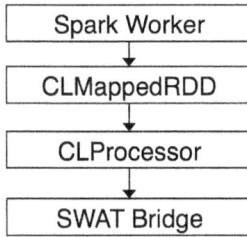

Figure 3: Example stack trace of entry point to SWAT Core.

1. OpenCL objects: This includes SWAT-specific items such as clAlloc allocators, as well as OpenCL-specific items like compiled kernels and OpenCL contexts.

2. Native Input Buffers: These are JVM handles on native, page-locked buffers allocated from clAlloc. Multiple page-locked buffers may be grouped into a single Native Input Buffer handle if they are required to serialize a given input type. For example, accumulating vectors from a `DenseVector` input iterator requires three native input buffers: one buffer to store the values of each vector, one buffer to store the length of each vector, and one buffer to store the offset of each vector in the values buffer.

3. JVM Input Buffers: These are small JVM objects that contain the logic to serialize items from an input iterator into backing Native Input Buffers. Sometimes it is necessary to store small temporary buffers in JVM Input Buffers. An actively buffering JVM Input Buffer is always backed by a Native Input Buffer in which it stores the accumulated and serialized input items.

4. Native Output Buffers: Page-locked host buffers that SWAT Bridge transfers the outputs of an OpenCL kernel into, asynchronously.

5. JVM Output Buffers: JVM objects backed by Native Output Buffers that expose an iterator interface which `CLProcessor` can use to deserialize and fetch output elements from Native Output Buffers.

Only one JVM input buffer and JVM output buffer are created by `CLProcessor`. Multiple native input and output buffers are created, but are limited to a fixed number to prevent out-of-memory errors caused by excessive native buffer allocation. Only a single JVM input or output buffer is necessary as different native buffers can be swapped in and out as the storage backing the JVM buffers' interfaces.

The CLProcessor uses two JVM threads: a dedicated reader thread and the main Spark thread. A reader thread is spawned by the main Spark thread when the SWAT RDD `compute` method is called. The reader thread retrieves an iterator for a given input partition. The reader thread is responsible for accumulating items from the input iterator, through the JVM Input Buffer, and into a Native Input Buffer. It then initiates the asynchronous input copies to the accelerator from the Native Input Buffer and launches an asynchronous kernel to process them, using the SWAT Bridge. Illustrative pseudocode for the reader thread is listed in Algorithm 1.

```
1  currentInputSeqNo = 0
2  lastSequenceNo = -1
3  done = false
4  jvmInputBuf = createJVMInputBuffer()
5  jvmInputBuf.setNativeInputBuf(fetchNativeInputBuffer())
6
7  while not done do
8      jvmInputBuf.accumulate(inputIter)
9
10     nextNativeInputBuf = fetchNativeInputBuffer()
11     jvmInputBuf.transferOverflowTo(nextNativeInputBuf)
12
13     jvmInputBuf.nativeInputBuf.copyToAccelerator()
14
15     currNativeOutputBuf = fetchNativeOutputBuffer()
16     bridge.setupOutputBuffers(currNativeOutputBuf)
17
18     kernelSequenceNo = currentInputSeqNo++
19     done = bridge.run(kernelSequenceNo)
20     if done then
21         lastSequenceNo = kernelSequenceNo
22     end
23 end
```

Algorithm 1: Pseudocode for SWAT Core reader thread.

The main Spark thread for the current partition first retrieves an output iterator from the SWAT RDD object's `compute` method and then repeatedly calls that iterator's `hasNext` and `next` methods to retrieve output items for the current partition, until `hasNext` returns false. `hasNext` checks that there are no remaining output items by verifying that the input iterator is finished, there are no pending OpenCL kernels, and that there are no pending output items left in any Native Output Buffers. `next`, on the other hand, either immediately returns an output item from a currently active Native Output Buffer or loads a new Native Output Buffer by waiting for the appropriate kernel launch to finish, based on a kernel sequence number. Illustrative pseudocode for the output iterator logic is listed in Algorithm 2.

```
1  currentOutputSeqNo = 0
2  jvmOutputBuffer = ∅
3
4  Procedure next
5      if jvmOutputBuffer == ∅ then
6          currNativeOutputBuffer =
7              bridge.waitForFinishedKernel(
8                  currentOutputSeqNo)
9          currentOutputSeqNo++
10         jvmOutputBuffer.fillFrom(currNativeOutputBuffer)
11     end
12     return jvmOutputBuffer.next
13
14 Procedure hasNext
15     return lastSequenceNo == -1 or
16         currentOutputSeqNo <= lastSequenceNo or
17         jvmOutputBuffer.hasNext;
```

Algorithm 2: Pseudocode for the SWAT Output Iterator.

Dataset	Size	# Items	Scala Type
Hyperlink	16 GB	1,289,970K	(Int, Int)
Census	14 GB	49,166K	DenseVector
ImageNet	1.3 GB	40,646K	(Int, DenseVector)

Table 2: Characteristics of each dataset.

4. EXPERIMENTAL EVALUATION

In this section we evaluate the performance gains and losses made using the SWAT framework. We start by considering its overall performance and scalability relative to Spark. We then look at task-level acceleration, i.e. how much faster the processing of a single RDD partition is in SWAT relative to Spark. Afterwards, we start looking at the underlying characteristics of selected applications running on SWAT to explain the higher level characteristics.

4.1 Experimental Setup

All benchmarks and metrics are evaluated on a hardware platform containing a 12-core 2.80GHz Intel X5660 CPU with 48GB of system RAM and two NVIDIA M2050 GPUs each with 2.5GB of device memory in each node. Nodes in this platform are connected by QDR Infiniband. Our experiments are limited to a maximum of nine nodes (one master, eight workers) by hardware availability. All experiments were run with 12 Spark executor threads in each node. The software platform consists of JDK 1.7.0_80, Scala 2.11.5, Spark 1.2.0, HDFS 2.5.2, and ICC 15.0.2. For the overall and task-level performance results, each benchmark was tested ten times at each node count. For the more detailed performance analysis, median runs were selected for study.

We use six benchmarks to evaluate SWAT:

1. PageRank: A graph algorithm that ranks nodes in the graph based on the nodes that link to them.

2. Connected: Connected components graph algorithm.

3. NN: A simple neural net implementation.

4. Fuzzy: A probabilistic clustering algorithm.

5. KMeans: An iterative clustering algorithm.

6. Genetic: A genetic, evolutionary algorithm. In this case, we use a genetic algorithm to find cluster centroids.

When writing these benchmarks for Spark, we chose to cache in-memory any RDD that was read more than once. We did this to keep the performance comparison fair, and believe it to be a reasonable choice. For example, the input points for the KMeans clustering algorithm are read on each iteration of the algorithm and so we mark them as cached. All applications were implemented using Spark's Scala API.

For these six benchmarks, we evaluate on three datasets. For PageRank and Connected we use the Hyperlink Graph available from the Web Data Commons [18]. For Fuzzy, KMeans, and Genetic we evaluate on the Census dataset available from the UCI Machine Learning Repository [6]. For NN we evaluate on a subset of the images in the ImageNet dataset [9]. The size of each dataset is listed in Table 2.

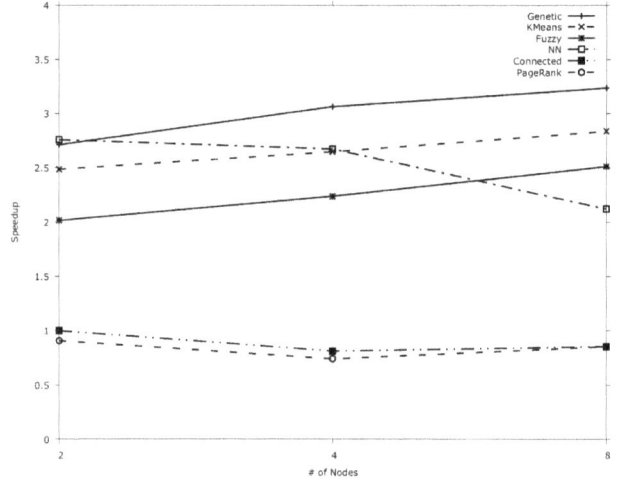

Figure 4: Overall speedup of each benchmark running on 1 master node and N worker nodes, for N = 2, 4, and 8.

4.2 Overall Speedup and Scalability

Figure 4 shows the overall speedup SWAT achieved relative to Spark on 2, 4, and 8 worker nodes. There are two clear categories of benchmarks: while Genetic, KMeans, Fuzzy, and NN all show speedups between 2× and 3.5×, PageRank and Connected either show no change, or slight slowdowns. We explain this through the characteristics of the applications: speedups are achieved when non-trivial computation is present in the application logic being accelerated by GPUs. For applications that are I/O bound on disk or network bandwidth and have small computational kernels, SWAT demonstrates no improvement. We support these claims in Sections 4.4, 4.5, and 4.6.

Figure 5 shows the scalability of each benchmark running on both Spark and SWAT when moving from two to eight executor nodes. Linear scalability would be denoted by a 4× speedup on the y-axis. At the scale of only eight executor nodes, it is difficult to make conclusions about the scalability of either framework. In general, neither consistently achieves linear scalability. However, these applications are not perfectly parallel and have collect or reduction stages which would make perfect scalability unlikely. Evaluating the scalability of the Spark framework is beyond the scope of this paper, but we observe no trends indicating a loss of scalability with SWAT.

We note that in Figure 5, the two applications with the worst scalability (PageRank and Connected) also demonstrated the lowest speedups in Figure 4. This poor scalability is caused by the same network and I/O bottlenecks that caused poor speedups when comparing SWAT to Spark.

4.3 Task-Level Speedup

Stepping down in the granularity of work being measured, recall that Section 2.1 defined a Spark task as the processing of a single RDD partition by a single transformation. When accelerated by SWAT, this includes all accelerator communication and computation. Figure 6 shows the average speedup for all different types of tasks in each benchmark. For most benchmarks, the task-level speedups are similar to the overall speedups. The primary outlier is NN:

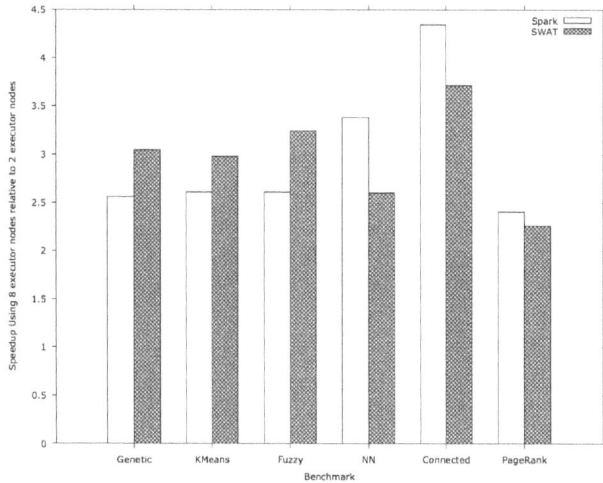

Figure 5: Speedup for each benchmark from two to eight nodes, using Spark or SWAT. This illustrates the scalability of each platform.

Some of its tasks show between 5 and 9× speedup, despite only achieving ∼2× speedup overall. Further investigation showed that the longest transformation of the NN benchmark consumes 26% of overall job time. Tasks in this stage only achieved a speedup of 1.11× when using the GPU, limiting the speedup achievable by Amdahl's Law. While each task consumed on average 48 seconds, only ∼1 second of each task was spent using the SWAT runtime. The remainder is spent fetching shuffle outputs at the start of each task.

4.4 SWAT Execution Timelines

Stepping down another level of granularity, we select five threads from a node running the PageRank and Genetic benchmarks and visualize their behavior using a custom SWAT profiling tool. We use these two benchmarks to study more fine-grain characteristics of the SWAT framework, as they are representative of the workloads that perform well or poorly on SWAT. We categorize the work performed in SWAT into three categories:

1. Input I/O, which includes deserialization and disk I/O.

2. OpenCL operations, which includes both data communication with and execution on the OpenCL device. Section 4.5 will dive deeper into the time spent in specific OpenCL operations, such as communication and execution.

3. Output I/O, which includes serialization and disk I/O.

Figure 7 shows the execution timeline for the PageRank benchmark, and Figure 8 shows it for the Genetic benchmark. Clearly, PageRank is dominated by input and output I/O while Genetic is dominated by computation. Combining these observations with Amdahl's Law explains the higher overall speedups achieved for the Genetic benchmark compared to the PageRank benchmark.

4.5 OpenCL Profiling

Finally, getting to the lowest work granularity, we use OpenCL event profiling [15] to analyze the time spent in

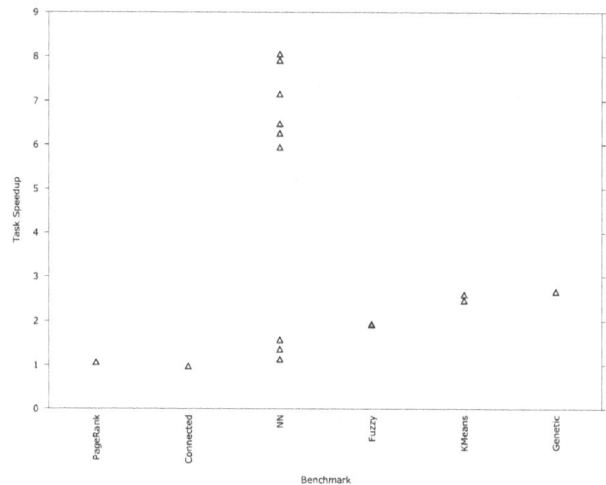

Figure 6: The task-level speedup averaged within each stage of each benchmark that is accelerated by SWAT. For example, KMeans runs two stages on the GPU and so we show two data points, each of which is the average speedup for all tasks in those stages.

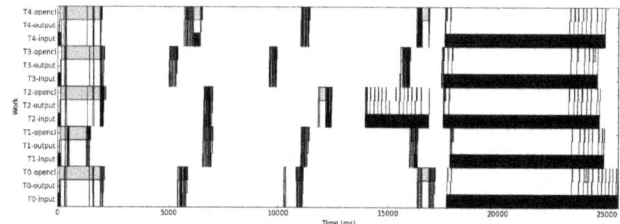

Figure 7: PageRank execution timeline. Light gray indicates input I/O, dark gray indicates OpenCL operations, and black indicates output I/O. No dark gray is visible at this time scale as little computation is performed in PageRank.

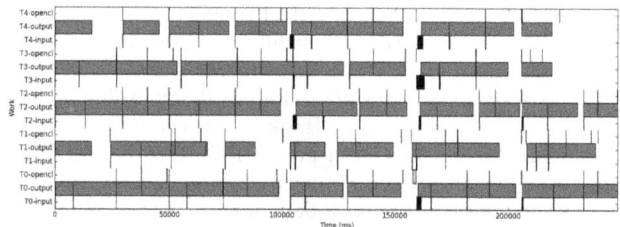

Figure 8: Genetic execution timeline. Light gray indicates input I/O, dark gray indicates OpenCL operations, and black indicates output I/O. Note that this figure is dominated by dark gray, indicating a large amount of time in OpenCL operations.

OpenCL operations (the dark gray bars in Figures 7 and 8). We subdivide OpenCL operations into data communication to the accelerator, computation on the accelerator, and data communication from the accelerator. OpenCL event profiling allows us to further split the time spent in each of these operations into:

1. Queued time: Time an operation spends in an OpenCL command queue on the host.

2. Submitted time: Time an operation spends submitted to the device driver, pending execution.

3. Run time: Time an operation spends running on the device.

Figure 9 plots the OpenCL profiling info for each benchmark. Each vertical bar represents the total time spent in a single node during a single job writing to the device, computing on the device, and reading from the device. Each of those operations is then subdivided into time those operations spend queued, submitted, and running. We can draw several conclusions from this plot.

PageRank spends much more time communicating to and from the device than actually running on it. The large amount of time the Write and Read portions spend in the Submitted state suggest high contention for the PCIe bus, forcing copies to wait before being able to execute. However, little time is spent in the Submitted stage for the Compute portion of PageRank, indicating that the device is poorly utilized and generally available.

Genetic, on the other hand, demonstrates long Submitted periods for all portions of the job: Write, Compute, and Read. This suggests high contention for both the GPUs and PCIe bus being shared by multiple JVM threads. While the different scales for the left and right y-axes make it difficult to see, we also observe that Genetic spends significantly more time in the Run stage of the Compute portion, relative to PageRank: 483,677.065 ns for Genetic versus 1,492.259 ns for PageRank.

4.6 Hardware Utilization

In addition to studying the performance of our application in terms of time-to-complete certain software operations, we also study how hardware utilization differs between Spark and SWAT. In particular, we look at CPU utilization and system memory utilization.

Figure 10 shows the change in CPU and memory utilization for the PageRank benchmark. Figure 11 shows the same information for the Genetic benchmark. Table 3 lists peak utilization information for all benchmarks.

We observe that the results in Figure 10 and Table 3 support the conclusion that PageRank is not a compute-bound benchmark, only achieving a peak CPU utilization of 55% when running on Spark. Similarly, Figure 11 and Table 3 show that Genetic is compute-bound, achieving a peak CPU utilization of 90% when running on Spark.

Performing a comparative study between Spark and SWAT, we note that CPU utilization drops by an average of 31% across all benchmarks when using SWAT, but system memory utilization increases by an average of 25%. Both of these results are expected. It is natural for the host utilization to drop if the main compute workload is now offloaded to an accelerator. We also expect system memory utilization to

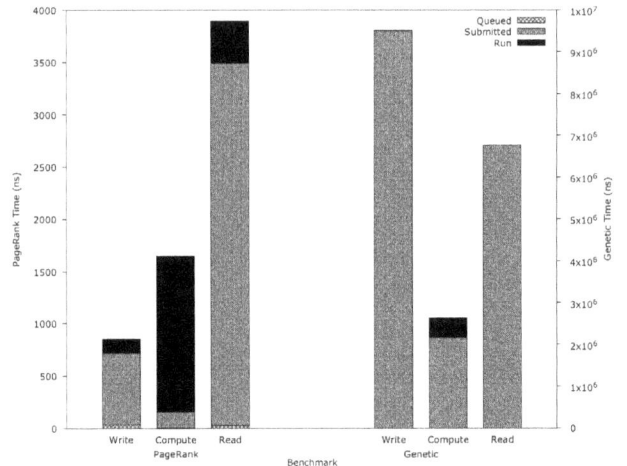

Figure 9: OpenCL event profiling information for PageRank and Genetic. Each vertical bar represents the total read, compute, or write time for a single benchmark. Each vertical bar is broken up into queued, submitted, and run times for that operation. PageRank is plotted against the left y-axis, Genetic is plotted against the right y-axis.

increase as SWAT allocates extra management data structures and host buffers for input and output accumulation.

Note that while there is an increase in system memory utilization with SWAT, the memory controls implemented as part of the SWAT Core are effective in keeping system memory utilization stable throughout the job: it does not oscillate or monotonically increase. In fact, it closely resembles the behavior of Spark's memory utilization, albeit with a constant factor added on top.

5. DISCUSSION AND CONCLUSIONS

In this work, we present work on an accelerated data analytics platform called SWAT that combines the distributed execution and high-level programming model of Apache Spark with the computational bandwidth of GPUs. Our approach uses code generation, an asynchronous & event driven runtime, dynamic GPU memory allocation inside & outside kernels, and a careful approach to resource management. Our performance evaluation in Section 4 shows that for compute-bound applications, our SWAT implementation achieves up to a 3.24× performance improvement, with no negative effects on scalability.

Some of the constraints we placed on this problem were important in shaping the solution. First, we wanted compatability with an existing and accepted framework out-of-the-box. That meant minimizing code change for existing applications and no access to framework-internal state. No existing work fulfills these constraints to our knowledge. Second, we wanted a minimalistic API that abstracted out all low-level details, leaving the runtime with more freedom to optimize. With a single method in our API and no custom data structures required, we satisfy this goal well. Third, we wanted to support the development of novel software applications and algorithms, requiring a code generation approach rather than the library-based approach that most related works have taken [8][14][17]. We see SWAT and

Benchmark	Peak CPU Utilization			Peak System Mem Utilization		
	Spark	SWAT	% Change	Spark	SWAT	% Change
PageRank	55%	50%	-9%	38%	49%	+27% (+12.96 GB)
Connected	28%	36%	-22%	81%	91%	+12% (+5.76 GB)
NN	89%	66%	-26%	77%	85%	+10% (+4.8 GB)
Fuzzy	92%	52%	-43%	30%	42%	+43% (+20.64 GB)
KMeans	85%	45%	-47%	37%	47%	+30% (+14.4 GB)
Genetic	90%	53%	-41%	37%	47%	+29% (+13.92 GB)
Average			**-31%**			**+25% (+12.00 GB)**

Table 3: Resource Utilization summary across all benchmarks

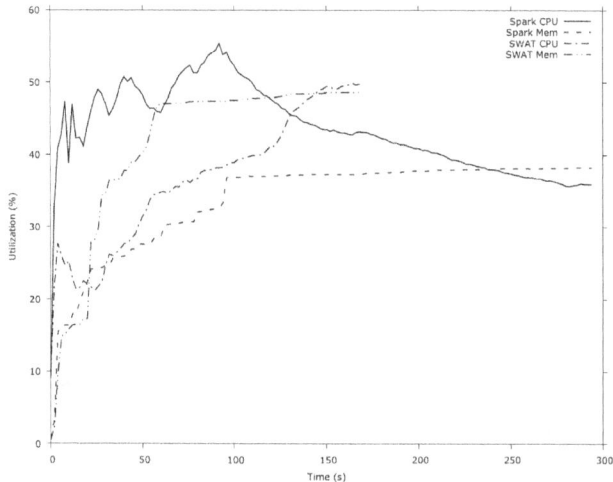

Figure 10: Host processor and memory utilization of the PageRank benchmark running on Spark and SWAT.

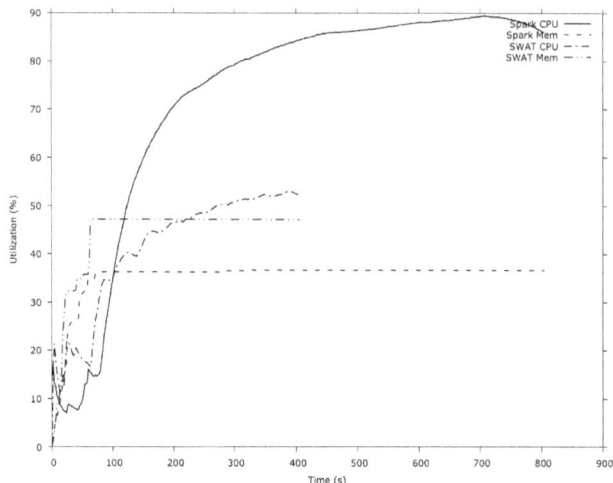

Figure 11: Host processor and memory utilization of the Genetic benchmark running on Spark and SWAT.

frameworks like it enabling domain experts to quickly develop novel and well-performing applications.

In our implementation, we emphasize tight resource management and minimize dynamic allocations by the framework on both the host and device to ensure that our framework is stable for long-running applications.

We also identify three hardware trends relevant to this work.

First, we see more accelerators packed into single nodes and the ratio of CPU cores to accelerators decreasing. With fewer threads sharing each accelerator, the device contention observed in Section 4.5 becomes less of a performance bottleneck.

Second, we also see higher performance interconnects between host and device, either in the form of higher bandwidth and lower latency buses (e.g. NVLink [19]) or system-on-a-chip solutions where the host and device physically share memory, like an AMD APU [3]. In more tightly coupled systems the data communication overheads for all heterogeneous applications are reduced, and we will see an increase in the domain of applications that can achieve performance improvement with SWAT. It is important to note that GPUs are not exclusively useful for compute-bound applications: in general, they also offer more memory bandwith than CPUs. The challenge today is that bandwidth-bound applications generally operate on large amounts of data, which must be transferred across a PCIe bus for the GPU to operate on. This leads to large communication overheads and nullifies any memory bandwidth benefits. Tightly coupled host-device systems reduce this problem.

Third, we see more researchers considering pairing power-efficient, lightweight host processors (e.g. Intel Atom, ARM) with GPUs to achieve high performance at low energy costs. In Section 4.6 we observed that using SWAT reduced CPU utilization by, on average, 31%. Most of our applications running on SWAT were only using ~50% of the available CPU cycles. It is possible that running this framework on a platform with lightweight CPU cores instead would yield energy gains without any loss in performance.

We plan to extend this work in a number of ways. We will investigate load-balancing across the JVM and GPUs. As we mentioned above, many of our SWAT applications show ~50% CPU utilization. It may be possible to do useful work in the JVM in parallel with GPU computation during those spare cycles.

We also will explore automatic device selection. In such a system, the framework would be responsible for determining that the JVM was the better execution platform for applications like PageRank and Connected, while the GPU should be used for NN, Fuzzy, KMeans, and Genetic. Past work has explored using historical performance data combined with current device load to do online prediction of task performance in Hadoop [11]. More recent work has looked at estimating task performance offline based on static kernel features using an SVM [2]. We plan to combine the lessons learned from these works to perform more accurate performance prediction for Spark tasks.

As a stress test for the SWAT runtime and API, ongoing work also focuses on porting an existing large-scale application, CS-BWAMEM [26], to use SWAT. We will continue to improve the performance, stability, and flexiblity of the open source release.

SWAT combines the strengths of Spark and GPUs into a unified and programmable framework. There are many exciting future directions for this work, and we see its design and performance characteristics as being complemented by ongoing and future hardware trends. We also believe SWAT to be the first ADA constructed on Spark to be sufficiently flexible for real world application development. SWAT continues the recent work on accelerated data analytics platforms by emphasizing compatibility, careful resource management, runtime asynchrony, and programmability.

6. ACKNOWLEDGMENTS

This work was supported in part by the Data Analysis and Visualization Cyberinfrastructure funded by NSF under grant OCI-0959097 and Rice University.

7. REFERENCES

[1] Apache Hadoop. http://hadoop.apache.org/.

[2] G. K. V. S. Akihiro Hayashi, Kazuaki Ishizaki. Machine-Learning-based Performance Heuristics for Runtime CPU/GPU Selection. In *12th International Conference on the Principles and Practice of Programming on the Java Platform, PPPJ*, 2015.

[3] AMD. AMD Accelerated Processing Units (APUs). http://www.amd.com/en-us/innovations/ software-technologies/apu.

[4] Apache. Project Tungsten. https://issues.apache.org/jira/browse/SPARK-7075.

[5] Apache. Spark: Lightning-fast cluster computing.

[6] A. Asuncion and D. Newman. Uci machine learning repository, 2007.

[7] M. M. Baskaran, J. Ramanujam, and P. Sadayappan. Automatic c-to-cuda code generation for affine programs. In *Compiler Construction*, pages 244–263. Springer, 2010.

[8] J. Canny and H. Zhao. Bidmach: Large-scale learning with zero memory allocation. In *BigLearning, NIPS Workshop*, 2013.

[9] J. Deng, W. Dong, R. Socher, L.-J. Li, K. Li, and L. Fei-Fei. Imagenet: A large-scale hierarchical image database. In *Computer Vision and Pattern Recognition, 2009. CVPR 2009. IEEE Conference on*, pages 248–255. IEEE, 2009.

[10] I. El-Helw, R. Hofman, and H. E. Bal. Glasswing: accelerating mapreduce on multi-core and many-core clusters. In *Proceedings of the 23rd international symposium on High-performance parallel and distributed computing*, pages 295–298. ACM, 2014.

[11] M. Grossman, M. Breternitz, and V. Sarkar. Hadoopcl2: Motivating the design of a distributed, heterogeneous programming system with machine-learning applications. In *IEEE Transactions on Parallel and Distributed Systems*.

[12] M. Grossman, S. Imam, and V. Sarkar. Hj-opencl: Reducing the gap between the jvm and accelerators. In *Proceedings of the Principles and Practices of Programming on The Java Platform*, pages 2–15. ACM, 2015.

[13] C. Hong, D. Chen, W. Chen, W. Zheng, and H. Lin. Mapcg: writing parallel program portable between cpu and gpu. In *Proceedings of the 19th international conference on Parallel architectures and compilation techniques*, pages 217–226. ACM, 2010.

[14] Y. Jia. Caffe: Convolutional architecture for fast feature embedding. In *Proceedings of the ACM International Conference on Multimedia*, pages 675–678. ACM, 2014.

[15] Khronos Group. clGetEventProfilingInfo. https://www.khronos.org/registry/cl/sdk/1.0/docs/ man/xhtml/clGetEventProfilingInfo.html.

[16] S. Lee, S.-J. Min, and R. Eigenmann. Openmp to gpgpu: a compiler framework for automatic translation and optimization. *ACM Sigplan Notices*, 44(4):101–110, 2009.

[17] P. Li, Y. Luo, N. Zhang, and Y. Cao. Heterospark: A heterogeneous cpu/gpu spark platform for machine learning algorithms. In *Networking, Architecture and Storage (NAS), 2015 IEEE International Conference on*, pages 347–348. IEEE, 2015.

[18] H. Mühleisen and C. Bizer. Web data commons-extracting structured data from two large web corpora. *LDOW*, 937:133–145, 2012.

[19] NVIDIA. NVIDIA NVLINK HIGH-SPEED INTERCONNECT. http://www.nvidia.com/object/nvlink.html.

[20] Reynold Xin. Project Tungsten (Spark 1.5 Phase 1). https://issues.apache.org/jira/browse/SPARK-7075, 2015.

[21] A. Sabne. Heterodoop: A mapreduce programming system for accelerator clusters. In *Proceedings of the 24th International Symposium on High-Performance Parallel and Distributed Computing*, pages 235–246. ACM, 2015.

[22] O. Segal, P. Colangelo, N. Nasiri, Z. Qian, and M. Margala. Sparkcl: A unified programming framework for accelerators on heterogeneous clusters. *arXiv preprint arXiv:1505.01120*, 2015.

[23] J. A. Stuart and J. D. Owens. Multi-gpu mapreduce on gpu clusters. In *Parallel & Distributed Processing Symposium (IPDPS), 2011 IEEE International*, pages 1068–1079. IEEE, 2011.

[24] The Apache Software Foundation. Spark MLlib. http://spark.apache.org/mllib/.

[25] S. Verdoolaege, J. Carlos Juega, A. Cohen, J. Ignacio Gómez, C. Tenllado, and F. Catthoor. Polyhedral parallel code generation for cuda. *ACM Transactions on Architecture and Code Optimization (TACO)*, 9(4):54, 2013.

[26] Yu-Ting Chen. Cloud-Scale BWAMEM. https://github.com/ytchen0323/cloud-scale-bwamem.

Consecutive Job Submission Behavior at Mira Supercomputer

Stephan Schlagkamp[1,2], Rafael Ferreira da Silva[2], William Allcock[3]
Ewa Deelman[2], Uwe Schwiegelshohn[1]
[1]Robotics Research Institute, TU Dortmund University, Dortmund, Germany
[2]University of Southern California, Information Sciences Institute, Marina Del Rey, CA, USA
[3]Argonne National Laboratory, Argonne, IL, USA
{stephan.schlagkamp,uwe.schwiegelshohn}@udo.edu, {rafsilva,deelman}@isi.edu,
allcock@anl.gov

ABSTRACT

Understanding user behavior is crucial for the evaluation of scheduling and allocation performances in HPC environments. This paper aims to further understand the dynamic user reaction to different levels of system performance by performing a comprehensive analysis of user behavior in recorded data in the form of delays in the subsequent job submission behavior. Therefore, we characterize a workload trace covering one year of job submissions from the Mira supercomputer at ALCF (Argonne Leadership Computing Facility). We perform an in-depth analysis of correlations between job characteristics, system performance metrics, and the subsequent user behavior. Analysis results show that the user behavior is significantly influenced by long waiting times, and that complex jobs (number of nodes and CPU hours) lead to longer delays in subsequent job submissions.

Keywords

User behavior, workload analysis, performance modeling.

1. INTRODUCTION

High Performance Computing (HPC) is mainstream for performing large-scale scientific computing [8, 12]. As a result, computing centers are devoting significant effort to satisfy the requirements of scientific applications, and provide high QoS. Understanding user reactions to the system performance is a key factor for improving user satisfaction, while improving the performance of scheduling systems [3]. Job schedulers often model workloads based on job requirements or historical performance data. However, using workload traces without the understanding of the user behavioral mechanisms may produce misleading results [18].

In this work, we aim to improve performance evaluation processes and testing environments by investigating the feedback effects between parallel job characteristics. We evaluate how system performance and job characteristics impact users' subsequent job submission behavior in HPC. We then extend and evaluate the definition of users' think time [2] (the timespan between a job completion and the submission of the next job), to assess the influence of system delays, and job complexity (number of nodes and CPU time) on the user behavior. We analyze a 1-year scheduling trace (2014) from the Mira supercomputer at ALCF to characterize the subsequent think time as a function of the job response time, as well as the think time response to queueing and processing time. Furthermore, we also analyze the think time in response to the slowdown and the job complexity. Our findings show that these components are strongly correlated and have a significant influence on user behavior. The main contributions of this work include (1) the characterization of a leadership supercomputer scheduling workload; (2) an evaluation of the think time definition for measuring delays in users' subsequent job submission behavior in HPC systems; (3) an in-depth analysis of correlations between subsequent think times, job characteristics, and system performance metrics; and (4) an analysis of the correlation of multidimensional metrics on user behavior.

2. BACKGROUND AND RELATED WORK

Although there is a plethora of works that analyze and suggest improvements to schedulers in HPC [3], there is a gap between theoretical results and their practical application [17]. This issue can be addressed by: assessing user behavior through cognitive studies, e.g., in the form of questionnaires—to investigate user reactions to high system utilization or acceptance for long waiting times, and user satisfaction [13,16]; or analyzing workload traces gathered from these systems, which can reveal aspects of user behavior related to system performance metrics and job characteristics. In [2], aspects of dynamic correlations between system performance, utilization, and the subsequent behavior are observed from analyzes of user behavior using HPC traces. These analyses have enabled: the development of models emphasizing aspects of the user behavior [10]; scheduling algorithms that leverage the knowledge about the users [19]; the analysis of workloads to characterize the submission behavior in the form of batches of jobs and user sessions [20]; and workload models and simulations to mimic the dynamic nature of user and system interaction [5, 15]. Several pa-

HPDC'16, May 31-June 04, 2016, Kyoto, Japan
© 2016 ACM. ISBN 978-1-4503-4314-5/16/05...$15.00
DOI: http://dx.doi.org/10.1145/2907294.2907314

Science Field	#Users	#Jobs	CPU hours (millions)	#TT Jobs
Physics	73	24,429	2,256	2,675
Materials Science	77	12,546	895	1,530
Chemistry	51	10,286	810	1,959
Computer Science*	75	9,261	96	—
Engineering	98	6,588	614	1,870
Earth Science	42	6,455	270	1,397
Biological Sciences	31	3,642	192	—
Other	40	5,575	565	—
Mira	487	78,782	5,698	14,145

*significant number of jobs run in *backfill* queue

Table 1: Characteristics of the Mira workload from Jan–Dec 2014, and number of subsequent jobs with positive think times: $0 < TT \leq 8$hrs.

pers have addressed computing workload characterization and modeling. In [6,7,9], analyses of grid, HPC, and HTC workload characteristics emphasized system usage, user population, and application characteristics. In [14], an analysis of a 5-years workloads from two Supercomputers at NERSC evaluates system performance metrics. The I/O behavior of the Intrepid Supercomputer at ALCF is shown in [1], while analyses of I/O workload traces from Intrepid and Mira are shown in [11]. Although these papers present a detailed analysis of system performance metrics, none of them have focused on the user behavior.

3. WORKLOAD CHARACTERIZATION

The analyses presented here are based on the workload from Mira, the IBM Blue Gene/Q system at ALCF. Mira is a 786,432-core production system with 768 TiB of RAM, and a peak performance of 10 PFlops. Each node is composed of 16 cores, and the minimum allocation per job is 512 nodes (8,192 cores). Mira's workload comprises 1-year computational jobs execution in 2014, which consists of 78,782 jobs, submitted by 487 users from 13 science domains. In total, these jobs consumed over 5.6 billion CPU hours. Table 1 shows the summary of the main characteristics of the dataset, and highlights the most important (by the number of jobs) science domain fields. Most of Computer Science jobs ($\sim$65%) consume less than the minimum allocation (i.e., 512 nodes or 8,192 cores), and have very short runtimes (less than 15 min), thus we see the low CPU hours consumption regardless the high number of jobs. Furthermore, about 25% of the computer science jobs ran in the backfill queue, which may bias user behavior—the uncertainty of the job start time is elevated. Therefore, Computer Science jobs are not considered in this study.

4. CHARACTERIZING THINK TIME

The user's *think time* quantifies the timespan between a job completion and the submission of the next job (by the same user) [2]. This metric is seen as capturing the influence of the system performance on user behavior (e.g., dissatisfied users may tend to throttle job submission, long queueing times may deviate the user's focus from their experiments, etc. [4,18]). In this paper, we analyze think time as a function of performance, i.e., response time (job walltime) and slowdown, and investigate whether waiting time or runtime have a more significant impact on the user behavior [2]. Additionally, we evaluate how job complexity (in terms of job

size and total CPU time) may also affect the think time behavior.

Think Time. Let s_j be the time when a job j is submitted, p_j the job processing time, and w_j the job waiting time. We define the job response time r_j as the sum of its waiting and processing times: $r_j = w_j + p_j$. Thus, we define the job completion time c_j as the sum of the job submission and response times: $c_j = s_j + r_j$. Job interarrival time is the timespan between two subsequent job submissions (j and j') by the same user. Two subsequent jobs are *overlapped* if job j has not finished before job j' is submitted ($c_j > s_{j'}$). Otherwise, they are considered *non-overlapped*, which are the set of jobs we focus on this paper. Therefore, we define think time TT as the timespan between the completion time of job j and the submission time of its successor j': $\mathrm{TT}(j, j') = s_{j'} - c_j$. For overlapping jobs, the think time is negative, thus we only consider subsequent job submissions of positive think time. Additionally, we only consider think times of less than eight hours, which is intended to represent subsequent job submissions belonging to the same working day. This threshold also eliminates biased user behaviors characterized by absent submissions for long periods of time followed by burst submissions for short periods (e.g., conference deadlines, allocation expiration, etc.). Table 1 also shows the number of subsequent jobs with positive think times for the studied science domains.

4.1 Analysis of Job Characteristics and Performance Parameters on Think Time

The analysis of think time behavior is often limited to the study of the impact of response time on user behavior. As response time is defined as a function of waiting and processing times, we evaluate how these components correlate with users' think times. Fig. 1a shows the average think times for subsequent jobs of Mira. All science fields follow the same linear trend, with slight differences for Engineering (for short response times) and Physics (for response times $\sim$5,000s). This difference is due to a few points that deviate from the averages. For Engineering, the peak is due solely to a pair of jobs that present a very high think time value of $\sim$8h. For Physics, a few points yield very low values (nearly instantaneous subsequent submissions). This behavior is typically due to the use of automated scripts or jobs that failed within a few seconds after submission. The analysis of think times in terms of processing time (a.k.a. runtime, Fig. 1b) and waiting time (Fig. 1c) shows that on average, the parameters have an equal influence on user behavior. This result lead to the conclusion that reducing queueing times would not significantly improve think times for long running jobs.

4.2 Analysis of Job Characteristics in Terms of Runtime and Waiting Time

The analysis of think times for subsequent job submissions of the Mira's trace showed that system performance metrics such as runtime and waiting time have a significant impact on user behavior. Hence, we investigate how job characteristics, in particular the job size and workload, combined with performance parameters impact think times. To this end, we conduct analyses using multidimensional metrics, i.e., we analyze the subsequent think time in response to, slowdown and job size. Note that the slowdown is itself another multidimensional metric defined as the factor between a job actual response time and its runtime:

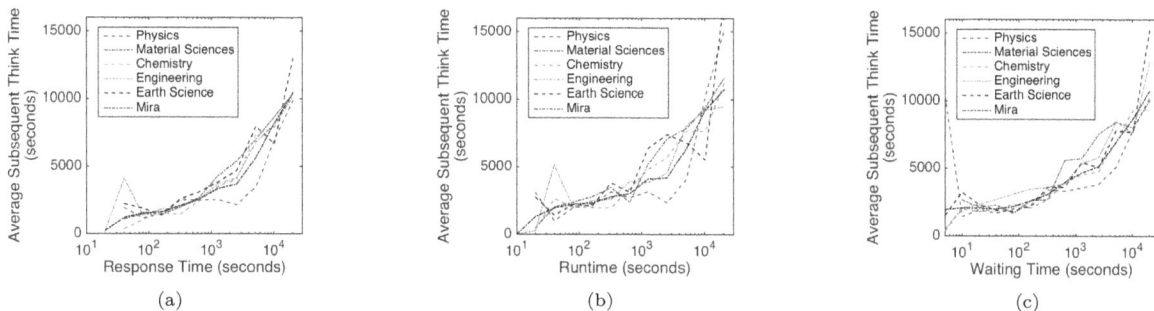

Figure 1: Average think times as a function of (a) response time, (b) runtime, and (c) waiting time.

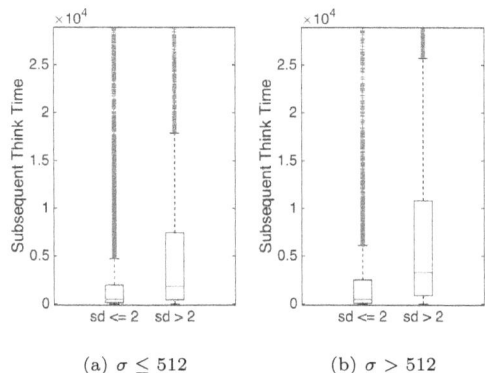

(a) $\sigma \leq 512$ (b) $\sigma > 512$

Figure 2: Influence of prevalent (sd $\leq$ 2) and non-prevalent (sd $>$ 2) runtimes on the users think times for (a) small and (b) large jobs in terms of job size (number of nodes). Note that sd denotes the slow-down, and whiskers are defined as 1.5 IQR.

$sd(j) = \frac{r_j}{p_j} = \frac{w_j + p_j}{p_j}$. The analyses conducted here use the job slowdown sd as a metric to separate jobs into two subsets: (1) *runtime-dominant*—the job runtime prevails the waiting time (sd $\leq$ 2); and (2) *wait-time-dominant*—jobs spend more time in queue than running (sd $>$ 2).

Fig. 2 shows the think time distribution according to job sizes. We divide the dataset into groups of small jobs that require the minimum amount of allocated nodes ($\sigma \leq 512$, Fig. 2a), which represent 49.2% of the total number of subsequent jobs, and large jobs requiring up to all available nodes (Fig. 2b). This threshold identifies the subset of jobs with low think time values ($<$ 1.5 hours). Several outliers characterize the datasets as heavy-tailed distributed, which is expected due to the natural variation of the user behavior and the large number of sampling data. Therefore, our analyses use the median as a robust metric to cope with outliers. In both scenarios, think times are relatively small when runtime prevails. The median think time is 507s for small jobs, and for large jobs 439s. The third quartile also yields low values (2,083s for small, and 2,361s for large jobs). Additionally, user behavior does not seem to be impacted by the job complexity (job size)—the average think times for both small and large jobs are of similar magnitude. Note that the third quartile values for *runtime-dominant* are below median values of *wait-time-dominant*. Prevailing waiting times may significantly affect user behavior, and the job size seems to influence the queueing time. For small jobs, the median think time is 2,478s, and for large jobs 4,276s. This result suggests that think time is not directly bound to job size, but the uncertainty produced by large waiting times. The

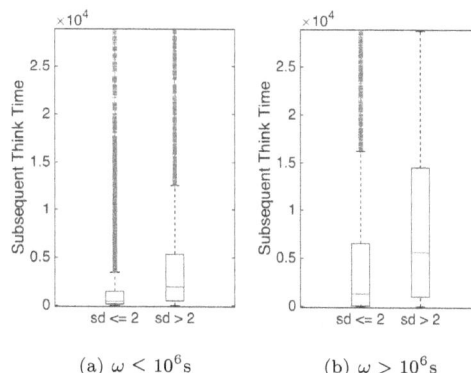

(a) $\omega \leq 10^6$s (b) $\omega > 10^6$s

Figure 3: Influence of prevalent (sd $\leq$ 2) and non-prevalent (sd $>$ 2) runtimes on the users think times for (a) small and (b) large jobs in terms of workload.

analysis of the job size parameter is limited to the number of nodes. On the other hand, the job workload ω (defined as the total CPU time of the job) also includes the time dimension. Fig. 3 shows the think time distribution in terms of workload. Small jobs are characterized by usage of less than ~277 CPU hours (10^6s), which identifies subsets with low think time values (under 1.5 hours). In contrast to the previous analysis, more complex jobs do yield higher think times. However, similar behavior is observed when the runtime or waiting time prevail. For *runtime-dominant*, small jobs have a median think time of 437s, and large jobs 1,305s. However, the third quartiles present a larger difference—1,478s for small jobs, and 6,544s for large ones. Waiting times have equivalent influence on the job size analysis. For small jobs, the median think time is 1,954s, and for large jobs 5,645s. These results indicate that (1) complex jobs require more think time to plan and release a new experiment (e.g., visualization and analysis on other systems); or (2) users do not have a full understanding of the expected behavior of their jobs, thus they lack of accurate estimate of the processing time. To validate the first assumption, an assessment of user behavior in the form of direct interview or questionnaires would be required [13], while the second assumption could be validated by investigating jobs that used a notification mechanism to alert the user of job completion.

4.3 Summary and Discussion

Our analysis of the user behavior has advanced the understanding of the think times between subsequent job submissions. Our findings sustain the premise that the job response time is the most significant factor influencing think time. However, not all elements constituting the response time have equivalent influence. Job characteristics (job size and workload) have a substantial impact on the queueing time a job will experience. Therefore, we argue that the think time definition should also consider job complexity. For large workloads, the job runtime also negatively influences the user behavior, despite short queuing times. This result suggests that users need more time to *think* about their experiment results and next steps, in particular for complex experiments. The analysis results contradict the assumptions made for the development of user-aware algorithms based on batches and sessions (e.g., CREASY scheduler [19]). For instance, CREASY considers response time as the main factor to increase steadiness within user sessions. However, further analysis suggests that other characteristics also impact the delays in subsequent job submission behavior. that other characteristics correlate Therefore, we argue that user-aware scheduling should not only consider response time, but also job characteristics such as the job complexity.

Although similar think time behaviors can still be identified in today's systems, the assumptions taken by this definition are restrictive and may lead to misleading conclusions. For instance, the 8hs threshold between subsequent job submissions limits the analysis for a small subset of the dataset (∼19% in this work), which may not capture all consecutive job submission behaviors of the system. The analyzed subset is mostly composed of jobs that require up to 512 nodes, which represents less than 10% of the total dataset. Thus, we argue that this definition does not scale to the complexity of today's applications and systems. Additionally, think time may also include the time that the user spends on other steps of the experiment—it is common to perform further computational analysis and visualization within an experiment using other systems. In this case, the time spent on these system should also be accounted for the think time. Therefore, we argue that a user-assisted analysis would significantly contribute to the understanding of this process. Finally, when simulating submission behavior one has to consider other job characteristics and system performance components beside the response time. For instance, probability based models [18], or linear models [15], which consider response time of jobs or batches to model inter-arrival times, would not produce accurate predictions.

5. CONCLUSION

In this paper, we have investigated the main factors influencing the users' response to system performance (think time). We analyzed over 78K jobs submitted by 450+ users to the Mira HPC system at ALCF. Analysis results show that job response times are linearly correlated to think times. Additionally, the analysis of the job complexity (number of nodes or workload) combined with slowdown unveil strong correlations between waiting time and the subsequent think time. Moreover, large workloads negatively influence user behavior. We acknowledge that the definition of think time may be restrictive and does not cover all edge cases. In the future, we intend to extend the current definition and explore new ones (based on concurrent activities) to evaluate how different assumptions of user behavior are influenced by performance metrics and job characteristics. We also intend to model think time as a function of job complexity from past job submissions. Future work will also include cognitive studies to unravel the real causes driving the user decisions, which cannot be obtained from statistical analysis.

Acknowledgements. This work was partly funded by DOE contract number ER26110, "dV/dt - Accelerating the Rate of Progress Towards Extreme Scale Collaborative Science", and #DESC0012636, "Panorama - Predictive Modeling and Diagnostic Monitoring of Extreme Science Workflows", and by the German Research Foundation, RTG 1855. This research used resources of the Argonne Leadership Computing Facility, which is a DOE Office of Science User Facility supported under Contract DE-AC02-06CH11357.

6. REFERENCES

[1] P. Carns et al. Understanding and improving computational science storage access through continuous characterization. *ACM TOS*, 7(3), 2011.

[2] D. G. Feitelson. Looking at data. In *IEEE IPDPS*, 2008.

[3] D. G. Feitelson. *Workload modeling for computer systems performance evaluation*. Cambridge University Press, 2015.

[4] D. G. Feitelson and A. W. Mu'alem. On the definition of on-line in job scheduling problems. *ACM SIGACT News*, 36(1), 2005.

[5] D. G. Feitelson and E. Shmueli. A case for conservative workload modeling: Parallel job scheduling with daily cycles of activity. In *IEEE MASCOTS*, 2009.

[6] R. Ferreira da Silva et al. Characterizing a high throughput computing workload: The compact muon solenoid (CMS) experiment at LHC. *Procedia Computer Science*, 51, 2015.

[7] R. Ferreira da Silva and T. Glatard. A science-gateway workload archive to study pilot jobs, user activity, bag of tasks, task sub-steps, and workflow executions. In *Euro-Par*. Springer, 2013.

[8] A. Geist and D. A. Reed. A survey of high-performance computing scaling challenges. *IJHPCA*, 2015.

[9] D. L. Hart. Measuring TeraGrid: workload characterization for a high-performance computing federation. *IJHPCA*, 25(4), 2011.

[10] C. B. Lee and A. Snavely. On the user–scheduler dialogue: studies of user-provided runtime estimates and utility functions. *IJHPCA*, 20(4), 2006.

[11] H. Luu et al. A multiplatform study of I/O behavior on petascale supercomputers. In *ACM HPDC*, 2015.

[12] D. A. Reed and J. Dongarra. Exascale computing and big data. *Communications of the ACM*, 58(7), 2015.

[13] J. Renker et al. Questionnaire for user habits of compute clusters (QUHCC). In *HCI International*. Springer, 2015.

[14] G. P. Rodrigo Álvarez et al. HPC system lifetime story: Workload characterization and evolutionary analyses on NERSC systems. In *ACM HPDC*, 2015.

[15] S. Schlagkamp. Influence of dynamic think times on parallel job scheduler performances in generative simulations. In *JSSPP*, 2015.

[16] S. Schlagkamp and J. Renker. Acceptance of waiting times in high performance computing. In *HCI International*. Springer, 2015.

[17] U. Schwiegelshohn. How to design a job scheduling algorithm. In *JSSPP*. Springer, 2014.

[18] E. Shmueli and D. G. Feitelson. Using site-level modeling to evaluate the performance of parallel system schedulers. In *IEEE MASCOTS*, 2006.

[19] E. Shmueli and D. G. Feitelson. On simulation and design of parallel-systems schedulers: are we doing the right thing? *IEEE TPDS*, 20(7), 2009.

[20] N. Zakay and D. G. Feitelson. On identifying user session boundaries in parallel workload logs. In *JSSPP*. Springer, 2013.

Scaling Spark on HPC Systems

Nicholas Chaimov   Allen Malony
University of Oregon
{nchaimov,malony}@cs.uoregon.edu

Shane Canon   Costin Iancu
Khaled Z. Ibrahim   Jay Srinivasan
Lawrence Berkeley National Laboratory
{scanon,cciancu,kzibrahim,jsrinivasan}@lbl.gov

ABSTRACT

We report our experiences porting Spark to large production HPC systems. While Spark performance in a data center installation (with local disks) is dominated by the network, our results show that file system metadata access latency can dominate in a HPC installation using Lustre: it determines single node performance up to $4\times$ slower than a typical workstation. We evaluate a combination of software techniques and hardware configurations designed to address this problem. For example, on the software side we develop a file pooling layer able to improve per node performance up to $2.8\times$. On the hardware side we evaluate a system with a large NVRAM buffer between compute nodes and the backend Lustre file system: this improves scaling at the expense of per-node performance. Overall, our results indicate that scalability is currently limited to $O(10^2)$ cores in a HPC installation with Lustre and default Spark. After careful configuration combined with our pooling we can scale up to $O(10^4)$. As our analysis indicates, it is feasible to observe much higher scalability in the near future.

CCS Concepts

•**Software and its engineering** → **Ultra-large-scale systems**; **Cloud computing**;

Keywords

Spark, HPC, Data Analytics

1. INTRODUCTION

Frameworks such as Hadoop [30] and Spark [32] provide a productive high level programming interface for large scale data processing and analytics. Through specialized runtimes they attain good performance and resilience on data center systems for a robust ecosystem of application specific libraries [14, 22, 5]. This combination resulted in widespread adoption that continues to open new problem domains.

This paper is authored by an employee(s) of the United States Government and is in the public domain. Non-exclusive copying or redistribution is allowed, provided that the article citation is given and the authors and agency are clearly identified as its source.

HPDC'16, May 31-June 04, 2016, Kyoto, Japan

ACM ISBN 978-1-4503-4314-5/16/05. . . $15.00

DOI: http://dx.doi.org/10.1145/2907294.2907310

As multiple science fields have started to use analytics for filtering results between coupled simulations (e.g. materials science or climate) or extracting interesting features from high throughput observations (e.g. telescopes, particle accelerators), there exists plenty incentive for the deployment of the existing large scale data analytics tools on High Performance Computing systems. Yet, most solutions are ad-hoc and data center frameworks have not gained traction in our community. In this paper we report our experiences porting and scaling Spark on two current very large scale Cray XC systems (Edison and Cori), deployed in production at National Energy Research Scientific Computing Center (NERSC) [2].

In a distributed data center environment disk I/O is optimized for latency by using local disks and the network between nodes nodes is optimized primarily for bandwidth. In contrast, HPC systems use a global parallel file system, with no local storage: disk I/O is optimized primarily for bandwidth, while the network is optimized for latency. Our initial expectation, was that after porting Spark to Cray, we can then couple large scale simulations using $O(10^4)$ cores, benchmark and start optimizing it to exploit the strengths of HPC hardware: low latency networking and tightly coupled global name spaces on disk and in memory.

We ported Spark to run on the Cray XC family in Extreme Scalability Mode (ESM) and started by calibrating single node performance when using the Lustre [7] global file system against that of an workstation with local SSDs: in this configuration a Cray node performed up to $4\times$ slower than the workstation. Unlike clouds, where due to the presence of local disks Spark shuffle performance is dominated by the network [25], file system metadata performance initially dominates on HPC systems. Perhaps expected by parallel I/O experts [21], the determining performance factor is the file system metadata latency (e.g. occurring in `fopen`), rather than the latency or bandwidth of read or write operations. We found the magnitude of this problem surprising, even at small scale. Scalability of Spark when using the back-end Lustre file system is limited to $O(10^2)$ cores.

After instrumenting Spark and the domain libraries evaluated (Spark SQL, GraphX), the conclusion was that a solution has to handle *both* high level domain libraries (e.g. Parquet data readers or application input stage) *and* the Spark internals. We calibrated single node performance, then we performed strong and weak scaling studies on both systems. We evaluate software techniques to alleviate the single node performance gap in the presence of a parallel file system:

- First and most obvious configuration is to use a local file system, in main memory or mounted to a single Lustre file, to handle the intermediate results generated during the computation. While this configuration does not handle the application level I/O, it improves performance during the Map and Reduce phases and a single Cray node can match the workstation performance. This configuration enables scaling up to 10,000 cores and beyond, for more details see Section 5.3. We have extended and released the Shifter [18] container framework for Cray XC with this functionality. Deploying Spark on Shifter has unexpected benefits for the JVM performance and we observe 16% performance improvements when running in memory on $\approx$ 10,000 cores.

- As the execution during both application initialization and inside Spark opens the same file multiple times, we explore "caching" solutions to eliminate file metadata operations. In Spark, the number of files used grows linearly with the number of cores, while the number of file opens grows quadratically with cores. We developed a layer to intercept and cache file metadata operations at both levels. A single Cray node with pooling also matches workstation performance and overall we see scalability up to 10,000 cores. Combining pooling with local file systems also improves performance (up to 17%) by eliminating system calls during execution.

On Cori we also evaluate a layer of non-volatile storage (`BurstBuffer`) that sits between the processors' memory and the parallel file system, specifically designed to accelerate I/O performance. Performance when using it is better than Lustre (by 3.5× on 16 nodes), but slower than RAM-backed file systems (by 1.2×), for *GroupBy*, a metadata-heavy benchmark. With `BurstBuffer` we can scale Spark only up to 1,200 cores. The improvements come from better `fopen` scalability, rather than read/write latency and illustrate the principle that optimizing for the tail is important at scale: the `BurstBuffer` median open latency is higher than Lustre's, but its variance is much smaller than on Lustre.

Besides metadata latency, file system access latency in `read` and `write` operations may limit scalability. In our study, this became apparent when examining iterative algorithms. As described in Section 6, the Spark implementation of PageRank did not scale when solving problems that did not fit inside the node's main memory. The problem was the interplay between resilience mechanisms and block management inside the shuffle stage in Spark, that generated a number of I/O requests that increased exponentially with iterations. This overwhelmed the centralized storage system. We fixed this particular case at the algorithmic level, but a more generic approach is desirable to cover the space of iterative methods.

Overall, our study indicates that scaling data analytics frameworks on HPC systems is likely to become feasible in the near future: a single HPC style architecture can serve both scientific and data intensive workloads. The solution requires a combination of hardware support, systems software configuration and (simple) engineering changes to Spark and application libraries. Metadata performance is already a concern for scientific workloads and HPC center operators are happily throwing more hardware at the problem. Hardware to increase the node local storage with large

NVRAM will decrease both metadata and file access overhead through better caching close to the processors. Orthogonal software techniques, such the ones evaluated in this paper, can further reduce metadata impact. In fact, at the time of the publication, our colleagues at NERSC have demonstrated Spark runs at $\approx 50,000$ cores using Shifter with our Lustre mounted local file system configuration. An engineering audit of the application libraries and the Spark internals will also eliminate many root causes of performance bottlenecks.

2. SPARK ARCHITECTURE

Apache Spark [32] and Hadoop [30] are open-source data analytics frameworks, designed to operate on datasets larger than can be processed on a single node while automatically providing for scheduling and load-balancing. They implement the Map-Reduce model [12] using an abstraction in which programs are expressed as data flow graphs. The nodes in the graph are of two types: *map operations*, which are purely local, and *reduce operations*, which can involve communication between nodes.

The traditional MapReduce framework [12] is limited to acyclic graphs, preventing efficient representation of iterative methods, and it uses data redundancy to provide resiliency. Spark can handle cyclic and acyclic graphs, and provides resiliency through *resilient distributed datasets* [31] (RDD), which carry sufficient information (lineage) to recompute their contents. In particular, the ability to express iterative algorithms accelerated Spark's adoption.

Programs are expressed in terms of RDDs derived from transformations of other RDDs (e.g. Map) and actions (e.g. Reduce). The application developer can choose to request that certain RDDs be cached in memory or saved to disk. The developer therefore has to make decisions based on tradeoffs between the costs of storage (in memory and time) and recomputation (in time). RDDs are lazily evaluated, which creates challenges [6] in attributing performance to particular lines or regions of code, as they do not execute until they are needed.

In Spark, the *Master* node executes a driver program, which creates the data flow graph by applying transformations and actions to RDDs, and partitions ownership of data to worker nodes within the cluster. When the result of an uncomputed RDD partition is needed, a *job* is created, consisting of multiple *stages*. Within a stage, only intra-partition communication can occur. All inter-partition communication happens at stage boundaries, through a process called *shuffling*, as shown in Figure 1. By deferring any computation until a result is needed, the scheduler can schedule work to compute only what is necessary to produce the result. In the event of the loss of a partition, only that partition needs to be recomputed.

2.1 Data Movement in Spark

Data movement is one of the performance determining factors in any large scale system. In Spark, data is logically split into *partitions*, which have an associated worker task. A partition is subdivided into *blocks*: a block is the unit of data movement and execution. Figure 2 shows the interaction of the Spark compute engine with the block and shuffle managers, which control data movement. The Block-Manager handles application level input and output data, as well as intermediate data within the Map stages. The Shuf-

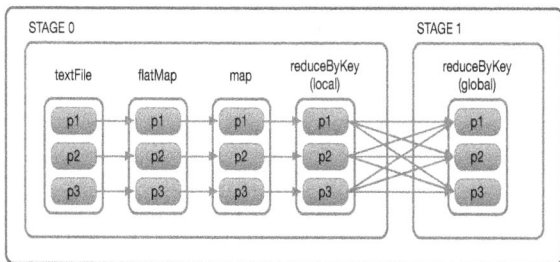

Figure 1: *Decomposition of a job into stages and tasks on partitions, with inter-partition communication limited to stage boundaries.*

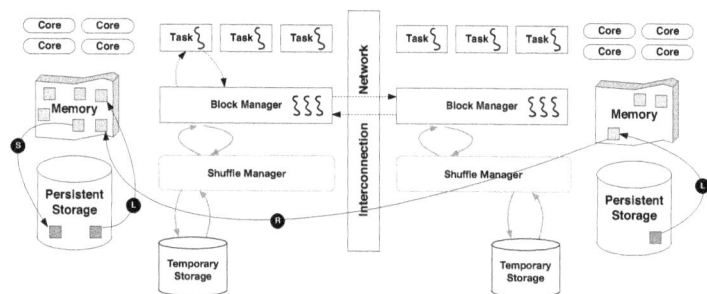

Figure 2: *Data movement in Spark and the interaction with the memory hierarchy.*

fleManager handles runtime intermediate results during the shuffle stage.

Data Objects and Naming: Spark manipulates data with global scope, as well as local scope. Application level data (RDDs) are using a global naming space, intermediate data blocks generated throughout execution have a local scope and naming scheme. Objects may exceed the capacity of the physical memory and need to be efficiently moved through the storage hierarchy; the typical challenge when managing naming schemes is mismatch with underlying system architecture. For instance, when global object is distributed (partitioned) across multiple storage spaces a long latency naming service may be needed to locate its physical location. Conversely, any locally named object stored in a physically shared storage may experience undue contention while servicing requests. A current research direction in the Spark community is providing an efficient global naming service, which can reduce network traffic. Note that the global file system in HPC installations provides global naming.

Vertical Data Movement: Vertical data movement refers to the movement through the entire memory hierarchy, including persistent storage. It is needed to move input data blocks into the memory for processing and for storing output data to the persistent storage. To minimize vertical movement for RDDs, Spark allows persisting data in the fast level of memory. As fast memory is capacity constrained, the Spark runtime assigns the task of moving objects across the memory hierarchy to a block manager. Whenever the working set size (input data or intermediate results) exceeds memory capacity, the block manager may trigger vertical data movement. The block manager may also decide to drop a block, in which case its later access may trigger additional vertical data movement for recomputation. Research efforts such as Tachyon [19] aim to reduce expensive (to storage) vertical data movement by replacing it with horizontal (inter-node) data movement. In network-based storage systems, a critical [4, 8] component to the performance of vertical data movement is the file setup stage (communication with the metadata servers).

Horizontal Data Movement - Block Shuffling: The horizontal data movement refers to the shuffle communication phase between compute nodes. Spark assigns the horizontal data movement to the shuffle manager and the block manager. A horizontal data movement request of a block could trigger a vertical data movement because a block may

not be resident in memory. Optimizing the performance of horizontal data movement has been the subject of multiple studies [29, 17, 20], in which hardware acceleration such as RDMA is used to reduce the communication cost. The benefit of these techniques is less profound on HPC systems with network-based storage [26] because the performance is dominated by vertical data movement.

2.2 System Architecture and Data Movement

Data centers have local storage attached to compute nodes. This enables fast vertical data movement and the number of storage disks scales linearly with the number nodes involved in the computation. Their bandwidth also scale with the number of compute nodes. The archetypal file system for data analytics is the Hadoop Distributed File System (HDFS) which aims to provide both fault tolerance and high throughput access to data. HDFS implements a simple coherency for write-once-read-many file access, which fits well the Spark and Hadoop processing models. In Spark with HDFS, global naming services are implemented in a client-server paradigm. A request is generated for the object owner, subject to the network latency. The owner services it, maybe subject to disk latency (or bandwidth) and the reply is subject to network latency (or bandwidth). Vertical data transfers access the local disk. Horizontal data are subject to network latency/bandwidth, as well as disk latency/bandwidth.

HPC systems use dedicated I/O subsystems, where storage is attached to a "centralized" file system controller. Each and all nodes can see the same amount of storage, and bandwidth to storage is carefully provisioned for the system as a whole. Given that these network file servers are shared between many concurrently scheduled applications, the servers typically optimize for overall system throughput. As such individual applications may observe increase in latency and higher variability. The Lustre [7] architecture, presented in Figure 3 is carefully optimized for throughput and implements a generic many-write-many-read coherency protocol. The installation consists of clients, a Metadata service (MDS) and Object Storage service. The Metadata service contains Metadata Servers, which handle global naming and persistence and the Metadata Targets which provide the actual metadata storage (HDD/SSD). In Spark with Lustre, global naming services access the metadata servers and are subject to network latency and MDS latency. Most existing Lustre installations in production (prior to Lustre 2.6) use a single MDS, only very recent installations [1, 10] use multi-

99

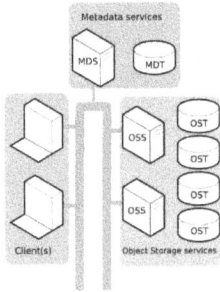

Figure 3: *Lustre architecture. (Courtesy of Intel Wiki.)*

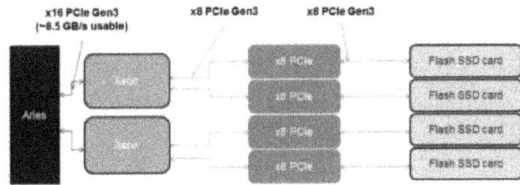

Figure 4: `BurstBuffer` *node architecture.(Courtesy of NERSC.)*

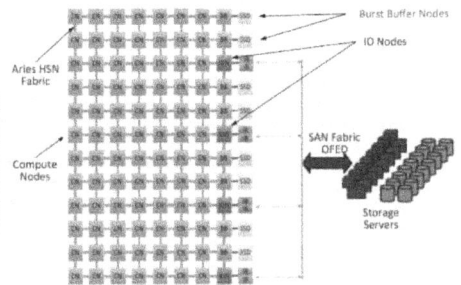

Figure 5: `BurstBuffer` *topology. (Courtesy of NERSC.)*

ple MDSes for improved scalability. Vertical data transfers are served by the Object Storage service, which contains the object Storage Server (OSS) and the Object Storage Target (OST), the HDD/SSD that stores the data. Bandwidth is provisioned in large scale installations by adding additional OSSes.

In our quest to introduce Spark into the HPC community there are two main questions to answer.

1. How does the differences in architecture between data centers and HPC influence performance? Previous performance studies of Spark in data center environments [25] indicate that its performance is dominated by the network, through careful optimizations to minimize vertical data movement and maximize the memory resident working set. Ousterhout et al. [23] analyzed the performance of the Big Data Benchmark [28] on 5 Amazon EC2 nodes, for a total of 40 cores, and the TPC-DS benchmark [24] on 20 nodes (160 cores) on EC2. These benchmarks both use Spark SQL [5], which allows SQL queries to be performed over RDDs. By instrumenting the Spark runtime, they were able to attribute time spent in tasks to several factors, including network and disk I/O and computation. They found that, contrary to popular wisdom about data analytics workflow, that disk I/O is not particularly important: when all work is done on disk, the median speedup from eliminating disk I/O entirely was only 19%, and, more importantly, when all RDDs are persisted to memory, only a 2-5% improvement was achieved from eliminating disk I/O. Upon introduction to HPC systems, we similarly need to understand whether access to storage or network performance dominates within Spark.

2. What HPC specific features can we exploit to boost Spark performance? Previous work optimizing data analytics frameworks on HPC systems [20, 17] proposes moving away from the client-server distributed paradigm and exploiting the global file name space already available or Remote Direct Memory Access (RDMA) functionality. Upon introduction to HPC systems, we are interesting in evaluating the potential for performance improvement of adopting such techniques into Spark. Besides providing an initial guide to system researchers, we are also interested in providing configuration guidelines to users and system operators.

We explore these questions using three benchmarks selected to cover the performance space: 1) *BigData Benchmark* uses SparkSQL [5] and stresses vertical data movement; 2) *GroupBy* is a core Spark benchmark designed to capture the worst case scenario for shuffle performance, it stresses both horizontal and vertical data movement; and 3)

PageRank is an iterative algorithm from GraphX [14] and stresses vertical data movement.

3. EXPERIMENTAL SETUP

We conducted our experiments on the Edison and Cori Cray XC supercomputers at NERSC [2]. Edison contains 5,576 compute nodes, each with two 2.4 GHz 12-core Intel "Ivy Bridge" processors. Cori contains 1,630 compute nodes, each with two 2.3 GHz 16-core Intel "Haswell" processors. Both systems use a Cray Aries interconnect based on the Dragonfly topology.

Cray provides a Cluster Compatibility Mode (CCM) for compute jobs requiring specialized services, such as secure connection, etc. CCM runs Linux and allows an easy path to configure Spark, but imposes limits on the number of nodes per job. More importantly, it disables network transfer mechanisms accelerated by the Aries hardware.

In this study, we ported Spark 1.5.0 to run on the Cray Extreme Scalability Mode (ESM) to allow better scaling of resources. In ESM, a lightweight kernel runs on the compute nodes and the application has full access to Aries. Spark 1.6 has been subsequently released: as file I/O patterns did not change the optimizations we describe in this paper remain applicable to it. We use one manager per compute node, based on YARN 2.4.1. This required additional porting efforts to allow TCP-based services. Compared to Spark's standalone scheduler, YARN allows better control of the resources allocated in each node. The Mesos [16] resource manager provides similar control as YARN, but requires administrative privilege. Job admission is done through a resource manager on the front-end node where Spark runs as a YARN client with exclusive access to all resources.

Both Edison and Cori use the Lustre file system. On Edison, the Lustre file system is backed by a single metadata server (MDS) and a single metadata target (MDT) per file system. On Cori, a master MDS is assisted by a 4 additional Distributed Namespace (DNE) MDSes. The DNEs do not yet support full functionality, and for all Spark concerns Cori performs as a single MDS system.

On Cori we also evaluate a layer of non-volatile storage (`BurstBuffer`) that sits between the processors' memory and the parallel file system, specifically designed to accelerate I/O performance. The NERSC hardware is based on Cray DataWarp and presented in Figures 4 and 5. The flash memory for Cray DataWarp is attached to Burst Buffer nodes that are packaged two nodes to a blade. Each Burst Buffer node contains a Xeon processor 64 GB of DDR3 memory, and two 3.2 TB NAND flash SSD modules attached over two PCIe gen3 x8 interfaces. Each Burst Buffer node is attached to a Cray Aries network interconnect over a PCIe gen3 x16 interface. Each Burst Buffer node provides approximately 6.4 TB of usable capacity and a peak of approximately 5.7 GB/sec of sequential read and write bandwidth. The `BurstBuffer` nodes can be accessed from the compute nodes in *private* mode and in *striped* mode. Ours is the first evaluation on such technology at scale. However, since the hardware is new and not tuned yet for production, the `BurstBuffer` results are only indications of its potential and it features; we expect them to evolve and improve.

We evaluate *BigData Benchmark*, *GroupBy* and *PageRank* in both weak and strong scaling experiments. Together they provide good coverage of the important performance factors in Spark. *BigData Benchmark* has inputs up to five nodes and we'll concentrate the node level performance discussion around it. *GroupBy* scales and we evaluate it up to 10,240 cores. For *PageRank* we have only small inputs available and evaluate it only up to 8 nodes. Each benchmark has been executed at least five times and we report mean performance. Some `BurstBuffer` experiments were very noisy and we report only the best performance.

4. SINGLE NODE PERFORMANCE

To calibrate initial performance, we evaluated a single node of Cori and Edison against a local workstation with fast SSDs: eight 3.5GHz Xeon i7-3770K cores with 1TB fast SSD. Figure 6 shows the performance of queries 1-3 of the Big Data Benchmark [28] using both on-disk and in-memory modes. The results are quite similar on Edison and Cori. As shown, a single node of Edison when running with eight cores and accessing the file system is roughly twice as slow than the workstation. When data is preloaded in memory, eight cores of Edison match the workstation performance; this is expected as the workstation contains server grade CPUs. When scaling up the Edison node and using all 24 cores, performance is still 50% slower than the workstation. This slowdown is entirely attributed to the file system; performance scales with cores when running with data preloaded in memory, as illustrated when comparing eight cores with the full node performance.

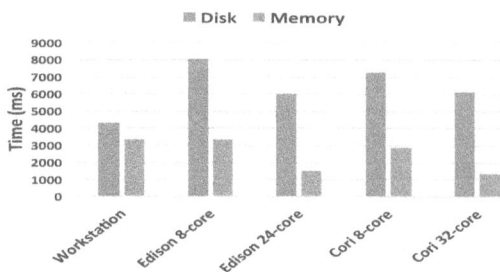

Figure 6: *BigData Benchmark performance on workstation and a single node of Edison and Cori. Input data is precached in memory or read from disk.*

To quantify the difference in I/O performance, we instrumented the Hadoop LocalFileSystem interface used by Spark to record the number of calls and the time spent in **open**, **read**, **write**, and **close** file operations. The time spent in **read**, **write**, and **close** operations did not significantly differ between the systems, while file **open** operations were *much* slower, as shown in Figure 7. On the workstation the mean file open time was 23 μs; on Edison it was 542 μs, almost 24 times greater. Some file open operations on Edison took an extreme amount of time to complete: in the worst case observed, a single file open operation took 324 ms.

The Big Data Benchmark illustrates the application level I/O bottlenecks. At this stage, the number of open operations is linear in the number of partitions. The dataset for Query 1 consists of a single directory containing one data file per partition in Parquet format: there are 3,977 partitions/files. Each file is accompanied by a checksum file used to verify data integrity. These all must be opened, so a minimum of 7,954 file opens must occur to run Query 1. The data format readers are designed to operate in series in a state-free manner. In the first step, the data and checksum files are opened and read, the checksums are calculated are compared, and the data and checksum files are closed, completing the first task. Then, each partition file is opened and the footer, containing column metadata, is read, and the partition file is closed, completing the second task. Finally, the partition file is opened again, the column values are read, and the partition file is closed again, for a total for four file opens per partition, or 15,908 file opens.

5. SCALING CONCERNS

On a data center system architecture with local disks, one does not expect file open (or create) time to have a large effect on the overall time to job completion. Thus, Spark and the associated domain libraries implement stateless operation for resilience and elastic parallelism purposes by opening and closing the files involved in each individual data access: *file metadata operations are a scalability bottleneck on our HPC systems.* Any effort scaling Spark up and out on an HPC installation has first to address this concern.

There are several Spark configuration alternatives that affect file I/O behavior. We were first interested to determine if the larger number of cores in a HPC node allows for a degree of oversubscription (partitions per core) high enough to hide the MDS latency. We have systematically explored consolidation, speculation, varying the number of partitions and data block sizes to no avail.

In the time honed HPC tradition, one solution is to throw bigger and better hardware at the problem. The first aspect is to exploit the higher core concurrency present in HPC systems. As the previous Section shows, increasing[1] the number of cores per node does improve performance, but not enough to mitigate the effects of the file system.

For the Lustre installations evaluated, metadata performance is determined by the MDS hardware configuration. Although Cori contains multiple MDSes, the current Lustre 2.6 version does not exploit them well[2] and performance for the Spark workload is identical to that of a single MDS. When comparing Cori with Edison, the former contains newer hardware and exhibits lower metadata access latency (median $270\mu s$ on Cori vs $338\mu s$ on Edison), still when using the

---

[1]Cori Phase II will contain Intel Xeon Phi nodes with up to 256 cores per node. This will become available circa Oct 2016 to early users.
[2]Supports a restricted set of operations that are not frequent in Spark.

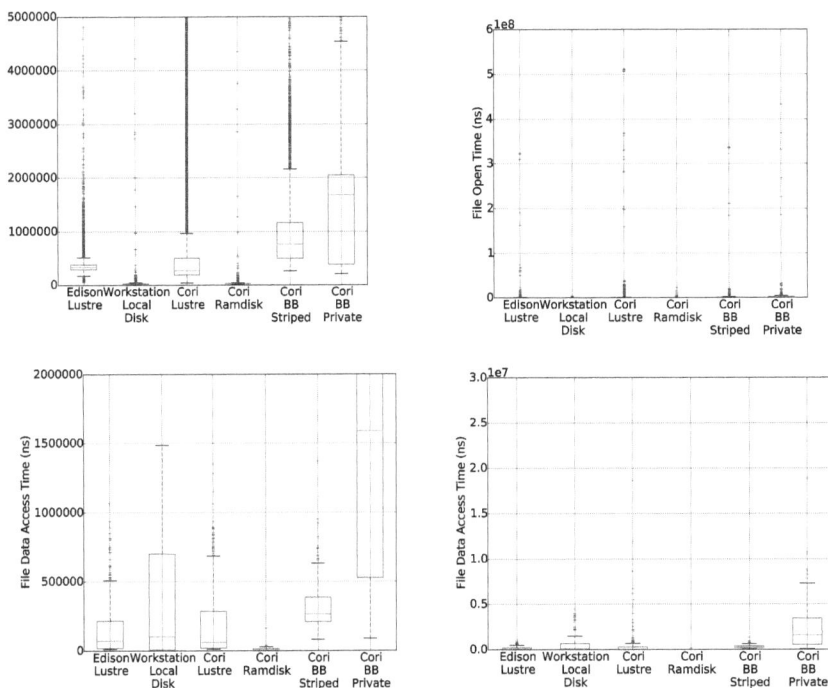

Figure 7: *Distribution of file I/O on the Lustre filesystem vs. a workstation with ext4 local disk, during the execution of Big Data. Left, median file open time is 24× higher on Lustre. Second, range of file open time, ≈ 14,000× larger on Lustre. Third, median of file read time for all BigData reads - latency similar between workstation and Lustre. Right, range of file open time - Lustre exhibits much larger variability than workstation.*

full node (32 and 24 cores) both are at best 50% slower than a eight core workstation. Enabling multiple MDSes will improve scalability but not the latency of an operation [10], thus over-provisioning the Lustre metadata service is unlikely to provide satisfactory per node performance.

A third hardware solution is provided by the `BurstBuffer` I/O subsystem installed in Cori. This large NVRAM array situated close to the CPU is designed to improve throughput for small I/O operations and for pre-staging of data. The question still remains if it is well suited for the access patterns performed by Spark.

Besides hardware, software techniques can alleviate some of the metadata performance bottlenecks. The first and most obvious solution is to use a memory mapped file system (e.g. `/dev/shm`) as the secondary storage target for Spark. Subject to physical memory constraints, this will eliminate a large fraction of the traffic to the back-end storage system. In the rest of this paper, we will refer to this configuration as `ramdisk`. Note that this is a user level technique and there are several limitations: 1) the job crashes when memory is exhausted; and 2) since data is not written to disk it does not provide any resilience and persistence guarantees.

HPC applications run in-memory so it may seem that `ramdisk` provides a solution. For medium to large problems and long running iterative algorithms Spark will fail during execution when using `ramdisk`, due to lax garbage collection in the block and shuffle managers. To accommodate large problems we evaluate a configuration where a local file system is mounted and backed by a Lustre file, referred to as `lustremount`. This requires administrative privilege on the systems and due to operational concerns we were initially

granted access to only one node. Based on the results of this study, this capability was added to Shifter [18], which is NERSC developed software that enables Docker containers to be run on shared HPC systems.

To understand scaling with large problems we develop a software caching layer for the file system metadata, described in Section 5.2. In the rest of this paper we refer to this configuration as `filepool`. This is a user level approach orthogonal to the solutions that mount a local file system. Since data is stored on Lustre, `filepool` provides resilience and persistence guarantees.

5.1 I/O Scaling in Spark

I/O overhead occurs due to metadata operations, as well as proper data access read/write operations. All these operations occur in both the application level I/O, as well as inside Spark for memory constrained problems or during the shuffle stage.

In Section 4 we have illustrated the impact of `fopen` metadata operations on the performance of *BigData Benchmark.*. There, the benchmark performed during the application input stage a number of open operations linear in the number of partitions $O(partitions)$. Big Data Benchmark did not involve a large amount of shuffle data.

Because Spark allows partitions to be cached in memory, slow reading of the initial data is not necessarily problematic, particularly in an interactive session in which multiple queries are being performed against the same data. Assuming that the working set fits in memory, disk access for input data can be avoided except for the first query. In this case, the `BurstBuffer` can be also used for data pre-staging.

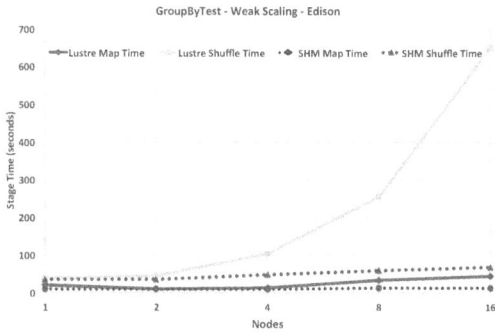

Figure 8: *Time for the map and reduce phases of GroupBy on Edison for Lustre and* `ramdisk` *as we use additional nodes to process larger datasets (weak scaling).*

In Figure 8 we show the scalability of the GroupBy benchmark up to 16 nodes (384 cores) on Edison for a weak scaling experiment where the problem is chosen small enough to fit entirely in memory.

GroupBy measures worst-case shuffle performance: a wide shuffle in which every partition must exchange data with every other partition. The benchmark generates key-value pairs locally within each partition and then performs a shuffle to consolidate the values for each key. The shuffle process has two parts: in the first (map) part, each node sorts the data by key and writes the data for each partition to a partition-specific file. This is the *local* task prior to the stage boundary in Figure 1. In the second (reduce) part, each node reads locally-available data from the locally-written shuffle files and issues network requests for non-local data. This is the *global* task after the stage boundary in Figure 1.

When running entirely in memory (`ramdisk`) performance scales with nodes, while scalability is poor when using Lustre. As illustrated, the Map phase scales on Lustre, while the Shuffle phase does not. For reference, on the workstation, mean task duration is 1,618 ms for `ramdisk` and 1,636 ms for local disk. On the Edison node, mean task duration was 1,540 ms for `ramdisk` and 3,228 ms for Lustre.

We instrumented Spark's Shuffle Manager component to track file I/O operations. During the write phase of the shuffle, a shuffle file is created for each partition, and each shuffle file is written to as many times as there are partitions. An index file is also written, which contains a map from keys to a shuffle file and offset. During the read phase, for each local partition to read and each remote request received, the index file is opened, data is read to locate the appropriate shuffle data file, which is then opened, read, and closed. The number of file open operations during the shuffle is quadratic in the number of partitions $O(partitions^2)$.

To enable load balancing, the Spark documentation suggests a default number of partitions as 4x the number of cores. On 16 nodes of Edison, with a total of 384 cores, then, we have 1,536 partitions, giving us 1,536 shuffle data files, each of which is opened 1,536 times during the write phase and another 1,536 times during the read phase, resulting in 4,718,592 file open. Not only is the number of file opens is quadratic in partitions, but the cost *per* file open also grows as we add nodes, as shown in Figure 9.

As the number of file I/O operations is linear with the number of partitions/cores during the application I/O and

quadratic during the shuffle stage, in the rest of paper we concentrate the evaluation on the shuffle stage.

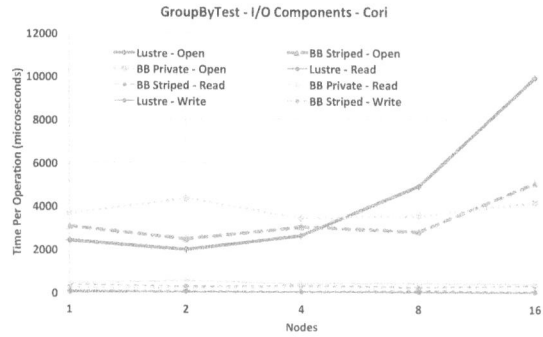

Figure 9: *Average time for a* `open`, `read`, *and* `write` *operation performed during the GroupBy execution with weak scaling on Cori.*

As for each read/write operation Spark will perform a file open, the performance ratio of these operations is an indicator of scalability. Figure 10 shows the performance penalty incurred by repeatedly opening a file, performing one read of the indicated size, and closing the file, versus opening the file once, performing many reads of the indicated size, and closing the file. Using many open-read-close cycles on a workstation with a local disk is 6× slower for 1 KB reads than opening once and performing many reads, while on Edison with Lustre, many open-read-close cycles is 56× slower than opening once and reading many times. Lustre on Cori is similar, while the Burst Buffers in striped mode reduce the penalty to as low as 16×. All of the filesystems available on our HPC systems incur a substantial penalty from open-per-read.

The scalability problems caused by the large number of file opens are exacerbated by the potentially small size of each read. Many data analytics applications have a structure in which many keys are associated with a small number of values. For example in PageRank, most write operations are smaller than 1KB. This reflects the structure of the data, as most websites have few incoming links. The data is structures as key-value pairs with a site's URL as the key and a list of incoming links as the value, so most values are short.

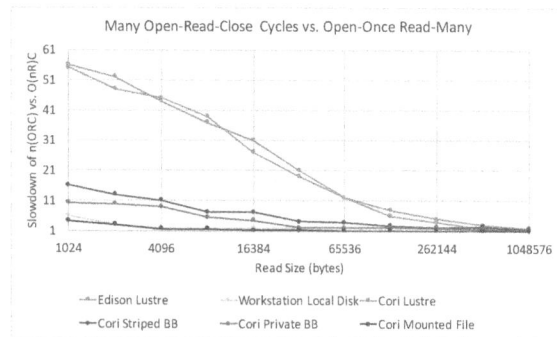

Figure 10: *Performance improvements from amortizing the cost of file opens. We compare one read per open with 100,000 reads per open.*

5.2 Improving Metadata Performance With File Pooling

For problems small enough to fit in the main memory, the ramdisk Spark configuration scales. However, in our experiments many large problems ran out of memory at runtime, particularly iterative algorithms where the block garbage collection inside the shuffle manager is not aggressive.

In order to accommodate large problems at scale we have simply chosen to add a layer for pooling and caching open file descriptors within Spark. All tasks within an Executor (node) share a descriptor pool. We redefine FileInputStream and FileOutputStream to access the pool for open and close operations. Once a file is opened, subsequent close operations are ignored and the descriptor is cached in the pool. For any subsequent opens, if the descriptor is available we simply pass it to the application. To facilitate multiple readers, if a file is requested while being used by another task, we simply reopen it and insert it into the pool.

This descriptor cache is subject to capacity constraints as there are limits on the number of Inodes within the node OS image, as well as site-wide Lustre limits on the number of files open for a given job. In the current implementation, each Executor is assigned its proportional number of entries subject to these constraints.

We evaluated a statically sized file pool using two eviction policies to solve capacity conflicts: LIFO and FIFO. For brevity we omit detailed results and note that LIFO provides best performance for the shuffle stage. As results indicate, this simple implementation enables Spark to scale.

Further refinements are certainly possible. Application I/O files can be easily distinguished from intermediate shuffle files and can be allocated from a smaller pool, using FIFO. Within the shuffle, we can tailor the eviction policy based on the shuffle manager behavior, e.g. when a block is dropped from memory the files included in its lineage are likely to be accessed together in time during recomputation.

Running out of Inodes aborts execution so in our implementation a task blocks when trying to open a file and the pool descriptor is filled at capacity. As this can lead to livelock, we have audited the Spark implementation and confirmed with traces that the implementation paradigm is to open a single file at a time, so livelock cannot occur.

5.3 Impact of Metadata Access Latency on Scalability

In Figure 11 we show the single node performance on Cori in all configurations. As shown, using the back-end Lustre file system is the slowest, by as much as 7× when compared to the best configuration. Both file system configurations improve performance significantly by reducing the overhead of calls to open files: ramdisk is up to ≈ 7.7× faster and lustremount is ≈ 6.6× faster than Lustre.

filepool also improves performance in all cases. It is ≈ 2.2× faster than Lustre, and interestingly enough is speeds up the other two configurations. For example, for *GroupBy* where each task performs $O(partitions^2)$ file opens, adding pooling to the "local" file system (e.g. ramdisk+filepool) improves performance by ≈ 15%. The performance improvements are attributed to the lower number of open system calls. For *PageRank* and *BigData Benchmark* the improvements are a more modest 1% and 2% respectively. As it never degraded performance, this argues for running in configurations where our filepool implementation itself or a user level file system is interposed between Spark and any other "local" file systems used for shuffle data management.

For all configurations the performance improvements are proportional to the number of file opens during the shuffle stage: *GroupBy* is quadratic in partitions while in *PageRank* it is a function of the graph structure.

In Figure 12 we show the scalability of *GroupBy* up to eight nodes (256 cores). We present the average task time and within it, distinguish between time spent in serialization (Serialization), disk access together with network access (Fetch) and application level computation (App). ramdisk is fastest, up to 6× when compared to Lustre. filepool is slower than ramdisk, but still significantly faster than Lustre, up to 4×. The performance differences between ramdisk and filepool increase with the scale: while system call overhead is constant, metadata latency performance degrades. When combining filepool with lustremount we observe performance improvements ranging from 17% on one node to 2% on 16 nodes.

In Figure 13 we present scalability for *PageRank* (left) and *BigData Benchmark* (right). As mentioned, the inputs for these benchmarks are not very large and we scale up to 8 nodes. The trends for *PageRank* are similar to *GroupBy* and we observe very good performance improvements from filepool and ramdisk. The improvements from combining pooling with ramdisk are up to 3%. In addition, when strong scaling *PageRank* the performance of ramdisk improves only slightly with scale (up to 25%), while configurations that touch the file system (Lustre and BurstBuffer) improve by as much as 3.5×. The gains are explained by better parallelism in the read/write operations during shuffle.

The performance of *BigData Benchmark* is least affected by any of our optimizations. This is because behavior is dominated by the initial application level I/O stage, which we did not optimize. This is the case where ramdisk helps the least and further performance improvements can be had only by applying the file pooling optimization or lustremount. *BigData Benchmark* illustrates the fact that any optimizations have to address in shuffle in conjunction with the application level I/O.

When using the Yarn resource manager we could not effectively scale Spark up to more than 16 nodes on either Edison or Cori. The application runs but executors are very late in joining the job and repeatedly disappear during execution. Thus the execution while reserving the initially requested number of nodes, proceeds on far fewer. After exhausting timeout configuration parameters, we are still investigating the cause.

For larger scale experiments we had to use the Spark standalone scheduler, results presented in Figure 12 right. While Yarn runs one executor (process) per node, the Spark manager runs one executor per core. The Lustre configuration stops scaling at 512 cores. The standalone scheduler limits the the performance impact of our file pooling technique: with Yarn we provide a per node cache while with the standalone scheduler we provide a per core cache. This is reflected in the results: while with YARN filepool scales similarly to ramdisk, it now scales similarly to Lustre and we observe speedup only as high as 30%. Note that filepool can be reimplemented for the standalone scheduler, in which case we expect it to behave again like ramdisk.

As illustrated in Figure 14 we successfully (weak) scaled ramdisk up to 10,240 cores. Lustre does not scale past 20

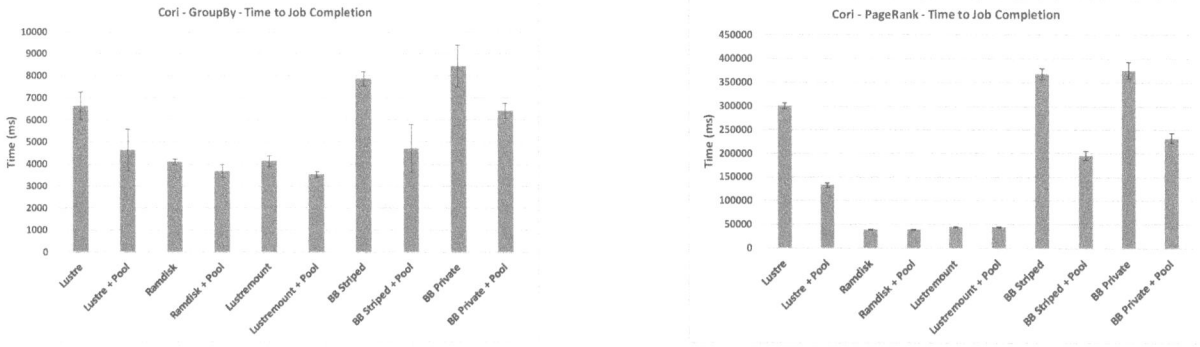

Figure 11: *GroupBy and PageRank performance on a single node of Cori.*

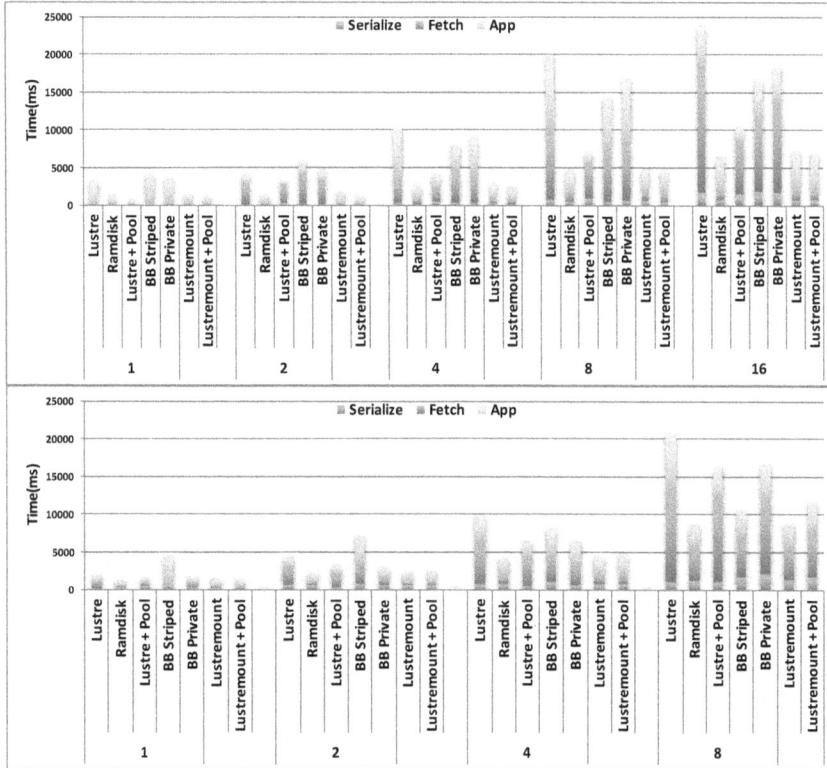

Figure 12: *GroupBy weak scaling on Cori up to 8 nodes (256 cores). Top: with YARN. Bottom: with the Spark standalone scheduler.*

nodes, where we start observing failures and job timeouts. When running on the `BurstBuffer` we observe scalability up 80 nodes (2,560 cores), after which jobs abort. Note that `BurstBuffer` performance is highly variable at scale and we report the best performance observed across all experiments.

Figure 15 compares Lustre, `ramdisk` and `lustremount`. To use `lustremount` on more than one node, we run Spark inside a Shifter user-defined image. With Shifter, each node mounts a single image containing JVM and Spark installations in read-only mode and a per-node read/write loopback file system. Because the JVM and Spark are stored on a file-backed filesystem in Shifter, file opens required to load shared libraries, Java class files, and Spark configuration files are also offloaded from the metadata server, improving performance over configurations where Spark is installed on the Lustre filesystem. Identically configured GroupBy bench-

marks running on `ramdisk` with Spark running in Shifter is up to 16% faster than than with Spark itself installed on Lustre. In addition, since the mount is private to a single node, the kernel buffer cache and directory entry cache can safely cache metadata blocks and directory entries. This can significantly reduce the number of metadata operations and improves performance for small I/O operations. For the `lustremount` implementation in Shifter initializes a sparse file in the Lustre file system for each node in the Spark cluster. These files are then formatted as XFS file systems and mounted as a loop back mount during job launch. Unlike using `ramdisk`, the `lustremount` approach is not limited to the memory size of the node and it doesn't take away memory resources from the application. Using `lustremount` we can scale up to 10,240 cores, with time to completion only 13% slower than `ramdisk` at 10,240 cores.

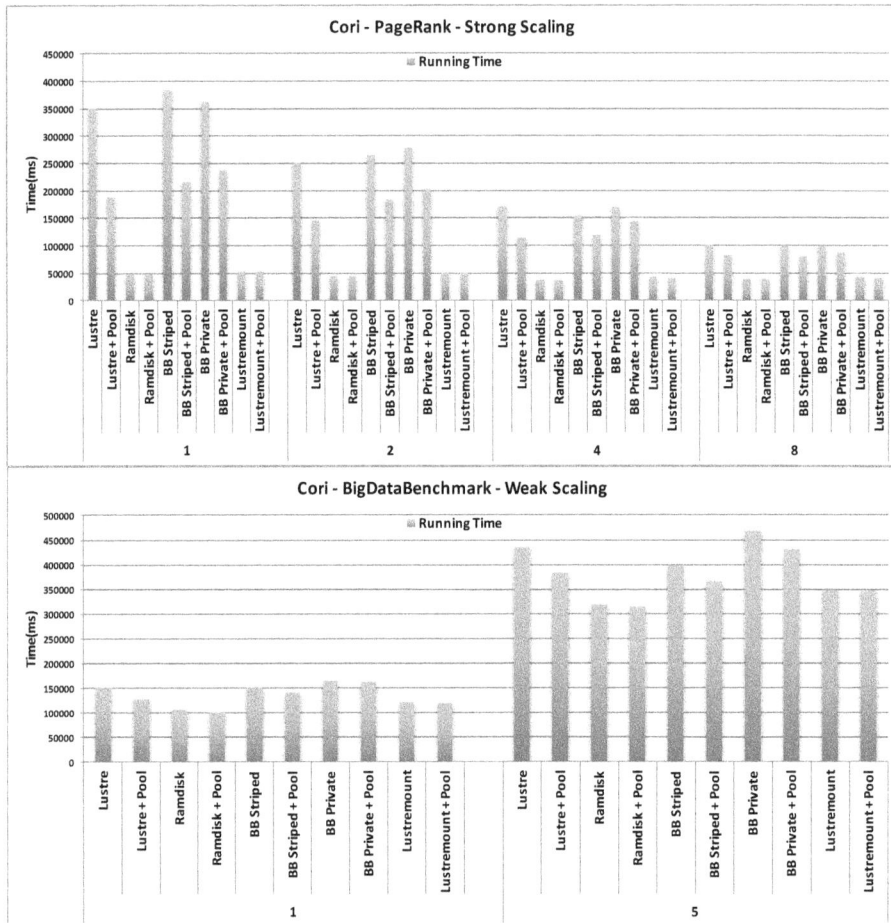

Figure 13: *PageRank and BigData Benchmark scaling on Cori, up to 8 nodes (256 cores).*

5.4 Impact of `BurstBuffer` on Scalability

The `BurstBuffer` hardware provides two operating modes, private where files are stored on a single blade (device) and striped where files are stored across multiple blades.

In Figure 7 we present the metadata latency and read operations latency for a single node run of *BigData Benchmark*. As illustrated, the mean time per operation when using the `BurstBuffer` is higher than the back-end Lustre in both striped and private mode. This is expected as interposing the `BurstBuffer` layer between processors and Lustre can only increase latency. On the other hand the variance is reduced 5× compared to Lustre. When comparing striped mode with the private mode for *BigData Benchmark* striped exhibits 15% lower variance than private.

Higher latency per operation affects performance at small scale and Spark single node performance with `BurstBuffer` is slightly worse than going directly to Lustre. On the other hand, lower variability translates directly in better scaling as illustrated in Figures 9 and 12. Up to 40 nodes (1,280 cores) `BurstBuffer` provides performance comparable to running in memory with `ramdisk`. As expected, the configuration with lower variability (striped) exhibits better scalability than private mode. This is a direct illustration of the need to optimize for the tail latency at scale.

6. IMPROVING SHUFFLE SCALABILITY WITH BETTER BLOCK MANAGEMENT

Even when running using a good configuration available, e.g. `filepool+ramdisk`, some algorithms may not scale due to the memory management within the shuffle manager, which introduces excessive vertical data movement. The behavior of the PageRank algorithm illustrates this.

In Figure 16 left we show the evolution of the algorithm for a problem that fits entirely in main memory on one node of Edison. We plot both memory usage and the duration of an iteration over the execution. As shown, execution proceeds at a steady rate in both memory and time. On the right hand side of the figure, we plot the evolution of the algorithm when the working set does not fit in the main memory. As illustrated, each iteration becomes progressively slower and each iteration takes double the amount of its predecessor. The same behavior is observed on the workstation, albeit less severe.

After investigation using the instrumentation framework already developed, we observed that during constrained execution the amount of data read from disk grows at a rate two orders of magnitude higher than during unconstrained execution. After further investigation, we attributed the root cause of the problem to the shuffle block manager. Whenever running out of memory, the block manager evicts the least recently used block. The first subsequent access to the evicted block triggers recomputation, which evicts another

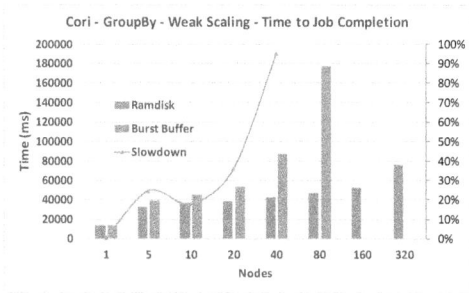

Figure 14: *GroupBy at large scale on Cori, up to 320 nodes (10,240 cores). Standalone scheduler. Series "Slowdown" shows the slowdown of* `BurstBuffer` *against* `ramdisk`, *plotted using the secondary right axis.*

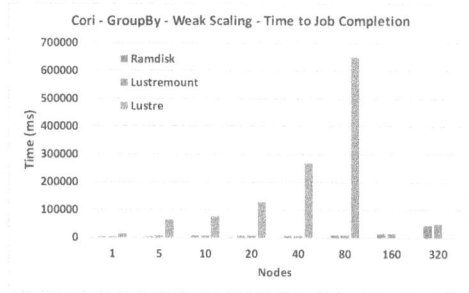

Figure 15: *GroupBy at large scale on Cori, up to 320 nodes (10,240 cores). Standalone scheduler. Lustre,* `ramdisk`, *and* `lustremount`.

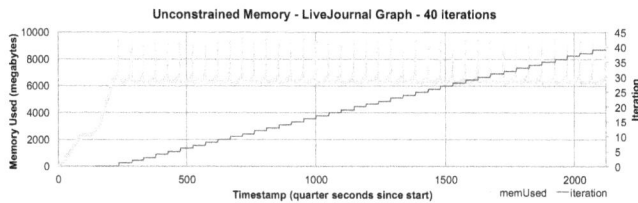

Figure 16: *PageRank performance on a single node of Edison. The amount of memory used during execution is plotted against the right hand side axis. The time taken by each iteration is plotted against the left hand side axis. Execution under constrained memory resources slows down with the number of iterations.*

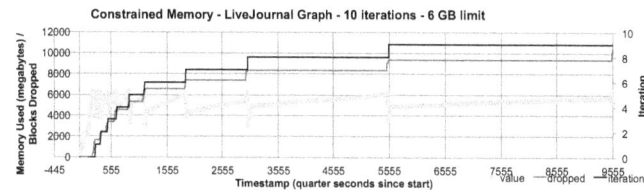

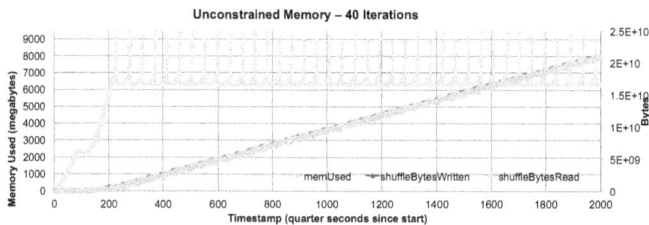

Figure 17: *PageRank IO behavior on a single node of Edison. The amount of memory used during execution is plotted against the right hand side axis. The amount of bytes read and written from disk is plotted against the left hand side axis. While memory usage stays constant, the amount of bytes read explodes under constrained memory resources.*

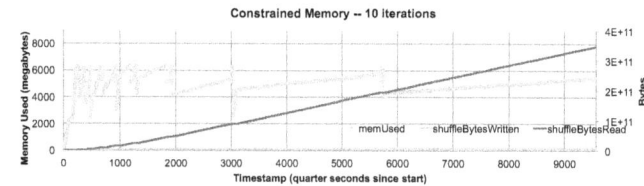

block needed for the partial solution which in turn triggers recomputation and eviction of blocks needed. This results in orders of magnitude increases in vertical data movement, as illustrated in Figure 17.

This behavior affects the scaling of iterative algorithms on all systems and it should be fixed. In the data center it is less pronounced as local disks are better at latency. As shown, it is very pronounced on our HPC systems. One lesson here is that because storage behaves differently, in particular for small requests, there exists incentive to specifically tune the shuffle block manager for HPC.

For the PageRank algorithm we have actually an algorithmic fix which involves marking as persistent the intermediate result RDDs from each iteration. This causes Spark to write them to the back-end storage. Upon eviction, a persistent block is read from storage instead of being recomputed. Figure 18 shows the performance of the fixed PageRank algorithm and we observe performance improvements as high as 11×. Note that all the performance findings in this paper are reported on this fixed algorithm. The original GraphX

implementation does not scale beyond a single node on our systems.

There are two possible generic solutions to this problem. First, we could implement a system which tracks how often shuffle data must be reread from disk and automatically persist partitions that depend on that data when a threshold is exceeded. Second, we could track the cost of recomputing and rereading the lineage of an RDD and, rather than evicting on a least-recently-used basis, instead evict the block which will have the lowest recompute or reread cost.

Note that we were initially interested in evaluating the `spark-perf` machine learning benchmark suite [3] for this study. Due to this problem with iterative algorithms, we postponed the evaluation to the time when we can consider the aforementioned fix in the shuffle manager.

7. DISCUSSION

Metadata latency and its relative lack of scalability is a problem common to other [4, 8] parallel file systems used in HPC installations. The shuffle stage is at worst quadratic

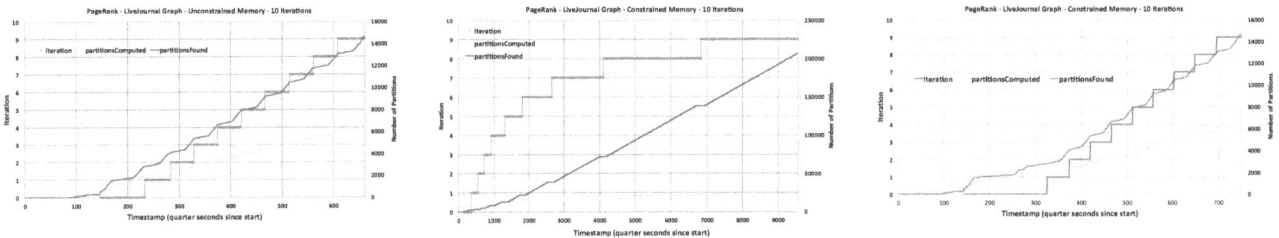

Figure 18: *Number of partitions read during the shuffle stage for PageRank. Left: execution with unconstrained memory. Right: when memory is constrained the number of partitions read from disk is one order of magnitude larger. Right: persisting intermediate results fixes the performance problems and we see a reduction by a order of magnitude in partitions read from disk.*

with cores in file open operations, thus metadata latency can dominate Spark performance. We believe our findings to be of interest to more than Cray with Lustre HPC users and operators. While Spark requires file I/O only for the shuffle phase, Hadoop requires file I/O for both map and reduce phases and also suffers from poor performance when run without local storage [26]. Our techniques may therefore also be applicable to Hadoop on HPC systems.

The hardware roadmap points towards improved performance and scalability. Better MDS hardware improves baseline performance (per operation latency), as illustrated by the differences between Edison and Cori. Multiple MD-Ses will improve scalability. The current usage of `Burst-Buffer` I/O acceleration on Cori, while it degrades baseline node performance, it improves scalability up to thousands of cores. Better performance from it can be expected shortly, as the next stage on the Cori software roadmap provides a caching mode for `BurstBuffer` which may alleviate some of the current latency problems. It may be the case that the `BurstBuffer` is too far from the main memory, or that it is shared by too many nodes for scales beyond $O(10^3)$. The HPC node hardware evolution points towards large NVRAM deployed inside the nodes, which should provide scalability with no capacity constraints.

As our evaluation has shown, software approaches can definitely improve performance and scalability. Besides ours, there are several other efforts with direct bearing. Deploying Spark on Tachyon [19] with support for hierarchical storage will eliminate metadata operations. In fact, we have considered this option ourselves but at the time of the writing the current release of Tachyon, 0.8.2, does not fully support hierarchical storage (missing append). We expect its performance to fall in between that of our configuration with a local file system backed by Lustre and `ramdisk+filepool`. Note also that our findings in Section 6 about the necessity of improving block management during the shuffle stage for iterative algorithms are directly applicable to Tachyon.

The Lustre roadmap also contains a shift to object based storage with local metadata. Meanwhile, developers [13, 26] have already started writing and tuning HDFS emulators for Lustre. The initial results are not encouraging and Lustre is faster than the HDFS emulator. We believe that the `lustremount` is the proper configuration for scalability.

The performance improvements due to `filepool` when using "local" file systems surprised us. This may come from the different kernel on the Cray compute nodes, or it may be a common trait when running in data center settings. As HPC workloads are not system call intensive, the compute node kernels such as Cray CNL may not be fully optimized for them. Running commercial data analytics workloads on HPC hardware may force the community to revisit this decision. It is definitely worth investigating system calls overhead and plugging in user level services (e.g. file systems) on commercial clouds.

Luu et al [21] discuss the performance of HPC applications based on six years of logs obtained from three supercomputing centers, including on Edison. Their evaluation indicates that there is commonality with the Spark behavior: HPC applications tend to spend 40% of their I/O time in metadata operations than in data access and they tend to use small data blocks. The magnitude of these operations in data analytics workloads should provide even more incentive to system developers to mitigate this overhead.

We are interested in extending this study with a comparison with Amazon EC2 to gain more quantitative insights into the performance differences between systems with node attached storage and network attached storage. Without the optimizations suggested in this paper, the comparison would have favored data center architectures: low disk latency provides better node performance and masks the deficiencies in support for iterative algorithms. With our optimizations (`filepool+lustremount`), single node HPC performance becomes comparable and we can set to answer the question of the influence of system design and software configuration on scalability. We believe that we may have reached close to the point where horizontal data movement dominates in the HPC installations as well. Such a comparison can guide both system and software designers whether throughput optimizations in large installations need to be supplemented with latency optimization in order to support data analytics frameworks.

8. RELATED WORK

Optimizing data movement in Map-Reduce frameworks has been the subject of numerous recent studies [29, 17, 20, 11]. Hadoop introduced an interface for pluggable custom shuffle [15, 29] for system specific optimizations. InfiniBand has been the target of most studies, due to its prevalence in both data centers and HPC systems. HDFS emulation layers have been developed for parallel filesystems such as PLFS [9] and PVFS [27]. These translate HDFS calls into corresponding parallel filesystem operations, managing read-ahead buffering and the distribution (striping) of data across servers. In Spark, only input and output data is handled through the HDFS interface, while the intermediate shuffle data is handled through the ordinary Java file API. Our work primarily optimizes intermediate shuffle data storage.

Optimizing the communication between compute nodes (horizontal data movement) has been tackled through RDMA-based mechanisms [29, 17, 20]. In these studies, optimized RDMA shows its best benefit when the data is resident in memory. Therefore, only the last stage of the transfer is carried out using accelerated hardware support. The client-server programming model is still employed to service requests because data are not guaranteed to be in memory. Performance is optimized through the use of bounded thread pool SEDA-based mechanism (to avoid overloading compute resources) [17], or through the use of one server thread per connection [29] when enough cores are available.

As we use network-attached storage, the bottleneck shifts to the vertical data movement. A recent study by Cray on its XC30 system shows that an improved inter-node communication support for horizontal movement may not yield significant performance improvement [26]. Note that this study for Hadoop also recommends using memory based file systems for temporary storage.

Optimizing vertical movement, which is one of the main motivation for the introduction of Spark, has been addressed by the file consolidation optimization [11] and by optimizations to persist objects in memory whenever possible. Our experiments have been performed with consolidation. We have analyzed the benefits of extending the optimization from per-core consolidation to per-node consolidation. As this will reduce only the number of file creates and not the number of file opens, we have decided against it.

9. CONCLUSION

We ported and evaluated Spark on Cray XC systems developed in production at a large supercomputing center. Unlike data centers, where network performance dominates, the global file system metadata overhead in `fopen` dominates in the default configuration and limits scalability to O(100) cores. Configuring Spark to use "local" file systems for the shuffle stage eliminates this problem and improves scalability to O(10,000) cores. As local file systems pose restrictions, we develop a user level file pooling layer that caches open files. This layer improves scalability in a similar manner to the local file systems. When combined with the local file system, the layer improves performance up to 15% by eliminating open system calls.

We also evaluate a configuration with SSDs attached closer to compute nodes for I/O acceleration. This degrades single node performance but improves out-of-the-box scalability from O(100) to O(1,000) cores. Since this is the first appearance of such system and its software is still evolving, it remains to be seen if orthogonal optimizations still need to be deployed with it.

Throughout our evaluation we have uncovered several problems that affect scaling on HPC systems. Fixing the YARN resource manager and improving the block management in the shuffle block manager will benefit performance.

Overall, we feel optimistic about the performance of data analytics frameworks in HPC environments. Our results are directly translatable to others, e.g. Hadoop. We scaled Spark up to O(10,000) cores and since, our NERSC colleagues have adopted the Shifter `lustremount` implementation and demonstrated runs up to 50,000 cores. Engineering work to address the problems we identified can only improve

its performance. All that remains to be seen is if the initial performance and productivity advantages of Spark are enough to overcome the psychological HPC barrier of expecting bare-metal performance from any software library whatsoever.

Acknowledgements

We would like to thank Douglas M. Jacobsen at NERSC for implementing the support for file mounts inside Shifter. This work has been partially supported by the US Department of Defense and by Intel through an Intel Parallel Computing Center grant to LBNL.

10. REFERENCES

[1] Cori Phase 1. https: //www.nersc.gov/users/computational-systems/cori/.

[2] National Energy Research Scientific Computing Center. https://www.nersc.gov.

[3] spark-perf benchmark. https://github.com/databricks/spark-perf.

[4] S. R. Alam, H. N. El-Harake, K. Howard, N. Stringfellow, and F. Verzelloni. Parallel i/o and the metadata wall. In *Proceedings of the sixth workshop on Parallel Data Storage*, pages 13–18. ACM.

[5] M. Armbrust, R. S. Xin, C. Lian, Y. Huai, D. Liu, J. K. Bradley, X. Meng, T. Kaftan, M. J. Franklin, A. Ghodsi, and M. Zaharia. Spark SQL: Relational data processing in spark. In *Proceedings of the 2015 ACM SIGMOD International Conference on Management of Data*, SIGMOD '15, pages 1383–1394. ACM.

[6] S. Babu and L. Co Ting Keh. Better visibility into spark execution for faster application development. In *Spark Summit*, 2015.

[7] P. J. Braam and others. *The Lustre storage architecture*.

[8] P. Carns, S. Lang, R. Ross, M. Vilayannur, J. Kunkel, and T. Ludwig. Small-file access in parallel file systems. In *IEEE International Symposium on Parallel Distributed Processing, 2009. IPDPS 2009*, pages 1–11.

[9] C. Cranor, M. Polte, and G. Gibson. HPC computation on Hadoop storage with PLFS. Technical Report CMU-PDL-12-115, Carnegie Mellon University, 2012.

[10] T. Crowe, N. Lavender, and S. Simms. Scalability testing of dne2 in lustre 2.7. In *Lustre Users Group*, 2015.

[11] A. Davidson and A. Or. Optimizing Shuffle Performance in Spark. UC Berkeley Tech. Report.

[12] J. Dean and S. Ghemawat. MapReduce: Simplified data processing on large clusters. 51(1):107–113.

[13] J. M. Gallegos, Z. Tao, and Q. Ta-Dell. Deploying hadoop on lustre storage: Lessons learned and best practices. Lustre User Group Meeting., 2015.

[14] J. E. Gonzalez, R. S. Xin, A. Dave, D. Crankshaw, M. J. Franklin, and I. Stoica. Graphx: Graph processing in a distributed dataflow framework. In *Proceedings of OSDI*, pages 599–613.

[15] A. Hadoop. Pluggable Shuffle and Pluggable Sort. https://hadoop.apache.org/docs/current/ hadoop-mapreduce-client/

hadoop-mapreduce-client-core/
PluggableShuffleAndPluggableSort.html.

[16] B. Hindman, A. Konwinski, M. Zaharia, A. Ghodsi, A. D. Joseph, R. Katz, S. Shenker, and I. Stoica. Mesos: A platform for fine-grained resource sharing in the data center. In *Proceedings of the 8th USENIX Conference on Networked Systems Design and Implementation*, NSDI'11, pages 295–308, Berkeley, CA, USA, 2011. USENIX Association.

[17] N. S. Islam, M. W. Rahman, J. Jose, R. Rajachandrasekar, H. Wang, H. Subramoni, C. Murthy, and D. K. Panda. High performance rdma-based design of hdfs over infiniband. In *Proceedings of the International Conference on High Performance Computing, Networking, Storage and Analysis*, SC '12, pages 35:1–35:35, Los Alamitos, CA, USA, 2012. IEEE Computer Society Press.

[18] D. M. Jacobsen and R. S. Canon. Contain this, unleashing docker for hpc. *Proceedings of the Cray User Group*, 2015.

[19] H. Li, A. Ghodsi, M. Zaharia, S. Shenker, and I. Stoica. Tachyon: Reliable, memory speed storage for cluster computing frameworks. In *Proceedings of the ACM Symposium on Cloud Computing*, pages 1–15. ACM.

[20] X. Lu, M. Rahman, N. Islam, D. Shankar, and D. Panda. Accelerating spark with RDMA for big data processing: Early experiences. In *2014 IEEE 22nd Annual Symposium on High-Performance Interconnects (HOTI)*, pages 9–16.

[21] H. Luu, M. Winslett, W. Gropp, R. Ross, P. Carns, K. Harms, M. Prabhat, S. Byna, and Y. Yao. A multiplatform study of I/O behavior on petascale supercomputers. In *Proceedings of the 24th International Symposium on High-Performance Parallel and Distributed Computing*, HPDC '15, 2015.

[22] X. Meng, J. Bradley, B. Yavuz, E. Sparks, S. Venkataraman, D. Liu, J. Freeman, D. B. Tsai, M. Amde, S. Owen, D. Xin, R. Xin, M. J. Franklin, R. Zadeh, M. Zaharia, and A. Talwalkar. MLlib: Machine learning in apache spark.

[23] K. Ousterhout, R. Rasti, S. Ratnasamy, S. Shenker, B.-G. Chun, and V. ICSI. Making sense of performance in data analytics frameworks. In *Proceedings of the 12th USENIX Symposium on Networked Systems Design and Implementation (NSDI)(Oakland, CA*, pages 293–307.

[24] M. Poess, B. Smith, L. Kollar, and P. Larson. Tpc-ds, taking decision support benchmarking to the next level. In *Proceedings of the 2002 ACM SIGMOD international conference on Management of data*, pages 582–587. ACM.

[25] R.-I. Roman, B. Nicolae, A. Costan, and G. Antoniu. Understanding spark performance in hybrid and multi-site clouds. In *6th International Workshop on Big Data Analytics: Challenges and Opportunities (BDAC-15)*, 2015.

[26] J. Sparks, H. Pritchard, and M. Dumler. The cray framework for hadoop for the cray XC30.

[27] W. Tantisiriroj, S. W. Son, S. Patil, S. J. Lang, G. Gibson, and R. B. Ross. On the duality of data-intensive file system design: reconciling hdfs and pvfs. In *Proceedings of 2011 International Conference for High Performance Computing, Networking, Storage and Analysis*, page 67. ACM, 2011.

[28] UC Berkeley AmpLab. Big data benchmark.

[29] Y. Wang, X. Que, W. Yu, D. Goldenberg, and D. Sehgal. Hadoop acceleration through network levitated merge. In *Proceedings of 2011 International Conference for High Performance Computing, Networking, Storage and Analysis*, SC '11, pages 57:1–57:10. ACM.

[30] T. White. *Hadoop: The Definitive Guide*. O'Reilly Media, Inc., 1st edition, 2009.

[31] M. Zaharia, M. Chowdhury, T. Das, A. Dave, J. Ma, M. McCauley, M. J. Franklin, S. Shenker, and I. Stoica. Resilient distributed datasets: A fault-tolerant abstraction for in-memory cluster computing. In *Proceedings of the 9th USENIX Conference on Networked Systems Design and Implementation*, NSDI'12, pages 2–2. USENIX Association.

[32] M. Zaharia, M. Chowdhury, M. J. Franklin, S. Shenker, and I. Stoica. Spark: cluster computing with working sets. In *Proceedings of the 2nd USENIX conference on Hot topics in cloud computing*, volume 10, page 10.

IBIS: Interposed Big-data I/O Scheduler

Yiqi Xu
Florida International University
11200 SW 8th St
Miami, FL 33199 USA
yxu006@cs.fiu.edu

Ming Zhao
Arizona State University
699 S Mill Ave
Tempe, AZ 85281 USA
mingzhao@asu.edu

ABSTRACT

Big-data systems are increasingly shared by diverse, data-intensive applications from different domains. However, existing systems lack the support for I/O management, and the performance of big-data applications degrades in unpredictable ways when they contend for I/Os. To address this challenge, this paper proposes *IBIS*, an Interposed Big-data I/O Scheduler, to provide I/O performance differentiation for competing applications in a shared big-data system. IBIS transparently intercepts, isolates, and schedules an application's different phases of I/Os via an I/O interposition layer on every datanode of the big-data system. It provides a new proportional-share I/O scheduler, SFQ(D2), to allow applications to share the I/O service of each datanode with good fairness and resource utilization. It enables the distributed I/O schedulers to coordinate with one another and to achieve proportional sharing of the big-data system's total I/O service in a scalable manner. Finally, it supports the shared use of big-data resources by diverse frameworks and manages the I/Os from different types of big-data workloads (e.g., batch jobs vs. queries) across these frameworks. The prototype of IBIS is implemented in Hadoop/YARN, a widely used big-data system. Experiments based on a variety of representative applications (WordCount, TeraSort, Facebook, TPC-H) show that IBIS achieves good total-service proportional sharing with low overhead in both application performance and resource usages. IBIS is also shown to support various performance policies: it can deliver stronger performance isolation than native Hadoop/YARN (99% better for WordCount and 15% better for TPC-H queries) with good resource utilization; and it can also achieve perfect proportional slowdown with better application performance (30% better than native Hadoop).

1. INTRODUCTION

Big data is an important computing paradigm that becomes increasingly used by many science, engineering, medical, and business disciplines for knowledge discovery, decision making, and other data-driven tasks based on processing and analyzing large volumes of data. These applications are built upon computing paradigms that can effectively express data parallelism and exploit data locality (e.g., MapReduce [9]) and storage systems that can provide high scalability and availability (e.g., Google File System [10], Hadoop HDFS [16]). As the needs of data-intensive computing continue to grow in various disciplines, it becomes increasingly common to use shared infrastructure to run such applications. First, big-data systems often require substantial investments on computing, storage, and networking resources. Therefore, it is more cost-effective for both resource users and providers to use shared infrastructure for big-data applications. Second, hosting popular data sets (e.g., human genome data, weather data, census data) on shared big-data systems allows such massive data to be conveniently and efficiently shared by different applications from different users.

Although computing resources (CPUs) are relatively easy to partition, shared storage resources (I/O bandwidths) are difficult to allocate, particularly for data-intensive applications which compete fiercely for access to large volumes of data on the storage. Existing big-data systems lack the mechanisms to effectively manage shared storage I/O resources, and as a result, applications' performance degrades in unpredictable ways when there is I/O contention. For example, when one typical MapReduce application (WordCount) runs concurrently with a highly I/O-intensive application (TeraGen), WordCount is slowed down by up to 107%, compared to when it runs alone with the same number of CPUs.

I/O performance management is particularly challenging for big-data systems because of two important reasons. First, big-data applications have complex I/O phases (e.g., rounds of map and reduce tasks with different amounts of inputs, intermediate results, and outputs for a MapReduce application), which makes it difficult to understand their I/O demands and allocate I/O resources properly to meet their performance requirements. Second, a big-data application is highly distributed across many datanodes, which makes it difficult to coordinate the resource allocations across all the involved nodes needed by the data-parallel application. For example, the performance of a MapReduce application depends on the received total storage bandwidth from all the nodes assigned to its map and reduce tasks.

This paper proposes *IBIS*, an Interposed Big-data I/O Scheduler, to provide performance differentiation for competing applications' I/Os in a shared big-data system. This scheduler is designed to address the above-mentioned two challenges. First, *how to effectively differentiate I/Os from competing applications and allocate the shared storage bandwidth on the individual nodes of a big-data system?* IBIS introduces a new I/O interposition layer upon the distributed file system in a big-data system, and is able to transparently intercept the I/Os from the various phases of applications and isolate and schedule them on every datanode of the system. IBIS also employs a new proportional-share I/O scheduler, SFQ(D2), which can automatically adapt I/O concurrency based on the storage load

HPDC'16, May 31-June 04, 2016, Kyoto, Japan
© 2016 ACM. ISBN 978-1-4503-4314-5/16/05. . . $15.00
DOI: http://dx.doi.org/10.1145/2907294.2907319

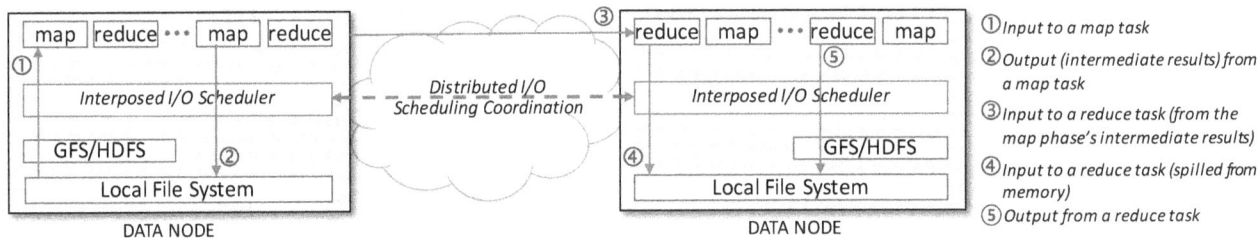

①	Input to a map task
②	Output (intermediate results) from a map task
③	Input to a reduce task (from the map phase's intermediate results)
④	Input to a reduce task (spilled from memory)
⑤	Output from a reduce task

Figure 1: Architecture of MapReduce-type big-data systems and the proposed IBIS-based I/O management

and achieve strong performance isolation with good resource utilization. Second, *how to efficiently coordinate the distributed I/O schedulers across datanodes and allocate the big-data system's total I/O service to the data-parallel applications?* IBIS provides a scalable coordination scheme for the distributed SFQ(D2) schedulers to efficiently coordinate their scheduling across the datanodes. The schedulers then adjust their local I/O scheduling based on the global I/O service distribution and allow the applications to proportionally share the entire system's total I/O service.

The IBIS prototype is implemented in Hadoop/YARN, a widely used big-data system, by interposing HDFS as well as the related local and network I/Os transparently to the applications, and it is able to support the I/O management of diverse applications from different big-data frameworks. It is evaluated using a variety of representative big-data applications (WordCount, TeraSort, TeraGen, Facebook2009 [6], TPC-H queries on Hive [17]). The results confirm that IBIS can effectively achieve total-service proportional bandwidth sharing for diverse applications in the system. They also show that IBIS can support various important performance polices. It achieves strong *performance isolation* for a less I/O-intensive workload (WordCount, Facebook2009, TPC-H) when under heavy contention from a highly I/O-intensive application (TeraGen and TeraSort), which outperforms native Hadoop by 99% for WordCount and 15% for TPC-H queries. This result is accomplished while still allowing the competing application to make good progress and to fully utilize the storage bandwidth ($< 4\%$ reduction in total throughput). IBIS can also achieve excellent *proportional slowdown* for competing applications (TeraSort vs. TeraGen) and outperforms native Hadoop by 30%. Finally, the use of IBIS introduces small overhead in terms of both application runtime and resource usages.

Overall, unlike most of the related works which focus on improving the I/O efficiency of big-data systems [8, 11], this paper addresses the problem of I/O interference and performance management in big-data systems, which is not adequately addressed in the literature. Although existing mechanisms such as cgroups [4] can be employed to manage the contention among local I/Os, as the results in this paper will show, they are insufficient due to the lack of control on distributed I/Os which are unavoidable for big-data applications. IBIS therefore complements the existing solutions for CPU and memory management of big-data systems, and provides the missing control knob for I/O management which is much needed by increasingly data-intensive applications. Compared to the few related works [20, 15, 19] that also studied the performance management of big-data storage, IBIS supports applications that are more challenging (with complex computing and I/O demands) and diverse (including both batch and query workloads).

The rest of the paper is organized as follows: Section 2 introduces the background and motivating examples; Sections 3, 4, and

5 describe the I/O interposition framework, SFQ(D2) scheduler, and distributed scheduling coordination of IBIS, respectively; Section 6 discusses the support for I/O management across different big-data frameworks; Section 7 presents the experimental evaluation; Section 8 examines the related work; Section 9 discusses the limitations and future work; and Section 10 concludes the paper.

2. BACKGROUND AND MOTIVATIONS

2.1 Big-data Systems

Typical big-data computing systems are often built upon a highly scalable and available distributed file system. In particular, Google File System (GFS) [10] and its open-source clone Hadoop Distributed File System (HDFS) [16] provide storage for massive amounts of data on a large number of nodes built with inexpensive commodity hardware while supporting fault tolerance at scale. A big-data application runs many tasks on these datanodes, which process the locally stored data in parallel via the I/O interface provided by such a distributed file system. In particular, the MapReduce programming model and associated run-time system are able to automatically execute user-specified map and reduce functions in parallel and handle job scheduling and fault tolerance [9]. Higher-level storage services such as databases (e.g., Hive [17]) can be further built upon the distributed file system and offer more convenient interfaces (e.g., SQL) for users to process the data. Therefore, this paper focuses on big-data storage systems of the GFS/HDFS kind.

Both the map and reduce phases of a MapReduce application can spawn large numbers of map and reduce tasks on the GFS/HDFS nodes to process data in parallel. They often have complex but well-defined I/O phases (Figure 1). A *map* task is preferably scheduled to the node where its input data is stored. It reads the input from GFS/HDFS (either via the local file system or across the network) and *spills* and *merges* key-value pairs onto the local file system as intermediate result. A *reduce* task starts by *copying/shuffling* its inputs from all the map tasks' intermediate results (either stored locally or across the network). It then *merges* the copied inputs, performs the *reduce* processing, and generates final output to GFS/HDFS. Each of the above phases can have different bandwidth demands for input and output. Moreover, given the same volume of data to a map or reduce task, it can take different amount of time to process the data depending on the application's computational complexity.

2.2 Big-data Resource Management

Existing big-data systems offer simple core resource management functions. Hadoop MapReduce [1] allocates CPU resources in terms of *slots* to map or reduce tasks, where the number of available slots is set according to the number of CPU cores in the system. Recent developments such as Mesos [12] and YARN [18] allow the

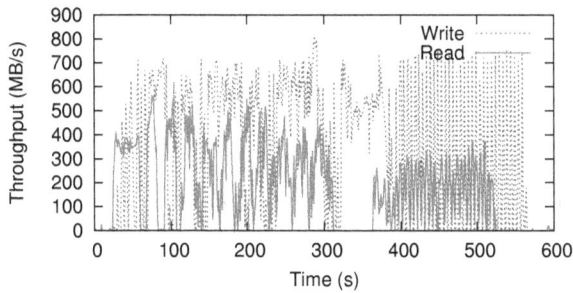

(a) TeraSort

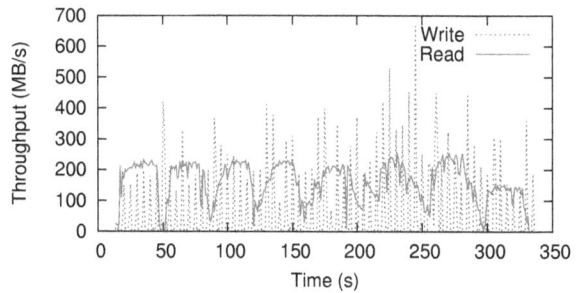

(b) WordCount

Figure 2: I/O demands of two classic MapReduce applications

allocation of both CPU and memory resources to competing big-data applications. The management of shared I/O bandwidth is still missing from existing solutions, which is however crucial to the performance of inherently I/O intensive big-data applications.

The performance management problem for big-data storage is not adequately addressed in the literature. Frosting [20] provides a scheduling layer upon HBase [3], but it treats the entire HBase stack as a single black box and it is thus difficult to achieve strong performance isolation and good resource utilization. PISCES [15] achieves fair-sharing of a key-value store by controlling the dispatching of simple requests to datanodes, and Cake [19] provides QoS support to HBase queries by controlling the queuing of simple requests. In comparison, IBIS is designed to manage the I/O performance for diverse big-data applications including those with much more complex and dynamic I/O demands. A detailed examination of the related work is presented in Section 8.

2.3 Motivating Examples

The lack of I/O management in big-data systems presents a serious hurdle for data-intensive applications to get their desired performance. In a MapReduce system, on every single datanode, the tasks from different MapReduce applications compete with one another across all their phases for HDFS, local file system, and network I/Os. Across the whole big-data system, these highly distributed applications also compete on many datanodes and their performance depends on the total amount of I/O services that they can get from all the involved nodes.

As an example of the diverse I/O demands of big-data applications, Figure 2 compares the I/O profiles of two classic MapReduce applications, *TeraSort* and *WordCount*, each running alone with the same allocation of CPU and memory resources. These profiles show that *TeraSort* has a much more intensive I/O workload than *WordCount*. *TeraSort* has intensive HDFS reads and local file system writes in the map phase and intensive HDFS writes in the reduce phase. *WordCount*'s output is much smaller than its input, but there are plenty of intermediate writes throughout the map and reduce phases.

With such diverse big-data applications, the lack of I/O management will lead to severe and unpredictable performance interference between the applications. As an example of the I/O contention's performance impact, Figure 3 compares the performance of WordCount when it runs alone to when it runs with another application (TeraGen, TeraSort, TeraValidate) while keeping its CPU allocation (half of the 96 CPU cores in the system) the same. Details of the experiment setup are provided in Section 7. The results show substantial performance degradation in WordCount, which confirms the significant performance impact caused by I/O contention (CPU cache contention is relatively insignificant to the per-formance of these data-intensive applications). This paper addresses this serious problem with an interposed big-data I/O scheduling approach, IBIS, which is presented in the rest of the paper.

3. INTERPOSED I/O SCHEDULING

The first question addressed by IBIS is *how to effectively differentiate the I/Os across the different phases of competing MapReduce applications on every datanode of a big-data system*. The general design of IBIS is based on the *virtualization* principles, where an indirection layer exposes the interfaces already in use by the big-data system to access storage, allowing applications to time-share the storage system without modifications, while enforcing performance isolation and differentiation among them.

A key design decision that needs to be made in a virtualization approach is choosing the proper abstraction to introduce the virtualization layer. In the context of a big-data system, there are multiple layers in the storage hierarchy, from the applications, to HDFS, and to local file system and storage devices. On one hand, introducing virtualization at a higher layer can make use of more application knowledge to help the implementation, but it is more tied to specific applications and loses control of how I/Os are executed by the underlying layers. On the other hand, introducing virtualization at a lower layer of the storage hierarchy allows more control of I/O executions and can support more diverse applications, but it has to deal with more primitive I/O operations and loses application semantics that are useful for I/O differentiation.

Considering this tradeoff, IBIS is introduced upon the GFS/HDFS layer of the MapReduce storage architecture (Figure 1). This design can make effective use of application information to differentiate I/Os, because applications access the shared storage mostly through the HDFS interface. It also has enough low-level I/O control by scheduling the dispatch of I/Os to local file systems. Interposing of the applications' direct local file system I/Os and network I/Os are done at other interfaces at the same level. The rest of this section details the interposition of these different types of I/Os used by a MapReduce application. All the modifications described below for implementing IBIS are made to Hadoop/YARN and do not require any change to applications.

Persistent I/Os are I/Os serviced by HDFS, where the inputs for map tasks are read from HDFS, and the outputs from reduce tasks are written to HDFS. Tasks use the *DFSClient* to interface with the *Data Node*, which represents an HDFS daemon, and Data Node converts the data requests, from both local and remote map tasks, to local file system I/Os. To differentiate I/Os from competing applications, the DFSClient interface is modified to carry application-specific information (job identifier and I/O service weight) as part of the header of each data request issued by the map/reduce tasks.

(a) HDD setup

(b) SSD setup

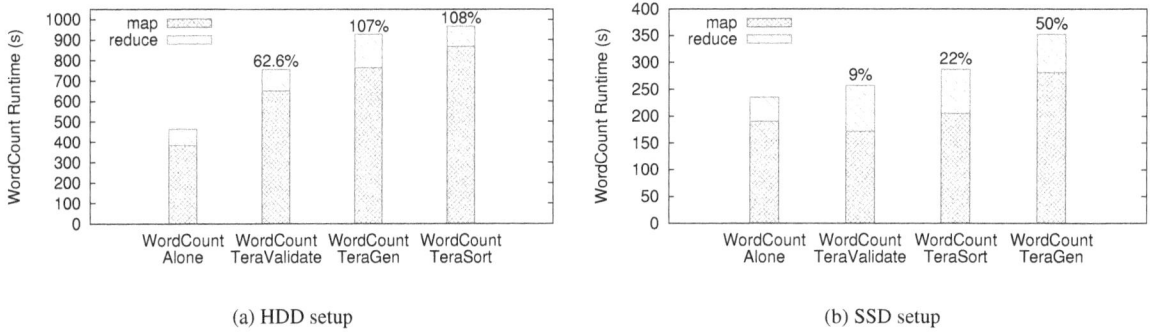

Figure 3: Runtime of WordCount when it runs alone vs. when it runs with another job on native Hadoop. The numbers on top of the bars are the slowdown w.r.t. the standalone runtime. The CPU allocation to WordCount is kept the same in all cases. Two different storage setups are considered, one with all hard disk drives (HDDs) and the other with all solid state drives (SSDs).

These requests are scheduled by the IBIS component implemented in Data Node, which maintains a request queue for its local storage and dispatches the queued requests according to the chosen scheduling algorithm and policy.

Intermediate I/Os are I/Os to a datanode's local file system (not HDFS) for storing temporary data. Both map and reduce tasks use the local file system for spilling and merging in-progress data. The intermediate I/Os can also influence an application's performance. For example, a sorting program can generate the same amount of intermediate data as its input. In IBIS, these intermediate I/Os are first tagged with the job identifier and I/O service weight and then routed to the IBIS component implemented within a local I/O scheduler, which can also reside in the Data Node daemon that runs on every datanode. IBIS schedules the intermediate I/Os in the same way as the persistent I/Os, following the same scheduling algorithm and policy.

Network I/Os occur during a shuffling phase between all the map tasks and reduce tasks. Because each reduce task's input is a partition of the map phase's outputs, it generally has to request a portion of the outputs from every map task. The data pulling thread launched by a reduce task is initiated with the job identifier and I/O service weight, which are carried over in the header of every HTTP-based data request. These requests are handled by the HTTP servlets which are implemented in the *Node Manager* daemons. Therefore, an IBIS scheduler is also implemented in the *Node Manager* to differentiate the network I/Os and schedule the corresponding local file system I/Os.

Note that IBIS does not rely on any bandwidth control from the network layer, and it is shown to be sufficient in the experiments because of two reasons: *1)* The storage is generally saturated before the network; *2)* By applying bandwidth control at the storage endpoints of the network I/Os, IBIS indirectly influences the contention on the network. However, IBIS can incorporate the network bandwidth control mechanisms such as OpenFlow [5] if they are necessary and available, which will be left for future work.

In all the above I/O phases, concurrent requests from different applications are differentiated by their unique application IDs. An application obtains its ID from the job scheduler, which is carried over to all of its parallel tasks and used by the tasks to tag their I/Os for HDFS, intermediate, and network data. For every shared I/O service, these requests are queued and dispatched by an IBIS scheduler according the algorithm presented in the next section.

4. PROPORTIONAL I/O SHARING

The second question addressed by IBIS is *how to allow the tasks from competing applications to proportionally share the I/O service of each datanode in a big-data system.* The interposed I/O scheduling framework in IBIS is flexible enough to support different algorithms. This paper focuses on algorithms that allow applications to proportionally share the I/O bandwidth, in the same way they share the CPU time proportionally (e.g., using the Hadoop Fair Scheduler [2]), so that it can provide the much needed, missing control knob for I/O allocation in big-data systems. Proportional resource sharing is defined as when the total demand is greater than the available resource, each application should get a *share* of the resource proportional to its assigned *weight*. Because only the relative values of weights matter to the bandwidth allocation, in the paper, the weight assignment to applications is often specified in terms of the *ratio* among the weights.

The proposed proportional-share scheduler is built upon the SFQ family of schedulers because of their computational efficiency, work-conserving nature, and theoretically provable fairness. SFQ schedules the backlogged requests from different applications using a priority queue, where each request's priority is positively affected by its application's weight and negatively affected by its cost (often estimated based on the size of the request). The scheduler can dispatch only one outstanding request, and it chooses the one with the earliest *start time* in the queue.

The SFQ(D) scheduler [13] is an extension of SFQ for proportional sharing of storage resources which are commonly capable of handling multiple outstanding requests concurrently. The level of concurrency that the shared storage resource supports is captured by the *depth* parameter D in SFQ(D). The scheduler follows the original SFQ algorithm to dispatch queued requests, but it allows up to D outstanding I/Os to be serviced concurrently by the underlying storage in order to take advantage of the available I/O concurrency.

The choice of D has important implications on both fairness and resource utilization for a real storage system. On one hand, a larger D allows more concurrent I/Os and a higher utilization of the storage, but it may hurt fairness because of the scheduler's work-conserving nature. A more aggressive workload can use up all the storage bandwidth and even overload it, delaying the I/Os from a less aggressive workload. On the other hand, a smaller D gives the scheduler a tighter control on the amount of I/O share that a more aggressive workload can steal from others, and allows the I/Os from a less aggressive workload to be serviced quickly when they arrive. It can thus improve fairness among the competing workloads but may lead to underutilization of the storage. So it is difficult to determine the optimal value of D statically, and it depends on the characteristics of the storage and workloads, some of which are also dynamic. It was in fact left as future work in the SFQ(D) paper [13].

To address the above problem, this paper introduces a new SFQ-based algorithm, *Dynamic Depth SFQ*, or *SFQ(D2)* in short. It employs a feedback controller to automatically and dynamically adjust the value of D online. The controller works periodically (e.g., every second), and decides the depth D_{k+1} for the next period $k+1$, based on the distance between the observed average I/O latency L_k of the previous period and the reference latency L_{ref}:

$$D_{k+1} = D_k + K \times (L_{ref} - L_k) \qquad (1)$$

where K is an integral gain factor which determines how aggressively the controller works to reach the target latency. Following this equation, the controller automatically optimizes the value of D as it steers the observed I/O latency towards the reference latency.

The controller chooses I/O latency as the target because its goal is to maximize the storage utilization without compromising the fairness among applications, and I/O latency directly reflects the I/O performance of applications and the I/O load of the underlying storage. The reference latency is decided offline by profiling the storage using a synthetic MapReduce workload with increasing I/O concurrency. Both the I/O latency and throughput are measured during the profiling, and the I/O latency observed before the storage starts to saturate is the reference latency for the controller. Such profiling needs to be done only once for a given storage setup. If the storage's read and write performance are asymmetric such as in SSDs, the profiling can give separate reference latencies for reads and writes. In this case, the L_{ref} and L_k in the controller become the weighted average of the read latencies and write latencies, with the weights being the percentages of reads and writes observed in the previous control period.

This SFQ(D2) scheduler works upon the interposition layer described in Section 3 on every datanode of the big-data system. Each scheduler independently adjusts D based on its local dynamics in the workloads and underlying storage, and dispatches up to D I/Os from its local queue to the storage. This scheduler is used to provide proportional sharing of all the important I/O services offered by a datanode, including HDFS I/Os, temporary data I/Os, and network I/Os.

5. DISTRIBUTED I/O SCHEDULING COORDINATION

The third question addressed by IBIS is *how to efficiently coordinate the distributed I/O schedulers across datanodes to support proportional sharing of a big-data system's total I/O service among competing applications*. A limitation of the IBIS scheduler described above is that a local scheduler's decision is made independently at each datanode, without accounting for information from other nodes. Local scheduling, based on only local knowledge, however, is not sufficient to deliver the desired performance differentiation from the perspective of the highly distributed big-data applications. The parallel nature of such an application requires it to get the necessary I/O service from all the nodes where its tasks are scheduled, and its performance depends on the total amount of I/O service that it gets from the system. Therefore, I/O management at the system level should support *total-service proportional sharing*, which means that the applications share the total I/O service from all the datanodes in the system proportionally to their assigned weights.

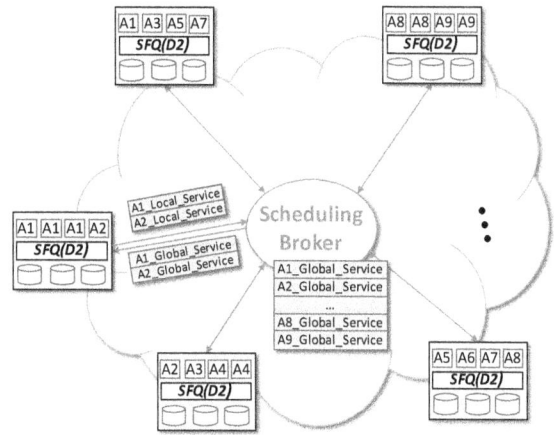

Figure 4: Architecture for distributed I/O scheduling coordination

The challenge to achieving total-service proportional sharing is that applications often get unevenly distributed I/O services from the involved nodes. The exact amount of service that an application gets from a particular node depends on the number of CPU slots that it gets on the node—which decides the I/O demands, and the applications running on the other slots of the same node—which decides the I/O contention. The number of slots that an application gets on a node in turn depends on the combination of, at any moment, the global CPU slot allocation policy, the application's data locality on the node, and the number of slots currently available on the node. Because of such uneven distribution of I/O service across the nodes, simply applying the same sharing ratio to each node and enforcing it using the local SFQ(D2) scheduler will not produce the same ratio of sharing of the total I/O service.

To address this challenge, IBIS enables the distributed SFQ(D2) schedulers to coordinate with one another and enforce total-service proportional sharing collaboratively. Every scheduler shares its local I/O service distribution—the applications that it serves and the amounts of services that they get locally, with the other schedulers. Based on the global I/O service distribution, every scheduler can then adjust its local I/O service distribution so that the total services that the applications get are proportional to their assigned weights. Specifically, IBIS follows the algorithm in DSFQ [21] to adjust local SFQ scheduling for total-service proportional sharing. When an SFQ(D2) scheduler considers the scheduling of a queued request, it delays the request's *start time* by the total amount of service that the corresponding application has received from all the other nodes. In this way, the local scheduler dispatches the requests from different applications according to their received total I/O services, not just the local services.

Another challenge that must be addressed by IBIS is how to efficiently coordinate a large number of distributed schedulers in a big-data system. If every scheduler has to broadcast its information to all the other schedulers, it can easily overwhelm the schedulers and the network as the system scales out. The DSFQ [21] work assumes a traditional remote I/O model, where the clients send their I/Os to remote datanodes and a coordinator can be interposed in between to gather and pass on the global I/O service information. But this approach does not apply to a big-data system, where computing tasks are shipped to the nodes where their data is stored and they process the data using primarily local I/Os.

To solve this problem, IBIS employs a centralized *Scheduling Broker* to facilitate the information exchange among the distributed

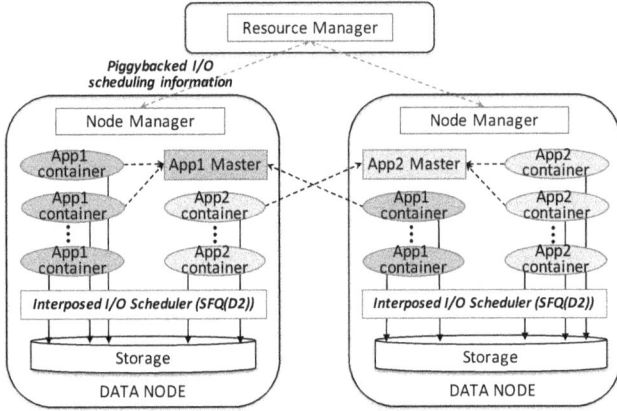

Figure 5: Integration of IBIS with YARN for supporting the I/O management of applications running on different big-data frameworks.

Table 1: The YARN configuration used in the evaluation

Key	Value
dfs.replication	3
dfs.block.size	134,217,728
fairscheduler.preemption	true, 5s

schedulers in a scalable manner (Figure 4). Every local scheduler $j \in \{1,\ldots,m\}$ sends its current I/O service distribution—a vector of *local* I/O service amount a_{ij} for each application $i \in \{1,\ldots,n\}$ that the scheduler j serves—to the broker periodically (e.g., every 1 second). Based on the information received from all the local schedulers, the broker summarizes the total I/O service $A_i = \sum_{j=1}^{m} a_{ij}$ for each application i in the system. It then responds to a local scheduler's message with the total I/O service distribution—a vector of *total* I/O service amount A_i for each application i that the local scheduler currently serves. Based on this total service information, the local scheduler can then adjust its scheduling as discussed above.

The overhead of this scheduling coordination scheme is small. The size of the messages between a local scheduler and the broker is bounded by the number of applications that the scheduler currently serves. The state that the broker needs to maintain is simply a vector of total I/O service amount for all the applications currently in the system. The frequency of coordination can be adjusted based on the desired granularity of fairness and the scale of the system—more frequent coordination reduces transient unfairness but increases the overhead; and vice versa. Hadoop/YARN already employs centralized managers, in particular the *Resource Manager* for coordinating the distributed *Node Managers*, which is shown to be scalable for managing thousands of nodes [18]. In fact, in the IBIS implementation, the I/O Scheduling Broker is embedded as part of the Resource Manager and the I/O scheduling coordination information is piggybacked on the existing communications between the managers to further reduce its overhead.

6. MULTI-FRAMEWORK I/O SCHEDULING

Big-data resources are increasingly shared by diverse computing frameworks [9, 17], as users have different data processing requirements as well as different preferences of programming models. No single framework is perfect for all big-data problems and all users. Solutions such as YARN [18] and Mesos [12] allow different frameworks to share the same set of resources and employ mechanisms such as containers [4] to allocate CPU cores and memory capacity to the resource-sharing applications. However, these resource management solutions still cannot provide strong performance isolation, because they do not support the allocation of shared I/O resources which the data-intensive applications have to compete for. As the experiments will show in Section 7.4, although containers do provide some level of I/O isolation, it is not

sufficient. Containers can control only the I/Os directly issued to the local file system, e.g., intermediate I/Os from MapReduce, but not the distributed I/Os, e.g., HDFS I/Os, which are serviced by a shared datanode server and cannot be differentiated using the container mechanism.

Thus, existing multi-framework resource management solutions still need IBIS to provide the missing I/O control knob for effective I/O bandwidth allocation. Specifically, in YARN, IBIS is seamlessly integrated in its *Application Master*, *Resource Manager*, *Node Manager*, and *Data Node* components (Figure 5). IBIS allows an application to specify its required total I/O bandwidth (e.g., 300MB/s) to its *Application Master*, in addition to the amount of required CPUs and memory (e.g., 64 CPU cores and 64GB RAM), in order to achieve its desired performance. The centralized *Resource Manager* collects the resource requests from the concurrent *Application Masters* and uses IBIS to determine the global, total-service I/O bandwidth allocation, in addition to allocating the CPUs and memory using an existing scheduler such as the Fair Scheduler. The *Resource Manager* then coordinates with the distributed *Node Managers* to enforce the resource allocations on every datanode. Each *Node Manager* uses the local *Data Node* to schedule the local I/Os according to the global, total-service I/O sharing target, similarly to how it uses containers to enforce the CPU and memory allocations to the local data processing tasks. Finally, the IBIS scheduler in *Data Node* interposes all the I/Os, as discussed in Section 3 and uses SFQ(D2) discussed in Section 4 to schedule the I/Os according to the given bandwidth allocation.

7. EVALUATION

7.1 Setup

The experimental evaluation was done on a cluster of nine nodes each with two six-core 2.4GHz AMD Opteron CPUs, 32GB of RAM, and two 500GB 7.2K RPM SAS disks, interconnected by a Gigabit Ethernet switch. All the nodes run the Debian 4.3.5-4 Linux with the 3.2.20-amd64 kernel and use EXT3 as the local file system. The evaluation was performed in YARN 2.7.0 with the IBIS prototype implemented in the *Resource Manager*, *Node Manager*, *Application Master*, and *Data Node* as described in Sections 3 and 6. Eight nodes are dedicated to run applications consuming up to 96 CPU cores and 192GB memory by their tasks, where each map task uses 1 CPU core and 2GB of memory and each reduce task uses 1 CPU core and 8GB of memory. One additional node runs the YARN *Resource Manager* and *Name Node* and the IBIS scheduling broker. The two disks on each node are used to store HDFS data and intermediate data separately. The configuration parameters of YARN and its Fair Scheduler used in the evaluation are listed in Table 1.

The evaluation compares the performance of IBIS to native Hadoop with YARN using a variety of benchmarks, including TeraGen (1TB output), TeraSort (50–400GB input), WordCount (50GB Wikipedia input), Facebook2009 [6], and TPC-H on Hive [17] (53GB input), which are explained in detail in the following experiments. For IBIS with the SFQ(D2) scheduler, the control period is set to 1 second.

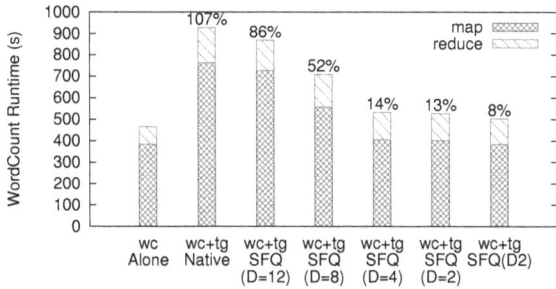

(a) Runtime of WordCount. The numbers on top of the bars are the slowdown w.r.t. the standalone runtime. The shuffling time of the first wave of reduce tasks is overlapped with the map phase and not shown in the bars. But the height of the bars reflects the total runtime.

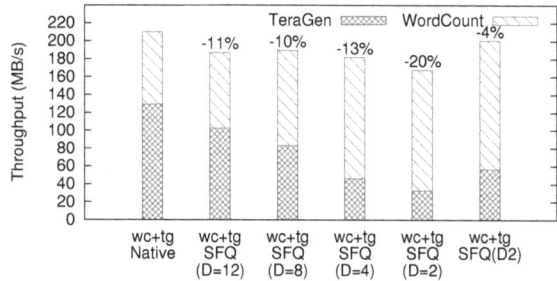

(b) Total throughput of WordCount and TeraGen. The numbers on top of the bars are the throughput loss w.r.t. the native case.

Figure 6: Performance of WordCount (*wc*) when it runs alone and against TeraGen (*tg*) in an HDD-based storage setup

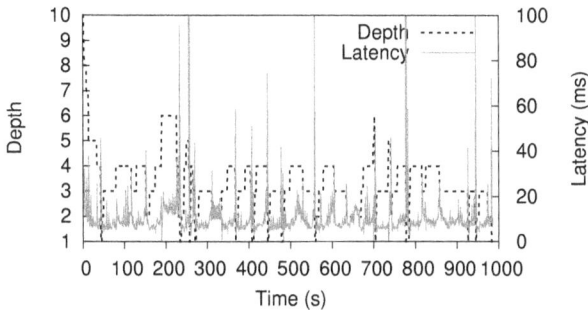

Figure 7: Adaptation of D by SFQ(D2) based on the observed I/O latency on one datanode

7.2 Performance Isolation (WordCount)

The first experiment evaluates whether IBIS is able to provide performance isolation to one application while it is under intensive I/O contention from others as in the motivating example discussed in Section 2.3. It is an important policy in many scenarios where the performance of an important big-data application must be guaranteed regardless of the contention from others. As in the motivating example, Figure 6a shows that when WordCount runs with Tera-Gen, it is slowed down by 107% due to I/O contention, compared to when it runs alone with the same CPU and memory allocation (48 CPU cores and 96GB RAM). Performance isolation is challenging to accomplish for WordCount because its I/O rate is much lower than TeraGen, while a work-conserving I/O scheduler tries not to underutilize the storage.

Figure 6a shows the results of IBIS from using both the classic SFQ(D) scheduler with a static value of D and the new SFQ(D2) scheduler which dynamically adjusts D. The sharing ratio between WordCount and TeraGen is set to 32:1 to favor WordCount, but Ter-aGen can always use the spare I/O bandwidth because the schedulers are work-conserving. Comparing the results from SFQ(D) with different D values, it shows that reducing D does give the scheduler a tighter control on I/O scheduling and achieves better performance isolation for WordCount, reducing its slowdown to as low as 13%. Comparing the results from SFQ(D) to SFQ(D2), it shows that the new scheduler achieves the best isolation for Word-Count with a runtime that is only 8% slower than when it runs alone, and it does so by automatically adjusting the value of D.

Note that the 32:1 sharing ratio is used here because the objective of this experiment is to restore the performance of WordCount without underutilizing the bandwidth. Lower sharing ratios would

favor WordCount less and result in worse performance of Word-Count while still being much better than the native case. For example, a sharing ratio of 2:1 restores WordCount's performance to 148% of its standalone runtime with SFQ(D=2) and 118% with SFQ(D2).

The excellent performance isolation from IBIS is accomplished while still allowing the competing application, TeraGen, to make good progress and fully utilize the underlying storage. To confirm this, Figure 6b compares the total throughput of WordCount and TeraGen when they run on native Hadoop without I/O management vs. when they run on IBIS. The native case has the highest total throughput, because TeraGen's I/Os are sent to storage as soon as they come without any control. In comparison, the number of outstanding I/Os is controlled by D in the schedulers of IBIS. The results show that IBIS can achieve good storage utilization in all configurations, where the best result is also from SFQ(D2) which is only 4% lower than the native case. This result is achieved while reducing WordCount's runtime slowdown from 107% to 8% as discussed above.

To provide a detailed view of how SFQ(D2) works, Figure 7 shows how it adapts D based on the observed I/O latency on one of the datanodes. It follows the equation for the feedback controller described in Section 4. The gain factor is set to 10^{-6}. The value of D is bounded between 1 and 12. Throughout the run the controller reacts quickly to the observed latency and adapts D quickly to sustain strong performance isolation with good resource utilization. Noticeable that at the 260th second and 790th second, the underlying storage system undergoes foreground flushing of the writes buffered in memory and causes the high spikes in I/O latency, while the controller still responds in a timely manner. Although IBIS does not have direct control of such lower-level dynamics, it can still effectively mitigate their impact by timely adapting the I/O concurrency. It is therefore able to sustain good performance isolation without having to modify the underlying storage layers which would be much more intrusive and expensive.

Although faster storage devices such as SSDs are increasingly considered by big-data systems, they cannot completely replace HDDs due to their limited capacity. Moreover, faster storage does not make the I/O contention problem go away; the increasing volume and velocity of big data will always demand I/O management. To confirm this, the same experiment is repeated on a different storage setup using SSDs (Intel 120GB MLC SATA-interfaced flash devices) to store both HDFS and temporary data on each datanode. The results in Figure 8a first confirm that WordCount is still severely interfered (50% slowdown) by TeraGen on native Hadoop due to I/O contention. They also confirm that IBIS still achieves

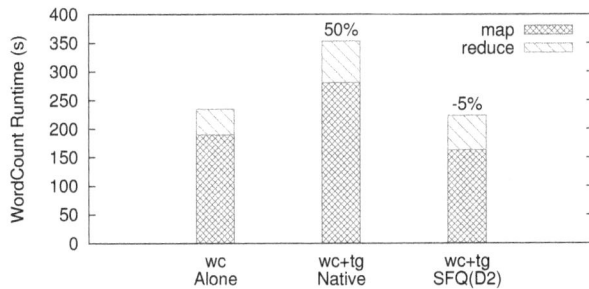

(a) Runtime of WordCount

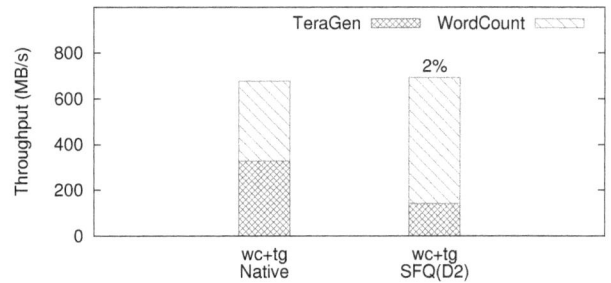

(b) Total throughput of WordCount and TeraGen

Figure 8: Performance of WordCount (*wc*) when it runs alone and against TeraGen (*tg*) in an SSD-based storage setup

strong performance isolation with excellent storage utilization for this faster storage setup. Interestingly, IBIS with SFQ(D2) achieves a better runtime for WordCount than when it runs alone, and a better total throughput for WordCount and TeraGen than native Hadoop. This can be explained by the read/write asymmetry of flash devices and the implicit promotion of reads in SFQ(D2). Writes are much slower than reads on flash devices and they can significantly slow down the reads that are scheduled after them. When intensive writes are received by the scheduler, it automatically reduces *D*, which gives the reads a better chance to establish backlogged requests and be dispatched before some of the writes, therefore achieving better overall performance. This unique characteristic of flash devices will be further studied in the future work to optimize the IBIS scheduler specifically for the use of SSDs in big-data systems.

7.3 Performance Isolation (Facebook2009)

The second experiment evaluates whether IBIS is also able to provide performance isolation to the Facebook2009 workload, which is far more diverse than WordCount. A total of 50 jobs are created using the SWIM workload generator [6], by sampling the historical Facebook job logs and emulating their computing and I/O phases. The samples are down-scaled to fit the size of this paper's testbed. The workload consists of diverse MapReduce applications, including both small and large jobs with different levels of I/O demands. Their input-to-shuffle ratio and shuffle-to-output ratio vary between 0.05 to 10^3 and 2^{-5} to 10^2 respectively. These ratios represent the relative data sizes between map input and shuffle input and between shuffle input and reduce output. Varying these ratios generates different levels of computation and I/O intensities for the various phases of the jobs.

The Facebook2009 jobs are run together with TeraGen on the native Hadoop (*Interfered*) and on IBIS using the SFQ(D2) scheduler with a bandwidth sharing ratio of 32:1 favoring Facebook jobs (*SFQ(D2)*). As a baseline, Facebook2009 is also run alone without I/O contention from others (*Standalone*). The CPU and memory resources allocated to Facebook2009 are kept to half of the total resources for all the cases.

Figure 9 compares the cumulative distribution of the Facebook2009 jobs' runtimes. In the *Standalone* case, 90% of Facebook2009 jobs finish within 120s. When they run together with TeraGen without I/O management in the *Interfered* case, they are impacted drastically by TeraGen, and no job finishes within 50s and 90% of them take up to 230s. In comparison, using *SFQ(D2)*, IBIS is indeed able to provide strong isolation to Facebook2009, and 90% of the jobs can finish within 138s. Comparing the average runtime of Facebook2009, it is reduced from 168s in the *Interfered* case to 115s un-

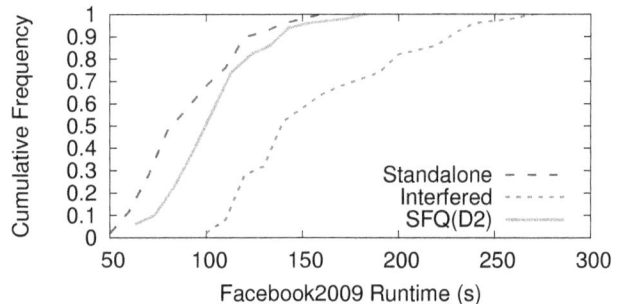

Figure 9: Cumulative distribution of Facebook2009 job runtimes

der *SFQ(D2)*, where the *Standalone* average runtime is 98s. Most of these jobs require only one wave of map and reduce tasks. Without an I/O scheduler, their I/Os are severely interfered by TeraGen and slowed down substantially. With IBIS, they are well isolated from TeraGen and can utilize the allocated storage bandwidth to achieve a performance close to the standalone case.

7.4 Multi-framework I/O Scheduling

The third experiment evaluates IBIS' ability to schedule I/Os and manage their performance for different big-data frameworks, Hive [17] and MapReduce, that share the same infrastructure. Specifically, this experiment considers TPC-H queries [7] as the benchmark for Hive. TPC-H represents decision support systems scanning large volumes of business data, executing queries with a high degree of complexity, and providing keys to important business questions. Hive is a data warehouse framework built upon Hadoop, to support the SQL query execution for data stored on HDFS. Its execution engine spawns a series of MapReduce jobs for query fulfillment, providing end users with much flexibility in data format adaptation and ease of use in a scalable cluster environment.

The experiment focuses on the TPC-H queries Q9 (*product type profit*) and Q21 (*suppliers who kept orders waiting*) which involve multiple intensive I/O phases including both HDFS and intermediate I/Os. Q9 reads 53GB of initial input from five tables stored on HDFS and generates 120GB of intermediate I/Os. Q21 reads 45GB of initial input from four tables on HDFS, and generates 40GB of intermediate I/Os. Both queries launch up to 15 sequential Hadoop jobs. Q9's final output is 5KB and Q21's final output is 2.6GB.

The TPC-H queries on Hive and TeraSort on MapReduce are run concurrently, each with half of the CPU cores and memory. Although the native YARN does not provide any support for I/O management, it is conceivable to extend it to use cgroups [4], which

118

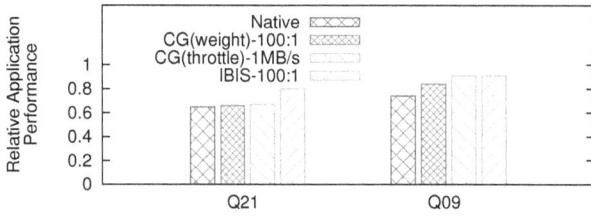

(a) Performance of TPC-H queries (Q9 and Q21) relative to their standalone runtimes

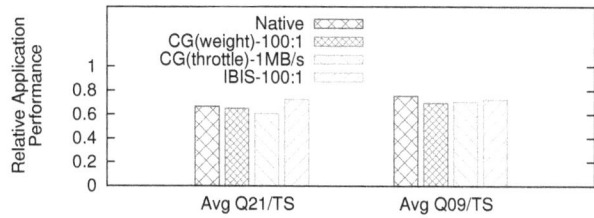

(b) The average relative performance of TPC-H and TeraSort

Figure 10: The performance interference and effectiveness of I/O scheduling for TPC-H on Hive and TeraSort on MapReduce that share the same infrastructure

YARN already uses to allocate CPUs and memory, to also manage I/O bandwidth allocation. To compare to this cgroups-based approach, YARN is extended to use the cgroups mechanisms to allocate shared I/O bandwidth between the two frameworks. This extended YARN can use both the proportional-sharing and throttling modes of cgroups to manage I/Os. In the proportional-sharing mode, the shared bandwidth is allocated to competing applications according to their assigned weights. In the throttling mode, a specific cap can be set to an application's bandwidth usage. Note that as discussed in Section 6, this approach as well as other similar ones can manage only the intermediate I/Os, but not HDFS I/Os; in contrast, IBIS is able to differentiate both local and distributed I/Os and schedule them according to the given performance policy.

Figure 10a shows the relative performance of the two TPC-H queries when running against TeraSort w.r.t. their standalone runtimes. For Q21, on *Native* YARN, the query experiences a 35.2% performance loss when compared to its standalone runtime. When using cgroups' two different modes with aggressive parameters to favor TPC-H—100:1 bandwidth sharing ratio in *CG weighted 100:1* and 1MB/s bandwidth cap on TeraSort in *CG throttled 1MB/s*, it can only improve the query performance by 1.2% and 2.5% respectively. In comparison, IBIS is able to improve the query performance to within 80% of its standalone performance, which is 15.2% better than native YARN and 12.7% better than cgroups. For Q9, the query experiences a 26% performance loss when running against TeraSort on *Native* YARN. Both cgroups' throttling policy and IBIS can restore the query performance to 91% of its standalone runtime, which is better than cgroups' proportional-share policy by 8%. The cgroups-based I/O throttling works better for Q9 than Q21, because Q9 has a higher level of intermediate I/Os which can be throttled by cgroups. However, throttling causes underutilization of storage and unnecessary slowdown of the competing application, TeraSort. Consequently, the performance of TeraSort is up to 16% worse when using cgroups throttling, compared to IBIS which is work-conserving.

To evaluate the overall system performance considering both competing frameworks, the experiment considers the *average relative performance* of the two applications, i.e., the average of each application's relative performance w.r.t. its own standalone performance. Figure 10b shows that when Q21 runs with TeraSort, the two applications experience a 26% performance loss in average on *Native* YARN, and the use of cgroups-based proportional bandwidth sharing does not improve it. The I/O throttling policy of cgroups makes it even worse because it is non-work-conserving and causes underutilization of the I/O bandwidth. In comparison, IBIS is able to achieve an average relative performance of 80%. For Q9, cgroups and IBIS achieve similar average relative performance, which is about 4% lower than *Native* because this query is more I/O intensive and incurs a higher overhead in I/O scheduling.

Considering the results from both figures, a multi-framework resource management solution such as YARN cannot provide strong performance isolation among competing applications due to the lack of I/O management. In comparison, IBIS is able to provide I/O isolation and when used in combination with YARN's CPU and memory management, it is able to protect the performance of a vulnerable application such as TPC-H while still allowing the competing, intensive application such as TeraSort to make good progress by using the available storage bandwidth.

7.5 Proportional Slowdown

The previous three experiments are designed to show IBIS' ability to support the performance isolation policy. Another important and commonly used policy is *proportional slowdown*, i.e., the relative performance of competing applications, w.r.t. their standalone performance, is proportional to their assigned weights. This policy is often used to achieve fairness for applications in terms of their performance, not their resource allocations. A big-data application's performance depends on both the available CPU cores and I/O bandwidth, and its use of CPU and I/O resources are correlated. Without control on the I/O bandwidth, it is possible to achieve proportional slowdown by limiting the CPU slots allocated to the more I/O-intensive application and indirectly throttling its I/O rate, so that the less I/O-intensive one can get more I/O bandwidth. Nonetheless, such a configuration leads to storage underutilization and suboptimal performance of the applications.

With IBIS, system administrators can tune both CPU slot and I/O bandwidth allocations together, and achieve proportional slowdown without wasting the resources. Ideally, this tuning should be done automatically without human intervention, which would require performance models of the big-data applications that can capture their CPU and I/O resource demands given different performance targets. How to create such models and use them to automatically tune the resource allocations are interesting research problems on their own and will be considered in the future work. This paper focuses on the problem of providing the necessary I/O control mechanisms to support a variety of performance policies such as performance isolation and proportional slowdown, which comes with a set of unique challenges discussed earlier and is tackled by the proposed IBIS framework. Without such control knobs enabled by IBIS, it would be difficult for either administrators or autonomic software to achieve the desired performance policy with efficient resource utilization.

In this experiment, *equal slowdown* of both TeraSort and TeraGen is the target policy, meaning that both applications should be

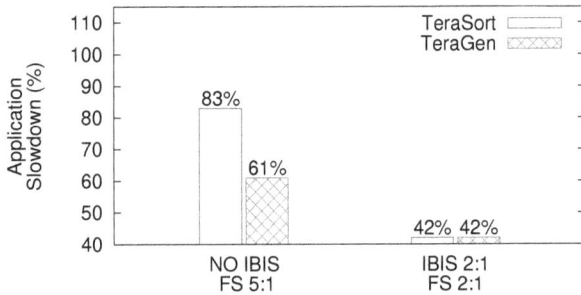

Figure 11: Performance slowdown of TeraSort and TeraGen using Hadoop Fair Scheduler (*FS*) based CPU slot allocations and IBIS-based I/O bandwidth allocations. The FS and IBIS ratios indicate the CPU and I/O shares, respectively, between TeraSort and Tera-Gen.

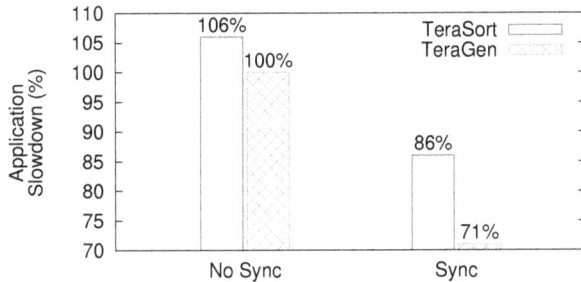

Figure 12: Performance slowdown of TeraSort and TeraGen when using IBIS *without* distributed scheduling coordination (*No Sync*) and *with* distributed scheduling coordination (*Sync*). The CPU sharing ratio of TeraSort vs. TeraGen is 1:1 and the I/O bandwidth sharing ratio is 32:1.

slowed down by the same percentage relative to their respective standalone runtime. Figure 11 shows the performance slowdown of these two applications. By adjusting only the CPU allocation using the Hadoop Fair Scheduler, the best equal slowdown that it can get is 83% slowdown for TeraSort and 61% for TeraGen. By using Fair Scheduler and IBIS to tune both CPU and I/O allocations together, it is able to get a perfect equal slowdown of 42%, which is 30% better than the average slowdown of the two applications when using Fair Scheduler only. These results therefore confirm that IBIS is also able to support the proportional slowdown policy and optimize the application performance under this policy.

7.6 Coordinated Scheduling

As discussed in Section 5, many factors decide the I/O service that an application gets from each datanode in a big-data system, including data distribution, slot allocation, task assignment, and competing applications, which all contribute to the uneven distribution of I/O services across the nodes. Without a mechanism for coordinating the distributed I/O schedulers and an algorithm to adjust local sharing ratios based on the global sharing policy, the total service that an application gets from the entire big-data system will diverge from the given target. This experiment evaluates the effectiveness of the proposed distributed scheduling coordination mechanisms (Section 5) for achieving total-service proportional sharing.

The experiment is conducted similarly to the previous one for achieving equal slowdown for TeraSort and TeraGen, but it considers two different IBIS setups where the distributed scheduling

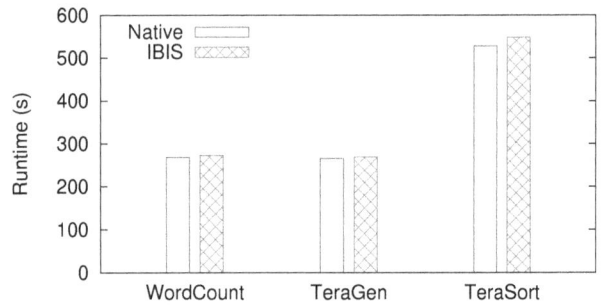

Figure 13: Runtime of WordCount, TeraGen, and TeraSort when each benchmark runs on native Hadoop (*Native*) vs. on *IBIS*

Table 2: CPU and memory usages of the YARN and IBIS daemons including the Resource Manager, Node Manager, and Data Node

Benchmark	Resource	Native	IBIS
WordCount	CPU	0.4%	0.5%
TeraGen	CPU	1.7%	5.1%
TeraSort	CPU	0.55%	0.65%
WordCount	Memory	1.2%	8.2%
TeraGen	Memory	2.0%	8.1%
TeraSort	Memory	1.6%	10.6%

coordination is disabled (*No Sync*) and enabled (*Sync*). The latter case should allow IBIS to find better equal slowdown because it can dynamically adjust local I/O service distribution based on global service distribution, which leads to better CPU and I/O resource utilization and better performance for both applications. Figure 12 shows the performance slowdown of TeraSort and TeraGen with respect to their own standalone runtimes. The average performance slowdown with *Sync* is 25% better than from *No Sync*, confirming the improvement made by the coordinated I/O scheduling.

7.7 Overhead

The last experiment evaluates the overhead of IBIS from several aspects. First, it studies the performance impact to a big-data application from IBIS-based I/O interposition and scheduling. WordCount, TeraGen, and TeraSort are all considered because each of them has distinct I/O patterns and demands. They are run separately with all the 96 CPU cores in the system. Figure 13 shows that the overhead of using IBIS is 1%, 2%, and 4% for WordCount, TeraGen, and TeraSort, respectively, in terms of runtime.

Second, the resource usages of IBIS are evaluated by tracking the total CPU and memory utilizations of the YARN Resource Manager, Node Manager, and Data Node, where the IBIS implementation is located. Table 2 lists the per-core CPU utilization and per-node memory utilization, which are reasonable compared to native YARN's resource usages.

Third, Table 3 summarizes the code development complexity in terms of lines of code categorized by the IBIS components. IBIS provides a flexible big-data I/O scheduling framework, and allows users to conveniently create new schedulers for different objectives. The amount of work required to develop a sophisticated scheduler on IBIS is only at the level of a thousand lines of code.

8. RELATED WORK

As storage performance becomes increasingly important to big-data applications, several recent works have studied this problem.

Component	Lines of Code
Interposition	2593
SFQ(D) Scheduler	734
SFQ(D2) Scheduler	1520
Scheduling Coordination	1705
Total	6552

Frosting [20] provides a scheduling layer upon HBase which dynamically controls the number of outstanding requests and proportionally shares the HBase storage among competing clients. However, it treats the entire distributed HBase storage stack as a single black box, and may underutilize the individual datanodes in order to provide any performance guarantee. In contrast, IBIS manages I/Os at the lower big-data file system layer and in a distributed manner, which can provide more effective I/O performance differentiation while making efficient use of the underlying storage resources.

PISCES [15] provides fair sharing of key-value storage by controlling requests dispatched to storage nodes according to the shares. In comparison, in a MapReduce-type big-data system an application's task distribution is driven by both CPU slot requirement and data locality, and its I/O demands are much more complex—including multiple phases of local and network I/Os, and diverse—with different intensities on the various types of I/Os. Hence, I/O management in a MapReduce system cannot be achieved by merely controlling task dispatching, and has to rely on both local I/O scheduling and global coordination which are part of the IBIS solution.

Cake [19] presents a two-level scheduling approach to meeting the performance goal of latency-sensitive applications (HBase) when they are consolidated with throughput-oriented applications (MapReduce), but it cannot provide any performance guarantee to the latter. In comparison, IBIS supports both types of applications.

Finally, a preliminary study of IBIS [23] presented the results from employing the traditional SFQ(D) scheduler for MapReduce applications only. This paper extends upon the initial results and includes a new scheduling framework that supports different types of big-data applications (both batch jobs and queries) and a new I/O scheduler SFQ(D2) that substantially outperforms SFQ(D).

Several works studied other orthogonal aspects of big-data storage: PACMan [8] manages memory-based caching of map task inputs to improve application performance; iShuffle [11] improves the performance of intermediate I/Os. However, they would still need a storage management solution like IBIS to provide performance isolation for the intermediate I/Os and the I/Os that trickle down the memory cache layer among concurrent applications.

I/O interposition is a technique often used to manage a shared storage resource that does not provide native knobs for controlling its competing I/Os. It has been employed in the related work to realize a proportional bandwidth scheduler for a shared file service [13], to create application-customized virtual file systems upon a shared network file system [25], and to manage the performance of a parallel file system based storage system [22]. Big-data systems present unique challenges to I/O management because of the complexity (different types of I/Os), diversity (different levels of intensity), and scale (many datanodes) of the I/O contention. These are addressed by the techniques embodied in IBIS, including holistic interposition of HDFS, local file system, and network I/Os, an adaptive proportion-share I/O scheduler, and scalable coordination of distributed I/O scheduling.

There are also related works on the performance management of other types of storage systems. Horizon [14] can provide global minimum throughput guarantee for a RAID storage system, but it requires a centralized controller to assign deadlines to requests, which is difficult to apply to a big-data system where I/Os are issued directly by local tasks on each datanode. A two-level scheduler [24] was proposed for meeting I/O latency and throughput targets, but it supports only local I/O scheduling, whereas a big-data system requires the distributed storage management provided by IBIS.

9. DISCUSSIONS

Overall IBIS can provide good performance isolation to various big-data applications. For WordCount, IBIS reduces the slowdown to merely 8% when it is under heavy I/O contention from a much more intensive job; but for a more latency-sensitive TPC-H query (Q21), it still shows a 25% slowdown despite the significant improvement over native YARN. Note that these results are achieved without underutilizing the shared storage bandwidth. Further improvement is possible by trading resource utilization for performance isolation. IBIS enables this tradeoff by adjusting its scheduler parameters (D in SFQ(D) and L_{ref} in SFQ(D2)) and choice of schedulers—in the extreme case, a non-work-conserving scheduler can provide strict performance isolation but may severely underutilize the storage.

This paper focuses on providing the missing control knob for managing I/Os in big-data systems, but it does not answer the question of how to automatically tune this new knob to meet an application's desired performance target—the results in Section 7 are from manually adjusting the scheduler parameters. A possible solution, which will be explored in the future work, is to build performance models for big-data applications that can map an application's resource allocations, including IBIS-based I/O bandwidth allocation, to its performance. Based on such models, admission control and resource allocation can be then done automatically given the desired application performance.

Although IBIS uses a centralized scheduling broker, its lightweight design promises good scalability. The broker handles only the forwarding of the global I/O service information to the local schedulers and let them decide how to schedule their local flows based on this information. In comparison, an alternative design that uses the broker to decide the scheduling of all the local flows in the system would not scale. The amount of information to be communicated between the broker and each local scheduler is also small, and it is piggybacked on the big-data system's existing heartbeat messages to further reduce its overhead. Therefore, the cost of global scheduling coordination does not grow significantly as the system size increases. Future work will consider the evaluation of IBIS on larger-scale testbeds to quantify its scalability.

Finally, the paper assumes that the big-data storage system is physical. A virtualized environment where the datanodes are hosted on virtual machines would present some new challenges. For example, several virtual datanodes may be sharing the same physical storage, and the scheduling decisions made by the IBIS schedulers running on these datanodes may be conflicting. As virtualized big-data systems gain wider adoption, this is also an interesting direction for future work.

10. CONCLUSIONS

Big-data systems are increasingly important platforms for efficient processing of large amounts of data for knowledge learning and sharing in various disciplines. Big-data applications are by nature I/O intensive, and their performance strongly depends on the I/O services that they get from the system. Existing big-data systems support only the allocation of CPUs and memory, which however does not provide any performance isolation on the shared storage. Moreover, it is challenging to achieve I/O performance management in a big-data system because of the intrinsic complexity of the application I/Os and the distributed nature of the system.

This paper presents IBIS, an Interposed Big-data I/O Scheduler, to address the above challenges and provide the much needed I/O performance differentiation to diverse big-data applications, possibly from different frameworks. IBIS is designed to transparently differentiate and schedule application I/Os on every datanode by interposing upon the distributed file system commonly used in big-data systems. It includes a new proportional-share I/O scheduler that can dynamically adjust I/O concurrency to optimize the trade-off between application fairness and resource utilization. It provides efficient coordination for the I/O schedulers distributed across the datanodes to cooperate and achieve proportional sharing of the big-data system's total I/O service. The results from an extensive evaluation confirm that IBIS can effectively address the severe I/O interference problem that existing big-data systems have and provide strong performance isolation with efficient resource usage.

11. ACKNOWLEDGMENTS

The authors thank the anonymous reviewers and the shepherd, Jon Weissman, for their helpful comments on the paper. This research is sponsored by National Science Foundation CAREER award CNS-125394 and Department of Defense award W911NF-13-1-0157.

12. REFERENCES

[1] Apache Hadoop. http://hadoop.apache.org/.
[2] Hadoop Fair Scheduler. https://hadoop.apache.org/docs/r2.7.1/hadoop-yarn/hadoop-yarn-site/FairScheduler.html.
[3] HBase. http://hbase.apache.org.
[4] Linux containers. https://linuxcontainers.org.
[5] OpenFlow. https://www.opennetworking.org/sdn-resources/openflow.
[6] Statistical workload injector for MapReduce (SWIM). https://github.com/SWIMProjectUCB/SWIM/wiki.
[7] TPC-H Benchmark Specification. http://www.tpc.org/tpch.
[8] G. Ananthanarayanan, A. Ghodsi, A. Wang, D. Borthakur, S. Kandula, S. Shenker, and I. Stoica. PACMan: Coordinated memory caching for parallel jobs. In *Proceedings of the 9th USENIX Conference on Networked Systems Design and Implementation*, 2012.
[9] J. Dean and S. Ghemawat. MapReduce: Simplified data processing on large clusters. In *Proceedings of the 6th Conference on Symposium on Opearting Systems Design and Implementation (OSDI'04)*, Berkeley, CA, USA, 2004. USENIX Association.
[10] S. Ghemawat, H. Gobioff, and S.-T. Leung. The Google file system. In *Proceedings of the Nineteenth ACM Symposium on Operating Systems Principles (SOSP'03)*, pages 29–43, New York, NY, USA, 2003. ACM.
[11] Y. Guo, J. Rao, and X. Zhou. iShuffle: Improving Hadoop performance with shuffle-on-write. In *Proceedings of the 10th International Conference on Autonomic Computing (ICAC'13)*, pages 107–117, San Jose, CA, 2013. USENIX.
[12] B. Hindman, A. Konwinski, M. Zaharia, A. Ghodsi, A. D. Joseph, R. Katz, S. Shenker, and I. Stoica. Mesos: A platform for fine-grained resource sharing in the data center. In *Proceedings of the 8th USENIX Conference on Networked Systems Design and Implementation*, 2011.

[13] W. Jin, J. S. Chase, and J. Kaur. Interposed proportional sharing for a storage service utility. In *Proceedings of the Joint International Conference on Measurement and Modeling of Computer Systems (SIGMETRICS'04)*, pages 37–48, New York, NY, USA, 2004. ACM.
[14] A. Povzner, D. Sawyer, and S. Brandt. Horizon: Efficient deadline-driven disk I/O management for distributed storage systems. In *Proceedings of the 19th ACM International Symposium on High Performance Distributed Computing (HPDC'10)*, pages 1–12, New York, NY, USA, 2010. ACM.
[15] D. Shue, M. J. Freedman, and A. Shaikh. Performance isolation and fairness for multi-tenant cloud storage. In *Proceedings of the 10th USENIX Conference on Operating Systems Design and Implementation*, pages 349–362, 2012.
[16] K. Shvachko, H. Kuang, S. Radia, and R. Chansler. The Hadoop distributed file system. In *Proceedings of the IEEE 26th Symposium on Mass Storage Systems and Technologies (MSST)*, pages 1–10. IEEE, 2010.
[17] A. Thusoo, J. Sarma, N. Jain, Z. Shao, P. Chakka, N. Zhang, S. Antony, H. Liu, and R. Murthy. Hive - A petabyte scale data warehouse using Hadoop. In *Proceedings of the 26th IEEE International Conference on Data Engineering (ICDE'10)*, pages 996–1005, March 2010.
[18] V. K. Vavilapalli, A. C. Murthy, C. Douglas, S. Agarwal, M. Konar, R. Evans, T. Graves, J. Lowe, H. Shah, and S. Seth. Apache Hadoop YARN: Yet another resource negotiator. In *Proceedings of the Fourth ACM Symposium on Cloud Computing*, 2013.
[19] A. Wang, S. Venkataraman, S. Alspaugh, R. Katz, and I. Stoica. Cake: Enabling high-level SLOs on shared storage systems. In *Proceedings of the Third ACM Symposium on Cloud Computing (SOCC'12)*, pages 14:1–14:14, New York, NY, USA, 2012. ACM.
[20] A. Wang, S. Venkataraman, S. Alspaugh, I. Stoica, and R. Katz. Sweet storage SLOs with Frosting. In *Proceedings of the 4th USENIX Conference on Hot Topics in Cloud Computing (HotCloud'12)*, Berkeley, CA, USA, 2012. USENIX Association.
[21] Y. Wang and A. Merchant. Proportional-share scheduling for distributed storage systems. In *Proceedings of the 5th USENIX Conference on File and Storage Technologies (FAST'07)*, Berkeley, CA, USA, 2007. USENIX.
[22] Y. Xu, D. Arteaga, M. Zhao, Y. Liu, R. Figueiredo, and S. Seelam. vPFS: Virtualization-based bandwidth management for parallel storage systems. In *Proceedings of the 28th IEEE Conference on Massive Data Storage (MSST)*, April 2012.
[23] Y. Xu, A. Suarez, and M. Zhao. IBIS: Interposed big-data I/O scheduler. In *Proceedings of the 22nd International Symposium on High-performance Parallel and Distributed Computing (HPDC'13)*, pages 109–110, New York, NY, USA, 2013. ACM.
[24] J. Zhang, A. Sivasubramaniam, Q. Wang, A. Riska, and E. Riedel. Storage performance virtualization via throughput and latency control. *ACM Transactions on Storage*, 2(3):283–308, Aug. 2006.
[25] M. Zhao and R. J. Figueiredo. Application-tailored cache consistency for wide-area file systems. In *Proceedings of the 26th IEEE International Conference on Distributed Computing Systems (ICDCS'06)*, 2006.

With Extreme Scale Computing the Rules Have Changed

Jack Dongarra
Innovative Computing Laboratory
EECS Department
University of Tennessee
dongarra@eecs.utk.edu

ABSTRACT

In this talk we will look at the current state of high performance computing and look at the next stage of extreme computing. With extreme computing there will be fundamental changes in the character of floating point arithmetic and data movement. In this talk we will look at how extreme scale computing has caused algorithm and software developers to changed their way of thinking on how to implement and program certain applications.

Biography

Jack Dongarra holds an appointment at the University of Tennessee, Oak Ridge National Laboratory, and the University of Manchester. He specializes in numerical algorithms in linear algebra, parallel computing, use of advanced-computer architectures, programming methodology, and tools for parallel computers. He was awarded the IEEE Sid Fernbach Award in 2004; in 2008 he was the recipient of the first IEEE Medal of Excellence in Scalable Computing; in 2010 he was the first recipient of the SIAM Special Interest Group on Supercomputing's award for Career Achievement; in 2011 he was the recipient of the IEEE IPDPS Charles Babbage Award; and in 2013 he received the ACM/IEEE Ken Kennedy Award. He is a Fellow of the AAAS, ACM

HPDC'16 May 31 - June 04, 2016, Kyoto, Japan

© 2016 Copyright held by the owner/author(s).

ACM ISBN 978-1-4503-4314-5/16/05.

DOI: http://dx.doi.org/10.1145/2907294.2926972

NVL-C: Static Analysis Techniques for Efficient, Correct Programming of Non-Volatile Main Memory Systems

Joel E. Denny[*]
Oak Ridge National Laboratory
dennyje@ornl.gov

Seyong Lee
Oak Ridge National Laboratory
lees2@ornl.gov

Jeffrey S. Vetter
Oak Ridge National Laboratory
vetter@ornl.gov

ABSTRACT

Computer architecture experts expect that non-volatile memory (NVM) hierarchies will play a more significant role in future systems including mobile, enterprise, and HPC architectures. With this expectation in mind, we present NVL-C[1]: a novel programming system that facilitates the efficient and correct programming of NVM main memory systems. The NVL-C programming abstraction extends C with a small set of intuitive language features that target NVM main memory, and can be combined directly with traditional C memory model features for DRAM. We have designed these new features to enable compiler analyses and run-time checks that can improve performance and guard against a number of subtle programming errors, which, when left uncorrected, can corrupt NVM-stored data. Moreover, to enable recovery of data across application or system failures, these NVL-C features include a flexible directive for specifying NVM transactions. So that our implementation might be extended to other compiler front ends and languages, the majority of our compiler analyses are implemented in an extended version of LLVM's intermediate representation (LLVM IR). We evaluate NVL-C on a number of applications to show its flexibility, performance, and correctness.

1. INTRODUCTION

NVM main memory hierarchies are playing an increasingly significant role in most computing systems, such as mobile, enterprise, and HPC architectures. Much of this trend is because NVM devices offers advantages over DRAM memory or magnetic hard disk drives (HDDs), in terms of power, density, performance, or cost [18, 10, 2, 20, 13, 9].

This trend is impacting system architecture and pertinent software (e.g., memory management in operating systems). Initially, these NVM devices have been integrated into ex-

isting systems in ways that hide the complexity from higher levels of software and applications: replacing a HDD with a solid-state disk (SSD) that uses NAND-Flash devices. This substitution greatly simplified the transition because the underlying complexity was hidden by the operating system and I/O subsystem, with relatively minor changes to the software stack. However, it becomes increasingly important to design software and applications that exploit the characteristics of these NVM devices. In the case of SSDs, the device drivers, operating systems, and I/O subsystems have been optimized for the underlying devices [5, 16, 15].

As the NVM technologies continue to improve, they become more credible for integration at other levels of the storage and memory hierarchy, such as either a peer or replacement for DRAM (see §2.1). In this case, scientists will be forced to redesign the architecture of the memory hierarchy, the software stack, and, possibly, their applications to gain the full advantages of these new capabilities [13].

Simply put, we posit that these new memory systems will need to be exposed to applications as first-class language constructs with full support from the software development tools (e.g., compilers, libraries) to employ them efficiently, correctly, and portably.

1.1 Key Contributions

In this paper, we present NVL-C: a novel programming system that provides language-level support for NVM main memory. More specifically, in NVL-C, we design, implement, and evaluate several novel static analyses and transformation techniques on these new constructs in order to provide support for efficient, portable, and correct execution of applications that contain NVM data structures. The key contributions of this paper are:

1. We design a novel and intuitive programming model (NVL-C) for NVM that facilitates efficient, portable, and correct execution.
2. We implement a prototype of this programming model using extensions to C and LLVM IR.
3. We describe novel static analyses and transformations in LLVM to support correct and efficient code generation for an underlying memory system including NVM.
4. We evaluate NVL-C on a set of applications to demonstrate its flexibility, performance, and correctness.
5. We identify two optimizations that significantly improve performance in our test applications: NVM pointer hoisting and aggregation of transaction data.

---

[*]Work performed while employed as Research Scientist I with the University of Tennessee Joint Institute for Computational Sciences.
[1]Pronounced "novel C".

HPDC'16, May 31-June 04, 2016, Kyoto, Japan
© 2016 ACM. ISBN 978-1-4503-4314-5/16/05...$15.00
DOI: http://dx.doi.org/10.1145/2907294.2907303

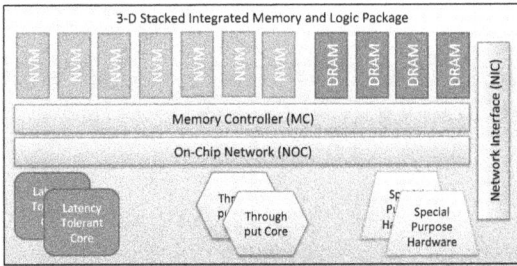

Figure 1: Expected architecture of future memory systems.

2. MOTIVATION AND NVL-C OVERVIEW

2.1 Emerging Memory Hierarchies

Contemporary NVM technology offers a useful compromise between the capabilities of DRAM and HDD [13, 18]. For example, computing systems use flash as SSDs through a POSIX file system interface, or through emerging interfaces, such as NVMe or NAND Flash Memory Interface (FMI). Often, these flash-based SSDs fully replace HDDs in mobile devices and laptops. While more expensive per byte than HDDs, flash is faster, so it reduces the performance bottleneck. However, like HDDs, flash is block-addressable and slower than DRAM, so it is still advantageous for systems to include DRAM banks as a form of volatile memory.

In contrast, future architectures, as illustrated in Figure 1, will include direct load/store interfaces to memory, bypassing the PCIe interface. Moreover, newer NVM technologies, such as PCM, STT-RAM, and ReRAM, promise to be byte-addressable and nearly as fast as DRAM. Thus, they are often described as storage-class memories (SCM). Like flash, SCM is also more power-efficient than DRAM. Unlike flash, SCM technologies are still immature and suffer from write endurance limitations and higher costs.

Eventually, NVM might be able to fully replace both HDD and DRAM. However, at least in the near future, we anticipate that NVM will continue to gradually replace HDD but complement DRAM, as in Figure 1.

2.2 Design Goals

Our design goals for providing programming support for NVM are as follows:

1. *Minimal, familiar, programming interface.* The interface to allocating, accessing, and managing NVM should be intuitively familiar to programmers and have minimal changes to existing language primitives or APIs. The interface must balance this simplicity against the requirements for efficiency, correctness, composability, and modularity. Moreover, the interface should provide concepts to share different types of memories.

2. *Pointer safety.* Programming systems for NVM involve new pointer types with new categories of pointer bugs [4]. Pointer safety constraints should be enforced to minimize or eliminate the occurrence of such bugs. Enforcement at compile time rather than at run time should be preferred when possible to maximize the pace of correct application development.

3. *Transactions.* The programming system must support transactions in order to avoid corruption of NVM in the case of application or system failure.

4. *High performance.* Code automatically inserted by the compiler to manage memory, to enforce safety con-

```
1   #include <nvl.h>
2   struct list {
3     int value;
4     nvl struct list *next;
5   };
6   void add(int k) {
7     nvl_heap_t *heap = nvl_open("foo.nvl");
8     nvl struct list *a
9       = nvl_get_root(heap, struct list);
10    nvl struct list *b
11      = nvl_alloc_nv(heap, 1, struct list);
12    b->value = k;
13    b->next = a->next;
14    a->next = b;
15    nvl_close(heap);
16  }
17  void remove(int k) {
18    nvl_heap_t *heap = nvl_open("foo.nvl");
19    nvl struct list *a
20      = nvl_get_root(heap, struct list);
21    #pragma nvl atomic heap(heap)
22    while (a->next != NULL) {
23      if (a->next->value == k)
24        a->next = a->next->next;
25      else
26        a = a->next;
27    }
28    nvl_close(heap);
29  }
```

Figure 2: NVL-C Linked List Example

straints, and to support transactions can entail a performance penalty. Programmer-specified performance hints and additional compiler passes should be implemented to reduce the overhead of such features.

5. *Modular Implementation.* To maximize flexibility and experimentation, the compiler and runtime should be designed modularly. At the core should be a common compiler middle-end implementation that is general enough to (1) be targeted by multiple compiler front ends for multiple high-level languages and (2) target multiple runtime implementations.

2.3 Programming Model Overview

Figure 2 presents an example of an NVM-stored linked list implemented in NVL-C. The type struct list is the list's node type. The add function inserts a node with value k at the beginning of the list. The remove function iterates the list and removes all nodes with value k. This example is based on a similar example presented by Coburn et al. for their NV-heaps system [4].

This example demonstrates some of the ways in which NVL-C addresses the design goals we enumerated in §2.2. First, notice that this NVL-C code is almost the same as the C code you might write for a linked list stored in volatile memory. The only required differences are (1) the nvl type qualifier to mark pointers into NVM and (2) the API function calls for memory management. Second, if NVL-C didn't require and enforce the nvl type qualifier, we could have accidentally coded the add function to call malloc instead of nvl_alloc_nv without receiving any warning from the compiler. As a result, we would accidentally link a volatile-memory-stored node into our NVM-stored linked list, producing a persistent dangling pointer at program termination. Finally, the remove function uses the NVL-C atomic pragma to declare the while loop as a transaction. The system then guarantees that, despite any power outages or other failures, either all or none of the nodes with value k are removed.

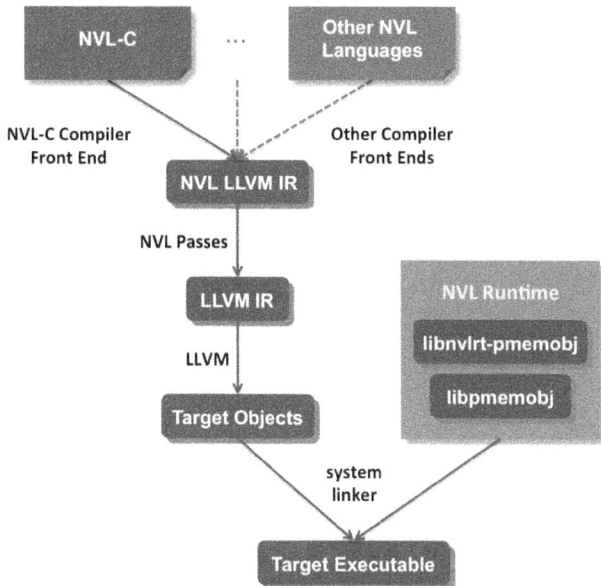

Figure 3: NVL-C System Implementation

2.4 Implementation Overview

As depicted in Figure 3, our NVL-C system implementation consists of a modular compiler and runtime that address our final design goal from §2.2. First, the NVL-C compiler front end's job is minimal: it validates the input NVL-C code and translates it to an extended version of LLVM IR. We use the term *NVL* instead of NVL-C to identify all remaining components of our NVL-C system implementation. The reason is that we designed those components to be shared with future implementations for other high-level languages, such as C++ or Fortran, if extended to support our NVM programming model. These components include the *NVL passes*, which are a set of LLVM passes that perform the bulk of the NVM-related compiler analysis and transformation work, and the *NVL runtime*.

Second, we have currently built our NVL runtime on top of Intel's libpmemobj library in order to use its NVM allocation functionality and transaction functionality [1]. However, we have encapsulated the interface of the NVL runtime in our libnvlrt-pmemobj library so that libpmemobj can easily be replaced by alternate runtime implementations in the future.

2.5 NVL-C Advantages

NVL-C is inspired by the NV-heaps system of Coburn et al. [4] and shares many of the same goals and programming model features. However, NVL-C also has a number of advantages, most of which stem from the fact that NVL-C is a language extension, not just a library:

1. *Improved interface*: whereas the NV-heap's programming interface is a C++ API, NVL-C's interface consists of a small set of C language extensions. As a result, NVL-C is easier to learn and program: instead of learning specialized macros, types, getters, and setters from a C++ templated class hierarchy, the user can program in familiar C syntax, allocate C types in NVM, and reference those allocations and their members with pointers. The difference in code readability can be seen by comparing Figure 2 with the NV-heaps linked list example [4].

2. *Compiler-supported*: whereas NV-heaps is implemented purely as a C++ library, NVL-C is supported by a compiler. Thus, NVL-C supports (a) additional safety constraints and diagnostics for common NVM programming errors, (b) compile-time enforcement of safety constraints that NV-heaps enforces at run time, (c) specialized compiler analyses and optimizations, and (d) implementation reuse for other high-level languages.

3. *Portable*: NV-heaps targets the fast, byte-addressable NVM technologies of the future, and NV-heaps assumes the theoretical hardware extensions of BPFS [5] for efficient durability support. In contrast, NVL-C is currently implemented on top of libpmemobj, which supports a wide range of persistent storage devices, from HDD to flash to future NVM, without special hardware extensions. Still, the focus is on future NVM.

Moreover, we have so far discovered two optimizations that can significantly improve performance: aggregation of transaction data (§3.9.2) and NVM pointer hoisting (§4.4). In this paper, we describe a novel interface for manually specifying the former optimization, but we are also exploring automation of both optimizations as part of our future work.

3. PROGRAMMING MODEL

3.1 Terminology

We use the terms *lvalue* and *rvalue* frequently in this section. By lvalue, we mean an expression that designates an object in memory, and we say that an lvalue is converted to an rvalue by a load of that object from memory. For example, given the declarations int i; and int *p;, then a subsequent expression i or *p is an lvalue that designates an integer stored in memory, and that integer is loaded to become an rvalue when i or *p is used as an operand in an expression, such as i+1 or *p+1.

3.2 The nvl and nvl_wp Type Qualifiers

NVL-C's most important C extension is the nvl type qualifier. Both syntactically and semantically, nvl is similar to any C type qualifier, such as const or volatile: it modifies the behavior of load and store operations on lvalues of so-qualified types. Specifically, for lvalues of nvl-qualified types, the objects designated by those lvalues are loaded from and stored to NVM. For brevity, we often use the term *NVM-stored* to describe such a type, lvalue, or object. NVL-C adds one other type qualifier, nvl_wp, that has the same syntax and semantics as nvl except that it designates weak pointers, which we describe in §3.7. For lvalues of types that are not qualified with nvl or nvl_wp, the objects designated by those lvalues are loaded from and stored to volatile memory instead. For example, Figure 2 line 19 declares a variable a, whose type is not NVM-stored, so a is stored in volatile memory. However, a is a pointer whose target type is NVM-stored, so the lvalue *a is NVM-stored.

3.3 Array and Struct Types

Generally in C and NVL-C, a type qualifier on an array type has the same meaning as that type qualifier on its element type. Thus, an array is NVM-stored if and only if either the array type or its element type is NVM-stored.

When accessing a member of an NVM-stored object of struct type, the compiler adds the nvl type qualifier to the type of the resulting member lvalue unless the member's

Pointer Class	Permitted
NV-to-V	no
V-to-NV	yes
intra-heap NV-to-NV	yes
inter-heap NV-to-NV	no

Table 1: Pointer Classes

type was declared NVM-stored. This behavior is similar to the way the resulting member lvalue would be const if the struct object were const. For example, in Figure 2, the `value` member of `struct list` is declared on line 3 with type `int`, but the type of the variable `a` declared on line 19 is `nvl struct list *`, so the type of the lvalue `a->value` is `nvl int`. Likewise, on line 26, the type of the lvalue `a->next` is `nvl struct list * nvl`.

3.4 Pointer Types

Generally in C and NVL-C, type qualifiers on pointer target types affect the behavior of load and store operations on the lvalues that result from dereferencing those pointers or, as in the example in §3.3, that result from accessing a member via those pointers. In the cases of the `nvl` and `nvl_wp` type qualifiers, the sizes of those pointers are also affected: as discussed in §4.2, pointers to NVM are wide.

Generally in C and NVL-C, it is a compile-time error to remove a type qualifier from a pointer's target type by means of a type conversion as that would break the behavior guaranteed by the type qualifier. For example, it is a compile-time error to assign a pointer of type `const struct list *` or of type `nvl struct list *` to a pointer of type `struct list *`. However, while some C compilers by default merely warn about violations of this constraint, the NVL-C compiler strictly enforces it for the cases of `nvl` and `nvl_wp`. Moreover, unlike C type qualifiers, it is also a compile-time error to *add* `nvl` or `nvl_wp` to a pointer's target type by means of a type conversion. These stricter constraints for `nvl` and `nvl_wp` are necessary because arbitrarily removing or adding them for a pointer target type could lead to load and store operations that are invalid for the memory addresses on which they're performed, producing persistent corruption of NVM data and segmentation faults.

As listed in Table 1, Coburn et al. identify several new pointer classes and two novel pointer safety constraints [4]. The first constraint does not permit what Coburn et al. call *NV-to-V pointers*, which are pointers from NVM to volatile memory. The justification is that, when a program terminates, all its volatile memory is cleared while NVM remains, so an NV-to-V pointer becomes a dangling pointer. While Coburn et al. state that their NV-heaps system enforces this constraint at run time, NVL-C enforces this constraint at compile time by constraining the use of the `nvl` and `nvl_wp` type qualifiers. Specifically, any NVM-stored pointer type must have an NVM-stored target type. For example, in Figure 2 line 4, if the pointer target type of the `next` member of `struct list` were declared without the `nvl` type qualifier, then the declaration of `a` on line 19 would be a compile-time error because the lvalue `a->next` would have type `struct list * nvl`, which is an NV-to-V pointer.

V-to-NV pointers are pointers from volatile memory to NVM. Like NV-heaps, NVL-C permits them. For example, Figure 2 line 19 declares the variable `a` as a V-to-NV pointer.

NV-to-NV pointers are pointers from NVM to NVM. For example, the pointer designated by the lvalue `a->next` is an NV-to-NV pointer. The second pointer safety constraint enforced by the NV-heaps system involves NV-to-NV pointers, and we discuss it in §3.6.

3.5 Loads and Stores

Generally in C and NVL-C, a load operation on an lvalue produces an rvalue of the same type except that top-level type qualifiers are removed because top-level type qualifiers have no meaning for rvalues. In the cases of the `nvl` and `nvl_wp` type qualifiers, this means that the object designated by an NVM-stored lvalue is loaded only into volatile memory, and there is no such thing as an NVM-stored rvalue. For example, as we explained in §3.3, in Figure 2 line 26, the type of the lvalue `a->next` that appears as the right-hand operand of the assignment operator is `nvl struct list * nvl`, so this lvalue is stored in NVM. Before the assignment is performed, a load is performed on that lvalue, and the resulting rvalue's type is `nvl struct list *`, so the rvalue is stored in volatile memory.

Storing to an NVM-stored lvalue is the reverse of loading: data is copied from volatile memory to NVM. For example, in Figure 2 line 24, the load for the right-hand operand of the assignment operator produces an rvalue of type `nvl struct list *`, and the left-hand operand is an lvalue of type `nvl struct list * nvl`.

3.6 NVM Allocations

NVL-C does not currently permit adding `nvl` or `nvl_wp` to variable declarations in order to convert their storage durations from automatic or static to persistent. For example, in Figure 2, it would be a compile-time error to `nvl`-qualify the type of the variable `a` on line 19 or of the function parameter `k` on line 17. Instead, NVL-C applications allocate NVM in the same manner as the NV-heaps system: via a hybrid of the traditional HDD and DRAM programming interfaces. First, NVM storage is always organized into separate *NVM heaps*, each identified by a unique file name. For this purpose, the constructs `nvl_heap_t`, `nvl_open`, and `nvl_close` are the NVM heap analogues of C's `FILE`, `fopen`, and `fclose` for normal files. An NVM heap can also be renamed, duplicated, or removed using file system commands. Second, NVM storage is always allocated dynamically within NVM heaps. For this purpose, `nvl_alloc_nv` is the NVM heap analogue of C's `malloc` function for the volatile heap.

For example, Figure 2 line 7 calls `nvl_open` to open the file `foo.nvl`, which must be an NVM heap. `nvl_open` maps the NVM heap's memory into the program's virtual address space and returns a pointer to an `nvl_heap_t`, a data structure that is stored in volatile memory to describe the NVM heap. On that `nvl_heap_t`, line 11 calls `nvl_alloc_nv` to dynamically create a new allocation within that NVM heap. The argument list specifies the number of elements and the type of each element, and the NVL-C compiler uses that type to compute the return type of this call as `nvl struct list *`. Line 15 calls `nvl_close` on that `nvl_heap_t` to close the NVM heap, unmap its memory, and free any volatile memory associated with it.

When an application opens an existing NVM heap using `nvl_open`, there are no V-to-NV pointers into that heap, so there is no way to access any NVM allocation or load any NV-to-NV pointer from the heap except via a distinguished allocation called the heap's *root*. The root can be set and get using the functions `nvl_set_root` and `nvl_get_root`. For example, line 9 contains a `nvl_get_root` call, whose return type is computed from the second argument as `nvl struct list *`. This example assumes that `nvl_set_root` has previously been called, and `nvl_get_root` would return a null pointer otherwise. Before closing a heap or before the application terminates, it is up to the programmer to ensure that all allocations in an NVM heap are reachable from the root if he wants those allocations to be retrievable later.

For each `nvl_get_root` or `nvl_set_root` call, the compiler computes a *type checksum* that includes all C- and ABI-level details of the root type, including type names, field widths, and signedness. Each `nvl_set_root` call records its type checksum alongside the root, and each `nvl_get_root` call fails if its type checksum does not match the previously recorded type checksum, thus preventing access to the heap using the wrong root type. Because all other allocations in a recently opened NVM heap are accessed via the root, checking the root type is sufficient to check their types. In our example, the heap consists entirely of a single linked list, and the root contains a pointer to the head node.

In §3.4, we described how NVL-C enforces the first of two pointer safety constraints that are also enforced by the NV-heaps system. We now describe how NVL-C enforces the second. As listed in Table 1, Coburn et al. divide NV-to-NV pointers into two categories: *intra-heap* and *inter-heap*, which identify whether the source and target NVM heaps are different [4]. Their second pointer safety constraint does not permit inter-heap NV-to-NV pointers. The justification is that there is no guarantee that the source and target NVM heaps will always be open or even exist at the same time. Moreover, when an NVM heap is reopened, it might be mapped to a different virtual address than when the pointer was created. Thus, the pointer would become a dangling pointer, and garbage collection schemes (see §3.7) would have difficulty tracking references to allocations. To address these problems, inter-heap NV-to-NV pointers could be expanded into arbitrarily large data structures that store NVM heap file names. However, programmers can develop such data structures themselves just as they would for references across any two files in a file system.

Like NV-heaps, NVL-C enforces the constraint against inter-heap NV-to-NV pointers at run time. Any V-to-NV pointer contains an identifier for the target NVM heap. When a V-to-NV pointer is stored to NVM, an NV-to-NV pointer is created, so this identifier is first checked against the identifier of the NVM heap into which the pointer is being stored. If the identifier fails to match, an inter-heap NV-to-NV pointer would be created, so a run-time error occurs. As long as this constraint is enforced, it is redundant for an NV-to-NV pointer to contain an identifier for the target NVM heap. That is, that identifier won't be needed again until the NV-to-NV pointer is loaded back into volatile memory to create a V-to-NV pointer. In that case, the required target NVM heap identifier is just the identifier of the NVM heap from which the NV-to-NV pointer is loaded.

3.7 Automatic Reference Counting

As part of their effort to protect against persistent corruption of NVM data, NV-heaps and NVL-C provide automatic reference counting. In the NV-heaps system, reference counts are stored per object whose type is a C++ class for NVM. However, NVL-C stores reference counts per NVM allocation. Because NVL-C permits NVM allocations of C types, such as arrays and structs, a reference count can then apply to multiple objects.

There are two reference counts for each NVM allocation, both of which must reach zero before the allocation is automatically freed. The first is for NV-to-NV pointers into the allocation, and the second is for V-to-NV pointers into the allocation. Each reference count is automatically incremented and decremented as associated pointers into the allocation are created and either overwritten or destroyed. The NV-to-NV reference count persists in NVM as long as the allocation does, but the V-to-NV reference count is effectively set to zero when the NVM heap containing the allocation is closed or when the application terminates.

If an NVM allocation is part of an NV-to-NV pointer cycle and is unreachable from the root of the NVM heap and from all V-to-NV pointers, then its NV-to-NV reference count can never reach zero, so it becomes a persistent memory leak. Thus, like the NV-heaps system, NVL-C provides both strong and weak pointers so that programmers can avoid pointer cycles. Because NV-to-V pointers are not permitted, it is impossible for V-to-NV pointers to appear in pointer cycles, so all V-to-NV pointers are strong pointers. NV-to-NV pointers whose types are `nvl`-qualified are strong pointers. NV-to-NV pointers whose types are `nvl_wp`-qualified are weak pointers. For example, in Figure 2, the type of the lvalue `a->next` is `nvl struct list * nvl`, which is a strong pointer. If we were to change the declaration of the `next` member of `struct list` on line 4 to have type `nvl struct list * nvl_wp`, then the lvalue `a->next` would be a weak pointer instead. Declaring a weak pointer is the only reason we have found to declare a struct member's type to be NVM-stored, and then all objects of that struct type must be NVM-stored.

For pointer types, strong vs. weak is the only difference between the `nvl` and `nvl_wp` type qualifiers. For other types, there is a major difference: `nvl_wp` is only permitted on pointer types or, as implied by §3.3, on array types whose element types are pointer types. Any other `nvl_wp`-qualified type is a compile-time error. In this respect, `nvl_wp` is similar to C's `restrict` type qualifier. It is fine to assign a strong pointer to a weak pointer and vice versa. In fact, every load of a weak pointer produces a strong V-to-NV pointer. Once the target allocation has been freed, loading the weak pointer produces a null V-to-NV pointer.

Every pointer to NVM must be initialized when allocated or else, when overwriting or destroying the pointer, it is not possible in general to determine whether the previous contents of the pointer are valid and thus whether a reference count must be decremented. This is true even for weak pointers because they are actually implemented as strong pointers to proxies for the target allocations. If an automatically or statically allocated V-to-NV pointer is not explicitly initialized at the time of allocation, the compiler can provide a null initialization. For example, Figure 2 line 19 provides an explicit initialization in the declaration of the V-to-NV pointer `a`. It is a compile-time error if a jump, such as a goto statement, bypasses the initialization of an automatically allocated V-to-NV pointer. This constraint is straight-forward to implement, and ISO C99 states a similar constraint for variably modified types.

```
1   #include <nvl.h>
2   void matmul(nvl_heap_t *heap, nvl float a[I][J],
3               nvl float b[I][K], nvl float c[K][J],
4               nvl int *i) {
5     while (*i<I) {
6       #pragma nvl atomic heap(heap) clobber(a[*i:N])
7       for (int ii=0; ii<N; ++ii, ++*i) {
8         for (int j=0; j<J; ++j) {
9           float sum = 0.0;
10          for (int k=0; k<K; ++k)
11            sum += b[*i][k] * c[k][j];
12          a[*i][j] = sum;
13  }}}}
```

Figure 4: NVL-C Matrix Multiply Example

3.8 Type Safety

Strong type safety in NVL-C can generally help to prevent persistent corruption of NVM data, and it is especially important for correct automatic reference counting. Void pointers, pointers casts, unions, variadic functions, and incomplete struct types are avenues in C to circumvent type safety, so NVL-C constrains their use for NVM-related types. These constraints do not affect normal C types, so NVL-C is still a superset of C. Due to space restrictions, we do not describe these type safety constraints in detail in this paper.

3.9 Transactions

NVL-C enforces run-time safety constraints, such as the constraint against inter-heap NV-to-NV pointers, by terminating the application when a constraint is violated. Applications can terminate prematurely due also to other application or system failures, such as segmentation faults or power loss. Premature termination can leave NVM in an inconsistent state. For this reason, it is important that NVL-C support grouping NVM writes into transactions. Our current implementation of transactions has several limitations (see §3.9.3). As the hardware and system software improves, we will continue to improve NVL-C language capabilities.

3.9.1 ACID Properties

In this section, we describe how a NVL-C transaction addresses ACID properties [7] for its NVM writes.

Atomicity. If a transaction does not commit before application termination, then the next time any application accesses the same NVM heap, all the transaction's NVM writes are first rolled back to restore NVM data to a consistent state. Atomicity entails an overhead in both time and space: old data to be overwritten must be backed up.

Consistency. This property is addressed by the way in which NVM writes are grouped into transactions. For this purpose, there are two kinds of transactions:

1. *Implicit transactions* are either built into the NVL runtime or inserted into application code by the compiler to satisfy internal consistency constraints of NVL-C. Most notably, when storing a pointer into NVM, there is an implicit transaction that includes storing all the pointer's fields, updating NV-to-NV reference counts, and freeing NVM allocations whose reference counts then reach zero.

2. *Explicit transactions* are specified by the NVL-C programmer via the nvl atomic pragma to satisfy any additional consistency constraints imposed by application requirements. All NVM writes appearing within the attached C block are considered part of the trans-

clause	requirements	access patterns
backup	backup, durable, wlock	rw, wr, wo
clobber	durable, wlock	wr, wo
readonly	rlock	ro

Table 2: Transaction Data Clauses

action. For example, the transaction starting at Figure 2 line 21 guarantees that the remove function removes either all or none of the linked list nodes of value k. Sometimes implicit transactions alone are sufficient to satisfy an application's consistency constraints. For example, in our linked list's add function, the implicit transaction for storing the pointer b to a->next on Figure 2 line 14 is sufficient because automatic reference counting ensures that the new node b is freed if the application terminates before then.

Isolation. In the future, we will extend NVL-C to automatically guarantee that transactions executing concurrently will leave NVM data in the same state as they would if they were to execute serially. We are confident NVL-C can be extended in this manner because NVL-C is conceptually based on NV-heaps, which offers this guarantee [4]. Nevertheless, it is already possible to combine NVL-C with existing parallel programming systems provided the programmer explicitly safeguards NVM data from concurrent access.

Durability. If a transaction commits before application termination, including power loss, then all its NVM writes are durably stored into NVM despite any processor caching or buffering. This property normally entails an overhead in time: any such caches or buffers must be flushed or synced.

3.9.2 Performance Hints

Consider a large matrix multiply that writes its result matrix to NVM. As a simple checkpointing mechanism to avoid losing significant progress in the event of premature application termination, the programmer could specify a transaction per N result rows, for some $N \geq 1$, as in Figure 4. That is, each transaction computes N rows, writes those rows to NVM, and increments an NVM-stored row counter N times so the application knows where to resume after premature application termination. Notice that the old data in the result matrix is irrelevant to the computation and thus to data consistency. Thus, the atomicity property in this case could be relaxed to say: if the transaction does not commit before application termination, then the next time the application accesses the same NVM heap, the transaction's writes to *only the row counter* are first rolled back to restore NVM data to a consistent state. Relaxing the atomicity property in this way is not necessary for correct behavior, but it avoids the backup overhead for the result matrix. However, result matrix writes still entail durability overhead. That is, row counter increments must not be committed if result matrix writes have not been durably stored.

We have devised several data clauses for the nvl atomic pragma that enable the programmer to provide performance hints for explicit transactions, such as eliminating backup overhead. These clauses are listed in Table 2. Each use of each clause specifies how the transaction is required to handle a specified segment of NVM. For example, the clause backup(arr[4:2]) specifies that, for elements 4 and 5 of the array arr, old data must be backed up and writes must be made durable. In our matrix multiply example, the backup clause is thus appropriate for the NVM-stored row counter. The `clobber` clause is the same as the `backup` clause except it does not back up old data, so it is appropriate for our matrix multiply example's result matrix. Notice that clause names reflect the handling of old data to be overwritten.

These clauses are also useful for aggregating actions on large contiguous NVM segments that the transaction accesses randomly. For example, in matrix multiply, rather than flush processor caches each time a transaction writes to a cell of its result matrix, it is usually more efficient to flush caches for all of the transaction's result matrix rows once at the end of the transaction. The `clobber` clause controls the granularity of such flushing, and the `backup` clause controls the granularity of backup logging. In the future when our transaction implementation supports the isolation property, the `readonly` clause will be useful for controlling the granularity of read locks on NVM segments that are read but never written by the transaction. The `backup` and `clobber` clauses will also control the granularity of write locks.

Table 2 also lists NVM access patterns to help guide the programmer's selection of appropriate clauses. The `backup` clause is the only clause that is appropriate for an NVM segment in which some bits are read before written (rw) by the transaction. That is, because old data there is used by the transaction, the old data must be backed up in case the transaction must be retried later. If no bits in an NVM segment are rw, but if some are written before read (wr) or only written (wo) by a transaction, then either the `backup` or `clobber` clause might be appropriate, depending on how the data there might be used elsewhere before the transaction is retried. The `readonly` clause is the only clause that is appropriate for an NVM segment that is only read (ro) by a transaction. Specifying a clause higher in this table for a NVM segment for which a clause lower in this table is actually appropriate will not harm behavior, but it might harm performance. The converse does not hold. The `nvl atomic` pragma also supports a `default` clause for specifying the default handling of an NVM segment not mentioned in the other clauses. If the `default` clause is not specified, the default is `backup`, which never harms behavior. NVL-C is free to ignore the default when, based on the access pattern for an NVM segment, it can safely improve performance.

3.9.3 Current Limitations

A couple of NVL-C's current limitations in its transaction support stem from its dependence on Intel's `libpmemobj` transaction support, which has similar limitations [1]. First, as mentioned above, NVL-C does not automatically guarantee the isolation property of ACID transactions. Second, an explicit transaction is limited to a single NVM heap, which must be specified explicitly. While `libpmemobj` does support dynamically nested transactions, we have not yet carefully addressed their relationship with the `nvl atomic` pragma's data clauses, which `libpmemobj` does not directly support.

4. IMPLEMENTATION

4.1 Compilation

As depicted in Figure 3, the compilation of NVL-C is divided into four stages, which we describe in this section.

Front end. In order to maximize analysis and optimization opportunities, all NVM-related constructs in the NVL-C programming interface, including all API function calls,

are recognized specially by the front end as compiler built-ins. The front end lowers NVL-C to *NVL LLVM IR*, which is standard LLVM extended with novel LLVM metadata, intrinsics, and address spaces that represent the same semantics as the NVM-related constructs from the NVL-C source. We implemented the reference front-end using an open-source C compiler called OpenARC [11].

NVL passes. Existing LLVM passes do not currently understand our LLVM IR extensions. However, we have created a new set of LLVM passes, which we call the *NVL passes*, to lower those extensions to standard LLVM IR before running any other LLVM passes. Lowering to standard LLVM IR is not the only responsibility of the NVL passes. That is, we have designed NVL LLVM IR to be semantically close to the source level so that the compiler front end's job is as minimal as possible, leaving the bulk of the NVM-related analysis and optimization work to the NVL passes. Thus, while we have already extended one C compiler front end to support NVL-C, we expect it to be straight-forward to extend other LLVM compiler front ends and high-level languages to support the NVL-C programming model as well.

LLVM. LLVM performs non-NVM-related optimizations and compiles the LLVM IR into target-specific object files.

Linking. NVL-C compilation does not require special linker support beyond linker support required by C. However, NVL-C applications must be linked with the NVL runtime. Currently, we have built the NVL runtime on top of Intel's `libpmemobj` library, version 0.4, in order to use its NVM allocation and transaction functionality [1]. However, we have encapsulated the interface of the NVL runtime in our `libnvlrt-pmemobj` library, and the compiler never targets `libpmemobj` directly. We have designed the NVL runtime in this way so that `libnvlrt-pmemobj` can be replaced with other versions of the NVL runtime that do not target `libpmemobj`, facilitating experimentation with other runtime implementations in the future.

4.2 Pointers

As with both NV-heaps and `libpmemobj`, NVL-C's pointers to NVM are wide. Specifically, NVL-C's V-to-NV pointers have three fields:

1. `heap`. This field contains the address of a volatile-memory-stored `nvl_heap_t` that contains volatile information about the V-to-NV pointer's target NVM heap, such as its base virtual address. In this way, the `heap` field implements what we described abstractly in §3.6 as the heap identifier, which we explained is redundant when the V-to-NV pointer is stored to NVM and thus becomes an NV-to-NV pointer. That's fortunate because, given that the `heap` field is a pointer into volatile memory, it will be invalid when the NVM heap is later reopened and a new `nvl_heap_t` is allocated.

2. `alloc`. This field is the heap-relative offset of the V-to-NV pointer's target NVM allocation. Because it is an offset not an absolute address, it never needs to be adjusted when an NVM heap is reopened and mapped to a different virtual address.

3. `obj`. This field is the allocation-relative offset of the V-to-NV pointer's target NVM object. As with the `alloc` field, because it's an offset, it does not need to be adjusted when an NVM heap is reopened.

The V-to-NV reference count for each NVM allocation is stored in a cuckoo hash table within the NVM heap's `nvl_heap_t`. The hash table key is the `alloc` field used in V-to-NV pointers to the allocation. On the other hand, the NV-to-NV reference count for an NVM allocation is stored within the allocation itself. Thus, given a V-to-NV pointer, our implementation uses its `heap` and `alloc` fields to look up the V-to-NV and NV-to-NV reference counts for the target NVM allocation in $O(1)$ worst case time.

When both the V-to-NV and NV-to-NV reference counts for an NVM allocation a reach zero, a must be freed. However, a might contain pointers to other NVM allocations, and so the NV-to-NV reference counts for those allocations must first be decremented. Unfortunately, the last pointer into a that was destroyed to cause a to be freed might be a pointer to some object o within a. While a can be located via that o pointer's `alloc` field, there is no means to determine the type of a. Without the type of a, how do we locate all pointers within a? Our solution is to take advantage of the redundant `heap` field in NV-to-NV pointers. That is, for NV-to-NV pointers, we rename the `heap` field to `nextPtrObj`, and our implementation uses it to form a linked list of pointers. Within any pointer within a, the `nextPtrObj` field contains the offset of the next pointer within a. The `nextPtrObj` field of the last pointer in a is null. The offset of the first pointer within a is stored in a field within a's header. Our implementation is careful not to overwrite these `nextPtrObj` fields when overwriting an NV-to-NV pointer with another NV-to-NV pointer.

Because V-to-NV reference counts are stored in volatile memory, when an NVM heap is closed or when the application terminates, all that heap's allocations' V-to-NV reference counts are destroyed. In the case of closing the heap, their V-to-NV reference counts are first set to zero, and any required frees are performed. However, as Coburn et al. note [4], when an application terminates without closing an NVM heap, any of that heap's allocations whose V-to-NV reference counts are non-zero but whose NV-to-NV reference counts are zero are leaked. To address this problem, our implementation maintains an NVM-stored doubly linked list of such allocations so it can free them the next time the heap is opened. Our implementation adds an entry for an allocation to this list whenever the allocation's NV-to-NV reference count reaches zero while its V-to-NV reference count is non-zero. Moreover, in each NVM allocation's header, our implementation records a pointer to its entry in that list so our implementation can efficiently remove its entry from the list if its NV-to-NV reference count becomes non-zero again.

4.3 NVL Passes

In this section, we describe in more detail the NVL passes, which we described in general terms in §4.1.

4.3.1 NVLAddTxs

The `NVLAddTxs` pass instruments NVL LLVM IR to implement transactions that are not built into the NVL runtime. That is, for any store instruction that writes at least one pointer into NVM but that is not enclosed in a transaction, this pass encloses that store instruction in an implicit transaction. For any store instruction that writes anything into NVM, if that store instruction is contained either in an implicit transaction or in an explicit transaction whose clauses do not suppress backup at that store instruction, this pass inserts instructions to perform backup. At the start of each transaction, this pass inserts instructions to perform

aggregated backup according to backup clauses. At the end of each transaction, this pass inserts instructions to ensure NVM writes are durable and to commit the transaction.

As described in §3.9, the programmer specifies an explicit transaction by attaching an `nvl atomic` pragma to a block of C code. The compiler front end must somehow mark the set of LLVM IR instructions generated from each such C block in order for the `NVLAddTxs` pass to properly identify the start and end of the transaction, identify contained store instructions, and implement the pragma's clauses. Using LLVM IR metadata and intrinsics to associate a C block's LLVM IR instructions with an attached pragma and its clauses is the purpose of our *basic block set* implementation for LLVM, which we described previously for FITL (Fault-Injection Toolkit for LLVM) [6]. We reuse that implementation in our NVL-C compiler front end and `NVLAddTxs` pass.

4.3.2 NVLAddSafety

The `NVLAddSafety` pass instruments NVL LLVM IR with run-time safety checks. To any store instruction that writes a pointer into NVM, this pass adds the interheap NV-to-NV pointer check we described in §3.4. To any NVM pointer comparison or subtraction instruction, this pass adds a check that the targets of the two pointer operands are not different allocations because such instructions are usually a sign of erroneous pointer arithmetic. This entire pass can be disabled in order to avoid the overhead of these run-time safety checks. Other run-time safety checks are performed by the NVL runtime, and we have not provided any means to disable them because their overhead is insignificant in comparison to the other operations performed by the runtime functions in which they appear.

4.3.3 NVLAddRefCounting

The `NVLAddRefCounting` pass instruments NVL LLVM IR with automatic reference counting. To any store instruction that writes a pointer into volatile memory or NVM, this pass adds an increment of the V-to-NV or NV-to-NV reference count for the target allocation of the pointer being written, and it adds a decrement for the target allocation of the pointer being overwritten. For V-to-NV reference counts, it also adds an increment where a new V-to-NV pointer is created in an LLVM register, and it performs a liveness analysis to determine where to add the corresponding decrement. To `nvl_alloc_nv` calls, it adds initialization of the `nextPtrObj` fields we described in §4.2. Other parts of automatic reference counting, including data structure extensions, are implemented within the NVL runtime and can be disabled via preprocessor macros when compiling the NVL runtime.

4.3.4 NVLLowerPointers

While the NVL passes mentioned in the previous sections instrument NVL LLVM IR with additional functionality, it is the `NVLLowerPointers` pass that finally lowers NVL LLVM IR to standard LLVM IR. Thus, `NVLLowerPointers` must be run after other NVL passes and before any non-NVL LLVM passes. The name of this pass is based on the fact that its primary function is to lower NVM pointers from typed LLVM IR pointers of special address spaces to their struct representation used within the NVL runtime.

Symbol	Description
ExM	Use persistent storage as if extended DRAM
ND	Skip runtime operations for durability
B	Basic NVL-C version w/o Safety, RefCnt, and transaction (T0, T1, ...)
S	Automatic pointer-safety checking
R	Automatic reference counting
T0	BSR + Enforce only durability of each NVM write
T1	BSR + Enforce ACID properties of each transaction
T2	T1 + aggregation using `backup` clauses
T3	T2 + skipping unnecessary backup using `clobber` clauses
T4	T3 at the granularity of each loop
CLFlush	Flush cache line to memory
MSync	Synchronize memory map with persistent storage

Table 3: Symbols Used in the Result Figures

4.4 Bare NVM Pointers

As explained in §4.2, our NVL-C implementation encodes an NVM pointer with multiple fields, which are required to enforce NVL-C's run-time safety constraints and to support automatic reference counting. Before a load or store operation can be performed on an NVM pointer, this encoding must be converted into an address encoding that is understood by the target architecture's load and store instructions. We refer to the resulting address encoding as a *bare NVM pointer* because it strips away all NVL-C metadata and exposes the same address encoding that is used for a normal pointer in C.

In our current implementation, the procedure to convert to a bare NVM pointer is simple: the base virtual address of the NVM heap is retrieved, the offset of the target allocation is added, and the offset of the target object is added. However, that procedure is many times longer than a single load or store instruction and is partially encapsulated in a `libpmemobj` API function that entails further overhead. For an application that spends much of its time performing NVM loads or stores, conversions to bare NVM pointers can then have a severe impact on performance. As part of our ongoing work, we have already found that seemingly minor tuning of this conversion procedure can dramatically alter the running time of some applications.

In applications like our matrix multiply in Figure 4, NVM loads and stores appear in a loop such that each conversion to a bare NVM pointer is a loop-invariant computation that can be hoisted before the loop so it is performed only once. We refer to this optimization as *NVM pointer hoisting* because it eliminates normal NVM pointers from the bodies of loops. Extending our NVL-C compiler to perform this optimization automatically is part of our future work. For our evaluation, we implement this optimization manually per application to measure its performance impact.

5. EVALUATION

5.1 Methodology

Because we are targeting future byte-addressable NVM systems, we have developed a multitier strategy to development and evaluation of NVL-C. To evaluate the performance of the proposed NVL-C system, we ported six applications into NVL-C versions: four kernel benchmarks (STREAM [12], MATMUL, JACOBI, and HASHTABLE) and two Department of Energy (DOE) proxy applications (XSBENCH [17] and LULESH [8]). The ported NVL-C applications were

executed on a machine with two eight-core Intel Xeon E5-2643s, 32 GB of DRAM, and a Fusion-io 1.65 TB MLC ioScale2 SSD connected via PCIe bus, running Scientific Linux Version 6.5. As a target device, we used the SSD, which is block-addressable. Because the NVL-C runtime works with both block-addressable and byte-addressable devices, we can also measure the performance of the NVL-C applications on SSD as if it were byte-addressable (*Byte-addressable NVM* mode in result figures), which gives us a rough idea of the expected performance of the SSD if it were byte-addressable, while measurements in a block-addressable mode show the actual performance. For a comparison, the same NVL-C applications were also executed using a RAMDisk, which is byte-addressable but volatile.

As explained in §4.3, the modular design of the NVL-C system allowed us to measure the overhead of each major component (e.g., safety checking, automatic reference counting, transaction, etc.).We also measured the performance effects of various optimizations, such as NVM pointer hoisting (in §4.4), aggregation of transaction data (`backup` clauses in §3.9.2), skipping unnecessary backup (`clobber` clauses in §3.9.2), and increasing the granularity of a transaction region. As a reference, the original C versions of the tested applications were executed only on a DRAM, and all NVL-C performance was normalized against the original DRAM-only versions (100% indicates the same performance as the DRAM-only version.). Table 3 explains the symbols used in the figures.

To verify transaction correctness, we created a synthetic checkpointing-recovery benchmark using NVL-C transactions and performed a stress test by randomly killing the running benchmark with `SIGKILL`. The stress test didn't produce any any data corruption or deadlock, but merely killing the application may not cover all the possible transaction issues, such as problems caused by power failures.

5.2 Application Results

STREAM: STREAM [12] is a synthetic benchmark to measure sustainable memory bandwidth and corresponding computation rate. STREAM consists of memory-bound kernels testing the streamed accesses of array data from/to the target memory device, and thus is suitable for the basic performance study of the NVL-C system. Figure 5 shows the measured performance of its TRIAD kernel on two target devices (SSD and RAMDisk), normalized to the performance of its original C version on a DRAM. In the figure, *ExM* shows the case where the target NVM is used as a secondary memory partition (i.e., extended volatile memory) ignoring any persistence-related issues such as transactions and safety checking, where no NVM pointers are used, and NVL-C provides functions similar to what NVMalloc [3] does on a local NVM. The ExM results in Figure 5a show that the tested SSD achieves performance comparable to DRAM. Figure 5b shows the performance on RAMDisk; because RAMDisk is byte-addressable, *MSync* overhead is negligible, and thus performance in the block-addressable mode is similar to that in the byte-addressable mode. Figure 5 indicates that in all tested devices, 1) the relative overheads for safety checking (*S*) and automatic reference counting (*R*) are negligible, 2) *NVM pointer hoisting* optimization (*Hoisting*) is critical to reduce overhead, while 3) supporting transactions incurs a huge performance penalty, as expected. To mitigate the transaction overhead, we increased the transaction granularity from per element write (*per elm*) to per whole array (*per loop*), which benefits more from transaction aggregation, achieving half of the DRAM performance on SSD in the byte-addressable mode (Figure 5a).

MATMUL: MATMUL is a locally developed dense matrix multiplication kernel. Figure 6a shows the normalized execution times on SSD, broken down into each major component. *T0* refers to a NVL-C version where only durability of its NVM writes is enforced (see 3.9.1). To enforce the durability, the NVL-C runtime performs two types of flush operations: flushing cache lines into the memory (*CLFlush*) and synchronizing buffers in the memory with the mapped file in the persistent storage (*MSync*). If the target NVM is byte-addressable, *MSync* may be skipped depending on the underlying file system supporting the NVM. *T1* shows the case where NVL-C transactions with ACID properties are enforced. As mentioned in §3.9.1, the current NVL-C runtime does not support the *isolation* property yet, but all the tested NVL-C applications are sequentially executed, and thus isolation is implicitly guaranteed. The figure shows that *T1* incurs more *MSync* overhead than *T0*, since *T1* involves more data synchronizations to durably store backup data to enforce atomicity. *T2* and *T3* show that transaction aggregation using `backup` or `clobber` clauses is quite effective in reducing *MSync* overhead. Figure 6b shows the overall performance on SSD when the *NVM pointer hoisting* optimization (*Hoisting*) is applied. The figure implies that the transaction aggregation is so effective that *T2* and *T3* perform similarly in both block-addressable and byte-addressable modes.

JACOBI: JACOBI is another locally developed benchmark that performs a stencil computation solving partial differential equations. JACOBI is more memory-intensive than MATMUL, and thus Figure 6c and 6d show that JACOBI incurs much more *MSync* and *CLFlush* overheads, resulting in significant slowdown and noticeable performance difference between block-addressable and byte-addressable modes. Nonetheless, transaction aggregation and skipping unnecessary backup are very effective, resulting in reasonable performance in the optimized version (*T3*).

XSBENCH: XSBENCH [17] is a mini-app representing a key computational kernel of the Monte Carlo neutronics application OpenMC, one of key DOE applications; XSBENCH calculates macroscopic neutron cross sections, a kernel which accounts for around 85% of the total runtime of OpenMC. XSBENCH deals with neutrons across a wide energy spectrum and materials of many different types, and thus it requires a very large read-only data structure holding cross section points for many discrete energy levels, which are suitable to be put on NVM. Figure 6e and 6f show the performance on SSD; because the major data structures are read-only, transactions have minimal overhead, resulting in overall performance comparable to the DRAM-only version in both block-addressable and byte-addressable modes.

LULESH: LULESH (Livermore Unstructured Lagrangian Explicit Shock Hydrodynamics) [8] is one of five challenge problems in the DARPA UHPC program and widely studied as an important DOE proxy application. Even though LULESH is a quite complex proxy application, it is well organized in a way that it distinguishes temporary variables that are initialized before use within a single iteration of the main loop from the variables with loop-carried true data dependencies or read-only variables, the latter of which are

good targets to be put on NVM. Therefore, we could easily create its NVL-C version by changing the memory allocation codes for the persistent or read-only global variables and adding NVM qualifiers to their declarations. Figure 6g and 6h show the performance on SSD; while the base NVL-C transaction versions (*T1*) suffer from very large transaction overheads, transaction aggregation and NVM pointer hoisting optimizations work together to effectively reduce the overall overheads. In LULESH, the backup skipping optimization in *T3* is not applicable since all persistent data are read-first, while the backup skipping optimization is applicable only to either write-only or write-before-read data (see §3.9.2).

HASHTABLE: HASHTABLE is another locally developed benchmark to measure the performance of typical key-value mapping operations, which are common in database and other data analytics domains. The benchmark consists of four kernels performing key-value pair insertion, update, read, and delete 1000 times, respectively. Figure 7 shows the performance on SSD and RAMDisk. Because the benchmark accesses key-value pairs randomly, transaction aggregation is not applicable. Moreover, skipping backup data is not applicable either, to maintain the consistency of the mapped data structure, which is required for database applications. Therefore, the figure shows that the NVL-C version on SSD suffers from significant overheads, mainly from the durability overhead in transactions (*CLFlush* and *MSync*), while that on RAMDisk achieves reasonable performance. To reduce the durability overhead in the block-addressable devices, special hardware extension [5] or extended low-level Linux primitives [14] will be necessary.

6. RELATED WORK

In anticipation of emerging NVM trends, previous research has described new programming systems that utilize NVM as fast and safe persistent storage, as our prior comprehensive surveys illustrate [13, 18]. In this section, we highlight several projects that bear interesting similarities to NVL-C.

First, NVL-C builds on the abstractions of NV-heaps, so we have compared NVL-C to NV-heaps throughout this paper [4]. A key focus of NV-heaps that drove our work is that, because data corruption persists across application termination and power loss, data corruption is inherently more dangerous for persistent NVM storage than for volatile storage, so extra safeguards are needed to protect data from application and system failures. We were unable to obtain the NV-heaps implementation for direct evaluation or extension.

Next, Mnemosyne is a compiler-supported, transactional, NVM programming system that targets future NVM technologies [19]. Unlike NVL-C, Mnemosyne modifies the Linux kernel, but it requires no hardware modifications like NV-heaps. Mnemosyne supports a type qualifier that is semantically similar to NVL-C's type qualifiers but that is used solely for compile-time warnings about mismatched pointer types. That is, the compiler does not instrument associated store instructions to provide automatic reference counting, and it does not enforce NVL-C's safety constraints, such as preventing NV-to-V pointers. A unique feature of Mnemosyne is that, in addition to dynamic allocations, it supports global variable declarations that persist across application termination. However, Mnemosyne assumes that traditional files are used for interchanging data among differ-

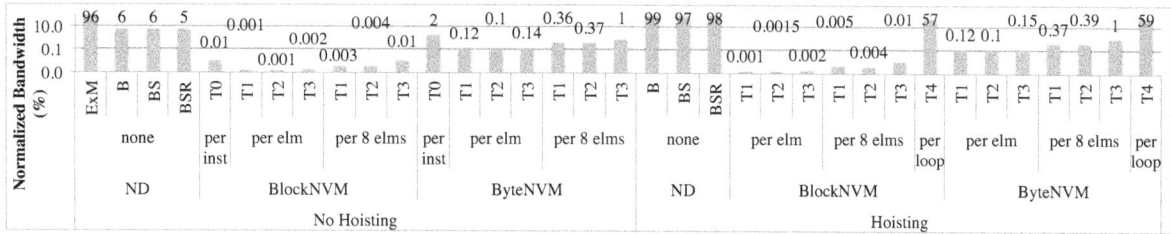

(a) SSD

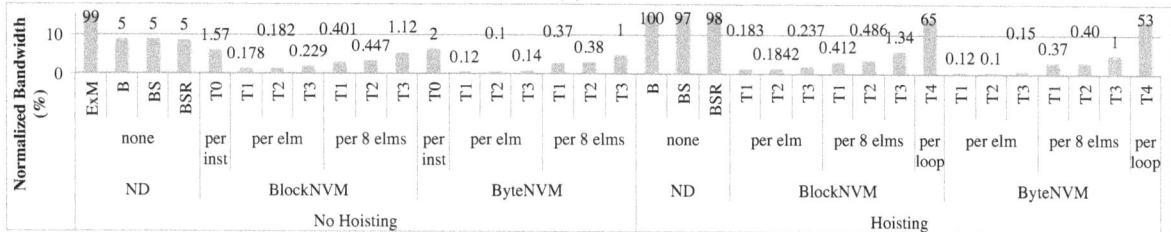

(b) RAMDisk

Figure 5: Bandwidth of STREAM TRIAD Normalized to DRAM-only Version

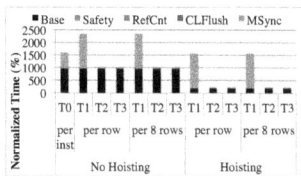

(a) MATMUL Decomposition

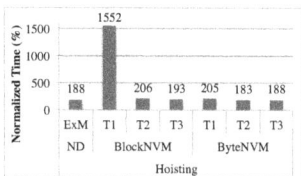

(b) MATMUL Performance

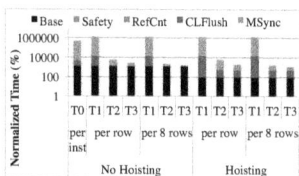

(c) JACOBI Decomposition

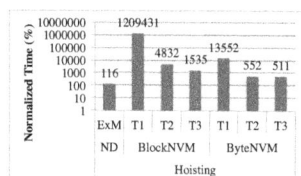

(d) JACOBI Performance

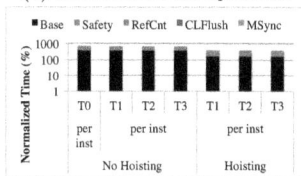

(e) XSBENCH Decomposition

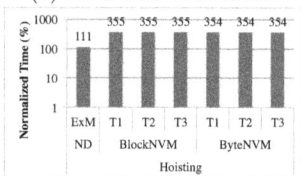

(f) XSBENCH Performance

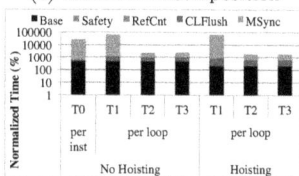

(g) LULESH Decomposition

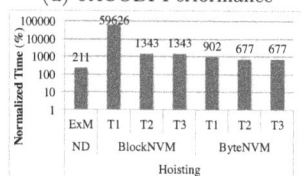

(h) LULESH Performance

Figure 6: NVL-C Benchmark Performance on SSD Normalized to DRAM-only Version

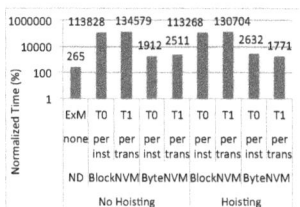

(a) Performance on SSD

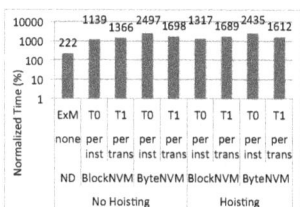

(b) Performance on RAMDisk

Figure 7: Normalized HASHTABLE Performance

ent applications, and it does not offer the file system interface that NVL-C offers for accessing arbitrary NVM heaps.

Another effort, NVMalloc, is a library that enables out-of-core computations to access aggregate NVM storage as a secondary memory partition [3]. Its focus is the distribution of SSD across compute nodes in extreme scale machines. Additionally, it exploits persistence for checkpointing both DRAM and NVM, but it does not offer transactions or NVL-C's other safeguards related to persistence.

Several systems propose low-level primitives on which NVL-C could be built instead of `libpmemobj` to guarantee atomicity and durability of updates to NVM data in the face of

application or system failures. BPFS is a file system that introduces a novel paging technique for targeting future NVM technologies, but it requires a set of theoretical hardware extensions, also assumed by NV-heaps [5, 4]. Park et al. extend low-level Linux primitives to create a simple interface for updates to `mmap`'ed files backed by any NVM device [14]. Specifically, they introduce a new `mmap` flag, `MAP_ATOMIC`, which specifies that writes to the `mmap`'ed file must not be durably stored to the underlying memory until an `msync` call completes successfully.

7. CONCLUSION

In this paper, we have presented NVL-C, a novel, transactional programming system that extends the familiar syntax of C to facilitate efficient and correct programming of emerging memory hierarchies including NVM. In comparison to existing NVM programming systems, NVL-C is more intuitive and flexible for the programmer, and it is more amenable to automated analysis, diagnostics, and optimizations because it is compiler-supported. The design is modular in order to maximize the ability to reuse implementation components among multiple compiler front ends, high-level languages, and runtimes in the future. The core of the compiler is an extension of LLVM, and we have currently built the runtime on Intel's `libpmemobj`. We have evaluated our prototype implementation by porting a number of kernel benchmarks and DOE proxy applications to NVL-C to make them recoverable across application or system failure. Our results demonstrate that performance is reasonable when two optimizations are employed: NVM pointer hoisting and aggregation of transaction data. Future work includes developing LLVM passes to automate such optimizations and extending transaction support.

8. ACKNOWLEDGMENTS

The authors thank Philip Roth (ORNL) for his help in administering the evaluation testbed, and FusionIO (now Western Digital/SanDisk) for providing our ioScale card.

This material is based upon work supported by the U.S. Department of Energy (DOE), Office of Science, Office of Advanced Scientific Computing Research. This manuscript has been authored by UT-Battelle, LLC under Contract No. DE-AC05-00OR22725 with the DOE. The United States Government (USG) retains and the publisher, by accepting the article for publication, acknowledges that the USG retains a non-exclusive, paid-up, irrevocable, worldwide license to publish or reproduce the published form of this manuscript, or allow others to do so, for USG purposes. The DOE will provide public access to these results of federally sponsored research in accordance with the DOE Public Access Plan (http://energy.gov/downloads/doe-public-access-plan).

9. REFERENCES

[1] NVM Library. [Online]. Available: http://pmem.io/nvml/. (Accessed January, 2016).

[2] A. Badam. How persistent memory will change software systems. *Computer*, 46(8):45–51, 2013.

[3] W. Chao, et al. NVMalloc: Exposing an aggregate SSD store as a memory partition in extreme-scale machines. In *Parallel & Distributed Processing Symposium (IPDPS), 2012 IEEE 26th International*, pages 957–968, 2012.

[4] J. Coburn, et al. NV-heaps: making persistent objects fast and safe with next-generation, non-volatile memories. In *Proc 16th Intl Conf Architectural support for programming languages and operating systems*, pages 105–118, Newport Beach, 2011. ACM.

[5] J. Condit, et al. Better I/O through byte-addressable, persistent memory. *Proc. ACM SIGOPS 22nd symposium on Operating systems principles*, pages 133–146, 2009.

[6] J. E. Denny, S. Lee, and J. S. Vetter. FITL: Extending LLVM for the Translation of Fault-injection Directives. In *Proceedings of the Second Workshop on the LLVM Compiler Infrastructure in HPC*, LLVM '15, pages 4:1–4:11, New York, NY, USA, 2015. ACM.

[7] T. Haerder and A. Reuter. Principles of transaction-oriented database recovery. *ACM Computing Surveys (CSUR)*, 15(4):287–317, 1983.

[8] I. Karlin, et al. LULESH programming model and performance ports overview. Technical Report LLNL-TR-608824, Lawrence Livermore National Laboratory (LLNL), Livermore, CA, 2012.

[9] B. Lee, et al. Phase-change technology and the future of main memory. *IEEE Micro*, 30(1):143, 2010.

[10] B. C. Lee, et al. Phase change memory architecture and the quest for scalability. *Communications of the ACM*, 53(7):99–106, 2010.

[11] S. Lee and J. Vetter. OpenARC: Open Accelerator Research Compiler for Directive-Based, Efficient Heterogeneous Computing. In *HPDC '14: Proceedings of the ACM Symposium on High-Performance Parallel and Distributed Computing, Short Paper*, june 2014.

[12] J. D. McCalpin. Memory bandwidth and machine balance in current high performance computers. *IEEE Computer Society Technical Committee on Computer Architecture (TCCA) Newsletter*, pages 19–25, Dec. 1995.

[13] S. Mittal and J. S. Vetter. A survey of software techniques for using non-volatile memories for storage and main memory systems. *Parallel and Distributed Systems, IEEE Transactions on*, PP(99):1–1, 2015.

[14] S. Park, T. Kelly, and K. Shen. Failure-atomic Msync(): A Simple and Efficient Mechanism for Preserving the Integrity of Durable Data. In *Proc 8th ACM European Conf Computer Systems*, EuroSys '13, pages 225–238, New York, NY, USA, 2013. ACM.

[15] S. Pelley, et al. Storage management in the NVRAM era. *Proc. VLDB Endow.*, 7(2):121–132, 2013.

[16] L. E. Ramos, E. Gorbatov, and R. Bianchini. Page placement in hybrid memory systems. *Proceedings of the international conference on Supercomputing - ICS '11*, pages 85–85, 2011.

[17] J. R. Tramm, et al. XSBench - The Development and Verification of a Performance Abstraction for Monte Carlo Reactor Analysis. In *PHYSOR 2014 - The Role of Reactor Physics toward a Sustainable Future*, Kyoto.

[18] J. S. Vetter and S. Mittal. Opportunities for nonvolatile memory systems in extreme-scale high performance computing. *Computing in Science and Engineering special issue*, 17(2):73–82, 2015.

[19] H. Volos, A. J. Tack, and M. M. Swift. Mnemosyne: Lightweight persistent memory. *ACM SIGPLAN Notices*, 46(3):91–104, 2011.

[20] H. Zhang, et al. In-memory big data management and processing: A survey. *IEEE Transactions on Knowledge and Data Engineering*, 27(7):1920–1948, 2015.

Automatic Hybridization of Runtime Systems

Kyle C. Hale   Conor J. Hetland   Peter A. Dinda
{kh,ch}@u.northwestern.edu, pdinda@northwestern.edu
Department of Electrical Engineering and Computer Science
Northwestern University

ABSTRACT

The hybrid runtime (HRT) model offers a plausible path towards high performance and efficiency. By integrating the OS kernel, parallel runtime, and application, an HRT allows the runtime developer to leverage the full privileged feature set of the hardware and specialize OS services to the runtime's needs. However, conforming to the HRT model currently requires a *complete* port of the runtime and application to the kernel level, for example to our Nautilus kernel framework, and this requires knowledge of kernel internals. In response, we developed Multiverse, a system that bridges the gap between a built-from-scratch HRT and a legacy runtime system. Multiverse allows existing, unmodified applications and runtimes to be brought into the HRT model without any porting effort whatsoever. Developers simply recompile their package with our compiler toolchain, and Multiverse automatically splits the execution of the application between the domains of a legacy OS and an HRT environment. To the user, the package appears to run as usual on Linux, but the bulk of it now runs as a kernel. The developer can then *incrementally* extend the runtime and application to take advantage of the HRT model. We describe the design and implementation of Multiverse, and illustrate its capabilities using the Racket runtime system.

1. INTRODUCTION

Runtime systems can gain significant benefits from executing in a tailored software environment. In previous work, we proposed one such specialized environment called the Hybrid Runtime (HRT) [10, 11]. In an HRT, a light-weight kernel

This project is made possible by support from the United States National Science Foundation through grant CCF-1533560 and from Sandia National Laboratories through the Hobbes Project, which is funded by the 2013 Exascale Operating and Runtime Systems Program under the Office of Advanced Scientific Computing Research in the United States Department of Energy's Office of Science.

framework (called an AeroKernel), a runtime, and an application coalesce into a single entity in which the runtime can enjoy full access to the underlying hardware, including features typically reserved for a privileged OS.

An AeroKernel can export functionality through a standard interface such as POSIX or through a custom interface. However, it exists solely for convenience, and the runtime may not even leverage the mechanisms it provides. Ultimately, the choices of proper execution model and abstractions to the hardware are left to the runtime. The runtime developers can build or choose the kernel abstractions they need. The motivation for an AeroKernel draws from the reliable performance of light-weight kernels [16, 15, 8], the philosophy regarding kernel abstractions of Exokernel [4], new techniques and ideas developed in multi-core OS research [17, 5], and the simplicity of other experimental OSes from previous decades [14, 18]. In this paper, we use our Nautilus AeroKernel, which we describe in more detail in Section 2.

Prior to the work and system we describe here, the implementation of an HRT consisted entirely of manual processes. HRT developers needed first to extend an AeroKernel framework such as Nautilus with the functionality the runtime needed. The HRT developers would then port the runtime to this AeroKernel manually. Readers interested in finer detail regarding this process can refer to our technical report [11]. While a manual port can produce the highest performance gains, it requires an intimate familiarity with the runtime system's functional requirements, which may not be obvious. These requirements must then be implemented in the AeroKernel layer and the AeroKernel and runtime must be combined. This requires a deep understanding of kernel development. This manual process is also iterative: the developer adds AeroKernel functionality until the runtime works correctly. The end result might be that the AeroKernel interfaces support a small subset of POSIX, or that the runtime developer replaces such functionality with custom interfaces.

While such a development model *is* tractable, and we have transformed three runtimes to HRTs using it, it represents a substantial barrier to entry to creating HRTs, which we seek here to lower. The manual porting method is *additive* in its nature. We must add functionality until we arrive at a working system. A more expedient method would allow us to *start* with a working HRT produced by an automatic process, and then incrementally extend it and specialize it to enhance its performance.

The Multiverse system we describe in this paper supports

just such a method using a technique called *automatic hybridization* to create a working HRT from an existing, unmodified runtime and application. With Multiverse, runtime developers can take an incremental path towards adapting their systems to run in the HRT model. From the user's perspective, a hybridized runtime and application behaves the same as the original. It can be run from a Linux command line and interact with the user just like any other executable. But internally, it executes in kernel mode as an HRT.

Multiverse bridges a specialized HRT with a legacy environment by borrowing functionality from a legacy OS, such as Linux. Functions not provided by the existing Aero-Kernel are forwarded to another core that is running the legacy OS, which handles them and returns their results. The runtime developer can then identify hot spots in the legacy interface and move their implementations (possibly even changing their interfaces) into the AeroKernel. The porting process with Multiverse is *subtractive* in that a developer iteratively removes dependencies on the legacy OS. At the same time, the developer can take advantage of the kernel-level environment of the HRT.

To demonstrate the capabilities of Multiverse, we automatically hybridize the Racket runtime system. Hybridized Racket executes in kernel mode as an HRT, and yet the user sees precisely the same interface (an interactive REPL environment, for example) as out-of-the-box Racket.

Our contributions in this paper are as follows:

- We introduce the concept of *automatic hybridization* for transforming runtime systems and their applications into HRTs, enabling them to run in kernel mode with full access to hardware features and the ability to adapt the kernel to their needs.
- We describe the design of Multiverse, an implementation of automatic hybridization that combines compile-time, link-time, run-time, and virtualization-based techniques.
- We demonstrate automatic hybridization with Multiverse by transforming the Racket runtime into an HRT.
- We evaluate the initial performance of Multiverse.

2. HRT AND HVM

Multiverse builds on our previously described work and systems [10, 11, 9] to define and support the hybrid runtime (HRT) model. We describe the key salient findings and components here.

The core premise of the HRT model is that by moving the parallel runtime (and its application) to the kernel level, we enable the runtime developer to leverage all hardware features (including privileged features), and to specialize kernel features specifically for the runtime's needs. These capabilities in turn allow for greater performance or efficiency than is possible at user-level. We developed a kernel framework, the Nautilus AeroKernel, to facilitate doing this. Nautilus runs on bare metal or under virtualization on x64 machines and the Intel Xeon Phi.

We have previously ported three runtimes to Nautilus, namely Legion [2], the NESL VCODE interpreter [3], and the runtime of a home-grown nested data parallel language. Using the HPCG (High Performance Conjugate Gradients) benchmark [13] developed by Sandia National Labs and ported to Legion by Los Alamos National Labs, we demonstrated speedups over Linux of up to 20% for the Intel Xeon Phi, and up to 40% for a 4-socket, 64-core x64 AMD Opteron 6272 machine.

Multiverse also builds on the Hybrid Virtual Machine (HVM), an extension to the open source (BSD) Palacios VMM [16]. HVM allows for the creation of a VM whose memory, cores, and interrupt logic are segregated so that one VM simultaneously runs two operating systems, the "Regular Operating System" (ROS) (e.g., Linux) and an HRT-based OS (e.g., Nautilus). The ROS runs on a partition of the cores and can see and touch only the ROS cores and the ROS subset of physical memory. In contrast, the HRT, while only allowed to run on its own distinct partition of the cores, has full access to all the memory, cores, and interrupt logic of the entire VM. The ROS and HRT can be booted and rebooted independently.

3. MULTIVERSE

The goal of Multiverse is to ease the path for developers of transforming a runtime into an HRT. We seek to make the system look like a compilation toolchain option from the developer's perspective. That is, to the greatest extent possible, the HRT is a compilation target. Compiling to an HRT results in an executable that is a "fat binary" containing additional code and data that enables kernel-mode execution in an environment that supports it. An HVM-enabled VM on Palacios is the first such environment. The developer can extend this incrementally—Multiverse facilitates a path for runtime and application developers to explore how to specialize their HRT to the full hardware feature set and the extensible kernel environment of the AeroKernel.

From the user's perspective, the executable behaves as if it were compiled for a standard user-level Linux environment. The user sees no difference between HRT execution and user-level execution.

3.1 Techniques

The Multiverse system relies on three key techniques: state split execution, event channels, and state superpositions. We now describe each of these.

Split execution. In Multiverse, a runtime and its application begin their execution in the ROS. Through a well-defined interface, the runtime on the ROS side can spawn an execution context in the HRT. At this point, Multiverse splits its execution into two components, each running in a different context; one executes in the ROS and the other in the HRT. The semantics of these execution contexts differ from traditional threads depending on their characteristics. In the current implementation, the context on the ROS side comprises a Linux thread, the context on the HRT side comprises an AeroKernel thread, and we refer to them collectively as an *execution group*. While execution groups in our current system consist of threads in different OSes, this need not be true in general. The context on the HRT side executes until it triggers a fault, a system call, or other event. The execution group then converges on this event, with each side participating in a protocol for requesting events and receiving results. This protocol exchange occurs in the context of HVM event channels, which we discuss below.

Figure 1 illustrates the split execution of Multiverse for a ROS/HRT execution group. At this point, the ROS has already made a request to create a new context in the HRT. When the HRT thread begins executing in the HRT side, exceptional events, such as page faults, system calls, and other exceptions vector to stub handlers in the AeroKernel

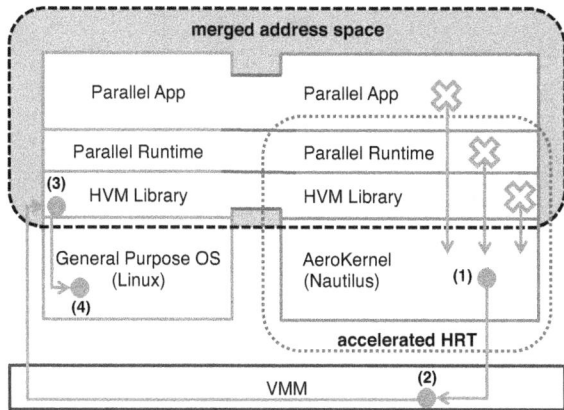

Figure 1: Split execution in Multiverse.

Item	Cycles	Time
Address Space Merger	~33 K	1.5 μs
Asynchronous Call	~25 K	1.1 μs
Synchronous Call (different socket)	~1060	48 ns
Synchronous Call (same socket)	~790	36 ns

Figure 2: Round-trip latencies of ROS↔HRT interactions.

(1). The AeroKernel then redirects these events through an event channel (2) to request handling in the ROS. The VMM then injects these into the originating ROS thread, which can take action on them directly (3). For example, in the case of a page fault that occurs in the ROS portion of the virtual address space, the HVM library simply replicates the access, which will cause the same exception to occur on the ROS core. The ROS will then handle it as it would normally. In the case of events that need direct handling by the ROS kernel, such as system calls, the HVM library can simply forward them (4).

Event channels. When the HRT needs functionality that the ROS implements, access to that functionality occurs over *event channels*, event-based, VMM-controlled communication channels between the two contexts. The VMM only expects that the execution group adheres to a strict protocol for event requests and completion.

Figure 2 shows the measured latency of event channels with the Nautilus AeroKernel performing the role of HRT. The first two calls are bounded from below by the latency of hypercalls to the VMM, while the remainder operate at memory synchronization speeds.

State superpositions. In order to forego the addition of burdensome complexity to the AeroKernel environment, it helps to leverage functions in the ROS other than those that lie at a system call boundary. This includes functionality implemented in libraries and more opaque functionality like optimized system calls in the vdso and the vsyscall page. In order to use this functionality, Multiverse can set up the HRT and ROS to share portions of their address space, in this case the user-space portion. Aside from the address space merger itself, Multiverse leverages other state superpositions to support a shared address space, including superpositions of the ROS GDT and thread-local storage state.

In principle, we could superimpose any piece of state visible to the VMM. The ROS or the runtime need not be aware of this state, but the state is nonetheless necessary for facilitating a simple and approachable usage model.

The superposition we leverage most in Multiverse is a merged address space between the ROS and the HRT. The merged address space allows execution in the HRT without a need for implementing ROS-compatible functionality. When a merged address space takes effect, the HRT can use the same user-mode virtual addresses present in the ROS. For example, the parallel runtime in the ROS might load files and construct a complex pointer-based data structure in memory. It can then invoke a function within its counterpart in the HRT to compute over that data.

4. EVALUATION

In this section we evaluate Multiverse using a hybridized Racket runtime system running a set of benchmarks from The Language Benchmark Game. We ran all experiments on a Dell PowerEdge 415 with 8GB of RAM and an 8 Core 64-bit x86_64 AMD Opteron 4122 clock clocked at 2.2GHz. Each CPU core has a single thread with four cores per socket. The host machine has stock Fedora Linux 2.6.38.6-26.rc1.fc15.x86_64 installed, and is configured for maximum performance in the BIOS. Benchmark results are reported as averages of 10 runs.

Experiments in a VM were run on a guest setup which consists of a simple BusyBox distribution running an unmodified Linux 2.6.38-rc5+ image with two cores (one core for the HVM and one core for the ROS) and 1 GB of RAM.

Racket

Racket [7, 6] is the most widely used Scheme implementation and has been under continuous development for over 20 years. It is an open source codebase that is downloaded over 300 times per day. Recently, support has been added to Racket for parallelism via futures [19] and places [20].

The Racket runtime is a good candidate to test Multiverse, particularly its most complex usage model, the incremental model, because Racket includes many of the challenging features emblematic of modern dynamic programming languages that make extensive use of the Linux ABI, including system calls, memory mapping, processes, threads, and signals. Readers can find more details on the various usage models of Multiverse in our technical report [12].

To evaluate the correctness and performance of our port, we tested it on a series of benchmarks submitted to The Computer Language Benchmarks Game [1]. We tested on seven different benchmarks: a garbage collection benchmark (binary-tree-2), a permutation benchmark (fannkuch), two implementations of a random DNA sequence generator (fasta and fasta-3), a generation of the mandelbrot set (mandelbrot-2), an n-body simulation (n-body), and a spectral norm algorithm.

Note that while this is an implementation of a high-level language, the actual execution of Racket programs involves many interactions with the operating system. These exercise Multiverse's system call and fault forwarding mechanisms.

Figure 3 compares the performance of the Racket benchmarks run natively on our hardware, under virtualization, and as an HRT that was created with the initial implementation of Multiverse. The overhead of the Multiverse case compared to the virtualized and native cases is due to the frequent interactions with the Linux ABI. Most of these in-

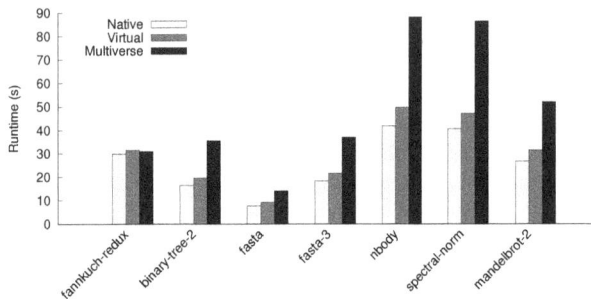

Figure 3: Performance of Racket benchmarks running Native, Virtual, and in Multiverse. Note that the Multiverse result is the result of Multiverse's automatic hybridization of Racket—it is the *starting point* for incremental enhancement within the HRT model.

teractions arise from page faults rather than system calls. In the Multiverse case, these are forwarded from the HRT to the ROS to be handled.

> It is worth reflecting on what exactly has happened here: we have taken a complex runtime system off-the-shelf, run it through Multiverse without changes, and as a result have a version of the runtime system that correctly runs in kernel mode as an HRT and behaves identically with virtually identical performance. To be clear, **all of the Racket runtime except Linux kernel ABI interactions is seamlessly running as a kernel.** While this codebase is the endpoint for user-level development, it represents a *starting point* for HRT development in the incremental model.

5. CONCLUSIONS AND FUTURE WORK

We introduced Multiverse, a system that implements *automatic hybridization* of runtime systems in order to transform them into hybrid runtimes (HRTs). We illustrated the design and implementation of Multiverse and described how runtime developers can use it as a tool for incremental porting of runtimes and applications from a legacy OS to a specialized AeroKernel.

To demonstrate its power, we used Multiverse to automatically hybridize the Racket runtime system, a complex, widely-used, JIT-based runtime. With automatic hybridization, we can take an existing Linux version of a runtime or application and automatically transform it into a package that looks to the user as if it runs like any other program, but actually executes on a remote core in kernel-mode, in the context of an HRT, and with full access to the underlying hardware. We evaluated the performance overheads of an unoptimized Multiverse hybridization of Racket and showed that performance varies with the usage of legacy functionality. Runtime developers can leverage Multiverse to start with a working system and incrementally transition heavily utilized legacy functions to custom components within an AeroKernel.

6. REFERENCES

[1] The computer language benchmarks game. http://benchmarksgame.alioth.debian.org/.

[2] M. Bauer, S. Treichler, E. Slaughter, and A. Aiken. Legion: Expressing locality and independence with logical regions. In *Proceedings of Supercomputing (SC 2012)*, Nov. 2012.

[3] G. E. Blelloch, S. Chatterjee, J. Hardwick, J. Sipelstein, and M. Zagha. Implementation of a portable nested data-parallel language. *Journal of Parallel and Distributed Computing*, 21(1):4–14, Apr. 1994.

[4] D. R. Engler, M. F. Kaashoek, and J. O'Toole, Jr. Exokernel: An operating system architecture for application-level resource management. In *Proceedings of the 15th ACM Symposium on Operating Systems Principles (SOSP 1995)*, pages 251–266, Dec. 1995.

[5] D. G. Feitelson and L. Rudolph. Gang scheduling performance benefits for fine-grain synchronization. *Journal of Parallel and Distributed Computing*, 16(4):306–318, Dec. 1992.

[6] M. Felleisen, R. B. Findler, M. Flatt, S. Krishnamurthi, E. Barzilay, J. McCarthy, and S. Tobin-Hochstadt. The Racket Manifesto. In T. Ball, R. Bodik, S. Krishnamurthi, B. S. Lerner, and G. Morrisett, editors, *1st Summit on Advances in Programming Languages (SNAPL 2015)*, volume 32 of *Leibniz International Proceedings in Informatics (LIPIcs)*, pages 113–128, Dagstuhl, Germany, 2015. Schloss Dagstuhl–Leibniz-Zentrum fuer Informatik.

[7] M. Flatt and PLT. Reference: Racket. Technical Report PLT-TR-2010-1, PLT Design Inc., 2010. https://racket-lang.org/tr1/.

[8] M. Giampapa, T. Gooding, T. Inglett, and R. W. Wisniewski. Experiences with a lightweight supercomputer kernel: Lessons learned from Blue Gene's CNK. In *Proceedings of Supercomputing (SC 2010)*, Nov. 2010.

[9] K. Hale and P. Dinda. Enabling hybrid parallel runtimes through kernel and virtualization support. In *Proceedings of the 12th ACM SIGPLAN/SIGOPS International Conference on Virtual Execution Environments (VEE 2016)*, April 2016.

[10] K. C. Hale and P. A. Dinda. A case for transforming parallel runtimes into operating system kernels. In *Proceedings of the 24th ACM Symposium on High-performance Parallel and Distributed Computing (HPDC 2015)*, pages 27–32, June 2015.

[11] K. C. Hale and P. A. Dinda. Details of the case for transforming parallel runtimes into operating system kernels. Technical Report NWU-EECS-15-01, Department of Computer Science, Northwestern University, Apr. 2015.

[12] K. C. Hale, C. Hetland, and P. A. Dinda. Automatic hybridization of runtime systems. Technical Report NWU-EECS-16-03, Department of Computer Science, Northwestern University, Mar. 2016.

[13] M. A. Heroux, J. Dongarra, and P. Luszczek. HPCG technical specification. Technical Report SAND2013-8752, Sandia National Laboratories, October 2013.

[14] G. C. Hunt and J. R. Larus. Singularity: Rethinking the software stack. *SIGOPS Operating Systems Review*, 41(2):37–49, Apr. 2007.

[15] S. M. Kelly and R. Brightwell. Software architecture of the light weight kernel, Catamount. In *Proceedings of the 2005 Cray User Group Meeting (CUG 2005)*, May 2005.

[16] J. Lange, K. Pedretti, T. Hudson, P. Dinda, Z. Cui, L. Xia, P. Bridges, A. Gocke, S. Jaconette, M. Levenhagen, and R. Brightwell. Palacios and kitten: New high performance operating systems for scalable virtualized and native supercomputing. In *Proceedings of the 24th IEEE International Parallel and Distributed Processing Symposium (IPDPS 2010)*, Apr. 2010.

[17] R. Liu, K. Klues, S. Bird, S. Hofmeyr, K. Asanović, and J. Kubiatowicz. Tessellation: Space-time partitioning in a manycore client OS. In *Proceedings of the 1st USENIX Conference on Hot Topics in Parallelism (HotPar 2009)*, pages 10:1–10:6, Mar. 2009.

[18] T. Roscoe. Linkage in the Nemesis single address space operating system. *ACM SIGOPS Operating Systems Review*, 28(4):48–55, Oct. 1994.

[19] J. Swaine, K. Tew, P. Dinda, R. Findler, and M. Flatt. Back to the futures: Incremental parallelization of existing sequential runtime systems. In *Proceedings of the ACM SIGPLAN International Conference on Object-Oriented Programming, Systems, Languages, and Applications (OOPSLA 2010)*, October 2010.

[20] K. Tew, J. Swaine, M. Flatt, R. Findler, and P. Dinda. Places: Adding message passing parallelism to racket. In *Proceedings of the 2011 Dynamic Languages Symposium (DLS 2011)*, October 2011.

Algorithm-Directed Data Placement in Explicitly Managed Non-Volatile Memory

Panruo Wu
U. of California, Riverside
pwu011@ucr.edu

Dong Li
U. of California, Merced
dli35@ucmerced.edu

Zizhong Chen
U. of California, Riverside
chen@cs.ucr.edu

Jeffrey S. Vetter
Oak Ridge National Lab
vetter@computer.org

Sparsh Mittal
Oak Ridge National Lab
mittals@ornl.gov

ABSTRACT

The emergence of many non-volatile memory (NVM) techniques is poised to revolutionize main memory systems because of the relatively high capacity and low lifetime power consumption of NVM. However, to avoid the typical limitation of NVM as the main memory, NVM is usually combined with DRAM to form a hybrid NVM/DRAM system to gain the benefits of each. However, this integrated memory system raises a question on how to manage data placement and movement across NVM and DRAM, which is critical for maximizing the benefits of this integration. The existing solutions have several limitations, which obstruct adoption of these solutions in the high performance computing (HPC) domain. In particular, they cannot take advantage of application semantics, thus losing critical optimization opportunities and demanding extensive hardware extensions; they implement persistent semantics for resilience purpose while suffering large performance and energy overhead. In this paper, we re-examine the current hybrid memory designs from the HPC perspective, and aim to leverage the knowledge of numerical algorithms to direct data placement. With explicit algorithm management and limited hardware support, we optimize data movement between NVM and DRAM, improve data locality, and implement a relaxed memory persistency scheme in NVM. Our work demonstrates significant benefits of integrating algorithm knowledge into the hybrid memory design to achieve multi-dimensional optimization (performance, energy, and resilience) in HPC.

1. INTRODUCTION

Extreme scale HPC systems are characterized by power constraints, massive parallelism, and large working set size. As a result, the DRAM-based main memory has remained a crucial bottleneck because of its relatively low capacity and large power consumption. Non-volatile memories (NVM), such as resistive RAM (ReRAM), spin-transfer torque RAM

(STT-RAM), and phase change memory (PCM), is expected to be able to revolutionize memory systems. They can have either better density (i.e., larger capacity per unit area) or lower stand-by power than DRAM, while being much faster than the traditional back-end storage. NVMs, however, have their own limitations: their write energy and access latency are typically larger than those of DRAM. Hence, NVM is usually combined with DRAM, forming a hybrid NVM/DRAM system to leverage the best characteristics of the two types of memories [15, 29, 32, 33, 34, 40, 37].

The hybrid main memory system, however, presents a challenge of effective data placement and movement across NVM and DRAM. Addressing this challenge is critical to optimize performance and energy efficiency of NVM. To exploit the persistence of NVM for resilience purpose, it is also desirable to manage data in NVM to support crash consistency, such that the application is resumable and re-computation is minimized after a system failure and reboot.

Most existing methods introduce hardware and software extensions to manage data placement in the hybrid main memory system. The hardware-based extensions treat DRAM as a transparent cache with customized caching policies to copy and migrate data [33, 32], or place DRAM and NVM side-by-side with the hardware-based monitoring mechanisms to capture memory access patterns and trigger data migration [40, 37, 34, 29, 15]. These hardware-based solutions, however, completely ignore application semantics. Due to the heuristic-based and reactive nature of their data movement algorithms, data migration in these works may trigger inefficient data movement with poor performance and low energy efficiency, and result in local optimum trap in adaptation.

On the other hand, the software-based extensions focus on implementing persistent semantics [30] for specific application domains, such as file systems [12], database [36], and key-value stores [11]. These designs, however, incur significant performance cost (120% increase in memory traffic and only 53% of the throughout of the pure DRAM-based system [41]) due to expensive logging [11, 36] or copy-on-write (COW) mechanisms [12, 35]. Although a recent work improves the performance [41], it cannot accommodate large-granularity persistent updates which are common in the HPC field. In general, most existing methods cannot work well for the HPC domain, because of the high-performance demands imposed in this domain.

In this paper, we re-examine the current hybrid memory designs from the HPC perspective, and aim to lever-

HPDC'16, May 31-June 04, 2016, Kyoto, Japan

© 2016 ACM. ISBN 978-1-4503-4314-5/16/05. . . $15.00

DOI: http://dx.doi.org/10.1145/2907294.2907321

age the knowledge of numerical algorithms to direct data placement. Compared to other domains, the numerical algorithms in HPC are highly structured and formalizable. Hence, many research efforts have focused on using numerical algorithm knowledge to address the problems of fault tolerance [14, 18, 9], performance optimization [23, 38], and energy efficiency [20, 17]. In this paper, we extend the usage of numerical algorithm knowledge into a new territory: by introducing algorithm semantics into data management, we identify three opportunities to improve performance, energy, and resilience (PER) of the hybrid memory.

First, algorithm-directed data placement (ADDP) enables optimization for specific numerical operations, commonly found in computational kernels of HPC applications. These operations include matrix transpose, regular scatter/gather using an indirection vector, and strided memory accesses. The current common practice to implement these operations can cause expensive data copy or low cache utilization because of data over-fetching for sparse data items. ADDP avoids those problems by explicitly controlling how data are accessed and cached in hybrid memory systems. This data control happens as a *side effect* of data movement in the hybrid memory system which avoids the data copy overhead.

Second, ADDP results in more aggressive data management than the existing solutions. Guided by the algorithm structure and bounded algorithm performance, ADDP is able to prefetch data from NVM to DRAM. Coupled with a direct memory access (DMA) mechanism for bulk data copy, data prefetching can be overlapped with computation, minimizing the negative impact of data management on performance. Furthermore, ADDP can trigger data migration from DRAM to NVM proactively to save limited DRAM space and save DRAM static energy.

Third, ADDP enables a relaxed memory persistency scheme to implement system resilience on NVM. The strict persistency approach, implemented by recent works [26, 30], maintains the program order of every write request. This, however, is also one of the fundamental reasons for its poor performance. By leveraging the algorithm knowledge, we demonstrate that the data persistency on NVM is only needed to be guaranteed at certain algorithm phases with the quantifiable cost of recomputation at system crashes. Hence, the relaxed persistency approach brings performance benefits manifested by high instruction execution performance and memory level parallelism. Also, the recomputation cost of ADDP is much smaller than that of a common HPC resilience technique (i.e., the checkpoint/restart).

We demonstrate the effectiveness of ADDP using three representative computational algorithms (conjugate gradient, fast Fourier transform, and LU decomposition). In this paper, we use PCM as an example of NVM, although our methodology is applicable to other hybrid NVM/DRAM systems also. In summary, this work makes the following contributions.

- We provide an *algorithm-managed* hybrid NVM/DRAM system to optimize across multiple dimensions (performance, energy, and resilience). We show that algorithm features, common numerical operations, and algorithm structures can be leveraged to direct data placement without extensive hardware changes. This result is important for building next-generation extreme-scale HPC systems where one often needs to strike

a balance between performance target and ownership cost.

- We propose a new relaxed memory persistence execution scheme on NVM. We reveal the correlation between data persistency and recomputation, and provide a new angle to examine the emerging memory persistency model [30] for NVM.

- We identify the necessary hardware support to implement ADDP. This hardware support includes a customized DMA mechanism for bulk data movement. In combination with the aggressive data management at the software level, the hardware support enables flexible algorithm control and productive programming experience.

- Our detailed evaluations show that ADDP provides higher performance (up to 49%) and energy efficiency of main memory (up to 25%), compared to a common data placement scheme without algorithm semantics. Further, write operations to PCM are significantly reduced (by up to 13x). Our approach incurs less than 2% performance overhead while achieving the same resilience as the checkpoint technique.

2. SYSTEM DESIGN

To enable algorithm-directed data placement, hardware and software must work in concert to support algorithm-specific optimizations. To avoid performance loss while improving energy efficiency, we must place write-intensive, frequently accessed data in the volatile memory (DRAM). Further, given the limited capacity of the volatile memory and large working set size of HPC applications, data in the volatile memory should be properly managed and timely migrated to the persistent memory (NVM) to save space and maximize the benefits of the volatile memory.

2.1 Hardware Design

The hardware design must accommodate three requirements to facilitate algorithm-directed data placement. *First*, the hardware design must support efficient, massive data movement. The massive data sets represented as data structures in a numerical algorithm often display uniform access pattern. For example, in the LU factorization algorithm, as the input matrix is iteratively decomposed, specific rows and columns of the input matrix can experience the same intensive update operations. These rows and columns can take 20% memory footprint of the algorithm. If they are identified as the candidates to migrate, massive data movement can occur. Similar examples can also be found in a large range of algorithm implementations based on well-structured stencils. *Second*, while the algorithm can direct critical data placement at the application level, we must relieve programmer from the burden of handling all data placement. Hardware is a solution to automatically direct data that cannot be guided by the algorithm. *Third*, to enable algorithm-directed data placement, hardware working with software must provide easy and direct access to the volatile memory and persistent memory. We organize DRAM and PCM to meet the second and third requirements, and introduce a DMA mechanism to meet the first requirement.

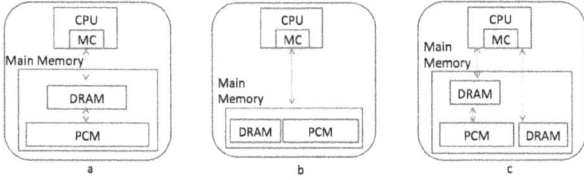

Figure 1: A logical view of main memory organizations

2.1.1 Main Memory Organization

Figure 1.c logically shows the memory organization in our hybrid memory system. This is in contrast to the convention memory organizations shown in Figure 1.a [33, 32] and Figure 1.b [40, 37, 34, 29, 15]. In Figure 1.a, DRAM is organized similar to an inclusive hardware cache invisible to the OS. The limitation of this approach is that DRAM space does not add to the overall memory capacity. Also, the hardware-managed DRAM cache is generally applied to all workloads, even those with poor locality (e.g., the sparse matrix vector multiplication), potentially losing performance and energy efficiency. In Figure 1.b, DRAM and PCM are combined into a large flat memory. To optimize performance and energy efficiency, the data placement in DRAM and PCM is determined by hardware or OS. Hardware or OS continuously monitors temporal memory access patterns to direct data placement. Notice that the architecture shown in Figure 1.a loses application semantics, and does not meet the third requirement to facilitate algorithm-directed data placement. Also, the architecture shown in Figure 1.b imposes significant burden of data management at the software side, and does not meet the second requirement.

Figure 1.c logically displays our design. With this design, DRAM is divided into two parts separately managed by software and hardware. In particular, one part of DRAM is used as an exclusive software-managed memory (SMM), and shares the same physical address space as PCM (but with different addresses). With the support of system software (Section 2.2), the application can explicitly direct which data blocks should be copied from PCM to SMM where the PCM-unfriendly computation will occur, or which data blocks should be migrated from SMM to PCM when the computation finishes or the SMM runs out of space. The other part of DRAM is used as an inclusive hardware LRU cache for PCM, similar to Figure 1.a. This hardware-managed DRAM cache is inevitable, because some data cannot be controlled by the application or is difficult to control by the application (e.g., stack frames and a third party library). The placement of these data must rely on conventional hardware based solutions without the need of application intervention.

To implement the hardware-managed DRAM cache in the above memory organization, we use a hardware design similar to [29, 33, 32]. In particular, the hardware-managed DRAM cache is organized similar to a traditional hardware cache. The hardware-managed DRAM cache is managed by an on-chip memory controller (MC) [29]. MC tracks whether data are located in the hardware-managed DRAM cache based on metadata (including tag, LRU, valid, and dirty bits). Each hardware-managed DRAM cache block has metadata. All metadata are stored in DRAM alongside data, but cached in MC to minimize metadata lookup latency [29]. Based on the retrieved metadata, a memory request is placed in either a DRAM scheduler or a PCM

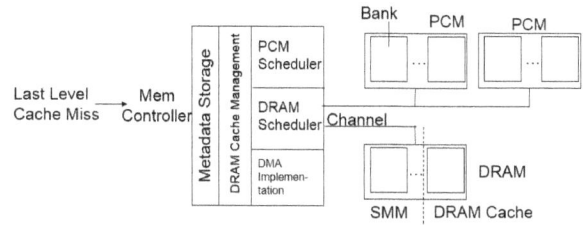

Figure 2: Our hybrid memory organization

scheduler in MC. After data arrive at MC, if they should be cached into (or evicted from) the hardware-managed DRAM cache, a migration request is inserted into the destination scheduler (either the DRAM scheduler or the PCM scheduler). The scheduler then writes data into the destination device.

Different from the existing hardware-based work, we treat SMM and PCM equally as the regular main memory. We use separate memory schedulers (one for PCM and the other for SMM and hardware-managed DRAM cache), because of the difference of memory timing constraints in DRAM and PCM. The hardware-managed DRAM cache and SMM are still composed of multiple banks organized as rows and columns of memory cells in the traditional manner, but they are separated at the granularity of memory bank. Figure 2 depicts important implementation details.

2.1.2 Massive Data Copy and Migration

To support algorithm-directed data placement and meet the first requirement, we introduce a DMA mechanism into MC to facilitate massive data copy and migration while minimizing data management overhead. We call data copy and migration collectively as *data management* in the later discussion.

DMA has been traditionally used to transfer data directly from the host memory to any input/output device without the host CPU intervention. We introduce DMA here to enable asynchronous data management between PCM and SMM. Asynchronous data management is a crucial performance optimization, especially when massive and frequent data management is desired in hybrid memory systems. In combination with algorithm direction at the user level, data management can overlap with computation, removing the data management overhead from the critical path.

An alternative for asynchronous data movement between memory devices without a dedicated DMA mechanism is to use helper threads. Although using helper threads for data movement is more flexible, we prefer the in-memory DMA for the following reasons. First, DMA frees CPU cores from moving the data by loading and storing, thereby increasing the system concurrency and possibly the performance. To use the DMA to move and transform data, CPU first initiates operations (in table 1) in the DMA and later checks the status of the operations. The DMA subsequently fulfills the data movements by scheduling memory access requests to MC. In contrast, the helper thread moves data by a series of load and store instructions executed by a CPU core. Those loads and stores go through the cache hierarchy, and the cache misses would result in memory access requests to MC. With bulk, non-sequential data movement, a high cache miss rate is expected. Whether DMA or a helper thread will perform better depends on the performance bottleneck of the application. For computation-intensive applications such as dense matrix operations and FFT where the computations are likely to be the performance bottleneck, offloading data movements to DMA would minimize the negative performance impact of using the helper thread. For other less computation-intensive applications where the bottleneck would likely be memory latency or bandwidth, the available cores may not be fully utilized, and the performance between DMA and the helper thread may not be significantly different. Second, using the helper thread, there are some negative side effects of moving data by loading into the processor and then storing into the memory. Both loads and stores may pollute the caches, and the stores may incur unnecessary fetches of cache lines from the memory. Non-temporal store with write-combining and non-temporal load with load buffer mitigates the problem, but can only work effectively when reads and writes are sequential. For non-sequential memory accesses, the useless bytes in a cache line would have negative performance and energy impacts. Third, the DMA within MC can be specialized to schedule memory accesses better using dynamic request information. For example, a larger internal buffer can be employed to support data transformations in the memory. In [7], the memory copy by DMA is demonstrated to be 20% faster than the best copy algorithm using CPU cores. In summary, we use in-memory data movement based on DMA rather than the helper thread for performance and energy optimization.

To implement the DMA operations, a set of registers are introduced into MC, similar to existing designs [21, 7]. In particular, we add a set of DMA control registers to record memory address, byte count, operation type (e.g., scatter and gather), and operation specific parameters (e.g., data distribution for scatter and gather) for data management. We also introduce status registers to track data management status for the DMA controller. The DMA controller performs data management. After being configured with the control registers, the DMA controller fetches a block of data from the source device to a copy/migration buffer, and then inserts a copy request into the destination scheduler which writes data from the copy/migration buffer into the destination device. The above process is repeated until the entire transfer is completed. Afterwards, the scheduler notifies the DMA controller of the completion of data management. The DMA controller then updates the control registers to indicate the DMA completion.

Different from the existing designs [21, 7], all DMA related registers are mapped into memory address space to fully enable DMA programmability at the application level (with the assistance of OS for virtual memory management). In particular, before triggering data management with DMA, the application initializes the control registers and launches DMA operations. The data involved in the DMA transfer is not available to use until the DMA completion notification is provided by the status register and read by the application. This application-managed DMA mechanism is critical for algorithm-directed data placement. Different from prior hardware-based data management in conventional hybrid memory systems, the statuses of massive data management (e.g., start and completion) are exposed, opening new opportunities for performance optimization at the application level. These opportunities include prefetching (from PCM to SMM) and proactive eviction (from SMM to PCM) to overlap data movement and computation. To implement

these two optimizations without DMA, one has to introduce thread-level parallelism (e.g., using a helper thread to manage data) and maintain thread synchronization.

Furthermore, motivated by vectored I/O DMA in networks, we introduce specific operations in DMA, including matrix transpose, strided memory accesses, and scatter/gather. These numerical operations are extremely common in HPC applications. For matrix transpose, the transpose happens as data are copied/migrated to the destination device, hence the transpose is treated as a *side effect* of data management, avoiding memory copy overhead in the traditional transpose implementation. For strided memory accesses, when sparse data items in PCM are copied from PCM to SMM, they can be collectively copied and packed in SMM. This improves on-chip cache utilization and improves performance. For scatter/gather operations, data copy from multiple memory areas can occur in a single DMA transaction, improving performance of data copy by leveraging memory level parallelism. These operations are initiated by specifying operation type in the DMA control registers.

Hardware Cost. The primary hardware cost includes the metadata storage for the implementation of the hardware-managed DRAM cache, and the DMA implementation (e.g., the DMA controller and registers). The metadata storage cost is the same as that in the existing hardware-based approach [29] (e.g., 8KB SRAM in MC), which is acceptable. For the DMA implementation, many previous works have proposed DMA with similar levels of complexity and sophistication [22, 3, 21, 7] with manageable area size. Our hardware cost is comparable to them.

2.2 Software Design

At the system software level, the DRAM cache is invisible and does not need any software support. PCM is treated as the main memory and managed by the traditional virtual memory management (VMM) in OS. SMM shares the same physical memory space with PCM, and is managed by VMM without paging. Paging is not supported by SMM, because the capacity-limited SMM tends to hold performance critical data and paging could significantly impact performance. From the programmer's view, SMM is just a pre-allocated memory space. The virtual address of the SMM space is mapped to the physical address of SMM by OS. In common programming practices, a global pointer can be employed to track the boundary of free SMM memory.

We also introduce a set of nonblocking memory operation APIs to enable algorithm direction and leverage DMA. These APIs are shown in Table 1. Here, *dma_memcpy* launches regular memory copy operations with DMA; *dma_stride*, *dma_gather*, *dma_scatter*, *dma_transpose*, and *dma_lacpy* perform optimized DMA operations as discussed in Section 2.1. Each of these DMA operations returns an ID. The request ID is used later to query the status of DMA or wait for its completion with *dma_wait* or *dma_test*. In addition, these DMA operations allow the programmer to customize data type with *dma_datatype*, especially for non-contiguous data in memory. The DMA primitives can be implemented in an operating system as system calls to read/write DMA registers. In general, we introduce limited extensions to the system software while introducing rich DMA semantics to enable algorithm directed data placement.

Table 1: APIs for managing and operating on SMM

API	Description
int **dma_memcpy**(void *src, void *dest, int count, DMA_Datatype datatype)	dest[i]=src[i] (i=0:count-1)
int **dma_stride**(void *src, void *dest, int count, int stride, DMA_Datatype datatype)	dest[i]=src[stride*i] (i=0:count-1)
int **dma_gather**(void *src, void *dest, int count, int *idx, DMA_Datatype datatype	dest[i]=src[idx[i]] (i=0:count-1)
int **dma_scatter**(void *src, void *dest, int count, int *idx, DMA_Datatype datatype)	dest[idx[i]]=src[i] (i=0:count-1)
int **dma_transpose**(void *src, void *dest, int dim1, int dim2, int m, int n, DMA_Datatype datatype)	dest[j+dim1*i]=src[i+dim2*j] (i=0:m-1,j=0:n-1)
int **dma_lacpy**(void *src, void *dest, int dim1, int dim2, int m, int n, DMA_Datatype datatype)	dest[i+dim1*j]=src[i+dim2*j] (i=0:m-1,j=0: n-1)
int **dma_wait**(int request, DMA_Status *status)	Wait for a DMA request to complete
int **dma_test**(int request, DMA_Status *status)	Test if a DMA request is completed

3. ALGORITHM-DIRECTED DATA PLACEMENT

In this section, we discuss details of the algorithms. While the algorithm details can vary from one algorithm to another, there are several common approaches for using algorithm knowledge to direct data placement. In this section, we first provide a general description of these approaches, and then show three case studies to explain how these approaches can be utilized in specific algorithms.

3.1 General Description

To improve performance and energy efficiency of the hybrid memory system, we rely on effective use of three techniques: (1) strategically placing data structures in SMM and PCM to avoid unnecessary thrashing in hardware-managed DRAM cache and expensive write in PCM; (2) using the asynchronous data movement primitives between SMM and PCM to overlap data movement and computation; (3) using hardware supported special data movement primitives (transpose, gather and scatter, etc) to efficiently move and transform data.

To implement (1), we leverage algorithm knowledge to determine the dynamic behavior of program based on the analysis of algorithm complexity and data criticality. Using algorithm knowledge, we always place performance- and algorithm-critical data into SMM. This is different from the existing approaches that direct data placement largely based on temporal access patterns. The direction of data placement based on the temporal access pattern can result in hardware-managed DRAM cache thrashing when the data access pattern changes across the execution of algorithm. Although the compiler-based data flow analysis and liveness analysis can also provide hints to implement (1), the complexity of inter-procedure analysis and alias analysis often underestimate data usage and skew the decision. As we show later, the effectiveness of (1) is especially pronounced in the first case study (i.e., the conjugate gradient algorithm).

To implement (2), we leverage algorithm knowledge to determine the best point to trigger proactive data movement. Using algorithm knowledge, we maximize the overlap between computation and data movement without impacting execution correctness. The effectiveness of (2) is especially pronounced in the second case study (i.e., the Fast Fourier Transform). To implement (2), we can also use general compiler and runtime techniques to direct data placement. For example, using a task-based programming model, we encapsulate computation and data movement into different tasks, and rely on runtime to determine the task scheduling and rely on task-level parallelism to improve performance. However, this method has two limitations. First, to ensure execution correctness, the task scheduling largely depends on data dependency analysis. However, a coarse-grained data dependency analysis (e.g., at the level of data array) can serialize task execution and reduce concurrency, while a fine-grained

data dependency analysis can bring large runtime overhead to track data dependency. Second, an algorithm implementation based on a task-based programming model sometimes requires restructuring of applications to address synchronization and consistency issues. By comparison, working at the algorithm level of abstraction provides succinct knowledge of data dependency at fine granularity. Further, it does not incur runtime overhead, and the cost of algorithm optimization can be easily amortized over frequent use of algorithm in large-scale applications. Note that the feasibility of the algorithm-level optimization is already demonstrated by well-known algorithm-level work (e.g, ScaLAPack [2] and PLASMA [1]).

To implement (3), we locate appropriate data movements in an algorithm, and then replace them with special hardware supported data movement primitives. While the compiler, with the assistance of user-annotation, may also implement (3), the identification of numerical operations and their optimization on a hybrid memory system still requires sufficient algorithm knowledge.

Implementation of persistency semantics for NVM implies that we exploit the non-volatility property of NVM to resume computation after system crashes. The key challenge in doing so is that after failure, the data state in PCM must be guaranteed to be *consistent*. Consistency means that the data in PCM represents a valid state in the fault free program execution. The data in PCM do not always constitute a consistent state due to the out-of-order processor and memory system and data buffering in volatile caches. Upon failure, the data in PCM could be in an invalid state. Implementing the persistency semantics for the HPC domain must meet two requirements: minimizing recomputation after application restarts and minimizing runtime overhead during fault free execution.

To meet the above requirements, we introduce a relaxed persistency scheme. We maintain the data consistency only at algorithm well-defined points. Hence, the persistency is not guaranteed between those points, forming the relaxed persistency [30]. In particular, as many numerical algorithms follow an iterative structure, we choose the end of each iteration to maintain persistency. This method avoids extensive logging or COW in the existing approaches [11, 36, 12, 35], and greatly reduces the runtime overhead. Furthermore, recomputation is bounded by only one iteration of the algorithm, much smaller than that of existing checkpoint/restart techniques that have recomputation at the granularity of a whole algorithm or a complete application phase with multiple algorithms.

Maintaining persistency at the end of each iteration means we ensure that the critical algorithm data is consistent in PCM at the end of each iteration. Furthermore, there should be one resumable state available at any time (not just at the end of each iteration), in case of application failures. To implement the above goal, we can simply employ a local checkpoint to create a persistent data copy in PCM. However, this will create significant performance overhead due to frequent checkpoint in the critical path of computation.

Different from checkpointing techniques, we leverage algorithm knowledge to implement data persistency as the algorithm updates the data. Using this method, we achieve the same resilience as provided by checkpoint, albeit with much smaller overhead.

To further explain our methodology, we categorize common numerical methods into three classes based on their iterative structure.

1. In-place streaming: data are processed in a streaming manner and transformed in-place and there is no dependency between iterations. Examples include 2D/3D FFT, and some structured grids.

2. Iterative without history: one iteration only depends on its last iteration, and the output of the iteration is overwritten by its next iteration (i.e., history is not preserved). This class includes most iterative solvers (CG, GMRES, MultiGrid) and time-step solvers.

3. Iterative with history: one iteration only depends on its last iteration, but different from the iterative without history, a part of the output of the iteration must be preserved across iterations. Many dense linear algebra methods fall into this class, such as right-looking LU decomposition.

For the first class of algorithms, since there is no inter-iteration dependency, as long as data is committed into PCM to ensure persistence at the end of iteration, the application is resumable from the data in the last iteration.

For the second class of algorithms, at each iteration we employ two versions of the data for read-write data structures[1]: one version is read-only and represents the most recent resumable state from the last iteration; the other version (also named as the *working version*) is read and written, and used for the computation of the current iteration. Once the current iteration is done, the working version is committed into PCM to ensure persistency, and then becomes the read-only version for the next iteration, while the other version becomes the working version. For this algorithm class, since history is not preserved across iterations, we can switch the two versions across iterations. This method is fundamentally different from checkpointing, since checkpointed data are never involved in computation and the application has to suffer from data copy overhead. In contrast, our method integrates the maintenance of data persistency into computation, and completely removes explicit data copy. We name our method, the *twin data* technique in the rest of the paper.

For the third class of algorithms, a similar two version scheme can be devised, but we must avoid overwriting the history when switching the two versions in PCM. We use algorithm knowledge to ensure that the essential data in the current working version has committed into PCM without overwriting the history data.

To implement the above relaxed persistency scheme, we must commit appropriate data to PCM. The data commit operation includes writing back dirty, on-chip cached data to PCM and writing dirty SMM data into PCM. This creates

---

[1]Read-only data always has persistency in NVM, and write-only data can leverage the method for the first algorithm class to maintain persistency.

runtime overhead, but the overhead is bounded and limited, given the small cache size and SMM size. Furthermore, as we switch the two versions, we pollute the on-chip caches, which creates further overhead. However, comparing with intensive computation within each iteration, the overhead at the end of each iteration can be easily amortized. We quantify the overhead in Section 5.

Discussion: The algorithm knowledge can estimate dynamic behaviors, identify data criticality, ensure execution correctness, and model performance. Based on the algorithm knowledge, we can perform optimizations that cannot be achieved by compiler and runtime. This has been demonstrated by the success of several highly optimized linear algebra packages [1, 2]. In fact, we expect compiler and runtime can help even further in identifying opportunities (e.g., read/write patterns and data dependency across iterations) to efficiently apply algorithm knowledge.

3.2 Case studies

In this section, we present cases studies on three representative numerical applications: conjugate gradient, fast Fourier transform, and LU decomposition for a matrix.

3.2.1 Conjugate Gradient

The conjugate gradient (CG) is one of the most commonly used iterative methods to solve the sparse linear system $Ax = b$ when the coefficient matrix A is symmetric positive definite. Figure 3 lists the algorithm pseudocode.

CG involves two sparse matrix vector multiplication (SpMV, lines 8 and 15), three vector updates (lines 11,12, and 14) and two vector inner products (lines 9 and 13) in every iteration of the method. In general, the algorithm computes successive approximation to the solution, computes residuals corresponding to the approximate solutions, and determines search directions to update both the approximate solutions and the residuals. Vector updates and vector inner products are lightweight, cache friendly and fast. The dominant kernel of CG is SpMV, which is also the kernel of many other iterative Krylov solvers. SpMV usually involves indirect indexing of an array. The access pattern of indirect indexing of an array exhibits very limited spatial and temporal locality.

To optimize performance and energy consumption, we note that in every iteration, the entire matrix A, which consumes the major memory footprint, can be read into the hardware-managed DRAM cache. As a result, the performance-critical vectors p, q, r, z will be evicted out of hardware-managed DRAM cache and written back to PCM. This unexpected data eviction can be triggered by the prior hardware-based data placement solutions based on temporal locality analysis, which causes performance loss. To prevent this undesirable effect, we pin the frequently updated vectors into SMM so that they will never be evicted to PCM and benefit from the fast read/write speed of DRAM.

To implement the relaxed persistency without checkpointing, we examine the read-write data structures within each iteration (i.e., the vectors q, p, r, z), and implement the twin data technique. As shown in Figure 3, in the original algorithm these vectors are updated at each iteration, and they are only dependent on the output from the last iteration. Hence CG is the second class of algorithm discussed in Section 3.1.

With the twin data technique, we create two sets of the vectors, and alternate between them when updating them

1: **ConjGrad**
2: Input: The sparse matrix A, right hand side b, and initial guess x
3: Output: The solution to $Ax = b$
4: Initialization: $q \leftarrow 0, z \leftarrow 0, r \leftarrow b - Ax, p \leftarrow r, \rho \leftarrow r.r$, where x is some initial guess
5: Data placement: p, q, r, z are placed in SMM.
6: **for** i=0,1,... **do**
7:    (commit $q, r, \alpha, \rho_0, \rho, p, z$)
8:    (q') $q \leftarrow Ap$
9:    $(\alpha')\alpha \leftarrow \rho/(p.q)$
10:    $(\rho_0')\rho_0 \leftarrow \rho$
11:    $(z')z \leftarrow z + \alpha p$
12:    $(r')r \leftarrow r - \alpha q$
13:    $(\rho')\rho \leftarrow r.r$
14:    $(p')p \leftarrow r + (\rho/\rho_0)p$
15:    Check convergence: $r = A.z$?
16:    (switch $q, r, \alpha, \rho_0, \rho, p, z$)
17: **end for**

Figure 3: Conjugate gradient algorithm. Capital letters such as A represent matrices; lowercase letters such as x, y, z represents vectors; Greek letters α, ρ represent scalar numbers. The purple operations inside parentheses are what happen in a version switching iteration. Blue text is the data placement optimization for performance and energy.

within the iteration. In particular, in each iteration we read from one set of the vectors and write the other set; in the next iteration we read from the other set and write the first set. By doing so, at any given time, there is always a set of consistent vectors available, i.e., the read-only set of the vectors. Using these consistent vectors and the read-only data structure (i.e., the sparse matrix A), the CG implementation is always resumable with the recomputation less than one iteration.

As a further optimization, we could switch the two versions every multiple iterations instead of every iteration to reduce runtime overhead. Also, using algorithm knowledge we notice that the vectors q, r can be re-generated from p, z. Hence we can exclude q, r from the implementation of the two versions to further reduce runtime overhead. However, the above optimization will result in larger recomputation after application failures.

3.2.2 Fast Fourier Transform

Fast Fourier Transform (FFT) is one of the most popular and widely used spectral methods [5]. It is used to compute the Discrete Fourier Transform (DFT) and its inverse. Given an input data grid $X(n1, n2, n3)$, a typical 3D FFT performs transformation and outputs the transformed X. In general, 3D FFT performs 1D FFT transformation on each of the three dimensions of the 3D data grid and 2D transpose. 2D transpose aims to transpose non-consecutive dimensions into consecutive dimensions to improve data locality. The pseudocode of 3D FFT is shown in Figure 4.

To improve performance and energy efficiency of 3D FFT, we optimize it using aggressive data management and the transpose DMA. In particular, the basic operations for 3D FFT are 2D transpose and 1D FFT, each of which has intensive write operations on the input data grid. Hence, the data grid must be copied into SMM for performance and energy efficiency reasons. When copying data from PCM to SMM, we leverage transpose DMA to implement data transpose as a side effect of data copy.

1: **FFT3D**
2: Input: a 3-D array $X(n_1, n_2, n_3)$, column major
3: Output: 3D DFT'ed $X(n_1, n_2, n_3)$
4: FFT along the x-axis:
5: **for** $k = 1, \ldots, n_3$ **do**
6:    FFT along 1st dimension on plane $X(:, :, k)$
7: **end for**
8: FFT along the y-axis:
9: **for** $k = 1, \ldots, n_3$ **do**
10:    Transpose the plane $X(:, :, k)$ into P
11:    FFT along 1st dimension on plane P
12:    Transpose the plane P back to $X(:, :, k)$
13: **end for**
14: FFT along the z-axis:
15: **for** $j = 1, \ldots, n_2$ **do**
16:    Transpose the plane $X(:, j, :)$ into plane P
17:    FFT along 1st dimension on plane P
18:    Transpose plane P back to $X(:, j, :)$
19: **end for**

Figure 4: 3D Fast Fourier Transform

Furthermore, we overlap data copy (i.e., transpose) with computation (1D FFT). Specifically, there are three loops in 3D FFT shown in Figure 4. According to the algorithm knowledge, within the second loop, the 1D FFT can start to work on the transposed data, even before the first 2D transpose is completed; the second 2D transpose can start to transpose the data processed by 1D FFT, even before the 1D FFT is completed. Hence, we can implement a pipeline of the two transposes and 1D FFT by partitioning SMM into three parts. Each part is in charge of either transpose or 1D FFT operation in a round-robin manner. Figure 5 generally depicts this execution paradigm for the second and third loops.

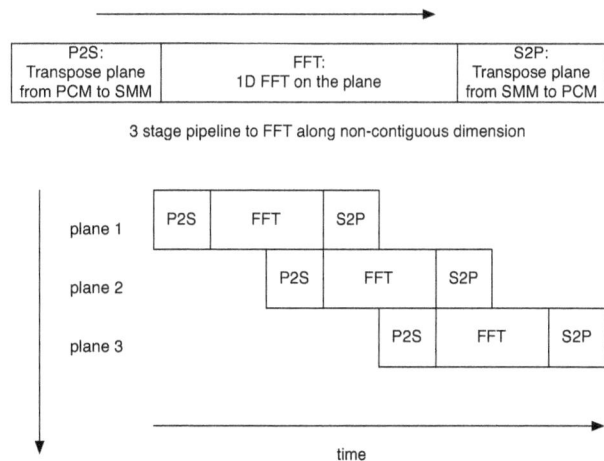

3 stage pipeline to FFT along non-contiguous dimension

Figure 5: Optimizing 3D FFT with transpose DMA and aggressive data management

To implement the relaxed persistency without checkpointing, we examine the read-write data structure, the data grid X. Since the data planes in X are processed one by one, FFT falls into the first algorithm class discussed in Section 3.1. At the end of each iteration in the three loops, we maintain persistency of X as a data plane is moved or transposed (using transpose DMA) from SMM to PCM. We also use a single variable to bookkeep the data plane position within X. Upon failure and reboot, the computation will be resumed based on the bookkeeping variable and persistent data planes. Note that implementing the above relaxed

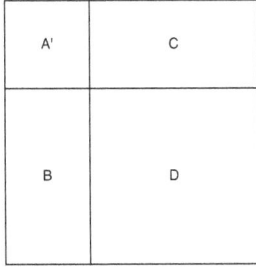

```
1: while A is not empty do
2:    Factorize the left NB columns A, B and update the top
      NB rows (C).
3:    Use updated panels from the previous step to update the
      trailing (right-bottom) matrix D ← D − BC.
4:    Move to work on the trailing matrix: A ← D
5: end while
```

Figure 6: Blocked right-looking LU factorization without partial pivoting

persistency does not increase data movement and computation, and does not alter the overlap between computation and data movement, therefore the run time overhead is minimized.

3.2.3 LU Decomposition

The LU decomposition is the standard algorithm to solve a general dense linear system. LU decomposition factors a general matrix A into the product of a lower triangular matrix (L) and upper triangular matrix (U) such that $A = LU$. To improve numerical stability, some LU algorithms employ partial pivoting. In the discussion below we do not consider partial pivoting because of page limitation, but our method is applicable to partial pivoting. Figure 6 generally describes the popular blocked right-looking LU algorithm.

For the right-looking LU algorithm, we do not have opportunities to improve performance and energy efficiency, however we can employ the twin data technique to achieve resilience improvement. Figure 7 depicts the memory snapshots when applying the twin data technique. Each memory snapshot corresponds to one step (i.e., one iteration) of LU. For the LU algorithm, the matrix A is a read-write data structure, and falls into the third algorithm class discussed in Section 3.1. At the beginning, we create a copy of the matrix A (see the memory snapshot 0), creating two instances of A (the new copy and the original one). Then the panel update is performed in one instance of the matrix A (the left one), and the updated area is highlighted in the figure (see the version 1 in the memory snapshot 1). If a failure happens during the transition from the memory snapshot 0 to 1, we can safely rollback to the version 0 (see Figure 7) from one instance of the matrix A (the right one particularly). After the step 1 is finished, the left matrix is committed to PCM to maintain persistency, and the right matrix becomes the working version. Afterwards, in the step 2 we read the panel from the left matrix but write to the right matrix shown in the snapshot 2. The algorithm continues the above process by alternating matrix update between the left and right instances.

With the above implementation, at any moment there is a resumable state existing in one of the two matrix instances. The recomputation after the system crashes is limited to one iteration. Note that we achieve the above resilience without

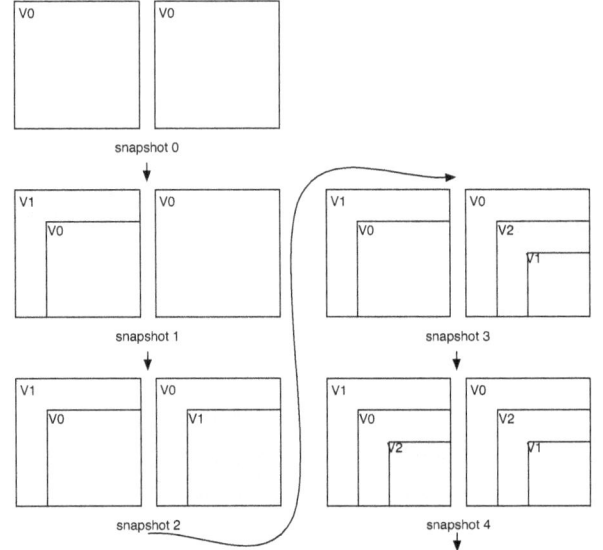

Figure 7: The implementation of the twin data technique for LU factorization. The updated areas are highlighted with yellow color.

intensive copying operations and with minimal changes to the original algorithm. In addition, at the end of LU, the final result is scattered between the two instances of the matrix. We must merge the two instances, but the merging operation is simple and the overhead is marginal comparing to the whole LU factorization.

4. EXPERIMENTAL METHODOLOGY

Our experiments are based on McSim [4], a PIN [27] based multi- and many-core cycle accurate simulation infrastructure. McSim provides event-driven timing simulation and models cores, caches, directories, on-chip networks and memory channels. We enhance the main memory model in McSim to support the hybrid DRAM/PCM simulation. The implementation of the new memory model allows configurable PCM/DRAM ratio and configurable memory organization. The new memory model also accounts for the microarchitecture of the DRAM and PCM devices. We further extend the implementation of the memory controller in McSim to implement DMA functionality.

Table 2 lists the detailed parameters and architecture configurations for the processor and memory system in our simulation. DRAM timing parameters are based on the Micron specification [28]; PCM timing parameters are based on [31, 10]. We calculate DRAM and NVM energy consumption based on the number of memory accesses broken down into row buffer hits, misses and the memory energy parameters listed in 2. This method is also utilized in [24, 41]. The memory energy parameters are listed in Table 2, and these parameters are based on [25, 8]. We collect performance and energy consumption results of the running phase of the numerical kernels, skipping the initialization phase.

To compare with the existing hardware-based solutions for data placement, we implement a hardware-managed DRAM cache in [33] as our baseline machine. This hardware-managed DRAM cache mechanism is one of the most common hardware-based data placement solutions. To distinguish this hardware-managed DRAM cache mechanism with the DRAM cache

Table 2: Simulation parameters

Processor	8-way super scalar, ROB size 64, instruction queue size 128
Memory organization	2 memory channels, 1 (DRAM) or 4 (PCM) ranks per channel, 8 banks per rank PCM 1GB, DRAM 32MB, SMM:DRAM cache=1:1 by default,
L1 Cache	split I/D caches, each 16KB, 4 ways, 64B block, private cache
L2 Cache	a unified 4MB cache, 16 ways, 64B block, shared cache
Memory Controller	64-entry Transaction Queue, 16-entry Command Queue, FR-FCFS, closed-page
Timing (cycles) [31, 10]	DRAM - tRCD: 14, tRAS: 34, tRP: 14, tRR: 1, tCL: 14, tBL: 4 tRRDact: 5 PCM - tRCD: 37, tRAS: 50, tRP: 14, tRR: 1, tCL: 10, tBL: 14, tRRDact: 3
Energy (pJ/bit) [40]	DRAM - Array read: 1.17, Array write: 0.39, row buffer read: 0.93, row buffer write: 1.02, background power: 0.08 PCM - Array read: 2.47, Array write: 16.82, row buffer read: 0.93, row buffer write: 1.02, background power: 0.08

employed in our system, we name the DRAM cache mechanism in [33] as the *pure DRAM cache*. Note that while the DRAM cache studied in [33] is abstract and geared towards exploiting the high density of PCM to reduce page faults, we are more interested in evaluating the hardware-managed DRAM cache idea in an HPC environment where the page fault is not a significant issue but the concurrency and latency of the hardware-managed DRAM cache are critical. Thus, we employ a highly optimized hardware-managed DRAM cache as our baseline. This DRAM cache has high hit concurrency (up to 64 concurrent requests), high associativity (32 way) without extended latency for tag matching, high miss concurrency (up to 64 concurrent requests). The implementation of such cache could be expensive but achieves excellent performance for HPC applications which are sensitive to the concurrency and latency of the cache. Hence, our hardware-managed DRAM cache is a high bar for evaluation, representing the best we can obtain from a transparent cache.

5. EVALUATION

We use CG (class B, CG.B) and FT (class A, FT.A) from NAS Parallel Benchmark (NPB3.3) suite, and LU from LAPACK [2] (the DGETRF input with a square matrix of size 1000) as algorithm implementation. Table 3 shows the memory system configurations for evaluation. Besides the baseline cache and ADDP, we also evaluate pure DRAM and pure PCM to reveal the implication of our designs and algorithm characteristics. All results are normalized to those of the baseline hardware-managed DRAM cache.

Table 3: Configurations of the memory system

Name	hardware-managed DRAM cache	DRAM SMM	Main memory	DMA
Baseline	Yes	No	PCM	No
ADDP	Yes	Yes	PCM	Yes
Pure DRAM	No	No	DRAM	No
Pure PCM	No	No	PCM	No
ADDP DRAM	Yes	Yes	DRAM	Yes

Performance: Figure 8 shows the execution time of CG.B and FT.A. The figure does not show the results for LU, because its implementation is highly optimized and bounded by computation, and can achieve 90% of the peak performance. The main memory system plays little role in determining the performance and hence, we do not optimize it. However, we will discuss the ADDP runtime overhead of LU in Figure 11.

Figure 8 shows that for CG our optimization scheme (i.e., placing the frequently updated vectors in DRAM SMM) reduces run time by 9% compared against the baseline. The performance improvement comes from eliminating the hardware-managed DRAM cache thrashing problem analyzed in Section 3.2.1. . The performance of ADDP is very close to that

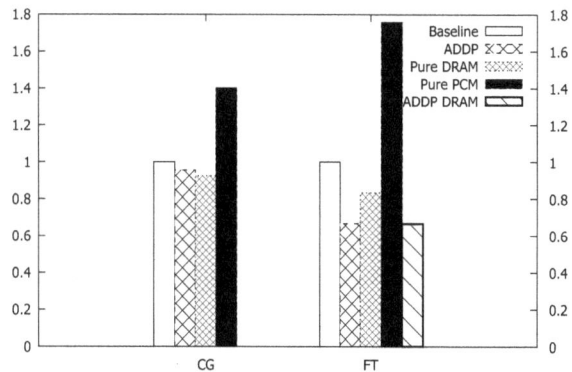

Figure 8: Execution time

of the pure DRAM system, and is much better than that of the pure PCM system. This demonstrates the effectiveness of ADDP for performance optimization.

For FT, we notice 49% performance improvement with ADDP over the baseline pure hardware-managed DRAM cache system. The significant performance improvement comes from successfully exploiting parallelism between processor and memory system with the DMA engine. ADDP in this case performs even better than a pure DRAM main memory system without DMA. To investigate the reason, we compare the performance of ADDP in the hybrid memory with that of ADDP in the pure DRAM system (labeled as *ADDP DRAM* in Figure 8 and Table 3). We found that the performance of these two approaches is very close. This result suggests that ADDP effectively removes the high latency of PCM access from the critical path by overlapping computation and data movement. Also, given the better performance of ADDP DRAM over the pure hardware-managed DRAM cache, we infer that there is significant parallelism untapped by the pure DRAM memory system. Hence, using DMA, we open new opportunities to improve performance.

To further understand the reasons why ADDP performs better than the baseline, we profile the data migration volume and hardware-managed DRAM cache miss rate. For ADDP, the hardware-managed DRAM cache miss refers to the cache miss happening in the inclusive hardware DRAM cache. From the figure 9, we notice that for CG the data migration volume reduces by 90%, which explains the performance benefit of CG. However, we do not see a significant difference between the baseline and ADDP for the cache miss rate. This is because the memory references to the read-only, input matrix A of CG (see the pseudocode in Figure 3) with a large memory footprint account for the major cache misses, while ADDP for CG does not optimize the data placement of A. For FT, we notice the significant reduction in both data

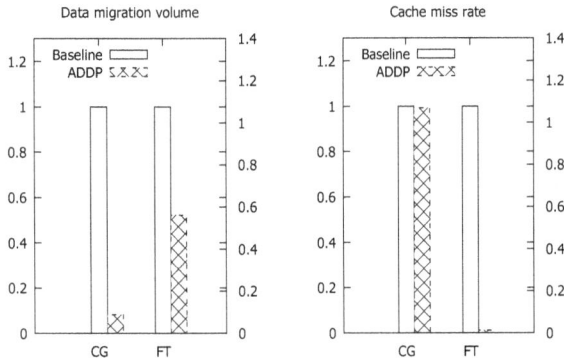

Figure 9: Data migration from DRAM to PCM and DRAM cache miss rate

migration and cache misses, which explains the big performance benefits of ADDP. The reduction in data migration and cache misses comes from our pipelined data management and optimized data transpose operations that avoid unnecessary data movement.

For both CG and FT, the performance difference between ADDP and pure DRAM is less than 12%. This performance gap is smaller than that achieved by the existing work [11, 36], demonstrating the feasibility of using ADDP for HPC.

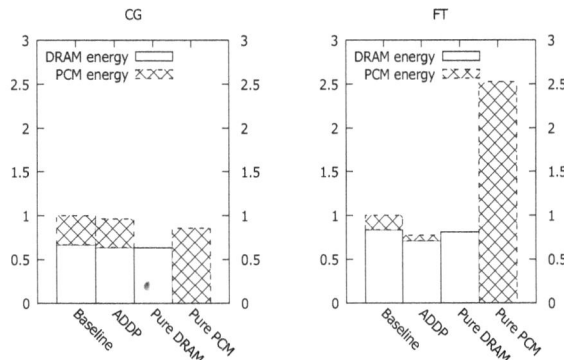

Figure 10: Dynamic energy of memory system

Energy: Figure 10 shows energy consumption of the main memory including both DRAM and PCM. For CG, we notice that in terms of energy consumption, the pure PCM is close to ADDP and the baseline cache, and is only second to the pure DRAM. In combination with the performance results, we conclude that for CG, we improve performance at the cost of slightly increased energy consumption on a hybrid memory system. However, comparing with the baseline, ADDP still successfully reduces energy consumption by 9.2%.

For FT, ADDP consumes the least energy, comparing with other three cases using PCM (25% energy saving comparing with the baseline case). With ADDP, we also have a high ratio of DRAM energy to PCM energy. This result is an indication of good caching effects—most memory accesses are served by DRAM. In contrast to CG, the pure PCM memory in FT consumes much more energy than the other cases, because FT is a write intensive application and writing PCM consumes much more energy than reading. In this

case, a hybrid DRAM/PCM system is beneficial for energy saving.

Resilience: To quantify the overhead of the relaxed persistency scheme, we compare the performance with and without the twin data technique. Figure 11 shows the results. As discussed in Section 3.1, the twin data technique can incur overhead when switching the two versions. In particular, the program must wait for the data in various volatile buffers to commit and become persistent in PCM; switching versions may also change the caching behavior because of the temporary expansion of working set. Note that employing the two versions does not change the locality property of the algorithm.

Figure 11 shows that the version switching overhead for the three algorithms is negligible (~1%), even if we switch the two versions at every iteration. This low overhead is due to the limited cache size and infrequent version switching. In the following analysis we assume there is negligible overhead in version switching, with up to one iteration re-computation when recovering from failures.

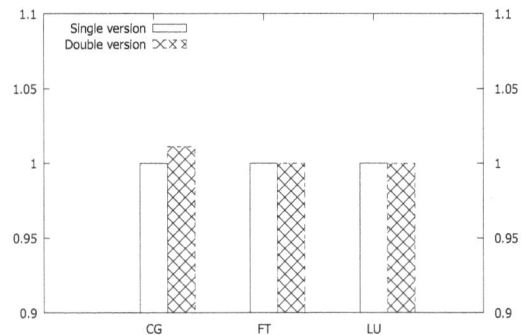

Figure 11: Version switching overhead of CG.B and FT.A based on ADDP

To further evaluate the effectiveness of our approach, we compare the twin data technique with a checkpointing technique. Given the lack of simulation capabilities for HPC checkpointing, we build an analytic model to make the comparison. The state-of-art checkpointing technique [16] employs PCM to implement a two level scheme. The first level is a global synchronous checkpoint that saves a consistent global state into stable global storage such as disks or neighboring PCM. The second level is a local synchronous checkpoint that saves the local state into local PCM. The paper leverages 3D stacking between DRAM and PCM to accelerate the local checkpointing while avoiding expensive global checkpoint with overhead around 6% [16].

The effective use of the twin data technique can serve the *functionality* of the local checkpointing, while avoiding the checkpointing overhead or the requirement of 3D stacking technology. Hence, we expect to see a dramatic reduction in checkpointing overhead.

To make the comparison relevant to HPC, we use the optimal checkpoint interval in [13]. The expected execution time of an application with checkpoint/restart can be decomposed into the following components:

$$T_{C/R}(\tau) = \text{solve time} + \text{dump time} + \text{rework time} + \text{recovery time}$$

$$= \frac{M}{p} e^{pR/M} (e^{(\tau+\sigma)p/M} - 1) \frac{T_s}{\tau}$$

$$(1)$$

where the solve time (T_s) is the original execution time of the computation, the dump time is the time to perform periodical dumping the state of the program to stable storage, the rework time is the work lost since the latest checkpoint, equivalent to the time elapsed when failure happens since last checkpoint, and the recovery time is the time required to be able to recompute from the latest checkpoint including reading the stored checkpoint data back, rebooting, re-initialization, etc. In the quantitative representation, M is the mean time to interrupt (MTTI) of a system component, p is the number of components, τ is the optimal checkpoint interval, σ is the time to do one dumping, and R is the time for one restart. The optimal checkpoint interval τ that minimizes $T_{C/R}$ can be found in [13].

With the twin data technique, since there is no checkpointing overhead, the execution time will consist of only the original solve time (T_s) and the recovery time (R). Using the same fault probability model as the checkpointing scheme, we calculate the expected execution time with the twin data technique as

$$T_{\text{twin}} = \text{solve time} + \text{recovery time}$$
$$= T_s e^{pR/M} \qquad (2)$$

Based on the above modeling, we compare the expected execution time of the state of the art checkpointing mechanism and the twin data technique. The ratio of the expected execution time is as follows, assuming the recovery times are the same for both techniques.

$$\frac{T_{C/R}}{T_{\text{twin}}} = \frac{M}{\tau p}(e^{(\tau+\sigma)p/M} - 1) \qquad (3)$$

Note that the ratio is always larger than 1, as $e^{(\tau+\sigma)p/M} - 1 \geq \frac{(\tau+\sigma)p}{M}$. As the scale ($p$) continues increasing exponentially, the ratio will grow very fast, even if we assume the optimal checkpoint interval τ for C/R. The above analysis demonstrates the performance benefits of introducing algorithm knowledge into the resilience design.

The above analysis assumes that the recomputation time is the same for ADDP and checkpointing. This is very conservative, because the recomputation with ADDP is bounded by one iteration, much smaller than that of checkpointing.

We further quantify and compare the performance of ADDP and the checkpointing mechanism with an example. We assume that a single dump (including the necessary coordination) is 0.5 minute, the MTTI of a single component (processor or socket) is 10 years, and the recovery time (including rebooting, re-initialization) is 1 minute. We use the model (1) to calculate the normalized execution time of C/R using the optimal checkpoint interval from [13], and model (2) to calculate the normalized execution time with the twin data technique. Figure 12 shows the performance. The figure reveals the lower execution time with the twin data technique and the rapidly increasing performance gap between the twin data and the checkpointing mechanism as the system scale becomes larger.

6. RELATED WORK

Some studies have considered hardware-based data placement for the hybrid memory system. Ramos et al. [34] rely on MC to monitor write intensity and popularity of memory pages, which is used to migrate pages between DRAM

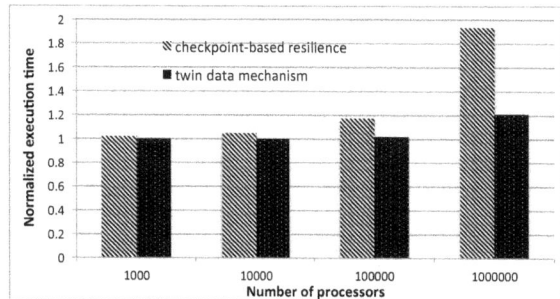

Figure 12: Overheads comparison: twin data vs. checkpoint

and PCM. Bivens et al. [6] and Qureshi et al. [33, 32] use DRAM as a set-associative cache that is logically placed between processor and PCM. Yoon et al. [40] place data based on row buffer locality in memory devices. Wang et al. [37] rely on static analysis and MC runtime monitoring to determine data placement on GPU. A key limitation of these approaches is that they rely heavily on hardware-based monitoring mechanisms and caching policies to direct data placement without awareness of application semantics. Hence, they can result in inefficient data copy/migration with poor performance and low energy efficiency, because the data management algorithms are generally based on memory access patterns monitored within a user-defined time period. Depending on the duration of the time period and other heuristic parameters to trigger data movement, these algorithms may not work well for a range of workloads and need to be disabled to avoid performance loss. By contrast, our technique takes a holistic view of algorithm structure and application data-access pattern and hence, it avoids the above problems in the traditional solutions. A few other works use software-based extensions to implement persistency semantics [12, 36, 11, 35]. However, these techniques cannot work well for HPC domain, due to their large overhead and limited support for massive data movement.

Numerical algorithms play crucial role in HPC and hence, several researchers have explored techniques for utilizing algorithm knowledge to improve application fault tolerance (e.g., [39, 9, 14, 18]), performance [23, 38, 19], and energy efficiency [20, 17]. Different from previous efforts, this paper demonstrates the significant benefits of using algorithm knowledge to direct data placement in the future hybrid memory system.

7. CONCLUSIONS

In this paper, we demonstrate that using algorithm knowledge, the data placement for hybrid memory can be optimized. Our approach provides valuable insights for using NVM for the future HPC systems. Based on algorithm direction, we reveal many opportunities to improve performance, energy efficiency, and implement a relaxed persistency scheme. The benefits are significant, demonstrating the feasibility to introduce algorithm semantics to address critical challenges of using the future hybrid memory systems.

Acknowledgement

The authors would like to thank the anonymous reviewers for their insightful comments and valuable suggestions. This work is partially supported by the U.S. Department of Energy, Office of Science, Advanced Scientific Computing Research, the NSF grants CCF-1553645, CCF-1305622, ACI-1305624, CCF-1513201, the SZSTI basic research program JCYJ20150630114942313, and the Special Program for Applied Research on Super Computation of the NSFC-Guangdong Joint Fund (the second phase).

8. REFERENCES

[1] The parallel linear algebra for scalable multi-core architectures (plasma). http://icl.cs.utk.edu/plasma/overview/index.html/.

[2] Scalable linear algebra package. http://www.netlib.org/scalapack/.

[3] Intel quickdata technology software guide for linux. http://www.intel.com/content/dam/doc/white-paper/quickdata-technology-software-guide-for-linux-paper.pdf, 2008.

[4] J. Ahn et al. McSimA+: A Manycore Simulator with Application-level+ Simulation and Detailed Microarchitecture Modeling. In *ISPASS*, 2013.

[5] K. Asanovic et al. The Landscape of Parallel Computing Research: A View from Berkeley. Technical Report EECS-2006-183, UC, Berkeley, 2006.

[6] A. Bivens et al. Architectural Design for Next Generation Heterogeneous Memory Systems. In *Int. Memory Workshop*, 2010.

[7] M. Calhoun. Characterization of Block Memory Operations. *Master Thesis, Rice University*, 2006.

[8] J. Chen et al. Energy-Aware Writes to Non-Volatile Main Memory. In *Workshop on Power-Aware Computing and Systems*, 2011.

[9] Z. Chen. Online-ABFT: An Online Algorithm Based Fault Tolerance Scheme for Soft Error Detection in Iterative Methods. *PPoPP*, 2013.

[10] Y. Choi et al. A 20nm 1.8V 8Gb PRAM with 40MB/s program bandwidth. In *ISSCC*, 2012.

[11] J. Coburn et al. NV-Heaps: making persistent objects fast and safe with next-generation, non-volatile memories. In *ASPLOS*, 2011.

[12] J. Condit et al. Better I/O Through Byte-Addressable, Persistent Memory. In *SOSP*, 2009.

[13] J. T. Daly. A higher order estimate of the optimum checkpoint interval for restart dumps. *Future Gen. Comp. Syst.*, 22(3):303–312, 2006.

[14] T. Davies and Z. Chen. Correcting Soft Errors Online in LU Factorization. In *HPDC*, 2013.

[15] G. Dhiman, R. Ayoub, and T. Rosing. PDRAM: A Hybrid PRAM and DRAM Main Memory System. In *DAC*, 2009.

[16] X. Dong et al. Leveraging 3D PCRAM Technologies to Reduce Checkpoint Overhead for Future Exascale Systems. In *SC*, 2009.

[17] R. Dorrance et al. A Scalable Sparse Matrix-Vector Multiplication Kernel for Energy-Efficient Sparse-Blas on FPGAs. In *FPGA*, 2014.

[18] P. Du et al. Algorithm-based Fault Tolerance for Dense Matrix Factorizations. In *PPoPP*, 2012.

[19] M. Faverge, J. Herrmann, J. Langou, B. R. Lowery, Y. Robert, and J. Dongarra. Designing LU-QR hybrid solvers for performance and stability. In *IPDPS*, 2014.

[20] E. Garcia et al. Optimizing the LU Factorization for Energy Efficiency on a Many-Core Architecture. In *LCPC*, 2013.

[21] R. Huggahalli, R. Iyer, and S. Tetrick. Direct Cache Access for High Bandwidth Network I/O. In *ISCA*, 2005.

[22] IBM. Cell broadband engine processor dma engines, part 1: The little engines that move data. http://www.ibm.com/developerworks/library/pa-celldmas.

[23] M. S. Lam, E. E. Rothberg, and M. E. Wolf. The Cache Performance and Optimizations of Blocked Algorithms. In *ASPLOS*, 1991.

[24] B. Lee, E. Ipek, O. Mutlu, and D. Burger. Architecturing Phase Change Mmemorhy as a Scalable DRAM Architecture. In *ISCA*, 2009.

[25] B. C. Lee, E. Ipek, O. Mutlu, and D. Burger. Architecting phase change memory as a scalable DRAM alternative. In *ISCA*, 2009.

[26] Y. Lu, J. Shu, L. Sun, and O. Mutlu. Loose-Ordering Consistency for Persistent Memory. In *ICCD*, 2014.

[27] C.-K. Luk et al. Pin: building customized program analysis tools with dynamic instrumentation. *Acm Sigplan Notices*, pages 190–200, 2005.

[28] Micron Technology. Calculating memory system power for ddr3. Technical Report TN-41-01, 2007.

[29] J. Meza et al. Enabling Efficient and Scalable Hybrid Memories Using Fine-Granularity DRAM Cache Management. In *IEEE CAL*, 2012.

[30] S. Pelley, P. M. Chen, and T. F. Wenisch. Memory Persistency. In *ISCA*, 2014.

[31] M. Poremba et al. NVMain: An Architectural-Level Main Memory Simulator for Emerging Non-volatile Memories. In *ISVLSI*, 2012.

[32] M. K. Qureshi et al. Enhancing Lifetime and Security of PCM-Based Main Memory with Start-Gap Wear Leveling. In *MICRO*, 2009.

[33] M. K. Qureshi et al. Scalable High-Performance Main Memory System Using Phase-Change Memory Technology. In *ISCA*, 2009.

[34] L. Ramos, E. Gorbatov, and R. Bianchini. Page Placement in Hybrid Memory Systems. In *ICS*, 2011.

[35] S. Venkataraman et al. Consistent and Durable Data Structures for Non-volatile Byte-addressable Memory. In *FAST*, 2011.

[36] H. Volos, A. J. Tack, and M. M. Swift. Mnemosyne: Lightweight Persistent Memory. In *ASPLOS*, 2011.

[37] B. Wang et al. Exploring Hybrid Memory for GPU Energy Efficiency through Software-Hardware Co-Design. In *PACT*, 2013.

[38] S. Williams et al. Optimization of Sparse Matrix-Vector Multiplication on Emerging Multicore Platforms. In *SC*, 2007.

[39] P. Wu et al. Fault Tolerant Matrix-Matrix Multiplication: Correcting Soft Errors On-line. *Scalable Algorithms for Large-Scale Syst.*, 2011.

[40] H. Yoon et al. Row Buffer Locality Aware Caching Policies for Hybrid Memories. In *ICCD*, 2012.

[41] J. Zhao et al. Kiln: Closing the Performance Gap Between Systems With and Without Persistence Support. In *MICRO*, 2013.

Self-configuring Software-defined Overlay Bypass for Seamless Inter- and Intra-cloud Virtual Networking

Kyuho Jeong
ACIS Lab - ECE Department
University of Florida
Gainesville, Florida, USA
kyuhojeong@acis.ufl.edu

Renato Figueiredo
ACIS Lab - ECE Department
University of Florida
Gainesville, Florida, USA
renato@acis.ufl.edu

ABSTRACT

Many techniques have been proposed to provide, transparently, the abstraction of a layer-2 virtual network environment within a provider, e.g. by leveraging Software-Defined Networking (SDN). However, cloud providers often constrain layer-2 communication across instances; furthermore, SDN integration and layer-2 messaging between distinct domains distributed across the Internet is not possible, hindering the ability for tenants to deploy their virtual networks across providers. In contrast, overlay networks provide a flexible foundation for inter-cloud virtual private networking (VPN), by tunneling virtual network traffic through private, authenticated end-to-end overlay links. However, overlays inherently incur network virtualization overheads, including header encapsulation and user/kernel boundary crossing. This paper proposes a novel system – **VIAS** (VIrtualization Acceleration over SDN) – that delivers the flexibility of overlays for inter-cloud virtual private networking, while transparently applying SDN techniques (available in existing Open-Flow hardware or software switches) to selectively bypass overlay tunneling and achieve near-native performance for TCP/UDP flows within a provider. Architecturally, VIAS is unique in how it integrates SDN and overlay controllers in a distributed fashion to coordinate the management of virtual network links and flows. The approach is self-organizing, whereby overlay nodes can detect that peer endpoints are in the same network and program bypass flows between OpenFlow switches. While generally applicable, VIAS in particular applies to nested VMs/containers across cloud providers, supporting seamless communication within and across providers. VIAS has been implemented as an extension to an existing virtual network overlay platform (IP-over-P2P, IPOP) by integrating OpenFlow controller functionality with distributed overlay controllers. We evaluate the performance of VIAS in realistic cloud environments using an implementation based on IPOP, the RYU SDN framework, Open vSwitch, and LXC containers across various cloud environment including Amazon, Google compute engine, and CloudLab.

HPDC'16, May 31-June 04, 2016, Kyoto, Japan
© 2016 ACM. ISBN 978-1-4503-4314-5/16/05...$15.00
DOI: http://dx.doi.org/10.1145/2907294.2907318

Keywords

SDN; OpenFlow; Cloud Computing; virtualization; P2P; overlay network

1. INTRODUCTION

Since the rise of multi-tenant clouds, the approach of providing virtualized computing resources such as virtual machines and containers has become key to an increasing body of distributed computing applications. Today, computing resources are readily available through multiple cloud service APIs and portals, and can be customized and instantiated from a template image dynamically. Cloud providers expose such virtual resources with a set of instance types, with discrete combinations of CPU, memory and storage capacities. While cloud platforms also offer virtual network capabilities (e.g. Amazon Virtual Private Cloud, OpenStack Neutron), these do not extend *across* multiple providers. Tenants who wish to benefit from the ability to choose the best offerings from multiple cloud providers, dynamically, must deal with different APIs and virtualization platforms (e.g. KVM, Xen), and providers who do not inter-operate in their virtual network capabilities. This paper proposes VIAS, a virtual network that addresses the challenge of providing a consistent virtual network abstraction across cloud instances deployed on multiple providers.

The increasing variety of cloud providers and the added flexibility of an extra layer of indirection from nested virtualization [21, 35, 2] are welcome news for tenants interested in deploying multi-cloud virtual infrastructures that seek to achieve high availability, geographical distribution, and to minimize cost/performance (while avoiding vendor lock-in) by selecting the best instance for a task from a variety of offerings of reserved and spot instances in the cloud market. Networking, however, becomes harder – it requires the coordinated configuration of virtual network interfaces, switches and routers across multiple instances. Furthermore, each cloud infrastructure has its own networking model and stack, and may be subject to connectivity constraints such as network address translation (NAT), in particular in private clouds. While tenants can use cloud APIs and Web interfaces *within* a provider to configure the network for their cloud instances (e.g. boto [1] or gcloud [9]), there is no inter-operability across providers. This leads to management complexity that is greatly compounded when tenants distribute their applications across clouds and expect elastic provisioning and management operations, such as VM migration, to work seamlessly.

Several applications can benefit from inter-cloud deployments. For instance, workflow management system such as Pegasus [5] can use heterogeneous resources to perform different tasks, and the best cost/performance resources may not be co-located in the same provider. In high-throughput applications such as parameter sweeps and bag-of-tasks, the most cost-effective computing resources, which are harvested upon the completion of a single task and reassigned to the other tasks [18], also may not be co-located.

Nonetheless, while applications can benefit from the flexibility cost/performance benefits of choosing resources across multiple providers, inter-cloud deployment can significantly increase the complexity of configuring, deploying and managing applications. Network virtualization provides a basis to address this challenge. Techniques for network virtualization based on overlay tunneling and encapsulation at endpoints, and Software-Defined Networking (SDN) at the network fabric have both been explored in related work, in different contexts.

Overlay networks have been applied to network virtualization (at layers 2 or 3) across cloud providers. For example, hSwitch [7] forms an overlay network by creating Generic Routing Encapsulation (GRE) tunnels across dispersed nested VMs. However, because it creates tunnels based on provided configuration files, the overlay topology is static, and dynamic joining/leaving of instances is complex to manage. The IP-over-P2P (IPOP [12]) overlay supports both layer 2 and 3 virtual private networking with peer-to-peer tunnels that are dynamically created and managed – even when nodes are behind NATs. Tunnels are created to reflect relationships stored in messaging or online social network services (e.g. an XMPP server), supporting overlay topologies such as unstructured social graphs and structured P2P networks [28]. IPOP has been used in the Kangaroo [21] inter-cloud platform-as-a-service system; however, its overlay processing hindered the performance of nested VMs across hosts within a provider. This paper directly addresses this performance limitation.

Another approach to network virtualization comes from the service providers. Techniques such as VLANs are not able to cope with the need for flexible configuration and isolation across large numbers of tenant address spaces, nor do they have sufficient range of virtual private address subnets [13]. The advent of SDN techniques and the OpenFlow standard have unlocked the potential to address these limitations and deploy network virtualization services at scale within service providers. However, while SDN-based solutions are becoming well-understood within the context of a *single* provider's infrastructure, SDN solutions *across* non-cooperating providers (e.g. different public/private clouds) are currently not feasible, as providers are not willing to allow external entities to exert control in their SDN infrastructure.

Overlays are scalable and general-purpose, but suffer from performance degradation within a data center, while SDN-based techniques are difficult to deploy across providers, because cloud resources (i.e. VMs) are managed by independent entities (possibly constrained by the presence of NATs), and establishing authenticated, encrypted links in the presence of dynamic instantiation and resource migration is complex, and requires coordination.

This paper presents VIAS, a novel approach that integrates overlay and SDN techniques to support flexible and high-performance virtual networking, in particular across

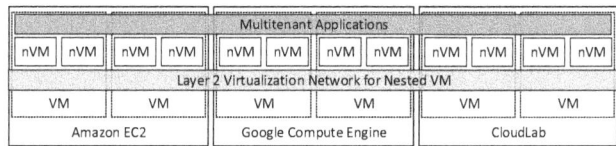

Figure 1: Illustration of layer-2 network virtualization for nested VMs across three cloud providers. The goal is to allow distributed applications (possibly multi-tenant) within nVMs to seamlessly communicate, as if they were connected to the same layer-2 segment – even though they are distributed across independently-managed providers.

tenant-managed nested virtualization instances distributed across cloud providers. It does so while exposing a network layer 2 abstraction to endpoints. VIAS supports the general case (the abstraction of a layer-2 virtual private networking linking instances across providers) by employing overlay networking as the substrate for virtualization, and optimizes for a common case (network flows among nodes within the same provider) by means of a novel performance enhancement technique of automatically detecting and programming fast bypath TCP/UDP flows using SDN APIs. Such SDN-programmed VIAS bypass removes the necessity of packet encapsulation and delivers virtualization performance near wire link speed. VIAS detects traffic-intensive TCP/UDP flows inside the overlay-encapsulated data traffic, and automatically switches over to the SDN fabric whenever such path can be programmed – such as when endpoints are within the same cloud provider.

The main contribution of this paper is a novel system that integrates distributed overlay network and SDN controllers to self-configure peer-to-peer virtual private overlay network tunnels across cloud providers, and transparently detect and program virtual network bypath flows within a provider. The system has been implemented by leveraging an existing overlay technique (IPOP) as a substrate, and integrating existing SDN programmable switches (Open vSwitch) to establish bypass flows. While it can generalize to different overlay tunneling and SDN targets, VIAS applies, in particular, to inter-cloud nested virtualization environments, where tenants can deploy software SDN switches (e.g. Open vSwitch) in their own instances. The paper demonstrates the functionality of VIAS within and across clouds, and evaluates the performance of our prototype in multiple cloud environments.

The rest of this paper is organized as follows: Section 2 elaborates on the use of overlay network and SDN as network virtualization solutions. Section 3 describes the general architecture of VIAS. Section 4 provides details on the design and implementation of a VIAS system. Section 5 presents results from the evaluation of our prototype in realistic cloud environments. Section 6 discusses related work, and Section 7 concludes the paper.

2. BACKGROUND

This section overviews techniques, issues and challenges that serve as a basis to motivate the design and uses of VIAS.

2.1 Network Virtualization

The purpose of VIAS is to provide a complete layer 2 abstraction to resources deployed across heterogeneous cloud services (as illustrated in Figure 1), without significant performance degradations. In general, there are two approaches to tackle this issue. The first relies on tenants deploying their own overlay network – which has the key advantage of not requiring any support from the underlying infrastructure. The other approach is to exploit SDN and/or network function virtualization (NFV) services provided by the cloud provider – which has the disadvantage of lack of interoperability across providers.

Overlay network: In overlay networks and VPNs (Virtual Private Network), the entire header and payload of a virtual network packet are encapsulated (and possibly encrypted and authenticated) by another layer to transfer the packet over public network links. Tunneling techniques such as L2TP, GRE or MPLS take advantage of encapsulation, which prepends an additional network header to the same or different OSI layer of the packet [27]. Tunnels can be built as stand-alone point-to-point links, or organized to form a topology, such as a mesh or structured P2P, that can be used for scalable overlay routing [34, 11, 12]. Overlay and tunneling techniques benefit from the flexibility of using encapsulation at the endpoints – which does not require changes to the infrastructure – but suffer from performance degradation. The additional encapsulation header is a source of overhead, limiting the effective maximum transmission unit (MTU) size. Furthermore, overlay processing adds computation overhead of dealing with encapsulation – possibly at the user level, as typical overlay networks are implemented as user-level processes.

SDN: Software Defined Networks initially emerged from the necessity of testing experimental protocols to overcome the difficulties of deploying new protocols on legacy hardware switches and routers [16]. Subsequently, the need for efficiently supporting large multi-tenant enterprise data centers, such as public and private clouds, has motivated the adoption of SDN techniques as an approach complementary to NFV (Network Function Virtualization) for data center network virtualization. Virtualization in cloud computing impacts the network performance because of its inherent sharing of processor resources. This can lead to negative impact on network performance and stability, such as exceptionally long delays and degraded throughput [31]. SDN and NFV techniques can mitigate performance degradations by migrating network virtualization processing overheads to network devices, and possibly lead to substantial reductions in operating expense for cloud and network service providers [10]. For example, VMware [13] supports network virtualization through both logically and physically deployed SDN nodes, providing a network virtualization platform (NVP) within a multi-tenant data center. NVP leverages software switches on VMware hypervisors at each server endpoint.

Typically, tunneling and SDN approaches are used in different network virtualization contexts – typically across (tunneling) and within (SDN) data centers. VIAS seeks to integrate these two approaches, by building a tunneled overlay network layer as a basis for layer-2 virtualization within and across providers, and by mitigating performance degradation by selectively applying SDN to establish a bypass path for intra-cloud TCP/UDP flows.

2.2 Nested Virtualization

While VIAS is generally applicable to any cloud infrastructure that exposes a virtual network interface (e.g. a tap device) and SDN switch (e.g. Open vSwitch), it complements, in particular, nested virtualization techniques. A nested virtualized environment inter-connected by VIAS enables users to deploy flexible inter-cloud virtual platforms that allow for a consistent application environment across different providers, and flexible fine-grain management of nested VM resources.

In its most general form, nested virtualization allows the capability of virtual machines to themselves host other virtual machines, in a recursive fashion. It builds upon the ability of "classic" VM monitors/hypervisors to expose the abstraction of a virtual machine at the instruction set architecture (ISA) layer, and can be supported if the underlying ISA follows the guidelines set forth in seminal virtualization work [20]. Initially applied in partitionable mainframe systems, nested virtualization became feasible in commodity server systems with the advent of virtualization extensions for the x86 architecture [30], and has been motivated by use cases in cloud computing [2].

While the most general form of nested virtualization allows a "classic" hypervisor to be instantiated within a virtual machine and supports completely unmodified software to run within VMs (e.g. instantiating KVM within VMware), the nested approach can also be applicable in other configurations, such as nested para-virtualized hypervisors (e.g. Xen on Xen [32]), trading off potential performance benefits with the additional requirement of software modifications in the kernel and/or applications. In particular, a form of nested virtualization that is appealing for deployment of software services in IaaS cloud computing platforms is to use the hypervisor of the cloud provider (e.g. Xen in Amazon EC2, KVM in Google compute engine, Hyper-V in Microsoft Azure) to deploy O/S containers (e.g. Linux LXC/Docker). This is the approach taken in Kangaroo [21]; the key advantage of this approach is performance, because containers are light-weight. The requirement to run software within containers poses a constraint, as nested instances need to use the same O/S kernel, but it is acceptable in many applications, as the adoption of container technologies continues to increase.

Different approaches to nested virtualization, as described above, yield different models of how virtual CPUs, memory and storage are allocated and managed. For instance, classic VMs expose virtual CPUs, physical memory, and block storage devices, while containers expose processes, virtual memory, and file systems at the O/S layer. Nonetheless, in general, nested virtualized systems typically expose a similar interface to the networking subsystem across multiple platforms. The lower-layer has Ethernet virtual network interface(s) provided and managed by a cloud provider's "outer" hypervisor; these are multiplexed among Ethernet virtual network interfaces managed/exposed by the tenant's "inner" virtualization stack.

Throughout this paper we use the term "nested VMs" (or "nVMs" in short) to refer broadly to any nested virtualization technique that exposes a layer-2 virtual network interface to each instance. In our evaluation, we focus on O/S containers as nVMs; nonetheless, the layer 2 virtual networking techniques in VIAS generally apply to any virtualized system that uses layer-2 Ethernet virtual interfaces.

2.3 Networking in Nested Containers

Nested virtualization supports virtual network interfaces for nested instances. For instance, Linux containers (LXC) expose one or more TUN/TAP devices for each container. By default, LXC also creates a Linux bridge on the host of a provisioned VM, and connects all virtual network interfaces of the nested VMs to this bridge. In this way, all the nested VMs attached to this bridge reside on the same layer-2 Ethernet segment. Because multiple nested instances share a single interface of the lower-layer hypervisor, it is necessary to assign and manage addresses, and multiplex access to the single interface using address translation. To this end, LXC also creates Network Address Translation (NAT) rules in the host machine, using iptables. To support automatic address assignment, LXC runs a lightweight DHCP server on the host machine. Thus, upon instantiation, each nested VM gets assigned a random IP address within a predetermined subnet range of (private) IP addresses. While not all nested virtualization technologies automate the process of providing a layer 2 network environment behind a virtual NAT, this behavior can be programmed using existing Linux devices and toolsets – a virtual bridge, iptables and dnsmasq.

2.4 NAT Traversal

In general, when deploying resources across clouds, tenants may be required to deal with private addresses and network address translation (NAT). First, public IPv4 addresses are scarce, and typically come with a price premium. For instance, EC2 provides by default a private IP address and a NAT-mapped public IP address, and charges extra for persistent public IP addresses (elastic IPs). Second, with deeper, nested virtualization, network interfaces provisioned by a cloud provided are further mutiplexed, as nested VMs are given private addresses. It is also possible that the VMs provisioned by a service themselves have private IP addresses that are translated by a NAT device, which is common in private clouds.

Consider, for instance, a tenant using a VM provisioned by a cloud provider (cVM1), and then instantiating nested instances (nVM1...nVMi) within cVM1. Each nVM is instantiated by the tenant, and hence has a virtual address that is private. While the nVMi instances can communicate within cVM1 through a virtual bridge or switch, in order to communicate across multiple instances (e.g. to nVMs hosted in other machines in the same provider, or on a different provider), it becomes necessary to map and translate addresses. In the absence of the ability to provision public addresses to nested VM instances (which is currently not offered by cloud providers), network virtualization techniques must deal with multiplexing and translation of nested/host addresses. This can, in principle, be accomplished through careful crafting of network rules by the tenant. However, this becomes complex and error-prone as the network increases in size and nodes are elastically added/removed from a tenant's infrastructure.

VIAS leverages the ICE [24], STUN [25] and TURN [15] protocols integrated in IPOP [12] to support dynamic NAT traversal, allowing (nested) cloud instances across different providers and behind one or more levels of NAT to establish P2P overlay links for tunneling. The key principle taken in VIAS is that NAT traversal is not considered as an exception, but rather a lowest-common denominator in estab-

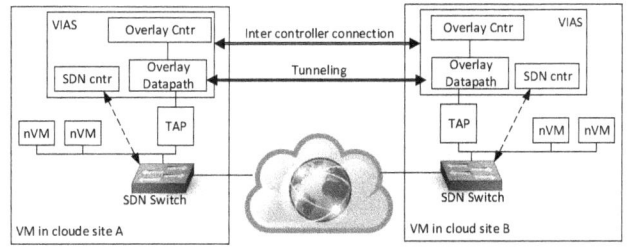

Figure 2: VIAS overview. VIAS main modules are user-level applications that are responsible for managing bypass flows (SDN cntr), setup and configuration of overlay tunnels (Overlay cntr), and encryption, encapsulation, tunneling and NAT traversal (Overlay datapath). The VIAS overlay datapath binds to an SDN switch port through a virtual network interface (tap), and the SDN controller module programs the switch. The SDN switches are commodity software/hardware devices programmed using OpenFlow APIs; they are also referred to as vias-nat-switch in the paper.

lishing inter-cloud overlay links. VIAS thus bootstraps from P2P links that can handle multiple levels of NATs across providers, and tunnel layer-2 virtual network traffic as the general case; for the particular case where P2P links are established within a single provider, the overhead of NAT traversal is side-stepped by identifying and establishing SDN bypass flows for TCP/UDP communication.

3. VIAS OVERALL ARCHITECTURE

The key design requirements in VIAS are: 1) to expose a layer-2 abstraction to unmodified applications, 2) to operate as a user-level application that can be deployed in any existing cloud instance, thus not requiring development of kernel modules, 3) to support private, encrypted tunnels in inter-cloud communications, and 4) to avoid the overhead of encapsulation and kernel/user crossings for TCP/UDP flows within a cloud provider. The VIAS architecture addresses these requirements by: fully supporting layer-2 tunneling through TLS/DTLS P2P overlay links as a baseline functionality implemented in user-level overlay software, and by automatically detecting and programming SDN switches to bypass TCP/UDP flows.

There are important reasons why VIAS bypasses TCP/UDP flows via SDN switches, but carries other virtual network traffic (e.g. ARP, ICMP) in tunnels. First, TCP/UDP are the transports used by the majority of cloud applications and the common case that needs to made fast. Second, cloud providers typically allow instances to communicate using TCP/UDP, but block layer-2 protocols (such as ARP); since we only assume SDN switches to be available at the endpoint at the minimum (e.g. software switches such as Open vSwitch in an instance), VIAS is not necessarily able to program the cloud provider's entire switch fabric.

With existing OpenFlow standard APIs and existing functionality in cloud platforms, bypass flows can be programmed by coordinated mapping/translation of TCP/UDP flow endpoints at SDN switches conencted to VIAS virtual network interfaces. To accomplish this, the VIAS architecture is structured as illustrated in Figure 2. It comprises of three main modules.

SDN Controller: This module acts as a controller for the SDN switches. In essence, it allows OpenFlow switches to retain conventional features (such as MAC learning) but, in addition, implements the distinctive features of VIAS: the abstraction of a layer-2 virtual network, and isolation of the virtual network from the host network. The VIAS SDN controller programs gateway and NAT functionalities on the SDN switch, such that virtual network endpoints can have a different subnet and private address range from the host network's. Those features are programmed using standard OpenFlow APIs, without any modifications to the switch, allowing the use of commodity hardware and software implementations of SDN switches. The main requirement is that the VIAS module is allowed to issue OpenFlow API calls to the switches. For brevity, we will refer to the SDN switches with these capabilities as *vias-nat-switch*.

The *vias-nat-switch* also implements VIAS overlay bypass to achieve high throughput for intra-cloud TCP/UDP flows. These flow bypass rules are programmed (also using OpenFlow APIs) to have higher priority than that of other flow rules. We give more details on the implementation (and limitations) of this vias-nat-switch and overlay bypass in Subsections 4.1 and 4.3.

Overlay datapath: Packets captured by the tap virtual network interface are handled by this module. This module runs as a user-space process that reads/writes from the tap device, and executes all low-level packet processing functions, such as prepending or translating network headers, as well as encryption and authentication. VIAS leverages the IPOP [12] overlay stack for this module. It reads the destination address to look up an overlay destination, prepends IPOP and UDP headers, then injects the packet to the WAN interface.

While the creation and termination of P2P overlay links are managed by the overlay controller, the metadata associated with each P2P overlay link (such as peer UID, IPv4 or MAC addresses) are used by the overlay datapath module to make forwarding decisions. Likewise, the necessary attributes of these headers (such as tunneling identifier and mapped IP and port numbers) are dynamically assigned by the overlay controller and programmed into the overlay datapath module. After the UDP header prepending, packets are ready to traverse through tunnels across the public Internet. We elaborate on the design and implementation of this module in Subsection 4.2.

Overlay Controller: The creation and termination of P2P links among overlay nodes, and the topology of the overlay network, are managed by this module. The VIAS overlay controller extends the IPOP overlay controller, which currently supports three types of topologies. One is an unstructured social network graph topology, where P2P links are created based on social links. A second topology is an all-to-all graph connecting all nodes, while the third topology is based on the Chord [28] structured P2P system. VIAS can use the all-to-all topology for small networks (tens of hosts), or the structured topology to scale to larger nodes. In the structured topology, each node identifier is based on SHA-1 of its virtual IP address, and identifier-based structured routing is performed when there is no direct P2P link connecting nodes. Structured topology policies, such as the number of successors or chord links, are configurable in the controller.

Overlay link/bypass flow management: The general approach taken by VIAS for the management (creation, monitoring, and tear-down) of links is as follows. First, overlay links are created by the overlay controller. Links may be created to enforce a topology invariant (e.g. left/right neighbors and chords in structured P2P), or on-demand based on traffic initiated by a peer. Second, for active links, their state is monitored (with respect to their traffic, and the transport addresses) by the overlay datapath module, and made available to the overlay controller. Building on overlay link monitoring mechanisms, the overlay controller defines policies for establishing a bypass TCP/UDP flow that takes into account: 1) the traffic between nodes, and 2) whether the two endpoints are within the same provider network, to initiate a link a request to create a bypass flow. The mechanisms to initiate a bypass flow are handled by the SDN controller module.

There are two instances where a bypass flow might be terminated: one is after VM migration, and another is if resources (available ports) are exhausted at the SDN switch. The policies to deal with bypass termination are left for future work, but mechanisms available to support these policies are monitoring of traffic per flow (which can be used to prioritize high-throughput traffic), and migration events (e.g. unsolicited ARP requests) to notify controllers to terminate a flow. In such events, the SDN controller can then clear out bypass rules, hence reverting all virtual network traffic to pass through overlay tunnels.

4. IMPLEMENTATION

In this section, we provide details of a VIAS prototype implementation, highlighting how each module is implemented and integrated. Moreoever, we explain how the transition between overlay and SDN virtualization takes place in VIAS. In Subsection 4.1, we elaborate on how the dynamic NAT feature offered by VIAS is programmed into the OpenFlow SDN switch. In Subsection 4.2, we explain tunneling and overlay virtualization along with various tunneling modes. Finally, in Subsection 4.3, we describe how VIAS detects flows and implements rules to bypass overlay virtualization by using SDN flow rules.

4.1 SDN Controller

As explained in Section 2.3, each nested VMs should be presented the full abstraction of a private layer 2 network, while still able to access the public Internet as if behind a NAT. To support this requirement, VIAS programs address translation rules using the OpenFlow controller, which makes Open vSwitch (or any other OpenFlow enabled devices) to work as a full-cone NAT router.

Through a configuration file, VIAS specifies a single switch port as its WAN interface (either by port number or interface name); the remaining switch ports are set as LAN ports. The controller also implements a gateway. Both the subnet range and the gateway IP address are statically assigned through VIAS configuration, and VIAS divides the address space of nested VMs from the cloud providers' address space. When packets are sourced from the LAN address range and destined beyond the gateway (i.e. the destination address is out of the range of LAN subnet), the controller programs a flow rule in the OpenFlow switch to perform full-cone NAT mappings.

For example, as in Figure 3, assume a nested nVM with IP address 192.168.1.2 tries to access a public server 4.2.2.2

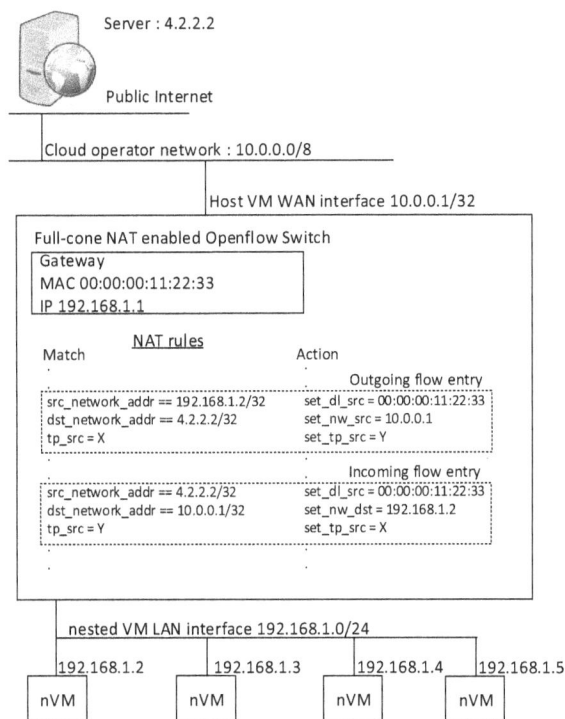

Figure 3: The VIAS SDN switch is programmed using Open-Flow to support NAT translation, in addition to "upcalls" to the overlay datapath and overlay bypass rules. This allows nVMs to access public Internet nodes through a layer-3 NAT gateway, in addition to exposing a virtual layer-2 network across all nodes connected to the overlay. In the example, an IP packet sent by nVM 192.168.1.2 to public server 4.2.2.2 triggers the programming of NAT rules by the VIAS SDN controller.

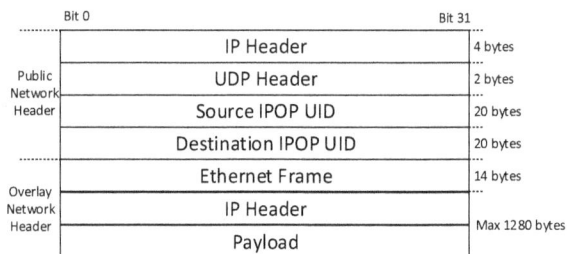

Figure 4: Packet encapsulation in IPOP.

through TCP with source port number X. Initially, the destination address of the very first packet does not match any existing flow rules in the switch. Note that this controller supports MAC address learning, such that it can learn and map each nVM MAC address to its respective port. Then, the metadata of this first packet is forwarded to the SDN controller through the OpenFlow API of ofp_packet_in. The SDN controller then checks the destination address; it can determine that the destination 4.2.2.2 is not in its LAN segment, but instead across the gateway. The SDN controller then randomly chooses port number Y from an available port number pool (which is also configurable). Finally, it makes two flow entries: one is an outgoing flow entry for streams from nested nVM to the public Internet, and the other is an incoming flow entry for the reverse stream. This can be done with series of ofp_match and ofp_actions.

Continuing in the example, the outgoing flow entry translates address from 192.168.1.2:X to 10.0.0.1:Y, replacing the source address of nested nVM to its WAN interface. The incoming flow entry translates destination address from 10.0.0.1:Y to 192.168.1.2:X, and injects the packets to the switch port of destination nested VM. The same technique can be applied to UDP streams.

Since the absence of ICMP echo identifier field in match of OpenFlow specification, ICMP protocol, which is widely used for echo request/reply (ping) message, cannot be NAT-ted. To this end, we forward every ICMP message to the controller, and NATting is performed in the SDN controller. While this approach increases the latency of ICMP messages, the functional behavior of the protocol is unaltered. Since ICMP is not used for traffic-intensive communications, this performance degradation is acceptable.

In the VIAS prototype, the SDN controller has been built upon the open-source RYU [26] SDN framework. The code (except the framework) is approximately 800 lines of Python code. For full backward compatibility, our implementation is based on OpenFlow specification version 1.0.

4.2 Overlay datapath and Overlay Controller

VIAS builds upon the IPOP codebase as a basis for the overlay datapath. In its current architecture, IPOP comprises of a packet processing/overlay datapath binary, and an overlay controller, which communicate through the Tin-Can API [12]. In essence, VIAS extends the IPOP overlay controller to support SDN bypass processing – we employ these two modules in VIAS as explained in Section 3.

In IPOP, nodes create direct P2P overlay links to tunnel virtual network traffic using the ICE protocol [24]. In order to bootstrap these direct P2P overlay links, an XMPP server is employed to assist in exchanging messages containing candidate endpoint information of peers – including the outer- and inner-most transport pairs, if nodes are behind multiple NATs. During this process, IPOP's overlay datapath module opens UDP ports ("hole-punching") on NATs to create P2P tunnels. Subsequently, peers communicate using these assigned UDP transports. The IPOP overlay header consists of two fields, which are the source and destination UIDs of overlay sender and receiver. The outer UDP and IP header are placed before the IPOP headers, resulting in the overall packet structure as shown in Figure 4.

In VIAS, each IPOP overlay link is considered as an OSI layer 2 tunnel. Each IPOP link is mapped such that multiple MAC addresses are bound to a link – which is akin to a layer 2 switch's MAC addresses bound to a port. The layer-2 overlay implements learning of MAC addresses by handling ARP request/reply messages in its LAN. IPOP checks the destination MAC address of the frame and injects the frame to the corresponding link. To bind the virtual network to VMs, IPOP uses virtual devices, including Linux bridge and Open vSwitch[17]. The tap interface is attached to this bind-

158

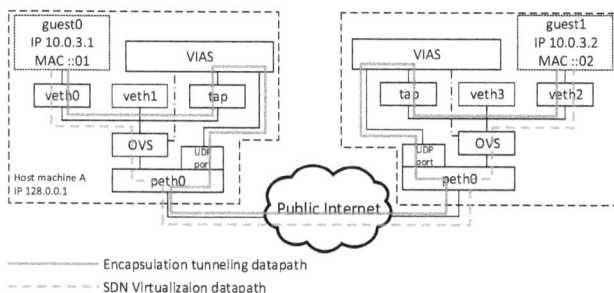

Figure 5: Packet datapath alternatives in VIAS. Initially, packets flow through the encapsulation tunneling datapath (solid line), through the overlay datapath module. Once a bypass flow is installed by the SDN controllers on both endpoints, the faster SDN virtualization datapath (dashed line) is used.

ing device and works as a bridge to the remote LAN virtual network.

For example, consider the usage scenario of Figure 5. The illustration shows two hosts running VIAS-enhanced IPOP. Each host contains multiple nested VMs (containers) with virtual network interfaces (veth#) attached to the Open vSwitch device. These guests are in the same layer 2 network, and are NATted by the host network stack to the physical interface (peth0).

When guest0 (veth0) attempts to send IP packets to guest1 (veth2), it first broadcasts an ARP request message. The VIAS-IPOP overlay datapath module picks this message through the tap device, and handles it as follows. First, the ARP message is encapsulated (Figure 4) and forwarded to all overlay links. At this stage, different overlay multicast approaches can be implemented by the overlay controller, depending on the overlay's topology. All the overlay nodes receiving the overlay-broadcast packet (e.g. the right-hand side of Figure 5) decapsulate the message and broadcast it to its L2 network (using the tap device). If there is no destination matching the ARP request message, the message is simply dropped. If the destination is in the network (e.g. veth2 in Figure 5), an ARP reply message is created by the guest, and the reply is sent back (with an unicast message) to the sender (e.g. guest0).

As part of this process, the overlay maps the MAC address it learned to the corresponding overlay link. All unicast MAC address frames captured by the overlay look up this mappings to determine along which overlay link to forward. VIAS mode can dynamically accommodate overlay topology changes by updating an MAC address and its overlay link bindings upon detecting an ARP frame. If we consider a usage scenario of VM migration from one host in a provider to another host in a different provider, the process can be automatically handled; there needs to be no network administrator involvement, since the ARP message from the migrated node itself incur updates the MAC-overlay link mapping on deployed overlay network.

4.3 Software-defined Overlay Bypass

As described in the previous section, the overlay virtualization process places several sources of overhead. At first,

there is the transition overhead of context switch between network kernel to user space. It also requires multiple copy operations when it sends packet from network kernel to user space. Moreover, since there is the need for additional prepending of overlay headers, the MTU size is smaller than that of the physical network. This overhead is the price paid to create overlay virtual networks linking nVMs across multiple providers, because tunneling, NAT traversal and encryption is required for virtual private networking. However, this overhead can be mitigated for nVMs *within the same provider*. To accomplish this, we bypass this encapsulation process on traffic-intensive TCP/UDP flows, as follows.

VIAS detects a traffic-intensive stream by monitoring traffic on overlay links, and can determine if an overlay path is possible by inspecting the overlay endpoints of a link whether they are within the same network. When VIAS determines that a bypass link should be created, it first allocates and assigns an available TCP (or UDP) port number pair for the outer address space. Then it establishes a mapping of inner address range to the outer address range with its port number. In OpenFlow, this can be programmed with a single flow add API call with *ofp_flow_mod* along a set of *ofp_match* and *ofp_action*.

On matched packet on ofp_match, the VIAS controller performs actions OFPAT_SET_DL_SRC and OFPAT_SET_DL_DST to replace the MAC address of nested VM and Open vSwitch to physical Ethernet (peth) and gateway of outer address space. Then it performs actions OFPAT_SET_NW_SRC and OFPAT_SET_NW_DST to replace inner IP addresses to outer address space. Finally, actions OFPAT_SET_TP_SRC and OFPAT_SET_TP_DST replace the inner transport number to outer transport number. The incoming traffic takes the same steps, but changes from public address space to private address space.

To illustrate this behavior, consider the example of a TCP stream depicted in Figure 6 alongside the flow rule example of Table 1. The example uses the private address space 10.0.3.0/24 for the inner address space for nested VMs, and public network addresses 128.0.0.0/24 (note that it is also possible to use private addresses for the outer address space, since VIAS supports NAT traversal). Initially, packets stream through encapsulation overlay datapath, VIAS prepending headers every packet. At certain threshold of traffic, VIAS triggers SDN bypass. First it extracts metadata of the stream, including the source/destination IP address (10.0.3.X) and port number (4000X). Then VIAS allocates and assigns an available port number (5000Y) to use as outer transport address. Next, VIAS programs inbound OpenFlow rules on the Open vSwitch SDN switch in host VM A. This inbounds rules translate outer transport (IP address and port number) to inner transport address. When VIAS programs an OpenFlow switch, it ensures the stream bypass rules have higher priority over other flow rules, so that the packet is not applied to other flow rules.

Soon after, VIAS sends a inter-controller RPC message through its P2P overlay link to the peer overlay node, passing along JSON-formatted metadata of the stream. This metadata sent through the inter-controller RPC API contains information such as outer transport address, inner transport address and transport type.

Upon receiving the message, the VIAS controller at host B programs inbound and outbound rules to its Open vSwitch

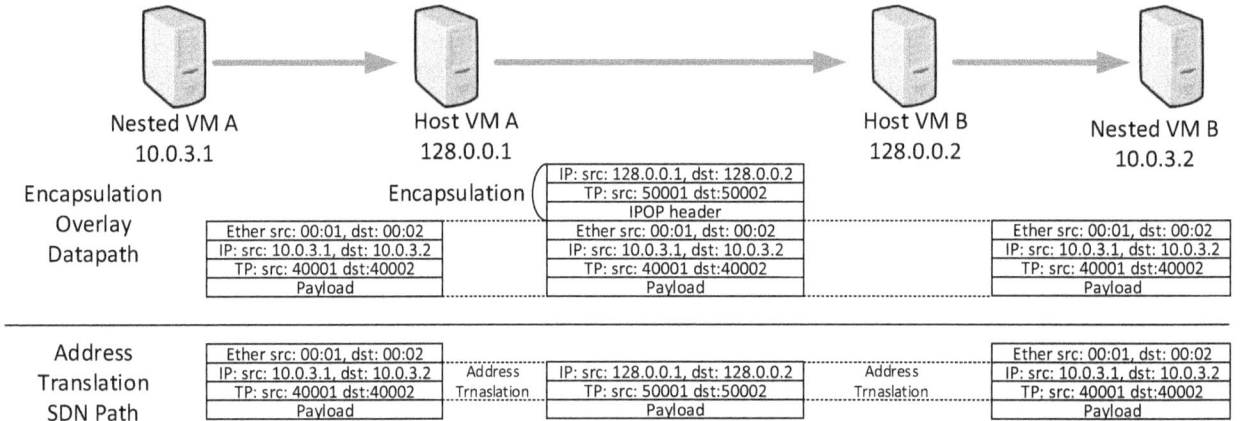

Figure 6: Virtualization comparison of datapath

Table 1: Stream Bypass Rule Example

		match	action
local host	outbound	nw_src=10.0.3.1, nw_dst=10.0.3.2, tp_src=40001, tp_dst=40002	set_nw_src=128.0.0.1, set_nw_dst=128.0.0.2, set_tp_src=50001, set_tp_dst=50002
	inbound	nw_src=128.0.0.2, nw_dst=128.0.0.1, tp_src=50002, tp_dst=50001	set_nw_src=10.0.3.2, set_nw_dst=10.0.3.1, set_tp_src=40002, set_tp_dst=40001
remote host	outbound	nw_src=10.0.3.2, nw_dst=10.0.3.1, tp_src=40002, tp_dst=40001	set_nw_src=128.0.0.2, set_nw_dst=128.0.0.1, set_tp_src=50002, set_tp_dst=50001
	inbound	nw_src=128.0.0.1, nw_dst=128.0.0.2, tp_src=50001, tp_dst=50002	set_nw_src=10.0.3.1, set_nw_dst=10.0.3.2, set_tp_src=40001, set_tp_dst=40002

SDN switch. The VIAS controller at host B then sends an acknowledgement RPC to host A through the overlay link, so that it makes sure that the outbound rule in local host is programmed only after all the other rules programmed. This ordering of events needs to be enforced to avoid packet loss during the setup of bypass rules. If we set local outbound rule before the other flow rules, the stream will have packets silently discarded by the SDN switch because of no matching rules. Finally, right after the final outbound rules are programmed in OpenFlow switches, the stream bypasses encapsulation and transfers packets through SDN switches on both endpoints.

This approach can be seen as an approach akin to NATs, as it provides the ability to map and translate addresses. However, unlike the conventional use of NAT, where each individual NAT is independently controlled, this scheme orchestrates the programming of mappings across controllers on both peer endpoints. VIAS essentially uses overlay link as control channels for coordination among the two peer SDN controllers to establish NAT mappings simultaneously across endpoints, allowing both nodes behind NATs to have a direct SDN flow that bypasses the overlay.

5. EVALUATION

In this section, we evaluate VIAS from three different perspectives. Firstly, in addition to providing overlay networking and bypass paths, VIAS acts as an OpenFlow-programmed SDN bridge and NAT for nested VMs. Typically, nested VMs create virtual network interfaces bound to a host Linux bridge and NAT behavior is implemented using iptables. To evaluate the VIAS SDN bridge/NAT, we compare the performance of Open vSwitch-based VIAS to the native Linux bridge/NAT implementation. The second evaluation considers the throughput delivered by VIAS for TCP streams between nested VMs within and across cloud providers. Thirdly, we use an application-layer benchmark (Redis) to evaluate end-to-end VIAS performance. For all experiments, we use Ubuntu Linux 14.04 LTS hosts provisioned from clouds, software SDN switches (Open vSwitch version 2.0.2), and LXC containers [14] inside the host to create nested instances. VIAS is implemented as extensions to IPOP 15.01 using RYU as a framework for OpenFlow handling.

5.1 VIAS Open vSwitch bridge/NAT

As pointed out in Section 4.1, OpenFlow is not capable to program flow rules to handle NATting of ICMP echo request/reply. Consequently, all ICMP echo request/reply packets are forwarded by the SDN switch to the VIAS controller: the controller itself handles NAT for ICMP packets by making an entry in a local table for every outgoing ICMP echo request message, using the ICMP echo identifier field as a key to this table. Even though the VIAS controller runs in the same host as Open vSwitch, ICMP handling incurs overheads.

We compare Open vSwitch NAT overhead with the native

Table 2: ICMP and TCP performance comparison between Linux NAT and NAT featured openvswitch of VIAS

	Test case	host VM		guest VM	
		ICMP	TCP	ICMP	TCP
S1	native	0.487 ms [±0.104]	5.24 Gbps [±0.421]	0.569 ms [±0.0611]	4.09 Gbps [±0.406]
	Open vSwitch	7.76 ms [±0.790]	4.87 Gbps [±0.577]	7.76 ms [±0.686]	3.86 Gbps [±0.518]
	percent change	1493 %	- 7.06 %	1264 %	-5.62 %
S2	native	41.7 ms [±0.269]	547 Mbps [±10.4]	41.7 ms [±0.514]	411 Mbps [±85.6]
	Open vSwitch	49.2 ms [±1.35]	527 Mbps [±48.9]	49.3 ms [±0.978]	398 Mbps [±83.1]
	percent change	17.9 %	-3.80 %	18.2 %	-3.16 %

Standard deviation is shown in square brackets

Linux bridge/NAT implemented by iptables in Table 2. In the experiment, host VMs are deployed in the CloudLab IG-DDC Cluster in Utah and are provisioned with 862MB of memory. We run 50 ping tests (ICMP echo) and 10 iperf throughput (TCP) tests and report the arithmetic mean (and standard deviation), considering a client in CloudLab and two different servers. One server (S1) resides in the same CloudLab cluster. The other server (S2) is provisioned as an m1.small instance with 2GB memory in the Chameleon cloud [3] in Texas.

As the results show, a latency overhead of about 7 ms is incurred in ICMP NAT handling, irrespective of the network distance to the server. This is because the overhead mostly comes from the inter-process communication between between Open vSwitch and the VIAS controller, and kernel/user context switch. This overhead is acceptable, as the ICMP echo message is typically used for network reachability checks and not for latency-sensitive applications.

The TCP iperf test results shows that the bridge/NAT throughput degrades about 3-7% compared to native Linux iptables. As Open vSwitch developers argue that the TCP performance is equivalent to that of Linux bridge [19], the slight performance degradation observed is due to the NAT rules programmed by VIAS. The NAT rules in the native Linux case are set by iptables and executed in Linux network kernel, while the VIAS NAT is implemented by flow rules inside Open vSwitch.

5.2 Microbenchmarks

This experiment evaluates the performance of VIAS for virtual network communication among nested VM instances. To this end, we have deployed VIAS on multiple cloud service platforms, including commercial and academic clouds. This allows the evaluation of functionality and performance for intra- and inter-cloud deployments across various geographical locations. We demonstrate that the nested containers separated by multiple NATs across multiple clouds are successfully connected by a virtual layer-2 network, and evaluate the performance of ARP, TCP, and ICMP protocols.

The following test cases are considered. The first case (CC) uses two Xen VMs deployed on CloudLab [4]. Each VM is provisioned with 862MB memory on CloudLab IG-DDC. The second case (AA) uses two Amazon EC2 instances of type t2.medium in the same zone (Oregon). Although Amazon does not provide specifications of network throughput of t2.medium (only mentioning that its low to

moderate), based on our link test in Figure 7, the performance levels are commensurate to an 1Gbps Ethernet link. The third case (GG) uses two Google compute engine instances of n1-standard-1 at US central zone. Host physical machine was provisioned on Intel(R) Xeon(R) CPU @ 2.30GHz and 3.7GB memory. In the fourth case (AA_dz), we run experiments also with t2.medium Amazon EC2 instances, but with VMs distributed across two availability zones (N. Virginia and Oregon) for comparison. Finally, the fifth case (AG_dz) considers two instances deployed across two different cloud service providers. One instance is on Amazon EC2 (t2.medium) at Oregon and the other instance is on Google compute engine (n1-standard-1) at US central.

Column *physical* is the latency between host VMs. The *overlay* column shows the latency between nested VMs. The traffic streams through overlay datapath from Linux bridge to tap device to P2P tunnel. The *VIAS* column shows the latency of overlay datapath with Open vSwitch and tap device. Note that, for the VIAS column, ARP and ICMP is forwarded to SDN controller, incurring additional latency.

ARP: The ARP latency is measured using iputils-arping and is shown on Table 3. The test is repeated 50 times, and the arithmetic mean and standard deviation are reported. The results for the AA, CC and GG case show that the overhead of ARP handling in overlay is less than 1.5 ms, while in VIAS, the latency overheads are in the range of 4-24ms, due to inter-process communication and SDN controller processing. Surprisingly, the results show an exceptionally long latency of ARP across host Xen VMs in one particular environment CC – the overlay and VIAS latencies are smaller than physical network. While we were not able to definitively determine the reason for this behavior, one observation is that the VIAS and the overlay paths use UDP as the protocol, whereas arping on the host VMs uses the ARP protocol. It is possible that the CloudLab platform handles ARP and UDP in different ways – since ARP traffic is relatively infrequent, the effects of delay in overall network performance are typically not significant. The ARP measurements in the AA case show that physical latency is lowest.

Naturally, geographically separated nested VMs (AA_dz and AG_dz) exhibit longer ARP latencies due to network distance; this is observed in the results summarized in the overlay column. Note that because the AA_dz and AG_dz instances are not in the same LAN segment, ARP traffic in the physical network is not supported, hence the physical column shows N/A. Furthermore, we could not evalu-

Table 3: ARP and ICMP latency comparison among conventional Linux implementation, overlay datapath and VIAS

Test	ARP [ms]			ICMP [ms]		
case	Physical	Overlay	VIAS	Physical	Overlay	VIAS
CC	432 [±243]	1.47 [±0.130]	24.4 [±0.102]	0.954 [±0.121]	1.17 [±0.0825]	15.4 [±1.20]
AA	0.693 [±0.0357]	1.42 [±0.0805]	4.00 [±0.120]	0.559 [±0.132]	0.970 [±0.149]	5.33 [±0.197]
GG	N/A	0.4207 [±0.126]	4.63 [±0.372]	0.421 [±0.126]	0.697 [±0.0843]	6.22 [±0.409]
AA_dz	N/A	84.5 [±0.243]	N/A	84.6 [±0.400]	92.5 [±0.169]	N/A
AG_dz	N/A	49.7 [±0.116]	N/A	50.7 [±0.101]	50.2 [±0.379]	N/A

CC: cloudlab AA:Amazon GG:Google compute engine AG:Amazon-Google dz:different zone. Standard deviation is shown in square brackets

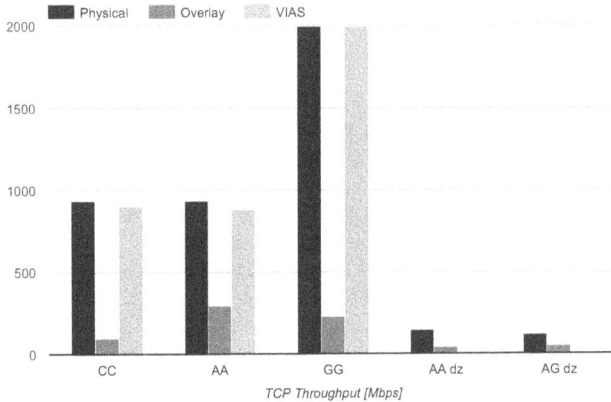

Figure 7: TCP performance comparison among physical, overlay datapath and VIAS bypass virtualization scenario

ate ARP in GG case, because Google compute engine does not provide layer 2 abstraction among instances deployed in the same zone, and thus the ARP protocol does not work. Nonetheless, the results demonstrate that, regardless of providers blocking L2 traffic within or across clouds, VIAS can present a L2 virtual network to nested VMs.

ICMP: ICMP echo latency is measured using the Linux ping command. We repeated the test 50 times, and report the arithmetic mean and standard deviation of the latency. The trend is similar with the ARP latency. The latency overhead is of the order of a few milliseconds across all test cases. Since the overhead only concerns in local kernel/user boundary crossing and local socket interface, the nested VM latency is not a function of the physical network's latency, but rather a constant overhead at the endpoints.

TCP: In Figure 7, TCP throughputs with different configurations between nested VMs across different cloud services are summarized. The iperf tool is used to test the maximum TCP throughput; tests were repeated 10 times, and the arithmetic means are shwon. For the physical column, iperf was executed on the host VM, while for the overlay and SDN bypass columns, iperf was executed on the nested VMs. Note that the VIAS bypass is not shown for experiments across cloud data centers, where tunneling is used instead.

The results show that encapsulation in user space has its peak throughput at around a few of hundreds Mbps, regardless of link layer bandwidth. This overlay performance

is a function of the host processor's performance, and overheads associated with packet handling and copying and O/S kernel-user context switch. In contrast, SDN virtualization achieves over 94% of the throughput of the physical network when endpoints are in the same data center (cases CC, AA and GG). Note that this experiment considers a software Open vSwitch that runs on the host VM, and does not use any assist from SDN hardware – though in principle VIAS can also program hardware-layer SDN switches, if available. Nonetheless, by eliminating O/S context switch and overlay packet handling through the VIAS SDN overlay bypass results in substantial performance improvements for network virtualization.

As described in Section 4.3, VIAS detects traffic-intensive TCP streams at runtime, and then automatically inserts bypass rules in the SDN fabric. Prior to completion of flow rule, TCP streams traverse the overlay datapath. Thus, there is a latency involved in the coordinated programming of flow rules in the SDN switch of both peer endpoints. This latency is a function of the round trip time between host VMs: we have measured the SDN bypass setup latency to be 13.5ms, 12.3ms and 2.63ms, respectively, in the CC, AA and GG cases. This latency is measured using the difference between the first packet and the last packet in the encapsulation path of each TCP stream.

5.3 Application Test

In this section, we show the virtualization performance at the application layer, using a round-trip latency sensitive application: Redis [22], a NoSQL, memory-based and key-value data structure storage system that is widely used. In the experiment, two host VMs are deployed in the CloudLab IG-DDC Cluster, provisioned with 862MB of memory. The test is done with the version 3.0.6 of Redis. The key length is 10 Bytes long and value length are set to 50 Bytes long, a common usage pattern of Redis [6]. For each run, clients make 1 million queries (50% sets and 50% gets). Every set packet size is 93 Bytes, and get return packets from the get are 36 and 57 Bytes, respectively.

Figure 8 shows the results of physical, overlay datapath, and VIAS SDN bypass cases. One important observation needs to be made – that the "Physical" case is one where when both Redis server and clients runs on the *host* VM, while in overlay datapath and SDN bypass cases, those run on *nested* containers. Each thread setup a single TCP stream with Redis server.

The throughput of VIAS SDN bypass is on par with the

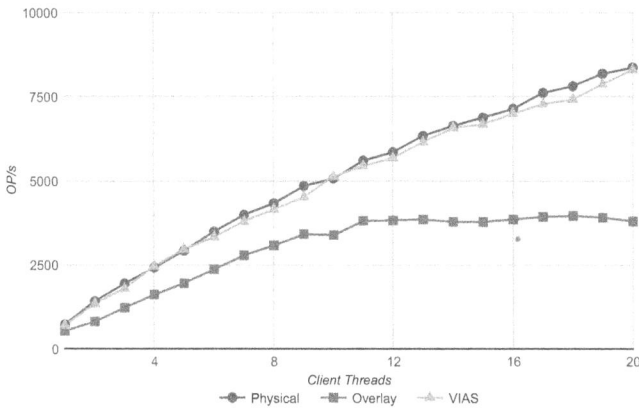

Figure 8: Redis simulation.

physical case, proportionally increasing the throughput as physical case with the increasing number of thread counts. On the contrary, overlay datapath throughput saturates around 4 KOP/S. The experiment shows that VIAS bypass performs significantly better than overlay encapsulation, and that it is capable to bypass multiple TCP streams simultaneously.

6. RELATED WORK

The idea of building user-level virtual networks for Grid-/cloud computing dates back to systems including Violin [11], VNET [29], and IPOP [8]. Violin proposed overlay virtual networks providing the abstraction of separate layer-2 networks for tenants. Violin was implemented without requiring any modifications on the VMM or the hosting network infrastructure, not only providing flexible user configurable network environment, but also reducing the threat of security risk from the host. VNET addressed a similar problem, focusing on the ability to inter-connect virtual machines across providers. This was accomplished by running VNET "proxies" on endpoints (e.g. VMs) at different sites, and tunneling L2 traffic over TCP/TLS links.

A limitation of these systems is performance – nowadays, cloud network infrastructure performance is 1Gbps or higher, making it challenging to deliver high-performance network virtualization at the application layer on commodity CPUs. VNET/P [34] addresses the performance gap by implementing a kernel module for layer 2 virtualization of guest VMs inside the VMM increasing the performance of virtual networks substantially by moving virtualization process from user space to a VMM module. It showed that it can achieve line speed performance virtualization in 1 Gbps network and 78% in 10 Gbps network. However, it requires changes to the VMM, which hinders deployment of this technique. VIAS seeks to also bypass user-level processing, but does so while reusing existing, unmodified systems by leveraging software SDN switches. Our experiments have shown that it is possible to deploy VIAS in existing cloud infrastructures (Amazon EC2, Google compute engine, CloudLab) without requiring any changes to VMMs nor VM images – VIAS only requires user-level software to be installed.

Another approach to minimize context switch between kernel and userspace is Netmap [23]. It eliminates the copy operation by using shared buffer and metadata between kernel and user space, showing that it achieves 20x speedups compared to conventional APIs. However, netmap relies on its own custom kernel module, again hindering the ability to deploy on commodity systems.

Instead of providing full virtual network to the users, VirtualWire [33] takes advantage of connect/disconnect primitives, which are assumed to be exposed by the cloud service provider. Their implementation requires changes to a Xen-blanket hypervisor, while VIAS can be deployed without changes to the VMM. Furthermore, VIAS makes no assumption about the primitives exposed by a provider to manage connectors – VIAS overlay links can be established even when cloud instances are constrained by NATs.

NVP [13] is closely related as it also shows combined version of tunneling and SDN fabric. It provides REST APIs to the tenants to expose network virtualization capabilities. Network elements such as switches and ports are presented to the tenants, and tenants build topology of their network. Then, tunnels and flow rules are created and programmed by NVP to each hardware and software OpenFlow switches to forward packets among VMs deployed intra and inter clouds. However, NVP is designed to support multiple tenants in a single cloud provider. Unlike VIAS, its techniques do not support inter-cloud network virtualization.

7. CONCLUSIONS AND FUTURE WORK

This paper presented the novel architecture of VIAS, and demonstrated its ability to automatically provide fast virtual network paths within a cloud provider via coordinated programming of SDN switches, while retaining the ability to dynamically establish inter-cloud virtual private network tunnel. The main contribution of this paper is a novel user-level approach to distributed, coordinated control of overlay and SDN controllers, supporting private inter-cloud and high-performance intra-cloud network virtualization flows.

VIAS leverages existing system-level VMM/kernel software without modifications, and has been demonstrated to work by extending existing overlay software (IPOP) and SDN platforms (RYU, Open vSwitch) in realistic cloud computing environments, including Amazon EC2 and Google compute engine. Results showed that VIAS can provide flexible layer 2 virtual network, in particular to nested virtualization environments, where tenants deploy containers across multiple providers.

While this paper has only quantitatively evaluated the use of VIAS with software virtual switches, the use of the OpenFlow standard allows VIAS to tap into hardware SDN resources, if available. In future work, we plan to offload the processing overhead of network virtualization from software to hardware OpenFlow devices.

8. ACKNOWLEDGMENTS

This material is based upon work supported in part by the National Science Foundation under Grants No. 1527415, 1339737 and 1234983, and by the Department of Defense award W911NF-13-1-0157. Any opinions, findings, and conclusions or recommendations expressed in this material are those of the author(s) and do not necessarily reflect the views of the National Science Foundation or the Department of Defense. The authors acknowledge the use of NSFCloud resources (CloudLab and Chameleon) for experiments.

9. REFERENCES

[1] AWS SDK for Python (Boto3). https://aws.amazon.com/sdk-for-python/.

[2] M. Ben-Yehuda et al. The turtles project: Design and implementation of nested virtualization. In *Proceedings of the 9th USENIX Conference on Operating Systems Design and Implementation*, OSDI'10, pages 1–6, Berkeley, CA, USA, 2010. USENIX Association.

[3] Chameleon. https://www.chameleoncloud.org/.

[4] CloudLab. http://cloudlab.us/.

[5] E. Deelman et al. Pegasus, a workflow management system for science automation. In *Future Generation Computer Systems Volume 46*, pages 17–35, 2015.

[6] W. Felter et al. An updated performance comparison of virtual machines and linux containers. IBM technical report RC25482 (AUS1407-001), 2014.

[7] A. Fishman et al. Hvx: Virtualizing the cloud. In *Presented as part of the 5th USENIX Workshop on Hot Topics in Cloud Computing*, Berkeley, CA, 2013. USENIX.

[8] A. Ganguly, A. Agrawal, P. O. Boykin, and R. Figueiredo. Ip over p2p: enabling self-configuring virtual ip networks for grid computing. In *Proceedings 20th IEEE International Parallel Distributed Processing Symposium*, pages 10 pp.–, April 2006.

[9] Google Cloud Platform. gcloud Tool Guide. https://cloud.google.com/sdk/gcloud/.

[10] E. Hernandez-Valencia et al. How will NFV/SDN transform service provider opex? *Network, IEEE*, 29(3):60–67, May 2015.

[11] X. Jiang and D. Xu. Violin: Virtual internetworking on overlay infrastructure. In *Parallel and Distributed Processing and Applications*, volume 3358 of *Lecture Notes in Computer Science*, pages 937–946. Springer Berlin Heidelberg, 2005.

[12] P. S. Juste et al. Tincan: User-defined p2p virtual network overlays for ad-hoc collaboration. *EAI Endorsed Transactions on Collaborative Computing*, 14(2), 10 2014.

[13] T. Koponen et al. Network virtualization in multi-tenant datacenters. In *11th USENIX Symposium on Networked Systems Design and Implementation (NSDI 14)*, pages 203–216, Seattle, WA, Apr. 2014. USENIX Association.

[14] Linux Containers. https://linuxcontainers.org/.

[15] R. Mahy et al. Traversal Using Relays around NAT (TURN): Relay Extensions to Session Traversal Utilities for NAT (STUN). RFC 5389, April 2010.

[16] N. McKeown et al. Openflow: Enabling innovation in campus networks. *SIGCOMM Comput. Commun. Rev.*, 38(2):69–74, Mar. 2008.

[17] Open vSwitch. http://www.openvswitch.org/.

[18] A. M. Oprescu and T. Kielmann. Bag-of-tasks scheduling under budget constraints. In *Cloud Computing Technology and Science (CloudCom), 2010 IEEE Second International Conference on*, pages 351–359, Nov 2010.

[19] B. Pfaff et al. The design and implementation of open vswitch. In *12th USENIX Symp. on Networked Systems Design and Implementation (NSDI 15)*, pages 117–130, Oakland, CA, May 2015. USENIX Assoc.

[20] G. J. Popek and R. P. Goldberg. Formal requirements for virtualizable third generation architectures. *Commun. ACM*, 17(7):412–421, July 1974.

[21] K. Razavi et al. Kangaroo: A Tenant-Centric Software-Defined Cloud Infrastructure. In *Proc. of the IEEE International Conference on Cloud Engineering*, Tempe, AZ, USA, United States, Mar. 2015.

[22] Redis. http://redis.io/.

[23] L. Rizzo. netmap: A Novel Framework for Fast Packet I/O. In *21st USENIX Security Symposium (USENIX Security 12)*, pages 101–112, Bellevue, WA, Aug. 2012. USENIX Association.

[24] J. Rosenberg. Interactive Connectivity Establishment (ICE): A Protocol for Network Address Translator (NAT) Traversal for Offer/Answer ProtocolsA Border Gateway Protocol 4 (BGP-4). RFC 5245, April 2010.

[25] J. Rosenberg et al. Session Traversal Utilities for NAT (STUN). RFC 5389, October 2008.

[26] Ryu SDN Framework. http://osrg.github.io/ryu/.

[27] T. Saad et al. Tunneling techniques for end-to-end VPNs: generic deployment in an optical testbed environment. In *Broadband Networks, 2005. BroadNets 2005. 2nd International Conference on*, pages 859–865 Vol. 2, Oct 2005.

[28] I. Stoica et al. Chord: A scalable peer-to-peer lookup service for internet applications. In *Proceedings of the 2001 Conference on Applications, Technologies, Architectures, and Protocols for Computer Communications*, SIGCOMM '01, pages 149–160, New York, NY, USA, 2001. ACM.

[29] A. I. Sundararaj and P. A. Dinda. Towards virtual networks for virtual machine grid computing. In *Proceedings of the 3rd Conference on Virtual Machine Research And Technology Symposium - Volume 3*, VM'04, pages 14–14, Berkeley, CA, USA, 2004. USENIX Association.

[30] R. Uhlig et al. Intel virtualization technology. *Computer*, 38(5):48–56, May 2005.

[31] G. Wang and T. Ng. The impact of virtualization on network performance of amazon ec2 data center. In *INFOCOM, 2010 Proceedings IEEE*, pages 1–9, March 2010.

[32] D. Williams et al. The xen-blanket: Virtualize once, run everywhere. In *Proceedings of the 7th ACM European Conference on Computer Systems*, EuroSys '12, pages 113–126, New York, NY, USA, 2012. ACM.

[33] D. Williams et al. VirtualWires for Live Migrating Virtual Networks across Clouds. IBM Research Report RC25378, 2013.

[34] L. Xia et al. VNET/P: Bridging the Cloud and High Performance Computing Through Fast Overlay Networking. In *Proc. of the 21st International Symposium on High-Performance Parallel and Distributed Computing*, HPDC '12, pages 259–270, New York, NY, USA, 2012. ACM.

[35] F. Zhang et al. Cloudvisor: Retrofitting protection of virtual machines in multi-tenant cloud with nested virtualization. In *Proc. of the Twenty-Third ACM Symposium on Operating Systems Principles*, SOSP '11, pages 203–216, New York, NY, USA, 2011. ACM.

Wiera: Towards Flexible Multi-Tiered Geo-Distributed Cloud Storage Instances

Kwangsung Oh, Abhishek Chandra, and Jon Weissman
Department of Computer Science and Engineering
University of Minnesota Twin Cities
Minneapolis, MN 55455
{ohkwang, chandra, jon}@cs.umn.edu

ABSTRACT

Geo-distributed cloud storage systems must tame complexity at many levels: uniform APIs for storage access, supporting flexible storage policies that meet a wide array of application metrics, handling uncertain network dynamics and access dynamism, and operating across many levels of heterogeneity both within and across data-centers. In this paper, we present an integrated solution called Wiera. Wiera extends our earlier cloud storage system, Tiera, that is targeted to multi-tiered policy-based single cloud storage, to the wide-area and multiple data-centers (even across different providers). Wiera enables the specification of global data management policies built on top of local Tiera policies. Such policies enable the user to optimize for cost, performance, reliability, durability, and consistency, both within and across data-centers, and to express their tradeoffs. A key aspect of Wiera is first-class support for dynamism due to network, workload, and access patterns changes. Wiera policies can adapt to changes in user workload, poorly performing data tiers, failures, and changes in user metrics (e.g., cost). Wiera allows *unmodified applications* to reap the benefits of flexible data/storage policies by externalizing the policy specification. As far as we know, Wiera is the first geo-distributed cloud storage system which handles dynamism actively at run-time. We show how Wiera enables a rich specification of dynamic policies using a concise notation and describe the design and implementation of the system. We have implemented a Wiera prototype on multiple cloud environments, AWS and Azure, that illustrates potential benefits from managing dynamics and in using multiple cloud storage tiers both within and across data-centers.

Keywords

Data Locality; Multi-DCs; Multi-tiered storage; Wide Area Storage; In Memory Storage

HPDC'16, May 31-June 04, 2016, Kyoto, Japan

© 2016 ACM. ISBN 978-1-4503-4314-5/16/05...$15.00

DOI: http://dx.doi.org/10.1145/2907294.2907322

1. INTRODUCTION

Today, the use of multiple geo-distributed datacenters (DCs) is commonly used to provide Internet services and applications to users that are distributed geographically. This mode of deployment not only reduces user-perceived latency by putting data close to users but also provides higher data availability and better fault tolerance by replicating data to multiple locations. Although this idea is simple, it introduces many complexities for the owner of the application and/or the data, 1) the number and location of replicas as a function of the desired consistency model, 2) degree of fault tolerance, 3) expected workload, and 4) metrics of interest such as user-perceived latency, cost, and so on. This is further complicated by the dynamics of the network environment, cloud services, and applications. Thus, static decisions or policies will not be effective. For example, application workload may vary over time with the storage system seeing a write-intensive pattern at first as new data is created and stored followed by a read-intensive pattern as that data is retrieved. This pattern is common in many data analytics applications. Similarly, the location of active users or the demand for data may change over time based on changing popularity, trends and user interests, especially for Internet services.

While some geo-distributed storage systems [3, 22, 1] have been proposed, they typically re-evaluate storage policies on very coarse time-scales such as hours-to-weeks and make assumptions that may not always be true (e.g., SPANStore assumes users are static). This results in policies that may be inadequate in a wide-area multiple-tier environment that spans different storage providers in which time-scales of change may be much shorter. Examples would include bursty demand due to flash crowds, temporary network outages, and changes in application access pattern type (reads vs. writes), all of which may occur at short time scales (seconds to minutes). Additionally, these systems generally do not exploit the wide diversity of storage characteristics available at different tiers of the cloud storage hierarchy both within and across data-centers and different providers. Different cloud providers offer multiple cloud storage services[1] with different characteristics such as durability, performance, and cost across their constituent DCs. Exploiting such diversity both within and *across* cloud storage providers can yield greater storage options and therefore greater benefits. Moreover, the number of DCs has been increasing continuously suggesting this opportunity will only grow. Ac-

---

[1] In this paper, we use the term storage tier and storage service interchangeably.

cording to datacentermap.com [10], there were 171 DCs as of Sep 2014 but 201 as of Dec 2015 within only the US West (California) region. So it seems clear that applications will have many more storage options to place data given the increased density of DCs. In a previous paper [15] we showed that applications can benefit by using multiple DCs within the same region.[2]

To address these challenges and opportunities, we present a new geo-distributed cloud storage system called Wiera (or Wide-area tIERA) that builds upon our Tiera cloud storage system [18]. Tiera provides storage instances that span the storage hierarchy within a single data-center for a single cloud provider. Wiera extends Tiera in multiple dimensions: to the wide-area across different data-centers, across different cloud providers, and enables policies that can respond to dynamism at short time scales (seconds to minutes). As with Tiera, the client is shielded from the underlying complexity introduced by multiple storage tiers across multiple DCs by a simple PUT/GET API and the encapsulation of storage policies. Wiera supports *global policies* by leveraging the local policy framework within each Tiera instance. A Wiera storage instance logically contains many Tiera instances distributed across the wide-area. We present the design and implementation of the Wiera system, show how a rich array of policies can be easily expressed in Wiera, and evaluate its performance on a live multi-cloud system to show its potential.

The key contributions of this paper are:

- The design and implementation of the Wiera system, an integrated geo-distributed cloud storage system that runs both within and across data-centers owned by different cloud providers.

- Mechanisms for easily specifying a rich array of global storage policies across a geo-distributed multi-tiered cloud storage environment including several common policies from the literature.

- First-class support for handling network and application dynamics within the storage policies to achieve user metrics (e.g., reduced cost, latency, and so on).

- Flexibility that allows *unmodified applications* to furhter reap benefits by replacing data/storage policies externalized at run-time.

- An empirical evaluation of the Wiera prototype in the Amazon AWS and Microsoft Azure clouds, showing that the use of non-local data-center storage tiers can result in: improved performance, reduced cost, and desired consistency at lower overhead.

The remainder of this paper is organized as follows. Section 2 provides a brief overview of Tiera upon which Wiera is built. Section 3 provides an overview of Wiera including its architecture and examples of global policies. Section 4 explains the implementation details of a Wiera prototype in the AWS (Amazon) and Azure (Microsoft) clouds. Section 5 discusses the results of our experimental evaluation. The results demonstrates that Wiera handles dynamics and achieves benefits by utilizing disparate storage tiers across multiple DCs and cloud providers. Section 6 reviews related work. Section 7 concludes the paper.

---

[2]We use the term region to represent a specific location e.g., US West, US East, and Europe West.

2. BACKGROUND

Wiera extends Tiera in multiple directions: wide-area (e.g., multiple data-centers, regions, and providers), dynamism, and global policies. We provide a brief description of Tiera as a background for understanding Wiera. Readers may consult the Tiera paper [18] for additional technical details.

2.1 Tiera Instance

Cloud service providers offer multiple storage tiers with different characteristics, performance, durability, and cost for storage. For example, Amazon provides ElastiCache (a caching service protocol compliant to Memcached), S3 (Simple Storage Service), EBS (Elastic Block Store), and Glacier as different cloud storage options. These storage services generally optimize one metric trading off others. For instance, an application can get better performance from ElastiCache but at high cost and low durability, compared to using S3. Thus, it is common to see applications seeking to obtain composite benefits from multiple cloud storage tiers, e.g., putting hot data in memory using ElastiCache for better performance and cold data in S3 for higher durability and reduced cost with much lower performance. However, accessing multiple storage tiers introduces significant complexities to the application because different tiers have different interfaces and different data models. At the same time, it creates a burden to specify and program policies to manage data across the different storage tiers to realize the desired metric(s). To address these problems, a Tiera instance encapsulates multiple cloud storage tiers and enables easy specification of a rich array of data storage policies to achieve desired tradeoffs. An important property of Tiera is that it can be inserted into an existing application framework with minimal or no code changes.

Two primary mechanisms—*event* and *response*—are used to express policies and manage data within the instance. An *event* is the occurrence of some condition and a response is the action executed on the occurrence of an event. Tiera supports different kinds of events such as *timer*, *threshold*, and *action* events. Tiera also supports *responses* such as *store*, *retrieve*, *copy*, *move*, *encrypt*, *compress*, *delete*, and *grow* to react to the events. New events and responses will be added in support of Wiera as we will show in Section 3.2.3. A Tiera instance is defined by specifying the following: the desired storage tiers, their capacities, and a set of events along with their responses. For example, Figure 1(a) and 1(b) show Tiera instances for low latency and for persistent data respectively. **LowLatencyInstance** (Figure 1(a)) uses two storage tiers, Memcached for performance and EBS for data persistence. For better performance, the instance will *put* data into memory first and then copy data back into EBS for persistence (write-back policy) responsive to a timer event. **PersistentInstance** (Figure 1(b)) trades performance for better data durability. This instance uses a small Memcached area to cache the most recently written data and copies data to EBS immediately when data is inserted into Memcached according to a *write-through* policy. This example also shows a simple backup policy which copies data into a more durable storage tier S3 if data in EBS is filled more than 50%. In this instance, an application may want to move data to Glacier instead of S3 not only for durable storage but also to reduce the price of cold data. Using these policies, the client of a Tiera instance is

```
Tiera LowLatencyInstance(time t) {
    % two tiers specified with initial sizes
    tier1: {name: Memcached, size: 5G};
    tier2: {name: EBS, size: 5G};

    % action event defined to always store data
    % into Memcached
    event(insert.into) : response {
        insert.object.dirty = true;
        store(what:insert.object, to:tier1);
    }

    % write back policy: copying data to
    % persistent store on a timer event
    event(time=t) : response {
        copy(what: object.location == tier1 &&
                    object.dirty == true,
            to:tier2);
    }
}
```

```
Tiera PersistentInstance(time t) {
    tier1: {name: Memcached, size: 5G};
    tier2: {name: EBS, size: 5G};
    tier3: {name: S3, size: 10G};

    % write-through policy using action event data
    % and copy response
    event(insert.into == tier1) : response {
        copy(what:insert.object, to:tier2);
    }

    % simple backup policy
    event(tier2.filled == 50%) : response {
        copy(what:object.location == tier2,
                to:tier3, bandwidth:40KB/s);
    }
}
```

(a) LowLatency Tiera instance.

(b) Persistent Tiera instance.

Figure 1: Tiera instance specifications.

shielded from the underlying complexity introduced by the multi-tiered cloud storage services.

2.2 Data Model

Data in Tiera is stored as objects[14] treated as an uninterpreted variable size sequence of bytes that can represent any type of application data, e.g., text files, tables, images, etc. Each object is immutable (i.e., cannot be modified) and can be accessed through a *globally* unique identifier that acts as the *key* to access the corresponding *value* stored. It is up to the application to decide the keyspace from which to select this globally unique identifier. Tiera exposes a simple PUT/GET API to allow applications to store and retrieve data. An object stored into Tiera cannot be edited, though an application can choose to overwrite an object. To support policy specification, Tiera provides several common attributes or metadata for each object such as: size, access frequency, dirty bit, modified time, location (i.e., which storage tier), and last access time. In addition, each object can be assigned a set of tags which enables an application to define object classes (those that share the same tag). The user can then easily specify policies that apply to all objects of a particular class. For example, an application could add a "tmp" tag to temporary file and a policy could dictate that objects with "tmp" tag are stored in inexpensive volatile storage. We have revised the Tiera data model to allow Wiera to manage multiple versions of an object as we will explain in Section 3.2.1.

3. WIERA OVERVIEW

In this section, we present an overview of Wiera, describing the Wiera architecture and data model, and mechanisms for defining global policies for managing data across multiple data centers.

3.1 Wiera Architecture

Wiera builds on top of Tiera in a geo-distributed setting: a *Wiera instance* consists of multiple Tiera instances running on multiple data centers. While *Tiera* is responsible for managing data on multiple storage tiers *within* a single DC, *Wiera* manages the data placement and movement

across multiple Tiera instances running on geo-distributed DCs. A Wiera instance simplifies the global data access for applications by hiding the complexities of accessing multiple Tiera instances. Wiera can launch and manage Tiera instances in multiple regions, and can enforce a global data management policy between them, as we will explain more fully in Section 3.3.

Figure 2 shows the Wiera architecture. Wiera consists of the following main components:

- The Wiera User Interface (WUI) provides an API to applications to manage Wiera instances (Table 1). The API allows applications to: launch multiple Tiera instances as part of a Wiera instance with a global policy specification, stop instances, and get the list of currently running instances.

- Global Policy Manager (GPM) creates a new policy for a Wiera instance. It stores metadata for the policy and executes a Tiera Instance Manager (TIM) to manage the Tiera instances which belong to the Wiera instance.

- Tiera Server Manager (TSM) manages Tiera servers at different locations, which spawn and remove Tiera instances based on application requests. For instance, if the application calls *startInstances* through WUI to start Tiera instances at Region 1 and Region 2, TSM will direct the Tiera servers in Region 1 and Region 2 to each spawn a new Tiera instance.

We will explain how these components work together in more detail in Section 4. Wiera also includes other components such as a network monitor, workload monitor, and data placement manager. The network monitor aggregates latency information for handling requests from each instance and latencies between instances. The workload monitor aggregates workload related information such as users' locations (number of requests from each instance), access patterns, and object sizes. Based on this aggregated information, a data placement manager could generate a dynamic global policy automatically. In this paper, we focus on defining different policies, and such automated policy generation is left as future work.

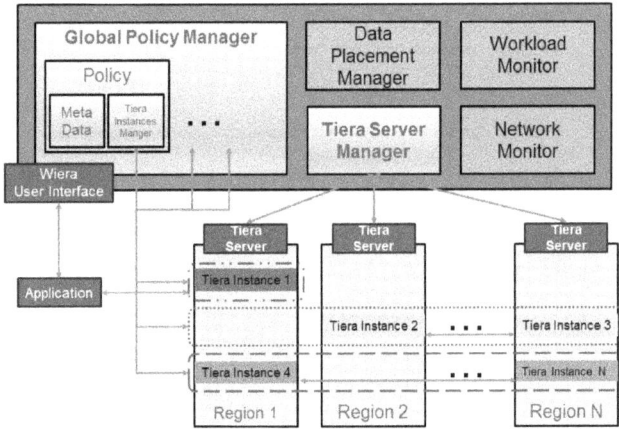

Figure 2: Wiera Architecture.

Table 1: Wiera Instance Management API

API	Arguments	Function
startInstances	wiera_instance_id, policy	Launch instances
stopInstances	wiera_instance_id	Stop instances
getInstances	wiera_instance_id	Get instances list

3.2 Changes and New Features in Wiera

As mentioned above, Wiera manages multiple geo-distributed Tiera instances. In order to handle data across multiple regions, we have extended the Tiera data model and policy mechanisms to support several key requirements: data replication and consistency across multiple locations; load balancing, locality-awareness, and fault tolerance; scalability of existing Tiera stores to multiple DCs; and modular construction of storage containers. In this section, we describe some of the changes and newly added features in Wiera.

3.2.1 Data Model Extension

In order to support low latency and fault tolerance, a Wiera instance can replicate data across multiple locations. Such replication could result in multiple copies of the same

Table 2: Wiera Object Versioning API

API	Arguments	Function
get	string key	Retrieve the latest version of object
getVersion	string key, integer version	Retrieve specific version of object
getVersionList	string key	Retrieve list of available version of object
put	string key, binary object	Store object
update	string key, integer version, binary object	Update specific version of object
remove	string key	Remove all version of object
removeVersion	string key, integer version	Remove specific version of object

data object in different locations, each with a potentially different state depending on the consistency model being used. As mentioned in Section 2.2, an object stored in Tiera is considered immutable, so that it cannot be modified but only overwritten. In order to support replication and consistency control, we have extended the Tiera data model to allow maintaining multiple versions of an object. Thus, modification of an existing object now results in the creation of a *new version* of the object. By default, an application will be provided with an appropriate object version based on its consistency policy (e.g., its local version for eventual consistency, the latest version for a primary-based consistency, etc.). An application can specify the object version number if it needs to access old versions. Old versions of objects will be stored until they are required to be garbage collected in the policy specification. Wiera exposes an object versioning API to applications as shown in Table 2.

3.2.2 Modular Instances

To provide *scalability and flexibility* to applications, a Tiera instance can specify another Tiera instance as a storage tier. This lets applications easily add pre-defined instances and easily extend Tiera instances to other regions where other Tiera instances are already running. For example, an application launches Tiera instances with a policy id (a) `RAW-BIG-DATA-INSTANCES`, for storing a big data size within a durable and cheap storage tier. Later, the application may launch other Tiera instances with a policy id (b) `INTERMEDIATE-DATA` which encapsulates `RAW-BIG-DATA-INSTANCES` as a read-only storage tier for retrieving raw data and local Memcached as another storage tier to store intermediate data for better performance. This can enable the modular assembly of complex storage containers.

3.2.3 New Events and Responses

In a geo-distributed setting, clients may access data from different regions. The placement and replication of data can have significant impact on the application's latency of access, load across different DCs, and consistency of data. Wiera provides a number of new events and responses to support different policies to manage data across multiple locations. Wiera adds three new *monitoring events*: (1) *LatencyMonitoring events* that occur when data access requests take longer than a specified latency threshold (and thus, may violate an application's latency requirements), (2) *RequestsMonitoring events* that occur when a Tiera instance gets more requests than other instances (and thus, may be overloaded), and (3) *ColdDataMonitoring events* that occur when certain data is not accessed more recently than a specified time threshold (and hence, is cold). To react to these newly added events, Wiera also adds new *responses*: (1) *forward* that forwards a request to another Tiera instance (e.g., for load balancing), (2) *queue* that enqueues a request for lazy update to other locations (e.g., to reduce on update traffic), and (3) *change_consistency* that changes the consistency model between Tiera instances at run-time to handle workload dynamics.

3.3 Defining Global Policies

The data model extensions as well as the new *events* and *responses* discussed above give more flexibility to applications to specify a number of global data management policies, including many that have been proposed in the literature [22, 3, 1]. In this section, we explain how various global policies can be specified by showing some examples. Wiera extends Tiera instance specification to define data placement policy *across* multiple Tiera instances. The desired storage tiers, their capacities, and the set of events along with corresponding responses for each instance are now specified using a Wiera policy. The application needs to specify the regions where instances will be running. Note that all global policies in this section are just examples to show how they can be easily specified. Applications can modify these policies or create a new policy based on their requirements. Note that instances running at different locations can have different local policy specifications as well. In this paper, however, we use the same specification everywhere for simplicity, unless noted otherwise. Further, due to space constraints, we show the specification of *put* operation in our examples, and *get* operation also can be specified similarly.

3.3.1 Data Consistency Policy

We begin by showing how a desired data consistency model between Tiera instances can be easily specified through in a global Wiera policy. Figures 3(a), 3(b), and 4 show three different consistency policies: Multiple Primaries Consistency, Primary Backup Consistency, and Eventual Consistency respectively.

In the MultiPrimariesConsistency policy (Figure 3(a)) specification, multiple locations maintain replicas of the data and every update to any replica is synchronously transmitted to all other replicas. This policy can be used for services in which strong data consistency is more important than *put* operation performance, e.g., flight booking system and banking system. The figure shows how this policy is implemented using the Wiera events and responses. Here, the same Tiera instances (LowLatencyInstance from Figure 1(a)) are created on multiple regions. When an application puts an object into an instance (normally the closest Tiera instance), it tries to get a *global lock* first for the key as specified in the global policy. Once it gets the lock for the key, it stores the object into the local Memcached storage tier first as was explained in Figure 1(a). Then it distributes the update to other instances that are part of the same Wiera instance. The lock is released upon getting a response from all other instances.

In the PrimaryBackupConsistency policy (Figure 3(b)), there is only one primary replica. Here, if a Tiera instance gets a *put* request from an application and the instance is not the *primary*, it will simply forward it to the *primary* instance. This policy is simpler than MultiPrimariesConsistency policy and can provide better performance since no global lock is required, but the *primary* instance can be a bottleneck for overall performance. The application can trade off its desired consistency with performance in this policy. For instance, to minimize *get* latency, the primary can send updates to other instances synchronously by using a *copy* response, so that all replicas are up-to-date. On the other hand, to improve *put* latency, updates could be transmitted asynchronously by the primary using *queue* response.

An EventualConsistency policy (Figure 4) is desired for better PUT/GET operations latency, e.g., for social network services like Facebook and Twitter. Here, a *put* operation simply stores the object to the local replica first and then queues the update for distribution to other replicas later in the background. Applications can specify how frequently

```
Wiera EventualConsistency() {
    ...

    %Eventual Consistency
    event(insert.into) : response {
        store(what:insert.oject, to:local_instance)
        queue(what:insert.object, to:all_regions)
    }
}
```

Figure 4: Eventual consistency policy.

queued updates need to be distributed. In this consistency model, there is no specific order of put operations from each instance, thus each instance needs to handle object version conflicts when update requests come in from other instances as we will explain in Section 4 in more detail.

3.3.2 Defining Dynamic Policies

Since the network, workload, and placement of replicas can be dynamic, it would be desirable to have a dynamic policy that can change its actions at run-time.

One example of such a dynamic policy would be one that can adjust the consistency model based on observed latencies of operations. While strong consistency is desirable for better user experience, achieving strong consistency can be expensive in a geo-distributed cloud environment due to high WAN latency. For example, in the MultiPrimariesPolicy (Figure 3(a)), the latency for a *put* operation will depend on the highest round trip latency from the primary initiating the update to any replica. For instance, consider a policy that maintains strong consistency as long as the latencies are low, but switches to a weaker consistency model such as eventual consistency if the latencies become high. Some shopping web applications (like amazon.com) may get benefits by having different policies, strong consistency for more important data (purchase transactions), eventual (or causal) consistency for browsing data. When all operations can be performed with low latency, strong consistency can be used for all data access. In the high latency case, browsing data can use eventual consistency for better user-perceived latency.

Figure 5(a) shows how Wiera can specify such a dynamic consistency policy. In this figure, an application specifies the latency threshold (800 ms) and the duration (30 seconds) for which this latency threshold is exceeded. Once the *put* operations violates both conditions, Wiera changes the global consistency policy to *eventual consistency* at run-time for better *put* operation latency. Similarly, while using the *eventual consistency* model, once Wiera detects that the latency for *put* operations can satisfy the conditions for the strong consistency, it will switch them back to *strong consistency* policy at run-time. The change of consistency policy is done in a manner that allows all operations in progress (or queued) to be applied first. All new requests from applications arrived at when the consistency is being changed will be blocked and queued until the change takes effect.

Consider another case in which handling dynamics is required. Assuming a single primary, if the workload changes over time (e.g., client locations change with time of day), then moving the primary replica closer to the users might be desirable [3]. Figure 5(b) shows how this can be achieved with Wiera for the PrimaryBackupPolicy. If the primary instance discovers that another instance received (and forwarded) more requests from an application than the pri-

```
Wiera MultiPrimariesConsistency() {
    Region1 = {name:LowLatencyInstance, region:US-West,
        tier1 = {name:LocalMemory, size=5G},
        tier2 = {name:LocalDisk, size=5G} }
    Region2 = {name:LowLatencyInstance, region:US-East
        tier1 = {name:LocalMemory, size=5G},
        tier2 = {name:LocalDisk, size=5G} }
    ...
    RegionN = {name:LowLatencyInstance, region:EU-West,
        tier1 = {name:LocalMemory, size=5G},
        tier2 = {name:LocalDisk, size=5G} }

    %MultiPrimaries Consistency
    event(insert.into) : response {
        lock(what:insert.key)
        store(what:insert.object, to:local_instance)
        copy(what:insert.object, to:all_regions)
        release(what:insert.key)
    }
}
```

(a) Multiple Primaries consistency policy.

```
Wiera PrimaryBackupConsistency() {
    % Same Tiera instances configuration
    % Primary instance is running on Region1
    Region1 = {name:LowLatencyInstance, region:US-West,
            primary:True}
    ...


    %PrimaryBackup Consistency
    event(insert.into) : response {
        if(local_instance.isPrimary == True)
            store(what:insert.object, to:local_instance)
            copy(what:insert.object, to:all_regions)
        else
            forward(what:insert.object, to:primary_instance)
    }
}
```

(b) Primary Backup consistency policy.

Figure 3: Primary-based consistency policies.

```
Wiera DynamicConsistency() {
    % In Multiple-Primaries Consistency
    % Put operation spends more time than
    % threshold required for specific amount of time
    event(threshold.type == put) : response {
        if(threshold.latency > 800 ms
            && threshold.period > 30 seconds)
            change_policy(what:consistency,
                    to:EventualConsistency);
        else if (threshold.latency <= 800 ms
            && threshold.period > 30 seconds)
            change_policy(what:consistency,
                    to:MultiPrimariesConsistency);
    }
}
```

(a) Changing consistency policy.

```
Wiera ChangePrimary() {
    % In Primary-Backup Consistency
    % If there is an instance which received more
    % requests than primary received from application.
    event(threshold.type == primary) : response {
        if(forwarded_requests_per_each_instance
            >= updates_from_primary
            && threshold.period = 600 seconds)
            chage_policy(what:primary_instance,
                    to:instance_forward_most)
    }
}
```

(b) Changing the primary in Primary Backup policy.

Figure 5: Defining dynamic policies.

mary, then Wiera will change the primary instance to the more heavily accessed replica. Once this change has been done, all requests will be forwarded to the new primary instance.

3.3.3 Achieving Desired Metrics

Applications can have different desired metrics such as performance, reliability, cost, etc. Wiera policies can be defined to achieve such desired metrics as well. While we focused on consistency policies above to achieve desired latencies in the presence of replication, another important metric could be cost.

Many internet applications see huge fraction of data which is accessed infrequently or not at all. For example, Facebook shows its data access patterns typically conform to a Zipfian distribution [11] in which only a small proportion of data is frequently accessed. One way for such an application to lower its cost could be to use cheaper but slower storage (e.g., Amazon S3 or Glacier) for its cold data while using more expensive, faster storage (e.g., MemCache or EBS) for hot data. Figure 6(a) shows how Wiera can allow applications to get benefits from such cheaper and durable storage tiers. In this policy, each instance has one cheaper storage tier. An application defines cold data by setting a threshold on elapsed time from the last access (120 hours). If an instance gets the event which notifies that there is any object has not been accessed for 120 hours, it is identified as cold and moved to the cheaper storage tier.

Another way to reduce cost could be by maintaining fewer replicas. This could reduce both storage costs as well as network bandwidth costs by reducing the update traffic, as cloud providers charge for all out-bound network traffic. As shown in our prior work [15], an application can achieve good performance even with fewer replicas by accessing nearby DCs' faster storage tier (e.g., Memcached) instead of a local slower tier (e.g., S3 or EBS). Figure 6(b) shows how Wiera can enable the reduction in the number of replicas by using the fastest storage tier in the centralized DC in a region. In this policy, all Tiera instances are running within the same region (US-WEST), and are forwarding requests to a primary instance. Thus instances in this region need not be concerned about data consistency which can reduce network traffic and cost. All non-primary instances could then be used as caches or for load balancing if needed. An application can reduce cost further by maintaining a single replica for cold data on centralized cheaper storage tier. That is, if the application allows instances to share the centralized cheaper storage tier for cold data, it can save even greater storage cost. We will explain how this can be achieved in Section 5.3 in more detail.

Using remote storage tiers may induce monetary network cost which should be considered. Wiera provides the flexibility for users to choose the right point in the cost-performance tradeoff. In a hybrid cloud environment, an application may not need to worry about the network cost. If much of the data flow happens from the private DC *into* a nearby pub-

```
Wiera ReducedCostPolicy() {
    ...
    RegionN = {name:PersistanceInstance, region:US-West,
        tier1 = {name:LocalDisk, size=5G}}
        tier2 = {name:CheapestArchival, size=5G}}

    %Data is getting cold
    event(object.lastAccessedTime > 120 hours) : response {
        move(what:object.location == tier1
            to:tier2, bandwidth:100KB/s);
    }
}
```

```
Wiera SimplerConsistency() {
    Region1 = {name:LowLatencyInstance, region:US-West-1,
                primary:True
        tier1 = {name:LocalMemory, size=30G}
        tier2 = {name:LocalDisk, size=30G}}
    Region2 = {name:ForwardingInstance, region:US-West-2}
    ...
    RegionN = {name:ForwardingInstance, region:US-West-N}

    %PrimaryBackup Consistency
    event(insert.into) : response {
        if(local_instance.isPrimary == True)
            store(what:insert.object, to:local_instance)
        else
            forward(what:insert.object, to:primary_instance)
    }
}
```

(a) Reducing cost by moving cold data to cheaper storage.

(b) Simpler consistency by using fastest storage tier within the same region.

Figure 6: Achieving desired cost metrics.

lic cloud DC, one could acquire better performance without any network cost as network traffic into DC is normally not charged.

4. IMPLEMENTATION

We now describe our implementation of the Wiera prototype (under 1000 lines of code written in python) and how Wiera components work together and with Tiera servers. We also describe additional features newly implemented in Tiera. To enable communication with applications, Wiera launches a Thrift server [4], a remote procedure call framework, that enables applications written in different languages to communicate with each other. Since Tiera instances now need to connect to Wiera and all other instances, we implement a communication component using Thrift in Tiera (under 500 lines of codes written in Java) while most of the Tiera code base remained unchanged. A global policy is implemented in the instance by hand-coding the event-response pairs into the Tiera's control layer. We implemented global policies that were explained in Section 3.3 (under 100 lines of codes written in Java per global policy). Note that Wiera mainly manages Tiera instances and their policies but is not involved in data movement. All data flow happens directly between Tiera instances as specified in the policies.

4.1 Wiera Communication

As described in Section 3.1, Wiera is composed of multiple components. Whenever a Tiera server (note, not a Tiera instance) launches, it connects to the *Tiera Server Manager* (TSM) first to let Wiera know that it is ready to spawn instances. Note: instances run within the Tiera server process for simplicity, but could easily run as a separate process for better fault tolerance. The TSM holds all information about Tiera servers and periodically sends a "ping" message to check on their health. The steps to initiate Tiera instances on multiple regions are as follows: 1) an application specifies the instances, their regions, and policies through the Wiera application interface, 2) when Wiera gets the request, the *Global Policy Manager* (GPM) creates a new policy with a *policy id* sent from the application and launches a new *Tiera Instance Manager* (TIM) to communicate with the Tiera instances which will be created, 3) the TSM asks the Tiera servers to spawn instances with storage tiers and local policy as specified in the request, 4) a Tiera server receives the request, spawns a new instance, and informs the instance

about the TIM address to which the new instance will connect, 5) the new instance runs a server with a unique port number to communicate with other instances. It then connects to the TIM and sends its own server information (port number for the application and port number for communicating between instances), 6) when the TIM accepts server information from its instances, it propagates information to all instances, 7) Wiera returns the list of instances and global policy ID to the application which sent the request, and 8) the application can connect to the closest instance (placed at the head of the list) and sends requests as in Tiera.

4.2 Global Lock and Conflicts Handling

If an instance is replicated it may need to obtain a global lock before distributing updates to all other instances. For example, if an application specifies MultiPrimariesConsistency (Figure 3(a)), it should get the global lock first for data consistency. For the global lock, Wiera relies on Zookeeper [13], an atomic messaging system that keeps all of the servers in sync, and we use Curator library [8] for using Zookeeper easily. When an instance gets updates from another instance, it will update the object as specified in the global policy. In MultiPrimariesConsistency, as an example, if an instance receives an update from another instance, it will simply update the object because the instance that sent the update has a global lock for the object and thus it does not need to be concerned about data consistency. However, in EventualConsistency (Figure 4), instances should check whether there is any write-write conflict between instances whenever they get updates from another instance. This is needed to avoid version conflicts because they do not hold the global lock for better write performance. To handle this, we add a new feature, which allows applications to have multiple object versions. Each object can have multiple versions with added metadata including version number, create time, access count, last modified time, and last accessed time. As in Tiera, all object metadata is stored and persisted using BerkeleyDB [16]. When instances distribute updates to other instances, they also send metadata including object version and last modified time. Thus, each instance that receives an update can decide whether it will accept the update based on the metadata version and last modified time. In the current implementation, we choose a simple strategy, last write wins. That is, updates will be accepted when they has a higher version number than the local object or when the update is newer (most recently written) than the local object if the versions are the same. We add new APIs for this feature as shown in Table 2.

4.3 New Events and Responses

As mentioned in Section 3.2.3, we added *events Latency-Monitoring*, *RequestsMonitoring* and *ColdDataMonitoring*, to Wiera to handle dynamics in the multiple cloud environment. *LatencyMonitoring* events are handled by a dedicated thread which waits to be signaled. The thread handling the application request will signal the dedicated thread to check the latency. The dedicated thread checks whether the conditions (a latency threshold and period of the violation) are met. If it is determined that all conditions are violated it will notify Wiera to handle it. In our example policy (Figure 5(a)), a *change_policy() response* request with a new desired consistency model will be issued to Wiera to change the consistency model.

RequestsMonitoring events are handled by the dedicated thread which waits to be signaled in the primary instance (or in all instances as specified by the policy). The thread which handles requests in the primary instance signals the dedicated thread to check the number of requests from both an application and other instances. If the thread detects that an instance has received more requests forwarded from other instances than it has directly received from the application, a *change_policy() response* request with a new *primary* instance will be issued to Wiera to change the primary instance.

ColdDataMonitoring events are handled by the dedicated thread in each instance. The dedicated thread will keep checking metadata to find any object not accessed for a specific amount of time. If it finds an object which has not been accessed, it will take the actions as specified in the policy. In our example policy, in Figure 6(a), it simply moves the object to the cheaper storage tier as a *response*.

4.4 Handling Failure

In the current implementation, an application can specify the required number of replicas to be available at all times. If a replica crashes, the system detects this via periodic heartbeat and creates a new replica if this threshold is not met. In addition, if the application observes that the closest instance is down then it tries to send requests to the second closest instance, and so on. In future work, we plan to develop mechanisms in Wiera in support of new reactive fault tolerance policies.

5. EXPERIMENTAL EVALUATION

We evaluated the Wiera prototype in the Amazon cloud and Azure. Wiera and Tiera instances were hosted on Amazon EC2 instances. For our experiments, we used EC2 t2.micro instances, 1 vCPU, 1GB of RAM, and 16GB of EBS storage for Wiera and Tiera servers unless mentioned otherwise. Wiera is running on the US East (Virginia) region and Zookeeper is also running with Wiera on the same instance (for global locking purposes). Tiera servers are running on multiple regions, US East (Virginia), US West (North California), Europe West (Ireland) and Asia East (Tokyo). The client workloads were generated using Yahoo Cloud Serving Benchmark [6] (YCSB) and our own benchmarks. We measure latency from the perspective of an application within a DC, with clients running on the same VM where the instances are running (thus no wide-area latency from users of

applications). Our experiments illustrate the following: (1) it is easy to change the data consistency model and configuration using Wiera to handle dynamics from applications and cloud services, (2) Wiera can enable applications to optimize for a particular metric in multi-cloud environments, and (3) Wiera can be easily used with an application without any modification. As mentioned in Section 4, Wiera is not a bottleneck in the data path. The performance overhead introduced by Tiera is very low (under 2%) as shown in the Tiera paper [18].

5.1 Changing Consistency

In this section, we show how Wiera changes consistency policy dynamically as specified in the *DynamicConsistency* policy (Figure 5(a)), using a *put* operation latency threshold of 800 ms and a period threshold of 30 seconds. In this experiment, instances are running in regions US West, US East, Europe West, and Asia East, and simulated applications send requests to instances in all the regions using workload A: an update heavy workload in YCSB [6].

We set instances to use *MultiplePrimariesConsistency* (Figure 3(a)) initially in which all *put* operations result in updates being distributed to all other instances synchronously. Figure 7 shows the latency for *put* operations in US West region[3]. The bold line in the figure indicates the application-perceived latency. Initially, the application sees around 400 ms which includes time for getting (and releasing) the global lock for a key, broadcasting updates to all other instances synchronously, and internal operations (write to local storage). We inject delays into an instance to simulate network or storage delay. In the figure, we can see that there are 3 simulated delays from (a) to (c). All of these delays cause the operation latency violation (800 ms), but only delays (a) and (b) cause a period threshold violation (30 sec). For delays (a) and (b), Wiera detects that both thresholds are violated, so it changes the consistency to *EventualConsistency* (Figure 4) to preserve application-perceived *put* operation latency which now becomes less than 10 ms. This is because instances don't need to get the global lock for the key and broadcasting updates is done in the background in *EventualConsistency*. Note that Wiera identifies the last delay (c) as being transient and hence, ignores it. When Wiera detects that there is no additional delay during the period threshold (30 seconds) i.e., points (1) and (2) in the figure, it changes the consistency model back to *MultiplePrimariesConsistency*. This result shows that Wiera can adaptively change consistency models to handle dynamics at run-time.

5.2 Changing Primary Instance

User location is another factor that may be important for data placement policy as shown in systems such as Volley [1] and Tuba [3]. Tuba shows that changing storage configuration can improve overall resource utilization and user-perceived latency. In this section, we show how Wiera can easily achieve the same goals as Tuba. To do this, we implement one of Tuba's policies: changing the *primary* instance based on user location.

In this experiment, instances are running on three regions: US West, Europe West, and Asia East. 10 clients are running per each region and the number of active clients are

---

[3]Note that we see a similar pattern of results from all regions, and we omit these results due to space constraints.

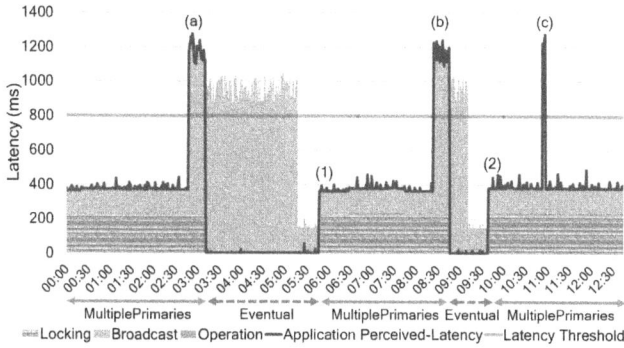

Figure 7: Changing consistency at run-time.

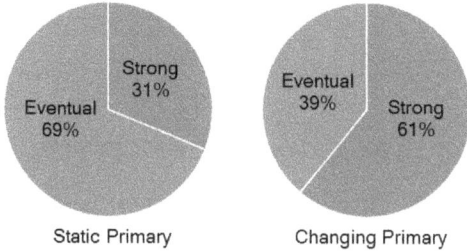

Figure 8: Percentage that applications can see the latest data (Strong) and outdated (Eventual) data.

modeled with a normal distribution to mimic the workload in different regions of the world. The mean of the normal distribution is 7.5 minutes and variance is set to 5 minutes. The number of active clients will increase and decease in the following order, Asia East, EU West and US West. Each simulated client sends requests to instances for each regions using workload A: Read mostly workload (5% put and 95% get) in YCSB [6]. We use the *queue response* mentioned in Section 3.3.2 to distribute updates asynchronously to other instances as Tuba does. We implement the Wiera ChangePrimary policy (Figure 5(b)). The difference as compared to Tuba is that Wiera changes the primary instance by comparing the number of *put* operations from clients and from other instances forwarded while Tuba used a cost model. Wiera could also adopt this cost model if desired. Initially, we set the primary instance to run on the Asia East region. The primary instance checks the *put* operation history (last 30 seconds) to find an instance which forwards more requests than the primary instance received from clients. We set the time period threshold to 15 seconds.

Figure 8 shows the chance that the clients will see the latest data (Strong) and outdated data (Eventual). With a static (no changing) primary location, 69% of *get* operations can return outdated data: clients that are not close to the primary instance can see outdated data since the updates are distributed asynchronously. Wiera reduces this to 39% when the the primary instance location is changed dynamically. That is, more clients now have a greater chance to obtain the latest version of the data from their closest instance. This pattern is similar to that shown for Tuba.

In addition, the overall application-perceived *put* operation latency is also decreased by changing the primary instance. Table 3 shows that an average *put* operation time for each region and overall average of all regions. With static

Table 3: Average put operation latency (in ms)

	EU West	US West	Asia East	Overall
Static	216.61	105.26	< 5	105.18
Changing	95.19	72.20	40.60	68.13

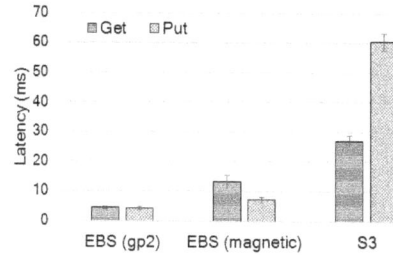

Figure 9: Operations Latencies for 4KB in US East.

primary location, the clients in Asia East can see low latency (<5ms) since they are always close to the *primary* instance, but clients in other regions need to wait a long time until *put* operations are forwarded to the *primary* instance. With changing of the primary instance, clients in all regions can have a greater chance that their closest instance will become the primary instance, so that the overall *put* operation latency can be decreased. These results show that Wiera can easily adopt policies hard-coded in other systems.

5.3 Reducing Cost Using Multiple Storage Tiers

Many internet services and applications have reported that their data access pattern follows Zipfian distribution e.g., Facebook [11], that is huge portion of data is accessed infrequently or not at all. Applications using cloud storage services, however, have to pay for the storage provisioned even for cold data whether it has been accessed or not. Even worse, the size of data will keep increasing but never decreasing while a large fraction of data will not be accessed. In this section, we will describe how an application can save the cost for storage with a new *ColdDataMonitoring* event explained in Section 3.2.3.

Within a DC, an application has various durable storage options with different performance. Figure 9 shows the latencies that the application can see from each storage tier through a Tiera instance. Table 4 shows the prices for provisioned storage, put/get requests, and network cost. Unsurprisingly, we see clear evidence that applications can get better performance from more expensive storage tiers. That is, EBS SSD (gp2-general purpose) ($0.1/GB) provides the

Table 4: Storage Tiers' Price in AWS (US East)

	EBS (SSD)	EBS (HDD)	S3	S3-IA	Cost/Unit
Storage	$0.1	$0.05	$0.03	$0.0125	GB/Month
Put req	$0	$0.0005	$0.05	$0.1	10,000 reqs
Get req	$0	$0.0005	$0.004	$0.01	10,000 reqs
Network	$0	$0	$0	$0	GB/Within a DC
Network	$0.09	$0.09	$0.09	$0.09	GB/To Internet

173

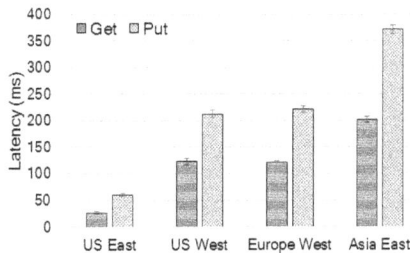

Figure 10: Operation Latency for S3 in US East from each region.

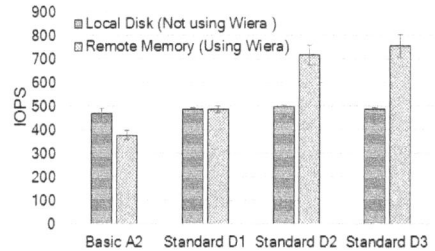

Figure 11: Performance (IOPS) comparison.

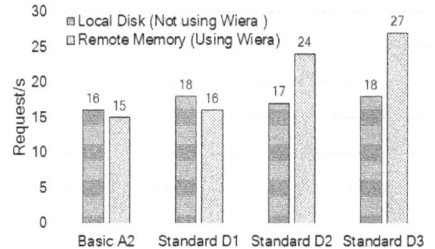

Figure 12: Throughput (request/s) comparison.

best performance and S3 ($0.03 or $0.0125 for S3-IA) provides the worst performance while EBS HDD (magnetic) ($0.05) is in between them. Note that since EBS uses the OS buffer cache, we see very low latency (<1ms) regardless of EBS type if there is enough memory on EC2. To see the native performance of EBS, we throttle the memory by running a memory-intensive application while doing the experiment.

Based on this cost and performance information, let's assume that an application sees that 80% out of 10TB data in EBS have not been accessed for 120 hours, in Figure 6(a) as an example. As a *response* for a *ColdDataMonitoring* event, each instance will move 8TB data into S3-IA and the application will save $700 (if data was stored in SSD) and $300 (if data was stored in HDD) per month for each instance. Of course, the application will see higher latency for cold data in S3-IA and pay a more expensive request cost than EBS, but this will happen very rarely as the data is cold. For the high *put* operation latency from S3-IA, the application can ignore this since all *put* operations will be done in other faster storage tiers as specified in the policy. Thus, the application can save the storage cost by moving cold data into cheaper storage without much penalty.

The application can save even greater storage cost if it allows instances to share the storage tier where the cold data is stored. That is, when Wiera detects that data is getting cold from all regions, it will ask the instance running on a single centralized region to move cold data into local S3-IA and will ask other instances running on other regions to remove cold data as a *response* for the *ColdDataMonitoring* event. If an instance running on a region other than the centralized one needs to read cold data, it will access the S3-IA storage tier located at the centralized region. Since S3-IA is a durable storage tier, the application doesn't need to consider data durability even with the reduced number of data replicas. Of course, the application needs to consider operation latency and network cost for the centralized storage tier. Figure 10 shows the operation latencies from all regions when all instances use S3-IA in US East region as a shared centralized storage tier. The highest *get* operation latency is around 200 ms when a request comes from Asia East. If this *get* latency is acceptable to the application, it can save $300 more (from our previous example, $100 per each region) by reducing the number of replicas for cold data. The high *put* operation latency also can be ignored since all *put* operations will be done in each region locally. In this example, the cost for requests becomes much more expensive by using a centralized storage tier, i.e., from free or $0.0005 to $0.01 per 10,000 *get* operation request,

and from free to $0.09 (or $0.02 between AWS) per GB for network as shown in Table 4. However, by definition, the access to cold data will be rare.

5.4 Exploiting Remote Storage Tiers

One of the benefits of Wiera is that it increases the range of storage tier options. In our previous work [15], we have shown that a *nearby* faster DC storage tier can provide better performance than a local but slower DC storage tier even with wide-area network latency. In this section, we will show how Wiera can let applications achieve better performance from non-local DC storage using both a benchmark (SysBench) and a real application case (RUBiS). Note that we have built our own POSIX-compliant file system using *Filesystem in User Space* (FUSE) [12] to run applications that require a POSIX interface to Wiera, so that all application requests are forwarded to Wiera through FUSE. Thus, applications that require a POSIX interface can run on top of Wiera *without any modification*.

5.4.1 Better Performance from Non-Local DC

In this experiment, we compare I/O performance between Azure's local disk without Wiera and AWS' memory with Wiera using SysBench [21], a system performance benchmark. We use Azure instances, Basic A2 (2 CPU, 3.5 GB of RAM), Standard D1 (1 CPU, 3.5GB of RAM), Standard D2 (2 CPU, 7GB of RAM) and Standard D3 (4 CPU, 14GB of RAM), and AWS EC2 t2.micro instance for non-local memory storage. First, we measure the native disk performance attached to Azure VMs. To avoid any cache (memory) influence, we turn host cache off for the disk attached and use the O_DIRECT flag for SysBench. This kind of setting is desired for some applications e.g., database systems (MySQL), to avoid double cache effects that may create cache misses. We then measure the *remote* memory (in AWS) performance through Wiera. In this setting, we deploy instances on AWS and Azure in the US East (Virginia) region where the latency between DCs is around 2 ms. We use *PrimaryBackup* consistency policy (Figure 3(b)) with synchronous update (*copy response*) and set an instance running on Azure to be the *primary* instance. We set the *primary* instance to have a disk storage tier only and set another instance on AWS to have memory storage tier. We set a *get* operation policy for all *get* operations to be forwarded to the instance on AWS. That is, if the *primary* instance receives *put* operations from SysBench, it puts data into local disk and sends the update to another instance on AWS synchronously. If the *primary* instance receives *get* operations from SysBench, it retrieves data from another instance on AWS i.e., *remote* memory instead of local disk.

We run the SysBench benchmark on Azure 10 times varying the VM size. Figure 11 shows results for each VM size. For the local disk performance, the figure shows the same performance ($\sim$ 500 IOPS) regardless of VM size. This is because Azure throttles the disk performance to 500 IOPS [4]. For the *remote* memory performance through Wiera, performance is sensitive to the VM size. Wiera can achieve a 44% performance improvement when the *primary* instance is running on Standard D2 and Standard D3 instances. Accessing non-local DC memory through Wiera may be affected by CPU performance but the fact that Basic A2 (2 CPUs) provides worse performance than Standard D1 (1 CPU) implies CPU is not a bottleneck in this experiment. We think that this is because Azure throttles the network performance between instances based on VM type and size as we have shown in our previous work [15]. These results shows that an application can achieve a desired goal (better performance) using *nearby* faster DC storage tiers through Wiera if network performance between DCs is not a bottleneck.

5.4.2 RUBiS on Wiera

We next explore running an *unmodified* web application, the popular open-source benchmark RUBiS [20], on Wiera. RUBiS is a multi-component web application that implements functions of an auction site EBay.com, selling, buying, bidding, commenting and so on. We use Apache and PHP for the front-end web server and MySQL for the back-end database. We use the same evaluation environment setup as in Section 5.4.1. All RUBiS components are hosted on an Azure VM.

For this experiment, MySQL uses two different storage settings: either *local* disk or *remote* memory through Wiera. We set the flag O_DIRECT (which prohibits MySQL to use the OS buffer) and reduce MySQL internal buffer size to the minimum (16MB) to see the performance from the native attached disk. The database was populated with information for 50,000 items and 50,000 customers. 300 simulated clients are hosted on a separate t2.micro EC2 instance on the same region (US East). The benchmark is run for 300 seconds, with 120 seconds for ramp-up and 60 seconds for ramp-down. Likewise, we vary VM size from Basic A2 to Standard D3. Figure 12 shows the throughput from each VM size. Similar to the SysBench results, we see low throughput from small instances (Basic A2 and Standard D1) and higher throughput (50% $\sim$ 80% improvement) from larger instances (Standard D2 and Standard D3) due to a reduction in network throttling. This experiment shows how easily an application can use Wiera to achieve desired (performance in this experiment) goal by accessing multiple storage tiers on multiple DCs *without any modification*.

6. RELATED WORK

Data Locality: Recent research [2] has shown that data locality within a DC is irrelevant, given the bandwidth of current DC networks. They show that accessing data from a remote node's memory within a DC can provide better performance than reading data from local disk. In our previous work [15], we show that data locality may also be irrelevant in multiple DCs environment, and accessing data over the network from the same or faster storage resource in a nearby DC can be faster than using a slower local storage tier. Wiera realizes many opportunities for utilizing cross-DC storage as a complete system.

In-Memory Storage: Many previous works utilize memory to improve performance. Cooperative Caching [9] tries to use idle remote node's memory to improve file system performance. Many recent storage systems, like Redis [19] and RAMCloud [17] aggregate memory resources from many nodes and present it as a common storage pool to applications. In this paper, we show that *unmodified* applications can get a performance benefit from these in-memory storage systems even in multi-DC environment through Wiera.

Wide Area Storage: Many previous storage systems utilize multiple DCs. Volley [1] performs automated data placement across distributed DCs using diurnal and weekly users' data access patterns to reduce user perceived-latency and to minimize costs associated with inter-DC traffic. Spanner [7] manages cross-data center replicated data and implements database operations while maintaining externally-consistent distributed transactions for their internal applications. These systems use a single cloud storage provider. In contrast, SPANStore [22] tries to utilize multiple cloud provider DCs rather than a single provider to get a higher DC density to deliver data closer to users with reduced cost, much like a content delivery network. Tuba [3] tries to achieved applications' desired goals while maximizing the utility delivered to read operations. They show that automatic reconfiguration of the storage system can yield substantial benefits such as higher overall resource utilization and better user-perceived latency. However, these storage systems do not adequately handle dynamics from the cloud infrastructure and applications because of their design choices, most notably, a lazy data placement policy decision. Our work tries to handle such dynamics using a combination of local policy, global policy, and multiple storage tiers across multiple DCs. In addition, Wiera provides a flexible substrate that enables the implementation of such existing data policies easily e.g., Wiera can support a time-varying user-specified data consistency model based on changes to access patterns and network conditions while most previous works only support a few hard-coded data consistency models.

Policy-Driven Storage: The policy architecture for distributed storage systems (PADS) [5] was proposed for system designers to construct a new distributed storage system easily. PADS provides a data plane that is a fixed set of mechanisms for storing, transmitting, and consistency information and control plane policy that specifies the system-specific policy for orchestrating flows of data among nodes. In our previous work Tiera [18], we explored building a storage framework that helps applications build a tiered storage system consisting of local DC memory resources for better performance, and persistent storage services like S3 or EBS for durability. Tiera supports dynamic policy modification e.g., addition/removal of tiers, adding new events and responses, at run-time. In this paper, we extend and utilize Tiera which focused on a single DC. We use storage tiers across multiple cloud providers to get additional benefits such as simpler consistency and reduced cost, and to handle dynamics from cloud infrastructures and applications at run-time.

Storage Tiering Features on Cloud Providers: Some cloud providers offer similar features but with significant limitations. For example, AWS S3 provides storage tiering between S3 and Glacier with limitations e.g., only from S3 to Glacier, data size (>128 KB), and duration (>30 days) and more. Google only supports deletion of old objects. Wiera provides diverse policies and more flexible features through our own custom implementation but without such limitations. Moreover, cloud providers don't provide guarantees on the consistent performance of their services and it is left to the applications to handle dynamics. Wiera makes this much easier for applications through a simple interface and support for changing policies.

7. CONCLUSION

In this paper, we introduced Wiera, an integrated geo-distributed cloud storage system that runs across multiple storage tiers, multiple data-centers, and multiple providers, to exploit storage options available to the application and user. The diversity of options is exploited by a flexible storage policy framework that can optimize across a wide array of metrics such as performance, cost, durability, reliability, in the face of network and application dynamics. Wiera is built upon the Tiera storage system to achieve far greater flexibility and adaptability including support for multiple levels of consistency based on current SLAs or performance goals. The results indicate that metrics such as reduced cost and higher performance are obtainable by exploiting the larger set of storage options. Lastly, the benefits can be obtained with minimal impact to existing applications as demonstrated by the *unmodified RUBiS application*.

8. ACKNOWLEDGMENT

We thank the anonymous reviewers and our shepherd, Thilo Kielmann, for their helpful comments. We acknowledge grant NSF CSR-1162405 that supported this research.

9. REFERENCES

[1] S. Agarwal et al. Volley: Automated data placement for geo-distributed cloud services. In *Proceedings of the 7th USENIX Conference on Networked Systems Design and Implementation*, NSDI'10, pages 2–2, Berkeley, CA, USA, 2010. USENIX Association.

[2] G. Ananthanarayanan et al. Disk-locality in datacenter computing considered irrelevant. In *Proceedings of the 13th USENIX Conference on Hot Topics in Operating Systems*, HotOS'13, Berkeley, CA, USA, 2011. USENIX Association.

[3] M. S. Ardekani and D. B. Terry. A self-configurable geo-replicated cloud storage system. In *Proceedings of the 11th USENIX Conference on Operating Systems Design and Implementation*, OSDI'14, pages 367–381, Berkeley, CA, USA, 2014. USENIX Association.

[4] Azure Virtual Machine. https://azure.microsoft.com/en-us/documentation/articles/virtual-machines-linux-sizes/.

[5] N. Belaramani et al. Pads: A policy architecture for distributed storage systems. In *Proceedings of the 6th USENIX Symposium on Networked Systems Design and Implementation*, NSDI'09, pages 59–73, Berkeley, CA, USA, 2009. USENIX Association.

[6] B. F. Cooper et al. Benchmarking cloud serving systems with ycsb. In *Proceedings of the 1st ACM Symposium on Cloud Computing*, SoCC '10, pages 143–154, New York, NY, USA, 2010. ACM.

[7] J. C. Corbett et al. Spanner: Google's globally distributed database. volume 31, pages 8:1–8:22, New York, NY, USA, Aug. 2013. ACM.

[8] Curator. http://curator.apache.org/.

[9] M. D. Dahlin et al. Cooperative caching: Using remote client memory to improve file system performance. In *Proceedings of the 1st USENIX Conference on Operating Systems Design and Implementation*, OSDI '94, Berkeley, CA, USA, 1994. USENIX Association.

[10] Data Center Map. http://www.datacentermap.com/.

[11] Flashcache at Facebook: From 2010 to 2013 and beyond. http://alturl.com/us4fi/.

[12] FUSE - Filesystem In User Space. https://github.com/libfuse/libfuse/.

[13] P. Hunt et al. Zookeeper: Wait-free coordination for internet-scale systems. In *Proceedings of the 2010 USENIX Conference on USENIX Annual Technical Conference*, USENIXATC'10, pages 11–11, Berkeley, CA, USA, 2010. USENIX Association.

[14] M. Mesnier, G. R. Ganger, and E. Riedel. Object-based storage. *Comm. Mag.*, 41(8):84–90, Aug. 2003.

[15] K. Oh et al. Redefining data locality for cross-data center storage. In *Proceedings of the 2Nd International Workshop on Software-Defined Ecosystems*, BigSystem '15, pages 15–22, New York, NY, USA, 2015. ACM.

[16] M. A. Olson, K. Bostic, and M. Seltzer. Berkeley db. In *Proceedings of the Annual Conference on USENIX Annual Technical Conference*, ATEC '99, pages 43–43, Berkeley, CA, USA, 1999. USENIX Association.

[17] J. Ousterhout et al. The case for ramclouds: Scalable high-performance storage entirely in dram. *SIGOPS Oper. Syst. Rev.*, 43(4):92–105, Jan. 2010.

[18] A. Raghavan, A. Chandra, and J. B. Weissman. Tiera: Towards flexible multi-tiered cloud storage instances. In *Proceedings of the 15th International Middleware Conference*, Middleware '14, pages 1–12, New York, NY, USA, 2014. ACM.

[19] Redis. http://redis.io/.

[20] RUBiS Web site. http://rubis.ow2.org.

[21] SysBench. https://github.com/akopytov/sysbench/.

[22] Z. Wu et al. Spanstore: Cost-effective geo-replicated storage spanning multiple cloud services. In *Proceedings of the Twenty-Fourth ACM Symposium on Operating Systems Principles*, SOSP '13, pages 292–308, New York, NY, USA, 2013. ACM.

MOS: Workload-aware Elasticity for Cloud Object Stores

Ali Anwar, Yue Cheng
Virginia Tech
Blacksburg, VA
{ali,yuec}@cs.vt.edu

Aayush Gupta
IBM Research – Almaden
San Jose, CA
guptaaa@us.ibm.com

Ali R. Butt
Virginia Tech
Blacksburg, VA
butta@cs.vt.edu

ABSTRACT

The use of cloud object stores has been growing rapidly in recent years as they combine key advantages such as HTTP-based RESTful APIs, high availability, elasticity with a "pay-as-you-go" pricing model that allows applications to scale as needed. The current practice is to either use a single set of configuration parameters or rely on statically configured storage policies for a cloud object store deployment, even when the store is used to support different types of applications with evolving requirements. This crucial mismatch between the different applications requirements and capabilities of the object store is problematic and should be addressed to achieve high efficiency and performance.

In this paper, we propose MOS, a Micro Object Storage architecture, which supports independently configured microstores each tuned dynamically to the needs of a particular type of workload. We also design an enhancement, MOS++, that extends MOS's capabilities through fine-grained resource management to effectively meet the tenants' SLAs while maximizing resource efficiency. We have implemented a prototype of MOS++ in OpenStack Swift using Docker containers. Our evaluation shows that MOS++ can effectively support heterogeneous workloads across multiple tenants. Compared to default and statically configured object store setups, for a two-tenant setup, MOS++ improves the sustained access bandwidth by up to 79% for a large-object workload, while reducing the 95th percentile latency by up to 70.2% for a small-object workload.

Keywords

Object store; Performance analysis; Resource management and scheduling

1. INTRODUCTION

Cloud object stores, such as Amazon S3, Google Cloud Store (GCS), OpenStack Swift and Ceph [34], have become the most widely used form of cloud storage in recent years. These stores combine key advantages such as high availability, elasticity and a "pay-as-you-go" pricing model, which allows applications to scale as the usage increases or decreases, and offers HTTP-based RESTful APIs for easy data management. The desirable features, coupled with the advances in virtualization infrastructure, are driving the adoption of cloud object stores by a myriad of applications. Examples range from web applications [14] that store image and video files, to backup services [3] that require large capacity for archival data, to big data analytics frameworks [17]. Similarly, object stores are increasingly being adopted by the HPC community [23] as they provide efficient metadata management and scalability that helps in extreme-scale high-end computing, and allows for seamless adaptation to a wide range of general purpose and scientific computing file system workloads [34].

A typical deployment of cloud object stores either opts to use a monolithic configuration or segmented storage setup [10] with a static configuration to handle different types of applications with evolving requirements. Using a monolithic configuration setup results in all applications experiencing the same service level, e.g., similar average latency per request, data transfer throughput, and queries per second (QPS). However, different applications entail extremely different latency and throughput requirements. For example, a social networking or photo sharing application requires low latency to support a highly-responsive user experience, whereas backup services can tolerate higher latency but require sustained high throughput. Some object stores provide static configuration of storage policies, e.g., Swift segmentation [10], to allow for segmenting the cluster. This static storage segmentation policy is limited to cover only the storage server layer of an object store. However, a typical object store setup also consists of additional layers such as proxy server and load balancer layer. End-to-end performance of an application depends on correct configuration at all these layers to meet its requirements, and not only the storage server. Thus, a comprehensive solution is needed.

From the cloud provider's perspective, supporting dramatically different workloads from different applications (tenants) using a single homogeneous configuration means that optimization opportunities are lost. Each different application represents a workload with different characteristics. For example, a photo sharing application such as Instagram would have a large number of small-medium sized files (e.g, KB- to MB-level image objects), with skewed access pattern where frequent read and write requests go for hotter/popular objects. In contrast, an enterprise backup application (e.g., Arq [1]) consists largely of write requests for large cold archive files with reads only sparsely arising. Us-

HPDC'16, May 31-June 04, 2016, Kyoto, Japan

© 2016 ACM. ISBN 978-1-4503-4314-5/16/05. . . $15.00

DOI: http://dx.doi.org/10.1145/2907294.2907304

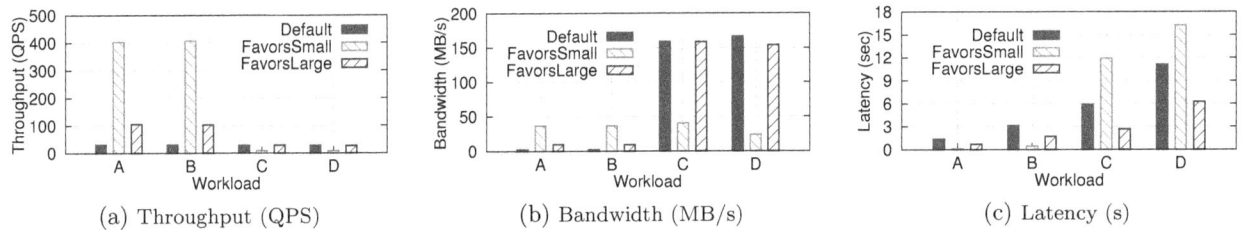

| (a) Throughput (QPS) | (b) Bandwidth (MB/s) | (c) Latency (s) |

Figure 1: Performance achieved under various object store configurations in a multi-tenant environment.

ing a homogeneous configuration prevents fine-tuning of the system to such varied needs and reduces overall system efficiency.

The situation is further complicated by the fact that due to regular system upgrades and introduction of new storage architectures, data centers hosting the object stores are becoming increasingly heterogeneous [21, 30]. However, with either the "one-size-fits-all" monolithic deployment or static storage segmentation policy driven partitioning, it is impossible to match specific types of hardware with the right type of application workload. For example, latency-sensitive small-object workloads would require low-latency storage devices and powerful CPU processing capacity, whereas large object write-only workloads can be supported with a combination of high network bandwidth across all layers (e.g., load balancer, proxy, and object servers etc.) and weaker CPU power. Under these scenarios, meeting SLA requirement for one of the workloads may require, (i) adding hardware resources that may not improve the performance for other workloads, and (ii) software tuning that may decrease the performance for other workloads.

Furthermore, the workloads seen by the object store are varied and fluctuate over time. Consider a scenario where the workload demand from one application (tenant) is spiking while the demand from another application that shares the same object store resources is dipping. In this situation, static policies need to be updated based on the changes experienced in the workload. This calls for a new object store architecture that can dynamically perform resource provisioning for driving online reconfiguration across multiple partitions of the object store.

Hence in this paper, we posit that compared to using a rigid object store *it is more beneficial to support multi-tenant workloads separately using dynamically configurable finer-grained object stores* on sub-clusters of available resources.

Motivational Study. To motivate our approach and demonstrate the need for differentiated object stores, we study different types of representative practical workloads as follows. We examine four different real-world applications that use cloud object storage as listed in Table 1. We deploy and evaluate OpenStack Swift in a multi-tenant environment using COSBench [35] as workload generator configured for the four types of studied workloads. Swift is a popular object store implementation provided by OpenStack that is increasingly becoming the *de facto* cloud computing software platform. In these tests, we use three different Swift configurations (setups)[1]. We run COSBench clients on designated machines to saturate Swift. Each benchmark is run for 15 minutes after

Workload	Workload characteristics			App. scenario
	Obj. size	Operation distribution		
A	1–128KB	G: 90%,	P: 5%, D:5%	Web hosting
B	1–128KB	G: 5%,	P: 90%, D:5%	Online game hosting
C	1–128MB	G: 90%,	P: 5%, D:5%	Online video sharing
D	1–128MB	G: 5%,	P: 90%, D:5%	Enterprise backup

Table 1: Different types of workloads and application scenarios used for testing the behavior of object stores. G: GET operation; P: PUT operation; D: DELETE operation.

all data is loaded into the store. We use two nodes as proxy servers in each of the configuration. To simulate datacenter heterogeneity, one of the proxy server has 32 cores while the other has 8 cores. The proxy server running on the 32-core machine is connected to the storage nodes via 1 Gbps interconnect, while the proxy server on the 8-core machine is connected via 10 Gbps interconnect. In addition, four 32-core machines are used as storage nodes. Each storage node has 3 SATA SSDs. The storage nodes are well-endowed and configured in such a way so as not to become a performance bottleneck for any of the studied configurations.

Default configuration: The default monolithic Swift setup is used where both 8-core and 32-core machines acted as proxy server. The workloads are handled by all resources and round robin DNS was used to distribute the requests to the proxies.

FavorsSmall configuration: The available resources are divided into two sub-object stores, one configured for workloads with small objects and the other for large objects. One 8-core machine (connected via 10 Gbps) served as proxy for WorkloadA and WorkloadB, and one 32-core machine connected via 1 Gbps network served WorkloadC and WorkloadD.

FavorsLarge configuration: One 32-core machine (connected via 1 Gbps) is used as proxy for WorkloadA and WorkloadB, while one 8-core machine (connected via 10 Gbps) is used as proxy for WorkloadC and WorkloadD.

Figure 1 shows the comparison of performance achieved under the studied configurations. As shown in Figure 1(a), separating proxy servers for different workloads improved the overall QPS by 700% and 225% for FavorsSmall and FavorsLarge, respectively, compared to the default Swift setup. It is interesting to note that even though FavorsSmall resulted in very high QPS for small objects of (WorkloadA and WorkloadB), it is not the best configuration as it significantly affects the MB/s (dropped by from 350% to 500%, as observed in Figure 1(b)) for workloads dominated with large object (WorkloadC and WorkloadD). On the other hand, in FavorsLarge the throughput for large objects remained same.

---

[1]The integrated Swift storage policies only support static storage node segmentation. In our motivational study we keep the storage node settings fixed and vary the proxy node settings. We do this

to highlight the need for a more comprehensive workload-aware scheme, which is the subject of this paper.

Similarly, the latency of `FavorsLarge` is also less than that achieved by the default configuration for all the workloads (Figure 1(c)). `FavorsSmall` provides best and worst latency for small and large object workloads, respectively. We also observe that switching to different network connections on proxy servers in `Default` configuration results in similar results. These results demonstrate the need for a comprehensive study of the impact of different configurations on performance to ensure efficient cloud object store design.

From our experiments, we infer the following. (i) Cloud object store workloads can be classified based on the size of the objects in their workloads. In case of small objects, cloud tenants are mostly interested in QPS and latency, whereas for large objects data throughput is considered more important. (ii) When multiple tenants run workloads with drastically different behaviors, they compete for the object store resources with each other, the workload dominated with small objects experiences a dramatic loss in performance. This is because the available network bandwidth is exhausted to transfer TCP packets containing payload for large objects, hence wasting the CPU power that would have been utilized to serve workloads with small objects on object storage nodes. That is why using a separate proxy server under `FavorsSmall` and `FavorsLarge` gives a fair chance to small object workloads to be properly handled by the storage nodes. Thus, cloud object stores need better resource management to ensure that tenants are treated equally.

Contributions. To this end, we propose MOS, a novel micro object storage architecture with independently configured micro-object-stores each tuned dynamically for a particular type of workload. We then expose these microstores to the tenants who can then choose to place their data in the appropriate microstore based on the latency and throughput requirements of their workloads. We further enhance our basic resource provisioning engine to build MOS++, which incorporates the container abstraction for fine-grained resource management, SLA awareness, and better resource efficiency.

Specifically, we make the following contributions:

- We evaluate the impact of conventional object storage configuration on performance and resource efficiency by conducting experiments on a local Swift testbed. Our observations stress the need to carefully evaluate the various configuration choices and develop simple *Rules-of-Thumb* that cloud providers can leverage for provisioning the object storage.

- We perform a detailed performance and resource efficiency analysis on identifying major hardware and software configuration opportunities that can be used to fine-tune object stores for specific workloads. Our findings indicate the need to re-architect cloud object storage specialized for the public cloud.

- Based on our behavior analysis, we design MOS, an object store that (i) dynamically provisions microstores, each configured with different combination of hardware and software options, and (ii) exposes the interfaces of microstores to the tenants to use according to application requirements.

- We extend our basic framework to MOS++ that uses container based approach to launch resources in a more fine-grained manner. MOS++ is SLA-aware, supports rapid deployment, portability across machines, offers a lightweight footprint, and simplifies maintenance.

- We implement a prototype of MOS++, and demonstrate that our approach results in improved performance (by up to 89.6% and 79.8% compared to the default monolithic and statically configured object store setup, respectively), as well as higher resource efficiency. Furthermore, we design a simulator to evaluate our solution under a large-scale 456-core cloud cluster setup. We also compare the performance of MOS with MOS++ to highlight advantages of our container based approach.

2. BACKGROUND AND RELATED WORK

Object Store Segmentation. Swift provides storage policies to support for segmenting the cluster through the creation of multiple object rings [10]. This feature is useful if a provider wants to offer different level of durability, performance, or storage implementation but does not want to maintain separate clusters. In contrast, MOS advocates to separately maintain clusters to incorporate segmentation across all layers. Furthermore, storage policies are static whereas MOS dynamically perform resource provisioning that can drive online reconfiguration across multiple partitions of the object store. Also, performance comparison of the Swift-based prototype of MOS with other object stores like Ceph will not be an apple-to-apple comparison as Ceph outperforms Swift [2] and they have significantly different architecture.

Workload-aware Elasticity. The focus of various recent research works have been on providing an elastic setup for cloud based storage. Lim et al. [29] propose an elastic storage system on HDFS for multi-tier application services. Similarly, ElasTraS [20] provides scalability and elasticity to the data store in clouds for optimizing transactional data access. MeT [19] focuses on systems metrics (CPU utilization, I/O wait and memory usage) that are critical for a NoSQL database. Skute [15] provides a fault-tolerance and scalable replication scheme for cloud storage. MOS differs from these works in that it focuses on providing best performance guarantee for heterogeneous multi-tenant workloads by exploiting automated elasticity for cloud object store.

Handling Cluster/Workload Heterogeneity. hatS [26] proposes a replication scheme for HDFS that integrates heterogeneous storage technologies into Hadoop. ϕSched [27] designs a cluster-heterogeneity-aware scheduler to improve the resource-application match. Walnut [16] suggests using a hybrid object strategy to support both small and large objects in an object store. CAST [17] and its extension [18] perform coarse-grained cloud storage (including object stores) management for data analytics workloads. In contrast, MOS explicitly partitions the conventional monolithic storage into multiple dynamically tuned microstores, each serving a particular type of workload.

Meeting SLA/SLO. SCADS [33] uses a steady-state performance model to predict whether a server can handle a particular workload, without violating a given latency threshold. SCADS reconfigures the storage system on-the-fly in response to workload changes driven by a performance model. Similarly, Papio [32] introduces a QoS-enabled function into the S3-based object store where it accepts an explicit performance request as an advanced reservation, and enables QoS in the access with the extended S3 RESTful interfaces. MOS differs from these works in that it: i) keeps track of

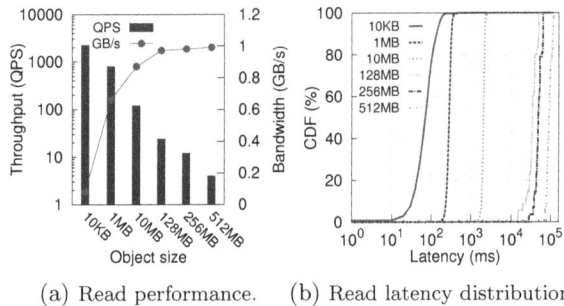

(a) Read performance. (b) Read latency distribution.

Figure 2: Impact of varying the object size on read performance. Note the log scale on the Y-axis of Figure 2(a) and the X-axis of Figure 2(b).

fine-grained resource usage; and ii) partitions the heterogeneous workloads and optimizes each individually based on tenants' SLA requirements while yielding higher overall performance and better resource efficiency.

Dynamic Resource Management. Mantle [31] is a programmable storage system that lets users inject custom balancing logic into Ceph [34]. This feature provides flexibility for allocating resources. Unlike Mantle, MOS automatically performs resource provisioning without burgeoning the users. [13] propose a fine-grained resource allocation mechanism based on metrics such as CPU utilization, I/O wait and memory usage that are critical for MapReduce workloads. Similarly, Lee et al. [28] design a heterogeneity-aware resource allocator and job scheduler for a cloud data analytics system. While these works provide heterogeneity-aware optimizations targeted at MapReduce workloads, MOS targets object stores and focuses on improving the performance of real-time request processing.

3. ANALYSIS

In this section, we present a detailed analysis of how object store behaves under various software and hardware configurations. Next, we use the study to develop *rules-of-thumb* for configuring object stores, which guide the design of MOS.

In the following analysis, we use a 32-core machine as a proxy node with two 32-core storage nodes each equipped with 3 SSDs (to eliminate the storage bottleneck), unless mentioned otherwise. For workloads dominated by small objects (at KB level) the metrics of interest are *throughput* in terms of queries per second (QPS) and response latency, while for workloads dominated by large objects (at MB–GB level), *bandwidth* in terms of MB/s or GB/s is more important.

Q1: How does object size impact performance? First, we analyze the impact of object size on performance in terms of throughput (QPS) and bandwidth (GB/s). While QPS captures the object-wise throughput performance, the bandwidth serves as an important metric reflecting byte-wise performance. As shown in Figure 2(a), increasing the object size results in the throughput decreasing drastically. Specifically, when the object size is increased from 10 KB to 10 MB, we observe the increasing tendency of the network bandwidth. When the object size is increased further to above 128 MB, the bandwidth only improves marginally (from 0.97 GB/s to 0.98 GB/s), implying that the NIC is saturated. Figure 2(b) plots the corresponding latency distribution at each studied object size. At large object sizes (10 MB–512 MB), the request response latency is more than

$100\times$ than that for small object sizes (10 KB–1 MB). From these tests, we can infer that, as long as the object size exceeds a certain threshold, network bandwidth becomes the limiting factor. Correspondingly, this again, explains why WorkloadA and WorkloadB achieve extremely poor performance when co-existing with WorkloadC and WorkloadD in §1. Hence, the tests demonstrate that, in a multi-tenant environment with mixed workloads, individual workloads should be partitioned and serviced through disjoint object stores to reduce mutual interference and performance impact.

Q2: How does proxy server configuration impact performance? Next, we study the effect of scaling proxy nodes on workload performance. We vary the computational capacity of the proxy node by increasing proxy's allotted CPU cores. Figure 3(a) shows the proxy tuning effect. As we increase the proxy workers in one proxy node the QPS is improved linearly until we reach 32 proxy workers. The observed CPU utilization reaches close to 85% (bounding the throughput) with both 32 and 64 proxy workers, implying that CPU becomes the bottleneck here. Adding one more proxy node (2x) almost doubles the performance (QPS increased from $2,200$ to $3,700$), clearly demonstrating that proxy's performance is constrained by the CPU capacity. Next, we repeat the test with large object workloads. As shown in Figure 3(b), the network bandwidth limit is reached as soon as the number of proxy workers reaches 4, with modest CPU utilization (about 25%) observed on the proxy node. This is because for large object workload, the performance becomes constrained by the network bandwidth before CPU can be saturated. Hence adding another proxy node (2x, i.e., doubling the available network bandwidth) results in linear increase in throughput. Thus, the takeaway is that a proxy's computational capacity can act as the bottleneck for workloads dominated with small objects, whereas the network bandwidth is the limiting resource for workloads dominated by large objects.

Q3: How does storage server configuration impact performance? Next, we study the effect of scaling object storage nodes on workload performance. As shown in Figure 3(c), the peak QPS for small object workloads is achieved with 16 object storage workers, which is exactly the same as the number of proxy workers launched to achieve this QPS (recall that two object storage nodes are deployed behind one proxy server node). This implies that the maximum performance can only be achieved when both the proxy and storage nodes are equipped with the same amount of CPU resources, which strengthens our observation that CPU capability is the limiting factor for small-object workloads. In contrast, for large-object workloads, the network limit is quickly reached with only 4 object storage workers. This is because, for large objects the performance is bottlenecked by the network (recall that each storage node has 3 SATA SSDs, thus disk bandwidth does not pose a limitation in our test).

Q4: How does network/storage affect performance? In our next test, we study the effect of varying storage device and network connectivity on workload throughput. Figure 4(a) shows that faster network interconnect (1 Gbps NIC → 10 Gbps NIC) results in only 12% increase in QPS for small object workloads with HDD as storage medium, and 70% increase when SATA SSD is used. This observation shows that small-object intensive workloads are more sensitive to the storage devices rather than the network

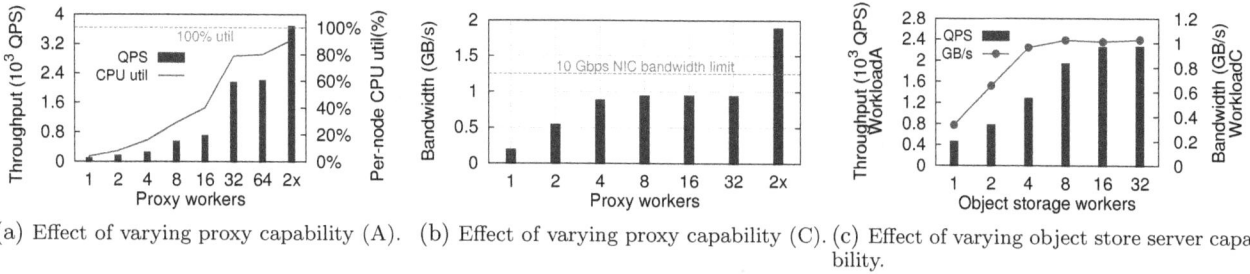

(a) Effect of varying proxy capability (A). (b) Effect of varying proxy capability (C). (c) Effect of varying object store server capability.

Figure 3: Studied software/hardware configuration options. In Figure 3(c), small-object workloads refer to bars (QPS) while large-object workloads refer to linepoints (GB/s). A: `WorkloadA`; C: `WorkloadC`.

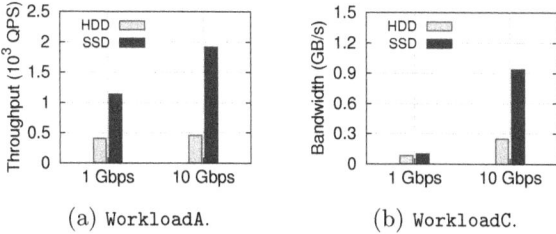

(a) `WorkloadA`. (b) `WorkloadC`.

Figure 4: Performance of the object store equipped with **homogeneous storage devices** as a function of the NIC bandwidth.

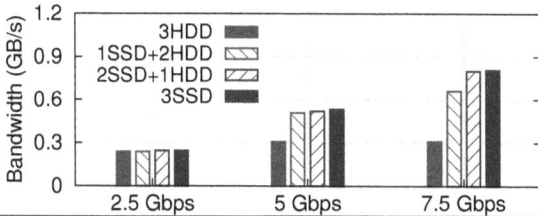

Figure 5: Performance of large-object workload with **heterogeneous storage devices** as a function of the NIC bandwidth. The corresponding bandwidth (GB/s) with 2.5 Gbps, 5 Gbps, and 7.5 Gbps are 0.31 GB/s, 0.62 GB/s, and 0.93 GB/s, respectively.

bandwidth. Thus, they may be efficiently handled using a lower-bandwidth network interconnect but by using high-bandwidth storage devices. On the other hand, increasing network interconnect improves performance by as much as 900% (using SSDs) in case for large-object intensive workloads (Figure 4(b)), which clearly indicates such kind of workloads can benefit from high-bandwidth network interconnects.

Q5: What is the impact of heterogeneous storage setup on performance of large-object workloads? Finally, we study the impact of heterogeneous storage configuration on large-object intensive workloads. Here, we limit the network bandwidth using Linux traffic control tool `tc`. We measure the performance of the object store under a large-object workload, with four setups: two heterogeneous setups 1 SSD + 2 HDD and 2 SSD + 1 HDD; and two homogeneous setups 3 HDD and 3 SSD as baselines. Figure 5 demonstrates that the choice of different storage device type combination changes based on the network bandwidth limit. We vary the network bandwidth limit to emulate the scenario where the network is partitioned in a multi-tenant environment. Note, when the network is limited to 2.5 Gbps, all four storage configurations achieve the same performance. Thus, the storage setup of choice under 2.5 Gbps is 3 HDDs. As the bandwidth limits increases to 7.5 Gbps, the 3 HDDs setup becomes the worst choice, especially when meeting

SLAs is critical. Here, the 2 SSD + 1 HDD setup is desirable as it achieves almost the same performance as the 3 SSD setup, but with a higher resource efficiency. These tests necessitate the need for a workload-aware resource provisioning mechanism that selects the most efficient and high performing options under dynamically changing workloads and tenant requirements.

Summary of Rules-of-thumb. It is fairly straightforward to manually tune the object stores by controlling all the other configuration variables. However, it is a challenging task to dynamically detect the workload shifts and meet the tenant goals while maximizing the resource efficiency at runtime, particularly when the service providers are faced with many software and hardware configuration options. To this end, we develop the following *rules-of-thumb* that are helpful in guiding the online/offline performance tuning of object stores as well as the design of MOS.

R1 Cloud object store design can benefit from (i) partitioning the monolithic object store architecture based on workload characteristics, and (ii) separately servicing interfering workloads in the multi-tenant environment. Object size distribution is a key factor for classifying workload characteristics.

R2 CPU capacity of proxy servers is the first-priority resource for small-object intensive workloads. CPU becomes a bottleneck much earlier than the network for such workloads.

R3 On the other hand, availabile network bandwidth plays a critical role in the performance of large-object intensive workloads.

R4 The number of CPU cores used in storage nodes can be safely configured based on the number of deployed proxy workers, given that the storage devices provide sufficient disk bandwidth. This rule can be modeled using the following equation:

$proxyCores = storageNodes * coresPerStorageNode$, e.g., one 32-core proxy node may require four 8-core storage nodes.

R5 The aggregated network bandwidth between proxy and storage nodes should be roughly the same as the link bandwidth used by cloud provider to connect to the proxies. Generally, this rule can be modeled as:

$bw_{proxies} = storageNodes * bw_{storageNode}$.

R6 A faster network cannot effectively improve QPS for small-object intensive workloads. For tenants who do not impose strict SLO requirements, the workload, if dominated with small objects, may be better served using a combination of low-bandwidth network (i.e., 1 Gbps NICs) with high-bandwidth storage devices (e.g., SSD delivering decent random and sequential I/O performance). This low-cost het-

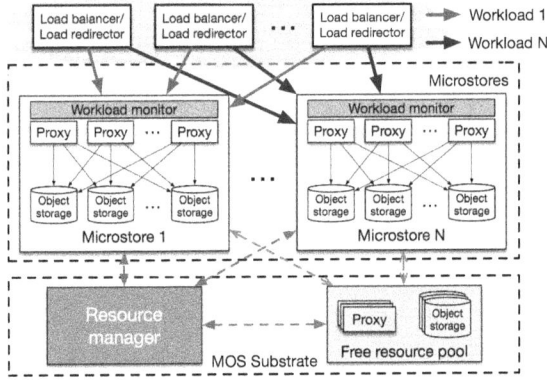

Figure 6: Overview of MOS architecture.

erogeneous resource combination can effectively meet tenants' requirement while improving data center cost efficiency.

R7 For large-object intensive workloads, we have to collectively consider the network bandwidth limits and the storage configuration. Given a certain network limit and SLA, a combination of slow and fast storage devices (e.g., HDD + SSD) may be able to serve the application needs in a resource efficient manner.

4. MOS FRAMEWORK

We design MOS based on the *rules-of-thumb* developed in §3, with the goal to address workload and datacenter resource heterogeneity. Instead of a conventional monolithic storage architecture, where all tenants/workloads share the storage resources using same or static configurations, MOS uses multiple object stores, which we refer to as microstores. To service changing workloads, MOS performs dynamic resource partitioning and provisioning, allowing each microstore within an object storage setup to run as a fully-functional object store unit. As pointed in our earlier motivational study, although the monolithic approach is simple to implement and configure, it is not necessarily resource efficient and can lead to wastage of CPU etc. resources.

Figure 6 shows the architecture of MOS, which consists of two layers: (1) **Microstores:** consists of multiple instances of object stores, a *microstore*, which is allocated a subset of proxy nodes and storage nodes that matches the requirements of application the microstore will support. (2) **MOS substrate:** consists of a resource manager that monitors the load on each microstore using a workload monitor and automatically reconfigures the resources assigned to the microstore to cope with workload shifts.

Microstores. A typical MOS deployment configures multiple instances of object store. Each instance comprises a subset of nodes in the cluster, and constitutes a unique microstore. Each microstore consists of two types of nodes: proxy nodes and storage nodes (each statically equipped with *hardware resources* such as CPUs, network interface cards (NICs) and storage devices, etc.). The proxy nodes are responsible for directing queries and managing the metadata for key space and replicas, etc. Whereas, the storage nodes store the object data in their local file systems and replicate the objects at multiple storage nodes for fault tolerance. The number of microstores configured in a deployment of MOS is specified by the service provider and will depend on the kinds of workloads that need to be supported. At any given

time during MOS's operation, the amount of resources allocated to each microstore is determined by its resource utilization. Such elasticity guarantees resource efficiency while delivering the needed performance.

MOS substrate. The MOS substrate layer consists of a central *Resource Manager* and the same number of *Workload Monitors* as the number of microstores. The main function of this layer is to perform online performance and resource utilization monitoring. The workload monitors are used to gather statistics of each running microstore, which are polled periodically by the resource manager to decide when and if a reconfiguration is warranted. The workload monitors also execute, as needed, online microstore reconfiguration commands issued by the Resource manager to meet tenants' demands. The resource manager manages the available pool of heterogeneous resources. It makes decisions about when and how to add or redistribute resources for the reconfiguration of a microstore in order to respond to workload shifts in the observed throughput and latency. We design the MOS framework in a modular fashion, where the core resource provisioning mechanism is configurable depending on tenants' needs.

Algorithm 1: MOS Resource Provisioning Algorithm.

Input: *microstores*: Microstore array, *free_pool*: free resource pool, $util_{low}$: low utilization threshold, $util_{high}$: high utilization threshold, *epoch*: configurable monitoring interval

begin
  $microstores.hw \leftarrow \text{init}(free\_pool)$
  while *true* **do**
    foreach *ms in microstores* **do**
      `// periodically collect monitoring stats`
      if $util_{low} \leq \text{util}(ms.hw) \leq util_{high}$ **then**
        $ms.firstTime \leftarrow true$
        continue
      else
        if $ms.firstTime$ **then**
          $ms.firstTime \leftarrow false$
          $ms.toChange \leftarrow 1$
        else
          $ms.toChange \leftarrow ms.toChange * 2$
        if $\text{util}(ms.hw) > util_{high}$ **then**
          `// to add in more resources`
          $ms.hw \leftarrow ms.hw + ms.toChange$
          `/* allocate resource from free resource pool */`
          $\text{alloc}(free\_pool, ms, ms.toChange)$
        else if $\text{util}(ms.hw) < util_{low}$ **then**
          `// to remove resources`
          $ms.hw \leftarrow ms.hw - 1$
          `/* return resource to free pool */`
          $\text{dealloc}(free\_pool, ms, 1)$
    $\text{sleep}(epoch)$

---

5. BASIC MOS

We first design a basic version of MOS. The goal of the basic version is to provide a coarse-grained dynamic resource management mechanism that can help achieve good resource utilization without worrying about SLA enforcement. The core of the basic MOS uses a greedy heuristic to perform resource provisioning based on online workload changes.

Basic MOS Algorithm. Algorithm 1 takes as input *microstores*, a vector of all microstores storing statistics such as hardware configuration, current load being served, and the resource utilization, e.g., CPU and network bandwidth utilization. Initially, the algorithm allocates the same amount of resources to each microstore conservatively. It then enters into the main loop, where the resource manager periodically (with configurable *epochs*) polls each microstore. In each iteration, if the resource utilization (fetched using util($ms.hw$)) of one microstore lies within a pre-defined threshold range (i.e., [$util_{low}$ $util_{high}$]), the algorithm simply moves to the next microstore. If the microstore is in suboptimal state, the algorithm decides to *quadratically* add or *linearly* remove resources. This is to ensure that the algorithm will not overshoot the de-allocation of resources, but can quickly respond to sudden workload increases.

6. ENHANCEMENTS: MOS++

There are two limitations of the basic MOS resource provisioning algorithm: (i) it is not SLA-aware; and (ii) it lacks the ability to perform fine-grained resource management. We address these shortcomings by designing support for container based deployment for object store in MOS to create MOS++. Containers greatly improve the flexibility for dynamic reconfiguration. For example, by leveraging containers, MOS++ can specify the number of CPU cores added to each microstore, support utilizing different types of storage devices in various configurations, and perform network partitioning.

Algorithm 2: MOS++ Resource Provisioning Algorithm (SLA-aware and Container-based).

Input: *free_pool*: free resource pool, sla_{low}: low SLA threshold, sla_{high}: high SLA threshold, $util_{low}$: low utilization threshold, $util_{high}$: high utilization threshold, $util_{thresh}$: % amount of time sampled in one epoch, *epoch*: configurable monitoring interval

begin
  | $ms \leftarrow$ init(sla, $free\_pool$)
  | **while** *true* **do**
    | | **if** $sla_{low} \leq ms.perf \leq sla_{high}$ **then**
    | | | **if** $util_{low} \leq ms.util \leq util_{high}$ **then**
    | | | | ∟ continue
    | | | **else**
    | | | | // fine-tune the ms config
    | | | | **if** $ms.util > util_{high}$ **then**
    | | | | | $ms.cont \leftarrow ms.cont + 1$
    | | | | | /* allocate resource from free resource pool */
    | | | | | ∟ alloc($free\_pool$, ms, 1)
    | | | | **else if** $ms.util < util_{low}$ **then**
    | | | | | $ms.cont \leftarrow ms.cont - 1$
    | | | | | /* return resource to free pool */
    | | | | | ∟ dealloc($free\_pool$, ms, 1)
    | | **else**
    | | | **if** sample($util_{low} \leq ms.util \leq util_{high}$) $> util_{thresh}$ **then**
    | | | | ∟ continue
    | | | **else if** $ms.perf > sla_{high}$ **then**
    | | | | // to remove containers
    | | | | $toChange \leftarrow$
    | | | | getContainers($ms.perf - sla_{high}$)
    | | | | $ms.cont \leftarrow ms.cont - toChange$
    | | | | ∟ dealloc($free\_pool$, ms, $toChange$)
    | | | **else if** $ms.perf < sla_{low}$ **then**
    | | | | // to add in containers
    | | | | $toChange \leftarrow$ getContainers($sla_{low} - ms.perf$)
    | | | | $ms.cont \leftarrow ms.cont + toChange$
    | | | | ∟ alloc($free\_pool$, ms, $toChange$)
    | ∟ sleep($epoch$)

Specifying SLAs. We consider latency-based SLAs with constraints for small-object intensive workloads and bandwidth based SLAs with constraints for large-object intensive workloads. Each SLA, which is associated with one object size attribute, has two parameters:

Notation	Description
E	Entities of the object store (proxy/object server)
cpu_{ij}^E	1 if CPU j is assigned to workload i, 0 otherwise
S	Disk storage type (PCIe/SATA SSD, HDD, etc.)
$disk_{ik}^S$	1 if Disk k is assigned to workload i, 0 otherwise
nw_i	Network bandwidth assigned to workload i

Table 2: Notations used in the LP model employed in MOS++.

- Average request response time (average latency) for small-object intensive workloads *OR* average bandwidth for large-object intensive workloads. For example, for a workload where 90% of all requests have a size of 10 KB , the average latency must be within a particular range, i.e., sla_{low} and sla_{high}, where sla_{low} is associated with the upper bound in terms of average latency and sla_{high} with the lower bound. Similarly, an SLA has a sla_{high} and sla_{low} associated with the upper and lower bound in terms of bandwidth, respectively, if the workload is large-object dominant, i.e., most objects with a size greater than 10 MB.

- Resource utilization: The fraction of time ($util_{thresh}$) the system resource utilization is within a specified range, e.g., $util_{low}$ and $util_{high}$.

The SLA requirement is met if *either one of the above two parameters is true*.

MOS++ Algorithm. Fine-grained resource allocation enables SLA-aware resource provisioning using Algorithm 2, which is an enhancement of Algorithm 1. In addition to the input parameters provided to the basic Algorithm 1, the enhanced algorithm takes three extra parameters: sla_{low}, low SLA threshold; sla_{high}, high SLA threshold; and $util_{thresh}$, fraction of time slots sampled during the period of one epoch.[2] In a workload, if the performance of a microstore goes above sla_{high}, resources are removed and reclaimed at per-container granularity from that microstore based on the suggested value provided by the function $getContainers(.)$. Conversely, resources are allocated and added into the microstore whose performance is observed to go below the sla_{low} value. We set a precondition of resource utilization as the second parameter for our SLA. Function $sample(.)$ periodically measures the resource utilization on a per-epoch basis. Again, the resources that need to be added are suggested by function $getContainers(.)$, which uses a linear programming (LP) optimizer to compute a near-optimal allocation plan.

Resource Provisioning Optimization. We define the amount of resources allocated to workload i as:

$$resource_i = \sum_j cpu_{ij}^E + \sum_l disk_{il}^S + nw_i . \quad (1)$$

The resource provisioning problem is modeled as an optimization problem to minimize the resources used for all workloads. Specifically, the objective is to:

---

[2]The sampling probability (%) is configurable. Each time slot is configured as 1% of the epoch. E.g., for an epoch of 5 minutes, a sampling time slot is 3 seconds.

$$minimize \sum_i resource_i \,, \qquad (2)$$

$$s.t. \ sla_i^{low} \leq \mathrm{cosperf}(resource_i) \leq sla_i^{high}, \forall i \,, \qquad (3)$$

$$0 \leq \sum_j cpu_{ij}^E \leq 1, cpu_{ij}^E = 0 \text{ or } 1, \forall i \,, \qquad (4)$$

$$0 \leq \sum_l disk_{il}^S \leq 1, disk_{il}^S = 0 \text{ or } 1, \forall i \,, \qquad (5)$$

$$0 < \sum_i nw_i \leq nw_{max} \,. \qquad (6)$$

Table 2 describes the notations used for representing the above model. Constraint 3 is used to guarantee that the SLA (the average response time for small-object workloads and the average bandwidth for large-object workloads) requirement is met. We profile the performance offline using an extensive stress test by iterating through nearly all possible resource configurations (§3). The estimated performance of a particular workload is estimated using function $cosperf(.)$, fed with the provisioned resources. Constraints 4 and 5 make sure that a CPU core or a storage drive can only be assigned to one workload. Similarly, Constraint 6 restricts the maximum network bandwidth (nw_{max}) that can be allocated to all the workloads. In the context of object stores, the CPU resources are allocated to two entities (denoted using E): proxies and object servers. While our model is general enough to cover many types of storage devices, we focus on three extant storage types (denoted using S) – PCIe/SATA SSDs, HDDs – in this work. The fairly small problem size implies that the optimization problem can be solved quickly, i.e., in seconds using CPLEX [8].

7. IMPLEMENTATION

Figure 7 shows the implementation details of MOS and MOS++. We build MOS on top of the Mesos [24] framework. The Mesos resource management is driven by the resource provisioning algorithms, i.e. Algorithm 1 or Algorithm 2. MOS launches Swift directly on the physical nodes serving as Mesos slaves. For MOS++ we extend Volt [11], a Mesos framework that can be used to launch containers on Mesos slaves.

For fine-grained resource allocation, we enforce the runtime constraints on resources while launching the Docker containers using the options provided by Docker [7]. The number of CPU cores is configurable for launching applications inside a container. Docker supports CPU core binding and disk size partitioning. For efficient disk utilization, we launch the object server containers with privileged mode, which enables the usage of devices attached to the host machine inside the container. We leverage this option to attach suitable storage devices for launched containers. To perform network partitioning, we use control groups (`cgroups`) [4] with Linux traffic control (`tc`) [9].

Container based deployment of Swift offers several advantages such as rapid deployment, portability across machines, easy sharing, lightweight footprint and simplified maintenance. All these advantages come at a cost of negligible or "close to zero" overhead [22]. To provide high availability, the Mesos cluster is launched with 3 masters with one acting as the leader and the rest on standby. In case of a master failure, a standby leader becomes the leader as a result of the election done by Zookeeper [25].

We have implemented our own proxy executor, object ex-

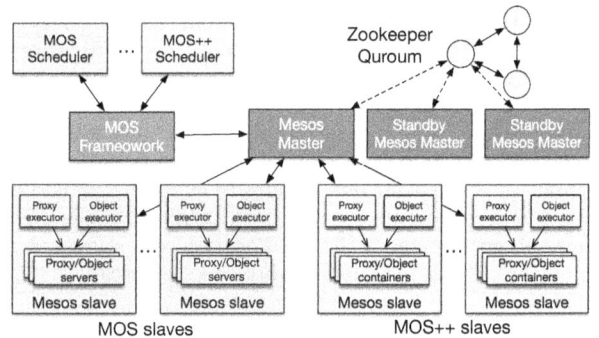

Figure 7: MOS modules and their interactions. Mesos provides support to launch Swift either directly on physical nodes or inside containers.

ecutor, and Python scripts to automate online reconfiguration of Swift in a distributed setup. The proxy executor is used to support dynamic reconfiguration of proxy servers inside the containers. The object executor performs online disk capacity management using the `swift-ring-builder` tool[3], whenever the storage configuration is updated. The code to build Docker container images and the Docker images for Swift proxy and object server are publicly available on Github [5, 6].

8. EVALUATION

We present the evaluation of MOS++ using both a prototype implementation and simulations. We first use the prototype to evaluate a number of object store setups under multi-tenancy in both static and dynamic workloads. This is followed by a simulation study of a large-scale system to compare MOS++ and MOS.

8.1 Prototype Evaluation

Experimental Methodology. We evaluate MOS++ using a 128-core local testbed. The testbed is connected using a 10 Gbps switch, with a maximum bandwidth of 40 Gbps. We emulate a two-tenant (client) environment, i.e., we run COSBench on two separate machines within the same subnet. We use `WorkloadA` (small-object read-intensive workload) and `WorkloadC` (large-object read-intensive workload) for this purpose. We compare MOS++ against two different object store setups – `Default`, where we use off-the-shelf monolithic configuration of Swift, and `Static`, where we statically configure two micro object stores designated for two tenants based on the rules-of-thumb of §3. The static approach is more advanced than the default segmentation policies [10] and serves as another point of comparison for our approach. Note that we focus on MOS++ for our prototype evaluation as it also encompass the basic design of MOS.

The `Default` setup is launched directly on the physical machines. `Static`, like MOS++, is launched inside containers. For `Static` setup, we tried several different overall configurations and selected the best one. Specifically, 75% CPU cores, 30% of NW bandwidth, and 100% PCIe SSD with 30% SATA SSD are assigned to `WorkloadA`. Accordingly, 25%

---

[3] Swift lazily migrates existing data replicas to newly added disks where new data can be instantly written and persisted. We leverage this feature to (i) control the I/O performance on new data that is written in newly added disks, and (ii) amortize the data migration cost.

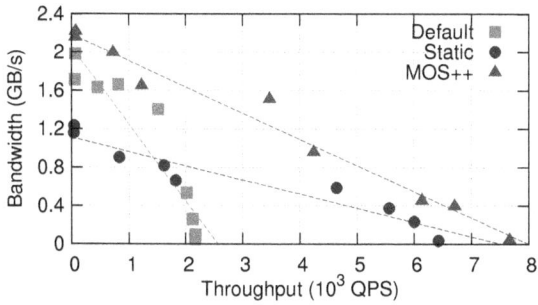

Figure 8: Overall throughput vs. bandwidth observed under different setups. Dotted lines are generated using linear regression, indicating the linear relationship between the overall throughput and bandwidth.

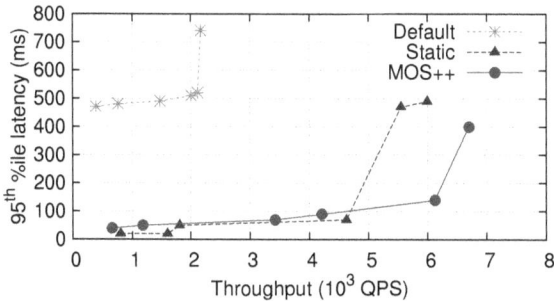

Figure 9: Throughput vs. 95th percentile latency under WorkloadA.

CPU cores, 70% NW bandwidth, and 70% SATA SSD are assigned to WorkloadC. MOS++ starts initially with the same configuration as Static throughout our evaluation. Regarding runtime parameters, we set sla_{low} to be proportional to the workloads' load and sla_{high} $2\times$ of sla_{low}. We set $util_{low}$ 65% and $util_{high}$ 85%. We set $epoch$ to be 3 minutes and $util_{thresh}$ as 80%.

Performance Evaluation. In our first set of experiments, we evaluate MOS++'s ability to handle heterogeneous varying workloads. We vary the COSBench processes from 2 to 1024 for WorkloadA to increase the throughput, while we decrease WorkloadC's load by varying the COSBench processes from 32 to 2. Figure 8 plots the overall performance of the two studied workloads in terms of both throughput (QPS) and bandwidth (MB/s). Default achieves significantly higher bandwidth compared to Static when WorkloadC dominates (the far left part on X-axis dimension). This is because the large-object workload consumes most of the network bandwidth to transfer packets containing payload for large objects. Guided by our rules-of-thumb, Static's statically provisioned micro store setup is able to balance the performance of both workloads to some extent. Hence, as WorkloadA gradually increases and eventually dominates, Static outperforms Default by as much as $2\times$. By leveraging workload-aware elasticity support, MOS++ combines the "best of both worlds", hence we see 10.4–89.6% improvement in overall throughput and 7.6–79.8% improvement in overall bandwidth, compared to both Default and Static. Thus, MOS++ is able to improve the overall performance for the two tenants with workloads exhibiting dramatically different characteristics.

Figure 9 depicts the 95th percentile read tail latency and throughput tradeoffs observed for WorkloadA. For WorkloadA, Default performs the worst and lies in the upper-left corner

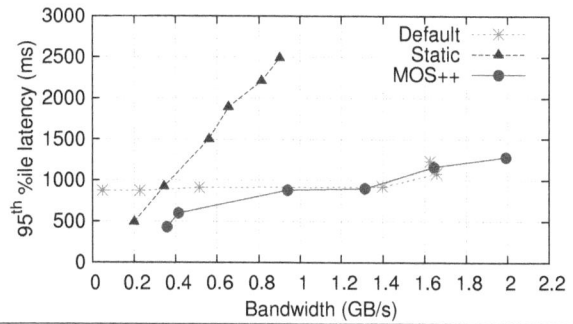

Figure 10: Bandwidth vs. 95th percentile latency under WorkloadC. Average latency results show similar trend.

of the scatter chart. Static achieves comparatively similar performance with MOS++ as WorkloadA starts to increase. By adapting to the increasing load and adding more CPU power for WorkloadA, MOS++ eventually outperforms Static at peak loads (the right-most two data points) by up to 11.7% in throughput and up to 70.2% in tail latency. Figure 10 shows a similar trend under WorkloadC. Under the large-object dominant workload, Static is bottlenecked by its statically allocated network resource and hence limits the bandwidth for WorkloadC. Accordingly, we observe up to 79% improvement in bandwidth and up to 50.6% reduction in tail latency, compared to Default. Thus, MOS++ is able to improve the performance for both tenants, and effectively remove the performance bottleneck observed in Default and Static setups.

Adaptivity and Efficiency Evaluation. In our next experiment, we evaluate the adaptivity and resource efficiency of MOS++. We use a dynamically changing heterogeneous workload, which is issued concurrently by two tenants – WorkloadA and WorkloadC. The workload is generated by COS-Bench and is composed of three stages. In Stage 1, the workload is dominated by large objects (WorkloadC). At around 40 min, Stage 2 begins with abrupt change in workload characteristics as the small-obj dominant workload (WorkloadA) instantaneously spikes and then gradually shifts down. This lasts for until around 200 min. Finally, at 230 min, in Stage 3 there is another abrupt change as WorkloadA once again increases and dominates. With these three stages concatenated together we capture the behavior of MOS++ both under abrupt as well as gradual change in a dynamically changing workload in a multi-tenant environment. Figure 11(a) and Figure 11(b) plot the average throughput change and the average read latency change[4] of WorkloadA, respectively. Figure 11(c) plots the average bandwidth change of WorkloadC. Besides, Figure 12 depicts the breakdown of a variety of resources used in our tests.

As Stage 1 begins, MOS++ achieves the same performance as Static. This is because MOS++ starts off with the same setup as Static. After around 5 min, MOS++ slightly outperforms Static by 12%, because MOS++ is SLA-aware and gradually reduces the network bandwidth originally allocated to WorkloadA and its performance reaches the highest after 5 min. Though Static achieves comparatively similar performance, it is not able to satisfy the SLA at 100% since its allotted network bandwidth is quickly saturated. In contrast, as observed in Figure 12, WorkloadC eventually uses up to 95% of all the available network resources (**R3** and **R5**

---

[4] We observed a similar trend for write latency.

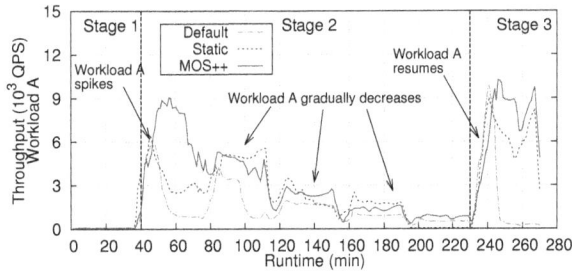

(a) Throughput under `WorkloadA`.

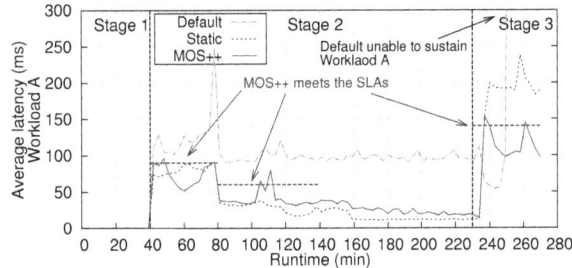

(b) Average latency under `WorkloadA`.

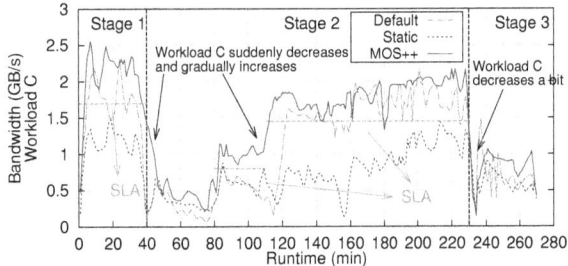

(c) Bandwidth under `WorkloadC`.

Figure 11: Performance of MOS++ and the baselines under a dynamically changing heterogeneous workload. Purple dashed lines represent tenant-defined SLAs in terms of average latency (sla_{low}) for `WorkloadA`. Orange dashed lines represent tenant-defined SLAs in terms of bandwidth (sla_{low}) for `WorkloadC`.

in §3). Accordingly, MOS++ detects nothing significant in `WorkloadA` and decides to free up the CPU resource originally allocated to `WorkloadA` (recall that MOS++ and MOS starts with the same configuration). This clearly demonstrates that, rather than reserving resources statically, MOS++ elastically reprovisions the resources to achieve better resource efficiency while meeting the SLA.

`Stage 2` instantaneously begins at around 40 min and then quickly spikes. At this time, MOS++ immediately start to react. Driven by the increasing `WorkloadA` and the specified SLA (90 ms average latency), MOS++ provisions proxies and object stores with more CPU cores. This can be observed in Figure 12 (**R2** and **R4**). Note in Figure 11(a), MOS++ improves the throughput of `WorkloadA` by up to 2.1× at around 60 min. As `WorkloadC`'s load decreases as `Stage 2` begins, MOS++ reduces the CPU cores allocated to `WorkloadC` and reassigns them to `WorkloadA`. Correspondingly, 58% of the network bandwidth allocated is reclaimed and marked as free and 21% is reallocated to `WorkloadA` (**R6**). `WorkloadA` spikes at around 60 min and gradually decreases while the `WorkloadC` slowly increases. Accordingly, MOS++ adapts by reclaiming the extra CPU resources that are not needed for the current load/SLA for `WorkloadA`, and grabs back the net-

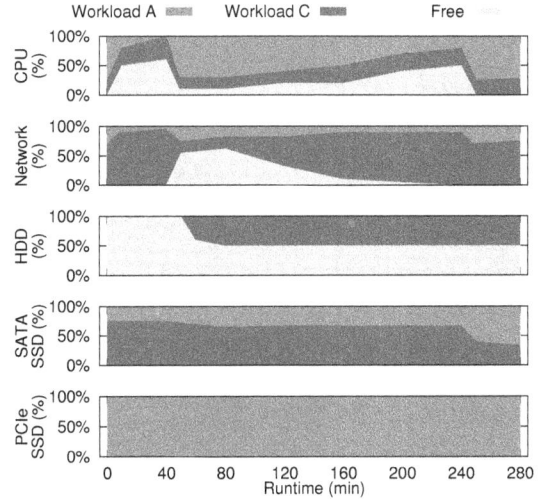

Figure 12: Resource allocation breakdown under dynamically changing heterogeneous workload.

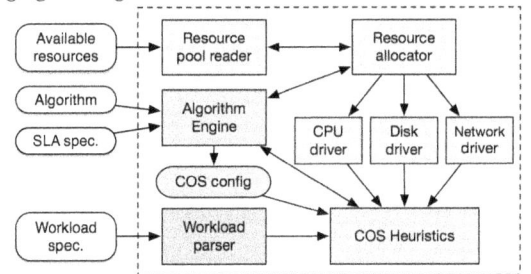

Figure 13: COSPerf architecture.

work resource, which gets eventually saturated by `WorkloadC` (Figure 11(c)). Note that MOS++ allocates 50% of the HDD capacity to `WorkloadC` at 80 min, since the optimizer detects that a combination of HDD+SSD yields the most economical setup provided the given SLA (**R7**). As shown in Figure 11(a), MOS++ maintains the highest performance for both tenants while being resource efficient, whereas both `Default` and `Static` fail to do so, which further demonstrates the superiority of MOS++.

`Stage 3` begins at around 230 min with a sudden spike of `WorkloadA` and about half drop in `WorkloadC`. `Default` is unable to sustain `WorkloadA`, because the network bandwidth is mostly used up by `WorkloadC`. Again, MOS++ maintains the best performance for both tenants featuring the SLA-awareness and workload adaptivity.

8.2 Comparison of MOS and MOS++

In our next set of experiments, we use a simulation study to compare MOS and MOS++ for a large-scale setup.[5]

COSPerf Simulator. We design and implement a cloud object store simulator (COSPerf) based on the rules-of-thumb discussed in §3. Figure 13 depicts the architecture of COSPerf. A resource parser takes as input available resources, and sort them based on capability/capacity. The resources from these pools are then fetched by the resource allocator for launching resource drivers including a CPU driver, a disk driver, and a network driver. Resource allocator is driven by the algorithm engine, which is used to simulate the resource provisioning algorithm that is provided as a configurable pa-

---

[5]For comparison of MOS with `Static` and the monolithic `Default` setup please refer to our short paper [12].

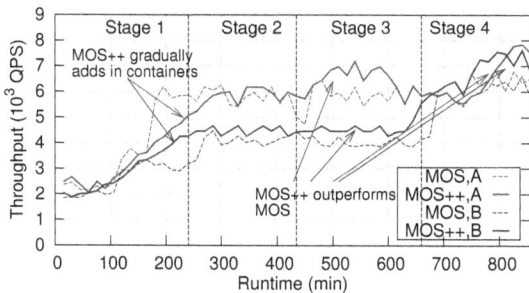

Figure 14: Throughput of MOS Vs. MOS++ under `WorkloadA` and `WorkloadB`.

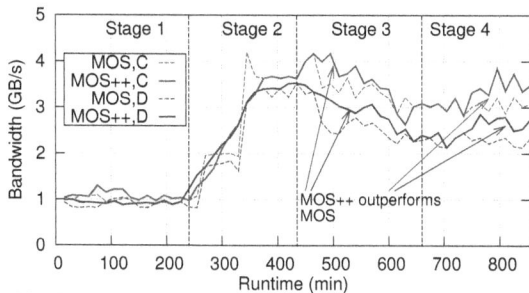

Figure 15: Bandwidth of MOS Vs. MOS++ under `WorkloadC` and `WorkloadD`.

rameter to COSPerf. The algorithm engine interacts with the resource allocator to keep track of the available resources and generates an object store configuration file. The algorithm engine also monitors the simulated performance of the launched microstores.

A cloud object store (COS) heuristics module takes workloads as input and predicts performance under a set of specified software/hardware configurations. The dynamic shifts in simulated performance due to online reconfiguration and workload changes are modeled and calculated by the COS heuristics module, which is built based on the extensive analysis and profiling of a real object store under various scenarios (§3). Thousands of experiments (each running for 15 minutes) were executed under varying load/configuration to further fine-tune our COS heuristics model.

Simulation Methodology. For simulation, we assume a pool of 50 server machines with diversified (heterogeneous) hardware configurations, including CPU, network, and storage devices. Specifically, we use the following pool of resources: (i) 3 32-core machines, 4 16-core, 31 8-core machines, and 12 4-core machines; (ii) 18 10 Gbps and 32 1 Gbps NICs; and (iii) HDD to SSD ratio was 70% to 30%. The workloads run for about 14 hours and we divide the workloads in four major stages. For analysis purposes, we focus on throughput in terms of QPS for small object workloads and bandwidth for large objects.

Simulation Evaluation. Figure 14 and Figure 15 show how MOS and MOS++ behave under dynamically-changing `WorkloadA-D`. The goal of our evaluation is to test under both abrupt and gradual change in a workload under multi-tenancy, which are emulated by our workloads. In `Stage 1`, as the load of small-object workloads (i.e., `WorkloadA` and `WorkloadB`) increases (as shown in Figure 14), MOS uses resources from the free resource pool to keep the resource utilization under control until the utilization stabilizes and falls back in the $[util_{low}, util_{high}]$ range. MOS++ also achieves the same goal but by allocating resources at a finer granular-

ity. As a result, we do not see a sudden spike in QPS. Instead the transition is smoother, which allows both `WorkloadA` as well as `WorkloadB` to almost linearly increase QPS. In addition to maintaining resource utilization within the acceptable range, MOS++ also makes sure that SLA requirements are met.

As `Stage 2` begins, the load of large-object workloads (i.e., `WorkloadC` and `WorkloadD`) increases. As shown in figure 15, both MOS and MOS++ start adding resources to accommodate the increasing demand on network bandwidth. Again, MOS++ keeps fine-grained track of the resources at per-container basis and just allocates the right amount of resources to meet the tenant requirements while maximizing the resource efficiency. Starting around 310 min, however, MOS ends up adding more resources than needed to microstore C and D. Though MOS is able to lower down the network utilization from 95% to 85%, it causes a spike in performance.

From the beginning of `Stage 3` up until around 500 min, both MOS and MOS++ end up utilizing all the resources due to the increasing demands from all tenants. As shown in Figure 14 and Figure 15, MOS++ outperforms MOS by up to 25% for `WorkloadA`, and up to 31% for `WorkloadD`. This is due to the following design choices we make in MOS++: (i) MOS++ allocates resources at the container granularity; and (ii) MOS++'s optimizer generates a better resource provisioning plan that yields higher performance by exploiting all the available resources. After 500 min, the load decreases for `WorkloadC` and `WorkloadD`. As a result, MOS and MOS++ reclaim resources from microstore C and D to the pool of free resources. Finally, in `Stage 4`, the load further increases for `WorkloadA` and `WorkloadB`. As a result, MOS and MOS++ utilize the resources freed up in `Stage 3` from `WorkloadC` and `WorkloadD`. At this point, both MOS and MOS++ quickly detects performance improvement opportunity for `WorkloadB` as the throughput of `WorkloadB` is still at a low level, while more resources are also added into `WorkloadA` with the goal to maintain the CPU utilization within the "sweet" range. Hence, tenants will not see performance lost as the workload shifts. MOS++ further improves MOS's performance on `WorkloadA` and `WorkloadB` by up to 33% and 26%, respectively. This, again, demonstrates the superiority of MOS++ in effectively utilizing the limited resources for maximizing performance improvement and meeting tenants' SLAs.

Table 3 presents a summary of the average performance by combining all stages for `WorkloadA-D`. The results show that for small-object workloads, MOS++ achieves 12.4% better performance

Workload	MOS	MOS++
A	4444 QPS	4994 QPS
B	3828 QPS	4429 QPS
C	2 GB/s	2.3 GB/s
D	1.6 GB/s	1.9 GB/s

Table 3: Average performance summary.

for `WorkloadA`, and 15.7% better performance for `WorkloadB`, compared to MOS. Similarly, average performance of MOS++ for large-object workloads is 15% higher for `WorkloadC` and 18.8% better for `WorkloadD` than that of MOS.

9. DISCUSSION

There are two limitations that are not fully addressed in our current implementation. First, although MOS supports multi-tenancy and heterogeneous workload separation, we limit the number of microstores to be launched based on workload characteristics (i.e., object sizes) to reduce the implementation complexity and reconfiguration overhead. Consequently, it limits the kinds of different workloads the system can effectively handle. Should a workload change its inherent characteristics, e.g., the object size distribution changes dramatically, and no longer fit well with any provisioned microstores, the system may end up doing reconfiguration thrashing. This in turn will lead to reduced performance. A possible solution is to perform online workload analysis and profiling at the load balancer/redirector side, and using the information to compute an optimal number of microstores and perform workload-to-microstore mapping on the fly. Such a dynamic detect-and-map system is part of our future work. Second, although MOS++ is able to meet the SLAs by leveraging offline workload profiling and online optimization, it does not currently consider the profit, i.e., revenue, for the service provider and tenant utility, i.e., $perf/\$$, while provisioning the microstores. A feasible yet simple cloud-profit-aware solution can be to enhance our optimizer by incorporating the cloud pricing model and monetary profit. This aspect is orthogonal to our work, but can be easily incorporated into the design if needed.

10. CONCLUSION

In this paper, we have presented an experimental analysis of cloud object store, and proposed a set of rules-of-thumb based on the study. The rules provide practical guidelines for service administrators and online resource managers to better tune object store performance to application needs. The resulting system, MOS, outperforms extant object stores in multi-tenant environments. Furthermore, we build MOS++ to enhance MOS by leveraging containers for fine-grained resource management and higher resource efficiency. Our experimentation reveals that it is possible to exploit the inherent heterogeneity within modern datacenters to better serve heterogeneous workloads across multiple tenants. Evaluation with our prototype implementation shows that MOS++ improves performance by up to 89.6% and 79.8% compared to the default monolithic and statically configured object store setup, respectively. We have implemented COSPerf, a cloud object store simulator, to further verify the design choices of MOS++. Results show that, by utilizing the same set of resources, MOS++ achieves up to 18.8% performance improvement compared to the basic MOS.

Acknowledgments. We thank the anonymous reviewers for their comments. This work was sponsored in part by the NSF under Grants CNS-1405697 and CNS-1422788.

11. REFERENCES

[1] Arq. https://www.haystacksoftware.com/arq/.
[2] Ceph vs Swift. http://goo.gl/rtvrvg.
[3] Cloud backup with HP cloud. http://goo.gl/43bC5W.
[4] Control groups. https://goo.gl/KkCXAR.
[5] Docker container image for Swift object server. https://hub.docker.com/r/alivt/swift-object.
[6] Docker container image for Swift proxy sever. https://hub.docker.com/r/alivt/swift-proxy.
[7] Docker run preferences. https://goo.gl/SoF9Pc.
[8] IBM CPLEX optimizer. http://goo.gl/BA95mC.
[9] Linux traffic control. http://goo.gl/E5aQdq.
[10] Swfit storage policies. http://goo.gl/hRrySo.
[11] Volt git repo. https://github.com/VoltFramework/volt.
[12] A. Anwar, Y. Cheng, A. Gupta, and A. R. Butt. Taming the cloud object storage with mos. In *ACM PDSW*, 2015.
[13] A. Anwar, K. Krish, and A. R. Butt. On the use of microservers in supporting hadoop applications. In *IEEE CLUSTER*, 2014.
[14] D. Beaver, S. Kumar, H. C. Li, J. Sobel, P. Vajgel, et al. Finding a needle in haystack: Facebook's photo storage. In *USENIX OSDI*, 2010.
[15] N. Bonvin, T. G. Papaioannou, and K. Aberer. A self-organized, fault-tolerant and scalable replication scheme for cloud storage. In *ACM SOCC*, 2010.
[16] J. Chen, C. Douglas, M. Mutsuzaki, P. Quaid, R. Ramakrishnan, S. Rao, and R. Sears. Walnut: a unified cloud object store. In *ACM SIGMOD*, 2012.
[17] Y. Cheng, M. S. Iqbal, A. Gupta, and A. R. Butt. Cast: Tiering storage for data analytics in the cloud. In *ACM HPDC*, 2015.
[18] Y. Cheng, M. S. Iqbal, A. Gupta, and A. R. Butt. Pricing games for hybrid object stores in the cloud: provider vs. tenant. In *USENIX HotCloud*, 2015.
[19] F. Cruz, F. Maia, M. Matos, R. Oliveira, J. Paulo, J. Pereira, and R. Vilaça. Met: workload aware elasticity for nosql. In *ACM EuroSys*, 2013.
[20] S. Das, D. Agrawal, and A. El Abbadi. Elastras: An elastic transactional data store in the cloud. *USENIX HotCloud*, 2009.
[21] C. Delimitrou and C. Kozyrakis. Paragon: Qos-aware scheduling for heterogeneous datacenters. In *ACM ASPLOS*, 2013.
[22] W. Felter, A. Ferreira, R. Rajamony, and J. Rubio. An updated performance comparison of virtual machines and linux containers. *IBM Research Report*, 2014.
[23] H. Greenberg, J. Bent, and G. Grider. Mdhim: A parallel key/value framework for hpc. In *USENIX HotStorage*, 2015.
[24] B. Hindman, A. Konwinski, M. Zaharia, A. Ghodsi, A. D. Joseph, R. H. Katz, S. Shenker, and I. Stoica. Mesos: A platform for fine-grained resource sharing in the data center. In *USENIX NSDI*, 2011.
[25] P. Hunt, M. Konar, F. P. Junqueira, and B. Reed. Zookeeper: Wait-free coordination for internet-scale systems. In *USENIX ATC*, 2010.
[26] K. Krish, A. Anwar, and A. R. Butt. hats: A heterogeneity-aware tiered storage for hadoop. In *IEEE CCGrid*, 2014.
[27] K. Krish, A. Anwar, and A. R. Butt. [phi] sched: A heterogeneity-aware hadoop workflow scheduler. In *IEEE MASCOTS*, 2014.
[28] G. Lee, B.-G. Chun, and R. H. Katz. Heterogeneity-aware resource allocation and scheduling in the cloud. In *USENIX HotCloud*, 2011.
[29] H. C. Lim, S. Babu, and J. S. Chase. Automated control for elastic storage. In *ACM ICAC*, 2010.
[30] J. Mars, L. Tang, and R. Hundt. Heterogeneity in "homogeneous" warehouse-scale computers: A performance opportunity. *IEEE CAL*, 2011.
[31] M. A. Sevilla, N. Watkins, C. Maltzahn, I. Nassi, S. A. Brandt, S. A. Weil, G. Farnum, and S. Fineberg. Mantle: a programmable metadata load balancer for the ceph file system. In *ACM SC*, 2015.
[32] Y. Tanimura, S. Yanagita, and T. Hamanishi. A high performance, qos-enabled, s3-based object store. In *IEEE CCGrid*, 2014.
[33] B. Trushkowsky, P. Bodík, A. Fox, M. J. Franklin, M. I. Jordan, and D. A. Patterson. The scads director: Scaling a distributed storage system under stringent performance requirements. In *USENIX FAST*, 2011.
[34] S. A. Weil, S. A. Brandt, E. L. Miller, D. D. Long, and C. Maltzahn. Ceph: A scalable, high-performance distributed file system. In *USENIX OSDI*, 2006.
[35] Q. Zheng, H. Chen, Y. Wang, J. Duan, and Z. Huang. Cosbench: A benchmark tool for cloud object storage services. In *IEEE CLOUD*, 2012.

IMPACC: A Tightly Integrated MPI+OpenACC Framework Exploiting Shared Memory Parallelism

Jungwon Kim
Oak Ridge National Laboratory
kimj@ornl.gov

Seyong Lee
Oak Ridge National Laboratory
lees2@ornl.gov

Jeffrey S. Vetter
Oak Ridge National Laboratory
vetter@ornl.gov

ABSTRACT

We propose IMPACC, an MPI+OpenACC framework for heterogeneous accelerator clusters. IMPACC tightly integrates MPI and OpenACC, while exploiting the shared memory parallelism in the target system. IMPACC dynamically adapts the input MPI+OpenACC applications on the target heterogeneous accelerator clusters to fully exploit target system-specific features. IMPACC provides the programmers with the unified virtual address space, automatic NUMA-friendly task-device mapping, efficient integrated communication routines, seamless streamlining of asynchronous executions, and transparent memory sharing. We have implemented IMPACC and evaluated its performance using three heterogeneous accelerator systems, including Titan supercomputer. Results show that IMPACC can achieve easier programming, higher performance, and better scalability than the current MPI+OpenACC model.

CCS Concepts

•Software and its engineering → Distributed programming languages; Concurrent programming languages; Source code generation; Runtime environments;

Keywords

MPI; OpenACC; Clusters; Heterogeneous computing; Programming models

1. INTRODUCTION

High Performance Computing (HPC) systems are becoming deeply hierarchical and heterogeneous. Instead of expensive shared memory systems, distributed memory systems, such as clusters that consist of low cost commodity servers, have become the mainstream in HPC architectures [9]. A typical cluster node is equipped with multi-socket, multi-core CPUs in a shared NUMA memory architecture. The addition of accelerators, such as NVIDIA/AMD GPUs, MICs

HPDC'16, May 31-June 04, 2016, Kyoto, Japan

ⓒ 2016 ACM. ISBN 978-1-4503-4314-5/16/05. . . $15.00

DOI: http://dx.doi.org/10.1145/2907294.2907302

(Intel Xeon Phi coprocessors), and FPGAs further increase the levels of the hierarchy and heterogeneity[48].

During this move to clusters in HPC environments, a distributed memory message passing model has played a pivotal role. The Message Passing Interface (MPI) is a message passing API, and it has been widely accepted as the de facto industry standard. This enables the HPC programmer to develop portable and scalable parallel applications using MPI, which can then execute on nearly all HPC systems.

Unlike MPI, there was no industry standard for accelerator programming models. Early on, each accelerator had its own programming language or methodology: CUDA for NVIDIA GPUs, Brook+ for AMD GPUs, LEO for MICs, and HDL for FPGAs. In order to achieve code portability, the Khronos Group introduced OpenCL as a standard for accelerator programming model. However, OpenCL does not provide ease of programming and performance portability because it exposes low-level hardware architecture to the programmers [41, 45].

Later, the OpenACC API [3] was designed to provide an easy, high-level, and portable way to develop parallel programs across a wide range of accelerators. OpenACC simplifies the accelerator programming through the use of directives, like the OpenMP API. Based on directives supplied by the programmers, OpenACC compilers automatically offload compute-intensive code to an accelerator, managing data movement between the host CPU and the accelerator. However, OpenACC and most of existing accelerator programming models are intra-node programming models, assuming node-scale systems (*host + accelerator*), where one or small number of accelerators are attached to the host CPU. This design, in turn, limits scalability [37].

In order to write portable and scalable applications for heterogeneous accelerator clusters, a hybrid *MPI+OpenACC* programming model can be feasible. It inherits the advantages, such as high performance, scalability, and portability from MPI and programmability and portability from OpenACC. However, this mixture of two orthogonal programming models introduces some inefficiencies and complexities including redundant data movement and excessive synchronization between the models.

In addition, a deeper hybrid programming model with MPI across nodes, shared memory parallel programming models, such as OpenMP within a node, and OpenACC for accelerators has some advantages over the flat MPI+OpenACC hybrid model[20, 35, 51]. It can exploit a shared memory parallelism in the system, such as data sharing, efficient buffer management without inter-process communication, and direct data transfer between accelerators on the same node[6, 43]. However, the deeper hybrid programming model exposes deeper memory and architecture hierarchy to the programmers, which is more complex and harder to program, resulting in lower productivity.

1.1 Contributions

In this paper, we propose *IMPACC* (*I*ntegrated *M*essage *P*assing *ACC*elerator programming), a novel programming framework for heterogeneous accelerator clusters; IMPACC tightly integrates MPI and OpenACC, while exploiting the shared memory parallelism in the system. IMPACC dynamically adapts the input MPI+OpenACC application onto the target heterogeneous system to fully exploit target system-specific features. This enables IMPACC to provide programmers with easier programming, higher performance, and better scalability than the current MPI+OpenACC model in heterogeneous accelerator cluster programming. This paper makes the following contributions:

- IMPACC integrates task creation in MPI and accelerator assignment in OpenACC adaptively to the target system. Also, the IMPACC runtime pins each task to certain CPUs in a NUMA-friendly way, considering its assigned accelerator in order to avoid undesired communication overhead.

- The IMPACC runtime maps the device memories of all available accelerators in a node onto the single *unified node virtual address space*. IMPACC implements an MPI task as a lightweight user-level thread, and the threaded-MPI tasks on the same node run on the single unified node virtual address space.

- IMPACC presents *unified MPI communication routines* that integrate MPI communication routines and OpenACC accelerator memory copy operations, with the help of the unified node virtual address space. It eliminates redundant communication both between tasks and between MPI and OpenACC, and it leads to low communication overhead.

- IMPACC provides *unified activity queue* that integrates non-blocking MPI communication to the OpenACC asynchronous activity queue in order to allow seamless streamlining of asynchronous intra-node/internode communication. It eliminates synchronization between two orthogonal streamlines of MPI and OpenACC, resulting in better programmability and scalability.

- IMPACC proposes *node heap aliasing technique*. It enables the MPI tasks that are in the same node and that have a producer-consumer relationship to share data transparently to the application while keeping their MPI semantics the same.

- The programmers can exploit full features of IMPACC, such as unified MPI communication routines, unified activity queue, and intra-node data sharing by adding OpenACC directive extensions for IMPACC (*#pragma acc mpi*).

- We show the effectiveness of IMPACC by implementing the compiler and runtime. We evaluate its performance with three heterogeneous accelerator clusters (two NVIDIA GPU-based clusters (*PSG*[8] and *Titan*[1]) and one Intel MIC-based cluster (*Beacon*[18])). The evaluation results demonstrate that IMPACC achieves ease of programming, high performance, and scalability on extreme-scale systems.

2. IMPACC ARCHITECTURE OVERVIEW

This section describes the architecture of IMPACC using a hierarchy of models: platform model, programming model, execution model, and memory model.

2.1 Platform Model

The platform model for IMPACC is a heterogeneous accelerator cluster as shown in Figure 1. Heterogeneous accelerator clusters have been widely used in HPC because they offer opportunities to greatly increase computational performance within a limited power budget. Nominally, a cluster consists of one or more compute nodes. The nodes are connected by an interconnection network (e.g., InfiniBand, custom interconnect). Typically, the nodes share storage through a high performance parallel file system like Lustre and GPFS.

Each node is equipped with multi-socket, multi-core CPUs in a shared NUMA memory architecture and augmented with one or more accelerators (e.g., NVIDIA/AMD GPUs, MICs, FPGAs). An accelerator communicates with the CPUs and other accelerators via a peripheral interconnect, such as PCIe and NVLink. For GPUs, the accelerator consists of multiple fully parallel execution units. Each execution unit is multithreaded, and each thread on the execution unit supports SIMD or vector operations. Especially, in order to exploit all available computing resources fully, IMPACC considers a set of CPU cores as an accelerator.

2.2 Programming Model

IMPACC uses MPI+OpenACC as its programming model to provide programmers with a practical way to write scalable, portable, and high-efficient HPC applications for heterogeneous accelerator clusters.

MPI is a message passing library used for distributed memory systems. It is designed primarily to support Single Program, Multiple Data (SPMD) model. Its autonomous task execution, good locality, and fine-grained control enable MPI to achieve high performance and good scalability in large-scale systems. MPI is widely recognized as the de facto standard for parallel HPC programming in industry and academia, and most existing HPC applications are written in MPI [11, 49].

Rewriting large legacy HPC applications for heterogeneous accelerator clusters using CUDA, OpenCL, or HDL can be difficult, if not impractical. It requires significant rewriting and restructuring of hundreds to thousands of lines, and reorganization of major data structures.

To address this challenge, OpenACC was designed as a high-level accelerator programming model to provide code and performance portability across a wide range of accelerators. The OpenACC API contains a set of directive-based extensions to standard languages that enable offloading of compute-intensive code to accelerators. Because OpenACC is a directive-based model, it requires few modification of the legacy application code, and little restructuring of the code, if any. Moreover, the modified OpenACC application can be run as the unmodified original application by ignoring the OpenACC directives at compilation time.

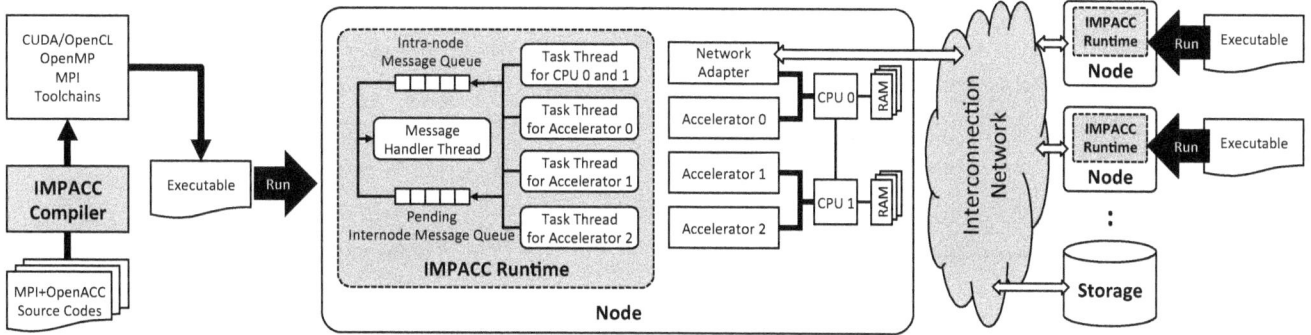

Figure 1: The Overview of the IMPACC Framework.

2.3 Execution Model

The IMPACC execution model exposes four levels of parallelism via *device*, *gang*, *worker*, and *vector* parallelism. Device parallelism follows the SPMD execution model. When IMPACC runs an MPI+OpenACC program on a heterogeneous accelerator cluster, the IMPACC runtime in every node launches the same number of program instances as the number of available accelerator devices in the node. The program instance is called an *MPI task*, or *task* for short. The IMPACC runtime implements a task as a lightweight user-level thread and assigns a distinct accelerator to each task as shown in Figure 1.

A task executes the host program in the input application on the host CPU with its attached accelerator device. Each task has its own unique id, called *rank*, throughout the whole running system. The tasks follow different execution paths to work on different data using the rank simultaneously in parallel. The device parallelism in IMPACC hides the hierarchy of nodes in the running cluster from the programmers, and thus it presents a flat-task view on the cluster.

A host program offloads compute intensive regions to the attached accelerator device. When a device executes a compute region, one or more gangs are launched on the device. Gang parallelism is coarse-grained. A gang has one or more workers. A worker is fine-grained and has a vector width. Vector parallelism is for SIMD or vector operations. Gang, worker, and vector parallelism are data parallelism. They are expressed as OpenACC *gang, worker, and vector* clauses, respectively.

2.4 Memory Model

The IMPACC memory model provides a single virtual address space, called *unified node virtual address space*, across the host system memory and device memories of all available accelerators in a node.

The IMPACC architecture assumes that the accelerator may be a discrete accelerator, such as an NVIDIA/AMD GPU, MIC and FPGA, or an integrated accelerator such as an AMD APU and a set of CPU cores. In the former case, the physical device memory on the accelerator is completely separate from the host memory. The IMPACC runtime dynamically maps their device memories in the unified node virtual address space. The host program performs all data movement between the host memory and device memory using OpenACC *data* constructs. A data construct allocates device memory and copies data between host and device memory. On the other hand, the integrated accelerator

shares one system memory with the host. In this case, there is no need for additional memory mapping by the runtime and explicit memory management by the host program, and the operations can be elided.

In IMPACC, all MPI tasks in a node share the same unified node virtual address space because an MPI task runs as a user-level thread. The IMPACC runtime exploits the shared memory parallelism between tasks on the same unified node virtual address space to optimize the intra-node MPI communications.

The IMPACC architecture hides shared memory address space from the tasks for code portability. Instead, the IMPACC architecture employs the distributed memory model across the tasks both within a node and across nodes. All data is private to each task, and there is no coherence between tasks. A task performs computation using its local data and communicates with other tasks by calling MPI communication routines explicitly. This local view of IMPACC memory model naturally leads to good locality, which is essential to achieve good scalability on large-scale systems.

3. IMPLEMENTATION

Figure 1 illustrates the overview of the IMPACC framework. The framework consists of two parts, the IMPACC compiler and the IMPACC runtime.

3.1 The IMPACC Compiler

The IMPACC compiler is a source-to-source translator. The compiler translates the compute-intensive codes augmented by *parallel* or *kernels* construct in the input MPI+OpenACC source codes into accelerator kernel codes written in CUDA C and OpenCL C. It also generates the host program that orchestrates the execution of the kernels on accelerators from the input source codes. The compiler translates all global and static variables in the host program source code to thread-local variables to make them private to each threaded-MPI task. The details of the compiler implementation are out of the scope of this paper.

3.2 Automatic Task-Device Mapping

In the current MPI+OpenACC model, the user should provide the total number of MPI tasks when executing the application. In order to run the same number of tasks as the number of available accelerators in the cluster, the number of total tasks should be the number of nodes multiplied by the number of accelerators per node. Then each task sets its accelerator by calling OpenACC runtime routine

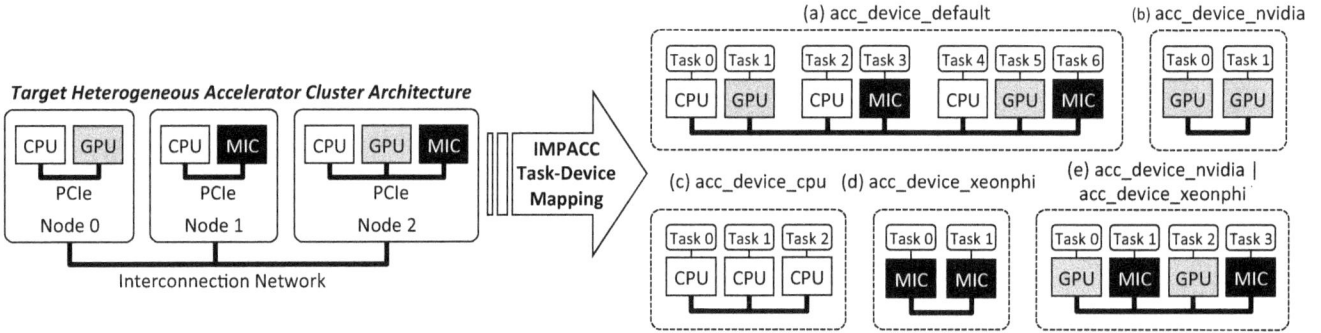

Figure 2: Automatic Task-Device Mapping in a Heterogeneous Accelerator Cluster with Different Nodes.

acc_set_device_num() with the local index of the accelerator. Typically the local index can be calculated by *MPI_rank % total_number_of_accelerators_per_node*.

This methodology assumes that the cluster consists of identical accelerator nodes; every node has the same number and same type of accelerators. When the target accelerator cluster consists of different accelerator nodes, the MPI task creation and OpenACC accelerator assignment are not simple.

In IMPACC, on the other hand, the user needs to provide the total number of nodes or the list of nodes when executing an MPI+OpenACC application. When the application is launched, the IMPACC runtime automatically creates the same number of MPI tasks as the number of all available or user's specified accelerators in the system. Users can specify the target accelerator types by setting an environment variable IMPACC_ACC_DEVICE_TYPE. Figure 2 (a), (b), (c), (d) and (e) shows the tasks created by the IMPACC runtime for the target heterogeneous accelerator cluster when the user specifies the target accelerator bit field type as acc_device_default, acc_device_nvidia, acc_device_cpu, acc_device_xeonphi, and acc_device_nvidia | acc_device_xeonphi, respectively.

The IMPACC runtime assigns a distinct accelerator to each task with a cluster-wide unique rank. Since the mapping between a task and an accelerator device is executed automatically by the IMPACC runtime, and thus the host program does not need to call acc_set_device_num(). The mapping is fixed during the application's lifetime, and the runtime ignores any additional acc_set_device_num() calls by the host program.

IMPACC does not provide any automatic mechanism for load balancing among different accelerators. Instead, the programmers can obtain the type of attached device to each task by calling a standard OpenACC runtime library routine, acc_get_device_type(). By using this device type information, the programmers can distribute the workload across the tasks manually.

3.3 NUMA-friendly Task-CPU Pinning

When multiple accelerator devices are equipped in a nonuniform memory access (NUMA) multi-CPU machine, it causes uneven data transfer performance between the CPUs and accelerators[39]. In Figure 1, the access distance between Accelerator 0 and CPU 0 is shorter than that of Accelerator 0 and CPU 1. The traffic in the former case traverses a PCIe between them. However, the latter case involves an additional traffic between CPU 0 and CPU 1 via an inter-

connect network such as Intel Quickpath Interconnect (QPI) and AMD HyperTransport (HT).

The IMPACC runtime identifies the CPU affinities of installed accelerators via *Linux sysfs (/sys/class/pci_bus)*. When the runtime creates the task threads for accelerators, it pins each task thread to the near CPU from its attached accelerator in order to avoid undesired communication overhead.

3.4 Unified Node Virtual Address Space

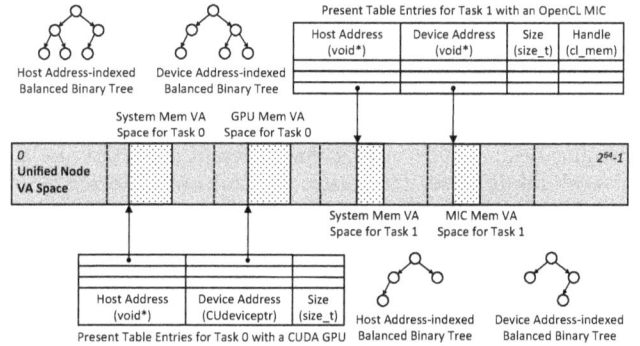

Figure 3: Present Tables for a CUDA GPU and an OpenCL MIC.

The *present table* in OpenACC maps host address ranges to corresponding device address ranges. The IMPACC runtime keeps a distinct present table for each task to avoid the access conflict between them. As shown in Figure 3, the runtime uses two balanced binary trees indexed by the host address and device address for a present table in order to reduce the worst-case search time.

A table entry in the present table stores the start address of host data, start address of the corresponding device data, and size of the data. When the runtime needs the device address associated with a host data, such as calling acc_deviceptr() from the host program, it searches the balanced tree indexed by the host address. The runtime searches the balanced tree indexed by the device address in the opposite case such as calling acc_hostptr().

The IMPACC runtime maps the host system memory and the device memories of all available accelerators in a node to the single *unified node virtual address space*. A physical system memory address is translated to a virtual memory address, with the help of operating system and MMU. When the accelerator is a CUDA-enabled GPU, then the IMPACC

192

runtime uses the *Unified Virtual Addressing (UVA)* technique that CUDA provides. UVA maps the allocated GPU memory into the host's virtual address space. The address of the allocated GPU memory is expressed as `CUdeviceptr` as shown in the present table for Task 0 with a CUDA GPU in Figure 3.

In OpenCL, a memory object is a handle to a region of accelerator device memory. That is, the memory object does not indicate the address of accelerator device memory directly like `CUdeviceptr` in CUDA. To allocate a memory region in an OpenCL-enabled accelerator, the IMPACC runtime calls `clCreateBuffer()` and gets an OpenCL memory object handle expressed by `cl_mem`. Then, the runtime reserves a virtual memory address space by calling `malloc()` with the same size of the OpenCL memory object. The obtained virtual memory address space represents the device-side mapped address space for host data.

The table entry for OpenCL-enabled accelerator has separate fields with a device address in an address pointer and a memory handle in cl_mem shown in the present table for Task 1 with an OpenCL MIC in Figure 3. The runtime uses the mapped device memory address to look up the entry in the present table. Then, it calls underlying OpenCL runtime routines with the cl_mem in the found entry and a corresponding offset. Typically, `malloc()` is implemented as lazy allocation[29], and thus the reserved memory space does not consume the physical system memory.

3.5 Unified MPI Communication Routines

With the help of unified node virtual address space and the present table, the runtime can detect the data location from a virtual memory address. This enables unified MPI communication routines to transfer data between tasks. A task can send from or receive to the device memory of its attached accelerator by calling the MPI communication routines with a device-mapped address pointer.

There are two ways to transfer data in the device memory in the IMPACC environment. First, the task calls MPI routines using the device address pointer directly as follows:

```
1  MPI_Send(acc_deviceptr(host_data), cnt, type, dst, tag, comm);
```

This methodology modifies the original MPI code to use OpenACC runtime routines `acc_deviceptr()`, and it leads to poor portability. For better portability, IMPACC introduces a novel OpenACC directive extension for MPI as follows:

```
1  #pragma acc mpi sendbuf(device)
2  MPI_Send(host_data, cnt, type, dst, tag, comm);
```

The new OpenACC directive extension (`#pragma acc mpi`), called *IMPACC directive*, indicates that the immediately following MPI call uses the device memory of host data in the send buffer argument. It is augmented by a directive, and thus the compiler can ignore it to run the unmodified original application, resulting in better portability. The syntax of IMPACC directive is:

#pragma acc mpi *clause-list new-line*

where *clause* is one of the following:

> sendbuf(*[device] [,] [readonly]*)
> recvbuf(*[device] [,] [readonly]*)
> async *[(int-expr)]*

The `sendbuf` and `recvbuf` clauses tell the compiler to use the device address of host data in the immediately following MPI call arguments and/or the buffers are read-only. When there is an `async` clause, the following non-blocking MPI call, such as `MPI_Isend()` and `MPI_Irecv()`, will be queued into an OpenACC asynchronous activity queue.

3.6 Unified Activity Queue

Figure 4 (a) shows a code snippet written in MPI+OpenACC. The program runs a kernel with `buf0` on the device and copies it to the system memory (line 2-3). Then the program sends `buf0` located in the system memory to another task (line 4) and receives `buf1` from the task (line 5). The program copies `buf1` from the system memory to the device memory and runs another kernel with `buf1` (line 6-7).

Figure 5 (a) shows the corresponding timeline graph for Figure 4 (a) code. The numbers in HOST-timelines in Figure 5 indicate that the code line numbers in Figure 4. The program runs six in-order operations; kernel - copyout - send - recv - copyin - kernel as shown in Figure 5.

In order to run the six operations sequentially, Figure 4 (a) uses synchronous APIs, such as OpenACC `kernels` construct, that has an implicit barrier at the end of the region, and blocking MPI communication routines. Synchronization operations are easy and safe to use, however it forces the host to wait until the completion of target operations as shown in Figure 5 (a). It leads to an undesirable waste of CPU cycles, resulting in poor CPU utilization. Furthermore, the synchronization can severely undermine scalability in the large-scale systems[44].

Figure 4 (b) shows an asynchronous version of Figure 4 (a). It uses MPI non-blocking communication routines and `async` clauses in `kernels` constructs. MPI non-blocking routines return immediately without waiting for the message to be sent or received.

In OpenACC, an accelerator has one or more *activity queues*. When there is an `async` clause on a `parallel`, `kernels`, `enter data`, `exit data`, or `update` directive, the host thread enqueues the parallel or kernels regions or data operations onto the device activity queue. The enqueued operations are processed independently and asynchronously on the device while the host thread continues its execution. The `async` clause may have a single nonnegative scalar integer expression argument. The argument is used to select the activity queue onto which to enqueue the operation on the accelerator.

With the help of MPI non-blocking communication and an OpenACC activity queue, Figure 4 (b) reduces the waste of CPU cycles as shown in Figure 5 (b). However, in order to synchronize two orthogonal streamlines across MPI and OpenACC, it still needs additional synchronization points such as `#pragma acc wait` and `MPI_Waitall()`. This leads to poor scalability.

IMPACC solves this synchronization issue by providing the *unified activity queue* to fully integrate MPI non-blocking communication and OpenACC activity queue. The users can enqueues MPI non-blocking communication routine calls to OpenACC activity queues. The IMPACC runtime completes the enqueued operations on an activity queue in order, while operations on different activity queues are active simultaneously and complete in any order.

```
1  /* (a) MPI+OpenACC Synchronous */
2  #pragma acc kernels loop copyout(buf0)
3  for (i = 0; i < n; i++) { buf0[i] = ...; }
4  MPI_Send(buf0, another_task);
5  MPI_Recv(buf1, another_task);
6  #pragma acc kernels loop copyin(buf1)
7  for (i = 0; i < n; i++) { ... = buf1[i]; }
```

```
1   /* (b) MPI+OpenACC Asynchronous */
2   #pragma acc kernels loop copyout(buf0) async(1)
3   for (i = 0; i < n; i++) { buf0[i] = ...; }
4   ...
5   #pragma acc wait(1);
6   MPI_Isend(buf0, another_task, &req[0]);
7   MPI_Irecv(buf1, another_task, &req[1]);
8   ...
9   MPI_Waitall(2, req);
10  #pragma acc kernels loop copyin(buf1) async(1)
11  for (i = 0; i < n; i++) { ... = buf1[i]; }
```

```
1  /* (c) IMPACC Unified Activity Queue */
2  #pragma acc kernels loop async(1)
3  for (i = 0; i < n; i++) { buf0[i] = ...; }
4  #pragma acc mpi sendbuf(device) async(1)
5  MPI_Isend(buf0, another_task, &req[0]);
6  #pragma acc mpi recvbuf(device) async(1)
7  MPI_Irecv(buf1, another_task, &req[1]);
8  #pragma acc kernels loop async(1)
9  for (i = 0; i < n; i++) { ... = buf1[i]; }
```

Figure 4: Synchronizations between MPI and OpenACC.

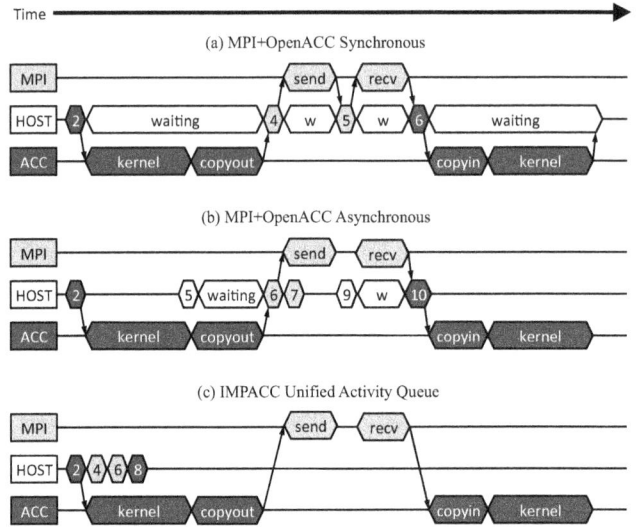

Figure 5: Synchronization Timeline.

The `async` clauses in the IMPACC directive and `async` clauses in the `kernels` constructs in Figure 4 (c) have the same queue number 1; these operations will be executed in-order by the runtime while the host thread is free from synchronization as shown in Figure 5 (c). It can improve the scalability of the system ultimately.

The unified activity queue also improves the programmability. In order to achieve the fully asynchronous communication, such as Figure 5 (c), in the current MPI+OpenACC model, it requires additional multithreaded programming to run a background thread that checks the status of non-blocking MPI requests or asynchronous OpenACC data transfers. This is much more difficult and error-prone than adding an `async` clause for the unified activity queue.

3.7 Handling MPI Communications

The IMPACC runtime runs a single *message handler thread* in each node as shown in Figure 1. The message handler thread handles all intra-node and pending fully asynchronous internode MPI communications. The message handler thread and task threads in each node share two in-order and lock-free multi-producer (task threads) single-consumer (message handler thread) queues, called *intra-node message queue* and *pending internode message queue*.

For the intra-node communication, when a task calls an intra-node MPI communication routine, the runtime creates a message command and enqueues the command into the intra-node message queue. The message handler thread matches a pair of a send message command and a receive message command in the intra-node message queue using their task ids and tags while guaranteeing their FIFO ordering. The message handler thread dequeues the matched pair of commands from the queue. The matched pair of message

commands represents a memory copy between host-to-host (HtoH), host-to-device (HtoD), device-to-host (DtoH), and device-to-device (DtoD) across the tasks depending on the locations of send and receive buffers.

The message handler thread fuses the matched two message commands into a single corresponding (accelerator) memory copy operation. We call it the *message fusion technique*. Figure 6 shows the differences between traditional MPI+OpenACC and IMPACC in the intra-node communication across tasks. In traditional MPI+OpenACC, a communication between tasks introduces inter-process communication and/or redundant host-to-host memory copy because a task is implemented as an OS process and runs on its private virtual address space.

On the other hand, the threaded-MPI tasks in IMPACC share a single unified node virtual address space, and the address of the send buffer and receive buffer in the matched MPI messages are located in the same linear virtual address space. Therefore, the runtime fuses two MPI messages into a single accelerator memory copy operation to eliminate the inter-process communication and redundant host-to-host memory copy as shown in Figure 6. Especially, when both send buffer and receive buffer reside in device memories, and the devices share the same upstream PCIe root complex, the runtime copies data directly between devices over the PCIe without the involvement of the CPU or system memory using the underlying vendor-specific features, such as NVIDIA GPUDirect[6] and AMD DirectGMA[4].

For the internode communication, the task threads call the underlying MPI communication routine in the system. When the data is located in the device memory, the runtime executes an additional memory copy between the device memory and the host system memory. If the underlying MPI library supports the direct accelerator memory access, such as Mellanox OFED GPUDirect RDMA[5], the runtime exploits it and transfers data directly from the device memory to a network adapter without staging through host memory.

The internode communication among the task threads depends on the multithreading support from the underlying MPI library. If the underlying MPI library supports

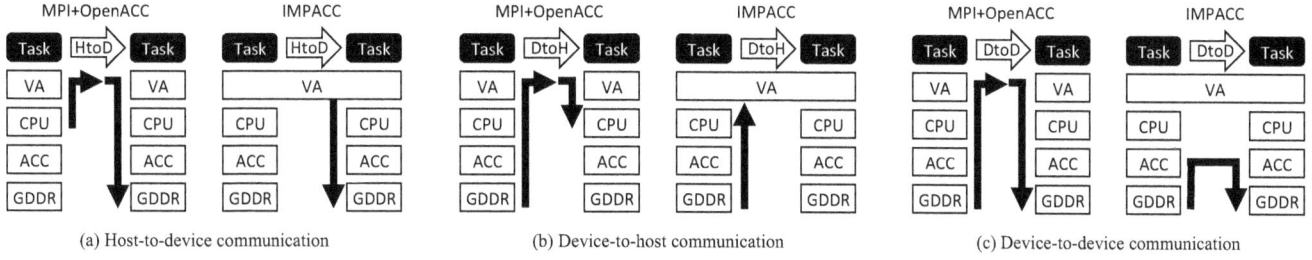

Figure 6: Message Fusion for Intra-node Communications. Two messages in MPI+OpenACC are fused into a single accelerator memory copy operation in IMPACC.

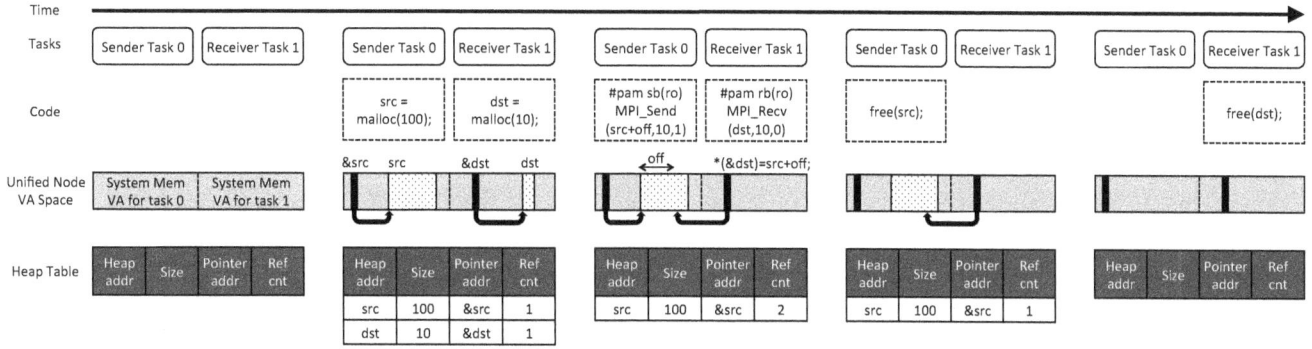

Figure 7: Node Heap Aliasing Example, where #pam sb(ro) and #pam rb(ro) refer to #pragma acc mpi sendbuffer(readonly) and #pragma acc mpi recvbuffer(readonly), respectively.

MPI_THREAD_MULTIPLE level, then multiple task threads can call MPI routines, with no restrictions. Typical state-of-the-art MPI libraries that provide MPI_THREAD_MULTIPLE level use fine-grained locking support to decrease the contention between threads[1, 7, 16].

If the underlying MPI library does not provide multi-threading support, then the IMPACC runtime serializes the internode communication for each node to achieve thread safety. Therefore, as the number of MPI tasks per node increases, the serialization of communication may induce overhead, and result in poor scalability. However, IMPACC keeps a small number of MPI tasks per node as the same number of accelerators available. These alleviate the scalability issue caused by lock contention and serializing internode communication between task threads.

To implement fully asynchronous internode communication across MPI and OpenACC, the sender task thread reads the data from its device memory by calling an asynchronous device memory copy operation, such as cuMemcpyAsync() in CUDA or clEnqueueReadBuffer() with CL_NON_BLOCKING flag in OpenCL. Then the task thread sets a notification callback function to the memory copy operation, using cuStreamAddCallback() in CUDA or clSetEventCallback() in OpenCL. The callback function is executed when the memory copy operation completes. It calls MPI_Isend() to send the data to the target task in the different node asynchronously. For better performance, the runtime internally uses the pre-pinned host memory.

Meanwhile in the receiver task side, the receiver task thread receives the data from the sender task using MPI_Irecv(). Then it creates a new *pending internode message command* and adds it to a *pending internode message queue*. The pending internode message command

contains the target address of the device memory and an MPI_Request object, MPI non-blocking communication request handle, to check its completion. The message handler thread checks the completions of pending commands in the internode pending message queue. When a pending command completes its non-blocking communication, the message handler thread calls cuMemcpyAsync() in CUDA or clEnqueueWriteBuffer() with CL_NON_BLOCKING flag in OpenCL to write data to the device memory and removes the pending command from the queue.

3.8 Intra-node Data Sharing

In the IMPACC framework, since the tasks on the same node share the unified node virtual address space, they can share data. The IMPACC directive has readonly attributes in the sendbuf and recvbuf clauses. There are five requirements to share data between tasks. First, the tasks should be on the same node. Second, the send buffer and receive buffer must be in the host heap memory. Third, every task calls MPI communication routines using the IMPACC directive with a readonly attribute. Fourth, the receiver task has no pointer variable that stores the receive buffer region before the MPI call. Last, the receive MPI call fully overwrites the receive buffer. When all these conditions are met, the IMPACC runtime enables the tasks to share the data between them using *node heap aliasing technique*. Node heap aliasing technique in IMPACC achieves data sharing among the MPI tasks that have a producer-consumer relationship transparently to the application while keeping their semantics the same.

Figure 7 shows an example. There are two tasks, Sender Task 0 and Receiver Task 1. Task 0 and Task 1 allocate heap src and dst with sizes of 100 and 10 respectively by

195

System	PSG	Beacon	Titan
Number of used (total) nodes	1 (16)	32 (48)	8,192 (18,688)
CPUs	2 × Intel Xeon E5-2698 v3	2 × Intel Xeon E5-2670	AMD Opteron 6274
Main memory size	256GB	256GB	32GB
Accelerators	8 × NVIDIA Kepler GK210	4 × Intel Xeon Phi coprocessor 5110P	NVIDIA Tesla K20x
Cores per accelerator	2,496 CUDA cores	60 x86 cores	2,688 CUDA cores
Accelerator core clock	875MHz	1.053GHz	732MHz
Memory per accelerator	12GB GDDR5	8GB GDDR5	6GB GDDR5
PCI Express	PCIe Gen3 x16	PCIe Gen2 x16	PCIe Gen2 x16
Interconnection	Mellanox InfiniBand FDR	Mellanox InfiniBand FDR	Cray Gemini interconnect
OS	CentOS 6.6	CentOS 6.2	Cray Linux Environment
Accelerator API	CUDA 6.5	Intel OpenCL 14.2	CUDA 6.5
MPI	MVAPICH2 2.0	Intel MPI Library 5.0	Cray MPICH2
MPI multithreading support	MPI_THREAD_MULTIPLE	MPI_THREAD_MULTIPLE	MPI_THREAD_MULTIPLE
C/C++ compiler	GCC 4.8.2	Intel C Compiler 15.0.2	Intel C Compiler 14.0.2

Table 1: The Target Heterogeneous Accelerator Systems.

calling `malloc()`. The IMPACC runtime hooks the heap-related routines, such as `malloc()`, `calloc()`, `realloc()`, `free()`, and etc., and it records the allocated heaps in the *Heap Table*. An entry in the Heap Table stores the allocated heap address, size, pointer address, and its reference count. Task 0 calls `MPI_Send()` augmented with an IMPACC directive with a readonly attribute (`#pragma acc mpi sendbuffer(readonly)`). Task 1 also calls `MPI_Recv()` with size 10 for the receive buffer augmented with an IMPACC directive with a readonly attribute (`#pragma acc mpi recvbuffer(readonly)`).

The message handler thread in the IMPACC runtime matches these two MPI communications and identifies that this intra-node communication meets all requirements for node heap aliasing. The message handler thread aliases the pointer of receive buffer (`dst`) to the send buffer address (`src + off`) and deallocates the original receive buffer heap region. Then, the message handler thread removes the corresponding heap table entry and increases the reference counter of the send buffer entry. After this sharing point, Task 1 shares the `src` heap region with Task 0 via `dst` pointer.

When a task calls `free()` to release the allocated heap region, the IMPACC runtime looks up the corresponding entry that contains the address of `free()` and decreases the reference count in the found entry. When the reference count becomes zero, it deallocates the heap region and removes the entry from the table.

MPI collective communications, such as `MPI_Bcast()`, in IMPACC also exploits node heap aliasing technique to eliminate redundant data movement. When the tasks call `MPI_Bcast()`, the IMPACC runtime sends the buffer in the root task to a task in every participated node. And then, the task that received the buffer sends the buffer to other tasks on the same node. At this time, if this data transfer meets the five requirements of the node heap aliasing technique, the tasks can share the buffer without additional memory copy.

4. EVALUATION

4.1 Methodology

Target systems. We evaluate the performance of IMPACC using three heterogeneous accelerator systems (*PSG*[8], *Beacon*[18], and *Titan*[1]). Table 1 summarizes the target systems.

Compiler and Runtime system. We have implemented the IMPACC compiler and runtime system. The IMPACC compiler is built on OpenARC[38], an open source OpenACC compiler framework. The accelerator part of the runtime is implemented with CUDA Driver API and OpenCL runtime.

Benchmark applications. We use four MPI+OpenACC applications: DGEMM, EP, Jacobi, and LULESH[33]. We compare their performance in our IMPACC framework with the legacy MPI+OpenACC implementations. In order to show the effectiveness of the runtime techniques proposed in the paper, we use the same IMPACC compiler for both cases to translate the OpenACC constructs to accelerator programs. The results show the performance gain from NUMA-friendly task-CPU pinning, intra-node/internode point-to-point and collective communication optimization, intra-node data sharing, and easier programming and better scalability from unified activity queue.

4.2 Results

NUMA-friendly Task-CPU Pinning. We measure the bandwidth of accelerator memory copies in order to show the effectiveness of NUMA-friendly task-CPU pinning in IMPACC. Bandwidth is measured using the transfers of blocks of data ranging in size from 64B to 1GB on the multi-socket CPUs systems: PSG and Beacon. A single task calls host-to-device (HtoD) or device-to-host (DtoH) memory copy with two configurations: NUMA-friendly and NUMA-unfriendly. We pin the task to the near CPU from the target accelerator in the NUMA-friendly configuration and pin the task to a far CPU in the NUMA-unfriendly configuration. Figure 8 demonstrates that our NUMA-friendly task-CPU pinning is effective for both HtoD and DtoH memory copies both on the NVIDIA GPU and Intel MIC systems. The NUMA-friendly configurations deliver higher bandwidth, up to 3.5 times, than NUMA-unfriendly configurations.

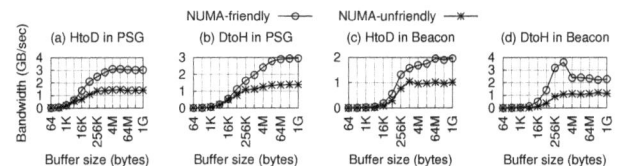

Figure 8: NUMA-friendly Task-CPU Pinning.

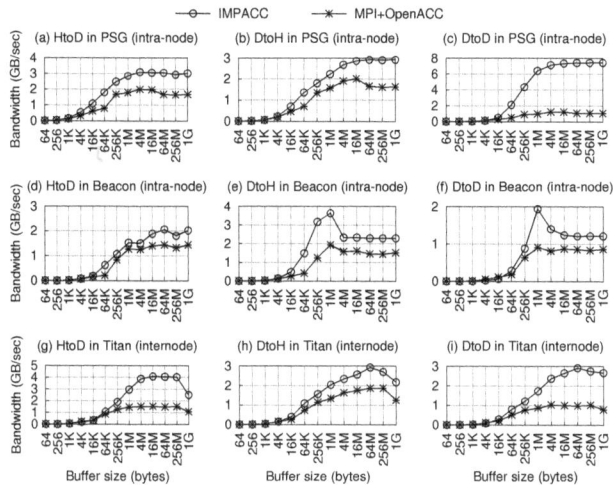

Figure 9: Point-to-point Communication Bandwidth.

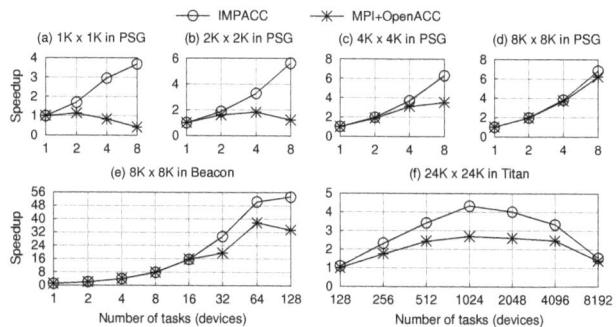

Figure 10: Speedup of DGEMM, normalized to MPI+OpenACC 1-task in PSG and Beacon, 128-tasks in Titan.

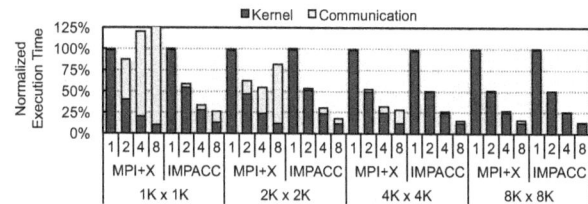

Figure 11: Execution Time Breakdown for DGEMM in PSG, normalized to MPI+OpenACC (noted as MPI+X) 1-task for each input. The x-axis represents the number of tasks (1, 2, 4, and 8) and the number of elements of the matrices.

Point-to-point Communication. Figure 9 shows the bandwidth of point-to-point communication between two tasks in IMPACC and MPI-OpenACC. We measure the bandwidth of intra-node point-to-point communication in PSG and Beacon and internode point-to-point communication in Titan. The IMPACC runtime eliminates the unnecessary host-to-host memory copy between the tasks on the same node as shown in Figure 6. IMPACC shows higher intra-node communication bandwidth than that of MPI+OpenACC as shown in Figure 9 (a) - (f). Especially, IMPACC shows almost eight times higher bandwidth than MPI+OpenACC in device-to-device intra-node communication in PSG (Figure 9 (c)) due to the direct transfer between devices via PCIe.

IMPACC also shows higher bandwidth in internode communications as shown in Figure 9 (g) - (i). This is because the IMPACC runtime internally exploits the Mellanox OFED GPUDirect RDMA from the underlying Cray MPICH2. It decreases the internode communication latency while eliminating the memory copy between the pinned CUDA buffer and the Mellanox HCA buffer.

DGEMM. DGEMM is a double-precision dense matrix-matrix multiplication, which computes the product of two matrices. We used square matrices for simplicity. The root task, whose rank is zero, sends the input sub-matrices to all of the other tasks, and then receives the output sub-matrices from them.

Figure 10 shows the strong scalability of DGEMM on the target systems. Figure 10 (a), (b), (c), and (d) show the speedup numbers of IMPACC and MPI+OpenACC over MPI+OpenACC with a single task in PSG. We vary the number of tasks (that is, number of devices) and the number of elements of the matrices from 1 to 8, and from 1K×1K to 8K×8K in powers of two, respectively. One DGEMM feature is that the ratio of computation ($O(N^3)$) to communication ($O(N^2)$) is proportional to $O(N)$. As shown in MPI+OpenACC implementation in Figure 10 (a), (b), (c), and (d), as the size of matrices increases, it shows better scalability because the large computation compensates the communication overhead.

On the other hand, IMPACC shows fair scalability for all input matrices even though MPI+OpenACC shows performance degradation with small-sized matrices. All tasks are on the same node, and the input matrices are read only. Therefore, IMPACC version exploits the node heap aliasing technique, and all the tasks share the root task's input matrices located in the unified node virtual address space. Also, higher point-to-point communication bandwidth in IMPACC decreases the communication overhead.

Figure 11 shows the normalized execution time breakdown for Figure 10 (a) - (d). The baseline is the total execution time of MPI+OpenACC version using a single task for each input. In the small input matrices, IMPACC dramatically reduces the communication overhead. As the size of matrices increases, the kernel execution time dominates the total execution time, and the communication overhead is hidden.

Figure 10 (e) shows the speedup numbers over the MPI+OpenACC version using a single task in Beacon. We vary the number of tasks from 1 to 128 in powers of two. A node contains 4 devices, and then 128 tasks run across 32 nodes. IMPACC shows similar performance to MPI+OpenACC until 16 tasks. However, IMPACC shows better performance than MPI+OpenACC from 32 tasks. As the number of tasks increases, the communication overhead increases because DGEMM broadcasts one of the input matrices to all tasks. IMPACC eliminates the redundant memory copy across the task on the same node in `MPI_Bcast()` using the node heap aliasing technique. Furthermore, IMPACC shows fair scalability up to 128 tasks even though MPI+OpenACC shows performance degradation in 128 tasks. This is because IMPACC version elimi-

197

nates all synchronization points, which undermine scalability, in the host program using the IMPACC unified activity queues. It only needs to add IMPACC directives along with `async` clauses.

Figure 10 (f) shows the speedup numbers over the MPI+OpenACC version using 128 tasks in Titan. We set the number of elements in the matrices to the maximum ($24K\times24K$) that 128 tasks can hold their sub-matrices in their device memories. Both IMPACC and MPI+OpenACC show performance degradation from 1024 nodes due to its communication overhead. However, IMPACC shows better performance than MPI+OpenACC up to 160% in 1024 nodes. This performance gain comes from exploiting the unified activity queues and higher internode communication bandwidth in IMPACC as shown in Figure 9 (g) - (i).

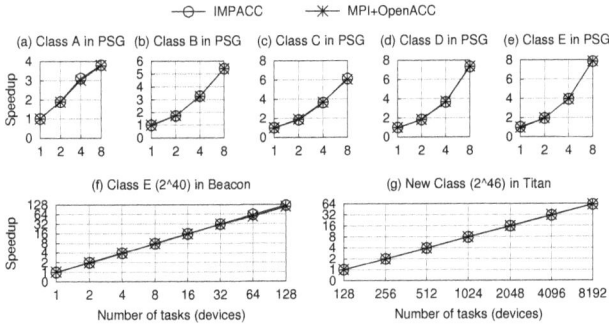

Figure 12: Speedup of EP, normalized to MPI+OpenACC 1-task in PSG and Beacon, 128-tasks in Titan.

EP. EP is Embarrassingly Parallel kernel in NAS parallel benchmarks[15]. It requires no communication between tasks except for the final reduction, and the kernel execution time dominates the total execution time.

We vary the input size from class A to class E in PSG as shown in Figure 12. In class D and E, EP shows almost linear scalability. However, in class A, B, and C, as the input size decreases it shows poor strong scalability. This is because, as the number of tasks increases, the kernel workloads to each task are reduced, and it lowers the device utilization.

Figure 12 (f) shows the speedup of class E on Beacon, and it shows a linear scalability. Figure 12 (g) shows the speedup of our new class, which is 64 times bigger than the NPB's biggest class (class E), over 128 tasks. Both IMPACC and MPI+OpenACC show linear speedups.

EP shows almost same performances in IMPACC and MPI+OpenACC for all experiments. IMPACC has no room to optimize performance for EP that has very little communication overhead.

Jacobi. The Jacobi iteration method is a stencil computation used to solve partial differential equations. We evaluate 2D Jacobi iteration for a square matrix and partition the matrix in one dimension for the given tasks. Communications between tasks are needed at block boundaries in order to receive values of neighbor points that are owned by another task.

Figure 13 (a), (b), (c), and (d) show speedup numbers of IMPACC and MPI+OpenACC over the MPI+OpenACC version with a single task in PSG. We vary the number of elements in mesh from $1K\times1K$ to $8K\times8K$. IMPACC shows better performance than MPI+OpenACC due to its op-

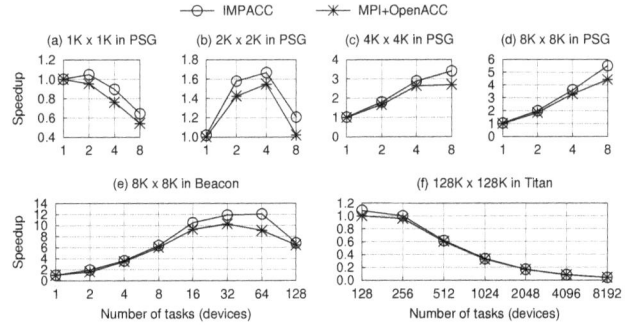

Figure 13: Speedup of Jacobi, normalized to MPI+OpenACC 1-task in PSG and Beacon, 128-tasks in Titan.

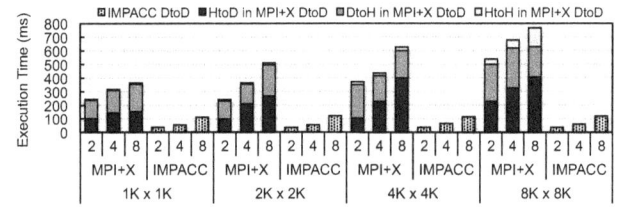

Figure 14: Device-to-Device Communication Time Breakdown for Jacobi in PSG. The x-axis represents the number of tasks (2, 4, and 8) and the number of elements in mesh.

timized intra-node communication using direct device-to-device memory copy.

Figure 14 shows the amount of total execution time for device-to-device communication between the tasks of Jacobi in PSG. As shown in Figure 6 (c), a device-to-device communication in IMPACC needs a single direct memory transfer between the devices via PCIe (noted as IMPACC DtoD in Figure 14). In MPI+OpenACC (noted as MPI+X), on the other hand, a device-to-device communication needs additional involvement of the host CPU and system memory (noted as HtoD, DtoH, and HtoH in MPI+X D2D). IMPACC significantly decreases device-to-device communication overhead, and thus allows for better performance.

Figure 13 (e) shows the speedup numbers in Beacon. The higher bandwidth in the intra-node point-to-point communication across the tasks in IMPACC is hidden with the small number of tasks because the kernel execution time dominates its total execution time. However, as the number of tasks increases, the kernel workload for each task decreases while the total amount of communication for each node does not change. Therefore, the communication overhead occupies the main part of its total execution time with a large number of tasks. As shown in Figure 13 (e) with 16, 32, and 64 tasks, IMPACC shows better performance than MPI+OpenACC due to its reduced communication overhead.

However, the communication overhead in Jacobi with a large number of tasks dominates its total execution ultimately, and it leads to poor scalability as shown in Figure 13 (e) with 128 tasks. Figure 13 (f) shows the strong scalability over 128 tasks in Titan. It shows worse performance as the

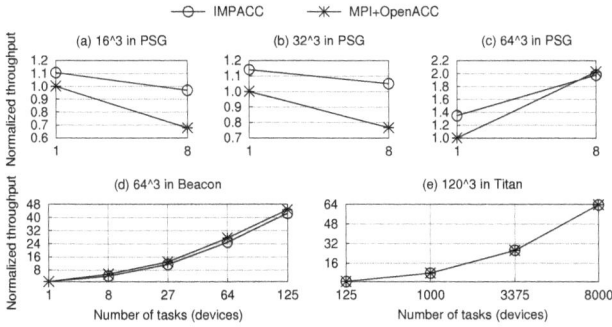

Figure 15: Performance Scaling of LULESH, normalized to MPI+OpenACC 1-task in PSG and Beacon, 125-tasks in Titan.

number of tasks increases due to its increasing communication overhead.

LULESH. LULESH is a shock hydrodynamics proxy application developed by Lawrence Livermore National Laboratory[33]. It solves the hydrodynamics equations on a staggered 3D spatial mesh. A task on the 3D sub-mesh computes on the volume of assigned elements ($O(N^3)$), and it transfers its surface elements in the mesh between its nearest neighbors in a Cartesian topology($O(N^2)$). And thus, computation-to-communication ratio is proportional to problem size ($O(N)$).

We run unmodified LULESH 2.0.2 MPI+OpenACC version[2] for both MPI+OpenACC and IMPACC, and thus all communications between tasks are host-to-host communications. Figure 15 shows the weak scalability for LULESH. Because LULESH requires that the number of tasks be a perfect cube, we vary the number of tasks to x^3 such as 1, 8, 27, 64, 125, 1000, 3375, and 8000. The graph titles in Figure 15 show the problem sizes for each task.

In a single node on PSG, IMPACC shows better performance than MPI+OpenACC due to the NUMA-friendly task-CPU mapping in a single task and message fusion technique that eliminates inter-process communication between tasks.

Beacon shows about 5% performance degradation in IM-PACC compared to MPI+OpenACC. This comes from the IMPACC runtime overhead. There is no room for IMPACC to optimize the host-to-host internode communication. Also, the task threads shift their intra-node communication onto the communication thread by inserting message commands into the intra-node message queues. It introduces additional creating message commands overhead and queue scheduling overhead, resulting in slightly lower performance. For large problem sizes, since kernel execution time dominates the total execution time, both IMPACC and MPI+OpenACC in Titan show similar performance and achieve almost linear scalability.

5. RELATED WORK

The primary goal of HPC programming models is to provide the programmers with easy programming and high performance. There are some papers that propose novel programming models for accelerator systems to achieve both of them. StarSs and OmpSs[14, 17, 23] present a directive-

based programming model for various accelerators such as Cell BE and multi-GPU. ADSM[27] provides a data-centric programming model that presents a shared address space between CPUs and accelerators. Haidar *et al.*[31] design algorithms and a programming model for dense linear algebra in accelerator systems. However, these approaches are limited to single node systems.

There have been efforts to provide novel unified programming models for heterogeneous architectures in both single-node and multi-node systems. Bueno *et al.*[19] present an implementation of OmpSs for GPU clusters. The runtime system automatically schedules the annotated codes with task directives to local or remote GPUs in the cluster. Phalanx[26] provides a synchronous task model supporting both coarse-grained and fine-grained parallelism. It also uses an IMPACC-like memory model to present a global address interface on multi-node systems. StarPU[12, 13] is a task programming library for heterogeneous architectures. Applications written in StarPU's language extensions submit computational tasks, with target device implementations, and StarPU schedules these tasks and associated data transfers on available devices. Cashmere[32] is a programming system for heterogeneous manycore clusters. It includes a framework to write and optimize kernels for different types of manycore devices, and it delivers automatic load balancing among them. HAM-Offload[40] defines a unified API to offload work to local and remote Intel Xeon Phi coprocessors in cluster environments. However, rewriting and restructuring the legacy HPC applications, that could contain tens or hundreds of thousands of lines, with new programming models requires a significant effort.

Some papers provide techniques that extend the target platform of existing programming models to heterogeneous accelerator clusters. SnuCL[34], LibWater[30], and rCUDA[22] extend the platform model of OpenCL and CUDA to the distributed clusters, respectively. However, their master-slave execution models do not scale well to the large-scale clusters due to the bottleneck of the centralized scheduling. Kwon *et al.*[36] presents a fully automated compiler-runtime system that translates and executes regular and repetitive OpenMP programs on clusters. However, their approach has some weakness, compared with hand-tuned MPI, due to the intrinsic limitations of static compiler techniques and runtime system overhead.

Exploiting shared memory parallelism in MPI implementations has been proposed by some work. HMPI[24] and ownership passing[25] share memory across MPI processes executing on the same node. TMPI[47] and MPI endpoint[21] relax the one-to-one relationship between MPI ranks and processes, and it enables the threads to act as MPI ranks. KNEM[28] provides MPI implementations with a scalable interface for performing kernel-assisted direct data transfers between local processes. However, to our best knowledge, no work has so far been published to exploit shared memory parallelism in MPI to expedite the accelerator data transfers.

MPI-ACC[10], MT-MPI[46], and some GPU-aware MPI implementations[5, 6, 42, 50] integrate MPI and accelerator programmings such as CUDA and OpenCL. However, they do not solve the synchronization issues between MPI and accelerator programmings, and/or inter-process communication overhead across MPI tasks as our approach does.

6. CONCLUSIONS

In this work, we propose IMPACC, a tightly integrated MPI+OpenACC framework for heterogeneous accelerator clusters. IMPACC starts with the observation that current MPI+OpenACC model has some inefficiencies and complexities to orchestrate two orthogonal programming models. IMPACC solves these problems by exploiting shared memory parallelism and the tight integration of MPI and OpenACC. IMPACC also proposes a new OpenACC directive extension to exploit the features of IMPACC, such as unified MPI communication routines, unified OpenACC activity queue, and node heap aliasing technique, easily and portably. We implement IMPACC and evaluate its performance with three accelerator systems. The evaluation results demonstrate that IMPACC achieves easier programming, higher performance, and better scalability than current MPI+OpenACC model.

7. ACKNOWLEDGMENTS

This research used resources of the Oak Ridge Leadership Computing Facility, which is a DOE Office of Science User Facility supported under Contract DE-AC05-00OR22725. This material is based upon work supported by the National Science Foundation under Grant Number 1137097 and by the University of Tennessee through the Beacon Project. Any opinions, findings, conclusions, or recommendations expressed in this material are those of the author(s) and do not necessarily reflect the views of the National Science Foundation or the University of Tennessee. The authors would like to thank NVIDIA for providing access to their PSG Cluster.

This material is based upon work supported by the U.S. Department of Energy, Office of Science, Office of Advanced Scientific Computing Research. This manuscript has been authored by UT-Battelle, LLC under Contract No. DE-AC05-00OR22725 with the U.S. Department of Energy. The United States Government retains and the publisher, by accepting the article for publication, acknowledges that the United States Government retains a non-exclusive, paid-up, irrevocable, world-wide license to publish or reproduce the published form of this manuscript, or allow others to do so, for United States Government purposes. The Department of Energy will provide public access to these results of federally sponsored research in accordance with the DOE Public Access Plan(http://energy.gov/downloads/doe-public-access-plan).

8. REFERENCES

[1] *Titan - Oak Ridge Leadership Computing Facility/Oak Ridge National Laboratory*, 2012. https://www.olcf.ornl.gov/titan/.
[2] *Livermore Unstructured Lagrangian Explicit Shock Hydrodynamics (LULESH) - Co-design at Lawrence Livermore National Laboratory*, 2013. https://codesign.llnl.gov/lulesh.php.
[3] *The OpenACC Application Programming Interface*, 2013. http://openacc.org.
[4] *AMD FirePro DirectGMA*, 2014. http://developer.amd.com/tools-and-sdks/graphics-development/firepro-sdk/firepro-directgma-sdk/.
[5] *Mellanox OFED GPUDirect RDMA*, 2014. http://www.mellanox.com/related-docs/prod_software/PB_GPUDirect_RDMA.PDF.
[6] *NVIDIA GPUDirect*, 2014. https://developer.nvidia.com/gpudirect.
[7] *MPICH: High-Performance Portable MPI*, 2015. http://www.mpich.org/.
[8] *PSG Cluster - NVIDIA Technology Center*, 2015. http://www.nvidia.com/nvtechcenter/.
[9] *TOP500 Supercomputer Sites*, 2015. http://www.top500.org/.
[10] A. M. Aji, J. Dinan, D. Buntinas, P. Balaji, W.-c. Feng, K. R. Bisset, and R. Thakur. MPI-ACC: An Integrated and Extensible Approach to Data Movement in Accelerator-based Systems. In *Proceedings of the 2012 IEEE 14th International Conference on High Performance Computing and Communication & 2012 IEEE 9th International Conference on Embedded Software and Systems*, HPCC '12, pages 647–654, 2012.
[11] K. Asanovic, R. Bodik, B. C. Catanzaro, J. J. Gebis, P. Husbands, K. Keutzer, D. A. Patterson, W. L. Plishker, J. Shalf, S. W. Williams, and K. A. Yelick. The Landscape of Parallel Computing Research: A View from Berkeley. Technical Report UCB/EECS-2006-183, EECS Department, University of California, Berkeley, Dec 2006.
[12] C. Augonnet, O. Aumage, N. Furmento, R. Namyst, and S. Thibault. StarPU-MPI: Task Programming over Clusters of Machines Enhanced with Accelerators. In *Proceedings of the 19th European Conference on Recent Advances in the Message Passing Interface*, EuroMPI'12, pages 298–299, 2012.
[13] C. Augonnet, S. Thibault, R. Namyst, and P.-A. Wacrenier. StarPU: A Unified Platform for Task Scheduling on Heterogeneous Multicore Architectures. In *Proceedings of the 15th International Euro-Par Conference on Parallel Processing*, Euro-Par '09, pages 863–874, 2009.
[14] E. Ayguadé, R. M. Badia, F. D. Igual, J. Labarta, R. Mayo, and E. S. Quintana-Ortí. An Extension of the StarSs Programming Model for Platforms with Multiple GPUs. In *Proceedings of the 15th International Euro-Par Conference on Parallel Processing*, Euro-Par '09, pages 851–862, 2009.
[15] D. H. Bailey, E. Barszcz, J. T. Barton, D. S. Browning, R. L. Carter, L. Dagum, R. A. Fatoohi, P. O. Frederickson, T. A. Lasinski, R. S. Schreiber, H. D. Simon, V. Venkatakrishnan, and S. K. Weeratunga. The NAS Parallel Benchmarks - Summary and Preliminary Results. In *Proceedings of the 1991 ACM/IEEE Conference on Supercomputing*, SC '91, pages 158–165, 1991.
[16] P. Balaji, D. Buntinas, D. Goodell, W. Gropp, and R. Thakur. Fine-Grained Multithreading Support for Hybrid Threaded MPI Programming. *Int. J. High Perform. Comput. Appl.*, 24(1):49–57, Feb. 2010.
[17] P. Bellens, J. M. Perez, R. M. Badia, and J. Labarta. CellSs: A Programming Model for the Cell BE Architecture. In *Proceedings of the 2006 ACM/IEEE Conference on Supercomputing*, SC '06, 2006.
[18] R. G. Brook, A. Heinecke, A. B. Costa, P. Peltz, V. C. Betro, T. Baer, M. Bader, and P. Dubey. Beacon: Deployment and Application of Intel Xeon Phi Coprocessors for Scientific Computing. *Computing in Science Engineering*, 17(2):65–72, Mar 2015.
[19] J. Bueno, J. Planas, A. Duran, R. M. Badia, X. Martorell, E. Ayguade, and J. Labarta. Productive Programming of GPU Clusters with OmpSs. In *Proceedings of the 2012 IEEE 26th International Parallel and Distributed Processing Symposium*, IPDPS '12, pages 557–568, 2012.
[20] F. Cappello and D. Etiemble. MPI Versus MPI+OpenMP on IBM SP for the NAS Benchmarks. In *Proceedings of the 2000 ACM/IEEE Conference on Supercomputing*, SC '00, 2000.
[21] J. Dinan, P. Balaji, D. Goodell, D. Miller, M. Snir, and R. Thakur. Enabling MPI Interoperability Through Flexible Communication Endpoints. In *Proceedings of the 20th European MPI Users' Group Meeting*, EuroMPI '13, pages 13–18, 2013.
[22] J. Duato, A. J. Pena, F. Silla, J. C. Fernandez, R. Mayo, and E. S. Quintana-Orti. Enabling CUDA Acceleration Within Virtual Machines Using rCUDA. In *Proceedings of the 2011 18th International Conference on High Performance Computing*, HIPC '11, pages 1–10, 2011.
[23] V. Elangovan, R. Badia, and E. Parra. Ompss-opencl programming model for heterogeneous systems. In *Languages and Compilers for Parallel Computing*, volume 7760 of *Lecture Notes in Computer Science*, pages 96–111. 2013.
[24] A. Friedley, G. Bronevetsky, T. Hoefler, and A. Lumsdaine. Hybrid MPI: Efficient Message Passing for Multi-core Systems. In *Proceedings of the International Conference on High Performance Computing, Networking, Storage and Analysis*, SC '13, pages 18:1–18:11, 2013.
[25] A. Friedley, T. Hoefler, G. Bronevetsky, A. Lumsdaine, and C.-C. Ma. Ownership Passing: Efficient Distributed Memory Programming on Multi-core Systems. In *Proceedings of the*

18th ACM SIGPLAN Symposium on Principles and Practice of Parallel Programming, PPoPP '13, pages 177–186, 2013.

[26] M. Garland, M. Kudlur, and Y. Zheng. Designing a Unified Programming Model for Heterogeneous Machines. In *Proceedings of the International Conference on High Performance Computing, Networking, Storage and Analysis*, SC '12, pages 67:1–67:11, 2012.

[27] I. Gelado, J. E. Stone, J. Cabezas, S. Patel, N. Navarro, and W.-m. W. Hwu. An Asymmetric Distributed Shared Memory Model for Heterogeneous Parallel Systems. In *Proceedings of the Fifteenth International Conference on Architectural Support for Programming Languages and Operating Systems*, ASPLOS XV, pages 347–358, 2010.

[28] B. Goglin and S. Moreaud. KNEM: A Generic and Scalable Kernel-assisted Intra-node MPI Communication Framework. *J. Parallel Distrib. Comput.*, 73(2):176–188, Feb. 2013.

[29] M. Gorman. *Understanding the Linux Virtual Memory Manager*. Prentice Hall PTR, 2004.

[30] I. Grasso, S. Pellegrini, B. Cosenza, and T. Fahringer. LibWater: Heterogeneous Distributed Computing Made Easy. In *Proceedings of the 27th International ACM Conference on International Conference on Supercomputing*, ICS '13, pages 161–172, 2013.

[31] A. Haidar, C. Cao, A. Yarkhan, P. Luszczek, S. Tomov, K. Kabir, and J. Dongarra. Unified Development for Mixed Multi-GPU and Multi-coprocessor Environments Using a Lightweight Runtime Environment. In *Proceedings of the 2014 IEEE 28th International Parallel and Distributed Processing Symposium*, IPDPS '14, pages 491–500, 2014.

[32] P. Hijma, C. J. H. Jacobs, R. V. v. Nieuwpoort, and H. E. Bal. Cashmere: Heterogeneous Many-Core Computing. In *Proceedings of the 29th of IEEE International Parallel and Distributed Processing Symposium*, IPDPS'15, pages 135–145, May 2015.

[33] I. Karlin. LULESH Programming Model and Performance Ports Overview. Technical Report LLNL-TR-608824, Lawrence Livermore National Laboratory, Dec 2012.

[34] J. Kim, S. Seo, J. Lee, J. Nah, G. Jo, and J. Lee. SnuCL: An OpenCL Framework for Heterogeneous CPU/GPU Clusters. In *Proceedings of the 26th ACM International Conference on Supercomputing*, ICS '12, pages 341–352, 2012.

[35] G. Krawezik. Performance Comparison of MPI and Three OpenMP Programming Styles on Shared Memory Multiprocessors. In *Proceedings of the Fifteenth Annual ACM Symposium on Parallel Algorithms and Architectures*, SPAA '03, pages 118–127, 2003.

[36] O. Kwon, F. Jubair, R. Eigenmann, and S. Midkiff. A Hybrid Approach of OpenMP for Clusters. In *Proceedings of the 17th ACM SIGPLAN Symposium on Principles and Practice of Parallel Programming*, PPoPP '12, pages 75–84, 2012.

[37] S. Lee and J. S. Vetter. Early Evaluation of Directive-based GPU Programming Models for Productive Exascale Computing. In *Proceedings of the International Conference on High Performance Computing, Networking, Storage and Analysis*, SC '12, pages 23:1–23:11, 2012.

[38] S. Lee and J. S. Vetter. OpenARC: Open Accelerator Research Compiler for Directive-based, Efficient Heterogeneous Computing. In *Proceedings of the 23rd International Symposium on High-performance Parallel and Distributed Computing*, HPDC '14, pages 115–120, 2014.

[39] J. Meredith, P. Roth, K. Spafford, and J. Vetter. Performance Implications of Nonuniform Device Topologies in Scalable Heterogeneous Architectures. *IEEE Micro*, 31(5):66–75, Sep 2011.

[40] M. Noack, F. Wende, T. Steinke, and F. Cordes. A Unified Programming Model for Intra- and Inter-node Offloading on Xeon Phi Clusters. In *Proceedings of the International Conference for High Performance Computing, Networking, Storage and Analysis*, SC '14, pages 203–214, 2014.

[41] P. M. Phothilimthana, J. Ansel, J. Ragan-Kelley, and S. Amarasinghe. Portable Performance on Heterogeneous Architectures. In *Proceedings of the Eighteenth International Conference on Architectural Support for Programming Languages and Operating Systems*, ASPLOS '13, pages 431–444, 2013.

[42] S. Potluri, D. Bureddy, K. Hamidouche, A. Venkatesh, K. Kandalla, H. Subramoni, and D. K. D. Panda. MVAPICH-PRISM: A Proxy-based Communication Framework Using InfiniBand and SCIF for Intel MIC Clusters. In *Proceedings of the International Conference on High Performance Computing, Networking, Storage and Analysis*, SC '13, pages 54:1–54:11, 2013.

[43] R. Rabenseifner, G. Hager, and G. Jost. Hybrid MPI/OpenMP Parallel Programming on Clusters of Multi-Core SMP Nodes. In *Proceedings of the 2009 17th Euromicro International Conference on Parallel, Distributed and Network-based Processing*, PDP '09, pages 427–436, 2009.

[44] S. L. Scott. Synchronization and Communication in the T3E Multiprocessor. In *Proceedings of the Seventh International Conference on Architectural Support for Programming Languages and Operating Systems*, ASPLOS VII, pages 26–36, 1996.

[45] S. Seo, G. Jo, and J. Lee. Performance Characterization of the NAS Parallel Benchmarks in OpenCL. In *Proceedings of the 2011 IEEE International Symposium on Workload Characterization*, IISWC '11, pages 137–148, 2011.

[46] M. Si, A. J. Peña, P. Balaji, M. Takagi, and Y. Ishikawa. MT-MPI: Multithreaded MPI for Many-core Environments. In *Proceedings of the 28th ACM International Conference on Supercomputing*, ICS '14, pages 125–134, 2014.

[47] H. Tang, K. Shen, and T. Yang. Compile/Run-time Support for Threaded MPI Execution on Multiprogrammed Shared Memory Machines. In *Proceedings of the Seventh ACM SIGPLAN Symposium on Principles and Practice of Parallel Programming*, PPoPP '99, pages 107–118, 1999.

[48] D. Tarditi, S. Puri, and J. Oglesby. Accelerator: Using Data Parallelism to Program GPUs for General-purpose Uses. In *Proceedings of the 12th International Conference on Architectural Support for Programming Languages and Operating Systems*, ASPLOS XII, pages 325–335, 2006.

[49] J. S. Vetter. *Contemporary High Performance Computing: From Petascale Toward Exascale*. Chapman & Hall/CRC, 2013.

[50] H. Wang, S. Potluri, M. Luo, A. K. Singh, S. Sur, and D. K. Panda. MVAPICH2-GPU: Optimized GPU to GPU Communication for InfiniBand Clusters. *Comput. Sci.*, 26(3-4):257–266, June 2011.

[51] X. Wu and V. Taylor. Performance Characteristics of Hybrid MPI/OpenMP Implementations of NAS Parallel Benchmarks SP and BT on Large-scale Multicore Supercomputers. *SIGMETRICS Perform. Eval. Rev.*, 38(4):56–62, 2011.

Improving GPU Performance Through Resource Sharing

Vishwesh Jatala
Department of CSE
IIT Kanpur
vjatala@cse.iitk.ac.in

Jayvant Anantpur
CDS, IISc, Bangalore
jayvant@hpc.serc.iisc.
ernet.in

Amey Karkare
Department of CSE
IIT Kanpur
karkare@cse.iitk.ac.in

ABSTRACT

Graphics Processing Units (GPUs) consisting of Streaming Multiprocessors (SMs) achieve high throughput by running a large number of threads and context switching among them to hide execution latencies. The number of thread blocks, and hence the number of threads that can be launched on an SM, depends on the resource usage–e.g. number of registers, amount of shared memory–of the thread blocks. Since the allocation of threads to an SM is at the thread block granularity, some of the resources may not be used up completely and hence will be wasted.

We propose an approach that shares the resources of SM to utilize the wasted resources by launching more thread blocks. We show the effectiveness of our approach for two resources: register sharing, and scratchpad (shared memory) sharing. We further propose optimizations to hide long execution latencies, thus reducing the number of stall cycles. We implemented our approach in GPGPU-Sim simulator and experimentally validated it on 19 applications from 4 different benchmark suites: GPGPU-Sim, Rodinia, CUDA-SDK, and Parboil. We observed that applications that underutilize register resource show a maximum improvement of 24% and an average improvement of 11% with register sharing. Similarly, the applications that underutilize scratchpad resource show a maximum improvement of 30% and an average improvement of 12.5% with scratchpad sharing. The remaining applications, which do not waste any resources, perform similar to the baseline approach.

Keywords

Register Sharing; Scratchpad Sharing; Warp Scheduling; Thread Level Parallelism

1. INTRODUCTION

Graphics Processing Units (GPUs) have been effectively used to accelerate large data parallel applications. GPUs consisting of Streaming Multiprocessors (SMs) achieve high throughput by concurrently executing a large number of threads to hide long latencies. The throughput achieved by a GPU depends on the amount of thread level parallelism (TLP) utilized by it. Recent studies [19, 31, 32, 34] focus on improving the throughput of GPUs by exploiting the TLP.

The amount of TLP utilized by a GPU depends on the number of threads resident on it. When an application is launched on a GPU, an execution configuration consisting of the number of thread blocks and the number of threads in a thread block is specified. The number of thread blocks that can actually be launched on an SM depends on the resource requirement, such as the number of registers and the amount of scratchpad memory needed by each thread block. If an SM contains R units of a resource and a thread block requires R_{tb} units to complete its execution, then the SM can launch at the most $\lfloor R/R_{tb} \rfloor$ thread blocks, utilizing $R_{tb} \times \lfloor R/R_{tb} \rfloor$ units. The remaining $R \bmod R_{tb}$ units are wasted.

In this paper, we propose a mechanism to share resources of SM and launch more thread blocks, effectively reducing resource wastage. In particular, we show how sharing of registers and sharing of scratchpad improves the throughput of SMs. It is observed [19] that increasing the number of threads benefits compute-bound applications, but may result in increased L1/L2 cache misses for memory-bound applications, thereby decreasing their performance. To overcome this, we propose an optimization, called *Owner Warp First (OWF)* that schedules the extra thread blocks and their constituent warps effectively. For the register sharing approach, we further propose two optimizations, viz., *Unrolling and Reordering of Register Declaration* and *Dynamic Warp Execution* that improves register utilization and minimizes the number of stall cycles observed by the additional thread blocks respectively.

We make the following contributions in this work:

1. To utilize the resources of GPUs effectively, we propose a novel resource sharing mechanism that enables launching of more thread blocks per SM.
2. We implemented our approach for two resources, i.e., registers and scratchpad. We propose optimizations to further improve the throughput of applications.
3. We implemented our approach using GPGPU-Sim and evaluated on 19 applications from GPGPU-Sim [7], Rodinia [9], CUDA-SDK [2], and Parboil [4] benchmarks. We observe that 8 of the applications, which underutilize the register resource, show an average improvement of 11% with register sharing approach. Similarly 7 applications, which underutilize the scratchpad resource, show an average improvement of 12.5% with scratchpad shar-

HPDC'16, May 31-June 04, 2016, Kyoto, Japan

© 2016 ACM. ISBN 978-1-4503-4314-5/16/05. . . $15.00

DOI: http://dx.doi.org/10.1145/2907294.2907298

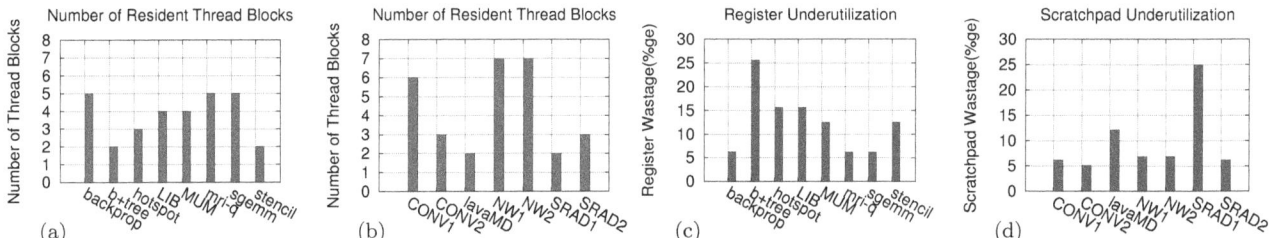

Figure 1: Number of resident thread blocks with (a) limited registers, (b) limited scratchpad. Underutilization of (c) registers, (d) scratchpad.

ing. While the remaining 4 applications, which do not waste any resources, perform comparable to the baseline approach.

The paper is organized as follows: Section 2 describes the background required for our approach. Section 3 motivates the need for sharing. Our approach is presented in Sections 4 and 5. Section 6 discusses hardware overhead for implementing our approach. Section 7 describes the experimental evaluation. Section 8 discusses related work, and Section 9 concludes the paper.

2. BACKGROUND

A typical NVIDIA GPU [1] consists of a set of Streaming Multiprocessors (SMs), and each multiprocessor has execution units called Stream Processors (SPs). CUDA [1] supports extensions to languages, such as C, to allow programmers to define and invoke parallel functions, called kernels, on a GPU. A kernel is invoked along with an execution configuration of threads that specifies the number of threads per thread block and the number of thread blocks.

The number of thread blocks that can reside on an SM depends on: (a) the number of registers used by a thread block and the number of registers available in the SM, (b) the amount of scratchpad memory used by a thread block and the amount of scratchpad memory available in the SM, (c) the maximum number of threads allowed per SM, and (d) the maximum number of thread blocks allowed per SM.

The threads in a thread block are further divided into a set of consecutive 32 threads called Warp. Each SM contains one or more warp schedulers which schedule a ready warp every cycle from a pool of ready warps. All threads in a warp execute the same instruction. Warp schedulers schedule instructions in-order and so, when the current instruction of a warp can not be issued, the warp is not considered to be ready. If no warp can be scheduled in a cycle, then that is a stall cycle. As the number of stall cycles increases, the run time goes up and the throughput decreases. Our approach increases the number of resident thread blocks by utilizing the wasted registers as well as scratchpad memory on each SM and hence increases the number of resident warps and also improves the warp schedulers to hide long latencies.

3. MOTIVATION

The problem of resource underutilization occurs in GPU because resources are allocated at thread block granularity. We analyzed several benchmark applications using the GPGPU-Sim [3] simulator[1]. For applications that are limited by register resource, we show the number of resident

[1]The GPU configuration is described in Table 1. The benchmark details are given in Table 2, Table 3 Section 7.

Table 1: GPGPU-Sim Architecture

Resource	GPU Configuration
Number of Clusters	14
Number of Cores/Cluster	1
Max Num of TBs/Core	8
Max Num of Threads/Core	1536
Number of Registers/Core	32768
Scratchpad Memory/Core	16KB
Warp Scheduling	LRR
Number of Schedulers	2
L1-Cache/Core	16KB
L2-Cache	768KB
DRAM Scheduler	FR-FCFS
GDDR3 Timings	$t_{RRD} = 6, t_{WR} = 12, t_{RCD} = 12,$ $t_{RAS} = 28, t_{RP} = 12, t_{RC} = 40,$ $t_{CDLR} = 5, t_{CL} = 12$

thread blocks per SM in Figure 1(a), and we show the percentage of registers that are unutilized per SM in Figure 1(c). Consider the application *hotspot*. Each thread for this benchmark needs 36 registers, and there are 256 threads in each block, so the number of registers required per thread block is 9216 (36 * 256). According to the configuration (Table 1), the number of registers available on an SM is 32768, so an SM can fit only 3 threads blocks ($\lfloor \frac{32768}{9216} \rfloor$). This results in wastage of 5120 registers per SM.

Similarly, in Figure 1(b) we show the number of resident thread blocks per SM for the applications that are limited by scratchpad resource, and in Figure 1(d) we show the percentage of scratchpad memory that remains unutilized per SM. Consider the application *lavaMD*. Each thread block for this benchmark needs 7200 bytes of scratchpad memory. According to the configuration in Table 1, the amount of scratchpad memory available per SM is 16384 bytes, hence an SM can fit 2 thread blocks. This results in 1984 bytes of scratchpad memory per SM remaining unutilized. Similar behavior is observed for other applications as well.

Applications that are constrained by their resource requirements may not only have low residency, but also waste resources of GPU. Our proposed approach reduces wastage of registers and scratchpad memory and increases the number of resident thread blocks. Our experiments show that these extra thread blocks help to hide long execution latencies and increase throughput.

4. RESOURCE SHARING

We can increase the number of thread blocks in an SM by allowing two thread blocks to share resources. For example, consider an application that has thread blocks of size 10 warps (320 threads), and a thread block requires 10K resource units to complete its execution. If an SM has 35K resource units, at most 3 thread blocks can be resident on

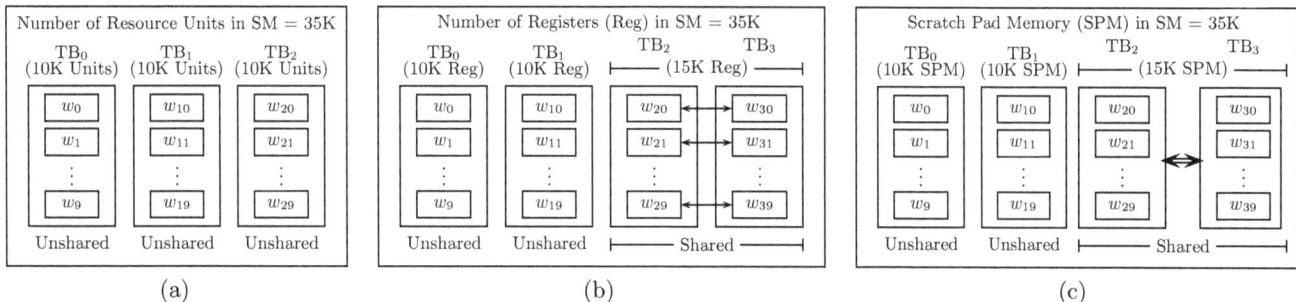

Figure 2: Approaches to Resource Allocation (a) Default Approach (b) Register Sharing (c) Scratchpad Memory Sharing

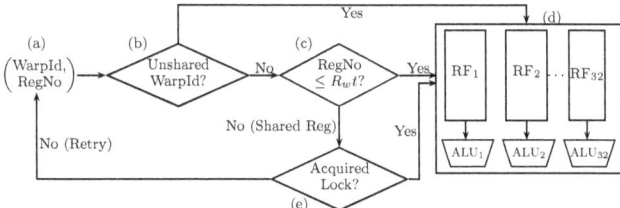

Figure 3: Register Access Mechanism

each SM by utilizing 30K resource units; the remaining 5K units are wasted. The schematic of this approach (baseline) is shown in Figure 2(a), where thread blocks TB_0, TB_1, and TB_2 are scheduled on an SM.

In order to reduce the wastage of resources, our approach allocates one more thread block (TB_3) in *sharing* mode with TB_2. Instead of allocating 10K resource units separately to each of the thread blocks TB_2 and TB_3, a total of 15K units for the two blocks are allocated as follows: each of TB_2 and TB_3 is allocated 5K units exclusively (*Private or Unshared Resource*), while the remaining 5K units (*Shared Resource*) are all allocated to TB_2 or TB_3 whoever needs *any one of these resources first*. The other thread block (which did not get the ownership of shared resources), when it needs *any* of the shared resources, waits till the owner block finishes.

We refer to any two thread blocks as *Shared Blocks* when they share resources exclusively (for example TB_2 and TB_3 in Figure 2(b)), and the warps of such thread blocks as *Shared Warps*. Thread blocks (warps) that do not participate in sharing are referred to as *Unshared Blocks* (*Unshared Warps*). We describe in detail our sharing approach for two types of resources (a) Registers, and (b) Scratchpad.

4.1 Register Sharing

The scenario in Figure 2(a) can be improved using our register allocation scheme shown in Figure 2(b), in which we allocate 10K registers to each thread block TB_0 and TB_1. The remaining 15K registers are shared between thread blocks TB_2 and TB_3 such that each pair of warps in these thread blocks are allocated 1.5K registers as described next. We refer to TB_0 and TB_1 as unshared thread blocks, whereas, TB_2 and TB_3 as shared thread blocks.

Consider the pair of warps W_{20} and W_{30} that participate in sharing. We allocate 0.5K registers (private or unshared registers) each to W_{20} and W_{30}. The remaining 0.5K registers are shared registers, that are allocated to these warps *together* in a shared but exclusive manner, i.e., only one of them can access the pool of shared registers at a time. For example, if warp W_{20} accesses any of the shared registers first, exclusive access to all the 0.5K shared registers is given to W_{20}, while W_{30} is prevented from accessing any of

those 0.5K shared registers till W_{20} finishes. This implies, W_{30} can continue its execution until its first access to any of the 0.5K shared registers and waits until the shared registers are released. Only after W_{20} finishes execution, W_{30} can access the shared registers and continue. This way, additional warps make *some* progress, which helps in hiding execution latencies.

To generalize this idea and to compute the increase in number of thread blocks, we will consider a GPU that provides R registers per SM. Also, consider a thread block that requires R_{tb} registers, and each warp in the thread block requires R_w registers to complete its execution. To increase the number of thread blocks that share registers with other existing thread blocks in the SM, we allocate $R_{tb}(1+t)$ (for any threshold $0 < t < 1$) registers to each pair of shared thread blocks, instead of allocating $2R_{tb}$ registers to them (in Figure 2(b), t is 0.5). Equivalently we allocate $R_w(1+t)$ registers per two warps from these thread blocks (i.e., one warp from each shared thread block in the pair), such that each of these warps can access $R_w t$ unshared registers independently, and they can access the remaining $R_w(1-t)$ shared registers only when granted access.

We allocate registers to a warp dynamically when it requires to access the registers on its first usage, and we deallocate them from the register file after the warp has finished its execution, as described in GPGPU-Sim [3]. Every unshared register is allocated as per the request, but the shared registers are allocated to only a warp that has exclusive access. To detect a register accessed by a warp as shared or unshared, and to efficiently access it from the register file unit, we modify the existing register file access mechanism as shown in Figure 3. When a warp (WarpId) needs to access a register (RegNo), we first check if the warp is an unshared warp, i.e., if it belongs to an unshared thread block (Figure 3, Step (b)). If it is an unshared warp, it can directly access the register from register file using a combination of (WarpId, RegNo). If WarpId is a shared warp, the accessed register is an unshared register if $RegNo \leq R_w t$ (Step (c)). This is because $R_w t$ number of unshared registers are allocated to each warp. If $RegNo > R_w t$, we treat the register as a shared register. A warp can access an unshared register directly from the register file, but it can access a shared register only when it gets exclusive access by acquiring a lock (Step (e)), otherwise it retries the access in another cycle[2].

Consider a scenario shown in Figure 4, where two thread blocks TB_1 and TB_2 are in shared mode. Assume that W_2 and W_3 have already acquired locks for accessing shared registers. Also, assume that the warps W_2, W_3 are waiting for

---

[2]The details of required additional storage units are described in Section 6.

205

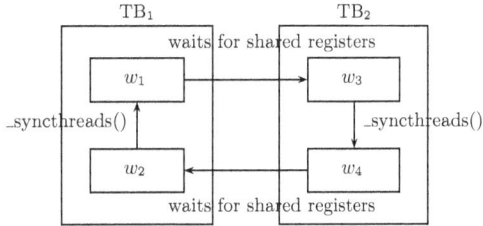

Figure 4: Deadlock in the presence of barrier instructions

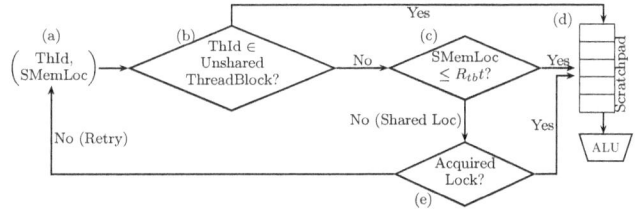

Figure 5: Scratchpad Access Mechanism

warps W_1 and W_4 respectively, to arrive at a barrier instruction (_syncthreads()). Now, if warp W_1 tries to acquire a lock to access shared registers from W_3, and W_4 tries to acquire a lock to access shared registers from W_2, then a deadlock occurs. To avoid deadlock, we always ensure that if thread blocks TB$_1$ and TB$_2$ share registers, then a warp from TB$_1$ (TB$_2$) can acquire a lock only when either (a) none of the warps from TB$_2$ (TB$_1$) have acquired a lock for the shared registers, or (b) the warps from TB$_2$ (TB$_1$) that have acquired exclusive access to the shared registers have finished their execution. For the above example, if warp W_3 already has acquired a lock, W_2 can not acquire a lock, avoiding the deadlock.

4.2 Scratchpad Sharing

Figure 2(c) shows an example of *Scratchpad Sharing*, where we consider a GPU that has 35K units of scratchpad memory per SM, and each thread block requires 10K units. To increase number of resident thread blocks with scratchpad sharing, we allocate 10K units to each TB$_0$ and TB$_1$; the remaining 15K scratchpad units are allocated together for thread blocks TB$_2$ and TB$_3$ such that each one gets 5K units in private mode and the remaining 5K units are accessed in exclusive mode, i.e., only one thread block can access it at a time[3]. Similar to Register sharing approach, we refer to TB$_0$ and TB$_1$ as unshared thread blocks, whereas, TB$_2$ and TB$_3$ as shared thread blocks.

When a thread from the shared thread block (say TB$_2$) needs to access a memory location from shared scratchpad, it gains an exclusive access by acquiring a lock. As long as TB$_2$ is running, no thread from TB$_3$ can access the shared scratchpad locations and hence the corresponding warps of TB$_3$ will have to wait for TB$_2$ to finish before they can proceed further. But warps of TB$_3$ that do not access the shared scratchpad locations can continue execution.

The implementation to support scratchpad sharing in GPGPU-Sim is shown in Figure 5. The steps for the shared scratchpad access follow the rules similar to the shared register access and are omitted for brevity. A deadlock can never occur with scratchpad sharing. Consider two thread blocks TB$_1$ and TB$_2$ that share scratchpad. When a warp from shared thread block (say TB$_1$) acquires a lock, no other warp from TB$_2$ is given access to the shared scratchpad region until TB$_1$ finishes its execution. So, only the warps from TB$_2$ that require accessing the shared resources wait for TB$_1$ to finish. Warps from TB$_1$ never wait for TB$_2$ to finish. Hence there is no deadlock cycle.

---

[3]Unlike register sharing, we can not distribute 1.5K scratchpad memory to each pair of warps because any thread within a thread block can access any scratchpad location allocated for that block.

4.3 Computing the Number of Thread Blocks to be Launched per SM

A naive method of sharing, where each thread block is sharing resources with some other thread block, may launch more thread blocks as compared to default (non-sharing) approach. However, the number of thread blocks that make progress (*effective thread blocks*) per SM can be less than that for non-sharing. For example, consider a scenario where 3 thread blocks are resident per SM without sharing. With naive sharing, it may be possible to have 4 thread blocks resident, such that block 1 shares resources with block 2; and block 3 with block 4. It can happen that block 2 and 4 start accessing shared resources causing blocks 1 and 3 to wait. Effectively only two thread blocks (blocks 2 and 4) will make progress in the naive sharing approach, whereas all 3 blocks can make progress in the non-sharing approach reducing the throughput. To avoid this, we describe a method to compute the total number of thread blocks (Shared + Unshared) to be launched per SM such that the number of effective thread blocks using sharing approach is no less than that of non-sharing approach. We use the following notations:

1. R: Number of units of resource available per SM,
2. R_{tb}: Number of resource units required by a thread block,
3. S: Number of pairs of thread blocks that are to be launched per SM in shared mode,
4. U: Number of thread blocks to be launched in an SM that do not share resources with any other thread block,
5. M: Maximum number of thread blocks to be launched in an SM,
6. t: Threshold for computing the number of resources that a thread block shares with another thread block. For a given threshold value t $(0 < t < 1)$ we allocate $(1+t)R_{tb}$ resource units per two shared thread blocks, in which $(1-t)R_{tb}$ resource units are shared.

Without sharing, we can launch up to $\lfloor R/R_{tb} \rfloor$ thread blocks in an SM, and all of them make progress. Whereas in our approach, if two thread blocks are launched in sharing mode, at least one thread block always makes progress. So, when S shared pairs are launched in an SM, at least S thread blocks always make progress. Also, if U unshared thread blocks are launched in the SM, they always make progress. Therefore, at least $S+U$ thread blocks always make progress with our approach. In order to keep the number of effective thread blocks in our approach to be same as that of no-sharing approach, we need the following relation to hold:

$$S + U = \left\lfloor \frac{R}{R_{tb}} \right\rfloor \qquad (1)$$

For each shared pair of thread blocks, we allocate $R_{tb}(1+t)$ resource units and for each unshared thread block, we allocate R_{tb} resource units. Since the total number of resource units available in the SM is R, we have:

$$U R_{tb} + S R_{tb}(1+t) \leq R \qquad (2)$$

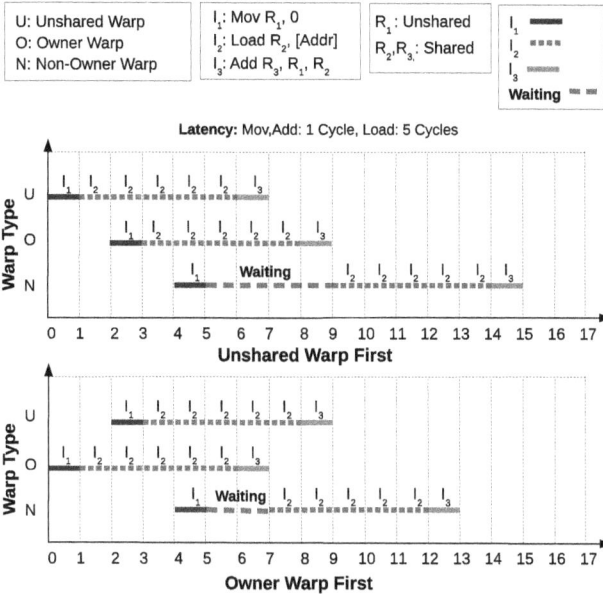

Figure 6: Warp Scheduling

The total number of thread blocks that can be launched in sharing approach is equal to the number of unshared thread blocks plus twice the number of shared pairs, i.e.,

$$M = U + 2S \qquad (3)$$

Using Equations 1, 2, and 3,

$$M = \left\lfloor \frac{R}{R_{tb}} \right\rfloor + \frac{1}{t}\left(\frac{R}{R_{tb}} - \left\lfloor \frac{R}{R_{tb}} \right\rfloor \right) \qquad (4)$$

Since the actual number of thread blocks that can reside in an SM also depends on other factors, such as (a) maximum number of resident threads per SM, and (b) maximum number of resident thread blocks per SM; the number of thread blocks that are launched in an SM by our approach is minimum of values obtained using the factors (a), (b), and the value M. When the number of thread blocks launched by our approach is more than that of baseline approach (i.e., $\left\lfloor \frac{R}{R_{tb}} \right\rfloor$), we enable our resource sharing approach; otherwise, we launch all the thread blocks in unsharing mode.

5. OPTIMIZATIONS

With the proposed resource sharing approach, each SM has unshared and shared warps, and scheduling these warps plays a very important role in determining the performance of applications. We propose an optimization called "Owner Warp First (OWF)" to schedule these warps effectively. If two thread blocks TB_i and TB_j are a shared pair, and at least one of the warps of TB_i waits for shared resources from TB_j, we call TB_j as *Owner Block*, and the warps that belong to TB_j are called *Owner Warps*. TB_i is called *Non-Owner Block* and warps of TB_i are called *Non-Owner Warps*. As soon as the owner thread block finishes its execution, it transfers its ownership to the non-owner thread block (i.e., the non-owner thread block becomes the owner), and a new non-owner thread block gets launched.

5.1 Scheduling Owner Warp First (OWF)

A warp scheduler in the SM issues a warp every cycle from a pool of ready warps. With our solution, the warps

can be categorized into three types viz., unshared, shared owner and shared non-owner. In register sharing, shared non-owner warps depend on the corresponding shared-owner warps to release registers, before they can make progress. Similarly, with scratchpad sharing, warps from non-owner thread blocks wait for owner thread blocks to complete their execution. Hence scheduling the warps plays a role in improving the performance of applications.

Consider a scenario shown in Figure 6. Assume that an SM contains 3 warps: unshared (U), shared owner (O), shared non-owner (N) warps, and each warp needs to execute three instructions (I_1, I_2, and I_3) as indicated in the figure. Assume that latency of Mov and Add instruction is 1 cycle, and the latency of Load instruction is 5 cycles. Also, assume that register R_1 is an unshared resource and R_2, R_3 are shared resources. If unshared warp is prioritized over owner warp (shown as *Unshared Warp First*), the unshared warp executes I_1 in the first cycle, and it starts execution of I_2 in the 2nd cycle. However, it can not start I_3 in the 3rd cycle because register R_2 of I_3 is dependent on the instruction I_2, and I_2 takes 5 cycles to complete the execution. If owner warp is prioritized over non-owner warp, it can start execution in the 3rd cycle. The non-owner warp which has the least priority can start its execution I_1 at the 5th cycle. However, it can not execute I_2 in the 6th cycle because it needs to acquire access to the shared resource R_2, which is held by its owner warp. Hence, it waits until the owner warp releases the shared resources (i.e., till the 9th cycle). The non-owner warp can resume its execution in the 10th cycle and can finish in 15 cycles.

To minimize the waiting time of the non-owner warps, we propose an algorithm, *Owner Warp First (OWF)*, that prioritizes warps in the order: shared owner, unshared, and shared non-owner. Giving the highest priority to shared owner warps helps finish them sooner, and hence the dependent shared non-owner warps can make progress. Since non-owner warps depend on their corresponding owner warps for shared resources, giving them low priority helps in hiding stalls when no other types of warps are are ready to run. In Figure 6 with OWF approach, owner warp can finish sooner, i.e., in 7 cycles. Similarly unshared warp, with second priority, can finish in 9 cycles. Since the non-owner has low priority, it can start executing I_1 in the 5th cycle. It can overlap the execution of I_2 with the unshared warp in the 8th cycle because its owner warp has released the shared resources. Further, it can finish the execution in 13 cycles as shown in the figure, thus improving the overall performance.

To leverage OWF optimization, we launch the additional thread blocks such that all the thread blocks in the SM will be initially arranged according to the order: owner, unshared, non-owner thread blocks. If we launch k thread blocks in addition to N original blocks (id: 0, ..., N-1), then thread block pairs with ids (0, N), (1, N+1), ..., (k-1, N+k-1) are launched as shared thread blocks, and thread blocks k to N-1 are launched as unshared thread blocks. Hence thread blocks with ids 0 to k-1 can become owner blocks, thread blocks k to N-1 become unshared blocks, and thread blocks N to N+k-1 become non-owner blocks.

5.2 Unrolling and Reordering of Register Declarations

In register sharing, non-owner warps need to wait for owner warps when they try to access shared registers. If

```
.reg .u32 $r<27>;            | .reg .pred $p0;
.reg .u32 $ofs<3>;           | .reg .u32 $o127;
.reg .pred $p<4>;            | .reg .u32 $r124;
.reg .u32 $r124;             | .reg .u32 $r16;
.reg .u32 $o127;             | .reg .u32 $r17;
...........                  | .reg .u32 $r9;
...........                  | .reg .u32 $r18;
...........                  | .reg .u32 $r10;
...........                  | ...........
                             | ...........
set.le.s32.s32 $p0/$o127,    | set.le.s32.s32 $p0/$o127,
     s[0x003c], $r124;       |      s[0x003c], $r124;
mov.u32 $r16, $r124;         | mov.u32 $r16, $r124;
mov.u32 $r17, $r124;         | mov.u32 $r17, $r124;
mov.u32 $r9, $r124;          | mov.u32 $r9, $r124;
mov.u32 $r18, $r124;         | mov.u32 $r18, $r124;
mov.u32 $r10, $r124;         | mov.u32 $r10, $r124;
/* Code here */              | /* Code here */

   (a) Normal Declarations       (b) Unrolled Declarations
```

Figure 7: Unrolling and Reordering of Register Declarations

the very first instruction issued by a non-owner warp uses a shared register, then the warp has to wait and can not start its execution until corresponding owner warp has released the shared register. In order to allow the non-owner warps to execute as many instructions as possible before stalling due to unavailability of shared registers, we unroll and reorder the register declarations. To illustrate this, consider the PTXPlus [3] code shown in Figure 7(a), which is generated by GPGPU-Sim [3] for the *sgemm* application from Parboil Suite [4]. The first instruction of the code accesses registers p0 and r124, which get the register sequence numbers as 31 and 35 according to the declaration. These registers are part of the shared registers for a certain threshold value t. Hence, a non-owner warp has to wait until the registers are released. To delay accessing the shared registers, we unroll and rearrange the order of the register declarations so that p0, r124 become unshared registers (i.e., they get the register sequence numbers as 1 and 3, as shown in Figure 7(b)). Hence the non-owner warps get to execute more number of instructions before they start accessing shared registers.

To implement this optimization, we converted the assembly code (PTXPlus) produced by GPGPU-Sim into an optimized assembly code. To achieve this, we first find an order of registers according to their first usage. Further, to ensure that unshared registers are used before shared registers, we modify the register declarations so that a register that has been used first is declared first. Finally, we modified the GPGPU simulator to use optimized PTXPlus code for simulating instructions. This optimization can be easily integrated at assembly level using CUDA compiler.

5.3 Dynamic Warp Execution

A study by Kayiran et. al. [19] shows that the performance of memory-bound applications can degrade with increase in the number of resident thread blocks. Executing additional thread blocks can increase L1/L2 cache misses, which leads to increase in the stall cycles. In register sharing, the additional warp (non-owner warp) resumes its execution as soon as its corresponding owner warp finishes, while in scratchpad sharing non-owner warps wait until its corresponding owner thread block finishes. In order to reduce the number of additional stalls due to the execution of non-owner warps in register sharing, we propose an optimization that can dynamically enable or disable execution of

long latency instructions (memory) issued by the non-owner warps.

To control the execution of memory instructions from the non-owner warps, we monitor the number of stall cycles for each SM. When executing memory instructions from non-owner warp leads to increase in the number of stalls, we decrease the probability of executing further memory instructions from the non-owner warps. To illustrate this, consider a GPU that has N SMs, all in sharing mode. Our approach disables execution of memory instructions for the non-owner warps, only on a specific SM (e.g. SM_0). Every other SM, SM_i for $i \in \{1 \ldots N - 1\}$, allows execution of memory instructions for the non-owner warps, and compares its stall cycles periodically with the stalls on SM_0. If stalls observed in the SM_i are more than the stalls appearing in SM_0, then the probability of executing memory instructions on SM_i from the non-owner warps is decreased by a predetermined value p. If the stalls in SM_i are less than that in SM_0, then the probability of executing memory instructions on SM_i from the non-owner warps is increased by the same value p. Thus, we reduce the number of stall cycles by controlling the execution of memory instructions.

After running several experiments, we selected the periodicity of monitoring to be 1000 cycles, which is to ensure that (a) the monitoring overhead is not high, and (b) sufficient number of stall cycles are observed. In our experiments, initially all the SMs (except SM_0) are allowed to execute all memory instructions, i.e., the probability of executing memory instructions from non-owner warp is 1. Depending on the stall cycles observed for an SM_i ($i \in \{1 \ldots N - 1\}$), this probability for SM_i is decreased or increased by $p = 0.1$, but is kept within interval $[0, 1]$ as a saturating counter.

6. HARDWARE REQUIREMENT

Figure 8 shows the modified architecture to implement our proposed resource sharing approach. There are mainly two changes in the scheduling logic. The first change is that the warp scheduler uses OWF policy to prioritize warps, using the owner information. The second change is the inclusion of resource access check. A warp is considered to be ready for issuing only when it can access the required resources (resource access check) and has all its operands available (scoreboard check). The resource access unit follows the resource access mechanism (Figure 3 and Figure 5), and uses some additional storage units (shown in grey color in Figure 8) to determine the access to resources.

Storage units required for register sharing:
1. Each SM requires a bit (shown as *ShSM* in Figure 8 in Additional Storage Units corresponding to Register Sharing) to specify whether sharing mode is enabled for it. This bit will be set when the number of thread blocks assigned to the SM using resource sharing is more than the default number of thread blocks per SM.
2. Each resident thread block stores its shared thread block id in the *ShTB* table, shown in the figure. If a thread block is in unsharing mode, its corresponding value is set to -1. For T thread blocks, $T\lceil \log_2(T + 1) \rceil$ (assuming ids 0 to T-1 for T thread blocks, we can use id T to represent -1) bits are required per SM.
3. Each warp requires a bit for specifying the owner information, which is stored in *Owner* table in the figure. This bit is set only when the warp is an owner warp. Hence, for W warps, W bits are needed.

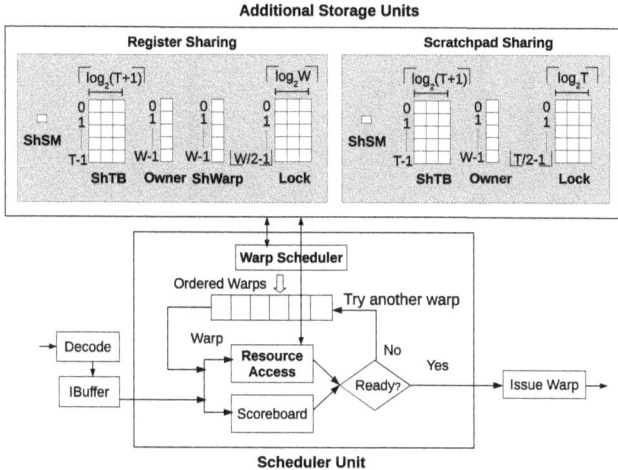

In the additional storage units, X dimension of each table refers to the number of bits, and Y dimension refers to the number of entries.

Figure 8: Modified Architecture for Resource Sharing

4. Each warp requires a bit to specify whether it is in sharing or unsharing mode (shown as *ShWarp* table in the figure). A warp is set to be in sharing mode, when its corresponding thread block is in sharing mode. For W warps in an SM, W bits are required. For a warp in shared mode, its corresponding shared warp can be identified using the sharer thread block id of its thread block and its relative position in the thread block.

5. Each pair of shared warps uses a lock variable to access the shared registers exclusively. The lock variable is set to the id of the warp which has gained access to the shared registers. This is maintained in the *Lock* table in the figure. If an SM has W warps, there can be a maximum of $\lfloor W/2 \rfloor$ shared pairs of warps in the SM. Hence, we need a total of $\lfloor W/2 \rfloor \lceil \log_2 W \rceil$ bits per SM.

Storage units required for scratchpad sharing:

1. Similar to register sharing, scratchpad sharing approach also requires *ShSM*, *ShTB*, and *Owner* tables as described above. These tables are shown in Figure 8 in Additional Storage Units corresponding to Scratchpad Sharing.

2. Each pair of shared thread blocks uses a lock variable to access the shared locations exclusively. The lock variable is set to the id of the thread block which has gained access to the shared scratchpad region. If an SM has T thread blocks, there can be a maximum of $\lfloor T/2 \rfloor$ shared pairs of thread blocks in the SM. Hence, we need a total of $\lfloor T/2 \rfloor \lceil \log_2 T \rceil$ bits per SM. Similar to register sharing, these values are maintained in the *Lock* table, shown in Figure 8 for scratchpad sharing.

The total amount of storage required (in bits) for a GPU with N SMs for implementing register sharing is:

$$(1 + T\lceil \log_2(T+1) \rceil + 2W + \lfloor W/2 \rfloor \lceil \log_2 W \rceil) * N$$

and for implementing scratchpad sharing is:

$$(1 + T\lceil \log_2(T+1) \rceil + W + \lfloor T/2 \rfloor \lceil \log_2 T \rceil) * N$$

For the architecture shown in Table 1, the additional storage required per SM is 273 bits for register sharing and 93 bits for scratchpad sharing.

Table 2: Set-1: Benchmarks limited by registers

Benchmark	Application	Kernel	Block Size	Registers per thread
Rodinia [9]	backprop	bpnn_adjust_ weights_cuda	256	24
Rodinia	b+tree	findRangeK	508	24
Rodinia	hotspot	calculate_temp	256	36
GPGPU-Sim [7]	LIB	Pathcalc_Portfo lio_KernelGPU	192	36
GPGPU-Sim	MUM	mummergpuKernel	256	28
Parboil [4]	mri-q	ComputeQ_GPU	256	24
Parboil	sgemm	mysgemmNT	128	48
Parboil	stencil	block2D_hybrid_ coarsen_x	512	28

In addition to storage units, the resource access unit requires two comparator circuits to implement the steps (b) and (c) shown in Figures 3 and 5. Similarly, it requires an arithmetic circuit to set the lock as shown in step (e).

7. EXPERIMENTS AND ANALYSIS

We implemented our approach using GPGPU-Sim V3.X [3]. Table 1 shows the baseline architecture used for comparison. We evaluated our approach on several applications from GPGPU-Sim [7], Rodinia [9], CUDA-SDK [2], and Parboil [4] benchmarks. Depending on the resource requirement of applications, we divided the benchmarks into three sets. Set-1 (Table 2) consists of applications whose number of thread blocks per SM are limited by registers. Set-2 (Table 3) has applications that are limited by scratchpad memory. Set-3 (Table 4) has applications that are limited neither by registers nor by scratchpad memory (i.e., they are limited either by the number of resident threads or the number of resident thread blocks). We choose Set-3 applications to ensure that our approach does not degrade the performance of applications that are neither limited by registers nor scratchpad memory. For each application in Table 2 and Table 3, we show names of the kernels used for evaluation and the number of threads per thread block. In Table 2, we report the number of registers per thread for each kernel, which GPGPU-Sim uses to compute the number of resident thread blocks, and in Table 3 we show the amount of scratchpad memory used by each thread block.

We use the value of threshold (t) to configure the percentage of resource sharing. For example, if each thread block requires R_{tb} units of resource, and we choose $t = 0.1$, then we allocate $1.1 * R_{tb}$ resource units per two shared thread blocks, which means 90% of resource units (R_{tb}) are used as shared resource units. So for a given threshold t, we can compute the percentage of resource sharing as $(1 - t) * 100$. We analyzed the performance of our approach for each application by varying t and chose the threshold value as 0.1 (i.e., 90% resource sharing) for our results (For details, see [16]).

We measure the performance of our approach using the following metrics, which are reported by GPGPU-Sim [3]:

1. The Number of Resident Thread Blocks: It indicates the number of thread blocks that are launched in an SM. We choose this metric to compare the amount of TLP that is present in an SM.

2. Instructions Per Cycle (IPC): It is the number of instructions that are simulated per core clock cycle. We use it to measure the performance of our modified GPU architecture with respect to benchmark applications.

3. Simulation Cycles: It is the number of cycles that a ker-

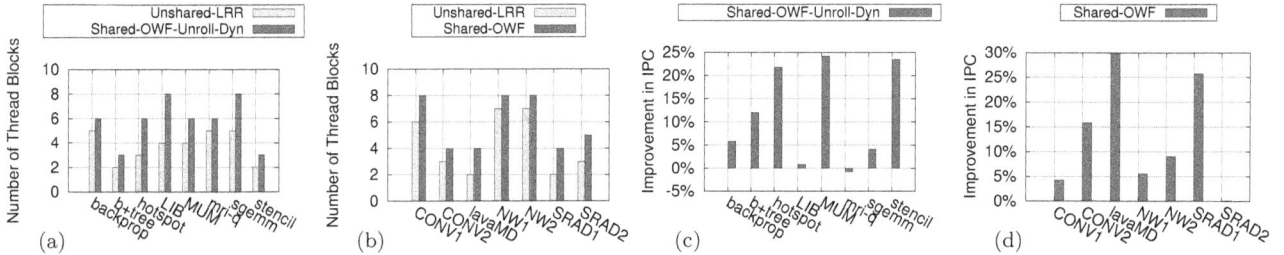

Figure 9: Comparing number of resident thread blocks of baseline approach with (a) Register sharing (b) Scratchpad sharing Performance comparison of (c) Register sharing (d) Scratchpad sharing with baseline approach

Table 3: Set-2: Benchmarks limited by scratchpad memory

Benchmark	Application	Kernel	Block Size	Scratchpad Size (bytes)
CUDA-SDK [2]	convolutionSeparable (CONV1)	convolution RowsKernel	64	2560
CUDA-SDK	convolutionSeparable (CONV2)	convolution ColumnsKernel	128	5184
Rodinia	lavaMD	kernel_gpu_cuda	128	7200
Rodinia	nw (NW1)	needle_cuda_shared_1	16	2180
Rodinia	nw (NW2)	needle_cuda_shared_2	16	2180
Rodinia	srad_v2 (SRAD1)	srad_cuda_1	256	6144
Rodinia	srad_v2 (SRAD2)	srad_cuda_2	256	5120

Table 4: Set-3: Benchmarks limited by threads or blocks

Benchmark	Application	Kernel	Limited by
Rodinia	backprop	bpnn_layer forward_CUDA	Threads
GPGPU-Sim	BFS	Kernel	Threads
Rodinia	gaussian	FAN2	Blocks
GPGPU-Sim	NN	executeSecondLayer	Blocks

nel takes to complete its simulation. We use this metric to measure performance of benchmarks applications with our modified GPU architecture.

4. Pipeline Stall Cycle: It is the cycle in which no warp can execute an instruction because the execution units are busy. This is to show that our approach can help in hiding the long latency instructions.

5. Idle Cycle: It is the cycle in which no warp is ready to execute next instruction. We choose this metric to show that the additional thread blocks launched by our approach help in minimizing the cycles in which SMs are idle.

7.1 Analysis of Set-1 and Set-2 benchmarks

7.1.1 Increase in the number of thread blocks

Figures 9(a) and (b) show that resource sharing helps in increasing the number of thread blocks launched for the applications. Figure 9(a) compares the effective number of thread blocks launched by register sharing approach (denoted as Shared-OWF-Unroll-Dyn) with that of baseline implementation (denoted as Unshared-LRR). For applications MUM, backprop, hotspot, and mri-q our approach is able to launch 6 thread blocks (i.e., 1536 threads), which is the limit on the number of resident threads per SM. Applications stencil and b+tree launch 3 thread blocks per SM, compared to 2 in the baseline approach. For applications LIB and sgemm our approach is able to launch 8 thread blocks per SM, which is the limit on the number of resident thread blocks.

In Figure 9(b), we compare the number of resident thread

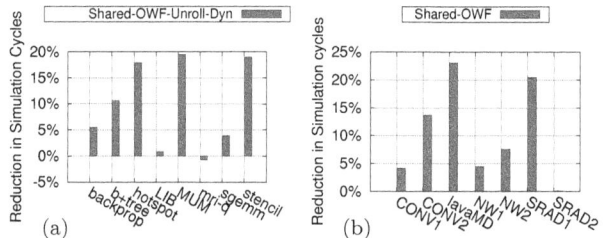

Figure 10: Percentage decrease in Simulation Cycles (a) Register Sharing (b) Scratchpad sharing

blocks launched by scratchpad sharing (labeled as Shared-OWF) with baseline approach. For applications CONV1, NW1, and NW2, we launch 8 thread blocks per SM, which is the limit on the number of resident thread blocks.

7.1.2 Performance analysis

Figure 9(c) shows the improvement in IPC with register sharing over baseline LRR (Loose Round Robin) implementation. We observe that applications show an average improvement of 11% with register sharing. Applications b+tree, hotspot, MUM, and stencil achieve significant speedups of 11.98%, 21.76%, 24.14%, and 23.45% respectively. Similarly Figure 9(d) shows the performance improvement in IPC with scratchpad sharing. We observe that applications show an average improvement of 12.5% with scratchpad sharing. CONV2, lavaMD, and SRAD1 achieve speedups of 15.85%, 29.96%, and 25.73% respectively. These applications leverage all our optimizations to perform better. The performance improvement in IPC for lavaMD is due to two reasons: (1) The number of resident thread blocks launched by our approach is twice that of baseline approach (2) No instruction that uses scratchpad memory location falls into shared scratchpad, hence all the additional thread blocks execute instructions without waiting for shared thread blocks. Though LIB launches 8 thread blocks per SM with register sharing, it improves only by 0.84%. It is due to increase in L2 cache misses caused by additional shared blocks. The benchmarks backprop and sgemm achieve modest improvements of 5.82% and 4.06% respectively with register sharing. Similarly, CONV1, NW1, and NW2 show improvements of 4.33%, 5.62%, and 9.03% respectively with scratchpad sharing. mri-q slows down by 0.72% because additional shared blocks increase L1 cache misses and hence increase the number of stalls. SRAD2 shows improvement only upto 0.1% because a barrier instruction placed next to shared scratchpad access limits the progress of shared threads that do not access any shared scratchpad location.

In Figures 10(a) and (b), we show the percentage decrease

in the number of simulation cycles with register and scratchpad sharing when compared to baseline approach. Since the number of instructions executed in our approach is same as that of the baseline approach, all the applications that show improvement in IPC in Figures 9(c) and (d) will take less the number of simulation cycles for completing their execution using our approach. That is why Figure 9 and Figure 10 show similar trend.

7.1.3 Effectiveness of optimizations

Figure 11(a) compares register sharing optimizations with baseline approach. We compare the results of register sharing when we do not use any optimization and use the existing baseline LRR scheduling policy (labeled Shared-LRR-NoOpt). Consider the application *hotspot*, it achieves a speedup of 13.65% even without using any optimization because the additional thread blocks launched by our approach help in hiding execution latencies. With register unrolling optimization (labeled Shared-LRR-Unrolled), we further see an improvement up to 15.18% because register unrolling enables threads to execute more instructions before they start accessing shared registers. Hence it can execute more instructions before it accesses shared registers. When we enable the dynamic warp execution (labeled Shared-LRR-Unrolled-Dyn), we see an improvement only upto 14.58% because it limits the execution of memory instructions from non-owner warps. However when we apply the OWF optimization (labeled Shared-OWF-Unrolled-Dyn), the application speeds further upto 21.76%. With OWF optimization, the priority of non-owner warps decreases compared to the other warps. Hence the memory instructions issued by non-owner warps do not interfere with the other warps, which minimizes the L1/L2 cache misses. We see that *b+tree* behaves similarly to *hotspot* in terms of performance gain by varying the optimizations.

MUM slows down by 0.15% when we do not use any optimization. We observe that increase in the resident thread blocks leads to increase in the number of memory instructions issued by non-owner warps, increasing L1 and L2 cache misses. Though we see an increase in the L1/L2 cache misses, the other instructions issued by the non-owner warps help in minimizing the stall cycles. With register unrolling optimization, we see a slight improvement (0.08%). When we apply the dynamic warp execution, it shows a speed up of 6.45%. From this, we analyze that dynamic warp execution reduces the additional stall cycles produced by issuing memory instructions from the non-owner warps. Further with OWF optimization, performance improves upto 24.14% because of the decrease in interference from non-owner warps.

LIB shows an improvement of 2% using sharing with no optimizations. We observe the same performance even with unrolling optimization because the number of instructions that use unshared registers before they start accessing shared registers is exactly the same as without optimization. With dynamic warp execution, we still observe the same since in this application all the owner warps have completed executing all instructions before any non-owner warp starts issuing any memory instructions. With OWF optimization, we observe a small degradation because of increase in the number of stall cycles compared to the LRR policy.

The benchmarks *sgemm*, *backprop*, and *stencil* achieve good improvements only when OWF optimization is enabled. Since instructions issued by non-owner warps exe-

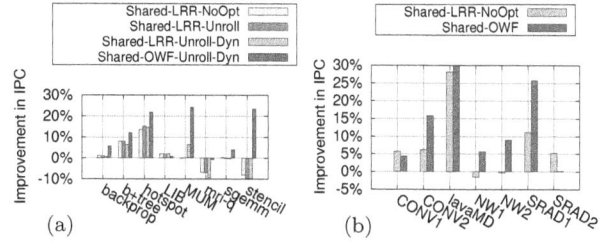

Figure 11: Performance analysis of optimizations for (a) Register Sharing (b) Scratchpad sharing

cute with the least priority, they do not interfere with other warps and hence minimize L1/L2 cache misses. We do not see any performance improvement with *mri-q* because the additional thread blocks increase L1 cache misses with our approach. However the slow down was reduced to 0.72% in the presence of all the optimizations.

To summarize, memory-bound applications, like *MUM*, take advantage of our sharing approach in the presence of dynamic warp execution and OWF optimizations. Whereas, compute-bound applications, like *hotspot*, perform better even without any optimizations, and they further improve with OWF optimization.

In Figure 11(b), we show the effect of OWF optimization on scratchpad sharing. *lavaMD* shows an improvement of 28% even without any optimization (labeled shared-LRR-NoOpt). It is because additional thread blocks do not access any memory location which belongs to shared scratchpad memory. *CONV1*, *CONV2*, *SRAD1*, and *SRAD2* applications show improvements of 5.68%, 6.21%, 11.1%, and 5.28% respectively without applying optimization, which is due to additional thread blocks that help in hiding the latencies.

With OWF optimization, *CONV2*, *NW1*, *NW2*, and *SRAD1* applications improve upto 15.85%, 5.62%, 9.03%, and 25.73% respectively. Since OWF optimization schedules the owner warps efficiently, it helps in minimizing stall cycles thus improving IPC value. *lavaMD* improves upto 30% since it has more benefit with sharing than OWF optimization. *CONV1* and *SRAD2* perform better when no optimization is applied because these applications go through extra cache misses (L1 and L2) and extra stall cycles with OWF optimization when compared to no optimization.

7.1.4 Comparison with other schedulers

In Figures 12(a) and (b), we show the performance improvement in the register sharing and the scratchpad sharing, respectively, over GTO (Greedy Then Old) scheduler. We observe that our approach shows an improvement upto 3.9% with register sharing and shows an improvement upto 30% with scratchpad sharing. *backprop* shows the same number L2 misses as the baseline GTO, but it has more L1 misses with our approach. In *stencil*, we observe extra L2 misses with our approach. *NW1* and *NW2* degrade with our approach because they have less number of stall cycles with GTO scheduler than our approach. Further, as shown in Figure 12(c) and (d) we observe an improvement upto 27.22% with register sharing and upto 27.08% with scratchpad sharing over the two-level scheduling policy.

7.1.5 Reduction in idle and stall cycles

In Figures 13(a) and (b), we report percentage decrease in the number of idle cycles and pipeline stall cycles when compared to the baseline approach. We observe that, all ap-

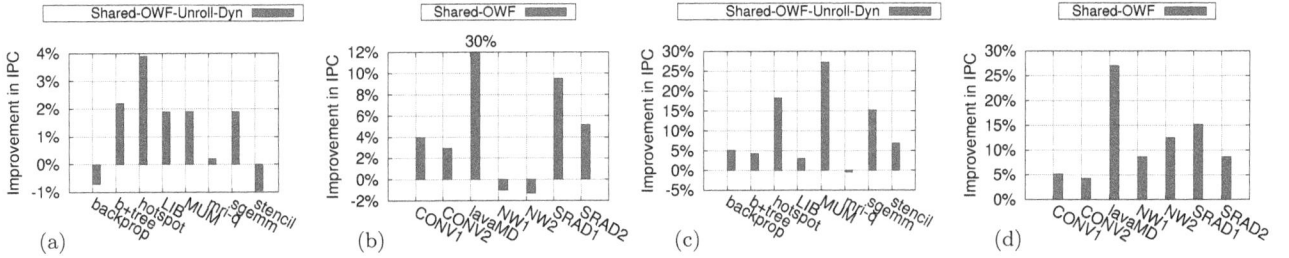

Figure 12: Performance comparison of (a) Register sharing (b) Scratchpad sharing with GTO (baseline) scheduler
Performance comparison of (c) Register sharing (d) Scratchpad sharing with 2-Level (baseline) scheduler

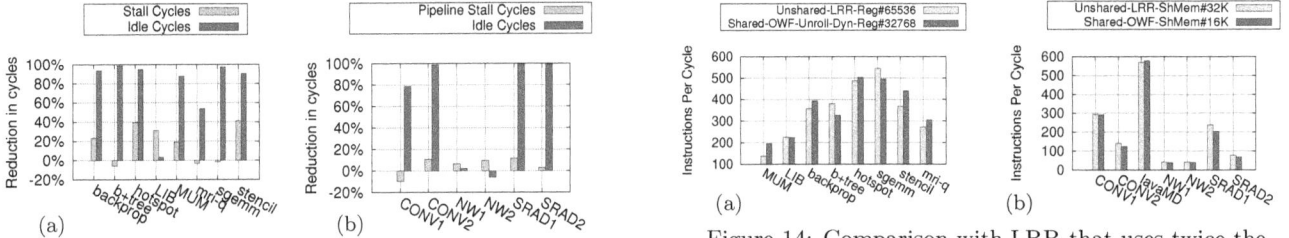

Figure 13: Percentage decrease in stalls and idle cycles for (a) Register Sharing (b) Scratchpad sharing . Note that lavaMD is not shown in (b) as it has zero stall cycles in baseline approach and 259 cycles in shared-OWF approach. It shows 49.5% decrease in idle cycles.

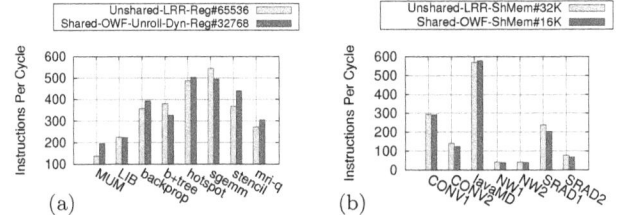

Figure 14: Comparison with LRR that uses twice the number of (a) Registers (b) Scratchpad

plications but one show reduction in the number of idle cycles (upto 99%). This is expected because with the increase in the number of thread blocks, number of instructions that are ready to execute also increase. For *MUM*, *LIB*, *backprop*, *hotspot*, and *stencil* the stall cycles also reduce with register sharing. Similarly for *CONV2*, *NW1*, *NW2*, *SRAD1*, and *SRAD2* applications, number of stall cycles reduce with scratchpad sharing. It indicates the additional thread blocks launched with our approach hide the long execution latencies in a better way. We observe an increase in the stall cycles for applications *b+tree* and *sgemm*. However, since the number of idle cycles have significantly reduced, overall we see a benefit with our approach. For *mri-q*, the number of stall cycles increases with our approach due to the increase in L1 cache misses. *lavaMD* shows an increase of 259 stall cycles because the additional threads wait for execution units (SP units) to become ready. For *CONV1* we see an increase in number of stalls with our approach due to L1 cache misses.

7.1.6 Resource savings

We also compare our approach against LRR Scheduler that uses twice the number of resources. In Figure 14(a), the baseline approach (labeled as Unshared-LRR-Reg#65536) uses 64K registers, whereas our approach uses only 32K registers. Even with an increase in the number of registers and hence an increase in the number of resident thread blocks in the baseline approach, our approach performs better in 5 out of 8 applications. *MUM* performs better with our approach, even though the number of thread blocks is same (6) in both the approaches because dynamic warp execution optimization helps minimizing the stalls produced by the additional thread blocks. *sgemm*, *b+tree*, and *LIB* perform better with the baseline approach due to an increase in the number of resident thread blocks and hence an increase in the number of active warps. In Figure 14(b), we compare scratchpad

sharing approach that uses 16K bytes of memory with that of baseline approach that uses 32K byes of memory. From the figure we observe that, performance of *CONV1*, *NW1*, and *NW2* is comparable to that of baseline approach because our approach can launch the same number of thread blocks as the baseline approach. *lavaMD* performs better than baseline approach because sharing helps in minimizing latencies. *CONV2*, *SRAD1*, and *SRAD2* degrade with our approach because number of resident thread blocks in our approach is less, and number of stall cycles in our approach is more compared to baseline approach.

7.2 Analysis of Set-3 benchmarks

The performance of register sharing and scratchpad sharing approach for the Set-3 applications (Table 4) is presented in Figures 15(a) and (b) respectively. As discussed earlier, these applications are not limited by the number of available resources but due to other factors such as the number of threads or thread blocks. We measure their performance when our approach uses (1) LRR scheduling policy, (2) GTO scheduling policy, and (3) OWF scheduling policy[4]. From Figures 15(a) and (b), we observe that our proposed resource sharing approach when used with LRR scheduling (labeled as Shared-LRR-Unroll-Dyn) performs exactly same as the baseline LRR scheduling (Unshared-LRR). Since the number of thread blocks launched by the applications are not limited by the resources, our approach does not launch any additional thread blocks, and all the thread blocks are in unsharing mode. Hence, it behaves exactly similar to the baseline approach. Similarly, our approach when used with the GTO scheduling policy (Shared-GTO-Unroll-Dyn), performs exactly same as the baseline approach that uses GTO scheduling policy without sharing (Unshared-GTO). Finally, we observe that with OWF scheduling policy (Shown as Shared-OWF-Unroll-Dyn), our approach is comparable to that of Unshared-GTO implementation. In OWF optimization, the warps are arranged according to the priorities of

---

[4]We do not use two-level scheduling policy because it cannot be directly integrated with our sharing approach.

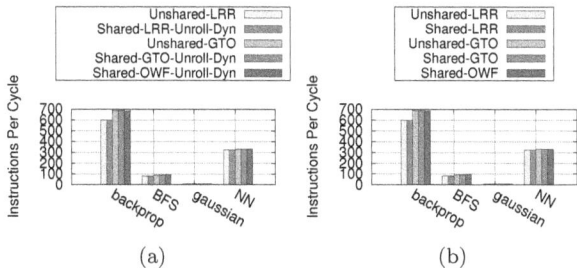

Figure 15: Performance analysis of Set-3 applications for (a) Register sharing (b) Scratchpad sharing

the owner, the unshared, and the non-owner warps. Since in this case, we do not launch any additional thread blocks, all the thread blocks are in unshared mode. Hence all the unshared warps are sorted according to their dynamic warp id. So the performance of Shared-OWF-Unroll-Dyn is similar to that of Unshared-GTO implementation.

From the results of Set-1, Set-2, and Set-3 benchmark applications we can say that, if the number of thread blocks launched by an application is limited either by registers or by scratchpad memory (as shown in Set-1 and Set-2), then they can leverage our sharing approach to improve their performance. When they are limited either by the number of resident threads or by the number of thread blocks, our approach does not launch any additional thread blocks, and they perform comparable to the baseline approach.

8. RELATED WORK

Xiang et. al. [32] discussed thread block level resource management. They proposed a hardware solution to launch a partial thread block when there are not enough resources to launch a full thread block. Their solution can have only one partial thread block running. The patented register management [31] uses the concept of virtual registers, which are more than the actual physical registers, and hence can launch more thread blocks than allowed by physical registers. This can be combined with our solution. Yang et. al. [34] proposed hardware and software solutions to the problem caused by allocation and deallocation of shared memory at the thread block granularity. Their solution is complementary to our approach. A compiler based co-ordinated register allocation [33] was proposed to improve the GPU performance by reducing the register spilling cost.

GPU register file virtualization [17] proposes techniques to share register space across warps. It uses compiler generated life time information to allocate dead registers to another warp. However, it is used for reducing the power consumption and not for improving performance. In contrast, our sharing approach focuses on improving the TLP thereby improving performance. Li et. al. [24] proposed a resource virtualization scheme to minimize the under utilization of system resources by sharing the GPU resources among multiprocessors. Their approach achieves speedup by overlapping multiple kernel executions on virtual GPU. Warped Register File [5] describes a solution to reduce power consumption in register file by turning off unallocated registers. Gebhart et. al. [14] proposed a unified memory for register, scratchpad, and primary cache, which partitions resources of SM as per the application need. It requires a lot of hardware changes to access unified storage.

Other techniques to improve GPU performance include re-ducing cache contention, improving DRAM bandwidth, hide long latencies, reduce energy consumption, etc. Rogers et. al. [29] propose a cache conscious wave front scheduling algorithm which makes use of intra-wave front locality detector, focusing on shared L1 cache. A Two level warp scheduler [27] proposed by Narasiman et. al. divides warps into groups and schedules the warps in each group in round robin manner to hide long latencies in a better way. Sethia et. al. [30] proposed a memory aware warp scheduling approach that prioritizes memory requests of a single warp when memory saturation occurs. Priority based cache allocation [23] was proposed to enable high throughput and better resource utilization. Gebhart et. al. [13] proposed energy efficient hierarchical register file storage and two level warp scheduler for high throughput processors. OWL [18] proposes techniques to improve cache contention and DRAM bank level parallelism. Lee et. al. [20] proposed alternative thread block scheduling mechanism to improve GPU performance and also proposed mixed concurrent kernel execution to improve resource utilization and performance. Warp criticality problem [22] has been addressed by scheduling critical warps more frequently than others. Also, Lee et. al. [21] proposed a coordinated solution to accelerate the execution of critical warps. Ma et al. [25] proposed an algorithm for shared memory allocation using integer programming framework. It maximizes the performance by maximizing the access to shared memory.

Other solutions to improve the throughput of GPUs are by handling branch and thread divergence. Fung et. al. [12] dynamically form warps to minimize branch divergence. The performance of this approach is dependent on the order in which the warps are issued to the pipeline. Thread block compaction [11] was proposed to reduce the divergence by regrouping to new warps at the divergent branch. Anantpur et. al. [6] proposed compiler based control flow linearization technique to handle branch divergence. Similarly other hardware and software techniques [8, 10, 15, 26, 28] were proposed to handle branch and thread divergence, and these are orthogonal to our approach.

9. CONCLUSIONS AND FUTURE WORK

We proposed sharing of some resources of SM to minimize their wastage by launching additional thread blocks in each SM. For effective utilization of these additional thread blocks, we proposed optimizations which further help in reducing the stalls produced in the system. We validated our approach for register sharing and for scratchpad sharing on several applications and showed improvements upto maximum 24% and average 11% with register sharing, and maximum 30% and average 12.5% with scratchpad sharing.

In future, we plan to incorporate traditional compiler analysis and optimizations into our approach. For example, live range analysis along with instruction reordering can be used to detect and release registers that are not used beyond a point. Such registers, if shared, can be used by the warp in the other thread block waiting for shared registers. Further, we plan to combine both the approaches to improve performance of applications that are limited by both registers and scratchpad memory. We also plan to extend our work to study the effect of various techniques such as, increasing the number of registers per thread, allocating temporary variables into available resources, and applying several cache replacement policies on our approach.

10. ACKNOWLEDGEMENTS

We thank the anonymous reviewers for their suggestions and comments. Vishwesh Jatala is supported by TCS Ph.D. fellowship. Jayvant Anantpur acknowledges the funding received from Google India Private Limited.

References

[1] CUDA C Programming Guide. https://docs.nvidia.com/cuda/cuda-c-programming-guide/.

[2] CUDA-SDK. http://docs.nvidia.com/cuda/cuda-samples.

[3] GPGPU-Sim. http://www.gpgpu-sim.org.

[4] Parboil Benchmarks. http://impact.crhc.illinois.edu/Parboil/parboil.aspx.

[5] M. Abdel-Majeed and M. Annavaram. Warped Register File: A Power Efficient Register File for GPGPUs. In *HPCA*, 2013.

[6] J. Anantpur and R. Govindarajan. Taming Control Divergence in GPUs through Control Flow Linearization. In *CC*, 2014.

[7] A. Bakhoda, G. Yuan, W. Fung, H. Wong, and T. Aamodt. Analyzing CUDA workloads using a detailed GPU simulator. In *ISPASS*, 2009.

[8] N. Brunie, S. Collange, and G. Diamos. Simultaneous Branch and Warp Interweaving for Sustained GPU Performance. In *ISCA*, 2012.

[9] S. Che, M. Boyer, J. Meng, D. Tarjan, J. Sheaffer, S.-H. Lee, and K. Skadron. Rodinia: A benchmark suite for heterogeneous computing. In *IISWC*, 2009.

[10] G. Diamos, B. Ashbaugh, S. Maiyuran, A. Kerr, H. Wu, and S. Yalamanchili. SIMD Re-convergence at Thread Frontiers. In *MICRO*, 2011.

[11] W. W. L. Fung and T. M. Aamodt. Thread Block Compaction for Efficient SIMT Control Flow. In *HPCA*, 2011.

[12] W. W. L. Fung, I. Sham, G. Yuan, and T. M. Aamodt. Dynamic Warp Formation and Scheduling for Efficient GPU Control Flow. In *MICRO*, 2007.

[13] M. Gebhart, D. R. Johnson, D. Tarjan, S. W. Keckler, W. J. Dally, E. Lindholm, and K. Skadron. A Hierarchical Thread Scheduler and Register File for Energy-Efficient Throughput Processors. *ACM Trans. Comput. Syst.*, 2012.

[14] M. Gebhart, S. W. Keckler, B. Khailany, R. Krashinsky, and W. J. Dally. Unifying Primary Cache, Scratch, and Register File Memories in a Throughput Processor. In *MICRO*, 2012.

[15] T. D. Han and T. S. Abdelrahman. Reducing Branch Divergence in GPU Programs. In *GPGPU-4*, 2011.

[16] V. Jatala, J. Anantpur, and A. Karkare. Improving GPU Performance Through Resource Sharing. CoRR, http://arxiv.org/abs/1503.05694, 2015.

[17] H. Jeon, G. S. Ravi, N. S. Kim, and M. Annavaram. GPU Register File Virtualization. MICRO, 2015.

[18] A. Jog, O. Kayiran, N. Chidambaram Nachiappan, A. K. Mishra, M. T. Kandemir, O. Mutlu, R. Iyer, and C. R. Das. OWL: Cooperative Thread Array Aware Scheduling Techniques for Improving GPGPU Performance. In *ASPLOS*, 2013.

[19] O. Kayiran, A. Jog, M. Kandemir, and C. Das. Neither more nor less: Optimizing thread-level parallelism for GPGPUs. In *PACT*, 2013.

[20] M. Lee, S. Song, J. Moon, J. Kim, W. Seo, Y. Cho, and S. Ryu. Improving GPGPU resource utilization through alternative thread block scheduling. In *HPCA*, 2014.

[21] S.-Y. Lee, A. Arunkumar, and C.-J. Wu. Cawa: Coordinated warp scheduling and cache prioritization for critical warp acceleration of gpgpu workloads. In *ISCA*, 2015.

[22] S.-Y. Lee and C.-J. Wu. CAWS: Criticality-aware Warp Scheduling for GPGPU Workloads. In *PACT*, 2014.

[23] D. Li, M. Rhu, D. R. Johnson, M. O'Connor, M. Erez, D. Burger, D. S. Fussell, and S. W. Redder. Priority-based cache allocation in throughput processors. In *HPCA*, 2015.

[24] T. Li, V. K. Narayana, E. El-Araby, and T. El-Ghazawi. GPU Resource Sharing and Virtualization on High Performance Computing Systems. In *ICPP*, 2011.

[25] W. Ma and G. Agrawal. An Integer Programming Framework for Optimizing Shared Memory Use on GPUs. PACT, 2010.

[26] J. Meng, D. Tarjan, and K. Skadron. Dynamic Warp Subdivision for Integrated Branch and Memory Divergence Tolerance. In *ISCA*, 2010.

[27] V. Narasiman, M. Shebanow, C. J. Lee, R. Miftakhutdinov, O. Mutlu, and Y. N. Patt. Improving GPU Performance via Large Warps and Two-level Warp Scheduling. In *MICRO*, 2011.

[28] M. Rhu and M. Erez. CAPRI: Prediction of Compaction-adequacy for Handling Control-divergence in GPGPU Architectures. In *ISCA*, 2012.

[29] T. G. Rogers, M. O'Connor, and T. M. Aamodt. Cache-Conscious Wavefront Scheduling. In *MICRO*, 2012.

[30] A. Sethia, D. A. Jamshidi, and S. Mahlke. Mascar: Speeding up GPU warps by reducing memory pitstops. In *HPCA*, 2015.

[31] D. Tarjan and K. Skadron. On demand register allocation and deallocation for a multithreaded processor, 2011. US Patent App. 12/649,238.

[32] P. Xiang, Y. Yang, and H. Zhou. Warp-level divergence in GPUs: Characterization, impact, and mitigation. In *HPCA*, 2014.

[33] X. Xie, Y. Liang, X. Li, Y. Wu, G. Sun, T. Wang, and D. Fan. Enabling Coordinated Register Allocation and Thread-level Parallelism Optimization for GPUs. In *MICRO*, 2015.

[34] Y. Yang, P. Xiang, M. Mantor, N. Rubin, and H. Zhou. Shared Memory Multiplexing: A Novel Way to Improve GPGPU Throughput. In *PACT*, 2012.

Parallel Execution Profiles

Zachary Benavides
Univ. of California Riverside
benavidz@cs.ucr.edu

Rajiv Gupta
Univ. of California Riverside
gupta@cs.ucr.edu

Xiangyu Zhang
Purdue University
xyzhang@cs.purdue.edu

ABSTRACT

Observing the relative behavior of an application's threads is critical to identifying performance bottlenecks and understanding their root causes. We present *parallel execution profiles* (PEPs), which capture the relative behavior of parallel threads in terms of the *user selected code regions* they execute. The user annotates the program to identify code regions of interest. The PEP divides the execution time of a multithreaded application into time intervals or a *sequence of frames* during which the code regions being executed in parallel by application threads remain the same. PEPs can be easily analyzed to compute execution times spent by the application in interesting *behavior states*. This helps user understand the severity of common performance problems such as excessive waiting on events by threads, threads contending for locks, and the presence of straggler threads.

CCS Concepts

•**Computing methodologies → Parallel computing methodologies;** *Parallel programming languages;*

Keywords

parallel behaviors; waiting; contention; load imbalance; stragglers; overhead; intrusion

1. INTRODUCTION

Understanding the runtime behavior of parallel programs is hard. Thus tools have been developed to understand parallel program behavior for performance debugging [1, 2, 4]. Existing works are aimed at specific metrics to identify performance bugs, e.g., normalized execution time, critical paths, slack etc. However, it is desirable to develop a single *versatile* framework that allows the user to capture a wide range of program behaviors and employ a variety of metrics to understand their causes. In addition, the framework should be *lightweight* and *accurate*. The instrumentation must be lightweight because its intrusive effects have the potential of altering the program's runtime behavior (e.g.,

HPDC'16, May 31-June 04, 2016, Kyoto, Japan
© 2016 ACM. ISBN 978-1-4503-4314-5/16/05. . . $15.00
DOI: http://dx.doi.org/10.1145/2907294.2907311

make contention appear or disappear). Sampling can be used to reduce runtime overhead [1]; however, it sacrifices the precision with which the runtime behavior is captured.

We present a framework for the collection and representation of runtime profiles of parallel executions that is versatile, accurate, and lightweight. Its key components are:

– **Code Region Annotations.** Our framework provides the user with an annotation mechanism using which code regions of interest are marked and named. This makes our system versatile as the user can select code regions of different types (e.g., code blocks, loops, functions, etc.) to match the needs for detecting interesting program behaviors (e.g., excessive waiting on events, locks with high contention, threads that are frequent stragglers).

– **Parallel Execution Profile Representation.** Code annotations guide the introduction of lightweight instrumentation via which *per thread local timestamped event traces* are collected while minimally perturbing the runtime behavior. Following program execution, the traces are converted into a novel representation called *Parallel Execution Profiles* (PEPs). A PEP divides the execution time of a multithreaded application into time intervals or a *sequence of frames* such that during each frame the code regions being executed in parallel by application threads remain the same. This representation is compact and precise. Interesting program *behavior states* involving multiple threads are characterized in terms of frames they generate.

– **Analyzing PEPs.** Since the PEP contains the activities of individual threads and their relative timing, a wide range of analyses to determine the frequencies and runtime durations of parallel behaviors can be determined. The user can build custom analyzers to identify performance bottlenecks and understand their root causes.

In our proposed approach, the user begins by developing a hypothesis for the cause of poor performance. Then, based upon this hypothesis, the user introduces annotations into the source code to identify code regions of interest. These annotations lead to instrumentation of the program that when executed produces timestamped traces for individual threads. The event traces are analyzed offline to generate a sequence of frames which describe what activities were performed by threads in parallel. Finally, the user constructs queries that reveal how often and for how long threads run in behavior states of interest, which reveals the absence or presence of the hypothesized performance problem. Moreover the above steps are applied iteratively till the program behavior is fully understood.

2. SELECTING CODE REGIONS

In this section we present easy to use annotations available to the user. The annotations provide the user with a great deal of flexibility in chosing regions that are assigned *names* so they can be distinguished from each other as follows:

– Marking region. The annotations #Region and #∼Region mark the entry and exit of the region respectively.

– Naming regions. As the user may mark multiple regions of interest, names are assigned to them to distinguish their executions from each other. For this purpose the user provides a *static name* in form a constant either on-entry or on-exit. A region can be a single-entry-single-exit or a single-entry-multiple-exit code region.

We observe that to identify performance problems it is useful to introduce a pair of related regions and analyzing their relative execution times – one region identifies the performance bottleneck and the other that helps evaluate the severity of the problem. In the rest of this section we illustrate the use of annotations through several examples.

Detecting wait time and lock contention. Figures 1 and 2 show two code fragments where region 1 has been introduced to capture the waiting time for a signal at a conditional wait and time spent in acquiring a lock before entering the critical section respectively. By introducing the surrounding region 0 in both cases, we can determine the time spent on waiting at the conditional relative to the execution time of the loop and time spent on acquiring the lock relative to the function's execution time.

Identifying straggler thread. Next let us consider the example of *barrier synchronization* where it is useful to identify the presence of a *straggler thread* causing excessive waiting at the barrier. Let's see how via appropriate region selection we can detect and find the cause of this behavior. By using the annotations shown on the left in Figure 3, we can determine the wait time for each thread at the barrier (region 1) as well as the total time spent in the loop (region 0). If it is found that all threads except one thread wait for a significant duration at the barrier, then that one thread is the straggler. By comparing the execution time of the loop (region 0) with the time spent at the barrier (region 1) we can see if barrier causes significant performance degradation.

Having detected the presence of a straggler, we can analyze to see if the same thread acts as a straggler or whether the straggler's identity varies. In the latter case, this behavior may be the result of variability in the amount of work performed by the loop body. This can be verified as follows. By using the modified annotation shown on the right where region 0 captures the time spent on the work performed during each loop iteration. If during an iteration, the thread identified as the straggler is also the one that spends the most time in region 0, then we know the cause is the nature of code in region 0.

Naming on exit. Finally, note that in the above examples, because we only considered single-entry single-exit regions, we were able to assign static names upon entry. However, for single-entry multiple-exit code regions where we want to treat each exit as forming a different region, we must name the region on exit since the region id is known at the exit point and not the entry point. For example, consider the function in Figure 4 with multiple return points. We use region ids 0 and 1 to distinguish different return points.

```
1   #Region(RID 0)
2   while (...) {
3       ...
4       #Region(RID 1)
5       cond_wait(&cond);
6       #~Region
7       ...
8   }
9   #~Region
```

Figure 1: Detecting wait time.

```
1   void f() {
2       #Region(RID 0)
3       ...
4       #Region(RID 1)
5       lock(&mutex);
6       #~Region
7       ...
8       shared++;
9       ...
10      unlock(&mutex);
11      ...
12      #~Region
13  }
```

Figure 2: Detecting lock contention.

```
1   #Region(RID 0)          1   for  (...) {
2   for  (...) {            2       #Region(RID 0)
3       //Loop body         3       //Loop body
4       ...                 4       ...
5       #Region(RID 1)      5       #~Region
6       barrier_wait ();    6       #Region(RID 1)
7       #~Region            7       barrier_wait ();
8   }                       8       #~Region
9   #~Region                9   }
```

Figure 3: Identifying straggler thread.

```
1   void f() {
2       #CodeRegion
3       if ( condition ) {
4           ...
5           #~CodeRegion(RID 0)
6           return;
7       }
8       else {
9           ...
10          #~CodeRegion(RID 1)
11          return;
12      }
13  }
```

Figure 4: Annotating a function with multiple exits.

3. PARALLEL EXECUTION PROFILE

In this section we first describe the per thread event trace that is generated when an annotated program is executed. Since event traces are thread local, they do not introduce any form of inter-thread synchronization, and thus do not perturb program behavior. Moreover, the overhead of trace collection is low because it uses lightweight instrumentation. Next we present a novel PEP representation that is derived offline, i.e. following program execution. The PEP representation consists of a series of frames. The local event trace of a thread tells us when the thread is executing a region of interest and when it is not. The frame sequence divides the application execution time into intervals where each frame captures the parallel behavior in terms of regions being executed by the threads in the interval.

Per Thread Event Trace represents the execution history of a single thread as a series of events and the times at which they took place. The event trace of thread t that begins execution at time s_t, ends execution at time e_t, and along the way encounters region entry and exit events $e_1 \cdots e_n$ at times $x_1 \cdots x_n$ is denoted as follows:

$$[t@s_t \rhd e_1@x_1 \rhd e_2@x_2 \rhd e_3@x_3 \rhd \cdots \rhd e_n@x_n \rhd]@e_t$$

The types of events captured by the event trace are:

- Thread creation and termination. A thread trace begins and ends with the events [tid and] marking the creation of thread identified by tid and its termination.

- Region entry and exit. Intervening events are either region entry or region exit that are of the form:

  - Named only on entry   → (rid ....);
  - Named only on exit   → (.... rid);

Figure 5 visually shows the event traces of a pair of threads $t1$ and $t2$ executing regions of examples presented in Figures 1 through 4 in the preceding section. When a thread does not execute a region of interest, we use the name ϕ.

Parallel Execution Profile (PEP) is represented in form of a sequence of frames where in each frame corresponds to the longest time interval over which, for all threads, the region being executed by each thread remains unchanged.

A frame is represented as follows where the time interval $[s, e)$ that it represents begins at s (inclusive) and ends at e (exclusive) and each $S(tid_i)$ represents the state of thread tid_i in terms of region(s) that it is executing.

$$[s, e) \to [S(tid_1)], [S(tid_2)], \ldots [S(tid_{n-1})], [S(tid_n)]$$

If thread tid is in an unnested region, then $S(tid)$ is one of the following: ϕ if thread tid is an unmarked region; and rid if thread tid is in a marked region. On the other hand if tid is nested in n regions, then $S(tid)$ has the following form: $S(tid) = [rid_1, rid_2, \cdots rid_n]$ where rid_1 is the outermost region and rid_n is the innermost region. The frames for executions of previously presented annotated code segments are shown in Figure 5.

Since PEPs give the global picture of the execution, unlike event traces that only describe individual threads, it is easy to characterize interesting behavior states in terms of the frames. For example, to detect a straggler thread we must

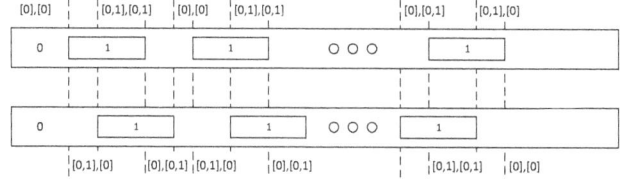

(a) Execution of regions in Figure 1.

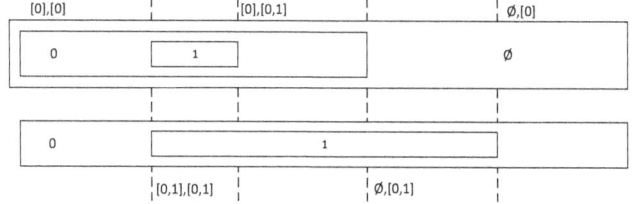

(b) Execution of regions in Figure 2.

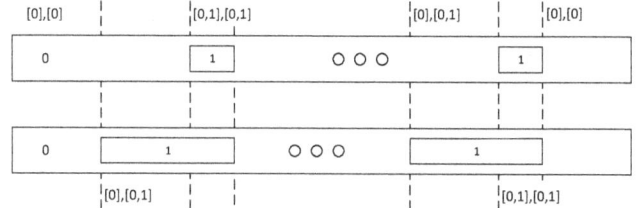

(c) Execution of regions in Figure 3 (left).

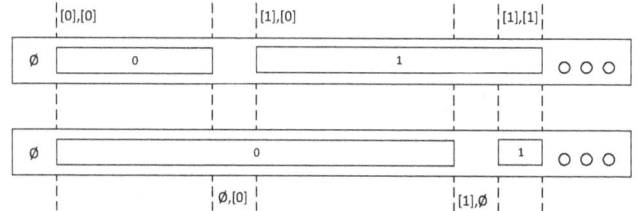

(d) Execution of regions in Figure 3 (right).

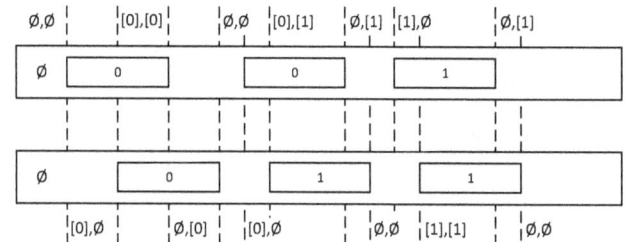

(e) Execution of regions in Figure 4.

Figure 5: Per Thread Event Traces Partitioned into a Sequence of Frames.

search for frames of the following form where region R_1 represents the loop body preceding the barrier and region R_2 represents the barrier itself.

$$[S(tid_1)], [S(tid_2)], \ldots [S(tid_{n-1})], [S(tid_n)]$$
$$\equiv$$
$$[R_2], [R_2], \ldots [R_2], [R_1]$$

Note that threads $T_1 \cdots T_{n-1}$ are waiting at the barrier while thread T_n is executing the code preceding the barrier. The duration for which threads $T_1 \cdots T_{n-1}$ wait at the barrier for thread T_n is simply given by $x_2 - x_1$. In the next section we will present additional examples that show how our query language allows user to easily analyze program behavior.

Performance Tuning Using PEPs. Next we illustrate the usage of PEPs to understand performance behaviors and tune performance for two commonly used parallel programming patterns involving *lock contention* and *stragglers*.

To illustrate the case of contention, we computed the total waiting time among application threads of the `body-track` benchmark from Parsec suite – the program was run with 16 threads and waiting was measured by annotating calls to `pthread_cond_wait`, `pthread_barrier_wait`, and `pthread_mutex_lock`. The contention was found to be quite high. In an attempt to alleviate this high contention, we reduced the number of threads by half, and measured the contention again. We found that the waiting time was reduced to 31.5% of original which translated into 2% reduction in overall execution time.

To illustrate the case of stragglers, let's examine the `swap-tions` benchmark from Parsec. In an older version of Parsec, this benchmark was arranged so that work was not ideally distributed amongst the worker threads. When the native input set containing 128 work items is split amongst 13 threads, 12 of the threads are given 9 items, and the 13th thread is given 20 items. This leads to one of the application threads acting as a straggler. When we amend the work distribution so that 11 threads are given 10 items and 2 threads are given 9 items, we realize a speedup of 1.45x.

4. RELATED WORK

A number of related works first introduce measures that assist in uncovering performance bottlenecks and then develop tools that efficiently collect runtime information for computing those metrics. [2] defines the notion of normalized processor time for a component as the ratio of the amount of processor time it consumes and the degree of parallelism. This metric is supported by the Quartz performance analysis tool. This approach essentially extends the gprof [5] style execution time profilers to handle multithreaded programs. [8] defines a metric called ParaShares as the normalized processor time with respect to weighted basic blocks. The key reason of using the above metrics for performance debugging is that the code which runs during periods of high parallelism has a smaller impact on overall execution time when optimized, than the code that runs during points of low parallelism.

Another popular technique for analyzing concurrent programs is based on the notion of a critical path that is defined to be the longest path through the program dependence graph that relates the activities of the program through their precedence relationships. In [7], the authors use hierarchical critical path analysis to build a tool for estimating the parallel speedup of each region in the program. [3] defines several new performance metrics based on critical path analysis with the intention of identifying performance problems, particularly load imbalance, in highly parallel systems. In [6] authors develop true zeroing which is a method for comparing performance metrics.

In [4] the authors present the Free Lunch profiler, a Java based tool for detecting lock contention. One of the most important contributions of this paper is the definition of what they call the free lunch metric, which is used to measure critical section pressure. Finally, there are also tools that make use of sampling and hardware performance counters to provide a highly scalable analysis [1].

5. CONCLUDING REMARKS

We presented a framework to capture and represent the runtime profile of a parallel application. Due to space limitations many important aspects of our work are not presented. First, the instrumentation for collecting event traces is lightweight and leads to modest execution time overhead of 0-7% for eight Parsec programs that were run on native inputs. Second, we support additional advanced annotations that allow capture of execution context of regions that is expressed in terms of dynamic names that are assigned to executed regions. Third, we have developed a rich query language that facilitates analysis of PEPs. The user can write complex queries that are implement to analyze PEPs automatically. Finally, we have carried out validation studies that demonstrate that our system captures runtime behavior with very high degree of precision.

Acknowledgments

This work is supported by NSF grants CCF-1524852 and CCF-1318103 to the University of California Riverside.

6. REFERENCES

[1] L. Adhianto, S. Banerjee, M. Fagan, M. Krentel, G. Marin, J. Mellor-Crummey, and N.R. Tallent. Hpctoolkit: Tools for performance analysis of optimized parallel programs. *Concurrency and Computation: P&E*, 22(6):685–701, 2010.

[2] T.E. Anderson and E.D. Lazowska. *Quartz: A tool for tuning parallel program performance*, In *SIGMETRICS Perf. Eval. Review*, 18(1):115–125, 1990.

[3] D. Bohme, F. Wolf, B.R. De Supinski, M. Schulz, and M. Geimer. Scalable critical-path based performance analysis. In *IPDPS*, pages 1330–1340, 2012.

[4] F. David, G. Thomas, J. Lawall, and G. Muller. Continuously measuring critical section pressure with the free-lunch profiler. In *OOPSLA*, 2014.

[5] S.L. Graham, P.B. Kessler, and M.K. Mckusick. Gprof: A call graph execution profiler. In *PLDI/CC*, pages 120–126, 1982.

[6] Jeffrey K Hollingsworth and Barton P Miller. Parallel program performance metrics: a comprison and validation. In *ACM/IEEE Supercomputing*, 1992.

[7] D. Jeon, S. Garcia, C. Louie, and M.B. Taylor. Kismet: parallel speedup estimates for serial programs. In *OOPSLA*, pages 519–536, 2011.

[8] M. Kambadur, K. Tang, and M.A. Kim. Parashares: Finding the important basic blocks in multithreaded programs. In *Euro-Par*, pages 75–86. Springer, 2014.

Faster and Cheaper: Parallelizing Large-Scale Matrix Factorization on GPUs

Wei Tan
IBM T. J. Watson Research Center
Yorktown Heights, NY, USA
wtan@us.ibm.com

Liangliang Cao[*]
Yahoo! Labs
New York City, NY, USA
liangliang@yahoo-inc.com

Liana Fong
IBM T. J. Watson Research Center
Yorktown Heights, NY, USA
llfong@us.ibm.com

ABSTRACT

Matrix factorization (MF) is used by many popular algorithms such as collaborative filtering. GPU with massive cores and high memory bandwidth sheds light on accelerating MF much further when appropriately exploiting its architectural characteristics.

This paper presents cuMF, a CUDA-based matrix factorization library that optimizes alternate least square (ALS) method to solve very large-scale MF. CuMF uses a set of techniques to maximize the performance on single and multiple GPUs. These techniques include smart access of sparse data leveraging GPU memory hierarchy, using data parallelism in conjunction with model parallelism, minimizing the communication overhead among GPUs, and a novel topology-aware parallel reduction scheme.

With only a single machine with four Nvidia GPU cards, cuMF can be 6-10 times as fast, and 33-100 times as cost-efficient, compared with the state-of-art distributed CPU solutions. Moreover, cuMF can solve the largest matrix factorization problem ever reported in current literature, with impressively good performance.

CCS Concepts

•Computer systems organization → Heterogeneous (hybrid) systems; •Computing methodologies → *Massively parallel algorithms; Factor analysis;*

Keywords

GPU; CUDA; matrix factorization; alternating least square (ALS); parallel algorithms; performance optimization

1. INTRODUCTION

Matrix factorization (MF) factors a sparse rating matrix R (m by n, with N_z non-zero elements) into a m-by-f and a f-by-n matrices, as shown in Figure 1. MF is widely

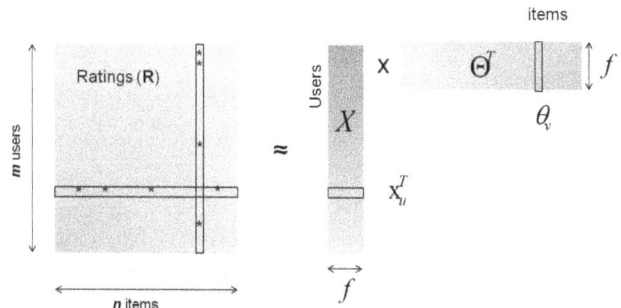

Figure 1: Matrix factorization.

used for collaborative-filtering-based recommendations [1] in e-commerce (e.g., Amazon) and digital content streaming (e.g., Netflix). Very recently, MF is also applied in text mining, deriving hidden features of words [2].

Given the widespread use of MF, a scalable and speedy implementation is very important. In terms of **scale**, many parallel solutions [3–5] aim at medium-sized problems such as the Netflix challenge [6]. However, industry-scale recommendation problems have evolved to two-orders-of-magnitude larger. Figure 2 shows the scale of MF problems, in terms of number of ratings and number of model parameters. As an example, Facebook's MF is with over 100 billion ratings, 1 billion users, and millions of items [7]. No existing system except [7] has tackled problems at this scale. In terms of **speed** to reach acceptable accuracy, recommendations need to evolve promptly in online applications. Current approaches use distributed frameworks, including MPI [5] based, Spark [8] and parameter server [9], to address large-scale MF problems. However, they require costly clusters (e.g., 50-node) and still suffer from long latency.

Recently, the GPU emerges as an accelerator for parallel algorithms [14, 15]. It has big compute power (typically 10x floating-point operations per second–flops vs. a CPU) and memory bandwidth (typically 5x vs. a CPU) [16], but with limited amount of control logic and memory capacity. Particularly, GPU's success in deep learning [17] inspires us to try GPUs for MF. In deep learning, the computation is mainly dense matrix multiplication which is **compute bound**. As a result, GPU can train deep neural network 10x as fast as CPU by saturating its flops. However, unlike

[*]Work done while the author was with IBM.

HPDC'16, May 31-June 04, 2016, Kyoto, Japan
© 2016 ACM. ISBN 978-1-4503-4314-5/16/05. . . $15.00
DOI: http://dx.doi.org/10.1145/2907294.2907297

[1]CCD++ [4], DSGD [10], DSGD++ [11], Facebook [7], Factorbird [9], Flink [12], Hugewiki [3], Netflix [6] SparkALS [8], and YahooMusic [13].

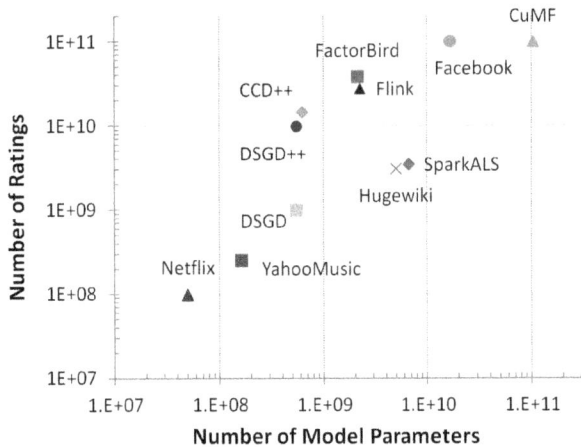

Figure 2: The scale of MF data sets[1]. Y-axis is the N_z of R, and x-axis is $(m+n) \times f$. CuMF can tackle MF problems of greater size, compared with existing systems.

deep learning, a MF problem involves sparse matrix manipulation which is usually **memory bound**. Given this, we want to explore a MF algorithm and a system that can still leverage GPU's compute and memory capability. We identified that, the alternating least square (ALS) algorithm [1] for MF is inherently parallel so as to exploit thousands of GPU cores. Moreover, compared with stochastic gradient descent (SGD), ALS has advantage when R is made up of implicit ratings and therefore no longer sparse [1].

Based on these observations, we design and implement **cuMF** (CUDA Matrix Factorization), a scalable ALS solution on one machine with one or more GPUs. CuMF achieves excellent scalability and performance by innovatively applying the following techniques on GPUs:

(1) On a single GPU, MF deals with sparse matrices, which makes it difficult to utilize GPU's compute power. We optimize memory access in ALS by various techniques including reducing discontiguous memory access, retaining hotspot variables in faster memory, and aggressively using registers. By this means cuMF gets closer to the roofline performance of a single GPU.

(2) On multiple GPUs, we add data parallelism to ALS's inherent model parallelism. Data parallelism needs a faster reduction operation among GPUs, leading to (3).

(3) We also develop an innovative topology-aware, parallel reduction method to fully leverage the bandwidth between GPUs. By this means cuMF ensures that multiple GPUs are efficiently utilized simultaneously.

The resulting CuMF is competitive in both speed and monetary cost. Table 1 shows cuMF's speed and cost compared with three CPU systems, NOMAD (with Hugewiki data) [5], Spark ALS [8], and Factorbird [9]. NOMAD and Spark ALS use Amazon AWS, and we pick an AWS node type similar to what Factorbird uses. CPU and GPU systems' cost is calculated by *(price per node per hr)*(#nodes)* (execution time)*, with unit price taken when submitting this paper[2]. CuMF runs on one machine with two Nvidia K80 (four GPUs devices in total) from IBM Softlayer, with an amortized hourly cost of $2.44. With faster speed and

[2]AWS price: https://aws.amazon.com/ec2/pricing/; GPU machine price: http://www.softlayer.com/gpu

Table 1: Speed and cost of cuMF on one machine with four GPUs, compared with three CPU systems on cloud.

Baseline	baseline config	#nodes	price /node/hr	cuMF speed	cuMF cost
NOMAD	m3.xlarge	32	$0.27	**10x**	3%
SparkALS	m3.2xlarge	50	$0.53	**10x**	1%
Factorbird	c3.2xlarge	50	$0.42	**6x**	2%

Note: Experiment details are in Section 5. NOMAD [5] uses Hugewiki data and AWS servers; it used m1.xlarge which is now superseded by m3.xlarge by Amazon. Factorbird's node is similar to AWS c3.2xlarge [9]. Speed is measured by wall-clock time when reaching the same accuracy.

Table 2: Notations

Name	Meaning	Range
R	sparse rating matrix: m by n	
X	low rank matrix: m by f	
Θ	low rank matrix: n by f	
m	vertical dimension of R	10^3 to 10^9
n	horizontal dimension of R	10^3 to 10^9
f	dimension of latent features	5 to 100s
N_z	number of non-zero entries in R	10^8 to 10^{11}
r_{uv}	R's value at position (u,v); $1 \leq u \leq m, 1 \leq v \leq n$	
$\mathbf{x}_u^T$	X's uth row; $1 \leq u \leq m$	
θ_v	Θ^T's vth column; $1 \leq v \leq n$	
R_{u*}	R's uth row; $1 \leq u \leq m$	
R_{*v}	R's vth column; $1 \leq v \leq n$	

Note: usually $N_z \gg m, n$ and $m, n \gg f$.

fewer machines, cuMF's overall cost of running these benchmarks is merely 1%-3% of the baseline systems compared. That is, cuMF is 33-100x as cost-efficient.

In summary, this paper describes a novel implementation of MF on a machine with GPUs and the set of exemplary optimization techniques in leveraging the GPU architectural characteristics. The experimental results demonstrate that with up to four Nvidia GPUs on one machine, cuMF is (1) competitive compared with multi-core methods, on medium-sized problems; (2) much faster than vanilla GPU implementations without memory optimization; (3) 6-10 times as fast, and 33-100 times as cost-efficient as distributed CPU systems, on large-scale problems; (4) more significantly, able to solve the largest matrix factorization problem ever reported.

This paper is organized as follows. Section 2 introduces matrix factorization and explains the two challenges in large-scale ALS, i.e., memory access on one GPU and scalability on multiple GPUs. Section 3 presents the memory-optimized ALS algorithm on a single GPU, to address the challenge in sparse and irregular memory access. Section 4 introduces the scale-up ALS algorithm to parallelize MF on multiple GPUs, to address the challenge in scaling to many GPUs. Section 5 shows the experiment results and Section 6 reviews related work. Section 7 concludes the paper.

2. PROBLEM DEFINITION

2.1 ALS algorithm for matrix factorization

Referring to the notations listed in Table 2, matrix factorization is to factor a sparse matrix R with two lower-rank, dense matrices X and Θ, such that $R \approx X \cdot \Theta^T$.

As shown in Figure 1, suppose r_{uv} is the non-zero element of R at position (u, v), we want to minimize the following cost function (1). To avoid overfitting we use weighted-λ-regularization proposed in [6], where n_{x_u} and n_{θ_v} denote the number of total ratings on user u and item v, respectively.

$$J = \sum_{u,v}(r_{uv} - \mathbf{x}_u^T \theta_v)^2 + \lambda(\sum_u n_{x_u}||\mathbf{x}_u||^2 + \sum_v n_{\theta_v}||\theta_v||^2) \quad (1)$$

Many optimization methods, including ALS [6], CGD [4], and SGD [3] have been applied to minimize J. We adopt the ALS approach that would first optimize X while fixing Θ, and then to optimize Θ while fixing X. Consider

$$\frac{\partial J}{\partial \mathbf{x}_u} = 0$$

and

$$\frac{\partial J}{\partial \theta_v} = 0$$

which lead to the following equation:

$$\sum_{r_{uv} \neq 0}(\theta_v \theta_v^T + \lambda I) \cdot \mathbf{x}_u = \Theta^T \cdot R_{u*}^T \quad (2)$$

together with:

$$\sum_{r_{uv} \neq 0}(\mathbf{x}_u \mathbf{x}_u^T + \lambda I) \cdot \theta_v = X^T \cdot R_{*v} \quad (3)$$

By this means, ALS updates X using eq. (2), and updates Θ using eq. (3), in an alternating manner. Empirically, ALS often converges in 5-20 iterations, with each iteration consisting of both update-X and update-Θ. In the rest of this paper, we explain our method using update-X. The same method is applicable to update-Θ.

The formalism of ALS enables solving in parallel so as to harness the power of GPU. Eqs. (2) and (3) shows that, the updates of each $\mathbf{x}_u$ and θ_v are independent of each other. This independent nature does not hold for SGD, which randomly selects a sample r_{uv}, and updates the parameters by:

$$\mathbf{x}_u = \mathbf{x}_u - \alpha[(\mathbf{x}_u^T \theta_v - r_{uv})\theta_v + \lambda \mathbf{x}_u]$$
$$\theta_v = \theta_v - \alpha[(\mathbf{x}_u^T \theta_v - r_{uv})\mathbf{x}_u + \lambda \theta_v] \quad (4)$$

Suppose there are two random samples r_{uv} and $r_{uv'}$ with the same row index u, their updates to $\mathbf{x}_u$ cannot be treated independently. Previous works on CPUs [3,5,10,11] all partition R into blocks with no overlapping rows and columns. Such a strategy works effectively on tens of CPU cores but is difficult to scale to a GPU with thousands of cores. As a result, we choose ALS instead of SGD for cuMF.

2.2 Challenges of speedy and scalable ALS

Table 3 lists the compute cost and memory footprint of solving X with eq. (2), using single precision. The calculation is divided into two phases, i.e.,

get_hermitian_x to obtain the left-hand Hermitian matrix $A_u = \sum_{r_{uv} \neq 0}(\theta_v \theta_v^T + \lambda I)$ and the right-hand $B_u = \Theta^T \cdot R_{u*}^T$, and

batch_solve to solve many equations $A_u \mathbf{x}_u = B_u$.

In line 3 of Table 3: *one item* in phase get_hermitian_x, to solve one row $\mathbf{x}_u$, obtaining A_u needs to calculate N_z/m

times[3] of $\theta_v \theta_v^T$s, each of which needs $f(f+1)/2$ multiplications. The cost of obtaining B_u is $(N_z + N_z f)/m + 2f$ [18]. In terms of memory, A_u uses f^2 floats, B_u uses f, Θ^T uses nf, and a row of R in Compressed Sparse Row (CSR) format uses $(2N_z + m + 1)/m$. In phase batch_solve, solving the linear equation $A_u \mathbf{x}_u = B_u$ does not need additional memory storage by using in-place solvers, but has an f^3 computation cost.

Challenge 1. On a single GPU, how to optimize sparse, irregular and intensive memory access.

Table 3 shows that, computation is bounded in both phases **get_hermitian_x** ($\mathcal{O}(N_z f^2)$) and **batch_solve** ($\mathcal{O}(mf^3)$). CUDA library cuBLAS [19] already provides dense solvers for phase batch_solve, so we focus on the get_hermitian_x phase. This phase is very costly, especially when $N_z \gg m$ and therefore $N_z f^2 > mf^3$. What is more troublesome is the *sparse, irregular* and *intensive* memory access in this phase. Details are as follows:

1. Access many columns θ_v subject to $r_{uv} \neq 0$ for every u. This access is *irregular* w.r.t. Θ^T, due to the sparseness of R. In each iteration to solve one $\mathbf{x}_u$ we need to access n_{x_u} columns (N_z/m, on average) spread **sparsely** and **discontiguously** across the n columns of Θ^T. For example, in the Netflix data set [6], one user rates around 200 items on average, leading to a discontiguous access of 200 columns from the total 17,770 in Θ^T.

2. Aggregate many $\theta_v \theta_v^T$s and $\mathbf{x}_u \mathbf{x}_u^T$s, is memory *intensive* due to the large number of θ_vs and $\mathbf{x}_u$s to aggregate. According to eq. (2), obtaining A_u needs to calculate many $\theta_v \theta_v^T$s and aggregate them. Therefore, each element in column vector θ_v is accessed frequently, and the partial aggregation result is updated frequently. To calculate $\theta_v \theta_v^T$ we need to read each element of θ_v f times; after obtaining a $\theta_v \theta_v^T$, to add it to $\sum_{r_{uv} \neq 0}(\theta_v \theta_v^T + \lambda I)$ we need to write $f(f+1)/2$, or f^2 elements if the downstream solver does not appreciate symmetricity.

Section 3 presents how cuMF tackles Challenge 1, with experiment results shown in Sections 5.2 and 5.3.

Challenge 2. On multiple GPUs, how to scale and minimize communication overhead.

When m, n, N_z and f get larger, ALS is bounded by the memory capacity of a single GPU. For example, the update-X iteration is to be bounded by memory footprint of m A_us (mf^2 without considering symmetricity), X^T (mf), Θ^T (nf) and R ($2N_z + m + 1$). The current Nvidia Maxwell and Kepler GPUs have 12 GB memory per device. Each device would only be able to load 3 billion (3×10^9) single precision floats. However, the smallest data set, i.e., Netflix, in Figure 2, has $m = 480K$. When $f = 100$, m Hermitian matrices are with size $mf^2 = 480K \times 100^2 = 4.8$ billion floats > 3 billion.

Previous CPU solutions already encountered and partially addressed this memory capacity issue. PALS [6] partitions X and R by rows, solving each partition in parallel by replicating Θ^T. However, this **model parallelism** is only feasible when Θ^T is small. SparkALS [8], the ALS implementation in Spark MLlib [20], also partitions X and R by rows, and then solve each partition X_i in parallel. Its improvement

---

[3]N_z/m is the average number of non-zero entries per row.

Table 3: Compute cost and memory footprint of ALS: the update-X step

		compute cost		memory footprint	
		A_u in (2)	B_u in (2)	A_u in (2)	B_u in (2)
get_hermitian_x	one item	$N_z f(f+1)/2m$	$(N_z + N_z f)/m + 2f$	f^2	$nf+f+(2N_z+m+1)/m$
	m_b items	$m_b N_z f(f+1)/2m$	$m_b(N_z + N_z f)/m + 2m_b f$	$m_b f^2$	$nf+m_b f+m_b(2N_z+m+1)/m$
	all m items	$N_z f(f+1)/2$	$N_z + N_z f + 2mf$	mf^2	$nf+mf+(2N_z+m+1)$
batch_solve	one item	f^3			
	m_b items	$m_b f^3$			
	all m items	mf^3			

Note: here we omit some minor computations and auxiliary data structures needed in eq. (2).

to PALS is that, instead of replicating Θ^T, it splits Θ^T into overlapping partitions $\{\Theta_i^T\}$, where Θ_i^T contains only the necessary θ_v columns for all $\mathbf{x}_u$s in X_i. This improvement still has several deficiencies:

1. Generating Θ_i^T from X_i is actually a graph partitioning task and time consuming.

2. Transferring each Θ_i^T to X_i involves much network traffic, especially when $N_z \gg m$.

3. Θ_i^T may still be too big to fit into a single GPU device, especially when $N_z \gg m$.

Section 4 presents how cuMF tackles Challenge 2, with experiment results shown in Sections 5.4 and 5.5.

3. MEMORY-OPTIMIZED ALS ON ONE GPU

3.1 The GPU memory hierarchy

To address **Challenge 1** "On a single GPU, how to optimize sparse, irregular and intensive memory access", we need direct control on GPU's memory hierarchy. We choose Nvidia GPUs because they provides a rich set of *programmable memory* of different characteristics, shown in Table 4. [4]

Table 4: Programmable GPU memory

Memory type	Size	Latency	Scope
global	large	high	application
texture	medium	medium	application, read-only
shared	small	low	thread block
register	small	lowest	thread; not indexable

Although the principles of memory optimization are generally known, the specific implementation of ALS on GPU is not trivial due to the following reasons:

1. GPU has a lower clock frequency than CPU (typically < 1 GHz vs. 2-3 GHz). If the massive parallelism in GPU is not fully utilized, cuMF is likely to be slower than the highly-optimized CPU implementations.

---

[4]There are *non-programmable memory* such as L1 and L2 cache. They also accelerate memory access but are not directly controllable by programmers. Therefore in cuMF we focus on the optimization by using the programmable memory.

2. Compared with CPU, GPU's global memory is smaller, e.g., 12 GB. In contrast, GPU has a much larger register file, e.g., 4 MB, which is largely ignored nowadays.

3. The control of register, shared, texture and global memory is complex. The global memory is large but slow, texture memory is read-only, and register and shared memory are not visible across GPU kernels (i.e., device functions). Moreover, registers are not *dynamically indexable*, which prevents them from being used for large arrays.

Due to these difficulties, without insight on both GPU hardware and algorithm specifics, an implementation can easily be bounded by memory capacity, latency or bandwidth, preventing us from harnessing the full power of GPU.

3.2 The base ALS algorithm

The base ALS algorithm 1 shows how to update X with eq. (2). The algorithm to update Θ is similar with all variables symmetrically exchanged. Algorithm 1 consists of two procedures: GET_HERMITIAN_X() and BATCH_SOLVE().

Algorithm 1 Base ALS: Update X
Input $R_{m \times n}$
Input $\Theta^T : [\theta_1, \theta_2, ..., \theta_n]_{f \times n}$
Output $X : [\mathbf{x}_1^T; \mathbf{x}_2^T; ...; \mathbf{x}_m^T]_{m \times f}$

1: **procedure** GET_HERMITIAN_X(R, Θ^T)
2:     **for** $u \leftarrow 1, m$ **do**
3:         $\Theta_u^T \leftarrow$ sub-matrix of Θ^T with cols θ_v s.t. $r_{uv} \neq 0$
4:         $A_u \leftarrow 0$
5:         **for all** columns θ_v in Θ_u^T **do**
6:             $A_u \leftarrow A_u + \theta_v \theta_v^T + \lambda I$
7:         **end for**
8:         $B_u \leftarrow \Theta^T \cdot R_{u*}^T$
9:     **end for**
10:     **return** $([A_1, A_2, ...A_m], [B_1, B_2, ..., B_m])$
11: **end procedure**

12: **procedure** BATCH_SOLVE($[A_1, A_2, ...A_m], [B_1, B_2, ..., B_m]$)
13:     **for** $u \leftarrow 1, m$ **do**
14:         $\mathbf{x}_u \leftarrow$ solve $A_u \cdot \mathbf{x}_u = B_u$
15:     **end for**
16:     **return** $[\mathbf{x}_1, \mathbf{x}_2, ...\mathbf{x}_m]^T$
17: **end procedure**

18: $(A, B) \leftarrow$ GET_HERMITIAN_X(R, Θ^T)
19: $X \leftarrow$ BATCH_SOLVE(A, B)

3.3 The memory-optimized ALS algorithm MO-ALS

Table 3 indicates that, GET_HERMITIAN_X() in Algorithm 1 is memory intensive. We observed that Lines 3-7, i.e., computing A_u, takes much of the overall execution time. To optimize the performance, we enhance Algorithm 1 by leveraging different types of GPU memory. We call this memory-optimized ALS algorithm **MO-ALS**, as described in Algorithm 2. The following lines in Algorithm 1 are enhanced in MO-ALS:

1. Reading from Θ^T in Line 3. Θ^T with dimension $f \times n$ is stored in global memory. When collecting the sub-matrix Θ_u^T from Θ^T, we use **texture memory** as the cache because: (1) this collecting process enjoys spatial locality, (2) Θ^T is read-only when updating X, and (3) different Θ_u^Ts can potentially re-use the same θ_vs cached in texture memory. As a result, this caching step reduces discontiguous memory access. This optimization is shown in Line 3 in Algorithm 2.

2. Storage of Θ_u^T in Line 3. We use one thread block with f threads to calculate each A_u, and use the per-block **shared memory** to store Θ_u^T, so as to speed up the subsequent read in Line 6. However, for each A_u, we are not able to copy the whole Θ_u^T into its shared memory space. This is because Θ_u^T is of size $f \times n_{x_u}$ and too big compared to the 48 or 96 KB per-SM[5] shared memory. If a single thread block consumes too much shared memory, other blocks are prohibited from launching, resulting in low parallelism. In order to achieve higher parallelism, we select a bin size bin, and for each $\mathbf{x}_u$ only allocate a share memory space $\Theta_u^T[bin]$ of size $f \times bin$. In practice we choose bin between 10 and 30, while n_{x_u} can be hundreds to thousands. We iteratively move a subset of Θ_u^T into $\Theta_u^T[bin]$ to be processed in the following step. This optimization is shown in Lines 5-10 in Algorithm 2.

3. Update of A_u in Line 6. Here we need to read a θ_v from $\Theta_u^T[bin]$, calculate the $f \times f$ elements of $\theta_v \cdot \theta_v^T$, and add them to global variable A_u. Obviously A_u is a memory hotspot. In order to speedup the aggregation in A_u, we choose **register memory** to hold $\sum_{\theta_v \in \Theta_u^T[bin]} \theta_v \theta_v^T$, and only update global memory A_u after we iterate over all columns in Θ_u^T. This reduces global memory access by a factor of n_{x_u}. This optimization is shown in Line 8 in Algorithm 2. More details are discussed in the following Section 3.4.

Figure 3 illustrates the memory usage of MO-ALS.

3.4 Enhanced utilization of registers

We exploit the GPU register file which is larger and has higher bandwidth compared to its shared memory [21]. For example, in the latest Nvidia Maxwell generation GPUs, each SM has a 256 KB register file and only 96 KB shared memory. However, while there is much focus on using shared memory [22], the use of registers is surprisingly ignored. This **under-utilization of registers** is mainly due to the fact that, register variables cannot be dynamically indexed. That is to say, you cannot declare and refer to an array in

---

Algorithm 2 MO-ALS: Memory-Optimized ALS; update X on one GPU.

$\mathcal{G}\{var\}$: var in global memory
$\mathcal{T}\{var\}$: var in texture memory
$\mathcal{S}\{var\}$: var in shared memory
$\mathcal{R}\{var\}$: var in register memory
Input $R_{m \times n}$
Input $\Theta^T : [\theta_1, \theta_2, ..., \theta_n]_{f \times n}$
Output $X : [\mathbf{x}_1^T; \mathbf{x}_2^T; ...; \mathbf{x}_m^T]_{m \times f}$

```
 1: procedure GET_HERMITIAN_X_MO(R, Θᵀ)
 2:     for u ← 1, m do
 3:         𝒯{Θᵤᵀ} ← sub-matrix of 𝒢{Θᵀ} with cols θᵥ s.t.
            rᵤᵥ ≠ 0
 4:         ℛ{Aᵤ} ← 0
 5:         while 𝒯{Θᵤᵀ} has more cols not processed do
 6:             𝒮{Θᵤᵀ[bin]} ← next bin cols from 𝒯{Θᵤᵀ}
 7:             for all cols θᵥ in 𝒮{Θᵤᵀ[bin]} do
 8:                 ℛ{Aᵤ} ← ℛ{Aᵤ} + 𝒮{θᵥ}𝒮{θᵥᵀ} + λI
 9:             end for
10:         end while
11:         𝒢{Aᵤ} ← ℛ{Aᵤ}
12:         𝒢{Bᵤ} ← 𝒢{Θᵀ} · 𝒢{Rᵤ*ᵀ}
13:     end for
14:     return 𝒢([A₁, A₂, ...Aₘ], [B₁, B₂, ..., Bₘ])

15:     (A, B) ← GET_HERMITIAN_X_MO(R, Θᵀ)
16:     X ← BATCH_SOLVE(A, B)
17: end procedure
```

---

register file[6]. In Algorithm 2, A_u is with size f^2 and to put it in register and access it, we have to declare f^2 variables instead of a single array. This makes the CUDA code hard to write. We use macro expansion in C to generate such a verbose paragraph of code. The snippet in Listing 1 demonstrates how the expanded code looks like when $f = 10$.

```
 1  get_Au_kernel()
 2  { ...
 3      //declare Au in registers
 4      float temp0 = 0, temp1 = 0, temp2 = 0,
 5      temp3 = 0, temp4 = 0, temp5 = 0,
 6      temp6=0, temp7=0, temp8=0, temp9=0;
 7      ...
 8      float temp90 = 0, temp91 = 0, temp92 = 0,
 9      temp93 = 0, temp94 = 0, temp95 = 0,
10      temp96=0, temp97=0, temp98=0, temp99=0;
11      //aggregate Au in register
12      for(k){
13          temp0 += theta[k*f]*theta[k*f];
14          temp1 += theta[k*f]*theta[k*f+1];
15          ...
16          temp98 += theta[k*f+9]*theta[k*f+8];
17          temp99 += theta[k*f+9]*theta[k*f+9];
18      }
19      //copy register to global memory
20      Au[0] = temp0;
21      Au[1] = temp1;
22      ...
23      Au[98] = temp98;
24      Au[99] = temp99;
```

---

[5]SM or SMX: stream multiprocessor. A GPU device usually consists of 10 to 15 SMs.

[6]An exception is that, the CUDA compiler may put very small (≤ 5) arrays on registers in loop unfolding.

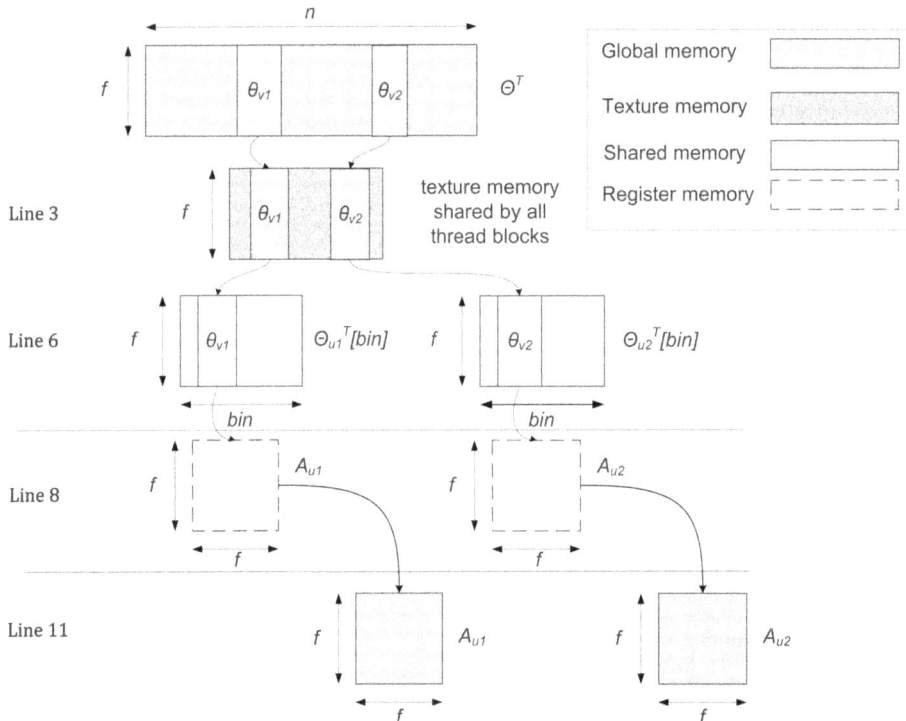

Figure 3: Illustration of memory usage in MO-ALS. Line numbers correspond to those in Algorithm 2. For simplicity, we solve two rows of X, i.e., $\mathbf{x}_{u1}$ and $\mathbf{x}_{u2}$, in parallel. In reality we solve as many rows of X as possible in parallel.

```
25  }
```
Listing 1: CUDA kernel code to use registers when f is 10

Limitation of MO-ALS. Algorithm 2 is able to deal with big X with one GPU, as long as Θ can fit into it. When X is big and Θ is small, we first load the whole Θ to the GPU, then load R and solve X in batches. However, this batch-based approach does not work when Θ cannot fit into a single GPU. This motivates us to scale to multiple GPUs on a single machine, as presented in Section 4.

4. SCALE-UP ALS ON MULTIPLE GPUS

Section 3 addresses **Challenge 1** regarding memory optimization on a single GPU. As problem size gets bigger, we need to address **Challenge 2**: "On multiple GPUs, how to scale and minimize communication overhead." This section presents a scale-up algorithm called **SU-ALS** which adds **data-parallelism** and **parallel-reduction** on top of MO-ALS.

4.1 The SU-ALS algorithm

In distributed machine learning, **model parallelism** and **data parallelism** are two common schemes [23]. Model parallelism partitions **parameters** among multiple learners with each one learns a subset of parameters. Data parallelism partitions the training **data** among multiple learners with each one learns all parameters from its partial observation. These two schemes can be combined when both model parameters and training data are large.

ALS is inherently suitable for model parallelism, as the updates of each $\mathbf{x}_u$ and θ_v are independent. As discussed in Section 2.2, both PALS and SparkALS employ only model

parallelism without considering data parallelism. To solve X in parallel, PALS and SparkALS partition X among multiple nodes. PALS broadcasts the whole Θ^T while SparkALS transfers a subset of it to each X partition. As pointed out by [4], both approaches are inefficient and may cause out-of-memory failure, when Θ^T is big and ratings are skewed.

To tackle large-scale problems, on top of the existing model parallelism, we design a data-parallel approach. A limitation of model parallelism is that, it requires all A_us in one partition $X^{(j)}$ ($1 \leq j \leq q$) to be computed on the same GPU. Consequently, a subset of Θ^T has to be transferred into that GPU. In contrast, our data-parallel approach distributes the computation of any single Hermitian matrix A_u to multiple GPUs. Instead of transferring all θ_vs to one GPU, it calculates a local A_u on each GPU with only the local θ_vs, and reduce (aka., aggregate) many local A_us later. Assume that there are p GPUs to parallelize on, we re-write eq. (2) to its data-parallelism form as:

$$A_u = \sum_{r_{uv} \neq 0} (\theta_v \theta_v^T + \lambda I) = \sum_{i=1}^{p} \sum_{r_{uv} \neq 0}^{GPU_i} (\theta_v \theta_v^T + \lambda I) \quad (5)$$

This approach is described in Algorithm 3 and illustrated in Figure 4.

Lines 2-4: partitions the input data. Θ^T is evenly split by columns into p partitions, X is evenly split by rows into q partitions, and R is split by rows and columns following the partition schemes of X and Θ^T.

Lines 5-7: copies $\Theta^{T(i)}$ to GPU_i ($1 \leq i \leq p$), in parallel.

Lines 8-20: loop over $\{X^{(1)}, X^{(2)}, ..., X^{(q)}\}$ and solve each $X^{(j)}$ partition in sequence ($1 \leq j \leq q$). Given more GPUs, this sequential loop can further be parallelized.

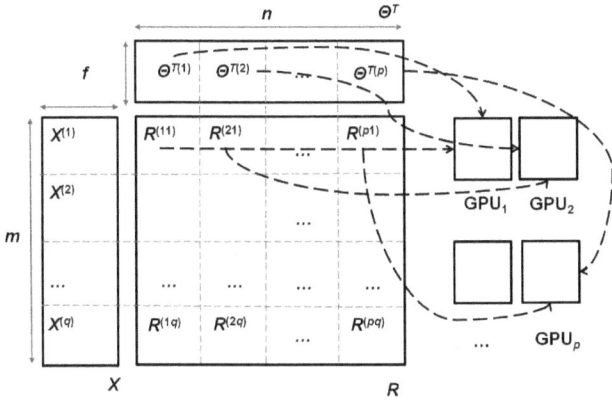

Figure 4: SU-ALS. Θ^T is partitioned evenly and vertically, and stored on p GPUs. X is partitioned evenly and horizontally, and solved in batches, achieving model parallelism. Each X batch is solved in parallel on p GPUs, each with Θ^T's partition on it, achieving data parallelism.

Algorithm 3 SU-ALS: Scale-Up ALS; update X on multiple GPUs.

1: Given p GPUs: GPU$_1$, GPU$_2$, ..., GPU$_p$.
2: $\{\Theta^{T(1)}, \Theta^{T(2)}, ..., \Theta^{T(p)}\} \leftarrow VerticalPartition(\Theta^T, p)$
3: $\{X^{(1)}, X^{(2)}, ..., X^{(q)}\} \leftarrow HorizontalPartition(X, q)$
4: $\{R^{(11)}, R^{(12)}, ..., R^{(pq)}\} \leftarrow GridPartition(R, p, q)$
5: **parfor** $i \leftarrow 1, p$ **do**   ▷ parallel copy to each GPU$_i$
6:     copy GPU$_i \leftarrow \Theta^{T(i)}$
7: **end parfor**
8: **for** $j \leftarrow 1, q$ **do**   ▷ model parallel
9:     **parfor** $i \leftarrow 1, p$ **do**   ▷ data parallel on GPU$_i$
10:        copy GPU$_i \leftarrow R^{(ij)}$
11:        $(A^{(ij)}, B^{(ij)}) \leftarrow$ Get_Hermitian_X_MO$(R^{(ij)}, \Theta^{T(i)})$
12:        synchronize_threads()
13:        $\{A_1^{(ij)}, A_2^{(ij)}, ..., A_p^{(ij)}\} \leftarrow A^{(ij)}$
14:        $\{B_1^{(ij)}, B_2^{(ij)}, ..., B_p^{(ij)}\} \leftarrow B^{(ij)}$
15:        $A_i^{(j)} \leftarrow \sum_{k=1}^{p} A_i^{(kj)}$
16:        $B_i^{(j)} \leftarrow \sum_{k=1}^{p} B_i^{(kj)}$
17:        $X_i^{(j)} \leftarrow$ Batch_Solve$(A_i^{(j)}, B_i^{(j)})$
18:     **end parfor**
19:     $X^{(j)} \leftarrow \{X_1^{(j)}, X_2^{(j)}, ..., X_p^{(j)}\}$
20: **end for**

Line 9-18: parallel loop over $\{\Theta^{T(i)}\}$ ($1 \leq i \leq p$) to solve $X^{(j)}$. Without sufficient number of GPUs, this **parallel for** loop can degrade to a **sequential** one.

Lines 11: on GPU$_i$ ($1 \leq i \leq p$), for each row $\mathbf{x}_u$ in $X^{(j)}$, calculate the A_u local to GPU$_i$ by only observing $\Theta^{T(i)}$ and $R^{(ij)}$:

$$A_u^i = \sum_{r_{uv} \neq 0}^{GPU_i} (\theta_v \theta_v^T + \lambda I) \tag{6}$$

Similarly, we calculate the local B_u matrix:

$$B_u^i = \Theta^{T(i)} \cdot (R_{u*}^{(ij)})^T \tag{7}$$

The collection of all A_u^is and B_u^is on GPU$_i$ are denoted as $(A^{(ij)}, B^{(ij)})$.

Line 12: a synchronization barrier to wait for all parfor threads to reach this step.

Lines 13-14: evenly partition $A^{(ij)}$ and $B^{(ij)}$ by rows of $X^{(j)}$. That is, $A^{(ij)}$ on GPU$_i$ is evenly divided into p portions:

$$A_1^{(ij)}, A_2^{(ij)}, ..., A_p^{(ij)}$$

$B^{(ij)}$ is partitioned in the same manner into:

$$B_1^{(ij)}, B_2^{(ij)}, ..., B_p^{(ij)}$$

Lines 15-16: **parallel reduce** p $A^{(ij)}$s and $B^{(ij)}$s into the global $A^{(j)}$ and $B^{(j)}$, on p GPUs. GPU$_i$ takes care of the reduction of partition i of all $A^{(kj)}$s ($1 \leq k \leq p$). See Figure 5 (a) for an example where $j = 1$ and $p = 4$: GPU$_1$ reduces $\{A_1^{(11)}, A_1^{(21)}, A_1^{(31)}, A_1^{(41)}\}$, GPU$_2$ reduces $\{A_2^{(11)}, A_2^{(21)}, A_2^{(31)}, A_2^{(41)}\}$, and so on. $B^{(ij)}$s are reduced in the same manner.

Line 17: solve the p partitions concurrently on p GPUs. GPU$_i$ solves the local partition $(A_i^{(j)}, B_i^{(j)})$ it reduces in *Lines 15-16*.

Line 19: collect p partitions $\{X_1^{(j)}, X_2^{(j)}, ..., X_p^{(j)}\}$ on p GPUs to obtain $X^{(j)}$.

4.2 Topology-aware parallel reduction to speed up SU-ALS

Parallel reduction. Refer to Lines 13-17 of Algorithm 3, $(A^{(j)}, B^{(j)})$ could have been reduced in one GPU (say, GPU$_1$) and $X^{(j)}$ solved there. However, this simple approach fails to parallelize either data transfer or computation. Moreover, multiple GPUs on a machine are usually connected through a PCIe bus. PCIe channels are full-duplex, meaning that data transfer in both directions can happen simultaneously without affecting each other. To leverage the bandwidth in both directions, we develop a parallel reduction scheme that evenly utilizes both incoming and outgoing channels of all GPUs, as shown in Figure 5 (a). Experiment on Hugewiki data set shows that this optimization is 1.7x as fast compared with the reducing-by-one-GPU approach. After this parallel reduction, *batch_solve* begins on p GPUs in parallel.
Topology-aware parallel reduction. Figure 5 (a) assumes a flat interconnection where all GPUs directly connect to a PCIe root. This assumption may not always hold. For example, in a two-socket machine with four GPUs, a typical configuration is that every two GPUs connect to one socket. Communications between the two GPUs in the same socket still go though the local PCIe bus, while communications between GPUs in different sockets go through the inter-socket connection. In this case, intra-socket transfers enjoy zero-copy and faster duplex PCIe channel, compared with inter-socket transfers. In such a topology, the scheme shown in Figure 5 (a) is not optimal.

Based on the GPU connection topology, we design a two-phase parallel reduction scheme shown in Figure 5 (b). In this scheme, each partition is first reduced intra socket (see the dash line). Afterward, the partial, intra-socket reduction results are moved across socket and generate the final reduction result (the solid line). Experiments show that this two-phase scheme enjoys an additional 1.5x speedup compared with the one-phase scheme shown in Figure 5 (a).

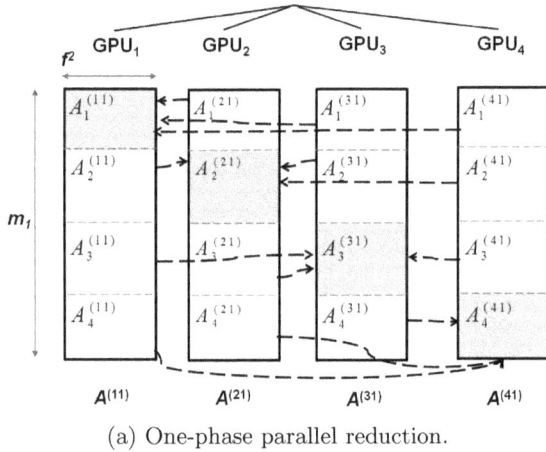

(a) One-phase parallel reduction.

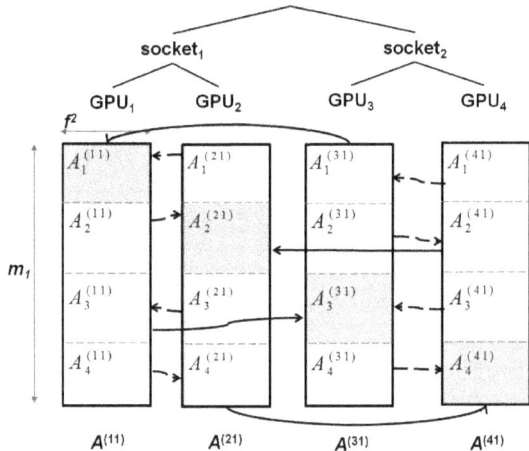

(b) Two-phase parallel reduction considering PCIe hierarchy: phase-1 (intra-socket) in dash lines; phase-2 (inter-socket) in solid lines.

Figure 5: Parallel reduce $A^{(ij)}$ in SU-ALS when $j = 1$ and $p = 4$. For $1 \leq i \leq p$, on GPU$_i$, $A^{(ij)}$ is evenly partitioned into p pieces: $A_1^{(ij)}, A_2^{(ij)}, ..., A_p^{(ij)}$. Afterward GPU$_i$ reduces all $A_i^{(kj)}$ across p GPUs ($1 \leq k \leq p$). This not only achieves parallel get_hermitian_x and batch_solve, but also leverages cross-GPU bandwidth efficiently.

4.3 How to partition?

Assume a single GPU's memory capacity is C. According to Algorithm 3, one GPU needs to hold $X^{(j)}$, $\Theta^{(i)}$, $R^{(ij)}$, $A^{(j)}$, and $B^{(j)}$. Therefore the choices of p and q are subject to (8).

$$\frac{m \times f}{q} + \frac{n \times f}{p} + |R^{(ij)}| + \frac{m}{q} \times f^2 + \frac{m}{q} \times f + \epsilon < C \quad (8)$$

ϵ is a headroom space for miscellaneous small variables. In practice, when $C = 12$ GB we choose $\epsilon = 500$ MB.
Here are some best practices in choosing p and q:

1. If $p = 1$ can satisfy (8), you can solve X in a single GPU in sequential batches. In this case SU-ALS is equivalent to MO-ALS.

2. When q increases and $p = 1$ satisfies (8), q should not

increase any more. At this time there is already no need to further partition X.

3. We usually start from p such that $\frac{n \times f}{p} \approx \frac{C}{2}$, and then choose the smallest q that satisfies (8).

4.4 Implementation of cuMF

This section describes selected details of cuMF. CuMF is implemented in C, using CUDA 7.0 and GCC OpenMP v3.0. It has circa 6,000 lines of code.

Out-of-core computation. As seen in Figure 2 and Table 5, rating and feature matrices can both have 100 billion entries. This goes far beyond the host and device memory limit. For such out-of-core problems, cuMF first generate a partition scheme, planning which partition to send to which GPU in what order. With this knowledge in advance, cuMF uses separate CPU threads to preload data from disk to host memory, and separate CUDA streams to preload from host memory to GPU memory. By this proactive and asynchronous data loading, we manage to handle out-of-core problems with close-to-zero data loading time except for the first load.

Elasticity to resources. Algorithm 3 is generic enough to cover many deployment scenarios where the number of GPUs are fewer or more than p or q. With more GPUs, the sequential **for** at *Line 8* can be parallelized; with fewer GPUs, the **parfor** at *Line 9* can be turned into a sequential for. This is similar to how MapReduce deals with resource elasticity: when there are fewer/more parallel tasks compared with task slots, tasks will be executed in fewer/more waves. By this design cuMF is able to solve ALS of any size.

Fault tolerance. Handling machine failure is straightforward in cuMF which uses a single machine. During ALS execution we asynchronously checkpoint X and Θ generated from the latest iteration, into a connected parallel file system. When the machine fails, the latest X or Θ (whichever is more recent) is used to restart ALS.

5. EXPERIMENTS

This section reports the performance evaluations on cuMF. We compare cuMF with multi-core solutions libMF [3] and NOMAD [5]. We also compare with distributed solutions including NOMAD (on multi-nodes), Factorbird [9], Spark ALS [8], and a Giraph based solution from Facebook [7]. We select these solutions because they either perform better than earlier studies [4, 10, 11, 24, 25], or are able to handle large data sets. Because none of existing GPU-based solutions [26, 27] can tackle big data sets, we do not compare with their results.

The goals of our experiments are to provide key insights on the following questions:

1. how would cuMF on a single GPU compare with highly optimized multi-core methods, such as libMF and NOMAD, on medium-size problems? (Section 5.2)

2. are the memory optimization done by MO-ALS effective? (Section 5.3)

3. is SU-ALS scalable with multiple GPUs? (Section 5.4)

4. with four GPUs on one machine, how would cuMF compare with multi-node methods on large-size problems? (Section 5.5)

Table 5: Data sets

Data Set	m	n	N_z	f	λ
Netflix	480,189	17,770	99M	100	0.05
YahooMusic	1,000,990	624,961	252.8M	100	1.4
Hugewiki	50,082,603	39,780	3.1B	100	0.05
SparkALS	660M	2.4M	3.5B	10	0.05
Factorbird	229M	195M	38.5B	5	0.05
Facebook	1B	48M	112B	16	0.05
cuMF	1B	48M	112B	100	0.05

5.1 Experiment setting

Data Sets. We use three public data sets, i.e., Netflix [6], YahooMusic [13] and Hugewiki [3] to measure the convergence speed. For large-size problems, we synthesize the data sets used by SparkALS [8], Factorbird [9] and Facebook [7]. For these three systems, we compare the per iteration latency because their convergence speed are not reported. We also synthesize a data set to the size that is beyond any previous attempts. That is, we use the rating matrix of the Facebook data set, with an enlarged f of 100 from the original 16. Characteristics of these data sets are shown in Table 5.

Hardware. Unless otherwise mentioned, we use one to four Nvidia Titan X GPUs, each with 3072 CUDA cores and 12 GB memory, on one machine. The machine is with two Intel Xeon E5 CPUs, 256 GB RAM, and the GPFS [28] as the file system.

Parameters. The f and λ values for each data set are given in Table 5. Feature matrices are initiated with random numbers in $[0,1]$. We focus on the speed and scalability of cuMF, and therefore did not spend much effort in hyperparameter tuning to achieve the best accuracy.

Evaluation. For Netflix, YahooMusic and Hugewiki, we evaluate the root-mean-square-error (RMSE) on test set. Performance of libMF and NOMAD is obtained from [3,5]. For SparkALS, Factorbird and Facebook, since the data is synthetic and no test RMSE is reported, we compare the per iteration run time.

5.2 MO-ALS on a single GPU

We run cuMF on one GPU, measure the test RMSE w.r.t. training time, and compare with NOMAD and libMF on one machine with 30 cores [5]. We choose these two for comparison because they are among the fastest multi-core solutions. In Figure 6, on both Netflix and YahooMusic, cuMF performs slightly worse than NOMAD at the beginning but slightly better later, and constantly faster than libMF. CuMF use ALS where each iteration takes much longer than SGD based methods. This makes it slower at the beginning. Nevertheless cuMF catches up quickly and outperforms soon afterward.

5.3 Benefit of using registers and texture memory in MO-ALS

We first measure the benefit of aggressively using registers in MO-ALS. Figure 7 compares cuMF's performance, with or without using register memory to aggregate A_u, on one GPU. On Netflix data, cuMF converges 2.5 times as slow (75 seconds vs. 30 seconds when RMSE reaches 0.92) without using registers. The result strongly supports the idea of ag-

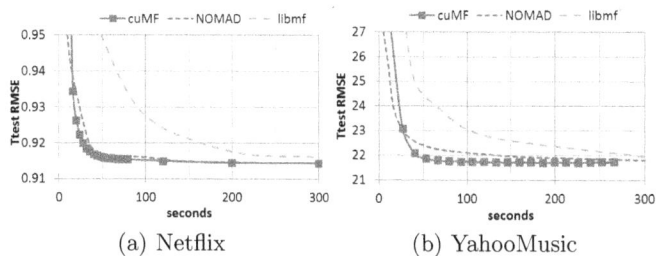

(a) Netflix (b) YahooMusic

Figure 6: Test RMSE convergence speed in terms of number of iterations: cuMF (with one GPU), NOMAD and libMF (both with 30 CPU cores).

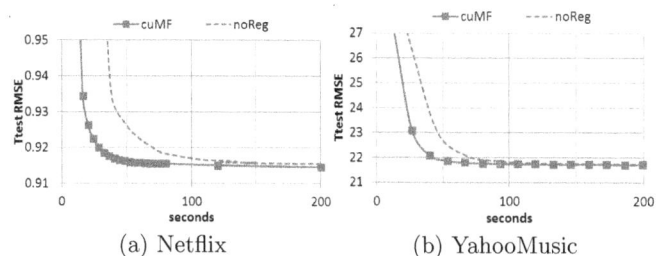

(a) Netflix (b) YahooMusic

Figure 7: The convergence speed of cuMF, with or without aggressively using registers on one GPU.

gressively using registers. Among all optimizations done in MO-ALS, using registers for A_u brings the greatest performance gain. Without using the registers, cuMF converges 1.7 times as slow on YahooMusic. YahooMusic has a smaller performance degradation without using registers than Netflix. This is because its rating matrix is more sparse. As a result, its GET_HERMITIAN_X() is less heavy-duty and occupy a smaller percentage of the overall run time.

Figure 8 compares cuMF's performance with or without using texture memory. Using texture memory, the convergence speed is 25% to 35% faster. The reason for the gain is due to the fact that Algorithm 2 updates Θ and X in an alternating manner, i.e., Θ is read-only when updating X, and X is read-only when updating Θ. This feature enables us to leverage the read-only texture memory in GPU to speed up memory access. Since YahooMusic data is more sparse, the penalty of not using texture memory is also smaller.

5.4 Scalability of SU-ALS on multiple GPUs

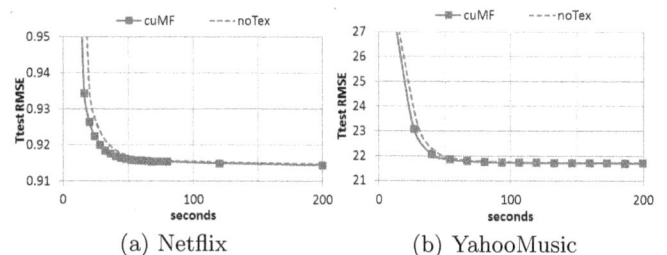

(a) Netflix (b) YahooMusic

Figure 8: The convergence speed of cuMF, with or without texture memory on one GPU.

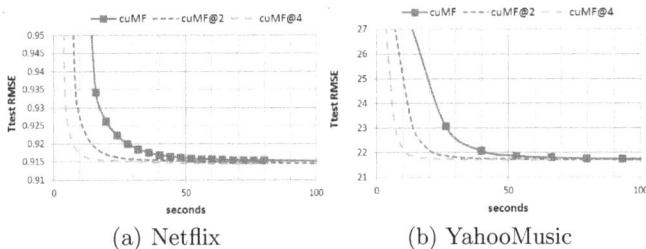

(a) Netflix   (b) YahooMusic

Figure 9: The convergence speed of cuMF on one, two, and four GPUs.

This section first studies how a problem with the fixed size data set can be accelerated with multiple GPUs. In both Netflix and YahooMusic, X and Θ can both fit on one GPU. As a result only model parallelism is needed. We run Netflix and YahooMusic data on one, two and four GPUs, respectively, on one machine. As seen from Figure 9, close-to-linear speedup is achieved. For example, the speedup is 3.8x when using four GPUs, measured at RMSE 0.92. Detailed profiling shows that, the very small overhead mainly comes from PCIe IO contention when multiple GPUs read from host memory simultaneously.

In contrast, NOMAD observed a sub-linear speedup on certain data sets, due to cache locality effects and communication overhead [5]. CuMF achieves better scalability due to the optimized memory access and inter-GPU communication. An advantage of cuMF is that, it consolidates massive computation on a single machine, so that it only uses PCIe connections which are faster than any existing network.

We also tested Hugewiki data on four GPUs. We compare with multi-node NOMAD (on 64-node HPC cluster and 32-node AWS cluster) because it outperforms DSGD [10] and DSGD++ [11]. Hugewiki is a relatively large data set where $m \approx 50M$, $n \approx 40K$, and $N_z \approx 3B$. When using X to solve Θ, X is too big to fit on one GPU. According to Algorithm 3 we partition X evenly into four GPUs and apply data parallelism. We use the two-phase parallel reduction scheme shown in Figure 5 (b), because our machine has two sockets each connecting to two GPUs. With all the intra- and inter-GPU optimizations, cuMF performs slightly better than NOMAD on a 64-node HPC cluster (again, with a slower start), and much better than NOMAD on a 32-node AWS cluster, as shown in Figure 10. This result is very impressive, as a 64-node HPC cluster is outperformed by only one node plus four GPUs. This indicates that cuMF brings a big saving in infrastructure and management cost.

5.5 Solve extremely large-scale problems

We conduct experiments on three extremely large problems. In this experiment we use four Nvidia GK210 cards on one machine. Each card is with 2496 CUDA cores (slightly fewer than Titan X) and 12 GB memory, and every two cards are encapsulated as one K80 GPU.

The results for the following experiments are shown in Figure 11. SparkALS [8] is a benchmark of Spark MLlib ALS. Its rating matrix is from the 100-by-1 duplication of the *Amazon Reviews* [29] data. It uses $50 \times$ m3.2xlarge AWS nodes with Spark MLlib 1.1, and takes 240 seconds per ALS iteration. We synthesize the data in the same way as [8], apply model parallelism solving X, and apply data parallelism

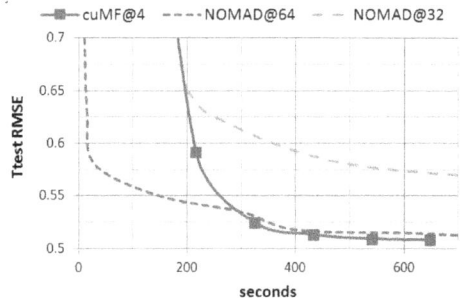

Figure 10: CuMF@4GPU, vs. NOMAD on a 64-node HPC cluster and a 32-node AWS cluster, with Hugewiki data. CuMF converges similar to NOMAD with 64 nodes, and 10x as fast as NOMAD with 32 nodes.

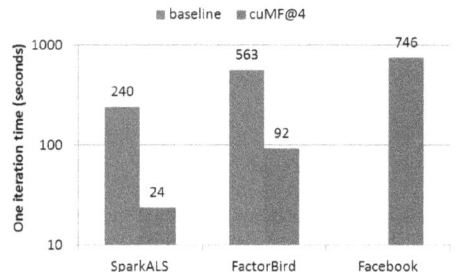

Figure 11: CuMF@4GPU on three very large data sets, compared with the their original implementations as baselines.

solving Θ. CuMF with four GPUs completes one iteration in 24 seconds, which is **ten times as fast** as SparkALS.

Factorbird [9] is a parameter server system for MF. It trains a data set ($m = 229M$, $n = 195M$, $f = 5$, and $N_z = 38.5B$) on a cluster of 50 nodes. We synthesize the data using the method described in [11]. We use only model parallelism in solving X and Θ because they both fit into one GPU. CuMF with four GPUs completes one iteration in 92 seconds. Factorbird needs 563 seconds per iteration, and with SGD it may need more iterations than ALS.

Facebook [7] recently revealed that its MF system deals with 1 billion users, millions of items and over 100 billion ratings. Given this hint we did a 160-by-20 duplication of the Amazon Review data, yielding a data set with $m = 1056M$, $n = 48M$, $f = 16$, and $N_z = 112B$. We use data parallelism to solve both X and Θ. Especially, when solving Θ, because X is huge ($1056M \times 16$ floats) and cannot fit on 4 GPUs, we change the **parfor** in Line 9-18 of Algorithm 3 into a **sequential for** with many batches. By doing this, cuMF completes one ALS iteration in 746 seconds. [7] does not report its speed on 50 Giraph workers, but we believe cuMF is competitive given the size of the problem and the low cost of one machine with GPUs. We further try a larger $f = 100$, and cuMF completes one iteration in 3.8 hours. To the best of our knowledge, this is by far the largest matrix factorization problem ever reported in literature.

As a summary, on two extremely large data sets, CuMF with four GPUs significantly outperforms the original distributed implementations. CuMF is also able to factorize the largest collaborative filtering matrix ever reported.

6. RELATED WORK

SGD, Coordinate Gradient Descent (CGD) and ALS are the three main algorithms for MF. This section firstly reviews the three algorithms and then the methods to parallelize them. Subsequently, we review GPU-based MF solutions.

6.1 MF algorithms

SGD based algorithms [1] have been often applied to matrix factorization. SGD handles large scale problems by splitting the rating matrix into blocks along with sophisticated conflict-avoiding updates. CGD based algorithms update along one coordinate direction in each iteration. [25] improved the default cyclic CGD scheme by prioritizing the more important coordinates. ALS algorithms [6,30] have advantages in easy to parallelize, converging in fewer iterations, and dealing with non-sparse rating matrices [1]. CuMF is based on ALS.

6.2 Parallel computing paradigms

Parallel SGD. SGD has been parallelized in environments including multi-core [3], multi-node MPI [5,11], MapReduce [10,24] and parameter-server [9,31]. These studies are inspired by HOGWILD! [32], which shows how to avoid expensive memory locking in memory sharing systems for some optimization problems with sparse updates. These methods partition the rating matrix into blocks with no overlapping rows or columns, and work on these blocks in parallel. They also use asynchronous communication, overlapping of communication and computation, and shared memory to achieve further speedup.

LibMF [3] is a very efficient SGD based library for matrix factorization on multi-cores. It has out performed nearly all other approaches on a 12-core machine. However, our experimental results show that libMF stops scaling beyond 16 cores, similar to the observation of [33]. Moreover, libMF is a single-machine implementation, which limits its capability to solve large-scale problems. NOMAD [5] extends the idea of block partitioning, adding the capability to release a portion of a block to another thread before its full completion. It performs similar to libMF on a single machine, and can scale out to a 64-node HPC cluster.

Parameter Server with SGD. More recently, the idea of "parameter server" [31, 34] emerges for extremely large-scale machine learning problems. In this paradigm, the *server nodes* store parameters, while the *worker nodes* store training data and compute on them. The parameter-server framework manages asynchronous communication between nodes, flexible consistency models, elastic scalability, and fault tolerance. Following this idea, Petuum [31] runs Netflix data on a 512 cores cluster using SGD. Factorbird [9] is a parameter server specifically implemented for matrix factorization, also based on SGD.

Parallel CGD. CCD++ [4] performs sequential updates on one row of the decomposed matrix while fixing other variables. CCD++ has lower time complexity but makes less progress per iteration, compared with ALS. In practice, CCD++ behaves well in the early stage of optimization, but then becomes slower than libMF.

Parallel ALS. As discussed in Section 2.2, PALS [6] and SparkALS [20] parallelize ALS by feature matrix replication and partial replication, respectively. These approaches does not work when feature matrices get extremely large. Face-

book [7] tackles this issue by feeding a feature matrix in parts to a node. For example, when solving X, X is partitioned disjointedly across nodes; Θ is also partitioned and rotated across the same set of nodes. When a Θ partition $\Theta^{(j)}$ meets X partition $X^{(i)}$, $X^{(i)}$ is updated by observing $\Theta^{(j)}$; $X^{(i)}$ completes an iteration of update after it meets all $\Theta^{(j)}$s. This is somewhat similar to SU-ALS but SU-ALS does not use rotation, as GPUs do not have sufficient memory to do rotation.

GraphLab [35] implements ALS in such a way that when Θ is big, it is distributed among multiple machines. When updating a $\mathbf{x}_u$ in a node, all needed θ_vs are fetched on-the-fly from all nodes. This involves a lot of cross-node traffic and puts a high requirement on network bandwidth.

6.3 GPU approaches

[26] employs GPU-based restricted Boltzmann machine for collaborative filtering, which gives relative performance compared with a CPU implementation on Netflix data. [27] implements both SGD and ALS on GPU to solve MF. It uses a mini-batch-based and sequential version of SGD, and a variant of ALS that adjusts (rather than re-calculates) the inverse of the Hermitian matrices in each iteration. They neither optimize the memory access to fully utilize GPU's compute power, nor scale to multiple GPUs to handle large-scale problems.

Compared with CPU-based approaches, cuMF has better performance with a fraction of hardware resources. Compared with GPU-based approaches, our optimization in memory access and parallelism yields higher performance and scalability.

7. CONCLUSION

Advances in GPU computing opens new possibilities to accelerate high performance parallel and large scale distributed applications. GPUs enable us to consolidate huge compute power and memory bandwidth on one or few machines, which may reduce the demand for big distributed clusters. This scale-up approach provides an alternative to the scaleout systems in distributed applications. Evidently, cuMF using a single machine with GPUs is faster and cheaper to solve matrix factorization, compared with distributed CPU systems. CuMF achieves this by optimizing memory access, combining data and model parallelism, and applying topology-aware parallel reduction.

In future work we plan to extend cuMF to deal with other sparse problems such as graph algorithms [36], and use it to accelerate Hadoop/Spark framework [15].

8. REFERENCES

[1] Y. Koren, R. M. Bell, and C. Volinsky, "Matrix factorization techniques for recommender systems," *Computer*, vol. 42, no. 8, pp. 30–37, 2009.

[2] J. Pennington, R. Socher, and C. D. Manning, "Glove: Global vectors for word representation," in *EMNLP*, 2014, pp. 1532–1543.

[3] Y. Zhuang, W. Chin, Y. Juan, and C. Lin, "A fast parallel SGD for matrix factorization in shared memory systems," in *RecSys*, 2013, pp. 249–256.

[4] H.-F. Yu, C.-J. Hsieh, S. Si, and I. S. Dhillon, "Scalable coordinate descent approaches to parallel matrix factorization for recommender systems," in *ICDM*, 2012, pp. 765–774.

[5] H. Yun, H.-F. Yu, C.-J. Hsieh, S. Vishwanathan, and I. S. Dhillon, "NOMAD: Non-locking, stochastic multi-machine algorithm for asynchronous and decentralized matrix completion," in *VLDB*, 2014, pp. 975–986.

[6] Y. Zhou, D. M. Wilkinson, R. Schreiber, and R. Pan, "Large-scale parallel collaborative filtering for the netflix prize," in *AAIM*, 2008, pp. 337–348.

[7] M. Kabiljo and A. Ilic, "Recommending items to more than a billion people," https://code.facebook.com/posts/861999383875667, 2015, [Online; accessed 17-Aug-2015].

[8] B. Yavuz, X. Meng, and R. Xin, "Scalable Collaborative Filtering with Spark MLlib," https://databricks.com/blog/2014/07/23/scalable-collaborative-filtering-with-spark-mllib.html, 2014, [Online; accessed 15-Aug-2015].

[9] S. Schelter, V. Satuluri, and R. B. Zadeh, "Factorbird-a parameter server approach to distributed matrix factorization," in *NIPS Workshop on Distributed Matrix Computations*, 2014.

[10] R. Gemulla, E. Nijkamp, P. J. Haas, and Y. Sismanis, "Large-scale matrix factorization with distributed stochastic gradient descent," in *KDD*, 2011, pp. 69–77.

[11] C. Teflioudi, F. Makari, and R. Gemulla, "Distributed matrix completion," in *ICDM*, 2012, pp. 655–664.

[12] T. Rohrmann, "How to factorize a 700 GB matrix with Apache Flink," http://data-artisans.com/how-to-factorize-a-700-gb-matrix-with-apache-flink/, 2015, [Online; accessed 15-Aug-2015].

[13] G. Dror, N. Koenigstein, Y. Koren, and M. Weimer, "The Yahoo! Music Dataset and KDD-Cup '11," in *KDD Cup 2011 competition*, 2012.

[14] S. J. Krieder, J. M. Wozniak, T. Armstrong, M. Wilde, D. S. Katz, B. Grimmer, I. T. Foster, and I. Raicu, "Design and evaluation of the gemtc framework for gpu-enabled many-task computing," in *HPDC*, 2014, pp. 153–164.

[15] A. Sabne, P. Sakdhnagool, and R. Eigenmann, "Heterodoop: A mapreduce programming system for accelerator clusters," in *HPDC*, 2015, pp. 235–246.

[16] J. L. Hennessy and D. A. Patterson, *Computer architecture: a quantitative approach*. Elsevier, 2011.

[17] A. Coates, B. Huval, T. Wang, D. Wu, B. Catanzaro, and N. Andrew, "Deep learning with COTS HPC systems," in *ICML*, 2013, pp. 1337–1345.

[18] Nvidia, "cuSPARSE," http://docs.nvidia.com/cuda/cusparse/#cusparse-lt-t-gt-csrmm2, 2015, [Online; accessed 4-Aug-2015].

[19] ——, "cuBLAS," http://docs.nvidia.com/cuda/cublas/, 2015, [Online; accessed 17-Aug-2015].

[20] X. Meng, J. K. Bradley, B. Yavuz, E. R. Sparks, S. Venkataraman, D. Liu, J. Freeman, D. B. Tsai, M. Amde, S. Owen, D. Xin, R. Xin, M. J. Franklin, R. Zadeh, M. Zaharia, and A. Talwalkar, "MLlib: Machine Learning in Apache Spark," *CoRR*, vol. abs/1505.06807, 2015.

[21] J. Canny, D. L. W. Hall, and D. Klein, "A multi-teraflop constituency parser using GPUs," in *EMNLP*, 2013, pp. 1898–1907.

[22] S. Ryoo, C. I. Rodrigues, S. S. Baghsorkhi, S. S. Stone, D. B. Kirk, and W.-m. W. Hwu, "Optimization principles and application performance evaluation of a multithreaded GPU Using CUDA," in *PPoPP*, 2008, pp. 73–82.

[23] J. Dean, G. S. Corrado, R. Monga, K. Chen, M. Devin, Q. V. Le, M. Z. Mao, M. Ranzato, A. Senior, P. Tucker, K. Yang, and A. Y. Ng, "Large scale distributed deep networks," in *NIPS*, 2012, pp. 1223–1231.

[24] B. Li, S. Tata, and Y. Sismanis, "Sparkler: Supporting large-scale matrix factorization," in *EDBT*, 2013, pp. 625–636.

[25] C.-J. Hsieh and I. S. Dhillon, "Fast coordinate descent methods with variable selection for non-negative matrix factorization," in *KDD*, 2011, pp. 1064–1072.

[26] X. Cai, Z. Xu, G. Lai, C. Wu, and X. Lin, "GPU-accelerated restricted boltzmann machine for collaborative filtering," in *ICA3PP*, 2012, pp. 303–316.

[27] D. Zastrau and S. Edelkamp, "Stochastic gradient descent with GPGPU," in *KI 2012: Advances in Artificial Intelligence*. Springer, 2012, pp. 193–204.

[28] IBM, "General Parallel Filesystem," http://www-01.ibm.com/support/knowledgecenter/?lang=en#!/SSFKCN_4.1.0.4/gpfs.v4r104_welcome.html, 2014.

[29] Stanford SNAP Lab, "Web data: Amazon reviews," https://snap.stanford.edu/data/web-Amazon.html, 2015, [Online; accessed 18-Aug-2015].

[30] I. Pillaszy, D. Zibriczky, and D. Tikk, "Fast ALS-based matrix factorization for explicit and implicit feedback datasets," in *RecSys*, 2010, pp. 71–78.

[31] H. Cui, J. Cipar, Q. Ho, J. K. Kim, S. Lee, A. Kumar, J. Wei, W. Dai, G. R. Ganger, P. B. Gibbons, G. A. Gibson, and E. P. Xing, "Exploiting bounded staleness to speed up big data analytics," in *USENIX ATC*, 2014, pp. 37–48.

[32] F. Niu, B. Recht, C. Re, and S. J. Wright, "HOGWILD!: A lock-free approach to parallelizing stochastic gradient descent," in *NIPS*, 2011, pp. 693–701.

[33] Y. Nishioka and K. Taura, "Scalable task-parallel sgd on matrix factorization in multicore architectures," in *ParLearning*, 2015.

[34] M. Li, D. G. Andersen, J. W. Park, A. J. Smola, A. Ahmed, V. Josifovski, J. Long, E. J. Shekita, and B.-Y. Su, "Scaling distributed machine learning with the parameter server," in *OSDI*, 2014, pp. 583–598.

[35] Y. Low, D. Bickson, J. Gonzalez, C. Guestrin, A. Kyrola, and J. M. Hellerstein, "Distributed GraphLab: a framework for machine learning and data mining in the cloud," in *VLDB*, 2012, pp. 716–727.

[36] F. Khorasani, K. Vora, R. Gupta, and L. N. Bhuyan, "Cusha: Vertex-centric graph processing on gpus," in *HPDC*, 2014, pp. 239–252.

GPU-Aware Non-contiguous Data Movement In Open MPI

Wei Wu
University of Tennessee
Knoxville, USA
wwu12@vols.utk.edu

George Bosilca
University of Tennessee
Knoxville, USA
bosilca@icl.utk.edu

Rolf vandeVaart
NVIDIA
Santa Clara, USA
rvandevaart@nvidia.com

Sylvain Jeaugey
NVIDIA
Santa Clara, USA
sjeaugey@nvidia.com

Jack Dongarra
University of Tennessee
Knoxville, USA
Oak Ridge National
Laboratory
Oak Ridge, USA
University of Manchester
Manchester, UK
dongarra@eecs.utk.edu

ABSTRACT

Due to better parallel density and power efficiency, GPUs have become more popular for use in scientific applications. Many of these applications are based on the ubiquitous Message Passing Interface (MPI) programming paradigm, and take advantage of non-contiguous memory layouts to exchange data between processes. However, support for efficient non-contiguous data movements for GPU-resident data is still in its infancy, imposing a negative impact on the overall application performance.

To address this shortcoming, we present a solution where we take advantage of the inherent parallelism in the datatype packing and unpacking operations. We developed a close integration between Open MPI's stack-based datatype engine, NVIDIA's Unified Memory Architecture and GPUDirect capabilities. In this design the datatype packing and unpacking operations are offloaded onto the GPU and handled by specialized GPU kernels, while the CPU remains the driver for data movements between nodes. By incorporating our design into the Open MPI library we have shown significantly better performance for non-contiguous GPU-resident data transfers on both shared and distributed memory machines.

CCS Concepts

•**Theory of computation** → *Distributed computing models;* •**Computer systems organization** → *Heterogeneous (hybrid) systems;* •**Computing methodologies** → Concurrent algorithms;

HPDC'16, May 31-June 04, 2016, Kyoto, Japan

© 2016 Copyright held by the owner/author(s). Publication rights licensed to ACM.

ACM ISBN 978-1-4503-4314-5/16/05... $15.00

DOI: http://dx.doi.org/10.1145/2907294.2907317

Keywords

MPI; GPU; datatype; non-contiguous data; hybrid architecture

1. INTRODUCTION

Throughput-oriented architectures, such as GPUs, are increasingly used for scientific applications because of their high efficiency in solving computationally intensive tasks at an unbeatable rate of power consumption. Evidence of this can be seen in the most recent Top500 list, where GPUs have become the most popular accelerators. GPUs are connected as peripheral devices via PCI-Express, and, for a long time, had a separate memory space than the host. Explicit memory copy directives were necessary to move data between host and GPU, before being available to CPU-based computations or communications. More recently, this memory separation has been fused with the introduction of the Unified Memory Architecture (UMA), allowing the host memory to be directly accessed from GPUs, and inversely, GPU memory to be directly accessed from CPUs – providing applications with transparent access to the entire memory, independent of the physical location of the memory.

MPI is a popular and efficient parallel programming model for distributed memory systems widely used in scientific applications. As many scientific applications operate on multidimensional data, manipulating parts of these data becomes complicated because the underlying memory layout is not contiguous.The MPI standard proposes a rich set of interfaces to define regular and irregular memory patterns, the so called derived datatypes (DDT). For example, the widely used linear algebra library ScaLAPACK [2] usually deals with sub-matrices and matrices with irregular shapes such as upper or lower triangular matrices. The DDTs provide a general and flexible solution to describe any collections of contiguous and non-contiguous data with a compact format. Once constructed and committed, an MPI datatype can be used as an argument for any point-to-point, collective, I/O, and one-sided functions. Internally, the MPI datatype engine will automatically pack and unpack data based on the type of operation to be realized, in an efficient way while hiding the low-level details from users. Thus, the scientific application developers do not have to manually pack and unpack data in order to optimize non-contiguous data transfers, but instead they can safely rely on the MPI runtime to make such operations trivial and portable. Several studies [12, 13] have shown that, at least when handling CPU-based data, recent MPI implementations have exhibited significant performance improvement for the handling of non-contiguous datatypes. As a result, applications taking advantage of the MPI datatypes express a drastic benefit in terms of performance, code readability and maintenance compared with codes that prefer a more handmade, application specific approach.

As GPUs have high computational capabilities, an increasing number of scientific applications migrate their computationally intensive parts to GPUs. Since the MPI standard [5] does not define interactions with GPU-based data, it is expected that application developers have to explicitly initiate data movements between host and device memory prior to using MPI to move data across node boundaries. Techniques such as GPUDirect [10] have been developed to enable direct GPU data movement between processes, i.e., without going through the host memory. Unfortunately, these optimizations were designed with a focus on contiguous data, leaving the most difficult operations, the packing and unpacking of non-contiguous memory patterns, in the charge of developers. To fully utilize the PCI-Express and the network, non-contiguous data must be packed into a contiguous buffer prior to wire transfer. There are effective packing/unpacking implementations for datatypes in host memory [12]. However, exposing the same level of support for a non-contiguous MPI datatype based on GPU memory remains an open challenge.

To address the lack of non-contiguous datatype support for GPUs, we present the design of a datatype engine for non-contiguous GPU-resident data, which is able to take advantage of the embarrassingly parallel nature of the pack and unpack operations and efficiently map them onto GPU threads. The GPU datatype engine is incorporated into the Open MPI [6] library, and takes advantage of the latest NVIDIA hardware capabilities, such as GPUDirect, not only to minimize the overheads but also to decrease the overall energy consumption. For contexts where GPUDirect is not available, we provide a copy-in/copy-out protocol using host memory as an intermediary buffer. All these approaches are using a light-weight pipeline protocol to allow pack and unpack operations to work simultaneously to reduce the overall communication time of non-contiguous data between MPI processes. Although this work is done using CUDA in the context of MPI, the ideas are generic and can be easily ported not only to different programming paradigms (OpenSHMEM and OpenCL), but also to other types of accelerators with computational capabilities.

The contributions of this paper are: a) a datatype engine designed for GPU-resident non-contiguous data, which adapts the parallelism of the pack/unpack operations to the parallelism available on GPUs; b) support for different communication protocols – for RDMA and copy in/out – to maximize the benefit from the capabilities available at the hardware level (GPUDirect); c) a light-weight pipeline mechanism to ensure all participants, the sender and the receiver, can be used simultaneously to prepare the data for transfer (pack and unpack); and d) to demonstrate the performance boost achieved by the techniques presented in this paper

while transferring widely used non-contiguous data memory layouts.

The rest of this paper is organized as follows. Section 2 introduces the related work. Section 3 outlines the design of the GPU datatype engine. Section 4 presents how the GPU datatype engine is integrated into Open MPI. Section 5 evaluates the performance in hybrid systems with four types of benchmarks. Section 6 concludes the paper and describes potential future work.

2. RELATED WORKS

2.1 GPU-Aware MPI

Heterogeneous systems feature several CPU cores and one or more GPUs per node. Writing efficient applications for such heterogeneous systems is a challenging task as application developers need to explicitly manage two types of data movements: intra-process communications (device to host) and inter-process communications. Recent versions of well-known MPI libraries such as MVAPICH2 [17] and Open MPI already provide some levels of GPU support. With these GPU-Aware MPI libraries, application developers can use MPI constructs to transparently move data, even if the data resides in GPU memory. Similar efforts have been made to integrate GPU-awarness into other programming models. Aij et. al. propose the MPI-ACC [1], which seamlessly integrates OpenACC with the MPI library, enabling OpenACC applications to perform end-to-end data movement. Lawlor presents the cudaMPI [8] library for communication between GPUs, which provides specialized data movement calls that translate to *cudaMemcpy* followed by the corresponding MPI call. Even though the paper discusses non-contiguous data support, the current implementation only includes support for vector types. For the PGAS programming model, Potluri et. al [11] extend OpenSHMEM to GPU clusters providing a unified memory space. However, as OpenSHMEM has no support for non-contiguous types, this implementation does not provide sufficient support to communicate non-contiguous GPU data. All these works focus on providing GPU-awarness for parallel programming models, and have been demonstrated to deliver good performance for contiguous data, but none of them provide full and efficient support for non-contiguous data residing in GPU memory.

2.2 MPI Datatype for Data Residing in GPU Memory

More recent works have focused on providing non-contiguous MPI datatype functionality for GPU data. Wang et. al. have improved the MVAPICH MPI implementation to provide the ability to transparently communicate non-contiguous GPU memory that can be represented as a single vector, and therefore translated into CUDA's two-dimensional memory copy (*cudaMemcpy2D*) [16]. A subsequent paper by the same authors tries to extend this functionality to many datatypes by proposing a vectorization algorithm to convert any type of datatype into a set of vector datatypes [15]. Unfortunately, indexed datatypes such as triangular matrices, are difficult to convert into a compact vector type. Using Wang's approach, each contiguous block in such an indexed datatype is considered as a single vector type and packed/unpacked separately from other vectors by its own call to *cudaMemcpy2D*, increasing the number of synchronizations and consequently decreasing the performance. Moreover, no pipelining or overlap between the different stages of the datatype conversion is provided, even further limiting the performance.

Jenkins et. al. integrated a GPU datatype extension into the MPICH library [7]. His work focuses on the packing and unpacking of GPU kernels, but without providing overlaps between data packing/unpacking and other communication steps. Both Wang and Jenkins's work require transitioning the packed GPU data through host memory, increasing the load on the memory bus and imposing a significant sequential overhead on the communications. All of these approaches are drastically different from our proposed design, as in our work we favor pipelining between GPU data packing/unpacking and data movements, and also take advantage, when possible, of GPUDirect to bypass the host memory and therefore decrease latency and improve bandwidth.

3. DESIGN OF THE GPU DATATYPE ENGINE

The datatype constructs provided by the MPI Standard [5] give one the capability to define contiguous and non-contiguous memory layouts, allowing developers to reason at a higher level of abstraction, thinking about data instead of focusing on the memory layout of the data (for the pack/unpack operations). MPI defines data layouts of varying complexity: *contiguous* a number of repetitions of the same datatype without gaps in-between; *vector* defines a non-contiguous data layout that consists of equally spaced blocks of the same datatype; *indexed* specifies a noncontiguous data layout where neither the size of each block nor the displacements between successive blocks are equal; *struct* consists of location-blocklength-datatype tuples, allowing for the most flexible type of non-contiguous datatype construction.

Many MPI-based libraries and applications are using datatypes to move the burden of handling non-contiguous data from users to the MPI library implementors. For example, in the 2D stencil application of the Scalable HeterOgeneous Computing benchmark (SHOC) [3], two of the four boundaries are contiguous, and the other two are non-contiguous, which can be defined by a *vector* type. In the LAMMPS application from the molecular dynamics domain [13], each process keeps an array of indices of local particles that need to be communicated; such an access pattern can be captured by an *indexed* type. Hence, MPI datatypes help application developers alleviate the burden of manually packing and unpacking non-contiguous data. Therefore, extending the same datatype support to GPU data is extremely important for efficient programming in heterogeneous systems.

Current networks are bandwidth-oriented instead of latency-oriented, and fewer large messages provide better bytes per second transfer rates. Thus, in the context of non-contiguous data transfers, instead of generating a network operation for each individual contiguous block from the non-contiguous type, it is more efficient to pack the non-contiguous data into a contiguous buffer, and send less – but larger – messages. The same logic can be applied when data resides in GPU memory. Considering sending/receiving non-contiguous GPU datatypes, the four solutions presented in Figure 1 are usually employed.

a) Copy the entire non-contiguous data including the gaps from device memory into host memory. Accordingly, the

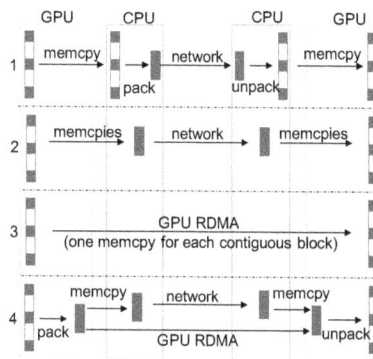

Figure 1: Four possible solutions for sending/receiving non-contiguous data residing in GPU memory.

data in host memory retains the same memory layout as the original, and the traditional CPU datatype engine can handle the pack/unpack operations. This solution provides good performance for memory layouts with little gaps, but cannot be generalized since it wastes a large amount of host memory for the intermediary copies, and has a potential degree of parallelism bounded by the CPU parallelism instead of taking advantage of the computational power of the GPU.

b) The second solution is to issue one device-to-host memory copy (*cudaMemcpy*) for each piece of contiguous data, packing the data into a single, contiguous buffer. Once packed, the resulting contiguous buffer is sent using a traditional approach. The receiver will also generate the required host-to-device memory copies to scatter the temporary contiguous buffer into the expected locations in device memory. The overhead of launching lots of memory copies degrades performance. Moreover, a memory copy of each small block of contiguous data is not able to utilize the bandwidth of PCI-Express even with the help of multiple CUDA streams. Hence, the performance of this approach is limited.

c) A small improvement upon the second solution, instead of going through host memory, it issues one device-to-device memory copy for each piece of contiguous data, and directly copies data into the destination device memory. Similar to the previous solution, this alternative suffers from the overhead of launching too many memory copies and the low utilization of PCI-Express. Also, this solution only works when the peers have identical memory layouts and the hardware supports direct device-to-device copy.

d) The last solution is to utilize the GPU to pack and unpack non-contiguous data directly into/from a contiguous GPU buffer. Then the contiguous GPU-based buffer can either be moved between GPUs with hardware support, or – in the worst case – through the host memory.

Among all of the above solutions, we believe the last to be the most promising. Compared with the CPU, the GPU has many light-weight cores and significantly larger memory bandwidth, which might be beneficial for GPU packing/unpacking as these operations can be made embarrassingly parallel. Since the kernel is offloaded into the GPU while the CPU is mostly idle (in an MPI call), it also provides the opportunity to pipeline pack/unpack with send/receive (discussed in Section 4). Moreover, this approach can be easily adapted to any hardware configuration: if GPUDirect is supported, we can bypass the host memory and use network RDMA capabilities, otherwise the copies to/from host memory can also be integrated in the pipeline, providing end-to-end overlap between pack/unpack and communications. In this paper, we present the design of a GPU datatype engine based on the 4th approach, taking advantage of CUDA *zero copy* and pipeline techniques to maximally the overlap between pack/unpack operations and communications.

In Open MPI, a datatype is described by a concise stack-based representation. Each stack element records type-specific parameters for a block, such as the number of contiguous elements in the block, the displacement of the first element from the beginning of the corresponding stack frame, and the number of blocks to be packed/unpacked. The most straightforward way to provide datatype support for GPU data would be to port the original (CPU-based) datatype engine into the GPU. However, porting the datatype stack to execute the pack/unpack operation on the GPU generates too many conditional operations, which are not GPU friendly. Thus, in order to minimize the branch operations executed by the GPU, we divided the pack/unpack operations into 2 stages. First, the host simulates the pack/unpack and generates a list of tuples <*source displacement, length, destination displacement*>. Because this list contains only relative displacements, it can be reused for a subsequent pack/unpack using the same datatype, and is therefore subject to caching optimizations. The second stage, which is represented by a kernel executing on a GPU, is using this list to execute – in parallel – as many of these pack/unpack operations as possible.

3.1 Vector Type

Other than *contiguous* datatype, *vector* is the most regular and certainly the most widely used MPI datatype constructor. A *vector* type is described by blocklengh and stride, where blocklength refers to the number of primitive datatypes that a block contains, and stride refers to the gaps between blocks. In our GPU datatype engine, we developed optimized packing/unpacking kernels specialized for a vector-like datatype. Similar to the 2 stages described above, the pack/unpack is driven by CPU. The pack kernel takes the address of the source and the destination buffers, blocklength, stride, and block count as arguments, and is launched in a dedicated CUDA stream. The operation is considered complete after a synchronization with the stream. The unpack kernel behaves similarly to the pack kernel.

While accessing global memory, a GPU device coalesces loads and stores issued by threads of a warp into as few transactions as possible to minimize DRAM bandwidth. Figure 2 shows the memory access pattern of GPU packing and unpacking kernels, forcing coalesced CUDA threads to access contiguous memory. Since device memory is accessed via 32-, 64-, or 128-byte memory-wide transactions [9], in order to minimize memory transactions, each thread theoretically should copy at least 4-bytes of data (128 bytes / 32 threads per warp). In our kernel, we force each thread to copy 8-bytes of data to reduce the number of total loops of each thread. In the case that data is not aligned with 8-

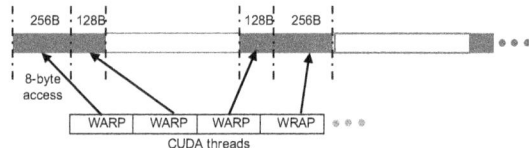

Figure 2: Access pattern of GPU pack/unpack kernels of *vector* type. The size of a CUDA block is a multiple of the warp size.

bytes, the block is divided into 3 parts: the prologue and epilogue sections follow the original alignment, while the middle one follows the 8-byte alignment.

3.2 Less regular memory patterns

Datatypes other than *vector* are more complicated, and cannot be described in a concise format using only blocklengh and stride, and instead require a more detailed description including the displacement. However, one can imagine that any type can be described as a collection of vectors, even if some of the vectors have a count of a single element. Thus, it would be possible to fall back on a set of vector-based descriptions, and launch a vector kernel (similar to 3.1) for each entry. This design is unable to provide good performance as many kernels need to be launched, overwhelming the CUDA runtime.

Instead, we propose a general solution by re-encoding a representation of any complex datatype into a set of work units with similar sizes as shown in Figure 3 by picking a reasonable work unit size. As described above, each entry is identified by a tuple <*source displacement, destination displacement, length*> named *cuda_dev_dist*. Together with the source and destination buffers, these entries are independent and can be treated in parallel. When entries work on the same length they provide a good occupancy. The incomplete entries can either be delegated into another stream with a lower priority, or treated the same as all the other entries. We choose to treat them equally to the other entries, allowing us to launch a single kernel and therefore minimize launching overhead. A more detailed procedure for the pack/unpack operations is as follows:

- First, convert the representation of the datatype from stack-based into a collection of Datatype Engine Vectors (DEVs), where each DEV contains the displacement of a block from the contiguous buffer, the displacement of the corresponding block from the non-contiguous data and the corresponding blocklength (the contiguous buffer is the destination for the pack operation, and the source for the unpack).

- The second step is to compute a more balanced work distribution for each CUDA thread. Limited by the number of threads allowed per CUDA block, a contiguous block of data could be too large to use a single CUDA block, resulting in reduced parallelism. To improve parallelism, a DEV is assigned to multiple CUDA blocks. Instead of copying the entire DEV into GPU memory and letting each CUDA block compute its working range, we take advantage of the sequentiality of this operation to execute it on CPU, where each DEV is divided into several *cuda_dev_dist* (called CUDA DEV) of the same size S – plus a residue if needed – and each one is assigned to a CUDA WARP. Similar to the vector approach, each CUDA thread accesses 8-bytes of data each time; to fully

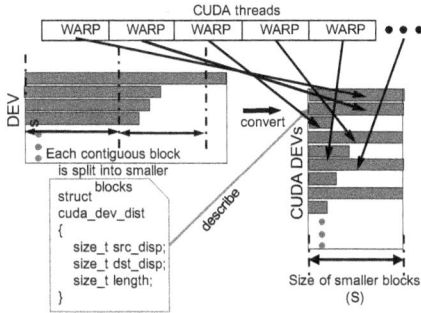

Figure 3: Access pattern of GPU pack/unpack kernels using the DEV methodology. The left *struct* describes a work unit for a CUDA WARP.

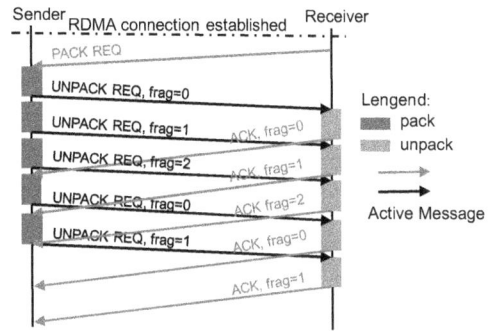

Figure 4: Pipelined RDMA protocol for send/receive of non-contiguous GPU-resident data.

utilize all threads of a WARP, the size S must be a multiple of 8 times the CUDA WARP size (32). Thus, the lower bound of S is 256 bytes; but since CUDA provides loop unrolling capability, we set the size S to 1KB, 2KB or 4KB to reduce the branch penalties and increase opportunities for instruction level parallelism (ILP).

- Last, once the array of CUDA DEVs is generated, it is copied into device memory and the corresponding GPU kernel is launched. When a CUDA block finishes its work, it would jump N (total number of CUDA blocks) on the CUDA DEVs array to retrieve its next unit of work.

Since any datatype can be converted into DEV, this approach is capable of handling any MPI datatype. However, without a careful orchestration of the different operations, the GPU idles when the CPU is preparing the CUDA DEVs array. To improve the utilization of both GPU and CPU, we pipeline the preparation of the array and the execution of the GPU kernel: instead of traversing the entire datatype, the CPU converts only a part of the datatype, then a GPU kernel is launched to pack/unpack the converted part into a dedicated CUDA stream. The CPU can then continue converting while the GPU is executing the pack/unpack kernel. As the CUDA DEV is tied to the data representation and is independent of the location of the source and destination buffers, it can be cached, either in the main or GPU memory, thereby minimizing the overheads of future pack/unpack operations.

4. INTEGRATION WITH Open MPI

This section describes how we integrated the GPU datatype engine with the Open MPI infrastructure. The Open MPI communication framework – outside the MPI API – is divided into three layers, with each one playing a different role. At the top level, the PML (point-to-point management layer) realizes the MPI matching, fragments, and reassembles the message data from point-to-point communications. Different protocols based on the message size (short, eager, and rendezvous) and network properties are available (latency, bandwidth, RMA support), and the PML is designed to pick the best combination in order to maximize network usage. Below the PML, the BML (BTL management layer) manages different network devices, handles multi-link data transfers, and selects the most suitable BTL for a communication based on the current network device where messages go through. The lowest layer, the BTL (byte transfer layer), is used for the actual point-to-point byte movement. Each

BTL provides support for a particular type of network (TCP, shared memory, InfiniBand, Portals, uGNI and so on), and mainly deals with low level network communication protocols where the focus is on optimally moving blobs of bytes. As different network devices have their own optimal communication protocols, the methodology of GPU datatype engine integration is realized at the level of the network device (the BTL). In this paper, we focus on the shared memory and InfiniBand BTL, and propose support for two types of protocols: RDMA and copy in/out. Of course, these protocols are adaptable to the GPU and network capabilities, and can be easily extended to other BTLs.

4.1 RDMA Protocol

NVIDIA's GPUDirect technology improves GPU to GPU communication by allowing data movement between GPU devices without going through host memory. According to [18], PCI-E bandwidth of GPU-GPU is larger than the one of CPU-GPU, therefore, RMDA GPU-GPU communication not only provides shortest data path between processes, but also has higher PCI-E utilization. In intra-node communications, CUDA IPC allows the GPU memory of one process to be exposed to the others, and therefore provides a one sided copy mechanism similar to RDMA. In inter-node communication, GPUDirect RDMA supports data exchange directly between the GPU and the network interface controller using PCI-E, enabling direct GPU data movement between nodes. Taking advantage of GPUDirect, a basic GPU RDMA protocol can be implemented as follows: sender packs a non-contiguous GPU datatype into a contiguous GPU buffer, and then exposes this contiguous GPU buffer to the receiver process. If the synchronization is done at the level of an entire datatype packing, the receiver should not access the data until the sender has completed the pack operation. The resulting cost of this operation is therefore the cost of the pack, followed by the cost of the data movement plus the cost of the unpack. However, if a pipeline is installed between the 2 processes, the cost of the operation can be decreased, reaching the invariant (which is the cost of the data transfer) plus the cost of the most expensive operation (pack or unpack) on a single fragment, which might represent a reduction by nearly a factor of 2 if the pipeline size is correctly tuned. This approach also requires a smaller contiguous buffer on the GPU as the segments used for the pipeline can be reused once the receiver completes the unpack and notifies the sender that its operation on a segment is completed. The Open MPI's PML layer is already capable of implementing message fragmentation and can send/receive them in a pipelined fashion. However, applying this pipelining feature directly for PML-based RDMA protocols is costly because PML is the top-level layer, and pipelining in this layer requires going through the entire Open MPI infrastructure to establish an RDMA transfer for each fragment. Starting an RDMA transfer requires the sender to send its GPU memory handle to the receiver for mapping to its own GPU memory space, which is a costly operation. With such an approach any benefits obtained from pipelining will be annihilated by the overhead of registering the RDMA fragments. To lower this cost, we implement a light-weight pipelined RDMA protocol directly at the BTL level, which only proposes a single one-time establishment of the RDMA connection (and then caching the registration).

The implementation of our pipelined RDMA protocol uses BTL-level *Active Message* [4], which is an asynchronous communication mechanism intended to expose the interconnection network's flexibility and performance. To reduce the communication overhead, each message header contains the reference of a callback handler triggered on the receiver side, allowing the sender to specify how the message will be handled on the receiver side upon message arrival.

Taking advantage of *Active Message* communications, the sender and receiver are dissociated, and they synchronize only when needed to ensure smooth progress of the pack/unpack operations. While the sender works on packing a fragment, the receiver is able to unpack the previous fragment, and then notify the sender that the fragment is now ready for reuse. Once the sender receives the notification from the receiver that a fragment can safely be reused, it will pack the next chunk of data (if any) directly inside. Figure 4 presents the steps of the pipelined RDMA protocol. Besides the address of a callback handler for invoking the remote pack or unpack functions, the header in our implementation also contains additional information providing a finer grain control of the pack/unpack functions (such as the index of the fragment to be used). In our RDMA protocol, the packing/unpacking is entirely driven by the receiver acting upon a GET protocol, providing an opportunity for a handshake prior to the beginning of the operation. During this handshake, the two participants agree on the type of datatype involved in the operation (contiguous or non-contiguous) and the best strategy to be employed. If the sender datatype is contiguous, the receiver can use the sender buffer directly for it's unpack operation, without the need for further synchronizations. Similarly, if the receiver datatype is contiguous the sender is then allowed to pack directly into the receiver buffer, without further synchronizations. Of course, based on the protocol used (PUT or GET), a final synchronization might be needed to inform the peer about the data transfer completion. The more detailed description of the pipelined RDMA protocol is as follows.

- **Sender:** detects if GPU RDMA is supported between the two MPI processes, and requests a temporary GPU-residing buffer from the datatype engine. It then retrieves the memory handle of this temporary GPU buffer, and starts the RDMA connection request providing the memory handle and the shape of the local datatype in a request message. It then waits until a pack request is received from the receiver. After finishing packing a fragment, an unpack request is sent to the receiver signaling the index of the fragment to be unpacked. In case the GPU buffer is full, or the pipeline depth has been reached, the

sender waits until it receives an acknowledgment from the receiver notifying that the unpacking is finished for a particular fragment that can be reused for the next pack. This stage repeats until all the data is packed.

- **Receiver:** upon receiving an RDMA request it maps the memory handle provided by the sender into its own memory, allowing for direct access to the sender's GPU buffer. After the RDMA connection is established, the receiver signals the sender to start packing, and then waits until it receives an unpack request from the sender. After finishing the unpacking of each fragment, the receiver acknowledges the sender, allowing the fragment to be reused. In the case where the sender and the receiver are bound to different GPUs, we provide the option to allow the receiver to allocate a temporary buffer within its device memory and move the packed data from sender's device memory into its own memory before unpacking. In some configurations, going through this intermediary copy delivers better performance than accessing the data directly from remote device memory.

4.2 Copy In/Out Protocol

In some cases, due to hardware limitations or system level security restrictions, the IPC is disabled and GPU RDMA transfers are not available between different MPI processes. To compensate for the lack of RDMA transfers we provide a copy in/copy out protocol, where all data transfers go through host memory. It is worth noting that this approach is extremely similar to the case when one process uses device memory while the other only uses host memory. Open MPI handles non-contiguous datatypes on the CPU by packing them into a temporary CPU buffer prior to communication. When GPU RDMA is not available, we forced Open MPI to always consider all data as being in host memory, and therefore it always provides a CPU buffer even for datatypes residing in device memory. When the datatype engine detects that the corresponding non-contiguous data is actually in device memory, it allocates a temporary GPU buffer (with the same or smaller size than the CPU buffer) for packing. Once this GPU buffer is full, the packed data is copied into the CPU buffer for further processing. This procedure repeats until the entire data is packed. A similar mechanism applies to unpack.

Unlike the RDMA protocol, extra memory copies between device and host memory are required. To alleviate the overhead of such memory transfer, pipelining can also be used by allowing the sender to partially pack the data, fragment after fragment, and allow the receive to unpack once it receives each packed fragment. Therefore, the pipelining becomes more complex, overlapping packing/unpacking on the GPU, with device-to-host data movement and intra-node communication. Another CUDA capability, *zero copy*, can be exploited to minimize the memory copy overhead. Instead of using the CPU to explicitly drive memory movement, the CPU buffer is mapped to GPU memory with the help of CUDA UMA, and then the data movement is implicitly handled by hardware, which is able to overlap it with pack/unpack operations. Overall, as indicated in the experimental Section 5, copy in/out protocol is a general solution suitable for most platforms, and delivers good performance – especially once integrated with a pipelined protocol.

Figure 5: Triangular matrix (red one) vs Stair triangular matrix (red and green one), width and height of stair *nb* is multiple of CUDA block size

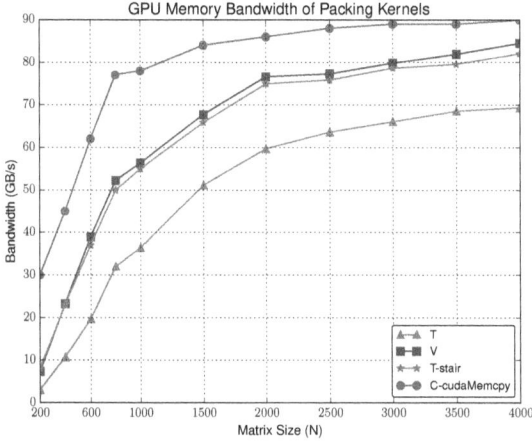

Figure 6: GPU memory bandwidth of packing kernels for sub-matrix and lower triangular matrix comparing with contiguous data of the same size. "T" represents triangular matrix, "V" represents submatrix, "C" represents contiguous matrix

5. EXPERIMENT AND EVALUATION

We evaluate our datatypes packing/unpacking methodology using four types of benchmarks. First, we investigate the performance of the GPU datatype engine. Second, we look at inter-process GPU-to-GPU communication through a non-contiguous data ping-pong test, and compare with MVAPICH2.1-GDR. Third, we figure out the minimal GPU resources required for GPU packing/unpacking kernels to achieve optimal overall performance when communication is engaged. Last, we analyze the impact on non-contiguous data transfer when access to the GPU resource is limited (the GPU is shared with another GPU intensive application). Experiments are carried out on an NVIDIA PSG cluster: each node is equipped with 6 NVIDIA Kepler K40 GPUs with CUDA 7.5 and 2 deca-core Intel Xeon E5-2690v2 Ivy Bridge CPUs; nodes are connected by FDR IB.

5.1 Performance Evaluation for Datatype Engine

In this section, we investigate the performance of our GPU datatype engine by using two commonly used datatypes: *vector* and *indexed*. These datatypes are representative of many dense linear algebra based applications, as they are the basic blocks of the ScaLAPACK data manipulation. More precisely, these types are represented as a sub-matrix and an (upper or lower) triangular matrix. Considering a submatrix with column-major format, each column is contiguous in memory, and the stride between columns is the size of the columns in the original big matrix, which follows the characteristic of a *vector* type (shown as "V" in the following figures). In the lower triangular matrix case, each column

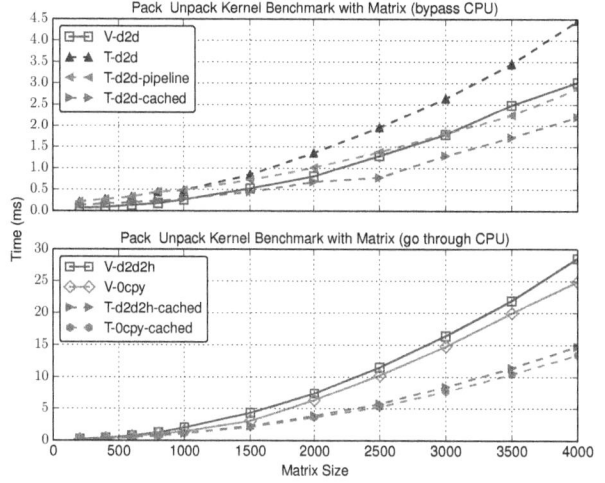

Figure 7: Performance of pack and unpack submatrix and lower triangular matrix varies by matrix size.

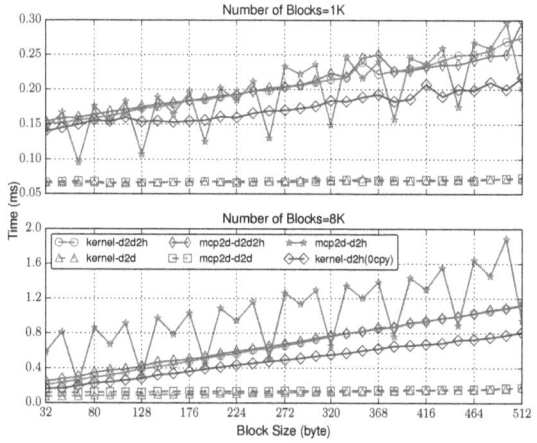

Figure 8: *vector* pack/unpack performance vs *cudaMemcpy2D*. "kernel" represents our pack/unpack kernels. "mcp2d" represents *cudaMemcpy2D*. "d2d" represents non-contiguous data packed into a GPU buffer. "d2d2h" represents "d2d" followed by a device-host data movement. "d2h" means non-contiguous GPU data moved directly into CPU buffer.

is contiguous in memory with a size smaller by one element than the size of the previous column; and the strides between consecutive columns are equal to the previous stride plus 1, which can be described by an *indexed* type (shown as "T" in the following figures). First, we evaluate the performance of our packing/unpacking kernels by measuring GPU memory bandwidth. Figure 6 presents the GPU memory bandwidth achieved from packing these two datatypes into local GPU buffer using our CUDA kernel compared with moving contiguous data of the same size using *cudaMemcpy*. *cudaMemcpy* is already the optimal implementation for moving contiguous GPU data, which can be treated as the practical peak of GPU memory bandwidth. Compared to *cudaMemcpy*, our GPU packing kernel is able to obtain 94% of the practical peak for a *vector* type. The memory instructions in the unpacking kernel are the same as the ones in the packing kernel – but in the opposite direction – and therefore the unpacking kernel delivers the same performance as packing kernels; this is not presented in the figure. For a triangular matrix, each column has a different size, which results in inefficient occupancy of the CUDA kernels; therefore, a GPU packing kernel is only able to achieve 80% of the GPU memory's peak bandwidth. In order to prove that the bandwidth difference between the sub-matrix and the triangular matrix is indeed from the less efficient GPU occupancy, the triangular matrix is modified to a stair-like triangular matrix (Figure 5). Thus, the occupancy issue can be reduced by setting the stair size *nb* to a multiple of a CUDA block size to ensure no CUDA thread is idle. Sure enough, it is able to deliver almost the same bandwidth as the *vector* type.

After studying the performance of the packing/unpacking kernels, we measure the intra-process performance of packing non-contiguous GPU-resident data to evaluate the GPU datatype engine. Because of the current limitation of GPUDirect, using an intermediate host buffer for sending and receiving over the network is better for large messages than direct communication between remote GPUs in an InfiniBand environment [14]. Thus, studying the case of going through host memory is also necessary. In the following benchmark, one process is launched to pack the non-contiguous GPU data into a local GPU buffer, followed by a data movement to copy the packed GPU data into host memory; and then, the unpacking procedure moves the data from host memory back into the original GPU memory with the non-contiguous layout. Accordingly, the time measurement of the benchmarks in this section contains two parts: "d2d" measures the time of packing/unpacking non-contiguous data into/from a contiguous GPU buffer; and "d2d2h" measures the time of packing/unpacking plus the round trip device-host data movements. We also apply *zero copy*, shown as "0cpy," to use the CUDA UMA to map the CPU buffer to GPU memory. In this case, the GPU to CPU data movement is taken care of by hardware implicitly. Since *zero copy* involves implicit data transfer, we are only able to measure its total time without having a separate in-GPU pack/unpack time to show in figures.

Figure 7 shows the results of a double precision sub-matrix and lower triangular matrix, with respect to matrix size. From the figure, a number of interesting trends can be observed. First, the pipelining discussed in Section 3.2 overlaps the preparation of the CUDA DEVs with GPU pack/unpack kernels, almost doubling the performance. If the CUDA DEVs are cached in GPU memory (shown as "cached"), the preparation cost can be omitted; therefore, by caching the CUDA DEVs, the packing/unpacking performance is improved when working on data types of the same format. Second, even though it takes the same time (if CUDA DEVs are not cached) to pack/unpack a sub-matrix and triangular matrix of the same matrix size on a GPU, one must note that the triangular matrix is half the size of a sub-matrix; therefore, compared with a vector approach, the overhead of CUDA DEVs preparation is significant – even with pipelining – which also demonstrates the importance of caching the CUDA DEVs. Since the MPI datatype describes data layout format, not data location, by spending a few MBs of GPU memory to cache the CUDA DEVs, the packing/unpacking performance could be significantly improved when using the

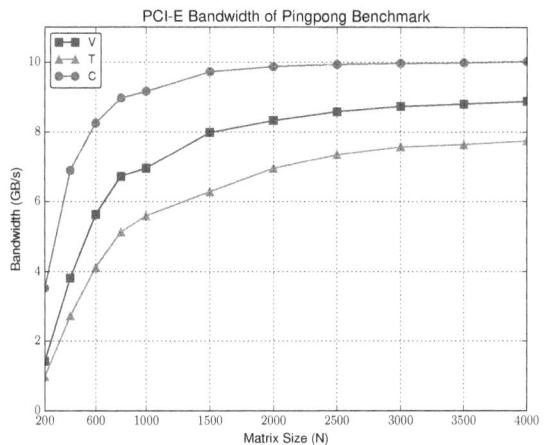

Figure 9: PCI-E bandwidth of vector and indexed data type comparing with contiguous data.

same data type repetitively. Third, since *zero copy* is able to overlap the device-host communication with the GPU kernel, it is slightly faster than explicitly moving data between device and host memory after/before pack/unpack kernels. In all remaining figures, the *zero copy* is always enabled if going through host memory is required.

Alternatively, CUDA provides a two-dimensional memory copy *cudaMemcpy2D* to move vector-like data. Figure 8 presents the comparison between our *vector* pack/unpack kernel and *cudaMemcpy2D*, when the numbers of contiguous blocks are fixed at 1000 and 8000, while block size varies covering both small and large problems. Since using our pack kernel to move vector-like non-contiguous GPU data is equivalent to initiating a device to host data movement using *cudaMemcpy2D*, we test it in three ways (device-to-device"mcp-d2d", device-to-device-to-host "mcp2d-d2d2h", and device-to-host "mcp2d-d2h"). As seen in the figure, the performance of *cudaMemcpy2D* between device and host memory highly depends on the block size: block sizes that are a multiple of 64 bytes perform better, while others experience significant performance regression – especially when the problem size increases. For non-contiguous data movement within a GPU, our kernels achieve almost the same performance as *cudaMemcpy2D*. Our DEV pack/unpack kernel is not compared with CUDA since CUDA does not provide any alternative function for irregular non-contiguous GPU data movement.

5.2 Full Evaluation: GPU-GPU Communication with MPI

In this section, we evaluate the performance of the GPU datatype engine integration with the Open MPI infrastructure. The performance is assessed using an MPI "ping-pong" benchmark. In a shared memory environment, the RDMA protocol over CUDA IPC is used to avoid extraneous memory copies between host and device. In a distributed memory setting, GPU data goes through host memory for communication. According to [14], even though the GPUDirect RDMA allows direct intra-node GPU data communication, it only delivers interesting performance for small messages (less than 30KB), which is not a typical problem size of GPU applications. Instead, when pipelining through host memory

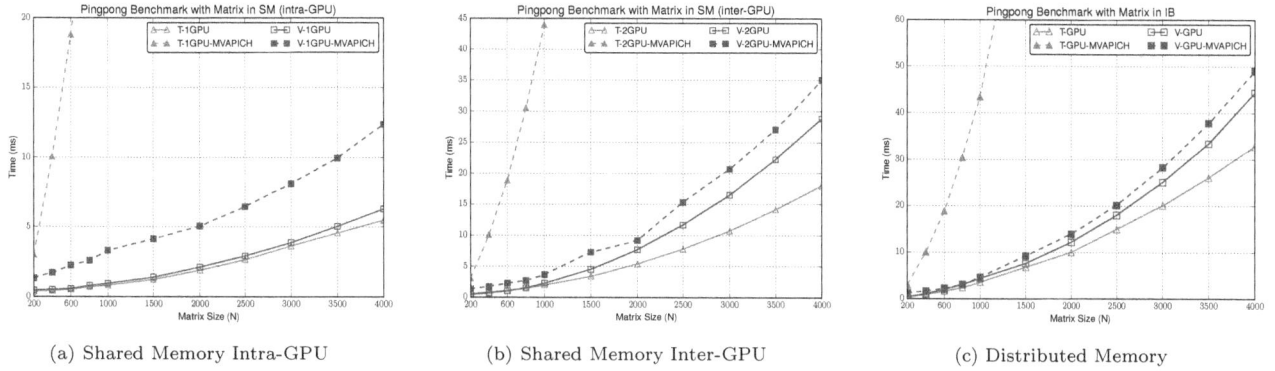

(a) Shared Memory Intra-GPU	(b) Shared Memory Inter-GPU	(c) Distributed Memory

Figure 10: Ping-pong benchmark with matrices. "V" refers to sub-matrix, "T" refers to triangular matrix.

and overlapping GPU pack/unpack kernels, the GPU-CPU data movement and inter-node data transfer performs better. Therefore, in a distributed memory environment, we always pipeline through host memory. Based on such a setup, packed GPU data always goes through PCI-E for communication no matter if it is in a shared or distributed memory environment; thus, PCI-E bandwidth could be a bottleneck of overall communication in a ping-pong benchmark. Similar to last section, we first evaluate the integration of the GPU datatype engine with OpenMPI by measuring PCI-E bandwidth achieved by *vector* and *indexed* datatypes, comparing data in contiguous format of the same size, with results shown in Figure 9. Thanks to the pipeline mechanism discussed in Section 4, we achieved 90% and 78% of the PCI-E bandwidth for *vector* and *indexed* types, respectively, by selecting a proper pipeline size.

Then, in the following ping-pong benchmarks, we explore both a shared memory ("SM") and a distributed memory (using InfiniBand "IB") environment under the following configurations with several commonly used data types, and compare them with the state-of-art MVAPICH2:

- "1GPU": both sender and receiver use the same GPU.

- "2GPU": sender and receiver use different GPUs. Data is sent over network (PCI-E or InfiniBand) to the receiver process.

- "CPU": the non-contiguous data is in host memory. This benchmarks the Open MPI CPU datatype engine.

5.2.1 Vector and Indexed Type

Figure 10 presents the ping-pong benchmark with regard to the matrix size in both "SM" and "IB" environments. As discussed in Section 4.1, in the "SM" environment with CUDA IPC support, we provide two options for unpacking in the receiver side: first, the receiver unpacks directly from the packed buffer in the remote GPU memory; second, the receiver process copies the packed buffer into a local GPU buffer prior to unpacking. The first option involves a lot of small chunks of data fetching from remote device memory, generating too much traffic and under-utilizing the PCI-E. In comparison, the second option groups small data into a big data movement between GPUs, minimizing the traffic on the PCI-E and becoming faster. Based on our experiment, by using a local GPU buffer, the performance is 5-10% faster than directly accessing remote GPU memory; so limited by the space, we always use the second option in later

benchmarks. The "1GPU" case omits the data movement between GPUs, being at least 2x faster than any "2GPU" case. Therefore, even though data is already packed to a contiguous format, the data transfer between GPUs over PCI-E is still the bottleneck of non-contiguous GPU data communication in an "SM" environment. Compared with MVAPICH2, our implementation is always significantly faster, independent of the datatype. Because of MVAPICH2's vectorization algorithm converting any type of datatype into a set of vector datatypes [15], each contiguous block in such an *indexed* datatype is considered as a single vector type and packed/unpacked separately, resulting in sub-optimal performance. As seen in the figure, their *indexed* implementation is slow, going outside the time range once the matrix size reached 1000.

In an "IB" environment, even though data is transitioned through host memory before being sent over the network, thanks to *zero copy*, the device-to-host transfers are handled automatically by the hardware, and this transfer is overlapped with the execution of the GPU pack/unpack kernels. In this environment we notice a significantly more desirable behavior from MVAPICH2, at least for the vector type. However, our approach achieves a roughly 10% improvement for the *vector* type. Similar to the *indexed* result of "SM" environment, the MVAPICH2 performance is quickly outside the range for matrices as small as 1500.

5.2.2 Vector-Contiguous

When using MPI datatypes, the sender and the receiver can have different datatypes as long as the datatype signatures are identical. Such features improve the application's ability to reshape data on the fly, such as in FFT and matrix transpose. In FFT, one side uses a *vector*, and the other side uses a *contiguous* type. Figure 11 shows the ping-pong performance with such datatypes of different sizes. As seen in the figure, taking the benefit of GPU RDMA and *zero copy*, our implementation performs better than MVAPICH2 in both shared and distributed memory environments.

5.2.3 Matrix Transpose

Matrix transpose is a very complex operation and a good stress-test for a datatype engine. With column-major storage, each column is contiguous in memory. A matrix can be described by a *contiguous* type or *vector* type if only accessing the sub-matrix. After the transpose, each column can be represented by a *vector* type with a block length of 1 element; consequently, the whole transposed matrix is a collection of N *vector* types. Figure 12 shows the bench-

239

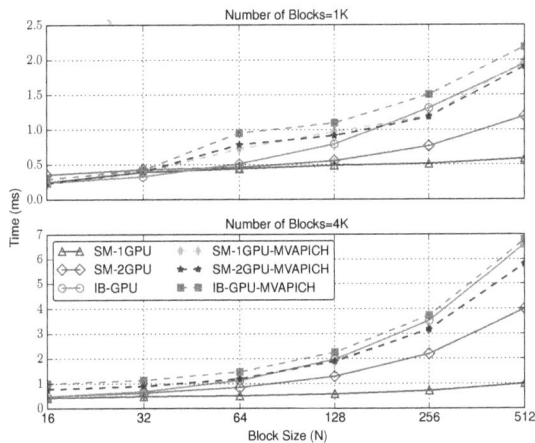

Figure 11: Ping-pong benchmark with vector and contiguous data type.

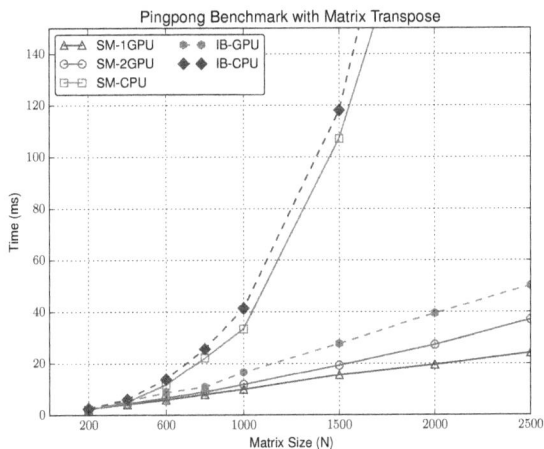

Figure 12: Ping-pong benchmark for matrix transpose in both shared and distributed memory environment.

mark for a matrix transpose depending on the matrix size. Since there is only 1 element in each block, the memory access is not following the coalesced rule, and the performance is not comparable with the regular *vector* type. However, such difficulty also occurs in the CPU implementation, benefiting from the parallel capability and high memory bandwidth, our GPU datatype implementation is at least 10x faster than the CPU version of Open MPI. Lacking stable support for such a datatype, MVAPICH2 crashed in this experiment and is not included in the figure.

5.3 GPU Resources of Packing/Unpacking Kernels

In previous benchmarks, GPU packing/unpacking kernels aggressively used CUDA's Streaming Multiprocessor (SM). Figure 6 shows that by using as many CUDA cores as possible, the kernels are able to achieve more than 80 GB/s of GPU memory bandwidth. However, in most cases, each MPI process is attached to a separate GPU; since GPUs are connected by PCI-E, then the communication bandwidth

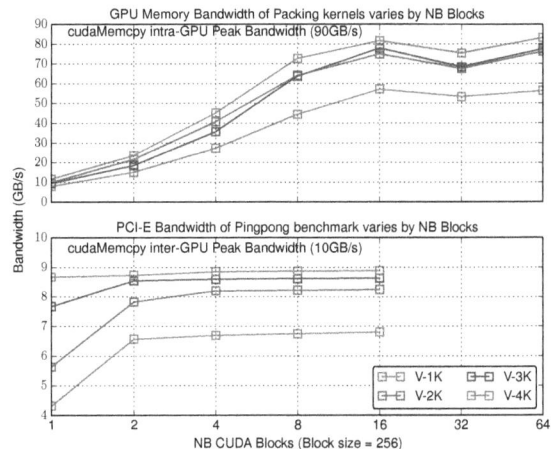

Figure 13: GPU memory and PCI-E bandwidth of pack/unpack sub-matrix "V" data types varies by number of blocks used for kernel launching. Matrix size varies from 1K to 4K.

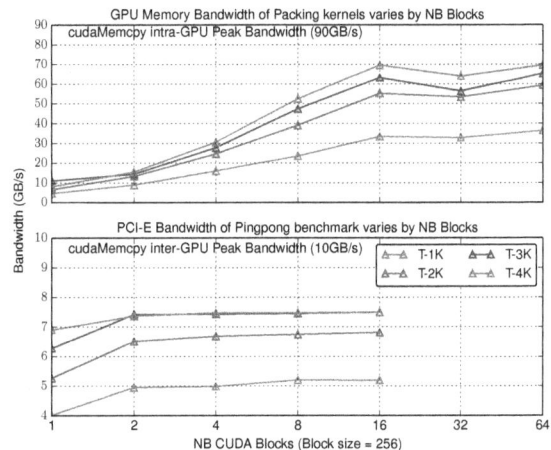

Figure 14: GPU memory and PCI-E bandwidth of pack/unpack triangular matrix "T" data types varies by number of blocks used for kernel launching. Matrix size varies from 1K to 4K.

is limited to the 10 GB/s available through PCI-E. In this section, we investigate the minimal resources required to fulfill the PCI-E bandwidth. The top figures of Figure 13 and Figure 14 present the GPU memory bandwidth of packing/unpacking kernels for sub-matrix "V" and triangular matrix "T" data types. NVIDIA's Kepler GPU has four warp schedulers per SM; therefore, in order to achieve the best GPU occupancy, the block size should be a multiple of 128 threads (32 threads per warp). In the benchmark, we use 256 threads per block. As seen in the figure, it requires 16 blocks to achieve the peak bandwidth, and achieves 10 GB/s (the peak of PCI-E bandwidth) by launching only 2 blocks in most cases. Hence, theoretically, by using no more than 2 blocks, the cost of packing/unpacking can be hidden by communication over PCI-E when pipelining is applied. Similarly, bottom figures of Figure 13 and Figure 14 illustrates that the PCI-E bandwidth of the same two data types varies

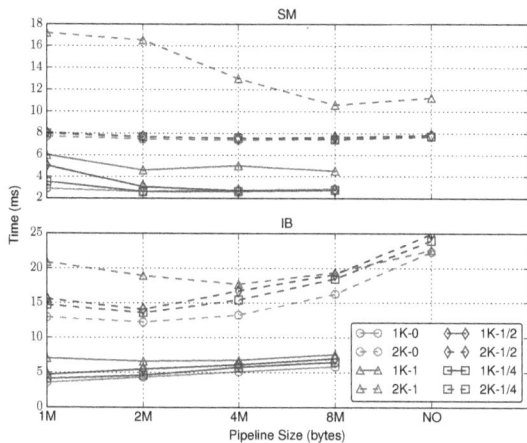

Figure 15: Ping-pong benchmark with partial GPU resources available. In the legend, the number after the matrix size is the ratio of GPU resources occupied.

by the number of blocks used for kernel launching. As seen in the figure, as we expected, the bandwidth becomes stable when using at least 2 CUDA blocks. The K40 GPU has 15 SMs, so in the worst case, one seventh of the GPU SMs are required to overlap the cost of packing/unpacking kernels with communications over PCI-E. In other cases when each MPI process is attached to the same GPU or future NVLink is introduced with higher bandwidth, our GPU datatype engine can be easily adapted by tuning CUDA blocks to fulfill bandwidth.

5.4 Pipeline and Resource Contention Effects

All previous benchmarks were executed under the assumption that the GPU resources are readily available for pack/unpack. As in some cases, overlapping communication with computation is possible, the application might be using the GPU while MPI communications with non-contiguous datatypes are ongoing. In this section, we investigate how resource contention affects the pack/unpack performance, as well as the pipelining discussed in Sec 4.

In this benchmark, we launch a special kernel to continuously occupy a fixed percentage of the GPU while executing the ping-pong benchmark. The grid size of the kernel varies to occupy full, half, or a quarter of the GPU resources; we then measure the ping-pong performance under these scenarios. The datatypes used are (*vector*) sub-matrices of size 1000 by 1000 and 2000 by 2000, since they are typical problem sizes for GPU applications in the linear algebra domain. The results are shown in Figure 15. Thanks to the pipelining methodology, a proper pipeline size improves the performance in both shared and distributed memory machines. However, as seen in the figure, with a small pipeline size the pack/unpack operations are divided into many small GPU kernels, and the scheduling of such kernels could be delayed by the CUDA runtime when the occupancy of the GPU is high. Our GPU pack/unpack kernels mainly contain memory operations without floating point operations, and they are memory bound. Therefore, as long as the GPU is not fully occupied, our pack/unpack methodology is not signifi-

cantly affected. By using a proper pipeline size, we limit the loss of performance to under 10%.

6. CONCLUSIONS

As heterogeneous compute nodes become more pervasive, the need for programming paradigms capable of providing transparent access to all types of resources becomes critical. The GPU datatype engine presented in this paper takes advantage of the parallel capability of the GPUs to provide a highly efficient in-GPU datatype packing and unpacking. We integrate the GPU datatype engine into the state-of-art Open MPI library, at a level of integration such that all communications with contiguous or non-contiguous datatypes will transparently use the best packing/unpacking approach. The different protocols proposed, RDMA, copy in/out, pipeline, and the use of novel technologies, such as GPUDirect, drastically improve the performance of the non-contiguous data movements, when the source and/or the destination buffers are GPU-resident. The described principles can be extended to other accelerators, and other types of networks in a simple manner. They can also be the basic blocks for defining and implementing concepts outside the scope of point-to-point constructs, such as collective and RDMA operations.

7. ACKNOWLEDGMENTS

This material is based upon work supported by the National Science Foundation under award #1339820. We would also like to thank NVIDIA for their support and for providing access to their resources.

8. REFERENCES

[1] A. M. Aji, J. Dinan, D. Buntinas, P. Balaji, W.-c. Feng, K. R. Bisset, and R. Thakur. MPI-ACC: An Integrated and Extensible Approach to Data Movement in Accelerator-based Systems. In *HPCC'12*, pages 647–654, Washington, DC, USA, 2012.

[2] L. S. Blackford, J. Choi, A. Cleary, E. D'Azeuedo, J. Demmel, I. Dhillon, S. Hammarling, G. Henry, A. Petitet, K. Stanley, D. Walker, and R. C. Whaley. *ScaLAPACK User's Guide*. Society for Industrial and Applied Mathematics, Philadelphia, PA, USA, 1997.

[3] A. Danalis, G. Marin, C. McCurdy, J. S. Meredith, P. C. Roth, K. Spafford, V. Tipparaju, and J. S. Vetter. The Scalable Heterogeneous Computing (SHOC) Benchmark Suite. In *GPGPU-3 Workshop*, pages 63–74, New York, NY, USA, 2010.

[4] T. Eicken, D. Culler, S. Goldstein, and K. Schauser. Active Messages: A Mechanism for Integrated Communication and Computation. In *ISCA'92*, pages 256–266, 1992.

[5] M. Forum. MPI-2: Extensions to the message-passing interface. In *Univ. of Tennessee, Knoxville, Tech Report*, 1996.

[6] E. Gabriel, G. E. Fagg, G. Bosilca, T. Angskun, J. J. Dongarra, J. M. Squyres, V. Sahay, P. Kambadur, B. Barrett, A. Lumsdaine, R. H. Castain, D. J. Daniel, R. L. Graham, and T. S. Woodall. Open MPI: Goals, concept, and design of a next generation MPI implementation. In *EuroMPI'04*, pages 97–104, Budapest, Hungary, 2004.

[7] J. Jenkins, J. Dinan, P. Balaji, T. Peterka, N. Samatova, and R. Thakur. Processing MPI Derived Datatypes on Noncontiguous GPU-Resident Data. *Parallel and Distributed Systems, IEEE Transactions on*, 25(10):2627–2637, Oct 2014.

[8] O. Lawlor. Message passing for GPGPU clusters: CudaMPI. In *CLUSTER'09.*, pages 1–8, Aug 2009.

[9] NVIDIA. NVIDIA CUDA Toolkit Documentation. http://docs.nvidia.com/cuda/index.html, 2015.

[10] NVIDIA. NVIDIA GPUDirect. https://developer.nvidia.com/gpudirect, 2015.

[11] S. Potluri, D. Bureddy, H. Wang, H. Subramoni, and D. Panda. Extending OpenSHMEM for GPU Computing. In *IPDPS'13*, pages 1001–1012, May 2013.

[12] R. Ross, N. Miller, and W. Gropp. Implementing Fast and Reusable Datatype Processing. In *Recent Advances in Parallel Virtual Machine and Message Passing Interface*, volume 2840 of *Lecture Notes in Computer Science*, pages 404–413. Springer Berlin Heidelberg, 2003.

[13] T. Schneider, R. Gerstenberger, and T. Hoefler. Micro-Applications for Communication Data Access Patterns and MPI Datatypes. In *EuroMPI'12*, pages 121–131, 2012.

[14] R. vandeVaart. Open MPI with RDMA support and CUDA. In *NVIDIA GTC'14*, 2014.

[15] H. Wang, S. Potluri, D. Bureddy, C. Rosales, and D. Panda. GPU-Aware MPI on RDMA-Enabled Clusters: Design, Implementation and Evaluation. *Parallel and Distributed Systems, IEEE Transactions on*, 25(10):2595–2605, Oct 2014.

[16] H. Wang, S. Potluri, M. Luo, A. Singh, X. Ouyang, S. Sur, and D. Panda. Optimized Non-contiguous MPI Datatype Communication for GPU Clusters: Design, Implementation and Evaluation with MVAPICH2. In *CLUSTER'11*, pages 308–316, Sept 2011.

[17] H. Wang, S. Potluri, M. Luo, A. K. Singh, S. Sur, and D. K. Panda. MVAPICH2-GPU: Optimized GPU to GPU Communication for InfiniBand Clusters. *Computer Science - Research and Development*, 26(3-4):257–266, 2011.

[18] L. Wang, W. Wu, Z. Xu, J. Xiao, and Y. Yang. BLASX: A High Performance Level-3 BLAS Library for Heterogeneous Multi-GPU Computing. In *ICS'16*, Istanbul, Turkey, 2016.

Implications of Heterogeneous Memories in Next Generation Server Systems

Ada Gavrilovska
Georgia Institute of Technology
ada@cc.gatech.edu

ABSTRACT

Next generation datacenter and exascale machines will include significantly larger amounts of memory, greater heterogeneity in the performance, persistence or sharing properties of the memory components they encompass, and increase in the relative cost and complexity of the data paths in the resulting memory topology. This poses several challenges to the systems software stacks managing these memory-centric platform designs. First, technology advances in novel memory technologies shift the data access bottlenecks into the software stack. Second, current systems software lacks capabilities to bridge the multi-dimensional non-uniformity in the memory subsystem to the dynamic nature of the workloads it must support. In addition, current memory management solutions have limited ability to explicitly reason about the costs and tradeoffs associated with data movement operations, leading to limited efficiency of their interconnect use. To address these problems, next generation systems software stacks require new data structures, abstractions and mechanisms in order to enable new levels of efficiency in the data placement, movement, and transformation decisions that govern the underlying memory use. In this talk, I will present our approach to rearchitecting systems software and services in response to both node-level and system-wide memory heterogeneity and scale, particularly concerning the presence of non-volatile memories, and will demonstrate the resulting performance and efficiency gains using several scientific and data-intensive workloads.

Biography

Dr. Ada Gavrilovska is a Senior Research Scientist at the College of Computing and the Center for Experimental Research in Computer Systems (CERCS) at Georgia Tech. Her research is centered on innovation of the systems software stack, driven by emerging hardware technologies, and focused on supporting data- and communication-intensive applications. Recent projects include systems software innovation in light of large-scale parallelism in multicores, platform-wide compute and memory heterogeneity, novel interconnect capabilities and increases in device-level computational resource density. Gavrilovska's research is supported by the National Science Foundation, the US Department of Energy, and industry grants, including from Cisco, HP, IBM, Intel, Intercontinental Exchange, LexisNexis, VMware, and others. She has published over eighty peer-reviewed papers, and edited a book "High Performance Communications: A Vertical Approach" (CRC Press, 2009). In addition to research, she also teaches courses on operating systems and high performance communications. She has a BS degree in Electrical Engineering from University Sts. Cyril and Methodius in Macedonia ('98), and a MS ('99) and PhD ('04) degrees in Computer Science from Georgia Tech.

HPDC'16 May 31 - June 04, 2016, Kyoto, Japan

© 2016 Copyright held by the owner/author(s).

ACM ISBN 978-1-4503-4314-5/16/05.

DOI: http://dx.doi.org/10.1145/2907294.2911993

Efficient Processing of Large Graphs via Input Reduction

[1]Amlan Kusum   [1]Keval Vora   [1]Rajiv Gupta   [2]Iulian Neamtiu

[1]Department of Computer Science, University of California, Riverside
{akusu001, kvora001, gupta}@cs.ucr.edu
[2]Department of Computer Science, New Jersey Institute Of Technology
ineamtiu@njit.edu

ABSTRACT

Large-scale parallel graph analytics involves executing iterative algorithms (e.g., PageRank, Shortest Paths, etc.) that are both data- and compute-intensive. In this work we construct faster versions of iterative graph algorithms from their original counterparts using input graph reduction. A large input graph is transformed into a small graph using a sequence of *input reduction* transformations. Savings in execution time are achieved using our *two phased processing model* that effectively runs the original iterative algorithm in two phases: first, using the reduced input graph to gain savings in execution time; and second, using the original input graph along with the results from the first phase for computing precise results. We propose several *input reduction transformations* and identify the *structural and non-structural properties* that they guarantee, which in turn are used to ensure the correctness of results while using our two phased processing model. We further present a *unified input reduction algorithm* that efficiently applies a *non-interfering* sequence of simple *local* input reduction transformations. Our experiments show that our transformation techniques enable significant reductions in execution time (1.25×-2.14×) while achieving precise final results for most of the algorithms. For cases where precise results cannot be achieved, the relative error remains very small (at most 0.065).

CCS Concepts

•Computing methodologies → **Parallel computing methodologies;** *Parallel programming languages;*

Keywords

Graph Processing; Input Reduction; Iterative Algorithms

1. INTRODUCTION

With the proliferation of data, parallel graph analytics has become a difficult task because it involves executing iterative algorithms on very large graphs. This has led researchers to explore acceleration strategies, some of which produce approximate results. There are two main strategies

HPDC'16, May 31-June 04, 2016, Kyoto, Japan

© 2016 ACM. ISBN 978-1-4503-4314-5/16/05. . . $15.00

DOI: http://dx.doi.org/10.1145/2907294.2907312

for approximate computing: *algorithmic* [5, 18, 1] and *code-centric* [21, 20, 29, 25, 2, 27]. The *algorithmic* approach is application specific and thus the ideas for one application may not transfer to others. The *code-centric* approach transforms the application so that at runtime it switches between code versions or skips computations to save time, albeit sacrificing accuracy. However, for applications whose behavior is input sensitive, intelligent skipping is difficult as the program *lacks global view* of input characteristics.

In this paper we present a general approach for accelerating *parallel vertex-centric iterative graph algorithms* that repeatedly process large graphs until convergence. Even though these algorithms are parallel, their execution times can be large for real-world inputs. Thus there is a great deal of benefit in approximating them to save processing time. The novel aspect of our two-phased approach is that it is *input data-centric*. In the first phase, the original (*unchanged*) iterative algorithm is applied on a smaller graph which is representative of the original large input graph; this step yields savings in execution time. In the second phase, the results from the smaller graph are transferred to the original larger graph and, via application of the original graph algorithm, *error reduction* is achieved, possibly converging to the *final accurate results*. The additional time required to process the reduced graph in the first phase (T_{phase1}) pays off as it is significantly lower than the savings achieved by the second phase ($T_{original} - T_{phase2}$); hence the overall processing time reduces from $T_{original}$ to $T_{phase1} + T_{phase2}$.

To reduce the size of input graphs, we propose light-weight vertex-level *input reduction* transformations whose application is guided by their impact on *graph connectivity* (i.e., the global structure of the graph). While there exist works [7, 17, 3, 18, 23, 35, 9, 8, 10] that reduce the size of graphs to accelerate processing, they mainly present algorithm-specific reduction techniques and mostly operate of regular meshes. [7, 17] present a multilevel graph partitioning algorithm where first a hierarchy of smaller graphs is created, then the highest level graphs are partitioned and then, these partition results are carefully propagated back down the hierarchy to achieve partitioning of the original graph. They use edge contraction or maximal independent set computation over dual graph which are suitable for relatively regular mesh structures but can be computationally expensive. [3, 9, 8, 10] also partition graphs via recursive edge contraction using maximal independent set computation to generate multinodes. In contrast, we identify light-weight, local and non-interfering transformations which are general (i.e., not algorithm-specific) and are suitable for reducing large irregular input graphs. Moreover, our reduction strategy is not hierarchical (multi-level) since our transformations are designed from the vertex's perspective and are applied at most once on each vertex. Other works like [23, 35] are specifically designed for certain problems (e.g., shortest paths) and require path-level or component-level transformations that involve computationally intensive pre-processing. Our transformations are vertex-level, light-weight, ans suitable for large irregular graphs.

Upon carefully studying various characteristics of vertex centric algorithms and properties of input reduction transformations, we show that it is possible to *achieve fully accurate results* for a subclass of graph algorithms, while remaining algorithms produce approximate solutions. In comparison to *algorithmic* works our approach is more general and in contrast to *code-centric* our approach has two advantages:

– *Input Data-centric Approximation:* via graph reduction, we achieve the effect of skipping computations like the *code-centric* approach. However, since skipping is achieved as a consequence of input graph reduction that is performed as a preprocessing phase, the decision of what to skip is sensitive to the structure of the input graph – graph *connectivity* guides the application of transformations.

– *Uncompromised Processing Algorithm:* our approach requires *no changes to the core graph analysis algorithm.* The original algorithm is used until convergence on the reduced graph and then on the full graph for error reduction. With careful choice of input transformations, the algorithm's capability can remain *uncompromised*, i.e., upon convergence the error reduction phase can give precise results.

We evaluate our two-phased processing technique in a shared memory environment using Galois [19], a state-of-the-art parallel execution and graph processing framework. Our experiments with six graph algorithms and multiple real-world graphs show that our techniques achieve an average speedup of 1.25×-2.14× while achieving precise final results for five benchmarks and approximate results for one with very low relative error (at most 0.065).

2. OVERVIEW OF OUR APPROACH

This section provides an overview of our two phased processing model. While graph reduction based processing strategies are used in various works like [7, 17], we focus on iterative general purpose graph algorithms and operate on a single reduced graph along with the original input graph (i.e., there are no multiple levels in the hierarchy). We use the vertex-centric programming model as it is intuitive and commonly used by many graph processing systems like GraphLab [15], GraphX [34], and Galois [19]. We consider directed graphs in our discussion; our approach easily simplifies to handle undirected graphs.

Given an iterative vertex-centric graph algorithm $i\mathcal{A}$ and a large input graph $\mathcal{G}$, the accurate results of vertex values $V_{\mathcal{G}}$ can be computed by applying $i\mathcal{A}$ to $\mathcal{G}$, that is:

$$V_{\mathcal{G}} = i\mathcal{A}(\mathcal{G})$$

To accelerate this computation, we use the following steps:

- Reduce input $\mathcal{G}$ to $\mathcal{G}'$: we transform the large input graph $\mathcal{G}$ into a smaller graph $\mathcal{G}'$ via multiple applications of an input reduction transformation $\mathcal{T}$.

- Compute results for $\mathcal{G}'$: we apply $i\mathcal{A}$ to $\mathcal{G}'$ to compute $V_{\mathcal{G}'}$. Computing on $V_{\mathcal{G}'}$ takes lesser time than on $V_{\mathcal{G}}$.

- Obtain results for $\mathcal{G}$: using simple mapping rules $m\mathcal{R}$s, we convert the results $V_{\mathcal{G}'}$ to $V_{\mathcal{G}}^1$. Then, via multiple application of update rules in $i\mathcal{A}$, we reduce the error in $V_{\mathcal{G}}^1$ and obtain the result $V_{\mathcal{G}}^2$.

Thus, our approach replaces computation $V_{\mathcal{G}} = i\mathcal{A}(\mathcal{G})$ by:

[INPUT REDUCTION]	$\mathcal{G}' = \mathcal{T}^{\Delta}(\mathcal{G})$
[PHASE 1]	$V_{\mathcal{G}'} = i\mathcal{A}(\mathcal{G}')$
[MAP RESULTS]	$m\mathcal{R} : V_{\mathcal{G}'} \to V_{\mathcal{G}}^1$
[PHASE 2]	$V_{\mathcal{G}}^2 = i\mathcal{A}(V_{\mathcal{G}}^1, \mathcal{G})$

where Δ is a parameter that controls the degree of reduction performed as it represents the number of applications of $\mathcal{T}$ to $\mathcal{G}$. Thus, the greater the value of Δ, the smaller the size of the reduced graph $\mathcal{G}'$. Depending on various properties of input reduction transformations $\mathcal{T}$ (Section 3.2) and the nature of iterative algorithm $i\mathcal{A}$, the computed values will be accurate, i.e., $V_{\mathcal{G}}^2 = V_{\mathcal{G}}$. However, we identify cases in which $V_{\mathcal{G}}^2$ may not be the same as $V_{\mathcal{G}}$ (Section 4) — the computed results are *approximate* for those cases.

2.1 Efficient Input Reduction Transformations

Given the iterative nature of algorithms considered, applying $i\mathcal{A}$ to $\mathcal{G}'$ as opposed to $\mathcal{G}$ is expected to result in execution time savings. However, these savings can be offset by the extra overhead due to application of input reduction transformations and result converting rules. Therefore we must ensure that these steps are simpler than the iterative computation that they aim to avoid. We do so by placing the following restrictions on the kind of transformation that is allowed (*local*) and the sequence of its application (*non-interfering*) permitted for reducing $\mathcal{G}$ to $\mathcal{G}'$.

A. Local transformation. Transformation $\mathcal{T}(v, \mathcal{G})$, where v is a vertex in $\mathcal{G}$, is a *local* transformation if its application only examines edges directly connected to v. The subgraph involving v and its edges is denoted as subGraph($\mathcal{T}(v, \mathcal{G})$).

$$\mathcal{G}_1 \leftarrow \mathcal{T}(v_1, \mathcal{G}); \quad \mathcal{G}_2 \leftarrow \mathcal{T}(v_2, \mathcal{G}_1) \quad \cdots$$
$$\cdots \quad \mathcal{G}_{\Delta-1} \leftarrow \mathcal{T}(v_{\Delta-1}, \mathcal{G}_{\Delta-2}); \quad \mathcal{G}' \leftarrow \mathcal{T}(v_\Delta, \mathcal{G}_{\Delta-1})$$

B. Non-interfering sequence. $\mathcal{T}^{\Delta}$, a sequence of Δ applications of local transformation $\mathcal{T}$ as shown above is *non-interfering* if and only if: vertices $v_1 \cdots v_\Delta$ are distinct vertices in $\mathcal{G}$; and each subGraph($\mathcal{T}(v_i, \mathcal{G})$) is contained in $\mathcal{G}$. Note that the above restrictions (local and non-interfering) ensure that input reduction is performed via a single pass over the original graph because:

- An edge $v_i \to v_j$ from $\mathcal{G}$ is only examined when considering the application of $\mathcal{T}$ to v_i or v_j; and

- Any vertex or edge created during one application of $\mathcal{T}$ cannot be involved in any other application of $\mathcal{T}$.

Thus, the cost of applying the transformation sequence is linear in the size of $\mathcal{G}$, i.e., the number of vertices and edges in it. Moreover, the cost of converting results is proportional to the size of the transformed portions of $\mathcal{G}$. In contrast, those computations over the transformed portions of $\mathcal{G}$ that we avoid would have required repeated passes due to the iterative nature of graph algorithms considered.

In conclusion, the restrictions on transformations and sequences ensure that the cost of applying them will be less than the cost of the computation they avoid, leading to net savings in execution time.

Algorithm 1 Iterative Vertex-Centric Graph Algorithm.

```
1:  function TPIA ( input G )
2:      G' ← ReduceGraph ( G, T, Δ )
3:      V¹_G ← IA(G')
4:      V²_G ← IAP2(V¹_G, G)
5:      return V²_G
6:  end function

7:  function ReduceGraph ( G, T, Δ )
8:      G' ← G
9:      for ( Vertex v : G ) do
10:         if ( NI ( subGraph(T(v,G)) ) then
11:             G' ← T(v,G')
12:             Δ ← Δ − 1
13:             if ( Δ == 0 ) then break end if
14:         end if
15:     end for
16:     return G'
17: end function

18: function IA ( input G )
19:     Initialize V_G & WorkQ
20:     while ( ! WorkQ.empty ) do
21:         v ← WorkQ.getFirst()
22:         if ( UpdateVals (v, V_G) ) then
23:             WorkQ.add ( outNeighbors (v) )
24:         end if
25:     end while
26:     return V_G
27: end function

28: function UpdateVals ( v, V_G )
29:     Updated ← false
30:     if  updateCheck ( v, inNeighbors (v) ) then
31:         update V_G[v]
32:         Updated ← true
33:     end if
34:     return Updated
35: end function

36: function IAP2 ( V¹_G, G )
37:     Initialize WorkQ
38:     for ( Vertex v : G ) do
39:         if ( v ∈ G' ) then
40:             V²_G ( v ) ← V¹_G ( v )
41:         else
42:             V²_G ( v ) ← initval ( )
43:             WorkQ.add ( v )
44:         end if
45:     end for
46:     WorkQ.add ( Vertex v s.t. v is affected by
47:         addition / deletion of edges)
48:     while ( ! WorkQ.empty ) do
49:         v ← WorkQ.getFirst()
50:         if ( UpdateVals (v, V_G) ) then
51:             WorkQ.add ( outNeighbors (v) )
52:         end if
53:     end while
54:     return V_G
55: end function
```

Algorithm 2 SSSP Algorithm.

```
1:  function TwoPhaseSSSP ( input G; srcVertex )
2:      ▷ V_G of a vertex v = length of the
3:      ▷      shortest path from srcVertex to v
4:  end function

5:  function ReduceGraph ( G, T, Δ, srcVertex )
6:      ▷ srcVertex is not part of applied T's
7:  end function

8:  function InitializeSSSP ( input G; srcVertex )
9:      ▷ Initialize V_G
10:     for ( Vertex v : G ) do V_G[v] ← ∞
11:     end for
12:     V_G[srcVertex] ← 0
13:     ▷ Initialize WorkQ
14:     WorkQ.add( outNeighbors(srcVertex) )
15: end function

16: function UpdateVals ( v, V_G )
17:     Updated ← false
18:     for ( Vertex v' : inNeighbors (v) ) do
19:         if V_G[v] > V_G[v'] + wt(v',v) then
20:             V_G[v] ← V_G[v'] + wt(v',v)
21:             Updated ← true
22:         end if
23:     end for
24:     return Updated
25: end function

26: function Phase2SSSP ( V_G', G )
27:     initval() assigns ∞ or results from phase 1
28: end function
```

2.2 Original and Two-Phased Algorithms

Next we summarize our approach by presenting the general form of an original iterative vertex-centric graph algorithm and its corresponding two phased version. In Algorithm 1, function IA represents the original algorithm whose application to graph G produces the accurate (V_G) result. Function TPIA is the two phased version that calls IA and IAP2 in first and second phases. Note that the processing logic in IAP2 (lines 48-53) is exactly the same as that in IA (lines 20-25). The result ($V²_G$) is obtained from the application of TPIA to G. The result obtained from TPIA might not be accurate; we discuss this in Sections 4.1 and 4.2.

ReduceGraph examines the vertices in G one at a time and if $T(v,G')$ is non-interfering with transformations already applied, then it is applied on v. The function NI enforces non-interference by ensuring that all vertices and edges in subGraph($T(v,G)$) are being examined for the first time. The algorithm terminates after applying Δ transformations. The function IAP2 copies results from vertices in G' to vertices in G for each vertex that is present in both graphs. The vertices in G that were eliminated in the process of creating G' are assigned initial values by initval(). Then, similar to IA, UpdateVals is applied to $V²_G$ until convergence.

2.3 Example: Single Source Shortest Paths

Algorithm 2 presents the two-phased version of the Single Source Shortest Paths (SSSP) algorithm. Only the code sequences that are specific to SSSP are shown while other code sequences from Algorithm 1 remain the same. The function UpdateVals() computes the shortest path for a vertex v based on its incoming edges.

(a) Original $\mathcal{G}$.   (b) Transformed $\mathcal{G}'$.

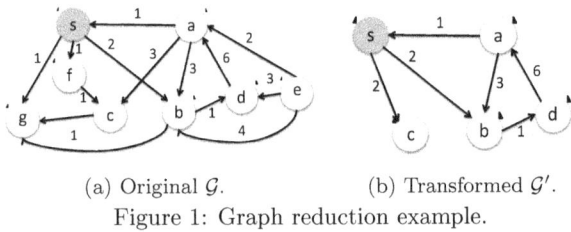

Figure 1: Graph reduction example.

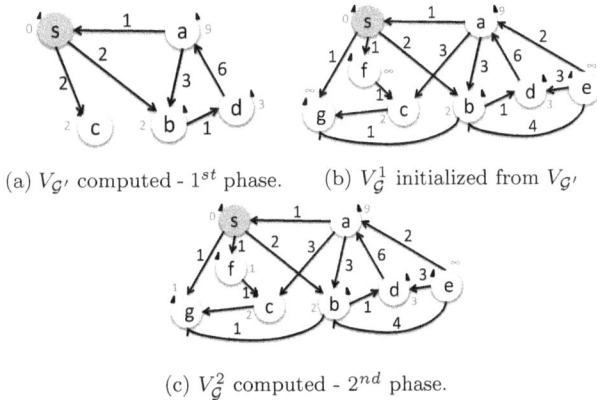

(a) $V_{\mathcal{G}'}$ computed - 1st phase.   (b) $V_{\mathcal{G}}^1$ initialized from $V_{\mathcal{G}'}$

(c) $V_{\mathcal{G}}^2$ computed - 2nd phase.

Figure 2: Two-phased SSSP processing on $\mathcal{G}$ & $\mathcal{G}'$.

Figure 1 illustrates graph reduction by converting $\mathcal{G}$ to $\mathcal{G}'$ and Figure 2 illustrates how the two-phased SSSP algorithm works on the example graph by first computing $V_{\mathcal{G}'}$ (Figure 2-a), then feeding these computed results to $V_{\mathcal{G}}^1$ (Figure 2-b), and then computing $V_{\mathcal{G}}^2$ (Figure 2-c). In this case a single application of UPDATEVALS in the second phase yields precise results (i.e., $V_{\mathcal{G}}^2 = V_{\mathcal{G}}$). In general, for large complex graphs and different applications, this may not be the case; however, the results computed in the first phase will accelerate the second phase.

3. INPUT REDUCTION

We present six transformations to reduce input graph and discuss their properties to gain useful programming insights.

3.1 Transformations for Input Reduction

Since many graph algorithms are super-linear in the number of edges, the goal of graph reduction is to reduce the number of edges in the graph. If all edges involving a node are eliminated, then so is the node. Figure 3 shows the transformations. The red dashed edges are the ones that are eliminated by the transformations. Algorithm 3 presents the algorithm which examines every vertex of the input graph ($\mathcal{G}$), and considers applicability of transformations.

$\mathcal{T}_1/\mathcal{T}_2$. If vertex v has no incoming/outgoing edges, its outgoing/incoming edges are removed and v is dropped.

$\mathcal{T}_3$. For every vertex v with a single incoming and a single outgoing edge, transformation $\mathcal{T}_3$ eliminates v and adds a direct edge between the other end vertices of v's edges. Thus, in a single step we bypass multiple nodes; however, for simplicity we consider bypassing a single node only. Note that $\mathcal{T}_3$ ensures that a path between two vertices v and w is preserved even though direct edges or intervening nodes are dropped.

$\mathcal{T}_4$. For a vertex v with high number of incoming edges,[1]

---

[1] An indegree threshold can be set while using $\mathcal{T}_4$ and $\mathcal{T}_6$. Based on our experiments, we set this threshold to be 1000.

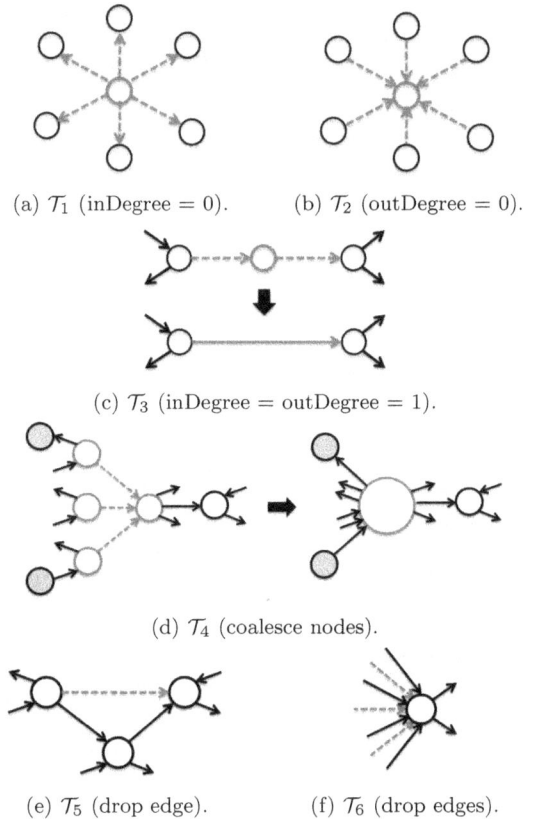

(a) $\mathcal{T}_1$ (inDegree = 0).   (b) $\mathcal{T}_2$ (outDegree = 0).

(c) $\mathcal{T}_3$ (inDegree = outDegree = 1).

(d) $\mathcal{T}_4$ (coalesce nodes).

(e) $\mathcal{T}_5$ (drop edge).   (f) $\mathcal{T}_6$ (drop edges).

Figure 3: Transformations for Input Reduction.

transformation $\mathcal{T}_4$ merges the vertices for those incoming edges with v. $\mathcal{T}_4$ achieves input graph reduction by coalescing directly connected nodes so that the edges connecting them are eliminated and a reduced graph with fewer edges is obtained. This approach does not reduce connectivity, rather it can introduce new directed paths that were not present in the original graph, hence increasing connectivity. As seen in Figure 3, $\mathcal{T}_4$ adds a path between the two gray vertices which is not present in the original graph.

$\mathcal{T}_5$. This transformation drops edge $v \rightarrow w$, if there exists a u such that $v \rightarrow u$ and $u \rightarrow w$. Effectively, for vertex v, $\mathcal{T}_3$ drops the outgoing edge $v \rightarrow w$ if a neighboring vertex of v is directly connected to w. As in $\mathcal{T}_3$, $\mathcal{T}_5$ ensures path preservation; however, $\mathcal{T}_5$ increases the hops/distance between connected vertices.

$\mathcal{T}_6$. Transformations $\mathcal{T}_1$-$\mathcal{T}_5$ can only be applied when their preconditions are satisfied. Thus, the amount of reduction obtained will depend upon the input graph's structural characteristics. In fact, in our experiments the input graph FT is greatly reduced by $\mathcal{T}_1$-$\mathcal{T}_5$ compared to the other graphs. Hence, we introduce transformation $\mathcal{T}_6$ which randomly eliminates incoming edges for a given vertex with high indegree.[1] In this case, the edges are dropped in proportion to the vertex's indegree. Since $\mathcal{T}_6$ can aggressively eliminate edges, it is applied when none of the previous transformations ($\mathcal{T}_1$-$\mathcal{T}_5$) can be used because the vertex does not satisfy their corresponding preconditions.

We classify $\mathcal{T}_5$ and $\mathcal{T}_6$ as *aggressive* transformations mainly because they do not fully preserve the structural similarity

Algorithm 3 Graph Reduction Algorithm.

```
 1: Algorithm TRANSFORM ( G(V, E) )
 2:    E' ← E
 3:    for ∀v ∈ V do
 4:       if ( inDegree(v) = 0 ) then
 5:          ▷ apply T₁ : drop v → *
 6:             E' ← E' \ outEdges(v)
 7:       elseif ( outDegree(v) = 0 ) then
 8:          ▷ apply T₂ : drop * → v
 9:             E' ← E' \ inEdges(v)
10:       elseif ( inDegree(v) = outDegree(v) = 1 ) then
11:          ▷ apply T₃ : bypass v
12:             E' ← (E' \ {u → v, v → w}) ∪ {u → w}
13:          where {u → v, v → w} ⊆ E'
14:       elseif ( all inNeighbors(v) are unchanged ) then
15:          ▷ apply T₄ : coalesce v and inNeighbors(v)
16:             E' ← COALESCE(G, E', v)
17:       end if
18:    end for
19:    if ( G requires further reduction ) then
20:       for ∀v ∈ V s.t. v is unchanged do
21:          if ( w ∈ outNeighbors(v) s.t. w is unchanged and
22:          outNeighbors(v) ∩ inNeighbors(w) ≠ ϕ ) then
23:             ▷ apply T₅ : drop v → w
24:                E' ← E' \ {(v → w)}
25:          elseif ( inDegree(v) > threshold ) then
26:             ▷ apply T₆ : drop some * → v
27:                E' ← E' \ R where R ⊆ inEdges(v)
28:          end if
29:       end for
30:    end if
31:    return E' of G'
32: end algorithm
33:
34: Algorithm COALESCE ( G(V, E), E', v )
35:    for ∀(w → v) ∈ inEdges(v) do
36:       E' ← E' \ {w → v}
37:       for ∀(u → w) ∈ inEdges(w) do
38:          E' ← E' \ {u → w}
39:          E' ← E' ∪ {u → v}
40:       end for
41:       for ∀(w → u) ∈ outEdges(w) do
42:          E' ← E' \ {w → u}
43:          E' ← E' ∪ {v → u}
44:       end for
45:    end for
46:    return E' of G'
47: end algorithm
```

Trans.	[V-ADD]	[V-SUB]	[E-ADD]	[E-SUB]	[C-MERGE]	[C-SPLIT]
T_1	✗	✓	✗	✓	✗	?
T_2	✗	✓	✗	✓	✗	?
T_3	✗	✓	✓	✓	✗	✗
T_4	✗	✓	✓	✓	✗	✗
T_5	✗	✗	✗	✓	✗	✗
T_6	✗	✗	✗	✓	✗	?

Table 1: Structural guarantees for each transformation. ✓ and ✗ indicate occurrence and non-occurrence of the corresponding property respectively, whereas ? indicates that the corresponding property may or may not occur.

mations as it efficiently applies the transformations by making a pass over the vertices in the graph. Since this is a conservative approach, we can run the algorithm to completion applying as many transformations from T_1-T_4 as possible in one pass (lines 3-18). If the expected reduction is not achieved, we use the aggressive transformations for further reduction (lines 19-30).

3.2 Transformation Properties

We consider each transformation and deduce strong guarantees about various properties of the transformed graph G' compared to that of the original graph G. These guarantees are categorized into two types: a) *Structural Guarantees* that determine a relation of structural properties, i.e., *edges*, *vertices* and *components*; and b) *Non-Structural Guarantees* that determine a relation of edge-weights.

Structural Guarantees. Consider six transformational properties that determine the relation of structural properties of G' with G when transformation T_k ($1 \le k \le 6$) is applied.

[V-ADD]: T_k results in vertex v s.t. $v \in G', v \notin G$.

[V-SUB]: T_k results in vertex v s.t. $v \in G, v \notin G'$.

[E-ADD]: T_k results in edge e s.t. $e \in G', e \notin G$.

[E-SUB]: T_k results in vertex e s.t. $e \in G, e \notin G'$.

[C-MERGE]: T_k results in a new component c s.t.
$c_1 \in G, c_2 \in G, c = c_1 \cup c_2, c \in G'$.

[C-SPLIT] T_k results in new components c_1 and c_2 s.t.
$c_1 \in G', c_2 \in G', c = c_1 \cup c_2, c \in G$.

It is easy to follow that T_1 and T_2 guarantee occurrence of [V-SUB], [E-SUB] and non-occurrence of [V-ADD], [E-ADD], [C-MERGE]. Also, [C-SPLIT] can occur when these two transformations are applied. Transformations T_3 and T_5 guarantee occurrence of [E-SUB] and non-occurrence of [V-ADD], [C-MERGE], [C-SPLIT]. T_3 also guarantees occurrence of [E-ADD] and [V-SUB], whereas T_5 also guarantees non-occurrence of [E-ADD] and [V-SUB]. Transformation T_4 guarantees occurrence of [V-SUB], [E-ADD], [E-SUB] and non-occurrence of [V-ADD], [C-MERGE], [C-SPLIT]. Finally, T_6 guarantees occurrence of [E-SUB] and non-occurrence of [V-ADD], [V-SUB], [E-ADD], [C-MERGE]. While dropping edges using T_6, [C-SPLIT] can occur.

Table 1 overviews all structural properties guaranteed by each of the transformations. Note that all transformations guarantee non-occurrence of [V-ADD] and occurrence of [E-SUB] which result in reduction of transformed graph sizes.

between the transformed graph and the original graph. In particular, T_5 can effectively increase the diameter of the input graph by spreading out vertices which are close to each other in the original graph, far apart in the transformed graph and hence, increasing the traversal cost. T_6, on the other hand, randomly drops edges from high-degree vertices which are typically important locations defining the graph structure. Care must be taken while reducing the graph using these transformations since the computed values from first phase using structurally dissimilar graphs can prove to be useless and hence, demand significant computation on the original graph in the second phase. Algorithm 3 achieves our objective of applying a *non-interfering* sequence of transfor-

Non-Structural Guarantees. Since transformations $\mathcal{T}_3$ and $\mathcal{T}_4$ guarantee occurrence of [E-ADD], correct edge weights need to be assigned to newly added edges for weighted graphs. We define two transformational properties which determine the relation of edge weights of $\mathcal{G}'$ with that of $\mathcal{G}$ when transformation $\mathcal{T}_k$ $(1 \leq k \leq 6)$ is applied. In the following expressions, $a \implies b$ means $b \in \mathcal{G}'$ is resulted from $a \in \mathcal{G}$.

[E-EQUAL] $\mathcal{T}_k$ results in edges e_1 and e_2, both with weights $w(e)$ s.t. $e_1 \in \mathcal{G}, e_1 \notin \mathcal{G}', e_2 \in \mathcal{G}', e_2 \notin \mathcal{G}, e_1 \implies e_2$.

[E-FUNC] $\mathcal{T}_k$ results in edges e_1, e_2 and e_3, with weights $w(e_1)$, $w(e_2)$ and $w(e_3)$ respectively s.t. $\{e_1, e_2\} \in \mathcal{G}, \{e_1, e_2\} \notin \mathcal{G}', e_3 \in \mathcal{G}', e_3 \notin \mathcal{G}, w(e_3) = func(w(e_1), w(e_2)), (e_1, e2) \implies e_3$.

[E-FUNC] represents the weight of the newly added edge as a function of weights of edges from the original graph that resulted in this new edge. For example, the new weight can be set as the *sum*, *minimum*, or *maximum* of the original edge weights ([E-SUM], [E-MIN], or [E-MAX] respectively).

Transformation $\mathcal{T}_3$ guarantees occurrence of [E-FUNC] and non-occurrence of [E-EQUAL]. For transformation $\mathcal{T}_4$, both [E-EQUAL] and [E-FUNC] can occur. As we will see in Section 4.1, we use [E-SUM] to benefit the exploratory and traversal based graph algorithms.

4. PROGRAMMING FOR TRANSFORMED GRAPHS

Using the transformation properties described in Section 3.2, we discuss properties of vertex-centric graph algorithms that permit them to benefit from the two-phased model.

4.1 Impact of Transformations on Vertex Functions

Since the aforementioned transformations change the structural and non-structural properties of the graph, it is important to determine the impact of these changes on how programmers should correctly express graph algorithms. Even though custom algorithms can be written so that computations performed on transformed graphs always lead to correct values, we eliminate this programming overhead by supporting the popular vertex centric programming for our two phased processing model.

Vertex-centric programming. In this model, algorithms are expressed in a vertex-centric manner, i.e., computations are written from the perspective of a single vertex. These computations, called *vertex functions*, are iteratively executed on all vertices in parallel, until all the vertex values in the graph stabilize. Vertex functions typically use the values coming from its incoming edges as inputs for computation. Hence, the newly computed value of a vertex depends on the values coming from its incoming edges. Moreover, the asynchronous nature of the graph algorithms requires computations over updates coming from incoming edges to be *commutative* and *associative* — this way, updates coming from different incoming edges can be processed in any order, e.g., the order of their arrival.

To guarantee correct answers at the end of computation, we need to reason about the behavior of vertex functions, first when applied on the transformed graph $\mathcal{G}'$, and later on the original graph $\mathcal{G}$. For illustration, we use two versions of the SSSP vertex functions, SSSP-IN and SSSP-SIN,

---

Algorithm 4 Variants of SSSP vertex functions.

```
1:  function SSSP-IN ( Vertex v )
2:      if ( v = source ) return 0; end if
3:          minPath ← ∞
4:      for ( Vertex u : inNeighbors (v) ) do
5:          if ( u.path + wt(u, w) < minPath ) then
6:              minPath ← u.path + wt(u, w)
7:          end if
8:      end for
9:      return minPath
10: end function
11:
12: function SSSP-SIN ( Vertex v )
13:     if ( v = source ) return 0; end if
14:         minPath ← v.path
15:     for ( Vertex u : inNeighbors (v) ) do
16:         if ( u.path + wt(u, w) < minPath ) then
17:             minPath ← u.path + wt(u, w)
18:         end if
19:     end for
20:     return minPath
21: end function
```

shown in Algorithm 4. Computations in SSSP-IN only depend on values coming from incoming neighbors, whereas those in SSSP-SIN depends on the previous value of the vertex in addition to the values coming from neighbors. The only difference between SSSP-IN and SSSP-SIN is the initialization of $minPath$ (line 3 and 14 marked in red); the rest of the functions are identical. Note that both of these variants produce correct results when used in the traditional vertex centric processing model. However, they behave differently when used in our two-phased processing model, in which only SSSP-IN leads to accurate results.

Let us evaluate each of the structural and non-structural properties which are affected by our transformations.

(A) [V-SUB] and [E-SUB]: [E-SUB] leads to computations being performed even when all the incoming edges of a vertex are not available. Such computations are equivalent to that in the staleness-based (i.e., relaxed consistency) computation model [31] where the edges can potentially contain stale values; in this case, missing edges can be viewed as edges with no new contribution. The same argument also holds true for [V-SUB] since the effect of vertex deletion is viewed as edge deletion by its neighbors, reducing to [E-SUB]. In both of these cases, SSSP-IN and SSSP-SIN produce an over-approximation of path distance when applied on $\mathcal{G}'$, compared to the precise distance computed on $\mathcal{G}$, i.e., $minPath(\mathcal{G}') \geq minPath(\mathcal{G})$. In the second phase when missing vertices and edges become available in $\mathcal{G}$, this approximation automatically gets corrected.

(B) [E-ADD], [E-EQUAL], and [E-FUNC]: Transformations resulting in [E-ADD] are introduced in order to preserve the connectivity in the graph which is essential for various traversal-based graph algorithms. Moreover, both [E-EQUAL] and [E-SUM] attempt to create edge-weights of newly added edges to represent an approximation of the distance between corresponding vertices in the original graph. This allows traversal algorithms to proceed with computations based on those newly added edges since the results for transformed graphs are close to the results for the original graph, and hence can accelerate processing over the orig-

Alg.	Vertex Function
SSSP	$v.path \leftarrow \min\limits_{e \in inEdges(v)}(e.source.path + e.wt)$
SSWP	$v.path \leftarrow \max\limits_{e \in inEdges(v)}(min(e.source.path, e.wt))$
CC	$v.component \leftarrow \min\limits_{e \in edges(v)}(e.other.component)$
PR	$v.rank \leftarrow 0.15 + 0.85 \times \sum\limits_{e \in inEdges(v)} e.source.rank$
GC	$change \leftarrow \bigvee\limits_{e \in edges(v)}(v.color == e.other.color)$ **if** $change == true$ **then:** $v.color \leftarrow c$: where $\forall_{e \in edges(v)}(e.other.color \neq c)$
CD	$\forall_{e \in edges(v)} frequency[e.other.community] += 1$ $v.community \leftarrow c$: where $frequency[c] = \max\limits_{i \in frequency}(frequency[i])$

Table 2: Various vertex-centric graph algorithms. SSSP, SSWP, CC, PR, and GC produce 100% accurate results.

inal graph in the second phase. However, care must be taken to ensure that algorithms which cannot tolerate such newly added relationships do run correctly; in such cases, the newly added edges can be eliminated dynamically from the computation. When [E-ADD] results from eliminating intermediate vertices such that there is a path between the end vertices in $\mathcal{G}$ (as in $\mathcal{T}_3$), correctness of both SSSP-IN and SSSP-SIN is guaranteed by [E-SUM].

However, $\mathcal{T}_4$, which results in [E-EQUAL], can add an edge between two vertices across which a directed path did not exist in $\mathcal{G}$. In this case, the approximation computed by SSSP-IN and SSSP-SIN can include calculated paths that are smaller than the true shortest paths. During the second phase using $\mathcal{G}$, SSSP-IN recovers from such approximation since the computation of a path does not depend on its own previous value, resulting in 100% accurate results.[2] On the other hand, computation in SSSP-SIN relies on the previously computed path value for the given vertex, and hence SSSP-SIN cannot recover from such approximate solution. In this case, instead of directly using [E-EQUAL], the edge weight for such newly added edges resulting in new paths can be set to ∞ ([**E-INF**]) which can guarantee 100% accurate results for SSSP-SIN as well.

(C) [C-SPLIT]: Finally, transformations resulting in [C-SPLIT] typically do not impact correctness since computations are performed locally at vertex-level. If the algorithm requires collaborative tasks at component level, they can be performed correctly in the second phase on the original graph. In our examples, both SSSP-IN and SSSP-SIN remain unaffected by [C-SPLIT].

Transformations beyond $\mathcal{T}_1$-$\mathcal{T}_6$. Note that our transformations can be used as fundamental building blocks to create more complicated transformations which can be applied to reduce the graph size. Conversely, the correctness of graph algorithms while using any new transformation $\mathcal{T}_x$ $(x > 6)$ can be argued by reducing the new transformation to one or many of the proposed set of transformations. If there exists a sequence of transformations among $\mathcal{T}_1$-$\mathcal{T}_6$ which produces the same transformed subgraph as that produced by $\mathcal{T}_x$, correct answers can be guaranteed at the end of computation using the transformed graph produced by $\mathcal{T}_x$. For some $\mathcal{T}_x$ which cannot be expressed as a sequence of proposed transformations, arguments using their structural and non-structural properties can be used to ensure correctness of results. Note that this relationship is *transitive* and hence, the newly proved $\mathcal{T}_x$ can be further used along with $\mathcal{T}_1$-$\mathcal{T}_6$ to prove correctness of results while using other new transformations.

4.2 Graph Algorithms

We now discuss how each of the graph algorithms used in this work will perform using our technique. Table 2 shows details about each of the seven vertex functions considered in this work. We will argue that PR, SSSP, SSWP, GC, and CC produce 100% accurate results whereas the same accuracy cannot be ensured by CD.

(A) Shortest & Widest Paths: As discussed in Section 4.1, when shortest path (SSSP) is computed on $\mathcal{G}'$, the transformations lead to an approximate solution which gets corrected in the second phase of processing when using SSSP-IN. For the widest path (SSWP), recall that [E-SUM] is a specialization of [E-FUNC] which can support a wide range of such traversal based algorithms. Hence, SSWP can be supported by ensuring that the weight of any newly added edge is the minimum of the edges whose removal caused the addition of this new edge ([E-MIN]). In this case, [E-MIN] ensures that the calculated path width in $\mathcal{G}'$ is always at most that of the equivalent path in $\mathcal{G}$.

(B) Connected Components: Since the main idea behind CC is that vertex values within a component are the same and those in different components are different, we determine its correctness using [C-MERGE] and [C-SPLIT] properties. All the transformations guarantee non-occurrence of [C-MERGE]; hence, values flowing in different components of the original graph will always be different in the transformed graph. When [C-SPLIT] occurs, vertices within the same component of the original graph can now belong to different components of the transformed graph, leading to different values flowing in the same original component. This approximation gets corrected when these vertices are re-grouped together into the same component in the second phase; the computation simply picks one of the vertex values to flow across the entire component.

(C) Graph Coloring: The underlying idea behind GC is to assign different colors to the end vertices of every edge while using minimal [3] set of colors to color all vertices. Hence, we determine its correctness using [E-ADD] and [E-SUB] properties. When [E-ADD] occurs, an edge connects two vertices in $\mathcal{G}'$, which were disconnected in $\mathcal{G}$. Even though this causes the two vertices to be assigned different colors, it does not violate the correctness of the solution: when the edge is removed in the second phase, the color assignment for one of these two vertices gets updated and is propagated throughout the graph. When [E-SUB] occurs, vertices which are connected by an edge in $\mathcal{G}$ become disconnected. This can cause the vertices to be assigned

---

[2]This is true for graph structures consisting of loops as well.

[3]Graph coloring is NP-complete and hence the constraint is usually relaxed to minimal colors which can be solved in polynomial time.

the same color when processing on $\mathcal{G}'$. However, during the second phase, these edges become available in $\mathcal{G}$ which re-processes the vertices and hence, the self-correcting nature of the algorithm detects and corrects the coloring inconsistency. This in turn ensures that different colors are assigned to connected vertices. Note that different executions of the same original graph coloring algorithm on the same graph can result in different color assignments and minimal number of colors, i.e., the set of correct solutions is not a singleton and hence, the solution computed by our two-phased approach is one of the solutions in the correct set because it adheres to the two constraints of the problem.

(D) PageRank: As shown in [6], PR converges to the correct solution regardless of the initial vertex values. With different initializations, the path to convergence changes. Since computations over $\mathcal{G}'$ provide an approximation of the final results, these results, when fed as initialization values for $\mathcal{G}$, cause the second phase to converge faster.

(E) Community Detection: CD detects communities in the graph by propagating labels that are most frequent among the immediate neighborhood of the vertices. Both [E-SUB] and [E-ADD] influence this computation since the frequency of labels get affected by edge addition/deletion, which leads to an approximation at the end of first phase. During the second phase when $\mathcal{G}$ becomes available, this approximation may not be fully corrected because individual corrections due to availability of original edges might not affect the highly approximate frequency calculated in previous iterations. This can lead to results which are not accurate.

Early Termination in First Phase. A key advantage of our approach is that none of the algorithms require processing over $\mathcal{G}'$ to converge to its final solution before moving on to $\mathcal{G}$. This is because the intermediate values produced while processing $\mathcal{G}'$ also represent a valid approximation of the final solution. Hence, to speed up the computation even further, we can employ *early termination* of first phase, where the computation does not wait to reach to its converged solution, and the available computed values are directly used in the second phase to process the original graph.

5. ANALYSIS & GENERALITY

We first theoretically analyze the performance benefits that can be achieved by our two-phased model and then discuss the generality of our approach to achieve similar benefits in different scenarios.

5.1 Analysis

Let P_G and P_T be the average execution times of a single iteration over G (original graph) and G_T (reduced graph) respectively. Further, let P_G^T be the average execution time of a single iteration over G in the second phase using computed results fed from G_T to G. Note that $P_G^T < P_G$. Moreover, since $|G_T| < |G|$, i.e., G_T has fewer edges than G, we know that $P_T < P_G$. In order to accelerate processing using the two-phased approach, we require:

$$I_1.P_T + I_2.P_G^T < I.P_G \tag{1}$$

where I_1, I_2, and I are the number of iterations in which G_T is processed in the first phase, G is processed in the second phase when computed results are fed from G_T, and G is processed in the original processing model, respectively. Upon rearranging Eq. 1 we get:

$$I_1.P_T < I.P_G - I_2.P_G^T \tag{2}$$

which conveys that in order to achieve benefits from our technique, the savings from the second phase ($I.P_G - I_2.P_G^T$) should be larger than the time spent in the first phase ($I_1.P_T$).

For example, if we want to accelerate the overall processing by 25%, we should have:

$$I_1.P_T + \frac{1}{4}.I.P_G = I.P_G - I_2.P_G^T$$

$$\implies \qquad I_1.P_T = \frac{3}{4}.I.P_G - I_2.P_G^T$$

$$\implies I_1.P_T < \frac{3}{4}.I.P_G \quad \rightsquigarrow \quad |G_T| < \frac{3}{4}.|G| \tag{3}$$

The above implication from processing times to graph sizes ($|G|$ and $|G_T|$) is an approximation that holds true as G_T is created primarily by dropping vertices and edges from G and hence, $I_1.P_T$ reduces proportionately compared to $I.P_G$.

Eq. 3 shows that if we want to accelerate the overall processing by 25% using our two phased processing technique, we must ensure that the reduced graph is reduced to at least 75% of the original graph. As we will see in our evaluation (Section 6), reducing the original graph by a quarter to a half of its original size practically allows up to 32% savings in execution times.

5.2 Generality

From the above analysis, it can be clearly seen that the savings in the overall processing times are largely dependent on $|G|$ and $|G_T|$, i.e., size of original and transformed graphs. This allows us to argue that the our technique is independent of the underlying processing environments, iterative algorithms, and input graphs.

Processing Environments. Processing large graphs in different environments incurs different overheads and since our technique eliminates significant amount of processing on the entire large graph, it can help alleviate some of these overheads. For example, processing large graphs on GPUs would require frequent transfer of subgraph information and computed values between host-memory and device-memory which is a significant overhead [11, 26]. Since our transformed graph is much smaller, bulk of this transfer gets eliminated in the first phase and is only performed for remaining few iterations in the second phase. Moreover, if the transformed graph fully fits in the GPU memory, absolutely no transfers are required in the first phase.

In a distributed processing environment, the overall performance is largely dependent on the communication of vertex updates between nodes [31]. Again, using our technique, much of the communication can be avoided in the first phase, hence reducing the overall communication overheads. Moreover, the transformed graph in the first phase can be processed on the subset of nodes in the cluster to reduce synchronization and communication overheads.

The applicability is similar in an out-of-core processing environment where the graph is resident on secondary storage [13, 22]. The first phase eliminates costly disk read and writes while reducing them in the second phase due to reduction in number of iterations.

Iterative Algorithms. The two-phased processing is suitable for iterative graph algorithms whose convergence is dependent on the values being computed. As shown in Section 6, the performance benefits are noteworthy for different kinds of graph algorithms: on one hand, traversal algorithms like SSSP/SSWP which require lesser computation and on other hand, algorithms like PR/GC/CD which require more computation to compute final solution. Also, the benefits achieved are higher for asynchronous graph algorithms [31] because correctness guarantees are stronger for those cases. Again, as deduced in the above analysis, the performance benefits of our technique are mainly due to reduction in the data-size that needs to be processed and is independent of the kind of processing being performed on the data.

Input Graphs. The proposed reduction and processing techniques are best suited for irregular graphs where the degree distribution across vertices is spread across a wider range, allowing various pre-conditions for our transformations to be satisfied [4]. As long as the input graph is large enough that reduction in its size achieves perceivable reduction in processing time, the two-phased processing model can be used to accelerate processing. As shown in Table 4, we use large real-world input graphs which are highly irregular and sparse for our evaluation on which our technique achieves reasonable benefits. Moreover, our transformations $\mathcal{T}_4$ and $\mathcal{T}_6$ are tunable so that they can be applied even to a graph on which no other transformations can be applied.

6. EVALUATION

We thoroughly evaluate our two-phased processing technique to show that our approach is *efficient* (savings in execution time), *scalable* (higher savings in execution with higher number of threads) and produces *accurate* results for most of the graph applications with low *time* overhead.

Benchmarks, Inputs and System. We consider six popular vertex centric graph algorithms, as shown in Table 2 and Table 3. We implemented the baseline and the two-phased version of each of the benchmarks in Galois [19], a state-of-the-art parallel execution framework.

Table 4 shows the details of the input graphs, their reduced versions and time taken for reduction. We use 4 input graphs, 3 of which are real-world graphs (Friendster, Twitter and UKDomain) from publicly available Konect repository [12]. The synthetic graph (RMAT-24) is a scalefree graph (a = 0.5, b = c = 0.1, d = 0.3) similar to the one

---

[4]Real-word graphs from various domains like social network analytics, web anaytics, mining, etc. are highly irregular.

Benchmark	Type
Single Source Shortest Path (SSSP)	
Single Source Widest Path (SSWP)	
PageRank (PR)	Accurate
Graph Coloring (GC)	
Connected Components (CC)	
Community Detection (CD)	Approximate

Table 3: Graph Algorithms.

Input Graph		Graph Size		Reduction
		#Nodes	#Edges	Time (sec)
Friendster	Original	68.3M	2.6B	5.63-9.37
(FT)	Reduced	41.9-51.8M	0.78-1.9B	
Twitter	Original	41.7M	1.5B	1.31-7.13
(TT)	Reduced	23.4-30.8M	0.4-1.1B	
UKDomain	Original	39.5M	936.4M	1.31-7.13
(UK)	Reduced	27.6-32.1M	280.9-702.3M	
RMAT-24	Original	17M	268M	0.05-0.34
(RM)	Reduced	11.6-13.5M	80.4-201M	

Table 4: Input Graphs.

used in [19]. To transform these graphs, we define a tunable parameter **Edge Reduction Percentage (ERP)** as:

$$ERP = \frac{|E_{\mathcal{G}'}|}{|E_{\mathcal{G}}|} \times 100$$

where $|E_{\mathcal{G}}|$ and $|E_{\mathcal{G}'}|$ are the number of edges in original graph $\mathcal{G}$ and the reduced graph $\mathcal{G}'$. We generate the reduced graphs with varying ERP (75%, 70%, 60%, 50%, 40% and 30%) using our transformation tool based on Algorithm 3.

Experiments were performed on a machine with 4 six-core AMD^{TM} 8431 processors (total 24 cores) and 32 GB RAM running Ubuntu 14.04.1 (kernel version 3.19.0-28-generic). The programs were compiled using GCC 4.8.4, optimization level -O3.

We evaluate the performance of following versions of the benchmark implementations:

- **Baseline:** based on the traditional processing model.
- **TP-X:** based on our two-phased processing model using reduced graphs with ERP = X%. Note that the execution times include the graph reduction times which are already presented in Table 4.

Unless otherwise specified, the benchmarks were run with 20 software threads.

Efficiency of Two-Phased Processing. Figure 4 show the speedups achieved by TP-X over Baseline for X $\in$ {30%, 40%, 50%, 60%, 70%, 75%}. As we can see, the speedups increase as ERP decreases from 75% to 40%; on an average, TP-75, TP-70, TP-60, TP-50 and TP-40 achieve a speedup of 1.23×, 1.27×, 1.41×, 1.51× and 1.53× respectively. This is because of the high savings achieved in the second phase while processing the original graphs. On an average for TP-75, TP-70, TP-60, TP-50, and TP-40, the savings achieved in the second phase are 84.88%, 83.08%, 80.65%, 77.99% and 73.71% respectively. These high savings allow tolerating the execution times of reduction and first phase over reduced graphs; the execution times normalized w.r.t. *Baseline* for the first phase of TP-75, TP-70, TP-60, TP-50, and TP-40 are 0.66, 0.61, 0.50, 0.42, and 0.36 respectively and for the reduction are as low as 0.01, 0.02, 0.03, 0.03, and 0.04 respectively. Since our reduction transformations are local and non-interfering, the cost of performing the input reduction is much lower than the savings achieved in processing.

As expected, the time taken to process the reduced graph in the first phase decreases as ERP decreases simply because the work done is typically proportional to the size of graph. On the other hand, the execution time in second phase increases as ERP decreases. This is mainly because an aggressively reduced graph with lower ERP is structurally less similar to the original graph compared to that reduced with a higher ERP. Hence, the values which are fed from reduced graph with lower ERP require more computation in the second phase in order to reach to maximum possible accuracy for the original graphs.

The savings achieved by our two-phased processing model increases as ERP decreases up to a certain limit. Across each of our benchmark-input-ERP combination, the maximum savings are observed for ERP around 40-50%. However, note that further decreasing ERP reduces the amount of savings achieved; with ERP = 30% the performance degrades and the average speedup drops to 1.41×. This is because the reduced graph with very low ERP becomes too small (i.e.,

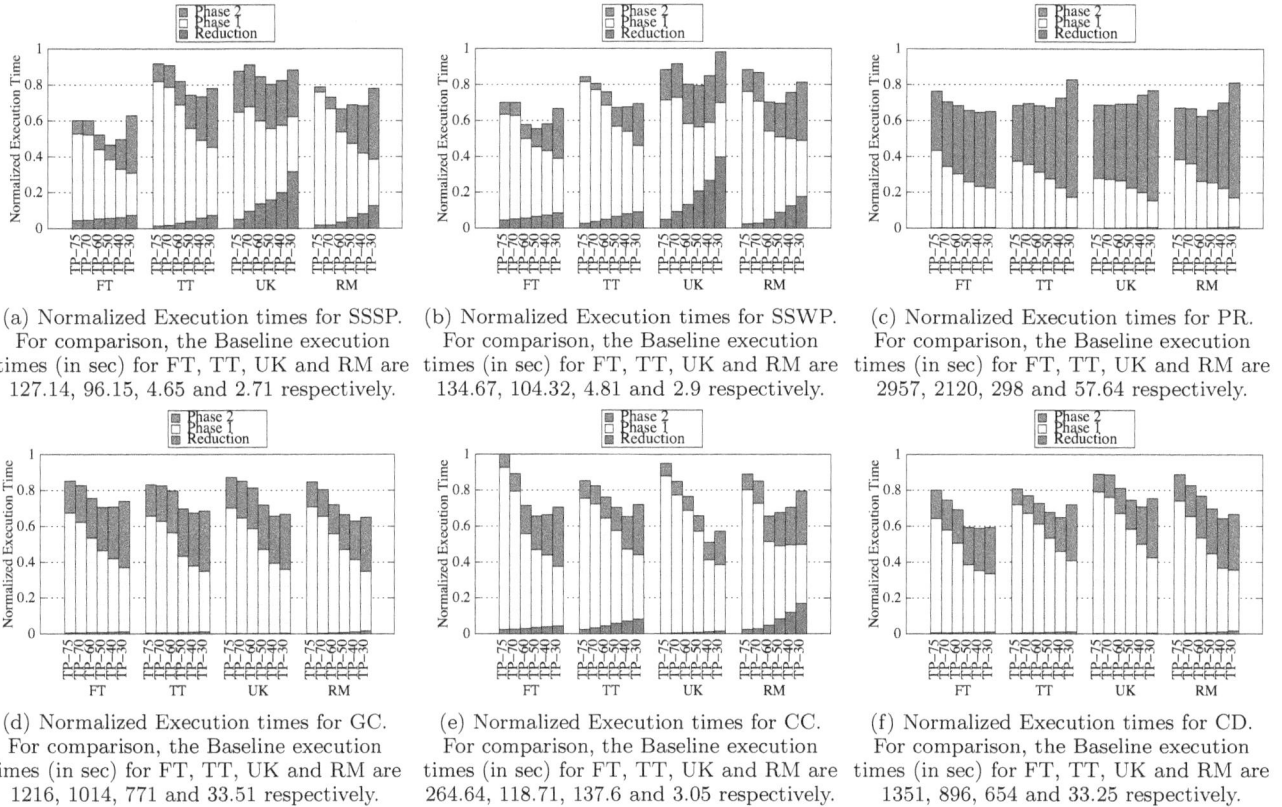

(a) Normalized Execution times for SSSP. For comparison, the Baseline execution times (in sec) for FT, TT, UK and RM are 127.14, 96.15, 4.65 and 2.71 respectively.

(b) Normalized Execution times for SSWP. For comparison, the Baseline execution times (in sec) for FT, TT, UK and RM are 134.67, 104.32, 4.81 and 2.9 respectively.

(c) Normalized Execution times for PR. For comparison, the Baseline execution times (in sec) for FT, TT, UK and RM are 2957, 2120, 298 and 57.64 respectively.

(d) Normalized Execution times for GC. For comparison, the Baseline execution times (in sec) for FT, TT, UK and RM are 1216, 1014, 771 and 33.51 respectively.

(e) Normalized Execution times for CC. For comparison, the Baseline execution times (in sec) for FT, TT, UK and RM are 264.64, 118.71, 137.6 and 3.05 respectively.

(f) Normalized Execution times for CD. For comparison, the Baseline execution times (in sec) for FT, TT, UK and RM are 1351, 896, 654 and 33.25 respectively.

Figure 4: Normalized execution time of two-phased execution for each benchmark-graph-ERP value.

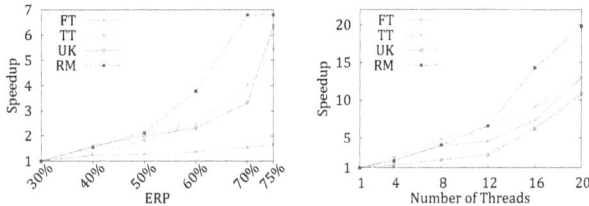

Figure 5: Scalability of Reduction Algorithm w.r.t. ERP (left) and number of threads (right) for TP-50.

structurally very dissimilar) compared to the original graph and the major burden of processing then moves over from first phase to second phase. As an extreme example, one can see that ERP = 0 means that no processing is required in the first phase whereas the second phase is exactly same as processing the original graph from the very beginning.

It is interesting to note that the benefits achieved from our two-phased approach are greater for FT graph (1.37-1.69×) mainly because it is larger than TT and UK graphs.

Scalability of Input Reduction. We study the scalability of our input reduction algorithm while 1) varying ERP from 30% to 75% with 20 threads; and, 2) varying number of threads from 1 to 20 for TP-50[5]. As we can see in Figure 5 (left), with increase in ERP the reduction algorithm runs faster than for ERP=30% mainly because there are fewer edges to be removed for higher ERP, and hence, the reduction algorithm only needs to traverse certain percentage of the graph to achieve the expected ERP. Moreover, Figure 5 shows that the reduction algorithm is scalable w.r.t. number of threads; this naturally follows from the requirement of the transformations to be local and non-interfering allowing them to be executed at vertex-level in parallel.

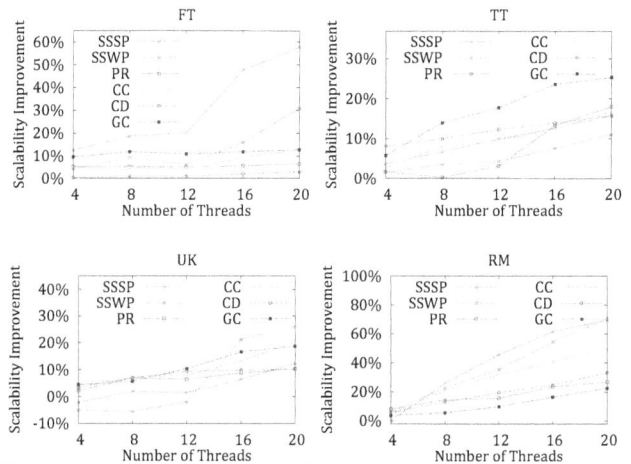

Figure 6: Improvement in scalability using the two-phased model with varying number of threads. For comparison, the Baseline execution times (in sec) for PR/SSSP with 1 thread for FT, TT, UK and RM are 24577/1674.43, 22307/1016.88, 3014.39/53.64 and 934.43/12.07.

Scalability of Two-Phased Processing. As shown in [19], the Baseline system scales well with increase in number of threads. To show the impact of our approach, Figure 6 shows the improvement in scalability achieved by TP-50[5] over Baseline while varying the number of threads from 1 to 20. Note that in Figure 6 the Baseline is also parallel, i.e., a data-point with t threads represents improvement achieved by our technique using t threads compared to baseline using t threads. As we can see in most cases, the improvements

---

[5] Since ERP = 50 performs best across most cases in our previous experiments, we only consider TP-50 to save space.

254

slowly increase as number of threads increase and the maximum improvements are achieved with 20 threads. We believe this is because the reduced graphs become denser compared to the original graphs and hence, the probability of the same vertex to be scheduled multiple times by different threads increases rapidly in TP-50 with increase in threads compared to that in Baseline. This in turn allows more merging of such multiple schedule requests of same vertices to single vertex computations. Moreover, the second phase mostly performs value corrections, hence, less contention is expected since probability of all neighboring vertices to be scheduled simultaneously is greatly reduced.

Memory Overhead. While the two phases can be processed separately, feeding values from the first phase to the next can incur expensive reads and writes which can offset the performance benefits achieved by our technique. Hence, it is crucial to maintain the reduced and the original graph in memory

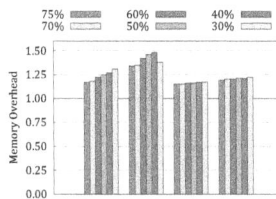

Figure 7: Increase in memory footprint.

and eliminate the explicit intermediate feeding by incorporating a unified graph which leverages the high structural overlap across the two graphs. Figure 7 shows the increase in memory when using a unified graph. On an average, the memory consumption increases by 1.25×; it goes higher for TT (1.34×-1.48×) mainly because the percentage of newly added edges in the transformed graphs is much higher (25%-40%) for TT compared to other graphs (2.7%-23%).

It is interesting to note that the overhead increases as ERP decreases. This is due to the impact of increase in the structural dissimilarity between the original and transformed graphs that requires representing the dissimilar components (i.e., newly added edges) separately for both graphs. Note that these overheads are tolerable compared to those incurred by representing both the graphs separately in memory which can be as high as 1.75×.

Relative Error for CD. As discussed in Section 4.2, the accuracy of results for CD could not be guaranteed. In order to determine how good the calculated results are, we define relative error as the ratio of vertices whose computed community values are different compared to the ideal results. Table 5 shows the relative error for CD across all input-ERP combinations. As we can see, the relative error is very small; the average relative error across all cases is 0.02 and the maximum relative error is only 0.065. In fact, the relative error for FT across ERP-60, ERP-70 and ERP-75 is very low (<1E-5). It is interesting to note that the error values decrease as ERP increases. This is mainly because with fewer reduction transformations being applied for higher values of ERP, the probability of merging communities in reduced graphs decreases.

Input	TP-30	TP-40	TP-50	TP-60	TP-70	TP-75
FT	0.017	0.002	0.001	<1E-5	<1E-5	<1E-5
TT	0.049	0.041	0.036	0.021	0.019	0.017
UK	0.065	0.023	0.017	0.013	0.012	0.011
RM	0.043	0.034	0.021	0.018	0.012	0.01

Table 5: Relative Error for CD.

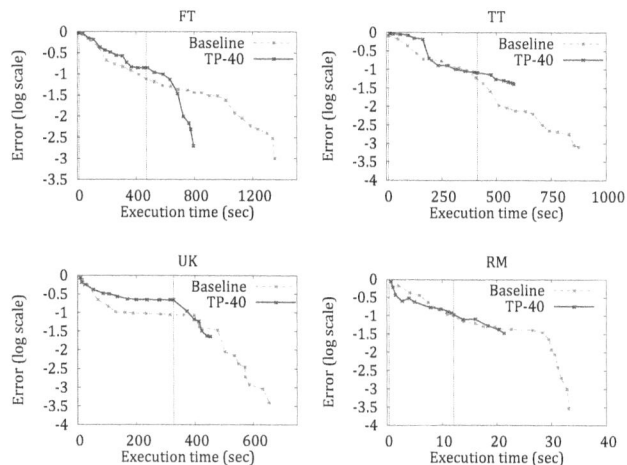

Figure 8: Relative Error (log scale) vs. Execution Time (sec) for CD: Baseline and TP-40. Note that the point at which the Baseline version terminates, i.e., relative error becomes zero, is not plotted due to use of log scale.

We further study how the relative error changes during execution by plotting it for TP-40 in Figure 8. The vertical dotted lines indicate different phases of execution; the first line (close to 0) indicates end of reduction process and the second line (in the middle) indicates the end of the first phase and the beginning of the second phase. As we can see, the relative error remains high during the first phase mainly because of vertices which are missing in the reduced graph. However, the relative error drops rapidly during the second phase due to availability of missing vertices and edges in the original graph. At the end of the first phase, the relative error for FT, TT, UK and RM remain at 0.014, 0.084, 0.22 and 0.12 respectively.

Contribution of Individual Transformations. Finally, we evaluate the effect of applying individual transformations one after the other on the overall performance. We define a transformation set $\mathcal{T}_{1-k}$ as the set of transformations starting from $\mathcal{T}_1$ up to $\mathcal{T}_k$. Hence, the transformation set $\mathcal{T}_{1-4}$ includes $\mathcal{T}_1$, $\mathcal{T}_2$, $\mathcal{T}_3$ and $\mathcal{T}_4$ whereas $\mathcal{T}_{1-1}$ only includes $\mathcal{T}_1$.

The reduced graphs for this set of experiments are generated using different transformation sets $\mathcal{T}_{1-k}$ ($1 \geq k \leq 4$). To clearly present the impact of transformations on both, the size of reduced graphs and the savings in execution time, we select ERP = 50% and only consider the SSSP benchmark. Figure 9 shows the speedups achieved for each of the graphs transformed using the transformation sets, compared to the Baseline. Since the transformations being applied have their pre-conditions which need to be satisfied, the actual ERP using a smaller transformation set can be higher than the requested ERP of 50%. Hence, we also present the actual ERP obtained using the transformation sets.

As we can see in Figure 9, $\mathcal{T}_1$, $\mathcal{T}_2$ and $\mathcal{T}_3$ collectively reduce only small portion of TT, UK and RM graphs; $\mathcal{T}_{1-3}$ achieves 95.26%, 96.58% and 99.39% ERP for TT, UK and RM respectively. Due to this, little to no savings are achieved until $\mathcal{T}_4$ is included in the transformation sets for which speedups of up to 1.34-1.55× are achieved. FT graph, on the other hand, is amenable to $\mathcal{T}_2$ and $\mathcal{T}_3$, allowing 50% ERP to be achieved for $\mathcal{T}_{1-2}$ and $\mathcal{T}_{1-3}$ too. Hence, the speedups achieved for those transformation sets are ~2.15×.

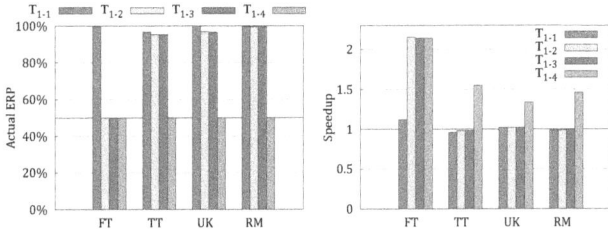

Figure 9: Actual ERP achieved (left) and speedups achieved (right) while using different transformation sets when ERP is set to 50%.

7. RELATED WORK

Graph processing has gained a lot of attention due to its applicability across various domains. Many graph processing frameworks have been developed for distributed ([16, 14, 31, 34, 24]), shared memory ([19, 28, 32]) and GPU based environments ([11, 26]). These frameworks include a parallel runtime that iteratively processes the input graph until all the graph values convergence. The computation is based on asynchronous or bulk synchronous model [30]. This traditional style of processing includes a single processing phase.

Multilevel transformation techniques. There is a body of work [7, 17, 3, 18, 23, 35, 9, 8, 10, 33] that reduces the size of graphs to accelerate processing. These works mainly rely on algorithm-specific reduction techniques and mostly operate of regular meshes. [7] presents a multilevel graph partitioning algorithm where first a hierarchy of smaller graphs is created, then the highest level graphs are partitioned and then, these partition results are carefully propagated back down the hierarchy to achieve partitioning of the original graph. It uses edge contraction where neighbors are unified into a single vertex which is suitable for relatively regular meshes. [17] uses the same three phases and relies on quality functions of the reduced (coarse) grids based on aspect ratio. Moreover, the reduction algorithm operates on the dual graph and uses maximal independent set computation which requires non-trivial processing. [3, 9, 8, 10] also aim to partition graphs via recursive edge contraction using maximal independent set computation and edge contraction to generate multinodes. In contrast, our work identifies light-weight, local and non-interfering transformations that are *general* (i.e., not algorithm-specific) and effective for *irregular* input graphs. Moreover, our reduction strategy is not hierarchical (multi-level) since our transformations are designed from the vertex's perspective and are applied at most once on each vertex. [33] processes queries by providing multiple levels of abstractions and refining the query to these abstraction levels. [23] is specifically designed for distance based algorithms like SSSP where they aim to achieve gate vertex sets which allow traversals to be constructed on the reduced graphs. [35] reduces by pruning weakest edges based on cost functions and which adhere to specific constraints related to connectivity maintenance. These works require path- or component-level transformations that are computationally expensive whereas our transformations are light-weight and hence effective for large graphs.

Beyond these works, various optimization techniques have been developed which attempt to accelerate processing at the cost of achieving approximate results. We divide the literature encompassing such approximation based graph processing techniques into two categories, discussed below. None

of these techniques provide correctness guarantees and hence the results of these techniques are always approximate.

Algorithm-specific approximation. Chazelle et al. proposed a technique for approximating the weight of minimum spanning tree in sublinear time by approximating the number of connected components [5]. The technique approximates the weight of the minimum spanning tree but it does not find the tree. Nanongkai [18] proposed an approximation technique to find SSSP and all-pair shortest path (APSP) by bounding the diameter of the graph. Bader et al. [1] proposed the approximation of Betweenness Centrality (BC) by employing an adaptive sampling technique. The algorithm samples a subset of vertices and performs SSSP on them selected, thus reducing the number of SSSP operations to determine BC. In contrast to sampling, our approach to input graph reduction is smarter as it considers graph connectivity and is more general as it is applied to a class of graph algorithms. In fact all of the above approximation techniques were developed for a single specific graph application. In contrast, *our technique applies to many iterative graph algorithms all using the same input reduction transformations.*

Compiler-based approximation. Researchers have focused on trading accuracy for execution time by skipping a task's execution or by choosing a specific implementation from multiple ones provided by the developer. Rinard proposed early termination [21] and task skipping [20] that are applied during execution. These techniques use a distortion model based on sampling to estimate the error introduced due to early termination or task skipping. The work does not provide an empirical justification for the distortion model and thus it is unclear if it will work for input graphs with different characteristics. Green [2] selects a specific implementation out of many different implementations provided by the developer while maintaining the quality of output. Hoffman et al. [29] proposed loop perforation where certain iterations of a loop are skipped to trade off accuracy for faster execution. The loops that are perforated are chosen with the help of training input and the error bound set by the user. This technique is not useful for different graph applications since it requires perforated loops to fall into one of the specified categories of the global patterns. *Our technique does not require loops to follow any such pattern and it does not perform any static or dynamic analysis of the application to achieve approximation.*

The Sage [25] compiler generates CUDA kernels that exploit GPUs to achieve approximation using different optimizations. The runtime system includes a tuning phase which selects the best optimization technique and a calibration phase to help maintain quality. Although we tested our methodology only for CPU systems, it can be easily applied for GPUs as we achieve approximation by reducing the input graph. Shang et al. [27] proposed auto-approximation of vertex-centric graph applications by automatically synthesizing the approximate version of an application. They combined different approximation techniques such as task skipping, sampling, memorization, interpolation and system function replacement for synthesizing the approximate version. Carbin et al. [4] proposed a language to specify approximate program transformations. *Our approach works without modifying the original implementation. Moreover input reductions, guided by impact on graph connectivity, customize the skipped computations to input characteristics.*

8. CONCLUSION

We proposed input reduction transformations and faster iterative graph algorithms that run in two phases: first, using the reduced input graph, and second using the original graph along with the results from first phase. We evaluated our two-phased model using Galois; our experiments with multiple algorithms and large graphs show that our technique reduces execution time by 1.25× to 2.14×.

Acknowledgments

The authors thank their shepherd, Shuaiwen Song, for his guidance in preparing the final version of this paper, as well as the anonymous reviewers for their feedback and suggestions. This work is supported by NSF grants CCF-1524852 and CCF-1318103 to the University of California Riverside.

9. REFERENCES

[1] D. A. Bader, S. Kintali, K. Madduri, and M. Mihail. Approximating Betweenness Centrality. WAW, 2007.

[2] W. Baek and T. M. Chilimbi. Green: A Framework for Supporting Energy-Conscious Programming using Controlled Approximation. *PLDI*, pages 198-209, 2010.

[3] S. T. Barnard and H. D. Simon. Fast Multilevel Implementation of Recursive Spectral Bisection for Partitioning Unstructured Problems. *Concurrency: Practice and experience*, 6(2):101–117, 1994.

[4] M. Carbin, D. Kim, S. Misailovic, and M. C. Rinard. Proving Acceptability Properties of Relaxed Nondeterministic Approximate Programs. *PLDI* 2013.

[5] B. Chazelle, R. Rubinfeld, and L. Trevisan. Approximating the Minimum Spanning Tree Weight in Sublinear Time. *International Colloquium on Automata, Languages and Programming*, 2005.

[6] A. Farahat, T. LoFaro, J. C. Miller, G. Rae, and L. A. Ward. Authority Rankings from HITS, Pagerank, and SALSA: Existence, Uniqueness, and Effect of Initialization. *SIAM J. Scientific Computing*, 27(4):1181–1201, 2005.

[7] B. Hendrickson and R. Leland. A Multilevel Algorithm for Partitioning Graphs. *ACM/IEEE Conference on Supercomputing*, 1995.

[8] G. Karypis and V. Kumar. Multilevel Graph Partitioning Schemes. *ICPP (3)*, pages 113–122, 1995.

[9] G. Karypis and V. Kumar. A Fast and High Quality Multilevel Scheme for Partitioning Irregular Graphs. *SIAM J. Sci. Comput.*, 20(1):359–392, Dec. 1998.

[10] G. Karypis and V. Kumar. Multilevel K-way Partitioning Scheme for Irregular Graphs. *JPDC*, 48(1):96–129, 1998.

[11] F. Khorasani, R. Gupta, and L. N. Bhuyan. Scalable SIMD-Efficient Graph Processing on GPUs. *PACT'15*.

[12] J. Kunegis. KONECT: The Koblenz Network Collection. WWW Companion, pages 1343-1350, 2013.

[13] A. Kyrola, G. Blelloch, and C. Guestrin. GraphChi: Large-scale Graph Computation on Just a PC. *OSDI*, pages 31-46, 2012.

[14] Y. Low, D. Bickson, J. Gonzalez, C. Guestrin, A. Kyrola, and J. M. Hellerstein. Distributed GraphLab: A Framework for Machine Learning and Data Mining in the Cloud. *VLDB Endowment*, 2012.

[15] Y. Low, J. E. Gonzalez, A. Kyrola, D. Bickson, C. E. Guestrin, and J. Hellerstein. GraphLab: A New Framework for Parallel Machine Learning. *arXiv preprint arXiv:1408.2041*, 2014.

[16] G. Malewicz, M. H. Austern, A. J. Bik, J. C. Dehnert, I. Horn, N. Leiser, and G. Czajkowski. Pregel: A System for Large-scale Graph Processing. *SIGMOD International Conf. on Management of Data*, 2010.

[17] I. Moulitsas and G. Karypis. Multilevel Algorithms for Generating Coarse Grids for Multigrid Methods. *Supercomputing*, pages 45–45, 2001.

[18] D. Nanongkai. Distributed Approximation Algorithms for Weighted Shortest Paths. *STOC*, pages 565-573, 2014.

[19] K. Pingali, D. Nguyen, M. Kulkarni, M. Burtscher, M. A. Hassaan, R. Kaleem, T.-H. Lee, A. Lenharth, R. Manevich, M. Méndez-Lojo, D. Prountzos, and X. Sui. The Tao of Parallelism in Algorithms. *PLDI*, pages 12-25, 2011.

[20] M. Rinard. Probabilistic Accuracy Bounds for Fault-tolerant Computations that Discard Tasks. *ICS*, pages 324-334, 2006.

[21] M. C. Rinard. Using Early Phase Termination to Eliminate Load Imbalances at Barrier Synchronization Points. *OOPSLA*, pages 369-386, 2007.

[22] A. Roy, I. Mihailovic, and W. Zwaenepoel. X-stream: Edge-centric Graph Processing using Streaming Partitions. *SOSP*, pages 472–488, 2013.

[23] N. Ruan, R. Jin, and Y. Huang. Distance Preserving Graph Simplification. *ICDM*, pages 1200–1205, 2011.

[24] S. Salihoglu and J. Widom. GPS: A Graph Processing System. *SSDBM*, pages 22:1-22:12, 2013.

[25] M. Samadi, J. Lee, D. A. Jamshidi, A. Hormati, and S. Mahlke. SAGE: Self-tuning Approximation for Graphics Engines. *MICRO-46*, pages 13-24, 2013.

[26] D. Sengupta, S. L. Song, K. Agarwal and K. Schwan. GraphReduce: Processing Large-scale Graphs on Accelerator-based Systems. *SC*, pages 28:1–12, 2015.

[27] Z. Shang and J. X. Yu. Auto-approximation of Graph Computing. *VLDB Endow.*, pages 1833-1844, 2014.

[28] J. Shun and G. E. Blelloch. Ligra: A Lightweight Graph Processing Framework for Shared Memory. *PPoPP*, pages 135-146, 2013.

[29] S. Sidiroglou-Douskos, S. Misailovic, H. Hoffmann, and M. Rinard. Managing Performance vs. Accuracy Trade-offs with Loop Perforation. *ESEC/FSE* 2011.

[30] L. G. Valiant. A Bridging Model for Parallel Computation. *CACM*, 33(8):103–111, 1990.

[31] K. Vora, S. C. Koduru, and R. Gupta. ASPIRE: Exploiting Asynchronous Parallelism in Iterative Algorithms using a Relaxed Consistency Based DSM. *OOPSLA*, pages 861-878, 2014.

[32] G. Wang, W. Xie, A. J. Demers, and J. Gehrke. Asynchronous Large-scale Graph Processing Made Easy. *CIDR* 2013.

[33] K. Wang, G. Xu, Z. Su and Y. D. Liu. GraphQ: Graph Query Processing with Abstraction Refinement—Scalable and Programmable Analytics over Very Large Graphs on a Single PC. *USENIX ATC*, pages 387–401, 2015.

[34] R. S. Xin, J. E. Gonzalez, M. J. Franklin, and I. Stoica. GraphX: A Resilient Distributed Graph System on Spark. *International Workshop on Graph Data Management Experiences and Systems*, 2013.

[35] F. Zhou, S. Malher, and H. Toivonen. Network Simplification with Minimal Loss of Connectivity. *ICDM*, pages 659–668, 2010.

DD-Graph: A Highly Cost-Effective Distributed Disk-based Graph-Processing Framework

YongLi Cheng[†]   Fang Wang[§†]   Hong Jiang[‡]   Yu Hua[†]   Dan Feng[†]   XiuNeng Wang[†]
[†]School of Computer, Huazhong University of Science and Technology, Wuhan, China
[†]Wuhan National Lab for Optoelectronics, Wuhan, China
[‡]Department of Computer Science & Engineering, University of Texas at Arlington, USA
{chengyongli,wangfang}@hust.edu.cn,hong.jiang@uta.edu,{csyhua,dfeng,xiunengwang}@hust.edu.cn
[§]Corresponding Author: Fang Wang

ABSTRACT

Existing distributed graph-processing frameworks, e.g., GPS, Pregel and Giraph, handle large-scale graphs in the memory of clusters built of commodity compute nodes for better scalability and performance. While capable of scaling out according to the size of graphs up to thousands of compute nodes, for graphs beyond a certain size, these frameworks usually require the investments of machines that are either beyond the financial capability of or unprofitable for most small and medium-sized organizations. At the other end of the spectrum of graph-processing frameworks research, the single-node disk-based graph-processing frameworks, e.g., GraphChi, handle large-scale graphs on one commodity computer, leading to high efficiency in the use of hardware but at the cost of low user performance and limited scalability. Motivated by this dichotomy, in this paper we propose a distributed disk-based graph-processing framework, called DD-Graph, that can process super-large graphs on a small cluster while achieving the high performance of existing distributed in-memory graph-processing frameworks.

Keywords

Cost-Effectiveness; High Performance; Super-Large Graphs

1. INTRODUCTION

With the rapid growth of data, there has been a recent surge of interest in processing large graphs in both academia and industry. Due to the fact that many graph algorithms exhibit irregular access patterns [2], most graph processing frameworks require that the graphs fit entirely in memory, necessitating either a supercomputer or a very large cluster to process large graphs [3,5].

Several graph-processing frameworks, e.g., GraphChi [1] and XStream [9], have been proposed to process graphs with billions of edges on just one commodity computer, by relying on secondary storage [1,9]. However, the performance of these frameworks is limited by the limited secondary storage bandwidth of a single compute node [4] and the significant

difference in the access speeds between secondary storage and main-memory [7]. Furthermore, the limited amount of storage of a single commodity computer can potentially limit the scale of the processed graphs, since graphs continue to grow in size [6].

The key difference between the distributed in-memory graph-processing frameworks and single-node secondary storage based graph-processing frameworks lies in the trade-off between the hardware cost and performance, with the former trading off hardware cost for performance while the latter doing the exact opposite. In this paper, we propose a highly cost-effective distributed disk-based graph-processing framework, called DD-Graph that has the salient feature of both the low hardware cost and high performance.

There are two key challenges in the design of a distributed external memory based framework, that is, the expensive communication in distributed in-memory graph-processing frameworks and the high disk I/O latency that the designers of external memory based graph-processing frameworks are most concerned about. By using a small cluster to hide the latencies of the communication and disk I/O intelligently, DD-Graph overcomes the two key challenges and thus reduces the overall runtime to the computation time of the compute nodes, achieving the comparable performance with existing distributed in-memory graph-processing frameworks.

The rest of the paper is structured as follows. Section 2 introduces DD-Graph framework. Experimental evaluations are presented in Section 3. We discuss related work in Section 4 and conclude the paper in Section 5.

2. DD-GRAPH FRAMEWORK

Key components and unique features of the DD-Graph framework are detailed in the subsections that follow.

2.1 Definitions

An input graph is partitioned into P subgraphs in preprocessing phase. A graph-computing job consists of N iterations. A **task** is defined as the execution process of a subgraph in one iteration, therefore there are $T = P \times N$ tasks, ordered as T_0, T_1, $\cdots$, $T_{P \times N-1}$. A task is decomposed into three stages: 1) loading subgraph from the disk, 2) computation, and 3) communication and saving results to the disk.

In the preprocessing phase, the edge values of each subgraph are organized into a local-edge data block, P-1 remote in-edge data blocks and P-1 remote out-edge data blocks intelligently. Each remote out-edge data block includes the values of all the out-edges whose destination vertices re-

HPDC'16, May 31-June 04, 2016, Kyoto, Japan
© 2016 ACM. ISBN 978-1-4503-4314-5/16/05...$15.00
DOI: http://dx.doi.org/10.1145/2907294.2907299

side within one of the remote subgraphs. Each remote in-edge data block includes the values of all the in-edges whose source vertices reside within one of the remote subgraphs. Since the out-edges of a given vertex are the in-edges of its neighbors, each remote out-edge data block is an exact copy of a remote in-edge data block of one of the other subgraphs. The local-edge data block is a special case because both the source vertices and destination vertices of the edges are in the same subgraph. This block-based edge-value organization method enables an efficient block-based communication model, described in the next subsection.

2.2 Architecture of DD-Graph

The DD-Graph architecture consists of a master node and M compute nodes. The master node schedules the tasks of the graph-computing job. Each compute node is responsible for managing and executing its assigned tasks. Without the loss of generality, we assume that there are three compute nodes, a graph is partitioned into six subgraphs, and a graph-computing job consists of two iterations. Thus, there are 12 tasks in total (T_0, T_1, $\cdots$, T_{11}). We describe the key components and unique features of the DD-Graph architecture as following.

Task Assignment: Tasks are assigned in order by using a hash of the task ID to select a compute node, the hash function is defined as $H(t) = t \bmod M$, where t is the ID of task t and M is the number of compute nodes. As shown in Table 1, the tasks T_0, T_3, T_6, T_9 are assigned to compute node 0, the tasks T_1, T_4, T_7, T_{10} are assigned to compute node 1, and the tasks T_2, T_5, T_8, T_{11} are assigned to compute node 2. Each compute node employs a *task queue* to store its tasks.

Table 1: Task Assignment.

Compute Node 0	Compute Node 1	Compute Node 2
T_0, T_3, T_6, T_9	T_1, T_4, T_7, T_{10}	T_2, T_5, T_8, T_{11}

Table 2: Subgraph Assignment.

Compute Node 0	Compute Node 1	Compute Node 2
S_0, S_3	S_1, S_4	S_2, S_5

Subgraph Assignment: Subgraphs are assigned in order by using a hash of the subgraph ID to select a compute node, with the hash function being defined as $H(s) = s \bmod M$, where s is the ID of subgraph s. As shown in Table 2, subgraphs S_0 and S_3 are assigned to compute node 0, subgraphs S_1 and S_4 are assigned to compute node 1, and subgraphs S_2 and S_5 are assigned to compute node 2. In order to avoid multiple copies of a subgraph, we impose a constraint condition that the number of subgraphs P is divisible by M.

Table 3: Associate Task with Subgraph.

Compute Node 0	Compute Node 1	Compute Node 2
$<T_0, S_0><T_3, S_3>$	$<T_1, S_1><T_4, S_4>$	$<T_2, S_2><T_5, S_5>$
$<T_6, S_0><T_9, S_3>$	$<T_7, S_1><T_{10}, S_4>$	$<T_8, S_2><T_{11}, S_5>$

Association between Task with Subgraph: Each task is associated with a subgraph by using a hash of the task ID to select a subgraph, with a hash function $H(t) = t \bmod P$, where t is the ID of task t and P is the number of the subgraphs. As shown in Table 3, for compute node 0, the tasks T_0, T_3, T_6, T_9 are associated respectively with Subgraphs S_0, S_3, S_0, S_3; for compute node 1, the tasks T_1, T_4, T_7, T_{10} are associated respectively with Subgraphs S_1, S_4, S_1, S_4; and for compute node 2, the tasks T_2, T_5, T_8, T_{11} are associated respectively with Subgraphs S_2, S_5, S_2, S_5.

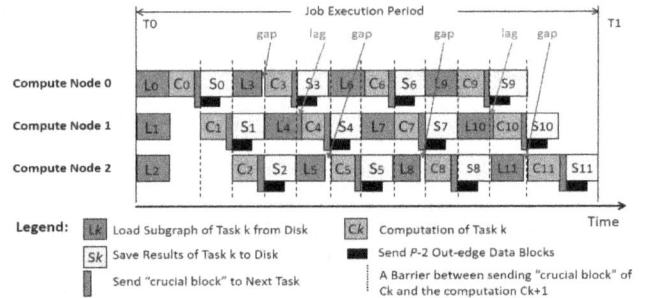

Figure 1: Job Execution Process.

Job Execution Process: As shown in Figure 1, all compute nodes start at time T0. Each compute node launches its first task from its *task queue* and loads the subgraph of that task. When the stage of loading subgraph has finished, the compute node either immediately executes the computation stage of the task t currently being launched or wait for a short time period for the arrival of the last remote out-edge data block, called the "crucial block", which is sent by the task *t-1*. The task T_0 is a special case because it is the first one. The short waiting time period indicates that the computation stage of task *t-1* has not finished. It can be eliminated by using more compute nodes. This is a trade-off between the system performance and hardware costs, as discussed in the following subsections.

In the computation stage, a user-defined **Update(v)** function is invoked for each vertex **v** in the subgraph in parallel. Inside **Update(v)**, the vertex **v** updates its state by its in-edge values and then updates its out-edge values. The in-edge values of vertex **v** were updated by the source vertices of the in-edges in the previous *P-1* tasks, and the out-edge values of vertex **v** will be used by the destination vertices of the out-edges in the subsequent *P-1* tasks.

Then, the compute node starts the block-based communication and result-saving processes simultaneously. In the block-based communication process, edge values are moved to implement the interactions between vertices, since the out-edges of a vertex are the in-edges of its neighboring vertices. The compute node sends *P-1* remote out-edge data blocks to the subsequent *P-1* tasks sequentially in order. Each of these *P-1* tasks updates the corresponding remote in-edge data block of its subgraph by using the received remote out-edge block. In the result-saving process, the compute node saves the local-edge data block and the vertex values of the subgraph currently being executed to the disk.

Finally, the compute node either repeats for the next task, or stops when it is demanded by the master node or the *task queue* is empty.

Number of Iterations: DD-Graph can run a fixed number of iterations by assigning N a fixed number. The graph-computing job can also proceed in an uncertain number of iterations until the convergence condition of the graph-computing job is met. In this case, a very large default value (such as 9999) of N is automatically assigned by DD-Graph.

2.3 Hardware Cost and Performance

DD-Graph overcomes two key challenges, including the high communication costs in distributed graph-processing frameworks and the high disk I/O latency in single-node external memory based graph-processing frameworks.

Minimizing Communication Cost: As illustrated in Figure 1, by using a small cluster, DD-Graph almost hides the communication latency by overlapping the communica-

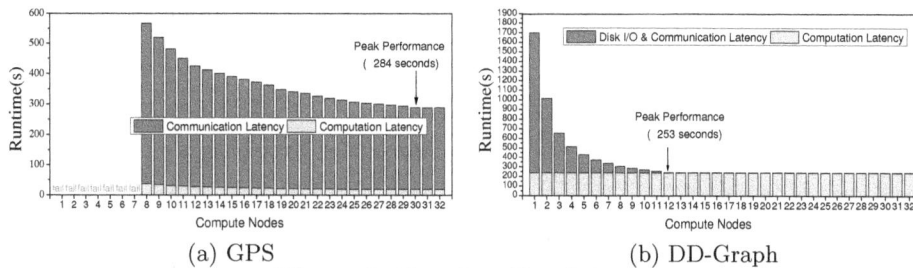

(a) GPS   (b) DD-Graph

Figure 2: Runtime Breakdown.

tion of each compute node with the computations of other compute nodes. Furthermore, in the communication process of each task, the compute node of the task only needs to send P-1 out-edge data blocks to the subsequent P-1 tasks sequentially in order. This communication model not only utilizes network bandwidth more efficiently but also depends weakly on the network bandwidth.

Hiding Disk I/O Latency: In order to mitigate the costly disk I/O latency [1], DD-Graph fully overlaps the processes of loading subgraph and saving results of a task with the computations of other physically distributed tasks.

By using a small cluster, the overall runtime is almost reduced to the computation time of compute nodes, achieving a comparable high-performance with Pregel-like distributed in-memory graph-processing frameworks, such as GPS [10].

2.4 Balancing Efficiency and Performance

There are *gaps* and *lags* during the execution process in DD-Graph, as shown in Figure 1. A *gap* represents an idle period between the loading subgraph stage and the computation stage of a task. For example, while L_3, the subgraph loading for the next task (Task 3), has finished, C_2, the computation of the current task (Task 2) has not finished, meaning that compute node 0 will be idle for a short period in which the computation stage of Task 3 waits for the computation stage of Task 2 to complete and the crucial block from Task 2. A *lag* signifies a short time span between two adjacent computations. For example, C_3, the computation of the current task (Task 3), has finished, but L_4, the subgraph loading for the next task (Task 4), has not finished, delaying the start of C_4. While *lags* bring extra latency between two adjacent computations and thus lengthen the overall run time, *gaps* result in the waste of computational resources and lead to efficiency loss.

More compute nodes bring more and longer *gaps* but fewer and shorter *lags*. The *lags* can be eliminated completely when the number of compute nodes is sufficiently large. In this case, DD-Graph reaches its peak performance. Inversely, fewer compute nodes result in fewer and shorter *gaps* but more and longer *lags*. DD-Graph can increase or decrease the *system scale* to tradeoff between performance and efficiency. In general, while the performance of DD-Graph increases with the *system scale*, its efficiency is inversely correlated to the *system scale*. The efficiency reaches a maximum value when *system scale*=1.

The *system scale* that achieves the peak performance depends on the specific graph algorithm since the computation time and load/store time vary from one graph algorithm to another. Even so, the peak-performance system scales are usually much smaller than those of existing distributed in-memory graph-processing frameworks while achieving the high performance of the latter, as shown in Section 3.

3. EXPERIMENTAL EVALUATION

In this section, we conduct extensive experiments to evaluate the performance of DD-Graph. Experiments are conducted on a 50-node cluster. Each node has two quad-core Intel Xeon E5620 processors with 32GB of RAM.

We implement four graph algorithms to evaluate DD-Graph: PageRank (PR), Community Detection (CD), Connected Components (CC) and RandomWalks (RW). We evaluate DD-Graph by using two real-world graph datasets and six synthetic graph datasets that are summarized in Table 4. We compare DD-Graph with two baseline frameworks. One is an up-to-date version of GPS, which is an open-source Pregel implementation from Stanford InfoLab [10]. The other is GraphChi, an open-source project from CMU [1].

Table 4: Summary of Graph Datasets.

DataSets	Vertices	Undirected Edges	Type
Twitter-2010	41×10^6	1.4×10^9	Social Network
UK-2007-05	106×10^6	3.7×10^9	Web
RMAT27	128×10^6	2×10^9	Synthetic
RMAT28	256×10^6	4×10^9	Synthetic
RMAT29	512×10^6	8×10^9	Synthetic
RMAT30	1×10^9	16×10^9	Synthetic
RMAT31	2×10^9	32×10^9	Synthetic
RMAT32	4×10^9	64×10^9	Synthetic

3.1 Hardware Cost & Performance

In order to have a clear understanding about how DD-Graph achieves high performance and low hardware costs, experiments are conducted to investigate the runtime breakdowns of DD-Graph and GPS. Each framework runs 10 iterations of PR on the Twitter-2010 graph repeatedly, with the number of compute nodes ranging from 1 to 32. We decompose the runtime of DD-Graph into two parts: (1) computation latency and (2) disk I/O & communication latency. The runtime of GPS consists of two parts: (1) computation latency and (2) communication latency.

Experimental results, shown in Figure 2, indicate that the computation latency of DD-Graph maintains a constant value when the system scale ranges from 1 to 32. The reason for this is that the computations of the physically distributed tasks are actually executed sequentially in time by DD-Graph. Due to the parallel execution of computations, the computation latency and communication latency of GPS are reduced gradually as the system scale increases from 8 to 30. However, the runtime of GPS maintains a constant value when the system scale ranges from 30 to 32. The reason is most likely the limited scalability of GPS. Note that GPS fails to execute the graph-computing job when system scale is less than 8. However, the disk I/O & communication latency of DD-Graph is reduced significantly when the system scale ranges from 1 to 12 and reaches the peak performance at the system scale of 12. The reason is that most of the communication and disk I/O time has been overlapped when 12 compute nodes are used. Although the computation la-

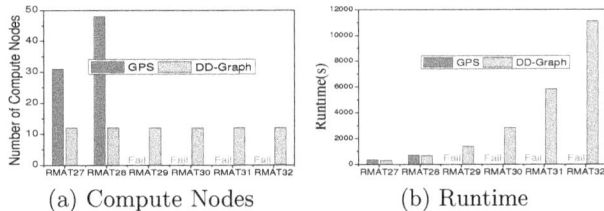

(a) Compute Nodes   (b) Runtime

Figure 3: Super-large Scale Graphs.

tency of DD-Graph is longer than that of GPS, the disk I/O & communication latency of DD-Graph is much shorter than the communication latency of GPS, leading to slightly shorter overall runtime of DD-Graph (i.e., 253 seconds vs. 284 seconds). Although there is a significant difference in the system scale, DD-Graph can achieve the high performance of GPS. We also repeat this experiment on CC, CD and RW respectively, and get the similar results.

3.2 Super-large Scale Graphs

We compare DD-Graph with GPS using a set of graphs, i.e., RMAT27, RMAT28, RMAT29, RMAT30, RMAT31 and RMAT32. Since the experimental results, shown in Section 3.1, indicate that DD-Graph can achieve its peak performance on 12 compute nodes for the PR graph algorithm. DD-Graph runs PR with these graphs respectively on the same 12-node cluster.

GPS first runs PR on the RMAT27 graph repeatedly, by increasing the system scale. GPS simply crashes when the system scale falls below 11, but as the system scale increases its runtime is reduced gradually and reaches the minimum value (340.6s) when 31 compute nodes are used. However, DD-Graph with only 12 compute nodes executes the same graph-computing job in 312.5 seconds. Experiments are repeated on RMAT28. Similarly, GPS reaches its peak performance (723.9s) when 48 compute nodes are used, while DD-Graph with only 12 compute nodes executes the same graph-computing job in 673.5 seconds. As shown in Figure 3(a), DD-Graph saves more compute nodes when handling RMAT28 than RMAT27. Furthermore, it can obtain slight performance improvements when handling both RMAT28 and RMAT27, as shown in Figure 3(b). These experimental results indicate that DD-Graph is more cost-effective when handling a larger graph than a smaller one.

As shown in Figure 3, GPS simply crashes when running on the 50-node cluster with RMAT29, RMAT30, RMAT31 and RMAT32, due to the out-of-memory problem. However, DD-Graph can process the RMAT29, RMAT30, RMAT31 and RMAT32 respectively on a cluster of 12 compute nodes.

3.3 Comparison with GraphChi

For fair comparison, DD-Graph is deployed on a single compute node. Each framework runs 10 iterations of PR on the graphs with different types and sizes. Experimental results indicate that DD-Graph can process the graphs of different sizes, and the runtimes of DD-Graph are similar to those of GPS when running on Twitter-2010, UK-2010-05, RMAT27, RMAT28 and RMAT29. However, GraphChi simply crashes when handling RMAT30 and RMAT31 graphs.

4. RELATED WORK

Chaos [8] scales X-Stream [9] out to multiple machines. This system reduces the disk I/O latency by using two measures. It avoids the random accesses by streaming completely unordered edge lists, aiming to improve the disk I/O performance. Within each machine, the disk I/O is par-

tially overlapped with computation. Chaos' system performance relies heavily on the high-bandwidth networks [8], while DD-Graph has the higher communication efficiency. The extreme requirement of network in Chaos is not easily met for most small and medium-sized organizations. Unlike Chaos, DD-Graph hides almost all of the communication latency and full I/O latency by overlapping the disk I/O and communication of each compute node with the computations of other compute nodes, thus achieving the higher performance but the lower hardware cost. Furthermore, Chaos adopts an edge-centric programming model while DD-Graph adopts the vertex-centric programming model that is more user-friendly.

5. CONCLUSION

This paper proposes DD-Graph, a distributed disk-based graph-processing framework. By scheduling the tasks of a graph-computing job on a small cluster, DD-Graph is capable of processing super-large scale graphs while achieving the high performance of Pregel-like distributed in-memory graph-processing frameworks. Extensive evaluation, driven by very large-scale graph datasets, indicates that the cost-effective advantage of DD-Graph makes it notably superior to the existing distributed graph-processing frameworks.

Acknowledgment

This work is supported in part by the National High Technology Research and Development Program (863 Program) of China under Grant No.2013AA013203 and National Basic Research 973 Program of China under Grant 2011CB302301. This work is also supported by State Key Laboratory of Computer Architecture (No.CARCH201505).

6. REFERENCES

[1] A. Kyrola, G. E. Blelloch, and C. Guestrin. Graphchi: Large-scale graph computation on just a pc. In *OSDI'12*.

[2] A. Lumsdaine, D. Gregor, B. Hendrickson, and J. Berry. Challenges in parallel graph processing. *Parallel Processing Letters*, 17(01):5–20, 2007.

[3] G. Malewicz, M. H. Austern, and etc. Pregel: a system for large-scale graph processing. In *Proc. ACM SIGMOD'10*.

[4] J. Malicevic, A. Roy, and W. Zwaenepoel. Scale-up graph processing in the cloud: Challenges and solutions. In *Proceedings of the Fourth International Workshop on Cloud Data and Platforms*. ACM, 2014.

[5] R. Pearce, M. Gokhale, and N. M. Amato. Faster parallel traversal of scale free graphs at extreme scale with vertex delegates. In *Proc. SC'14*.

[6] R. Pearce, M. Gokhale, and N. M. Amato. Multithreaded asynchronous graph traversal for in-memory and semi-external memory. In *Proc. SC'10*.

[7] R. Pearce, M. Gokhale, and N. M. Amato. Scaling techniques for massive scale-free graphs in distributed (external) memory. In *IPDPS'13*.

[8] A. Roy, L. Bindschaedler, J. Malicevic, and W. Zwaenepoel. Chaos: Scale-out graph processing from secondary storage. In *Proc. ACM SOSP'15*.

[9] A. Roy, I. Mihailovic, and W. Zwaenepoel. X-stream: edge-centric graph processing using streaming partitions. In *Proc. ACM SOSP'13*.

[10] S. Salihoglu and J. Widom. Gps: A graph processing system. In *Proc. ACM SSDBM'13*.

Evaluation of Pattern Matching Workloads in Graph Analysis Systems

Seokyong Hong
North Carolina State
University
Raleigh, NC 27695, USA
shong3@ncsu.edu

Sangkeun Lee
Oak Ridge National
Laboratory
Oak Ridge, TN 37831, USA
lees4@ornl.gov

Seung-Hwan Lim
Oak Ridge National
Laboratory
Oak Ridge, TN 37831, USA
lims1@ornl.gov

Sreenivas R. Sukumar
Oak Ridge National
Laboratory
Oak Ridge, TN 37831, USA
sukumarsr@ornl.gov

Ranga Raju Vatsavai
North Carolina State
University
Raleigh, NC 27695, USA
rrvatsav@ncsu.edu

ABSTRACT

Graph data management and mining became a popular area of research, and led to the development of plethora of systems in recent years. Unfortunately, a number of emerging graph analysis systems assume different graph data models, and support different query interface and serialization formats. Such diversity, combined with a lack of comparisons, makes it complicated to understand the trade-offs between different systems and the graph operations for which they are designed. This study presents an evaluation of graph pattern matching capabilities of six graph analysis systems, by extending the Lehigh University Benchmark to investigate the degree of effectiveness to perform the same operation over the same graph in various graph analysis systems. Through the evaluation, this study reveals both quantitative and qualitative findings.

1. INTRODUCTION

The emergence of graph analysis created a maze with numerous new systems [9], similar to other big data analysis sectors such as NoSQL databases [2]. A few major differences among such systems include system architectures (e.g., standalone and distributed), graph data models (e.g., *RDF* and *property graph*), graph serialization formats (e.g., *N-Triple*, *JSON*, and *GraphML*), and query interface (e.g., query languages and APIs). In order to decide which system is the most suitable for a specific purpose, a user may need to perform ad-hoc evaluations by converting his datasets into multiple different formats to load them into different systems and writing queries using different query languages. For data scientists, a full investigation into each graph analysis system is time consuming, error-prone, and a distraction

HPDC'16, May 31-June 04, 2016, Kyoto, Japan

© 2016 ACM. ISBN 978-1-4503-4314-5/16/05...$15.00

DOI: http://dx.doi.org/10.1145/2907294.2907305

from the original goal, that is, deriving insights from the data.

The goal of this study is to provide an evaluation of various graph analysis systems. Among graph analysis operations, this study particularly focuses on *graph pattern matching*. Graph pattern matching is an important graph problem in its own right [4]. In addition, graph pattern matching forms an essential part of graph analysis in discovering knowledge for many critical and practical missions such as fraud detection for online payment companies [8] and health insurance claims [1]. In order to achieve our objective, it is inevitable for us to rely on a benchmark suite which supports a variety of data serialization formats based on different graph models and query languages while keeping the structural characteristics of benchmark datasets the same. The lack of suitable benchmark suites propelled us to generate one by extending the popular benchmark suite for evaluating triple-stores, *Lehigh University Benchmark (LUBM)*. Using our own evaluation methodology, we present the benchmark results of the same graph pattern matching operations over the same graphs for six graph analysis systems containing both databases and graph processing systems. We also present qualitative analysis of each graph analysis system.

The rest of this paper is organized as follows: § 2 presents our evaluation method. § 3 describes our experimental evaluation results, along with detailed description of our evaluation environment. § 4 concludes this study, suggesting the future work.

2. EVALUATION METHODOLOGY

Comparisons of heterogeneous graph processing systems require supports for several graph representation models and a variety of data serialization formats along with different query languages while keeping structural characteristics the same. However, the lack of adequate benchmark suites drove us to extend one of well-known RDF benchmark suites, LUBM. The reasons that we chose the suite are twofold: (1) it suites really well for evaluating systems with graph pattern matching and (2) it is a *de facto* standard for evaluating RDF and NoSQL graph database systems in the industry [7].

Data generation for property graph: LUBM generates datasets in two web ontology languages: OWL and

Parameter	Value
dfs.replication	3
dfs.blocksize (in byte)	268435456
spark.driver.memory	5g
spark.executor.memory	40g
spark.executor.extra.JavaOptions	-XX:+UseG1GC
spark.shuffle.memoryFraction	0.3
spark.storage.memoryFraction	0.5

Table 1: Parameters for HDFS and Spark

DAML+OIL. However, those serialization formats are not widely supported by property graph-based graph analysis systems. Therefore, we extended the data generator so that it produces data in different serialization formats: N-Triple, GraphML, and JSON.

Characteristics of generated graphs: we generated datasets of universities(U) = 100 - 10K. The U100 dataset has 2M nodes and 6M edges and the U10K dataset has 217M nodes and 661M edges. Data size, the number of nodes and edges, and the number of triangles are proportional to the number of universities while all nodes reside in a single connected graph.

Query translation for property graph: the original benchmark query set is written in SPARQL which is the default language for RDF database systems. However, property graph-based systems provide different query languages and there exists no such a standard for those systems. Therefore, we rewrote the original queries in different languages: Cypher (Neo4j), Gremlin (TitanDB), Scala (GraphX), and Python (NetworkX). We selected nine queries from the original benchmark queries, taking the approach proposed in [5].

Characteristics of pattern queries: each benchmark query contains more than one representative graph patterns: neighborhood, chains, stars, triangles, and multi-edges. The queries have different selectivity patterns. The selectivity of Q4, Q5, Q7, Q8, and Q12 increases linearly as U increases while Q6, Q9, and Q14 show an almost constant pattern. Q2 shows an almost constant selectivity from U100 to U1K but it increases from U1K to U10K.

3. EVALUATION RESULTS

3.1 Evaluation environments

In this experiment, we used three different computer systems: a standalone desktop, a 9-node in-house cluster, and a shared-memory system. The desktop has an i5 1.3GHz quad-core processor, 16GB DDR3 RAM, and a 250GB solid state disk and was used for benchmarking standalone graph analysis systems (NetworkX 1.9.1, Jena Fuseki 1.1.1 with TDB, and Neo4j 2.2.3 community edition). For Java-based systems (Jena and Neo4j), we configured the JVM maximum heap size to 80% of the physical memory.

For distributed systems, we used 9 machines from CADES (Compute And Data Environment for Scientists) [6] at Oak Ridge National Laboratory. We configured a VM instance per machine, which has 32 virtual CPUs, 64GB RAM, and 500GB locally attached hard disks and used Hadoop Distributed File System (HDFS) for the underlying storage. On top of HDFS (packaged in Hadoop 2.4.0), we used Titan 0.5.1 with HBase 1.0 as the backend storage and three nodes of zookeeper quorum with all default parameters. We employed GraphX packaged in Spark 1.3.1. We configured HDFS and Spark as shown in Table 1. For both HBase and Spark (GraphX), we used eight worker nodes (region servers for HBase). As a shared-memory system, we used uRiKA [3]

which is built around a parallel supercomputer architecture. The system supports up to 8,192 hardware threads, a 2TB shared-memory, and 125TB Lustre file system.

3.2 Quantitative performance evaluation

Data loading time: NetworkX did not show comparable data loading performance among standalone graph analysis systems and could not load more than U100. Jena showed the best loading time, resulting in 16 - 29% better performance than Neo4j. However, it could not load U500 due to heap memory error. For the number of universities ≥ 3K, we stopped the loading Titan after 12 hours. As with many property graph-based systems, the Titan graph database internally allocates IDs for nodes and edges. Titan allocates a block of IDs ahead of creating entities. However, when the graph is large, those pre-allocated IDs are depleted too soon compared to the ingestion rate of back-end storages. Thus, the loading is bottlenecked by ID allocation. Also, the use of HBase backend contributed to linear increase of loading time. It is principally because of the design principle of HBase; when inserting a new entry, it firstly fills a region in one region server. When the region size exceeds a pre-configured limit, the region splits. Then, if the number of regions in the region server exceeds the pre-configured limit, it finds a new region in another region server. Therefore, the loading process did not fully utilize multiple region servers when we load graph in bulk. In uRiKA, multiple processors dedicated to I/O enabled concurrent data loading and database creation in its shared memory. This parallelized I/O and data processing capability enabled the best data loading performance out of the five graph analysis systems.

Changes on data size after loading: when loaded on NetworkX, the size of graph data increased tremendously (627% with U100) since it maintains labels along with their attributes as objects in hierarchical dictionaries. In case of Jena and Neo4j, the input data additionally occupied 25 - 88% more storage space for storing metadata and additional data structures. On Titan, the occupied storage size, however, decreased around 89%. This is because Titan maintains edges in a compressed way, and serializes and compresses graph data when loaded into HBase. On uRiKA, the input size-to-storage size ratios remained same regardless of graph size.

Query execution times: we examined the graph analysis systems to check their pattern matching performance with our benchmark suite. Figure 1 compares the execution times for processing individual pattern matching queries. As we mentioned previously, NetworkX failed to load U ≥ 200, which did not allow to run queries over those datasets. It is notable that NetworkX performs in-memory analysis avoiding expensive disk I/Os but it did not show superior performance for most of the queries than other systems even with the smallest dataset. Its loop-based graph iterations along with inefficiency on its programming interface degrade the advantage of in-memory analysis. Among standalone systems, Jena processed many of the queries relatively well and showed comparable performance against Q2, Q6, Q12, and Q14 while Neo4j showed the best performance against Q7 and Q8. For distributed and high performance analysis platforms, uRiKA was superior to the others for most of the queries with U ≥ 1K. For Q6 and Q12 with some datasets, GraphX showed slightly better performance but the difference was negligible. uRiKA also showed better performance

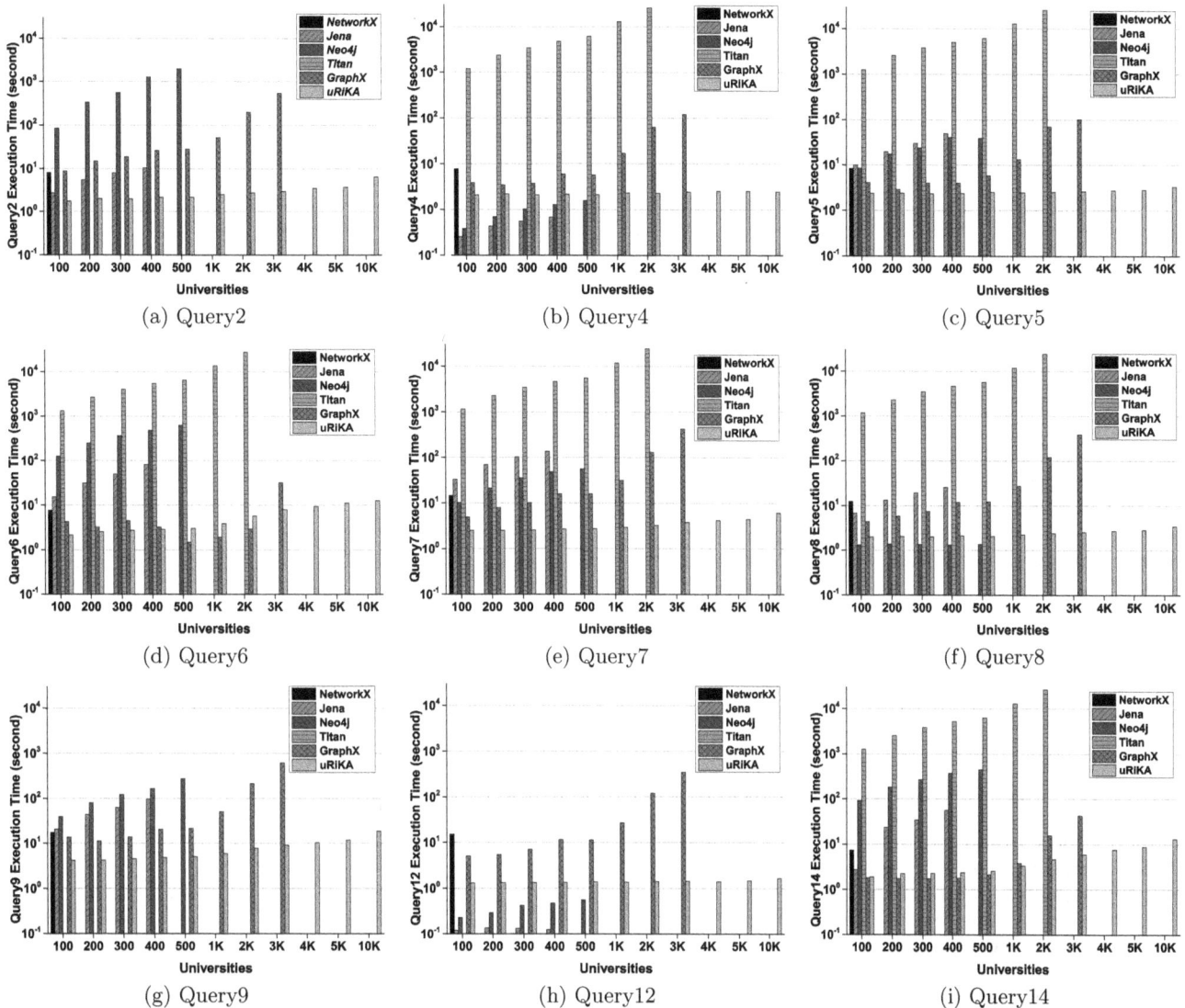

(a) Query2	(b) Query4	(c) Query5
(d) Query6	(e) Query7	(f) Query8
(g) Query9	(h) Query12	(i) Query14

Figure 1: Query execution times in log scale: note that standalone systems (Neo4j, NetworkX, and Jena), distributed systems (GraphX and Titan), and shared-memory system (uRiKA) used different hardware. Query 2, 9, and 12 are not implemented in Gremlin (refer to 3.3). We averaged execution times after cache warm-up periods.

for Q2, Q5, Q6, Q7, Q9, and Q14 with U < 1K even than standalone analysis systems; however, for Q4 and Q12, Jena outperformed uRiKA with those datasets. We omitted Q2, Q9, and Q12 for Titan due to a limitation of Gremlin query language. Titan showed excessively slower performance than the other systems including standalone systems for the other six queries.

3.3 Qualitative evaluation

We discuss several qualitative observations from extending the LUBM benchmark suite and conducting benchmarks on the graph analysis systems.

Data serialization and loading: support for various serialization formats with corresponding data loaders is a fundamental requirement for dealing with graph data from heterogeneous sources. In RDF, there exist several serialization formats and Jena could support those serialization formats. However, we observed that uRiKA only supports a limited set of serialization formats: N-Triple and N-Quad. Many of the property graph-based systems sup-

port GraphML natively or with third-party plugins. However, GraphX does not support GraphML and there exists no available extension. We notice that it is not trivial to implement a GraphML loader optimized for GraphX-like distributed graph analysis systems. The major difficulty is that simply partitioning GraphML data over multiple nodes results in loss of required information. First, GraphML locates metadata about node and edge properties at a separate location in a single file. Next, it uses XML notation where each element is described over multiple lines and elements are structured in a nested manner. This pre-processing adds additional costs to the pattern matching query [10]. Instead, we chose Property Graph/JSON as a serialization format for GraphX and implemented a corresponding data loader.

Expressiveness of query languages: for graph pattern matching, Cypher and SPARQL have the best expressiveness in that they expose intuitive ways for users to list interesting structural constraints in declarative ways. On the other hand, Gremlin has several limitations on expressing graph pattern queries compared to Cypher and SPARQL. First, Gremlin users should consider not only structural constraints but also orders in which nodes and edges are traversed. This is because Gremlin is designed based on the principle of graph traversal rather than graph pattern matching. Next, it is not trivial and sometimes not possible to write complex pattern queries to retrieve results in a desired fashion. For example, Q9 finds triangles by traversing graphs as students→professors→courses→students and returns the URI attribute of retrieved students. Although we can retrieve the result set with the same size (which implies that the same patterns have been identified), it was not trivial to save or print out results as triangular patterns as the original query intends – a collection of URIs in the form of student, professor, and course in a single line from three vertices in the matched subgraphs, instead of URI only from students. It is primarily because each traversal operation in Gremlin finds vertices and, thus, `sideEffect` only outputs properties of vertices at the current step, instead of expressing properties of vertices from matched subgraphs. In this work, our goal was to evaluate the ability to obtain the same analysis results, which should include the time to retrieve the result set and present to users. As a result, this study omitted to implement query 2, 9, and 12 in Gremlin.

NetworkX and GraphX provide general programming environments as querying interfaces, Python and Scala, respectively. In NetworkX, the programming interface results in several nested loops and one-by-one comparisons for finding graph elements that match structural constraints in subgraphs. On the other hand, GraphX provides additional graph processing primitives that can be utilized for graph pattern matching tasks (e.g., *triplets* and *join*), which allow a declarative way to express graph patterns to some extent.

Optimization issues: Cypher and SPARQL are declarative query languages, which can decouple query optimization tasks from query writing tasks. However, we observed that the query processing engine in Jena produces different query plans based on the order of triple patterns in queries, which significantly affects query execution time. Therefore, this burdens users to optimize their queries before execution. In case of Gremlin, there are multiple ways to traverse a given graph pattern, each of which results in different query selectivity. Titan does not change user-defined traversal orders being aware of selectivity. Therefore, users are responsible for optimizing queries by finding optimal traversal orders. In addition, complex graph patterns often break traversals. That is, they cannot be traversed in a *"connecting-the-dots"* manner and require to jump to previously visited nodes. This also requires intermediate states at certain points to be recorded during traversals. Hence, Gremlin users need to explicitly represent such decisions in their queries by using a set of relevant primitives. In NetworkX, complex graph pattern matching queries produce several nested loops. Since the size and the level of each loop along with the number of loops can increase computational complexity, minimizing the overall cost is users' responsibility. In GraphX, triplets are mapped to triples in SPARQL and join operation links triples by their nodes. With the use of such primitives, graph patterns which have multiple edges and long chains produce multiple join operations in their query representation. In such cases, a typical optimization is ordering joins to minimize query processing costs. However, still, the order of performing joins is on users' hand.

4. CONCLUSION

This study presented a comparison between a number of heterogeneous graph analysis systems with evaluation procedures for pattern discovery capability of those systems. For future work, as a graph analysis pipeline often involves both graph pattern matching and exploratory graph analysis (graph mining), it might be interesting to study the efficiency of performing both tasks in one system or in a combination of systems. In addition, it will be desirable to devise a principled approach to synthesize more realistic graphs or to fit a graph generative model to an empirical graph. We envision that this study will serve as a guide for data scientists to select the optimal graph analysis tool for their graph pattern matching workloads and for data system designers to advance graph analysis systems.

5. ACKNOWLEDGMENTS

This manuscript has been authored by UT-Battelle, LLC under Contract No. DE-AC05-00OR22725 with the U.S. Department of Energy. The United States Government retains and the publisher, by accepting the article for publication, acknowledges that the United States Government retains a non-exclusive, paid-up, irrevocable, world-wide license to publish or reproduce the published form of this manuscript, or allow others to do so, for United States Government purposes. The Department of Energy will provide public access to these results of federally sponsored research in accordance with the DOE Public Access Plan (http://energy.gov/downloads/doe-public-access-plan).

6. REFERENCES

[1] V. Chandola, S. R. Sukumar, and J. C. Schryver. Knowledge discovery from massive healthcare claims data. In *Proceedings of the 19th ACM SIGKDD*, KDD '13, 2013.

[2] B. F. Cooper, A. Silberstein, E. Tam, R. Ramakrishnan, and R. Sears. Benchmarking cloud serving systems with ycsb. In *Proceedings of the 1st ACM Symposium on Cloud Computing*, SoCC '10, 2010.

[3] Cray. urika-gd. http://www.cray.com/products/analytics/urika-gd.

[4] D. Dominguez-Sal, N. Martinez-Bazan, V. Muntes-Mulero, P. Baleta, and J. L. Larriba-Pey. A discussion on the design of graph database benchmarks. In *Performance Evaluation, Measurement and Characterization of Complex Systems*, pages 25–40. Springer, 2011.

[5] A. Gubichev and M. Then. Graph pattern matching - do we have to reinvent the wheel? In *Second International Workshop on Graph Data Management Experiences and Systems, GRADES, co-located with SIGMOD/PODS*, 2014.

[6] Oak Ridge National Laboratory. Materials scientists use ornl's cades to transform big data to 'smart data' for rapid image analysis. {http://www.ornl.gov/ornl/highlights/materials-scientists-use-ornls-cades}.

[7] Oracle. Oracle spatial and graph: Benchmarking a trillion edges rdf graph. http://download.oracle.com/otndocs/tech/semantic_web/pdf/OracleSpatialGraph_RDFgraph_1_trillion_Benchmark.pdf.

[8] PayPal. Graph mining for fraud detection. http://lanyrd.com/2015/big-data-techcon/sdkcqp/.

[9] N. Satish, N. Sundaram, M. M. A. Patwary, J. Seo, J. Park, M. A. Hassaan, S. Sengupta, Z. Yin, and P. Dubey. Navigating the maze of graph analytics frameworks using massive graph datasets. In *Proceedings of the 2014 SIGMOD*, SIGMOD '14, 2014.

[10] Sujoe Bose. Efficient processing of large and complex xml documents in hadoop. http://www.slideshare.net/Hadoop_Summit/bose-june26-405pmroom230cv3-24148869.

SMT-Aware Instantaneous Footprint Optimization

Probir Roy, Xu Liu
Department of Computer Science
College of William and Mary
{proy, xl10}@cs.wm.edu

Shuaiwen Leon Song
High Performance Computing Group
Pacific Northwest National Laboratory (PNNL)
Shuaiwen.Song@pnnl.gov

ABSTRACT

Modern architectures employ simultaneous multithreading (SMT) to increase thread-level parallelism. SMT threads share many functional units and the entire memory hierarchy of a physical core. Without a careful code design, SMT threads can easily contend with each other for these shared resources, causing severe performance degradation. Minimizing SMT thread contention for HPC applications running on dedicated platforms is very challenging because they typically spawn threads within Single Program Multiple Data (SPMD) models. Since these threads have similar resource requirements, their contention cannot be easily mitigated through simple thread scheduling. To address this important issue, we first vigorously conduct a systematic performance evaluation on a wide-range of representative HPC and CMP applications on three mainstream SMT architectures, and quantify their performance sensitivity to SMT effects. Then we introduce a simple scheme for SMT-aware code optimization which aims to reduce the memory contention across SMT threads. Finally, we develop a lightweight performance tool, named *SMTAnalyzer*, to effectively identify the optimization opportunities in the source code of multithreaded programs. Experiments on three SMT architectures (i.e., Intel Xeon, IBM POWER7, and Intel Xeon Phi) demonstrate that our proposed SMT-aware optimization scheme can significantly improve the performance for general HPC applications.

Categories and Subject Descriptors

C.4 [**Performance of systems**]: Measurement techniques, Performance attributes; D.2.8 [**Metrics**]: Performance measures.

Keywords

SMT, Memory Hierarchy, Instantaneous Footprint, SMT-Aware Optimization, Locality, Performance Tools

1. INTRODUCTION

Modern architectures employ simultaneous multithreading (SMT, also known as fine-grained threads) [37] to support many hardware threads. These SMT-based architectures have become increasingly popular, leveraged by seven of the top ten supercomputers in the world today [1]. Unleashing their maximum computing power has become critical for the future missions towards Exascale computing.

In this paper, we refer to the hardware threads on the same physical core as *SMT threads*. SMT threads can avoid CPU stalls and improve the throughput of a physical core. If one SMT thread stalls in execution pipeline, instructions from other SMT threads can be switched in so that the execution can continue without additional overhead. With the trend of increasing thread-level parallelism on chip, more SMT threads have been integrated to a single physical core. For example, Intel Xeon Phi [16] has four SMT threads per core and IBM POWER8 [13] has eight SMT threads per core, both of which double the SMT thread number compared to their previous generation.

Unlike threads on different physical cores, SMT threads share many functional units in the execution pipeline such as instruction issuing slots, load store queues, integer and floating units. Moreover, they share the entire memory subsystem including all levels of cache, prefetchers, and bandwidth. Without a careful code design, SMT threads can easily contend for these shared resources, causing significant performance degradation.

Previous studies [38, 7, 25, 30, 8] analyzed the performance impact of resource sharing between SMT threads. To minimize resource contention, they characterize thread execution and schedule them to the same physical core if they have different resource requirements. This co-scheduling approach works well for mixed workloads running on an SMT architecture, because their threads usually have different resource requests. However, this scheme does not work well for HPC applications which usually run on a dedicated system without sharing resources with co-running applications. Moreover, HPC applications often use Single Program Multiple Data (SPMD) models which create threads with similar characteristics and resource requests. Therefore, such simple thread co-scheduling cannot minimize SMT thread contention for HPC applications that possess similar resource requirements across threads.

In this paper, we propose an SMT-aware optimization scheme to reduce the contention among SMT threads at the source code level for HPC applications. The underlying intuition in our code optimization technique is that threads should collaboratively work on a small data set rather than on a large or multiple data sets. This can be achieved by altering the typical parallel strategy widely used in modern threading models, such as OpenMP [28] and Pthread [4]. Our novel optimization method contrasts and complements the existing approaches based on thread scheduling by developing the first code transformation technique intended to improve the performance for HPC codes running on SMT architectures.

The application of a practical SMT-aware optimization has three major challenges. First, to apply appropriate optimizations, we need to be able to identify the major performance bottlenecks in an SMT architecture. Second, the optimization itself should not be overly complex and should be easy for developers or compilers to adopt and apply. Third, there must be some accompanying technique to explicitly, automatically and accurately highlight the locations in source code where such an optimization should take place in order to achieve the best performance. To address these challenges, this paper makes the following contributions:

- We systematically evaluate the performance impact of SMT on a wide-range of representative HPC and CMP applications on three mainstream SMT architectures. We derive new latency-based metrics to quantify their performance in the memory subsystem. Based on the analysis, we discover that SMT shows inconsistent memory behaviors across applications.

- We introduce a simple but effective code transformation scheme to reduce the contention among SMT threads in the memory hierarchy. To the best of our knowledge, this is the first work on *unconventional* code-level optimization for SMT thread execution. Specifically, we introduce *false sharing* between SMT threads to improve the inter-thread locality.

- We develop a performance tool named *SMTAnalyzer* that can help identify SMT optimization opportunities in existing multithreaded programs. SMTAnalyzer monitors execution of unmodified binaries, collects performance data with low overhead, and provides insights to guide SMT-aware optimizations.

We evaluate our proposed optimization scheme on three modern SMT architectures: Intel Xeon, Intel Xeon Phi, and IBM POWER7. Under the guidance of SMTAnalyzer, we are able to significantly improve the performance for several widely-used and highly-optimized HPC applications.

We organize this paper as follows: Section 2 explores the performance impact of SMT on various applications. Section 3 describes our SMT-aware optimization scheme. Section 4 illustrates the design and implementation of SMTAnalyzer. Case studies under the guidance of SMTAnalyzer are demonstrated in Section 5. Section 6 reviews previous work and distinguishes our approach. We conclude this work in Section 7.

2. PERFORMANCE IMPACT OF SMT: OBSERVATIONS AND ANALYSIS

In this section, we study the performance impact of SMT by analyzing the execution behaviors of parallel applications on modern SMT architectures. To better quantify such impact, we investigate a broad spectrum of 31 widely-used and often highly-optimized benchmarks from chip multiprocessing (CMP) research (i.e., PARSEC [3]), popular HPC

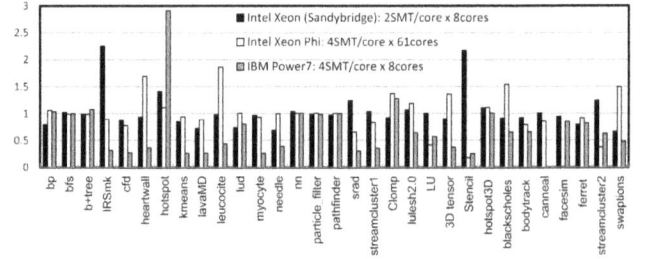

Figure 1: Runtime Ratio (SMT/NONSMT) for applications on Intel SandyBridge, Intel Xeon Phi, and IBM Power7. Two PARSEC benchmarks encounter compilation issues: `facesim` on Xeon Phi and `canneal` on Power7. They are shown as 0 in the figure.

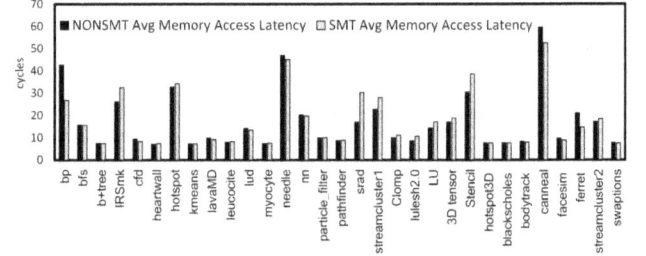

(a) Average memory access latency (L) swing from NONSMT to SMT on Intel Xeon.

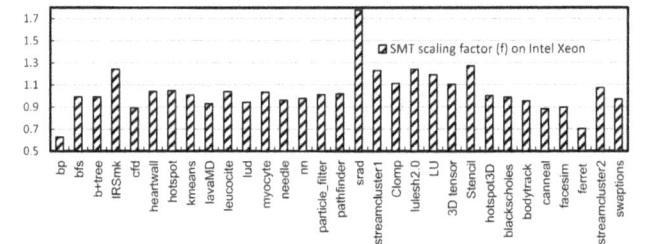

(b) SMT Scaling Factor $(F) = L_{SMT}/L_{NONSMT}$

Figure 2: Memory performance affected by SMT effects on Intel Xeon: (a) Average memory access latency (L) swing from NON-SMT to SMT; (b) SMT Scaling Factor (F).

suites (i.e., Rodinia [5] and NPB [2]), and HPC application benchmarks (i.e., Sequoia Benchmark [18]). They cover a variety of execution patterns including data sharing, locality, inter-thread communication, synchronization, and on-/off-chip traffic. We list all the benchmarks that we investigated from each suite as the following:

- Rodinia Benchmarks: `bp`, `bfs`, `b+tree`, `cfd`, `heartwall`, `hotspot`, `kmeans`, `lavaMD`, `leucocite`, `lud`, `myocyte`, `needle`, `nn`, `particle_filter`, `pathfinder`, `srad`, `streamcluster1`, `hotspt3D`.

- Sequoia Benchmarks: `Clomp`, `lulesh2.0`, `IRSmk`.

- PARSEC Benchmarks: `blackscholes`, `bodytrack`, `canneal`, `facesim`, `ferret`, `fluidanimate`, `streamcluster2`, `swaptions`.

- NAS Benchmark Suite: `LU`.

- Microbenchmarks: `3D tensor`, `Stencil`.

We evaluate these benchmarks on three SMT architectures that are commonly deployed in modern HPC systems: Intel Xeon (SandyBridge), Intel Xeon Phi, and IBM Power7.

Processor Type	SMT per core	caches shared by SMT per core	L1	L2	L3	Memory
Intel Xeon E5-4650 2.70GHz,	2	$L2, $L1	32KB private	256KB private	20MB/8cores shared	64GB, 8 cores 51.2 GB/s
Intel Xeon Phi 1.24GHz	4	$L2 (Ring Structure), $L1	32KB private	512KB private	No L3	16GB, 61 cores 352 GB/s
IBM Power7 3.7 GHz	4	$L2, $L1	64KB private	4MB private	32MB/8cores shared	64GB, 8 cores 68.2 GB/s

Table 1: Architecture features of the three platforms under investigation.

(L, F)	Benchmarks	Characterization
(high, high)	srad, streamcluster1, Lulesh2.0, IRSmk, LU, 3D tensor, Stencil, streamcluster2, hotspot, Clomp	potentially sensitive to mem-centric SMT optimizations
(high, low)	lud, needle, bfs, nn, bp, canneal, ferret	not clear if they can further benefit from SMT optimizations
(low, high)	leucocite, heartwall, pathfinder, myocyte	little benefit from mem-centric SMT optimization
(low, low)	b+tree, cfd, kmeans, lavaMD, particle_filter, hotspot3D, blackscholes, bodytrack, facesim, swaptions	good memory performance with SMT enabled

Table 2: Categorization based on the degree of potential performance benefits from reducing the SMT-induced overhead.

Each of them has different architectural features and SMT capabilities, as shown in Table 1. To prevent the non-uniform memory access (NUMA) impact from interfering with our observations, we only experiment on one socket in the IBM Power7 and Intel Xeon platforms (i.e., both have 8 cores per socket). Random noise in the results is reduced through the average measurement of repetitive runs.

2.1 Runtime Ratio Analysis

We first quantify the overall performance impact of applying SMT on benchmarks using a general runtime ratio which is calculated as $\frac{Runtime\_SMT}{Runtime\_NONSMT}$. We run the benchmarks on all the three SMT architectures to evaluate their SMT impact, shown in Figure 1. We compute the runtime ratio for each benchmark running with their maximum SMT capability.

From the figure, we observe that a majority of the benchmarks are not close to achieving their expected speedups on all three architectures when SMT threads are enabled. In many cases, they gain no speedup or even perform worse. For instance, on the Intel SandyBridge platform, the average runtime ratio across 31 applications is 1.038 while doubling the threads. Only 18 out of 31 benchmarks achieve some degree of speedup, 13% on average. Among them, swaptions is the only benchmark that achieves close to 2x speedup. The other 13 benchmarks either exhibit little to no performance improvement, or have significantly worse performance than the baseline (e.g., hotspot, srad, IRSmk, Lulesh, Stencil and streamcluster2). Although the root causes of this negative performance impact could be a combination of factors at both the computation (e.g., competing for shared resources in execution pipelines) and memory levels, this work primarily focuses on addressing the bottlenecks in the *memory hierarchy* (i.e., private and shared layers) introduced by the SMT effects, which include both suboptimal data locality and scalability issues.

2.2 General Memory Performance Analysis

We further investigate how SMT impacts different benchmarks in the memory hierarchy. We apply the *average memory access latency* as the metric for evaluating the memory-level bottlenecks caused by the SMT effects. We prefer the latency-based metric over hit rate because it reflects the performance change more accurately for SMT architectures which are typically latency-oriented. For example, even if one case has much worse overall performance than the other due to its significant L1 bandwidth contention, they can still have the same L1 hit rate.

We denote the *average memory access latency* for an application as L. L can be calculated as the aggregate latency for accessing the memory subsystem divided by the number of memory accesses, i.e., $L = (\sum_{i=1}^{n} L_i)/n$, where n represents the number of memory accesses. To obtain an accurate estimation of L, precise and lightweight measurement mechanism is required. Among the three SMT architectures, only Intel SandyBridge provides such capability through Precise Event-Based Sampling (PEBS) [14] (see Section 4.1 for more discussion). We use the aggregate sampled latency divided by the number of memory samples to approximate L.

Figure 2(a) shows the values of L with SMT enabled (L_{SMT}) and with SMT disabled (L_{NONSMT}) for 31 benchmarks. We can observe that L_{NONSMT} for some benchmarks are already high (e.g., bp, canneal, needle, IRSmk and hotspot), indicating significant memory-level bottlenecks before applying SMT. Additionally, enabling SMT introduces higher L for 17 benchmarks, 10 of which are observed with an over 10% L increment. More interestingly, applying SMT actually reduces L for the other 14 benchmarks, indicating that the data locality between SMT threads on the same core (i.e. inter-thread sharing) is improved and this performance benefit even surpasses resource contention in the memory hierarchy. This unique finding inspires our SMT-aware optimization on memory in Section 3.

2.3 Benchmark Categorization

To understand which benchmark can potentially benefit from reducing SMT-induced overhead, we adopt the differential analysis theory from [23] to construct a metric describing SMT effects with different focus and evaluation standards. We name it *SMT Scaling Factor (F)*, where $F = \frac{L_{SMT}}{L_{NONSMT}}$. Figure 2(b) shows the F value for each benchmark.

We combine L_{NONSMT}, short as L, and F to create an evaluation tuple (L, F) for categorizing the benchmarks in terms of SMT-optimization sensitivity, shown in Table 2. In this table, benchmarks are classified into four categories based on their (L, F) values: (low, low), (low, high), (high,low) and (high, high). For the Intel Xeon architecture, we treat L as high if it exceeds 10 cycles (Figure 2(a)) since the average memory access latency with no contention for

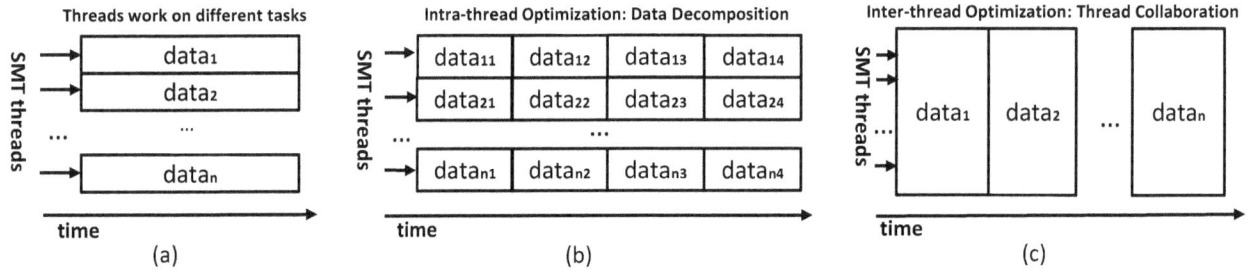

Figure 3: Three parallel execution schemes: (a) Default parallel execution: all threads work on different data to enjoy "embarrassingly parallelism"; (b) Reducing instantaneous footprints through intra-thread optimization: data decomposition; (c) Reducing instantaneous footprints through inter-thread optimization: thread collaboration.

the architecture is around 7 cycles. We also treat F as low if $F < 1.05$. The category (low,low) indicates the scenario that SMT does not introduce memory bottlenecks. The category (low,high) indicates that there is probably little benefit from further SMT-oriented optimization, since L is too low. Benchmarks in (high, high) category not only perform worse with SMT threads but also have the high base latency L, which makes them good candidates for SMT-aware optimizations. The category (high, low) includes several interesting cases, which either are sensitive to SMT and their Ls are improved with SMT (e.g., bp, canneal, ferret); or react little to the SMT effects (e.g., lud, needle, bfs, and nn) but still with high L. It is unclear if these applications can further benefit from SMT-aware optimizations, requiring a deeper investigation.

Based on this categorization, we narrow our focus down to only the benchmarks from (high, high) and (high, low) categories, since their performance can be potentially improved by reducing SMT-induced contention in the memory hierarchy. Note that although the accurate (L, F) values cannot be directly obtained for benchmarks running on IBM Power7 and Intel Xeon Phi due to the profiling limitations in hardware (refer to Section 4.1), coarse-grained approximation using performance counters suggests a similar categorization for (high, high) and (high, low) with ferret, IRSmk, and streamcluster2 moving in between the two categories.

2.4 Fine-Grained Analysis in Memory Layers

Table 3 shows the latency inflation in different memory layers on the three architectures for the benchmarks falling into the (high, high) category. The table confirms that SMT effects result in significant memory-level contention for these benchmarks, including cache-level contention caused by limited bandwidth and hardware resources (e.g., limited cache space, limited entries for LFB and TLB), and large memory footprint incurred by a large number of threads. Based on these findings, we propose our SMT-aware optimization techniques to reduce memory contention in the next section.

3. SMT-AWARE CODE OPTIMIZATION

From our analysis in Section 2, optimizing the memory subsystem by reducing the contention in cache space and bandwidth is critically important for SMT architectures. We propose a term *instantaneous footprint* to characterize the contention among SMT threads (defined as the hardware threads on the same physical core), as follows.

Definition 1 (Instantaneous Footprint) *We define instantaneous footprint of a program context (loops, functions,*

APPs	Latency Increase (↑) and Decrease (↓)		
	Intel Xeon	Xeon Phi* (miss impact)	Power7*
srad	L1 hit ↑ 62% TLB miss ↑104x	↑102%	L2 hit ↑5% L3 hit ↑8% Local_mem hit ↑5%
streamcluster1	LFB hit ↑69%	↑33%	L2 hit ↑3x L3 hit ↑23%
Lulesh 2.0	L1 hit ↑11% L2 hit ↑170% LFB hit ↑60%	↑113%	L3 hit ↑24% Local_mem hit ↑17%
NAS LU	LFB hit ↑87% L2 hit ↑115%	↑65%	L2 and L3 hit ↓
3D Tensor	L3 miss ↑24%	↑34%	L2 hit ↑15% L3 hit ↑17%
Stencil1	LFB hit ↑48% L1 hit ↑13%	↑160%	L2 hit ↑23% L3 hit ↑9% Local_mem hit ↑26%
Clomp	L1 hit ↑7% LFB hit ↑10%	↑13%	L2 hit ↑50% L3 hit ↑15%
hotspot	L2 hit ↑8x L3 hit ↑45% mem_bus ↑110%	↓0.5%	L2 hit ↑1.5x

*Unlike Xeon, Xeon Phi and Power7 require workarounds from performance counters to approximate latency inflation for a subset (not all) of memory layers. For instance, L1 miss latency can be estimated through the limited hardware events available on Xeon Phi: Estimated Latency Impact = (CPU_CLK_UNHALTED − EXEC_STAGE_CYCLES − DATA_READ_OR_WRITE) / DATA_READ_OR_WRITE_MISS.

Table 3: Latency inflation of the major memory bottlenecks (based on F and latency contribution of individual memory component) for (high, high) applications on the three architectures.

or the whole program) as the memory bytes required by all the SMT threads at a specific time point.

A large instantaneous footprint potentially leads to high memory contention, as loading these data concurrently competes for cache space and bandwidth. As an example shown in Figure 3(a), threads are working on n different data sets, which may cause increased thread contention due to the large instantaneous footprint (i.e., as high as n data sets). This parallelization is widely used in multithreaded applications with modern programming models, such as OpenMP [28], Pthread [4], and Cilk [11]. While this can benefit from "embarrassing parallelism", it could also introduce severe contention in the memory subsystem. To reduce the contention, we propose two techniques to shrink the instantaneous footprint with code transformation in Section 3.1, and then use empirical analysis to show their applicability for the real optimization in Section 3.2. Finally, we discuss some limitations of our proposed methods in Section 3.3.

3.1 Instantaneous Footprint Reduction

As shown in Figure 3(b) and (c), we propose two methods to reduce instantaneous footprint, including intra-thread optimization through *data decomposition* and inter-thread optimization through *thread collaboration*.

Intra-thread Optimization. Figure 3(b) shows the basic idea of enhancing intra-thread memory utilization and data locality through data decomposition. Instead of loading the entire data set of each thread to compete for the memory subsystem, we can decompose the data set of each thread into several (e.g., 4 in the figure) small pieces and load them one by one. Thus, the instantaneous footprint across all the threads is reduced to a quarter of the original footprint. For example, as a concrete software-level intra-thread optimization, we regroup n arrays in a loop from structure of arrays (SoA) to array of structure (AoS). In the SoA loop, the instantaneous footprint is n cache lines per iteration, because a thread needs to load a cache line from each array for the computation. However, in the AoS loop, the instantaneous footprint is reduce to $\frac{n}{8}$ cache lines with the assumption that all the arrays contain eight-byte double elements and the cache line size is 64 bytes. Thus, we consider array regrouping as a viable option for reducing the large instantaneous footprint on SMT architectures.

It is worth noting that reducing instantaneous footprint through intra-thread optimization is often complex and sometimes impossible for every loop, since data layouts with different access patterns may not be easily matched between hot loops to obtain good intra-thread locality. Details about array regrouping in highly threaded codes can be found in our previous work [22]. For the rest of the section, we will mainly focus on discussing the inter-thread optimization in SMT architectures.

Inter-thread Optimization. When intra-thread optimization is not feasible or effective, inter-thread optimization can be applied. Figure 3(c) demonstrates the basic idea of inter-thread optimization. As shown in the figure, all the threads collaboratively work on the same data set and then move on to the next upon completion, reducing the instantaneous footprint to $\frac{1}{n}$ of the default parallelization mode in Figure 3(a). Note that such parallelization mode may incur thread synchronization more often. However, the synchronization between the SMT threads occurs in L1 cache as L1 hits, whose cost is much smaller than the gain from the inter-thread optimization that reduces cache miss significantly (see the evaluation in Section 3.2). As a concrete inter-thread optimization, increasing sharing, even *false sharing* between SMT threads can effectively reduce the instantaneous footprint across these threads. In the next section, we elaborate on this idea with empirical studies.

3.2 False Sharing among SMT Threads

3.2.1 General Finding

False sharing is a well-known performance contention in multithreaded programs [19]. Assume that each thread runs on a distinct core with its own private cache. False sharing occurs when threads simultaneously access logically-independent data in the same cache line, and where at least one of the accesses is a write. Usually it causes significant performance degradation because threads keep invalidating cache lines and incur many coherence cache misses. False

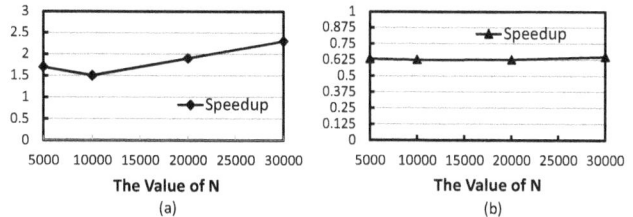

Figure 4: Speedups for the SMT-aware optimization on (a) Listing 1 and (b) Listing 2.

```
1 #pragma omp parallel for <schedule(static,1)>
2   for (int i=0; i<N; i++)
3     for (int j=0; j<N; j++)
4       B[j][i] = A[i][j];
```

Listing 1: Threads have no intra-thread locality on array B. We can enhance inter-thread locality to improve performance.

sharing can be avoided by placing the data required by different threads into different cache lines.

Counter-intuitively, false sharing does *not* hurt the performance of SMT threads, which share the private cache to that core. False sharing degrades performance only if threads running on different physical cores, because cache line invalidations and coherence misses only occur between private caches of different cores. Unlike threads in the traditional multicore architectures, SMT threads share all levels of cache within the same physical core. Therefore, false sharing between SMT threads does not hurt performance. This matches the observation we had in Figure 2(a) (although true and false sharing could both occur there). Based on this insight, we discover the following finding, which serves as the foundational knowledge for reducing instantaneous footprint via inter-thread optimization in SMT architectures:

> ***Key Finding:*** *Introducing false sharing but not breaking the original intra-thread locality can significantly improve performance for SMT threads.*

3.2.2 Empirical Evaluation of the Finding

We empirically illustrate how to use this finding in the optimization and assess its performance gain. Several simple OpenMP [28] microbenchmarks are developed here for evaluation purposes. OpenMP is one of the most popular multithreading models and provides intuitive parallel structures suitable for our investigation. However, the same finding and conclusion can also be applied to other thread models, such as Linux Pthread [4], TBB [34], and Cilk [11]. The experiments for this evaluation are conducted on the POWER7 machine listed in Table 1 with four SMT threads bound to the same physical core. All the code examples used in this section are compiled with gcc-4.9.

Listing 1 shows an OpenMP parallel loop nest for matrix transposition. Referencing array B has long strides, leading to poor spatial locality in each thread. The original code (with no blue keywords) also has no inter-thread reuse because the OpenMP library assigns a chunk of i loop iterations to each thread by default: all threads access different segments of B. It is worth noting that improving the intra-thread locality of the loop via loop transformation is not easy because interchanging the loop nest improves B but hurts A.

We apply a simple SMT-aware optimization to introduce false sharing across threads. We add the blue keywords in Listing 1 to let OpenMP runtime library dispatch ad-

```
1  #pragma omp parallel for shared(array) <schedule(static,1)>
2    for (int i=0; i<N*N; i++)
3      array[i]++;
```

Listing 2: `array` has intra-thread locality in the loop.

```
1  #pragma omp parallel for shared(matrix)
2    for (int i=0; i<N; i++)
3      ...
4      for (int k=0; k<N; k++)
5        ...
6        for (int j=0; j<N; j++)
7          matrix[i][...][j][...][k] = ...;
```

Listing 3: A multi-level loop nest with poor intra-thread locality in `matrix`.

```
1  <#pragma omp parallel>
2  {
3    for (int i=0; i<N; i++)
4      ...
5      <#pragma omp for shared(matrix) schedule(static,1)>
6      for (int k=0; k<N; k++)
7        ...
8        for (int j=0; j<N; j++)
9          matrix[i][...][j][...][k] = ...;
10 }
```

Listing 4: Inter-thread optimization for the loop nest. The blue code highlights the transformation.

```
1  #pragma omp parallel shared (matrix)
2  {
3    // n is the number of physical cores in the system
4    int n = omp_get_num_threads()/SMT_NUM;
5    int DN = N/n; // suppose N is dividable by n
6    int t = omp_get_thread_num(); // thread ID
7    int dt = t/SMT_NUM;
8    int rt = t%SMT_NUM;
9    for(int i= dt*DN+rt; i<(dt+1)*DN; i+=SMT_NUM)
10     for (int j=0; j<M; j++)
11       B[j][i] = A[i][j];
12 }
```

Listing 5: Code transformation to ensure B is only falsely shared by the SMT threads on the same physical core, avoiding any false sharing between threads running on different physical cores. `SMT_NUM` is the number of SMT threads on a core.

jacent loop iterations to each thread, in an interleaved manner. Therefore, threads (falsely) share the elements of B in the same cache line to reduce the instantaneous footprint of B from four cache lines (because we have four hardware threads per core) to one cache line. Figure 4(a) shows the speedup of the code after this optimization. The x axis illustrates the values of the loop trip count N and the y axis shows the speedup of the optimized code over the original case. From the figure, we find that enhancing inter-thread locality with false sharing can achieve significant speedups as N increases. We also examine the hardware performance counters to understand the causes of the speedups. For the case of $N = 30,000$, the optimized code has 8% more instructions than the original case, mainly due to the extra iteration scheduling in the OpenMP library. However, the optimized code reduces L1, L2, and L3 cache misses by 15%, 70%, and 67%, respectively.

The code example in Listing 1 has no reuse in array B inside each thread due to the long accessing stride, so increasing false sharing between SMT threads can significantly improve performance. However, if the code transformation breaks the temporal or spatial reuse that originally exists within the thread, it may suffer from performance degradation. Listing 2 shows such an example. Since the threads stream `array` with a unit stride, they have good intra-thread spatial locality in their own chunk of loop iterations. If we interleave loop iterations to different SMT threads (shown in the blue keywords), the performance degrades. Figure 4(b) illustrates the degradation. Regardless of the array size, the interleaved version has about a 40% longer execution time than the original code. The main reason is that interleaving loop iterations add more parallel overhead from the OpenMP runtime library to the execution. Moreover, it prevents each thread to benefit from the good intra-thread locality and causes memory-bandwidth underutilization. The performance counters show that the interleaved loops result in 83%, 49%, and 9% more L1, L2, and L3 cache misses respectively than the original case.

3.2.3 Generalizing the Optimization Scheme

To generalize the idea, we extend our optimization method to deep loop nests and multiple physical cores.

Deep loop nests: We consider the multi-level loop nest in Listing 3, which has poor intra-thread locality. The loop does not iterate the right-most k dimension of `matrix` in the inner-most loop, so all the accesses to `matrix` suffer from non-unit stride. To enhance the inter-thread locality, we apply the SMT-aware optimization, as shown in Listing 4. Instead of parallelizing the outer-most loop, we parallelize

the k loop by interleaving its iterations to threads, which effectively introduces false sharing between SMT threads.

Multiple physical cores: Enhancing inter-thread locality with false sharing should only happen between SMT threads. For threads running on different physical cores, false sharing should be avoided because it can cause significant execution slow down [19]. We explicitly schedule thread and parallel loop iterations, as shown in Listing 5, which is an example code transformation for Listing 1. We explicitly divide the entire B into n disjoint chunks, where n is the number of physical cores. Each chunk is assigned to one core to avoid false sharing between cores. To process each chunk, SMT threads interleave the accesses to the elements to introduce the false sharing between threads within a core. This OpenMP parallel region uses software thread ID (obtained from `omp_get_thread_num()`) and thread affinity set by an environmental variable to guarantee that each hardware thread executes the desired iterations of the outer i loop. With this optimization, running on 32 hardware threads in our POWER7 machine achieves a 1.5× speedup. Moreover, the L1, L2, and L3 cache misses are reduced by 39%, 53%, and 46%, respectively. *It is worth noting that such explicit thread scheduling beyond simply adding* `schedule(static,1)` *is a more general use case of our inter-thread optimization.*

3.2.4 Summary

We summarize our findings related to the inter-thread optimization as follows:

- False sharing between SMT threads does not hurt performance. Thus, it is not harmful to introduce false sharing in SMT-aware optimizations.

- Exploiting inter-thread locality between SMT threads can significantly improve performance, even via false sharing. However, the code transformations cannot be applied to the memory accesses that already have intra-thread locality.

- The performance gains from enhancing inter-thread locality come from a significant instantaneous footprint reduction, resulting in miss rate reduction at different cache levels.

Through the findings, we have illustrated a simple but effective SMT-aware optimization: explicit iteration scheduling of parallel loops to different SMT threads. This inter-thread optimization complements the intra-thread optimization, i.e., array regrouping, for reducing the instantaneous footprint across threads.

3.3 Limitations and Challenges

There are a few limitations for our technique. First, transforming from SoA to AoS is not always possible and beneficial, as arrays may have different access patterns. Second, explicitly introducing false sharing may not work for irregular memory accesses, as it may be difficult to understand their random and complex patterns. Thus, although our SMT-aware optimization (including both intra- and inter-thread) for reducing instantaneous memory footprint is powerful, it is not applicable to every data layout and parallel loop. For example, if we interleave every parallel loop in NAS LU, a case study program in this paper, we get more than 20% performance degradation. The reason is that some loops in LU have good intra-thread locality, which does not benefit from our SMT-aware optimization. It motivates the needs of a performance tool to identify the potential data structures and parallel loops for optimization, especially for a program with thousands of lines of code. We describe SMTAnalyzer in Section 4 to address these challenges.

4. SMTANALYZER

SMTAnalyzer has three unique capabilities: (1) it is a compiler-independent tool and works with unmodified binaries, (2) it provides rich information to guide SMT-aware optimizations, and (3) it incurs very low overhead. These capabilities make it applicable to real massively parallel applications. SMTAnalyzer employs the methods from our previous work [22] to identify poor-intra thread locality (e.g., long accessing strides and multiple memory streams) and arrays that can be regrouped for intra-thread optimization. In this section, we mainly focus on the design of SMTAnalyzer for pinpointing inter-thread optimization opportunities.

According to the findings described in Section 3, a code section that potentially benefits from the inter-thread optimization should meet the following three requirements. First, it is a parallel loop that has regular access patterns across iterations, so one can control memory access patterns by dispatching loop iterations to threads. Such dispatching can enhance inter-thread sharing between SMT threads and avoid false sharing between threads on different physical cores. Second, the loop is hot and memory bound. Since our SMT-aware optimization reduces memory contention, applying it to such loops may lead to significant whole-program speedups. Third, access patterns in the loops have poor intra-thread locality to benefit from our inter-thread optimization.

In this section, we describe the design and implementation of SMTAnalyzer. Section 4.1 describes the background knowledge of hardware sampling mechanisms utilized by SMTAnalyzer. Section 4.2 describes the method SMTAnalyzer uses to identify parallel loops and quantify their 'hotness' and memory intensiveness. Section 4.3 shows the method used by SMTAnalyzer to analyze loop access

patterns. It filters out irregular access patterns that cannot be optimized by our scheme.

4.1 Hardware Sampling Support

Modern microprocessors employ performance monitoring units (PMU) to provide insights into an application's behavior. The PMU periodically generates interrupts as samples during an application's execution. It can effectively associate work (e.g., instructions executed), resource consumption (e.g., cycles), and inefficiency (e.g., latency) with code regions. Such asynchronous sampling serves as the foundation of SMTAnalyzer's analysis of program execution. SMTAnalyzer uses these performance events to identify hot loops with significant memory accesses.

In addition, PMUs on recent processors support address sampling, which collects instruction and data address pairs to associate memory references with the data that they touch. In modern Intel Xeon architectures, SMTAnalyzer can leverage Precise Event-Based Sampling (PEBS) [14] supported by PMUs. PEBS provides the following insights:

- It can record the memory address read or written by a sampled memory access instruction.

- It can glean memory related metrics. Such information is useful for understanding the performance of memory accesses (e.g., collection of L in Figure 2(a)).

- It can capture the precise instruction pointer for each sample to avoid "skid" [6] on processors with out-of-order cores. This information guarantees precise measurement.

SMTAnalyzer uses the information collected by address sampling to attribute samples to both code regions and data objects [21]. SMTAnalyzer's analyses are based on these two attribution techniques, which are described as follows:

Code-centric attribution: SMTAnalyzer analyzes a loop's access pattern by aggregating all the samples that are taken in the loop. Because PMU triggers memory access samples that include instruction pointers (IP), SMTAnalyzer can associate samples with instructions that can be further aggregated to the loop level.

Data-centric attribution: SMTAnalyzer allows the analysis of access patterns for each data object referenced in the loop, so it attributes samples to data objects. Because PMU captures the effective address accessed by each memory access sample, SMTAnalyzer leverages this address to associate the sample with the memory range allocated statically or dynamically for a data object. SMTAnalyzer inherits the data-centric attribution from HPCToolkit [21].

4.2 Identifying Hot Parallel Loops

SMTAnalyzer using its code-centric attribution to first identify hot parallel loops with significant memory accesses. SMTAnalyzer can easily identify loops parallelized by OpenMP, because OpenMP compilers convert the parallel loops into outline functions. However, some other threading models, like Pthread, do not create outline functions associated with parallel loops. In this case, SMTAnalyzer parses the machine code for a program, builds a control flow graph (CFG) for each procedure, and then uses interval analysis [12] to identify loops in each procedure's CFG. If multiple threads execute the same loop, SMTAnalyzer marks the loop as a parallel loop.

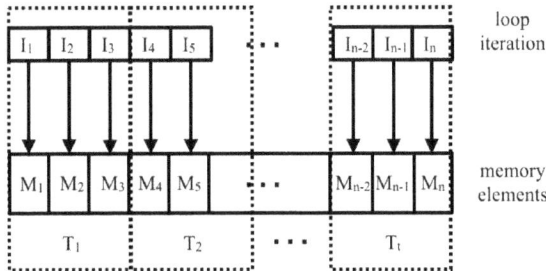

Figure 5: Relax iteration-dependent patterns to thread-dependent patterns: instead of associating memory elements with iterations, we associate them with threads.

SMTAnalyzer measures the memory access latency consumed in each parallel loop to identify the hot ones, which narrows down the analysis to only the parallel loops with intensive memory accesses. In addition, SMTAnalyzer associates the average memory access latency obtained from PEBS with each loop that is investigated. Loops with high average memory access latencies are memory bound and suffer from poor locality. The threshold to determine which loops have high latencies in a program varies with the underlying architectures.

4.3 Analyzing Memory Access Patterns

Our SMT-aware optimization enhances inter-thread locality via explicitly allocating loop iterations to threads. It is effective only if access patterns can be controlled via assigning threads to different loop iterations for execution. We call such access pattern *iteration-dependent*. The iteration-dependent patterns are always regular. In contrast, irregular access patterns, such as random or indirect accesses lead to iteration-independent patterns. Changing the loop iteration assignments for applications with such patterns may not improve their inter-thread locality. SMTAnalyzer uses its code- and data-centric attributions to identify parallel loops with iteration-dependent access patterns.

Usually, analyzing access patterns involves heavyweight code instrumentation for memory accesses and loop iterations, incurring unaffordable overhead in execution. Instead, SMTAnalyzer employs a lightweight method to identify parallel loops with iteration-dependent access patterns. To avoid the instrumentation to each loop iteration, SMT-Analyzer relaxes the iteration-dependent patterns to *thread-dependent patterns*. To avoid instrumentation to all the memory accesses, SMTAnalyzer only monitors part of them using PEBS described in Section 4.1.

4.3.1 Problem Relaxation

For a simplified explanation, Figure 5 shows a loop iteration-dependent access pattern for array in Listing 2. The elements of array are referenced in each iteration in an ascending order. We find that iteration-dependent patterns can be relaxed to thread-dependent patterns to avoid monitoring each loop iteration. For parallel loops, threads are usually assigned a block of iterations for execution, as the dashed rectangles shown in Figure 5. Therefore, instead of correlating memory references with each iteration, we can associate ranges of memory references with each thread. This relaxation provides the possibility of using sampling to identify parallel loops with iteration-dependent patterns.

4.3.2 Sampling-Based Pattern Analysis

SMTAnalyzer samples memory accesses in each thread to identify whether access patterns are thread-dependent. For the analysis, SMTAnalyzer needs two pieces of information for each sample: (1) which parallel loop the sample belongs to, and (2) which data object the sample accesses. SMTAnalyzer uses the code- and data-centric attribution described in Section 4.1 to obtain (1) and (2), respectively.

For each sampled memory access m to a data object x in the parallel loop l, SMTAnalyzer computes its relative access offset o in x with Equation 1. In the equation, m_a is the memory address accessed by m; x_{begin} and x_{end} are the boundaries of the memory range allocated for x.

$$o = \frac{m_a - x_{begin}}{x_{end} - x_{begin}} \qquad (1)$$

Because m_a is always smaller than x_{end}, o is always between [0,1]. At the loop l level, SMTAnalyzer clusters o of all the sampled accesses by computing a [min, max] interval of o per thread and reveals how x is accessed in each thread. Figure 6(a) shows two access pattern examples. The left pattern illustrates that each thread works on the segments in a cyclic distribution, while the right pattern shows that each thread accesses a segment of the data object. They match the pre-transformation access patterns for B in Listing 1 and array in Listing 2, respectively. Figure 6(b) shows an example output of SMTAnalyzer by plotting the [min, max] intervals across threads to represent the right pattern of Figure 6(a). These regular access patterns imply that they are both thread-dependent and furthermore, iteration-dependent. It is worth noting that SMTAnalyzer may not accurately report the memory chunk boundary accessed by each thread, because the sampling technique does not monitor every memory address accessed by each thread. However, from our experiments, such inaccuracy does not affect the results of the pattern analysis.

In contrast, if a thread references the offset of a data object randomly, the algorithm will not recognize its access pattern as thread-dependent. SMTAnalyzer will then reason that memory accesses in the loop cannot be optimized by the proposed transformation. *SMTAnalyzer highlights hot, regular parallel loops with poor intra-thread locality as the final candidates for the inter-thread SMT optimization.*

5. CASE STUDIES

Benchmarks: To evaluate the effectiveness of our SMT-aware optimization and SMTAnalyzer for instantaneous footprint reduction, we investigated all the benchmarks categorized as (high, high) and (high, low) from Table 2 with large inputs. SMTAnalyzer does not pinpoint significant optimization opportunities in all the benchmarks studied in these two categories. For instance, further code analysis through STMAnalyzer suggests that neither Clomp nor hotspot in (high, high) is an ideal candidate for our SMT-aware optimization. Although STMAnalyzer identifies that Clomp has bad intra-thread locality (i.e., parallel loop:328-338), it performs pointer chasing which hinders itself from performing SMT-aware optimization. Additionally, hotspot is observed with unit stride memory accesses, but it has no temporal reuse which causes high memory access latency even without SMT effects. For lud in (high, low), stride analysis shows that its loop accesses to key data objects with

Benchmarks	Suite	Code Analysis from SMTAnalyzer			SMTAnalyzer Overhead	
		bottleneck region	% of total latency	OPT method	total time (s)	overhead
lulesh2.0	Sequoia [18]	lulesh.cc: 604-609	3.6%	inter-thread	389.9	+3.1%
IRSmk	Sequoia [18]	rmatmult3.c: 86-103	78.6%	intra-thread	116.7	+3.2%
needle	Rodinia [5]	needle.cpp:185-187	20%	inter-thread	37.4	+2.99%
srad	Rodonia [5]	srad.cpp:136-167	80.1%	intra-thread	599.2	+2.47%
LU	NAS [2]	rhs.f:318-328	8.4%	inter-thread	148.1	+10.6%
Stencil	Micro	stencil.c:16-21	95.7%	inter-thread	481	+1.55%
3D tensor	Micro	mt.c: 22-22	69.4%	inter-thread	96	+2.4%
streamcluster2	PARSEC [3]	streamcluster.cpp:653	14.1%	inter-thread	120.7	+15.2%

Table 4: The analysis results reported by SMTAnalyzer. SMTAnalyzer pinpoints problematic loops with only 5.2% overhead on average.

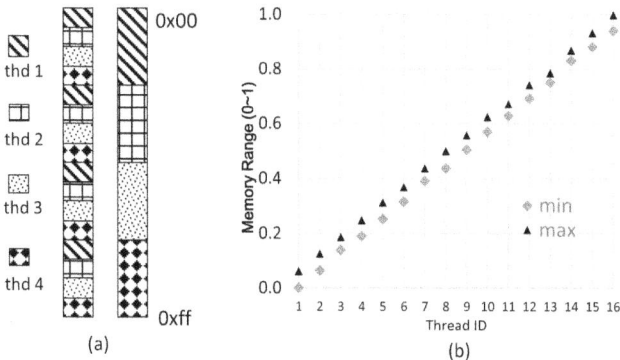

(a)   (b)

Figure 6: Figure 6(a) shows two possible thread-dependent patterns identified by SMTAnalyzer. The left and right patterns match the pre-transformation access patterns for B in Listing 1 and array in Listing 2, respectively. Figure 6(b) shows the output of SMTAnalyzer on the pattern shown in the right of Figure 6(a), across the memory address touched by 16 threads.

Benchmarks	Optimization techniques	Speedups
lulesh2.0	Enhance False sharing	1.43×
IRSmk	Array regrouping	4.86×
needle	Enhance False sharing	2.37×
srad	Array regrouping	1.74×
LU	Enhance False sharing	1.36×
Stencil	Enhance False sharing	10.9×
3D tensor	Enhance False sharing	1.44×
streamcluster2	Enhance False sharing	6.72×

Table 5: Speedups of the benchmarks running on SMT architectures after applying our optimization. We report the best speedup across different SMT architectures. The detailed analysis is described in the following sections.

a hybrid pattern using both unit stride and non-unit stride. Thus, it is not suitable for our proposed optimization. Finally, the eight selected benchmarks for further analysis are shown in Table 4.

Evaluation Platforms: The evaluation is conducted on three SMT architectures shown in Table 1. All the benchmarks are evaluated with the full SMT capabilities on these platforms. Without specific mention in the individual case studies, experiments are run with 8 cores × 2 SMT threads on Intel Xeon, 8 cores × 4 SMT threads on IBM POWER7, and 61 cores × 4 SMT threads on Intel Xeon Phi. We compile all the benchmarks using `icc 13.0.0` on Intel Xeon Phi, and `gcc 4.9` on Intel Xeon and IBM POWER7, with the highest optimization-level flag.

Code Analysis: As discussed in Section 4.1, SMTAnalyzer uses PEBS to conduct monitoring on the Intel Xeon platform. During the profiling runs on Intel Xeon, the benchmarks are run with 2 hardware threads per core on

```
1  #pragma omp parallel for private(j,k) schedule(static,1)
2  for (i = 0; i < N; i++)
3      for (j = 0; j < N; j++)
4          for (k = 0; k < N; k++)
5              tensor_a[i][j][k] = tensor_b[k][j][i];
```

Listing 6: Optimization for the 3D tensor transposition.

```
1  #pragma omp parallel for shared(array) schedule(static,1)
2  for (int i=T; i<N-T; i++)
3      for (int j=T; j<N-T; j++)
4          for (int k=0; k<T; k++)
5              R[i][j] = matrix[i][j]+matrix[i-k][j]+matrix[i][j-k]
6                      +matrix[i+k][j]+matrix[i][j+k];
```

Listing 7: Optimization for the 2D Stencil computation.

8 cores. Because POWER7 and Xeon Phi do not provide necessary PMU sampling capabilities such as PEBS to support SMTAnalyzer, we use the analysis insights from Intel Xeon to optimize the benchmarks and then apply them to the other two platforms.

Table 4 summarizes the analysis results from SMTAnalyzer. SMTAnalyzer reports the locations of problematic loops in source code, percentage of memory access latency caused by these loops over the entire program, and optimization suggestions. SMTAnalyzer incurs an average of 5.2% runtime overhead. Additionally, the memory space consumed by SMTAnalyzer is less than 32 MB. Table 5 reports the optimization techniques we utilized to reduce instantaneous footprint and the best speedups obtained from our Intel Xeon, Xeon Phi, and IBM POWER7 platforms. In the rest of this section, we conduct individual case study for the benchmarks in Table 4, show the code transformations on the problematic loops reported by SMTAnalyzer, and quantify the speedups on all the three SMT architectures.

5.1 3D Tensor Transposition

Listing 6 shows a transposition on three-dimensional tensors. SMTAnalyzer identifies that both `tensor_a` and `tensor_b` in the parallel loop have iteration-dependent accesses. Figure 6(b) shows the access pattern analysis output from SMTAnalyzer. Moreover, `tensor_b` has poor locality as it has a long accessing stride. Therefore, we can apply the SMT-aware optimization to enhance the inter-thread locality on `tensor_b` via introducing (false) sharing. The blue code in Listing 6 shows the transformation sufficient for this purpose to enhance sharing on `tensor_b` between SMT threads on the same core. It is worth noting that interleaving the outer-most loop does not hurt intra-thread locality of `tensor_a` because each thread still works on continuous elements of `tensor_a` in k loop. We evaluate this benchmark with the full thread capability on all the three platforms. This simple optimization achieves a 1.05× speedup (1.06× at loop) on POWER7, a 1.44× speedup (2.49× at loop) on

```
1  for (i=0;i<iter;i = i + SMT) {
2      change += pgain(feasible[x+(pid%SMT)], points, z, k, pid, barrier);
3  }
4  ...
5  pgain(long x, Points *points, double z, long int *numcenters, int pid,
           pthread_barrier_t* barrier)
6  {
7  ...
8      k1 = ((int)(pid / SMT)) * bsize;
9      k2 = k1 + (bsize * SMT);
10     for ( i = k1; i < K2; i++ ) {
11         float x_cost = dist(points->p[i], points->p[x], points->dim)
12         ...
13     }
14 ...
15 }
```

Listing 8: A parallel loop that applies inter-thread optimization (explicit thread scheduling to make false sharing only between SMT threads) in StreamCluster.

```
1  #pragma omp parallel for private(jj,ii,i)
2  for (kk = kmin; kk < kmax; kk++) {
3      for (jj = jmin; jj < jmax; jj++) {
4          for (ii = imin; ii < imax; ii++) {
5              i = ii + jj * jp + kk * kp;
6              b[i]=ABCD[i].dbl*xdbl[i]+ABCD[i].dbc*xdbc[i]+ABCD[i].dbr*xdbr[i]+
7              ABCD[i].dcl*xdcl[i]+ABCD[i].dcc*xdcc[i]+ABCD[i].dcr*xdcr[i]+
8              ABCD[i].dfl*xdfl[i]+ABCD[i].dfc*xdfc[i]+ABCD[i].dfr*xdfr[i]+
9              ABCD[i].cbl*xcbl[i]+ABCD[i].cbc*xcbc[i]+ABCD[i].cbr*xcbr[i]+
10             ABCD[i].ccl*xccl[i]+ABCD[i].ccc*xccc[i]+ABCD[i].ccr*xccr[i]+
11             ABCD[i].cfl*xcfl[i]+ABCD[i].cfc*xcfc[i]+ABCD[i].cfr*xcfr[i]+
12             ABCD[i].ubl*xubl[i]+ABCD[i].ubc*xubc[i]+ABCD[i].ubr*xubr[i]+
13             ABCD[i].ucl*xucl[i]+ABCD[i].ucc*xucc[i]+ABCD[i].ucr*xucr[i]+
14             ABCD[i].ufl*xufl[i]+ABCD[i].ufc*xufc[i]+ABCD[i].ufr*xufr[i];
15         }
16     }
17 }
```

Listing 9: A parallel loop that applies intra-thread optimization (array regrouping) in IRSmk.

```
1  do j = jst, jend
2  !$omp do schedule(static,1)
3      do i = ist, iend
4          do k = 1, nz
5              utmp(1,k) = u(1,i,j,k)
6              utmp(2,k) = u(2,i,j,k)
7              utmp(3,k) = u(3,i,j,k)
8              utmp(4,k) = u(4,i,j,k)
9              utmp(5,k) = u(5,i,j,k)
10             utmp(6,k) = rho_i(i,j,k)
11         end do
12         ...
13     end do
14 !$omp end do
15 end do
```

Listing 10: An candidate loop nest for SMT-aware optimization identified by SMTAnalyzer in LU.

Intel Xeon Phi and a 1.03× speedup (1.11× at loop) on Xeon throughout the application.

5.2 Stencil computation

Listing 7 shows an example two-dimensional stencil computation. It uses k neighbors on each dimension in the matrix to compute an element. Thus, this 2D stencil code has good spatial locality on the x-axis direction but poor spatial locality along the y-axis direction. SMTAnalyzer identifies that the loop has poor locality due to the long access stride incurred by matrix[i-k][j] and matrix[i+k][j].

We use SMT-aware optimization to interleave iterations of the i loop to enhance the inter-thread locality for matrix[i-k][j] and matrix[i+k][j]. Moreover, the transformation does not hurt the intra-thread locality for matrix[i][j], matrix[i][j-k], and matrix[i][j+k]. The SMT-aware optimization shows 1.28× and 1.25× speedups on POWER7 and Xeon Phi, respectively, running with 32 hardware threads. Additionally, it can achieve up to 10.9× speedups on Xeon Phi while running on 244 threads (i.e., 61 cores). The optimization obtains a mild 1.03× speedup running with 16 hardware threads on Intel Xeon.

5.3 StreamCluster

StreamCluster from PARSEC is used to solve online clustering problems. SMTAnalyzer identifies the problematic loop of StreamCluster, as shown in Listing 8. Accessing to different fields of point incurs significant contention in the memory hierarchy between SMT threads. To increase inter-thread sharing and reduce the instantaneous footprint, we modify the loop to have SMT threads working on the adjacent memory blocks, as shown in Listing 8. Note that this optimization is similar to the one shown in Listing 5 by explicitly controlling the thread and work allocation according to our inter-thread optimization. This SMT-aware optimiation speeds up the loop by 6.72× on POWER 7 and 1.14× on Intel Xeon.

5.4 IRSmk

IRSmk solves a diffusion equation on a three-dimensional block-structured mesh. The loop kernel performs matrix multiplication in a three nested level. SMTAnalyzer identifies that this parallel loop has significant memory access latency. Further code analysis shows that there are 27 streams in the loop. Although threads have regular access patterns with unit access stride, too many streams per thread contend for cache and interfere prefetchers, causing bad intra-thread locality. We apply array regrouping to this loop nest by converting multiple streams into one, as shown in List-

ing 9. The new array layout successfully reduces instantaneous memory footprint in the loop from 27 to 4 cache lines per iteration and achieves 4.86×, 4.83×, and 2.92× speedups on POWER7, Xeon Phi, and Xeon, respectively.

5.5 NAS LU

LU, a computational fluid dynamic appliaction, is a lower-upper Gauss-Seidel solver. SMTAnalyzer reports a problematic parallel loop nest that calculates *zeta-direction flux differences*. This loop has iteration-dependent access patterns and poor spatial locality due to the long stride of accessing array u [1]. This piece of code from rhs.f computes right hand sides from the z dimension. This parallel loop accounts for around 10% of total LU execution time. According to our SMT-aware optimization, we move the OpenMP parallel directives to the loop that iterates the inner-most dimension i of array u, as shown in the Listing 10. The optimization obtains 1.36× and 1.22× speedups for this loop nest on IBM POWER7 when running with 4 and 8 hardware threads, respectively.

5.6 SRAD

SRAD is an image processing benchmark based on partial differential equation. SMTAnalyzer identifies a hot parallel loop in SRAD with significant memory access latency and suggests to regroup the arrays to reduce instantaneous footprint. Listing 11 shows the code after the array regrouping, which leads to 1.43× and 1.74× speedups on the full thread capability of POWER7 and Xeon, respectively. It is worth noting that our SMT-aware optimization hurts performance of SRAD running on Xeon Phi. The reason is that the AoS data layout suggested by our intra-thread optimization breaks the code vectorization that is significantly important on Xeon Phi as it supports 512-bit SIMD instructions. Unlike IRSmk, the benchmark we obtain speedup on

---

[1]LU is a Fortran program, whose memory layout is column major.

```
1  #pragma omp parallel for shared(J, cnswe, rows, cols, iN, iS, jW, jE)
          private(i, j, k, Jc, G2, L, num, den, qsqr)
2  for (int i = 0 ; i < rows ; i++) {
3    for (int j = 0; j < cols; j++) {
4      ...
5      cnswe[k].dN = J[iN[i] * cols + j] - Jc;
6      cnswe[k].dS = J[iS[i] * cols + j] - Jc;
7      cnswe[k].dW = J[i * cols + jW[j]] - Jc;
8      cnswe[k].dE = J[i * cols + jE[j]] - Jc;
9      G2 = (cnswe[k].dN*cnswe[k].dN + cnswe[k].dS*cnswe[k].dS
10       + cnswe[k].dW*cnswe[k].dW + cnswe[k].dE*cnswe[k].dE) / (Jc*Jc);
11
12     L = (cnswe[k].dN + cnswe[k].dS + cnswe[k].dW + cnswe[k].dE) / Jc;
13
14     num = (0.5*G2) - ((1.0/16.0)*(L*L)) ;
15     ...
16   }
17 }
```

Listing 11: A parallel loop that has many memory access streams in SRAD. SMTAnalyzer suggests to use intra-thread optimization for SRAD.

```
1  #pragma omp parallel for firstprivate(numNode) schedule(static,1)
2  for( Index_t gnode=0 ; gnode<numNode ; ++gnode ) {
3    ...
4    for (Index_t i=0 ; i < count ; ++i) {
5      Index_t ElemId = nodeElemCornerList[start+i] ;
6      Index_t CornerId = Find_Pos(nodelist, gnode, ElemId);
7      nodefx += f_elem[ElemId][xDir][CornerId] ;
8      nodefy += f_elem[ElemId][yDir][CornerId] ;
9      nodefz += f_elem[ElemId][zDir][CornerId] ;
10   }
11   ...
12 }
```

Listing 12: A candidate loop nest for SMT-aware optimization identified by SMTAnalyzer in LULESH.

```
1  #pragma omp parallel for shared(input_itemsets) firstprivate(i,max_cols,
          penalty) private(idx, index) schedule(static,1)
2
3  for( idx = 0 ; idx <= i ; idx++){
4    index = ( max_cols - idx - 2 ) * max_cols + idx + max_cols - i - 2 ;
5    input_itemsets[index]= maximum( input_itemsets[index-1-max_cols]+
          referrence[index],
6    input_itemsets[index-1]       - penalty,
7    input_itemsets[index-max_cols] - penalty);
8 }
```

Listing 13: Optimizing the parallel loop that has long strided accesses in Needle.

Xeon Phi with array regrouping, the problematic loop in SRAD has only four streams, causing mild cache contention and prefetcher interference. Thus, the gain of contention reduction is difficult to trade off the vectorization loss. The trade-offs between the footprint reduction and vectorization is out of the scope and will be studied in our future work.

5.7 LULESH

LULESH, an application benchmark developed by Lawrence Livermore National Laboratory (LLNL), is an Arbitrary Lagrangian Eulerian code that solves the Sedov blast wave problem in 3D. SMTAnalyzer pinpoints a parallel loop in LULESH as a candidate for the SMT-aware optimization. This loop, shown in Listing 12 accounts for 3.6% of total memory access latency. SMTAnalyzer reports that the accesses to f_elem are iteration-dependent, although from the static code analysis, f_elem is accessed indirectly via ElemId and CornerId. The access pattern of f_elem across threads is similar to the one in Figure 6(b), but chunks have overlaps accessed by adjacent threads. Moreover, SMTAnalyzer reports a non-unit stride of accessing f_elem in the loop. The reason for the long stride is that ElemId, the left-most index is also updated in the inner loop body besides CornerId, the right-most index. Therefore, this parallel loop in LULESH qualifies all the conditions for the SMT-aware optimization. We can interleave iterations of the gnode loop to let threads work on adjacent f_elem elements for better inter-thread locality. This SMT-aware optimization leads to $1.21\times$ and $1.43\times$ speedups for this loop on POWER7 and Xeon Phi, respectively.

5.8 Needle

Needle is a bioinformatics application that performs dynamic programming. SMTAnalyzer pinpoints a problematic parallel loop shown in Listing 13. Memory analysis from Table 3 shows that Needle incurs high memory access overhead due to the increasing TLB misses for L2 hit when running with SMT. The reason can be inferred from the loop, which accesses array input_itemsets using a long stride, indicating inferior intra-thread locality. If the SMT threads are assigned consecutive idx, the inter-thread sharing increases. Thus, we perform the inter-thread optimization to reduce its instantaneous footprint, resulting in a $2.37\times$ speedup at loop level on Intel Xeon.

5.9 Discussion

To understand the performance behaviors in the memory hierarchy, we capture the cache miss events with hardware counters. Figure 7 quantifies the miss reduction due to our SMT-aware optimization at different cache layers on the three architectures. The data is collected on the whole-program level. We can observe that the benchmarks that obtain significant speedups enjoy cache miss reduction, such as 3D tensor transposition, Stencil, IRSmk, Needle, and StreamCluster. This shows that our SMT-aware optimization for instantaneous footprint reduction can efficiently improve the memory-level performance. However, for LU and LULESH2.0 on Intel Xeon and Xeon Phi, cache misses do not improve much and even get worse. The reason is that the optimized loops in these benchmarks are not hot enough and optimizing them does not show a high impact in the caches miss reduction of the entire program. Moreover, introducing the extra code by controlling thread and work allocation adds extra instructions and pollutes caches, resulting in higher cache misses.

It is also worth noting that the observed speedups are not consistent across different SMT architectures. Some benchmarks, e.g., Needle, LULESH, LU, and SRAD, obtain mild or even no speedups on one architecture but significant speedups on the others. Moreover, the number of physical cores involved in the experiments also impacts the performance gain. For example, LU can achieve speedups running with one or two physical cores on POWER7, but no speedups with more cores. A possible reason is that inter-core behaviors may influence the gains from the SMT-aware optimization. Such influence on performance may become dominant in some cases when the core number increases. Studying detailed characterization of the inter-core influence across different SMT architectures is a strong interest of our future research.

6. RELATED WORK

Thread optimization on SMT architectures: There is some previous work [38, 7, 25, 30, 10, 9] focusing on scheduling different workloads on SMT architectures. Workloads with different resource requirements are put on the same physical core and executed by its SMT threads due to minimal contention. The common drawback of these approaches is treating programs as black boxes. They change the execution environment rather than the code itself. Al-

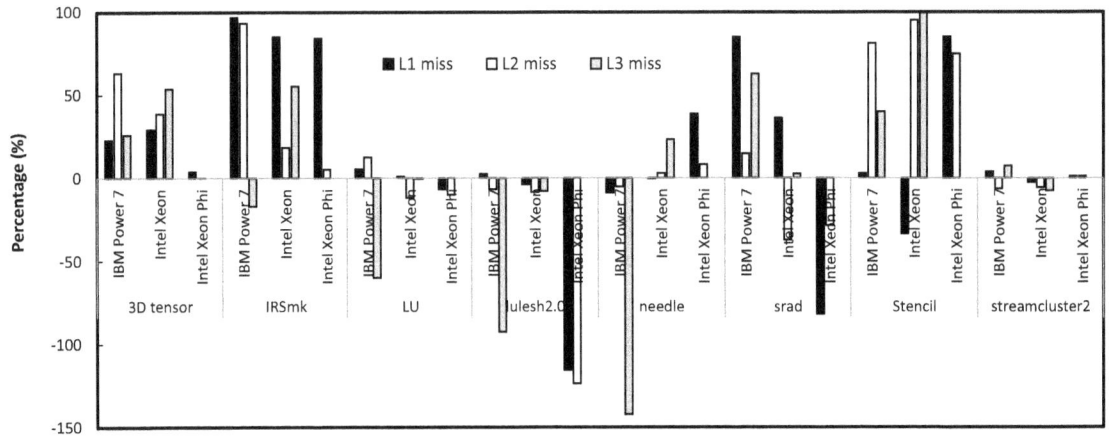

Figure 7: The miss reduction due to our SMT-aware optimization at different cache layers on different SMT architectures. The positive numbers represent cache miss reduction, while the negative values are cache miss increase.

though these methods can avoid contention, they omit the optimization opportunities in the source code. Moreover, they do not achieve an appreciable performance improvement for HPC applications coded with Single Program Multiple Data (SPMD) models, because all threads have similar resource requests. A more recent work [32] characterizes the HPC benchmarks on SMT architectures and leverages machine learning methods to predict the performance with SMT enabled. However, this work does not provide any specific optimization method for SMT architectures.

Code optimization for shared caches: Some recent studies introduce code transformations to enhance thread sharing for programs running on multi-core systems to avoid thread contention, through adapting code to make threads share data non-uniformly [39]. Moreover, fine-grained control of data placement [20, 17, 24, 31] in source code can significantly reduce memory contention in multi-socket systems. Finally, some previous studies leveraged cache partitioning [29] and cache bypassing [36] to reduce thread contention in shared cache. However, the code transformations introduced in these approaches target programs running on multi-core and multi-socket architectures, rather than SMT architectures. Our work contrasts and compliments these approaches by developing the first code transformation technique intended to improve the performance of HPC applications running on SMT architectures. The most related work to ours is the code transformation to optimize SMT execution. Nikolopoulos [27] leverages specific tiling techniques to partition shared cache and avoid contention between SMT threads. Unlike our approach, his method does not target instantaneous footprint reduction to avoid memory contention through a general systematic optimization scheme. Moreover, there is no tool associated with his method to guide optimization.

Lightweight performance tools: There are a few tools that guide source code transformations to minimize thread contention in the shared memory hierarchy. Memphis [26], MemProf [17], and HPCToolkit [20] identify thread contention on shared data in multi-socket systems. They can associate the performance losses with data objects due to threads from different sockets congesting the memory bus. MACPO [33], ThreadSpotter [35], PTU [15], and Predator [19] pinpoint false sharing between threads running on multi-core systems. To the best of our knowledge, there is

no existing performance tool like SMTAnalyzer that directly identifies opportunities in source code for SMT-aware optimizations.

7. CONCLUSIONS

In this paper, we first vigorously conduct systematic performance analysis to characterize SMT performance impacts on a wide range of benchmarks, and quantify their detailed memory-level contention on three mainstream SMT architectures (i.e., Intel Xeon, Intel Xeon Phi, and IBM Power7). Based on these architecture-level analysis, we introduce the concept of *instantaneous footprint*, which serves as a good indicator for memory contention in SMT architectures. We then propose a simple yet effective scheme to reduce instantaneous footprint including both intra- and inter-thread SMT-aware optimizations. To reduce the optimization efforts, we develop SMTAnalyzer, a performance tool that identifies SMT-aware optimization opportunities in multi-threaded programs with low overhead. Guided by SMTAnalyzer, we optimize several widely-used SMT-sensitive applications on three platforms, and the results indicate that our proposed techniques can significantly improve the performance of these programs through drastic reduction on memory contention.

Acknowledgements

This research was supported by the National Science Foundation (NSF) under Grant No. 1464157 and DOE CENATE (66150) project. The Pacific Northwest National Laboratory is operated by Battelle for the U.S. Department of Energy under contract DE-AC05-76RL01830.

8. REFERENCES

[1] Top 500 lists. http://www.top500.org/lists/2015/11, Nov. 2015.

[2] D. H. Bailey et al. The NAS parallel benchmarks – summary and preliminary results. In *Proc. of SC*, 1991.

[3] C. Bienia. *Benchmarking Modern Multiprocessors*. PhD thesis, Princeton University, January 2011.

[4] D. R. Butenhof. *Programming with POSIX threads*. Addison-Wesley Longman Publishing Co., Inc., Boston, MA, USA, 1997.

[5] S. Che et al. Rodinia: A benchmark suite for heterogeneous computing. In *Proc. of IISWC*, 2009.

[6] P. J. Drongowski. Instruction-based sampling: A new performance analysis technique for AMD family 10h processors, Fall 2010.

[7] S. Eyerman and L. Eeckhout. Probabilistic modeling for job symbiosis scheduling on smt processors. *ACM Trans. Archit. Code Optim.*, 9(2), June 2012.

[8] S. Eyerman and L. Eeckhout. The benefit of SMT in the multi-core era: Flexibility towards degrees of thread-level parallelism. In *Proc. of ASPLOS*, 2014.

[9] J. Feliu, J. Sahuquillo, S. Petit, and J. Duato. L1-bandwidth aware thread allocation in multicore SMT processors. In *Proc. of PACT*, 2013.

[10] J. Feliu, J. Sahuquillo, S. Petit, and J. Duato. Addressing bandwidth contention in SMT multicores through scheduling. In *Proc. of ICS*, 2014.

[11] M. Frigo, C. E. Leiserson, and K. H. Randall. The implementation of the Cilk-5 multithreaded language. In *Proc. of PLDI*, Montreal, Quebec, Canada, 1998.

[12] P. Havlak. Nesting of reducible and irreducible loops. *ACM Trans. Program. Lang. Syst.*, 19(4):557–567, 1997.

[13] IBM Corp. POWER8 Processor. In *Hot Chips: A Symposium on High Performance Chips*, 2013.

[14] Intel Corporation. Intel 64 and IA-32 architectures software developer's manual, Volume 3B: System programming guide, Part 2, Number 253669-032, June 2010.

[15] Intel Corporation. Intel Performance Tuning Utility 4.0 Update 5. https://software.intel.com/en-us/articles/intel-performance-tuning-utility, October 2012. Last accessed: Aug. 10, 2014.

[16] J. Jeffers and J. Reinders. *Intel Xeon Phi Coprocessor High Performance Programming*. Morgan Kaufmann Publishers Inc., San Francisco, CA, USA, 1st edition, 2013.

[17] R. Lachaize, B. Lepers, and V. Quéma. MemProf: A memory profiler for NUMA multicore systems. In *Proc. of USENIX ATC*, 2012.

[18] Lawrence Livermore National Laboratory. LLNL Sequoia Benchmarks. https://asc.llnl.gov/sequoia/benchmarks. Last accessed: Dec. 12, 2013.

[19] T. Liu et al. PREDATOR: Predictive false sharing detection. In *Proc. of PPoPP*, 2014.

[20] X. Liu and J. Mellor-Crummey. A tool to analyze the performance of multithreaded programs on NUMA architectures. In *Proc. of PPoPP*, 2014.

[21] X. Liu and J. M. Mellor-Crummey. A data-centric profiler for parallel programs. In *Proc. of the 2013 ACM/IEEE Conference on Supercomputing*, Denver, CO, USA, 2013.

[22] X. Liu, K. Sharma, and J. Mellor-Crummey. ArrayTool: a lightweight profiler to guide array regrouping. In *Proc. of PACT*, Edmonton, Alberta, Canada, 2014.

[23] X. Liu and B. Wu. ScaAnalyzer: A tool to identify memory scalability bottlenecks in parallel programs. In *Proc. of the 2015 ACM/IEEE Conference on Supercomputing*, Austin, TX, USA, 2015.

[24] Z. Majo and T. R. Gross. Matching memory access patterns and data placement for NUMA systems. In *Proc. of CGO*, 2012.

[25] S. Manousopoulos et al. Characterizing thread placement in the IBM POWER7 processor. In *Proc. of IISWC*, 2012.

[26] C. McCurdy and J. S. Vetter. Memphis: Finding and fixing NUMA-related performance problems on multi-core platforms. In *Proc. of ISPASS*, 2010.

[27] D. Nikolopoulos. Code and data transformations for improving shared cache performance on SMT processors. In *High Performance Computing*. 2003.

[28] OpenMP Architecture Review Board. OpenMP application program interface, version 4.0. http://www.openmp.org/mp-documents/OpenMP4.0.0.pdf, July 2013.

[29] A. Pan and V. S. Pai. Imbalanced cache partitioning for balanced data-parallel programs. In *Proc. of MICRO-46*, 2013.

[30] S. Parekh, S. Eggers, H. Levy, and J. Lo. Thread-sensitive scheduling for SMT processors. Technical report, University of Washington, Department of Computer Science and Engineering, 2000. Available as http://www.cs.washington.edu/research/smt/papers/threadScheduling.pdf.

[31] G. Piccoli et al. Compiler support for selective page migration in numa architectures. In *Proc. of PACT*, 2014.

[32] L. Porter et al. Making the most of smt in hpc: System- and application-level perspectives. *ACM Trans. Archit. Code Optim.*, 11(4):59:1–59:26, Jan. 2015.

[33] A. Rane and J. Browne. Enhancing performance optimization of multicore chips and multichip nodes with data structure metrics. In *Proc. of PACT*, Minneapolis, MN, USA, 2012.

[34] J. Reinders. *Intel Threading Building Blocks*. O'Reilly, Sebastopol, CA, 2007.

[35] Rogue Wave Software. ThreadSpotter manual, version 2012.1. http://www.roguewave.com/documents.aspx?Command=Core_Download&EntryId=1492, August 2012. Last accessed: Dec. 12, 2013.

[36] A. Sandberg, D. Eklöv, and E. Hagersten. Reducing cache pollution through detection and elimination of non-temporal memory accesses. In *Proc. of SC, 2010*, 2010.

[37] D. M. Tullsen, S. J. Eggers, and H. M. Levy. Simultaneous multithreading: Maximizing on-chip parallelism. In *Proc. of ISCA*, 1995.

[38] V. Čakarević et al. Characterizing the resource-sharing levels in the UltraSPARC T2 processor. In *Proceedings of MICRO*, 2009.

[39] E. Z. Zhang et al. Does cache sharing on modern CMP matter to the performance of contemporary multithreaded programs? In *Proc. of PPoPP*, 2010.

BAShuffler: Maximizing Network Bandwidth Utilization in the Shuffle of YARN

Feng Liang
Department of Computer Science
The University of Hong Kong
loengf@connect.hku.hk

Francis C.M. Lau
Department of Computer Science
The University of Hong Kong
fcmlau@cs.hku.hk

ABSTRACT

YARN is a popular cluster resource management platform. It does not, however, manage the network bandwidth resources which can significantly affect the execution performance of those tasks having large volumes of data to transfer within the cluster. The shuffle phase of MapReduce jobs features many such tasks. The impact of underutilization of the network bandwidth in shuffle tasks is more pronounced if the network bandwidth capacities of the nodes in the cluster are varied.

We present BAShuffler, a bandwidth-aware shuffle scheduler, that can maximize the overall network bandwidth utilization by scheduling the source nodes of the fetch flows at the application level. BAShuffler can fully utilize the network bandwidth capacity in a max-min fair network. The experimental results for a variety of realistic benchmarks show that BAShuffler can substantially improve the cluster's shuffle throughput and reduce the execution time of shuffle tasks as compared to the original YARN, especially in heterogeneous network bandwidth environments.

Keywords

YARN; MapReduce; Shuffle; Network Scheduling

1. INTRODUCTION

YARN (Hadoop Version 2) [13] is a fault-tolerant, highly reliable and scalable distributed computing platform for big data processing. YARN exercises a fine-grain control over a cluster's resources, including memories and CPU cores but not the network bandwidths that are available to the cluster nodes. In reality, many tasks running on YARN may need to transfer non-trivial amounts of data among themselves, which happens when executing the shuffle phase of MapReduce [7] and Spark [14]. The performance of these tasks can be largely affected by the network bandwidths allocated to them (by some scheduling of the communication flows). It has been reported that for "shuffle-heavy" jobs, the data shuffling time can take up to as much as 70% of the overall

execution time [5]. Optimizing the shuffle performance is thus of paramount importance for these shuffle-heavy jobs.

In MapReduce, the worker of a reduce task needs to fetch the map outputs from a set of mappers via a limited number of TCP flows. The shuffle phase in YARN by default would try to evenly distribute the load on the network by randomly selecting the source node (which corresponds to one or more pending flows) when such a fetch occurs. If the links connecting all the nodes in the cluster are more or less equal in terms of bandwidth and if the number of network connections is large, this random source selection (RSS) policy could prevent some nodes/links from becoming a bottleneck. Obviously, however, without monitoring the ongoing connection allocations in the cluster, and based on which to select a source node to schedule its flows, the RSS approach cannot offer any bandwidth guarantee to the selected flows. In the case where the network is heterogeneous in terms of its links' capacities, RSS would very likely lead to suboptimal performance in scheduling all the flows in a shuffle.

We propose BAShuffler, a network bandwidth aware shuffle scheduler, that can maximize the network bandwidth utilization during the shuffle phase. BAShuffler operates at the application level, without changing the underlying network and the MapReduce interfaces. BAShuffler applies the Partially Greedy Source Selection (PGSS) method to select the appropriate source nodes that can maximize the network bandwidth utilization. PGSS estimates the bandwidth utilization via the notion of max-min fairness in TCP communication. We use examples to illustrate how PGSS works and can increase the bandwidth utilization in different scenarios, for both homogeneous and heterogeneous networks. Our experiment results on a physical cluster show that BAShuffler can significantly increase the shuffle throughput and reduce the total job completion time by up to 29% for shuffle-heavy jobs as compared to the original YARN.

2. APPLICATION-LEVEL SCHEDULING

2.1 Application- vs. Network-Level Design

To improve shuffle performance, a solution can be devised to operate at the network level or the application level. At the network level, ideas such as performance isolation [8] and fair sharing of network resources [12] can provide performance guarantees for the shuffle fetch flows. However, as the flows belonging to one shuffle are correlated in semantics and the shuffle phase cannot finish until its last flow finishes, optimization by scheduling the network based on the granule

HPDC'16, May 31-June 04, 2016, Kyoto, Japan
© 2016 ACM. ISBN 978-1-4503-4314-5/16/05...$15.00
DOI: http://dx.doi.org/10.1145/2907294.2907296

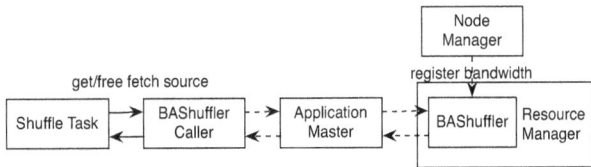

Figure 1: Architecture of BAShuffler

of individual flows may not always lead to improved shuffle performance.

The "coflow" model [6] was proposed to allow scheduling the network based on the granule of a collection of application-level correlated flows. But nevertheless, neither coflow nor any other pure network-level model can actually possess any knowledge about the runtime status of the shuffle phase due to information the gap between the network level and the application level. The application level can only create a limited number of fetch flows at a time (5 per reduce task by default) due to system limits, and the remaining map outputs are left pending until there are available fetch workers later, which is unknown to the network level (or any coflow there). Minimizing the completion time of a coflow is NOT the same thing as minimizing the shuffle completion time.

To obtain the optimal scheduling solution that minimizes the shuffle completion time, the scheduler needs to consider both the application-level runtime status (all the available map outputs and their target destinations) and network-level information (the network fabric, routing, bandwidth allocation, etc.). However, it is too costly to implement such a scheduler because it will need to gather/distribute a large amount of information from/to both the application level and the network level. The overhead of the cross-layer communication between the application level and the network level could be prohibitive.

Application-level shuffle scheduling has the advantage that it can readily obtain the true runtime status of the shuffle. Although it cannot do anything to improve the operation of the underlying network, it can observe and predict the behavior and performance of the network, and then schedule the shuffle flows accordingly based on these observations and the predicted values (e.g., by using max-min fairness in the TCP network) to obtain a near-optimal solution.

2.2 Max-Min Fairness in TCP

The max-min fair (MMF) allocation behavior of TCP communication is the converged state achieved by the AIMD (Additive Increase, Multiplicative Decrease) congestion control algorithm used by TCP [9]. The MMF policy of TCP has been extensively analyzed and verified in the literature [4]. Although it cannot accurately model the exact behavior of TCP communication, the MMF model is acceptable and appropriate for approximating the network behavior, and can lead to useful conclusions in various application settings. By the notion of MMF, the current bandwidth allocated to each TCP flow can be estimated, given the knowledge of the topology, the capacities of the links and the routing paths of the flows.

With the recent progress in research on full bisection bandwidth topologies [2, 11], it is reasonable to simplify the datacenter fabric as a non-blocking switch [5, 3]. In this case, the bottleneck links of the flows would then lie in the access layer which is directly connected to the nodes. When work-

---

Algorithm 1: Partially Greedy Source Selection

Input : Sources; Pattern: the sources and destinations the allocated flows in the cluster
Output: Selected
Heaviest ← the heaviest-loaded source nodes in Sources
MaxBandwidth ← 0
foreach *Source* ∈ *Heaviest* **do**
   Util ← the MMF bandwidth utilization of the whole cluster after adding Source to Pattern
   if *Util > MaxBandwidth* **then**
     MaxBandwidth ← Util
     Selected ← Source
   end
end
add Selected to Pattern
update the load count of Selected

---

ing out the MMF allocation of the TCP flows, the network topology and the paths of the data flows can be ignored, and only the bandwidth capacities of the links in the access layer and the source and destination nodes of the TCP flows need to be considered. The non-blocking switch abstraction largely simplifies the estimation of the MMF bandwidth allocation. In the rest of the paper, we hold the assumption that all bottleneck links are in the access layer.

3. BASHUFFLER

3.1 Architecture of BAShuffler

BAShuffler is implemented and embedded in YARN, and its architecture is shown in Fig. 1. When a shuffle task needs to schedule a new fetch, it sends a source selection request to BAShuffler which is housed in the Resource Manager and makes scheduling decisions using the Partially Greedy Source Selection (PGSS) algorithm. The PGSS algorithm is introduced below and the details of the design of BAShuffler can be found in the extended version [10] of this paper.

3.2 Partially Greedy Source Selection

The algorithm of PGSS is presented in Algorithm 1. PGSS assigns every node a *load count*, which indicates how many fetch flows will be created from this node in the immediate or near future. When a shuffle begins, PGSS assumes that there will be a new fetch flow later from every map task. Therefore, it increments the load count of each potential pending source node by the number of map tasks in the node. When PGSS needs to select a source from the pending nodes, it zeros in on the set of source nodes that have the largest remaining load counts ("partial") and selects the one that gives that maximum MMF bandwidth utilization ("greedy").

The advantage of selecting the source from the heaviest loaded nodes is that this incurs a small scheduling overhead. Suppose that the number of nodes in the cluster is N, the number of existing flows in the network is F, the number of pending sources is $M(M \leq N)$, and the number of the heaviest-loaded nodes is $K(K \leq M)$. Given that the time complexity for obtaining the MMF bandwidth utilization of the specific network from a communication pattern is $O(N + F)$, the time complexity of PGSS is $O(K \times (N + F))$ for scheduling each request, instead of $O(M \times (N + F))$ if all the pending sources are considered.

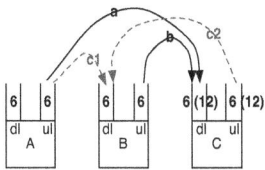

(a) Uneven Pattern   (b) Even Pattern

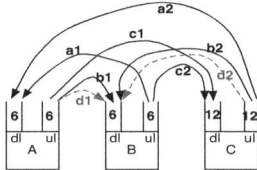

Figure 2: Scenarios of Selecting the Source in Different Flow Patterns

Table 1: MMF Bandwidth Allocation of Uneven Flow Pattern in Homogeneous Network

Selected Flow	a	b	c1	c2	Overall
Nil	3	3	-	-	6
c1	3	3	3	-	9
c2	3	3	-	6	12

Table 2: MMF Bandwidth Allocation of Uneven Flow Pattern in Heterogeneous Network

Selected Flow	a	b	c1	c2	Overall
Nil	6	6	-	-	12
c1	3	6	3	-	12
c2	6	6	-	6	18

3.3 Applying PGSS

We illustrate how PGSS is applied when selecting a source based on the notion of MMF allocation in both homogeneous and heterogeneous network settings, corresponding to the capacities of the access layer links being the same or different, respectively.

Fig. 2 depicts two scenarios of either uneven or even flow pattern, where even means that the numbers of flows into or out of all the nodes are the same, and uneven otherwise. In the homogeneous network setting, the three nodes, A, B, and C, have the same uplink and downlink bandwidth capacities, which are 6, 6 and 6, respectively; whereas in the heterogeneous setting, there capacities are 6, 6 and 12, respectively. The solid arrows represent the existing fetch flows and the dashed arrows represent the new flows that can be selected. Now, a fetcher in Node B becomes available and PGSS needs to decide a source node (A or C) to fetch the data. Assume that both Node A and Node C are the heaviest-loaded nodes.

3.3.1 Homogeneous Network

For the homogeneous network setting, the MMF bandwidth allocation of each flow before or after the selection of a new flow is shown in Table 1, where "Nil" in an entry means before the source selection. Different selection decisions can lead to different MMF bandwidth allocations and overall bandwidth utilizations. PGSS will select Node C as the source, which gives 33% higher overall bandwidth utilization than if Node A is selected. Note that the RSS policy of YARN will have a 50% probability of selecting the source node "A".

3.3.2 Heterogeneous Network

For the heterogeneous network setting, RSS gives rise to an even poorer bandwidth utilization than in the case of a homogeneous network, regardless of whether the flows are evenly allocated across the network or not.

Table 3: MMF Bandwidth Allocation of Even Flow Pattern in Heterogeneous Network

	a1	a2	b1	b2	c1	c2	d1	d2	Overall
Nil	3	3	3	3	3	3	-	-	18
d1	3	3	2	2	2	3	2	-	17
d2	3	3	2	2	4	3	-	2	19

For the uneven flow patterns in Fig. 2(a) with the heterogeneous network setting, the MMF allocation of each flow is shown in Table 2 The overall bandwidth utilization difference between selecting Flow c1 and Flow c2 is amplified in the heterogeneous network (3:2), when compared to the homogeneous network (4:3). PGSS will always select the source (Node C) that brings about the maximum bandwidth utilization.

In the homogeneous network, if the communication pattern of the flows is exactly even, selecting any source node for fetching will make no difference in the overall bandwidth utilization. However, in the heterogeneous network, selecting the right source node can lead to a higher bandwidth utilization.

Fig. 2(b) depicts the scenarios of the even flow pattern, and the capacities of the links follow the heterogeneous network setting. The MMF allocation of the flows before and after selecting the new flows (dashed arrows) is shown in Table 3. Surprisingly but it does happen that the overall MMF bandwidth utilization drops if Flow d1 is selected. PGSS selects Flow d2 to guarantee the maximum bandwidth utilization.

4. EVALUATION

We run BAShuffler in a physical testbed with the heterogeneous network setting. The cluster contains 18 computer nodes, one of which assumes the role of the name node of HDFS, and another one acts as the resource manager of YARN. The remaining 16 nodes are configured as both the data nodes of HDFS and the node managers of YARN. All the 18 nodes are connected to an internal non-blocking switch with GbE ports. To create the heterogeneous network capacities, among the 16 node managers, the bandwidth capacities of the uplinks and downlinks of 8 nodes are manually limited to 160 Mbps, by using the traffic control tool "tc", and the remaining 8 nodes keep to their physical uplink and downlink bandwidth capacity, which is 320 Mbps.

The benchmarks and datasets used are from a realistic MapReduce benchmark suite [1]. We use mainly the shuffle-heavy applications because we want to evaluate the performance of BAShuffler when the shuffle workload can saturate the network most of the time. The sizes of the datasets of the benchmarks are listed in Table 4. Unless specified otherwise, the number of fetchers in each shuffle task is 5 (the default value).

4.1 Shuffle Throughput

The metric of the overall shuffle throughput reflects the cluster's overall bandwidth utilization along the time axis. The overall shuffle throughput is depicted as the cumulative completion ratio of the overall shuffle workload. Fig. 3 shows the cumulative completion ratios of RSS and PGSS in various benchmarks, where PGSS clearly outperforms RSS in all the benchmarks. The overall shuffle throughput improvement is the result of maximizing the overall bandwidth

Table 4: Benchmark Dataset Size (GB)

Benchmark	Input	Shuffle	Output
Terasort	190	190	190
InvertedIndex	200	42	34
SequenceCount	300	180	150
RankedInvertedIndex	150	175	153

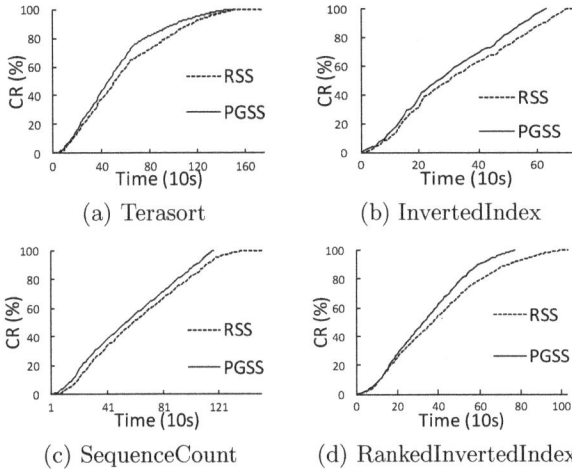

(a) Terasort   (b) InvertedIndex

(c) SequenceCount   (d) RankedInvertedIndex

Figure 3: Cumulative Completion Ratio (CR) of the Overall Shuffle Workload of RSS and PGSS in Various Benchmarks along the Time

utilization, e.g., the shuffle throughput speedup due to PGSS is about 12% in the Terasort benchmark.

4.2 Completion Time

The reduce completion time is the duration from the time when all the map tasks have finished to the time when the job finishes. Fig. 4 depicts the reduce completion time speedup and the job overall completion time speedup by PGSS as compared to RSS with different numbers of fetchers in each shuffle task. Different numbers of fetchers will create different degrees of traffic congestion in the network. As the benchmarks are reduce-heavy, where the shuffle phase can occupy a major portion of the overall workload, in most cases, BAShuffler not only improves the reduce phase, but also the overall completion time of the jobs rather decisively. For example, in the RankedInvertedIndex benchmark with 5 fetchers, PGSS shortens the reduce completion time by 29% and the overall completion time by 21%. In some cases, the speedup of PGSS is not obvious (e.g., Terasort with 6 fetchers in Fig. 4(a)) which is because the reduce completion time of RSS is already the minimum among all the fetcher settings.

5. CONCLUSION

In this paper, we describe BAShuffler which we implement in YARN to improve the shuffle performance. It schedules the source nodes of the shuffle flows at the application level in order to maximize the overall max-min fairness bandwidth utilization. BAShuffler can significantly increase the shuffle performance especially when the network is heterogeneous in the capacities of its links.

Acknowledgement This work is supported in part by a Hong Kong RGC CRF grant (C7036-15G).

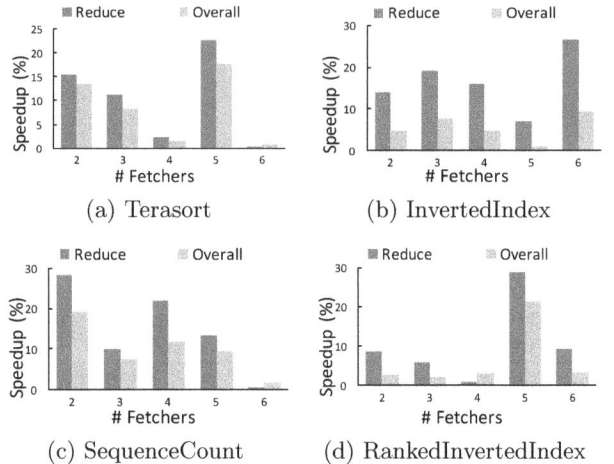

(a) Terasort   (b) InvertedIndex

(c) SequenceCount   (d) RankedInvertedIndex

Figure 4: Reduce Completion Time Speedup and Job Overall Completion time Speedup of PGSS

6. REFERENCES

[1] F. Ahmad, S. Lee, M. Thottethodi, and T. Vijaykumar. Puma: Purdue mapreduce benchmarks suite. 2012.

[2] M. Alizadeh, T. Edsall, S. Dharmapurikar, R. Vaidyanathan, K. Chu, A. Fingerhut, F. Matus, R. Pan, N. Yadav, G. Varghese, et al. Conga: Distributed congestion-aware load balancing for datacenters. In *SIGCOMM*, 2014.

[3] M. Alizadeh, S. Yang, M. Sharif, S. Katti, N. McKeown, B. Prabhakar, and S. Shenker. pfabric: Minimal near-optimal datacenter transport. *SIGCOMM*, 2013.

[4] D.-M. Chiu and R. Jain. Analysis of the increase and decrease algorithms for congestion avoidance in computer networks. *Computer Networks and ISDN systems*, 17(1):1–14, 1989.

[5] M. Chowdhury, M. Zaharia, J. Ma, M. I. Jordan, and I. Stoica. Managing data transfers in computer clusters with orchestra. In *SIGCOMM*, 2011.

[6] M. Chowdhury, Y. Zhong, and I. Stoica. Efficient coflow scheduling with varys. In *SIGCOMM*, 2014.

[7] J. Dean and S. Ghemawat. Mapreduce: simplified data processing on large clusters. *Communications of the ACM*, 2008.

[8] A. Greenberg, J. R. Hamilton, N. Jain, S. Kandula, C. Kim, P. Lahiri, D. A. Maltz, P. Patel, and S. Sengupta. Vl2: a scalable and flexible data center network. In *SIGCOMM*, 2009.

[9] V. Jacobson. Congestion avoidance and control. In *SIGCOMM*, 1988.

[10] F. Liang and F. C. M. Lau. Bashuffler: Maximizing network bandwidth utilization in the shuffle of yarn. http://i.cs.hku.hk/%7Efliang/paper/BAShuffler.pdf.

[11] R. Niranjan Mysore, A. Pamboris, N. Farrington, N. Huang, P. Miri, S. Radhakrishnan, V. Subramanya, and A. Vahdat. Portland: a scalable fault-tolerant layer 2 data center network fabric. In *SIGCOMM*, 2009.

[12] A. Shieh, S. Kandula, A. Greenberg, C. Kim, and B. Saha. Sharing the data center network. In *NSDI*, 2011.

[13] V. K. Vavilapalli, A. C. Murthy, C. Douglas, S. Agarwal, M. Konar, R. Evans, T. Graves, J. Lowe, H. Shah, S. Seth, et al. Apache hadoop yarn: Yet another resource negotiator. In *SOCC*, 2013.

[14] M. Zaharia, M. Chowdhury, T. Das, A. Dave, J. Ma, M. McCauley, M. J. Franklin, S. Shenker, and I. Stoica. Resilient distributed datasets: A fault-tolerant abstraction for in-memory cluster computing. In *NSDI*, 2012.

Master of Puppets: Cooperative Multitasking for In Situ Processing

Dmitriy Morozov
Lawrence Berkeley National Laboratory
dmitriy@mrzv.org

Zarija Lukić
Lawrence Berkeley National Laboratory
zarija@lbl.gov

ABSTRACT

Modern scientific and engineering simulations track the time evolution of billions of elements. For such large runs, storing most time steps for later analysis is not a viable strategy. It is far more efficient to analyze the simulation data while it is still in memory. In this paper, we present a novel design for running multiple codes in situ: using coroutines and position-independent executables we enable cooperative multitasking between simulation and analysis, allowing the same executables to post-process simulation output, as well as to process it on the fly, both in situ and in transit. We present Henson,[1] an implementation of our design, and illustrate its versatility by tackling analysis tasks with different computational requirements. Our design differs significantly from the existing frameworks and offers an efficient and robust approach to integrating multiple codes on modern supercomputers. The presented techniques can also be integrated into other in situ frameworks.

1. INTRODUCTION

Many scientific fields rely on simulations to produce models and predictions. Typical examples are astrophysics and cosmology, climate studies, plasma physics, and neural simulations, where the number of computational elements, for example, dark matter particles or neural synapses, reaches into the trillions. A single time snapshot from such runs is tens of terabytes. In this regime, the traditional approach of running a CPU-intensive simulation, saving many outputs to disk, and analyzing them later is hopelessly inefficient.

To make matters worse, while there are several HPC centers around the world that allow scientists to obtain time allocations large enough to produce such simulations, there is virtually no way to apply for petabytes of disk storage for their output. Therefore, a significant challenge for computational science is how to efficiently run simulation and analysis codes *in situ*, without saving (most of) the data to disk. This problem is the main motivation of our work.

[1] https://github.com/mrzv/henson

HPDC'16, May 31-June 04, 2016, Kyoto, Japan

DOI: http://dx.doi.org/10.1145/2907294.2907301

Even if there was disk space, it would be impractical to save a large number of time steps — the slowdown due to I/O would be high. At the same time, the data could be analyzed while it's still resident in memory: many forms of analysis produce output orders of magnitude smaller than the input — halo catalogs or light cones in cosmological simulations; changes in average temperatures over time in climate simulations; cumulative energy distributions for particles in plasma simulations — making it both possible and sensible to save the results of the analysis, while either abandoning the simulation data completely, or storing only a few snapshots.

It may seem that the supercomputers' restrictions and the desire to share memory force simulation and analysis codes to be tightly coupled by being compiled into a single executable. In this paper we show that tight coupling is not required. The codes can remain separate yet execute on the same nodes. Crucially, they can share the same memory and data without any changes to their memory management facilities.

2. COOPERATIVE MULTITASKING

Our solution depends on two ingredients: position-independent executables and coroutines.

Position-independent executables. To let multiple executables share memory, as well as to avoid limitations of some supercomputers, such as the absence of fork on IBM BG/Q systems, we can compile our codes as *position-independent executables*. The resulting binaries are both executables and dynamic libraries.

If one compiles an analysis code as a position-independent executable, one can launch it as a standalone process to analyze a snapshot of a simulation saved on disk. But it also becomes possible to load the code inside a different process, using the dlopen/dlsym facilities of libdl to get the address of its main. Listing 1 presents the relevant code snippet.

```
typedef  int   (*MainType)(int argc, char *argv[]);
void*    lib   = dlopen(fn.c_str(), RTLD_LAZY);
MainType lib_main = (MainType) dlsym(lib, "main");
```

Listing 1: dlopen/dlsym example.

Loading simulation and analysis executables inside one process has a significant advantage. All the routines share the same address space — there is no process isolation enforced by the operating system. Therefore, they can exchange data by simply passing pointers to each other, without any changes to their memory management facilities. Achieving such zero-copy regime with executables running as separate processes is considerably more complicated.

Coroutines. Once the `main` functions are in memory, we need to switch control between them. It is possible for the simulation to call the analysis code directly, as a subroutine. But this puts a restriction on the analysis, which wouldn't exist if we used separate processes: when returning back to the simulation, the analysis would inevitably lose its state, both the stack and the program counter.

What we face is a classical problem with subroutines: they have a single entry point, and, when returning, they lose their stack frame. This problem has an elegant solution. *Coroutines*, a generalization of subroutines, described in detail in the first volume of Knuth's monograph [1, Section 1.4.2], maintain their state across invocations. Switching from one coroutine to another changes the execution context, including the stack pointer, program counter, registers, etc. As a consequence, not only is the coroutine's data preserved, but when we switch back to it, the execution resumes exactly where it left off.

There are C++ libraries that provide the coroutine functionality. By default, Henson uses `libcoro`,[2] included in its distribution, which allows us to create an independent context for each executable. The switches between contexts happen *cooperatively*, when either simulation or analysis explicitly returns control via a `yield` function, described in more detail in the next section.

3. HENSON

We now describe a system, Henson, built on the principles of the previous section. Henson consists of three parts: the application that controls the execution flow between the different codes, referred to as *puppets* inside the application; a small C library that the puppets must link (the library wraps `libcoro` and provides functions to control execution and data exchange); and auxiliary tools (as well as examples) to simplify transition from in situ to in transit analysis regimes.

Controller. `henson`, the application, controls execution. The user specifies what codes to run and how to run them in a script. A sample script appears in Listing 4. The first lines define puppets used in the code. The text after the equals sign is interpreted as a command line: the first word is the executable, while the rest of the symbols are parsed and passed to the `main` function. Once the puppets are loaded, the script specifies how to alternate execution between them.

Puppets. Listing 2 gives an example of a puppet; it illustrates a typical time step of a simulation. After the computation is finished, the simulation exposes its data to other puppets by calling `henson_save_*`, and yields control back to `henson` by calling `henson_yield`. These functions are provided by `libhenson`, the C library that all the puppets must link.

Henson provides a shared table that maps strings to values. When a puppet saves an array, it does not actually copy any elements, but rather stores the pointer and array metadata in the table. An array stores the address of its first element, the size of individual elements, their number, and the stride between elements; see Listing 2 for an example.

Having read this metadata, analysis code can access the respective arrays directly. Listing 3 shows a skeleton of the analysis code. Analysis itself may choose to yield execution

---

[2] http://software.schmorp.de/pkg/libcoro.html

to `henson`, for example, if its output may need to be processed by another code.

```
double redshift; size_t count, dtype, stride;
float *x, *y, *z;
henson_load_double("redshift", &redshift);
henson_load_array("x", &x, &dtype, &count, &stride);
henson_load_array("y", &y, &dtype, &count, &stride);
henson_load_array("z", &z, &dtype, &count, &stride);
// analyze the data
henson_save_pointer("analysis-data", analysis_data);
henson_yield();
```

Listing 3: Analysis skeleton.

Execution groups. Henson supports multiple execution groups, each specified as a separate `while`-loop in the script. Listing 4 defines two execution groups, `producer` and `consumer`. When launching `henson`, a user may specify on the command line how many processors to allocate to each execution group.

Henson supports multiple execution groups to allow in transit analysis, where data moves from one group to another, running on a separate set of processors. To identify those processors, group names are helpful inside puppets: a puppet may request an MPI inter-communicator that connects the processors of its local execution group with those of a remote group by calling `henson_get_intercomm(remote_group_name)`. In Listing 4, group names (`producer` and `consumer`) are passed to `send` and `receive` puppets precisely for this reason.

MPI. Henson initializes MPI, so puppets should not repeat the initialization individually. Similarly, each puppet should restrict its communication to an MPI intra-communicator within its execution group. The latter can be obtained with an explicit call to `henson_get_world`, but `libhenson` also includes MPI wrappers (built on top of the PMPI interface). These wrappers, when running under Henson, disable MPI initialization and transparently replace `MPI_COMM_WORLD` by the result of `henson_get_world` in all operations. These wrappers allow the same codes to run independently or under Henson, both with a single or multiple execution groups, with no changes.

Data flow. Individual puppets don't have to be simulation or analysis codes, they can also be routines that exchange data between execution groups. Henson includes two tools, `send` and `receive`, which not only serve as examples of such puppets, but are also useful for real applications. `send` looks up the names in the shared table and sends their contents to the remote group; `receive` receives the remote data and inserts them into the local table. Both tools can communicate between execution groups with different numbers of processors.

The two routines can be run in synchronous or asynchronous mode; `--async` flag in Listing 4 indicates the latter. In synchronous mode, the two routines wait for each other, so each time step of the simulation is sent over to the analysis. In the asynchronous mode, `send` checks if `receive` has requested more data, in which case it fulfills the request. When the temporal resolution of the simulation is finer than what the analysis needs, the asynchronous mode has the obvious advantage: simulation and analysis proceed at their own pace, pausing to exchange data only when necessary.

The advantage of our design is that simulation and analysis don't require any changes to accommodate different execution

```
while (/* main time loop */)
{
    // ... (simulation time step)
    henson_save_double("redshift", z);
    henson_save_array("x", &P[0].Pos[0], sizeof(float), count, sizeof(struct particle_data));
    henson_save_array("y", &P[0].Pos[1], sizeof(float), count, sizeof(struct particle_data));
    henson_save_array("z", &P[0].Pos[2], sizeof(float), count, sizeof(struct particle_data));
    henson_yield();
}
```

Listing 2: Time step in a cosmological simulation puppet. Particle quantities are stored in `struct particle_data`. Our analysis uses only positions; we set element size to `sizeof(float)`, while using the size of `particle_data` as the stride. `count` is the number of particles on the local processor.

```
sim       = ../../L-Gadget3/L-Gadget3 $gadget_settings(gadget-defaultx256)
tess      = ./tess -w _ _ _ _ _ 0. 0. 0. $max_x(100.) $max_y(100.) $max_z(100.)
entropy   = ./entropy _ $entropy_out(entropy-256.txt)
lightcone = ./lightcone 1 1 1 0.524 lightcone.out

send      = ../henson/tools/send     --async consumer x,y,z:array t:size_t redshift:double
receive   = ../henson/tools/receive  --async producer x,y,z:array t:size_t redshift:double

producer while sim:
    sim
    lightcone
    send

consumer while receive:
    receive
    *tess
    entropy
```

Listing 4: Henson script to (asynchronously) exchange data between execution groups, `producer` and `consumer`. The two while-loops execute in parallel; `send` and `receive` puppets move data between the processors on demand.

regimes: simulation posts pointers to data in a shared table, analysis reads them from the table, but each one is oblivious to what happens when they are not running. This allows other puppets (like `send` and `receive` above) to move data between different nodes, enabling the in transit analysis, illustrated in Listing 4. At the same time, the simulation and analysis codes require no changes to run in situ; the user simply modifies the script to replace two execution groups by one, as in Listing 5.

```
world while sim:
    sim
    lightcone
    *tess
    entropy
```

Listing 5: In situ version of the script in Listing 4, with identical puppet definitions omitted.

4. EXPERIMENTS

To evaluate Henson, we conducted a series of experiments at the National Energy Research Scientific Computing Center (NERSC) on Edison, a Cray XC30 with 5,576 nodes, each with 24 cores (Intel Ivy Bridge 2.4 GHz) and 64 GB RAM.

We ran several N-body simulations using Gadget [2], a widely used code for modelling the evolution of cosmic structure, which we modified to save in Henson's data table, after every time step, several internal variables, including particle positions and redshift, and to call `henson_yield`. Listing 2 shows all the necessary changes, copied directly from our modified version of Gadget. For reference, it takes Gadget approximately 8.5 seconds to save on disk all particle positions for a single time step, when using 4096 processors. The simulation takes on average 0.6 seconds for a single time step using 4096 processors.

Tessellation. Most our analysis uses Voronoi tessellations. We use `tess`, a tessellation code that implements the algorithm of Peterka et al. [3] In cosmology, Voronoi tessellations can be used to estimate mass density from N-body simulations, for example, as particle mass divided by its Voronoi cell volume. After normalization, we can treat the result as a probability density function and compute its information entropy using `entropy` code.

We always run `tess` and `entropy` on the same nodes, but we try two different regimes for placing the `tess–entropy` pair and the simulation. In the first case, we run all three in situ, on the same set of nodes, with all data transfers between codes occurring by passing pointers using Henson data facilities. Because the `tess–entropy` analysis of a single time step takes a lot longer than the simulation, and because we don't need to analyze every time step, we try a *fair* scheduling regime. An auxiliary puppet times how long `tess–entropy` took to analyze the last time step. It then blocks analysis until the simulation has run for at least as long. At this point it transfers control back to analysis, timing its performance.

The second regime is in transit. Simulation and `tess–entropy` analysis are placed into two separate execution groups, as shown in Listing 4. In this case, the total number of processors is split evenly among them, but one can adjust the split with a command-line parameter to `henson`. The simulation and analysis communicate asynchronously using `send` and `receive` tools: the analysis requests the data from the simulation only when it's ready to analyze it.

Light cone. We also use a particle filtering code, `lightcone`, which constructs the cosmic structure as it would be observed at a fixed space–time location. Light cones are traditionally produced by saving enough time steps from a simulation and then stacking them in redshift shells. Doing this in situ is

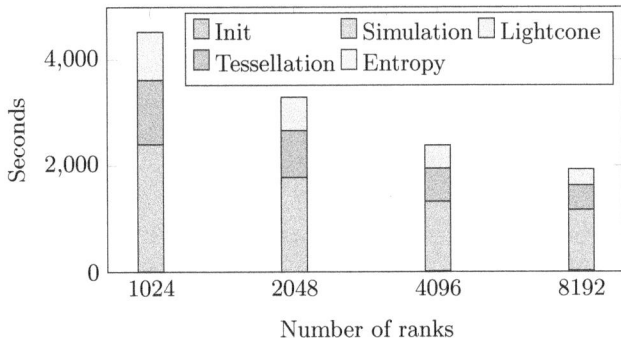

Figure 1: Gadget–tess–entropy pipeline run in situ. Init and Lightcone times are so small that they are imperceptible in the plot.

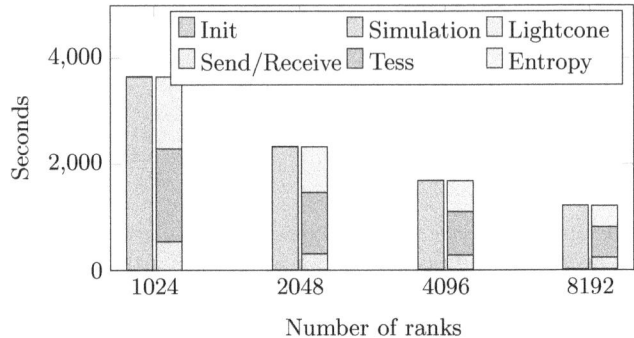

Figure 2: Gadget–tess–entropy pipeline run in transit. Init, Lightcone, and Send times are so small that they are imperceptible in the plot.

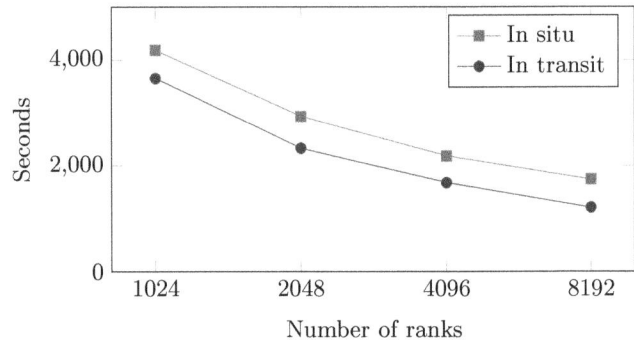

Figure 3: Simulation and analysis scaling comparison in situ vs. in transit. In situ analysis time is normalized to match the number of steps analyzed in transit.

both more computationally efficient and more accurate, since the resulting light cone has shells as fine as the simulation time steps.

The analysis is simple: it requires a single pass over the data and accumulates those particles that match a particular criterion, saving them to disk once the simulation ends its run. We run `lightcone` in situ with the simulation because it requires little memory or time overhead. In this regime, less than a second is spent on the analysis during an hour-long simulation run.

Evaluation. Figure 1 shows the results of the (fair) in situ runs, where Gadget simulates 2001 time steps. We note that (1) Henson initialization is negligible, taking less than 25 seconds on 8192 cores; (2) the time spent in analysis (`tess` and `entropy`) never exceeds the time in simulation, balance achieved by the fair scheduling; and (3) more and more time steps are analyzed in the time it takes to simulate 2001 time steps, from 213 steps using 1024 cores to 353 steps using 8192 cores — analysis scales better than the simulation.

Figure 2 shows the results of in transit runs, where half of the processors are dedicated to the simulation, and the other half to the analysis. Again, Gadget simulates 2001 time steps. The first thing to note is that communication on the simulation side (`send` time) is negligible: from 6.97 seconds for 1024 cores down to 1.60 seconds for 8192 cores. In other words, in this regime Gadget has virtually no overhead; the processors dedicated to it spend almost all of their time simulating the universe. This makes scheduling predictable.

On the other hand, communication on the analysis side (`receive` time) is significant: when analysis finishes, it returns control to `receive`, which signals to the `send` that it is ready for more data. Such a request is processed once the simulation completes its current time step and passes control to `send`. The wait times accumulate over the course of the simulation.

It may seem that in situ analysis is performing better since more time steps get analyzed. But it also takes longer. To get a meaningful comparison of the two, we estimate how long the simulation and analysis would run in situ if they were to analyze the same number of time steps as in transit (using the same total number of cores). Specifically, we calculate $s + (t + e) \cdot (i_2/i_1)$, where s, t, and e are the in situ simulation, tessellation, and entropy times, and i_1 and i_2 are the number of steps analyzed in situ and in transit, respectively. We compare the results to the total running time of the in transit simulation (and, by construction, analysis); see Figure 3.

As the figure illustrates, despite the communication overhead, in transit analysis performs better. Although surprising

at first, there is a simple explanation: neither simulation, nor analysis scale perfectly. When running in situ, both have to use twice as many processors as they would in transit. The higher overheads slow the execution. But in other examples, like `lightcone`, in situ is more efficient. This highlights the importance of a flexible system, like the one presented, that seamlessly supports different execution regimes.

Acknowledgements

We would like to thank Matthew Wolf and Patrick O'Leary for helpful discussions, and Wes Bethel for his support. We are grateful to our colleagues, Wes Bethel, Peter Nugent, Tom Peterka, and Rollin Thomas, for providing feedback on draft versions of this paper. Calculations presented in this paper used resources of the National Energy Research Scientific Computing Center (NERSC). Both NERSC and the authors were supported by the Office of Science of the U.S. Department of Energy under Contract No. DE-AC02-05CH11231. ZL was in part supported by the SciDAC program funded by the U.S. Department of Energy.

5. REFERENCES

[1] D.E. Knuth. *Fundamental Algorithms. The Art of Computer Programming 1.* Addison–Wesley, 1997.

[2] V. Springel. The Cosmological Simulation Code GADGET-2. *Monthly Notices of the Royal Astronomical Society*, 364:1105–1134, 2005.

[3] T. Peterka, D. Morozov, and C. Phillips. High-Performance Computation of Distributed-Memory Parallel 3D Voronoi and Delaunay Tessellation. In *Proceedings of the SC*, pages 997–1007, 2014.

Author Index

www.ingramcontent.com/pod-product-compliance
Lightning Source LLC
hersburg PA
LSHW061342210326
00035B/5858